The Prehistory of the Netherlands

Volume 2

The Prehistory of the Netherlands

Volume 2

Edited by

L.P. Louwe Kooijmans

P.W. van den Broeke

H. Fokkens

A.L. van Gijn

AMSTERDAM UNIVERSITY PRESS

The publication of this book was made possible by grants from:
- the Netherlands Organisation for Scientific Research (NWO)
- Archol BV, Leiden
- The Prince Bernhard Cultural Foundation (PBCF)

Cover illustration: Flint arrowhead from the Middle Bronze Age burial at Wassenaar, c. 1700 BC, see feature L, p. 459 (photo J. Pauptit, Faculty of Archaeology, Leiden University).

Cover design: Studio Jan de Boer BNO, Amsterdam
Lay-out: Perfect Service, Schoonhoven

ISBN 90 5356 160 9 (both volumes)
ISBN 90 5356 806 9 (volume 1)
ISBN 90 5356 807 7 (volume 2)
NUR 682

Contents Volume 1

Contents Volume 2

Conclusion

Note on the dates used in this book

Dates before 50,000 are based on various physical dating techniques, other than radiocarbon, and expressed as 'years ago'.

Dates in the period 50,000-10,000 years ago are based on uncalibrated radiocarbon dates and expressed as 'years ago' or 'years BP' (= Before Present).

Dates in the last 10,000 years are based on calibrated radiocarbon dates and expressed as 'years BC'. Only these dates can be equated with calender or solar years.

See chapter 1, section 'periods and dates' for the principles of radiocarbon dating.

Part IV

Increasing diversity

The introduction of the custom of burying cremated remains in urnfields and an innovation in pottery traditions represent remarkable changes that took place around 1100 BC. These changes can be followed in greater detail than the replacement of bronze by iron as a raw material for weapons and tools, which was to take place a few centuries later. This transition to a new type of metal and the related changes in trade relations coincided with the end of the custom of burying hoards of metal objects. What is still a mystery to us is the emergence of a social elite in the eastern rivers area in the 7th century BC. This elite can hardly have obtained its exotic prestige objects by virtue of its economic basis, which comprised little more than the products of crop cultivation and animal husbandry, produced at small farms that were organised in a pattern of – constantly shifting – dispersed settlement, comprising isolated farmsteads and hamlets. In the Early Iron Age new ecological zones were exploited for the first time: the coastal peat marshes in the west and the salt marshes in the north. These new environments will have implied limitations with respect to the range of crops at the least, and probably also a heavy reliance on animal husbandry. The resultant dependence on the hinterland, which will undoubtedly have been a source of friction, may explain the appearance of small fortified settlements on the sands of Drenthe around the beginning of the Christian era. From written evidence more than from archaeological observations we know that battles were being fought and that tribes were on the move in the southern part of the Netherlands in this period. These battles and mass migrations form the prelude to the Roman domination and the end of the prehistoric period.

21 Late Bronze Age and Iron Age: introduction

Peter van den Broeke

ENVIRONMENT AND SETTLEMENT

A combination of elements

By the Middle Bronze Age the Netherlands consisted almost entirely of sandy soil and peat, in more or less equal proportions. This was to change very little, and only in the northern half of the country, until the end of prehistory. However, geological processes in the areas of Holocene sedimentation did lead to major changes in the settlement pattern. The main cause of these changes was a new marine transgression (the Dunkirk I phase), which affected the groundwater level and the drainage of the rivers. On the higher Pleistocene grounds developments were less drastic, involving only sand drifts, which – not by chance – affected the most intensively used parts of the sandy regions.

The above phenomena do not seem to have been caused by major climatic changes, although it is believed that the transition from the Sub-Boreal to the Sub-Atlantic, which took place in the Late Bronze Age, was marked by a change to a somewhat wetter and cooler climate (see chapter 3).

We know for certain that various changes took place in the vegetation in the first millennium BC. In the forests, beech and hornbeam became more prominent, at the expense of hazel, oak and birch in particular.[1] The forests on the sandy soils declined, as a result of clearing, exhaustion of the soil and pasturing. This process was precipitated by a decrease in the soil's mineral content, caused largely by leaching. Infertile heathlands increasingly dominated the landscape, if not yet to the same extent as in historical times. Heather became a characteristic feature of the coastal landscape, too, in the many places where raised bogs had developed on top of the fen peats.[2]

The lushest vegetation was to be found along the rivers, whose banks supported rich forests. The treeless landscape of the salt marshes forms the other extreme of the widely varied spectrum of environments that were occupied in late prehistoric times.

The connection between the environment and habitation

After 1200 BC the Dunkirk O transgression phase was succeeded by a regression phase that was to last for several centuries. The peat growth that had started behind the long uninterrupted coastal barrier that closed off the coast of the western Netherlands continued at a steady pace, in accordance with the rise in the groundwater level. Although the latter rose only slowly, conditions in the salt marshes of Westfrisia became so wet that this formerly densely occupied area was almost completely abandoned around 800 BC. Later on, the gradual submersion of the land and peat growth forced the occupants of the sandy soils on the western periphery of the plateau of Friesland and Drenthe to move elsewhere, too.[3]

Further north, the coastal barriers (what are now the Frisian Islands) provided little protection against the encroaching sea. There, floods during a first, regional phase of the Dunkirk I transgression moved large parts of the coastal barrier further inland and created new inlets in the Late Bronze Age. The continuous supply of sediments led to the formation of a wide zone of new salt marshes, also in largely unprotected coastal regions (Groningen). With time, those salt marshes became fit for occupation, too, and in the Early Iron Age the first colonists moved onto the attractive pastures that had formed on them.[4] The number of settlements increased considerably during the Iron Age. However, the occupants of these salt marshes were forced to raise the level of their settlement sites to protect themselves against floods. The resultant *terpen* dominated the flat, treeless landscape, which may consequently rightly be described as a *terpen* landscape.

In the western Netherlands the impact of the encroaching sea was not felt until around the beginning of the Iron Age, when the seawater penetrated into the coastal peat zone via the existing estuaries and washed away the sediment that had been deposited in former tributary tidal channels and creeks, thus creating new inlets. This process, and the formation of the Striene/Bernisse arm of the Scheldt, which emptied into the Meuse estuary, led to the drainage of the coastal peat. In the Early Iron Age the first colonists ventured onto this peat, settling mainly around the estuaries.[5] With a few interruptions, especially in the Late Iron Age, when parts of the coastal peat were covered with a layer of clay, this landscape remained fit for occupation until in the Roman period (fig. 21.1).

The floods and sedimentation in the coastal zone coincided with major floods in the rivers area in the central part of the Netherlands. There, too, clay was deposited over large areas and the rising groundwater level made for poorer occupation conditions. Nevertheless, many settlements, most from the Iron Age, have been found on stream ridges and higher sand ridges in this area.

The changes that took place in the landscape of the Pleistocene sands are largely the consequences of human occupation, on which they in turn had an – adverse – effect. By making clearances in the forests, by laying fields fallow, and probably also by peat cutting, the inhabitants created opportunities for the wind to get more hold on the surface. On the plateau of Friesland and Drenthe in particular this led to frequent sand drifts after the Middle Bronze Age, which of course also affected the areas under cultivation. This same phenomenon was to make life more difficult for the occupants of the dunes along the North Sea.[6]

fig. 21.1

In the Iron Age the first colonists settled on the peat expanse bordering the North Sea. The oldest evidence of large-scale peat exploitation in the Netherlands dates from that same period. The pits from which the peat was dug stand out clearly at this site near Monster as the clay with which they were filled in the Middle Iron Age or earlier contrasts markedly with the dark surrounding peat.

DEVELOPMENTS AT THE END OF
THE SECOND MILLENNIUM BC

According to the evidence currently available, no fundamental changes seem to have taken place in settlement patterns or the economy at the transition from the Middle Bronze Age to the Late Bronze Age. All the same, the attested innovations in burial practices and pottery traditions are sufficient grounds for drawing a line at this transition. The changes observable in the Netherlands are only a faint reflection of what was taking place in Central Europe, where the custom of inhumation had come to an end around the middle of the 2nd millennium BC already. In the Urnfield culture and the related Polish/German Lausitz culture that subsequently emerged, cremation was the common form of burial. The urns in which the cremated remains were buried were often accompanied by a wide range of grave goods. These urns were buried in clustered graves, which ultimately evolved into the so-called urnfields. Most of the burial pits were no longer covered with barrows, as had been customary in the previous period; at most, a low mound was thrown up over the urn.

This custom of burying cremated remains in urnfields spread to the Lower Rhine region, too. In this area, however, cremation was no new development. In the southern part of the Netherlands this form of burial had in fact been practised for several centuries already; the burial of remains in groups was not new either (Haps, Toterfout-Halve Mijl). There is no evidence for an increase in the number of grave goods in the Lower Rhine region; the only new element is the single accessory vessel, usually quite small, that was buried together with the urn. The remains continued to be buried beneath a mound surrounded by a peripheral structure, the only difference being that the dimensions of the round mounds decreased. The only really conspicuous change observable in the Netherlands is the differentiation in the funerary *monuments*; this manifested itself in the northern part of the Netherlands earlier than in the southern part.

Whether these developments reflect changes in ways of thinking we do not yet know. The number of figurative representations found in the Netherlands is far too small to allow any comparisons with the representations of sun symbols, ships and birds that have been found in many places in Central Europe and southern Scandinavia and that are believed to have played a part in cults and myths.

Cremation remained the common form of burial until in the Roman period, although the evidence for cremation burials after the Early Iron Age becomes increasingly scarce.

The most striking change is actually that which took place in pottery production. The coarse, more or less uniform and virtually undecorated pottery of the Middle Bronze Age period B gave way to a wide range of different types, many of which were burnished and beautifully decorated. Clear parallels of types from western Central Europe (the Rhenish-Swiss-eastern French branch of the Urnfield culture) have been found in the southern part of the Netherlands in particular. As far as the range of types and decorative motifs are concerned, the pottery that was produced in the Netherlands was still to undergo many changes until the Roman period, but none of those changes could be termed as drastic as those that took place at the beginning of the Late Bronze Age.

CULTURAL UNITS

After the beginning of the Late Bronze Age the marked geographical differences in burial practices that had characterised the previous period became less pronounced. Nevertheless, a certain cultural discrepancy remained between, roughly speaking, the northern and southern half of the Netherlands. The cultural traditions of the western Netherlands have a few elements in common with those of the coastal zone in the north of the Netherlands, such as the three-aisled layout of the farms and possibly also the specific coastal burial practice, but otherwise the same north/south distinction characterising the settlement pottery of the rest of the Netherlands is also observable in the western Netherlands. The line dividing the distribution areas of the two pottery styles does not coincide with the course of the major rivers in the central Netherlands. For example, the distinctive Marnian pottery based on northern French types that was produced in the southern part of the Netherlands in the 5th century BC has also been encountered to the north of the Rhine, in the eastern part of the Netherlands. The rivers do not seem to have prevented contacts between the two regions. On the contrary, they will have been important trade arteries.

The distribution patterns of many of the objects that made their way into the Netherlands via trade or exchange show the same north/south division. We can use the metal objects as a guide in tracing the contacts they represent. The northern half of the country shows close cultural and exchange connections with northern Germany and Denmark, whereas the southern half was oriented far more towards Central Europe and – until in the Late Bronze Age – western France and Britain. These connections explain why Montelius' Scandinavian chronological framework, which extends to the end of the Early Iron Age, is often used for the northern part of the Netherlands. The Central European chronological and cultural terms Hallstatt (Ha) and La Tène (LT) are more commonly used for the part of the Netherlands to the south of the Rhine; the former culture was succeeded by the latter around 475 BC.

The degree of cultural uniformity varied with time. This is at least the impression created by the pottery, which was on the whole produced and distributed on a local level. Distinct regional styles can be distinguished within the pottery that was produced after the Early Iron Age. We cannot yet say to what extent the distribution areas of those regional pottery styles correspond to the tribal territories distinguished by Caesar and Tacitus around the beginning of the Christian era.[7]

fig. 21.2

The terms most commonly employed to refer to the cultures of the Late Bronze Age and the Iron Age in the Netherlands. The chronological boundaries between the archaeological cultures which Waterbolk (1985b) and Verlinde (1987) distinguished in the northern part of the Netherlands have been adjusted on the basis of recently acquired evidence.

years BC	period	culture		
		north		south
		Waterbolk	Verlinde	
12	Roman Period	Fries (Frisian)		
	Late Iron Age			
250	Middle Iron Age		Zeijen	
500	Early Iron Age	Zeijen		
800	Late Bronze Age	Sleen	Ems	Niederrheinische Grabhügelkultur
1100	Middle Bronze Age	Elp	Elp	Hilversum

(Urnfield Period spans Early Iron Age and Late Bronze Age rows)

480

The geographical and chronological cultural differences outlined above have found only little expression in the cultural terminology used in the Lower Rhine region. The earliest cultural units are the Ems culture[8] and the *Niederrheinische Grabhügelkultur*.[9] It is no coincidence that the final dates of the periods spanned by those cultures coincide with the final date of the urnfield period, as both are based exclusively on evidence from funerary contexts. In chronological terms, the Ems culture partly overlaps the Elp, Sleen and Zeijen cultures distinguished by other archaeologists (fig. 21.2);[10] its distribution area comprises the northeastern part of the Netherlands and the adjacent parts of Lower Saxony and Westphalia. The other terms have so far been used only for the northeastern part of the Netherlands (fig. 21.3).

The *Niederrheinische Grabhügelkultur* covers the eastern and southern parts of the Netherlands and the adjacent parts of Germany and Belgium. The term suggests that the area in question had a distinct cultural identity of its own; some archaeologists, however, class this area as the northwesternmost extension of the distribution area of the Urnfield culture.[11] Even when we consider the burial evidence in isolation it is not really possible to make any sharp cultural distinctions between the northern and southern parts of the Netherlands in this period.[12]

As far as the Middle and Late Iron Age are concerned, cultural units have been distinguished for the northern part of the Netherlands only. Waterbolk later simplified the chronological sequence he had set up for this region[13] by combining the proto-Frisian and Frisian cultures he had originally distinguished as the successors of the Zeijen culture into a single, Frisian, culture. The spatial limits of these cultures, which have never been strictly defined, are based mainly on the distribution area of the Ruinen-Wommels I-IV pottery types.

Due to the lack of grave goods from the entire Late Bronze Age and the Iron Age, little is known about the culture of the western Netherlands.[14] Several groups of settlement pottery have recently been identified on the basis of differences in stylistic features,[15] but they have much smaller distribution areas and show much less internal variation than the aforementioned cultures. As these cultures, some of which comprise exclusively burial evidence, have so far been only very summarily described, they will be rarely mentioned in the following chapters. In most cases geographical and chronological indications will suffice to define the relevant contexts.

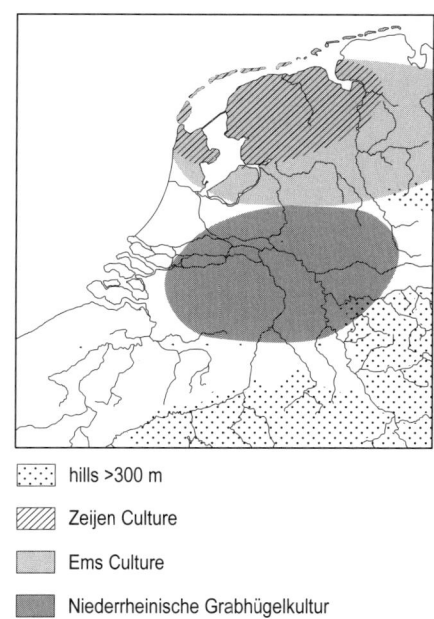

hills >300 m

Zeijen Culture

Ems Culture

Niederrheinische Grabhügelkultur

fig. 21.3
The geographical centres of archaeological cultures of the Late Bronze Age and Early Iron Age.

CHRONOLOGY

Dating problems

Although dendrochronological dates are now available, the chronology of the late prehistory of the Netherlands is still based substantially on a combination of stratigraphical evidence, ^{14}C dates and typological sequences of metal artefacts and pottery.

Only when, in the nineteen-eighties, a high degree of accuracy was obtained in the calibration of ^{14}C dates was it realized what little validity ^{14}C dates actually have for the chronology of the last phases of prehistory. Some archaeologists somewhat exaggeratedly spoke of 'the first millennium BC radiocarbon disaster'.[16] Owing to substantial fluctuations in the concentration of ^{14}C in the atmosphere between *c.* 800 and 400 BC, it is impossible, or very difficult, to place results between *c.* 2550 and 2400 BP within the indicated time span of four centuries. This is also the reason why we still don't know exactly when the first colonists moved onto the salt marshes. The available evidence cannot help us answer this question either, partly because of the still uncertain chronology of the Ruinen-Wommels I pottery.[17]

As far as the southern part of the Netherlands and the adjacent areas are concerned, the recent definition of a fine-scaled chronological sequence based on pottery assemblages from Oss-Ussen[18] has to some extent extenuated the problem of the undifferentiated section of the calibration curve. The quantitative approach that had to be used in defining this chronological sequence has also been applied to evidence from the western Netherlands.[19] Consequently, we are now able to present a more detailed description of the developments that took place in the Early and Middle Iron Age in the aforementioned two areas than of the contemporary developments in the other parts of the Netherlands.

Some period limits

In the northern part of the Netherlands and the adjacent part of Westphalia the beginning of the Urnfield period has on typological grounds been fixed around the transition from Hallstatt A1 to A2 (= the transition from Montelius' phase III to IV). Dendrochronological evidence has shown that in Central Europe this transition is to be dated before 1100 BC.[20] Several ^{14}C dates of between c. 3000 and 2950 BP[21] suggest dates in the 12th century at the latest, possibly earlier, for the oldest monuments. Further south, in the area extending up to the loess region, the oldest urnfield monuments are of a later date, from around the transition from Hallstatt A2 to B1, c. 1050 BC (2900-2850 BP).[22]

Only in the south of the Netherlands do the innovations in pottery coincide with changes in burial rites. In the northern urnfields the new pottery tradition was firmly established only around 1100 BC (2900 BP), i.e. after the introduction of the new funerary monuments.[23] In the general chronological chart (fig. 1.10) we have therefore fixed the beginning of the Late Bronze Age at the average date of 1100 BC.

It is difficult to define exact dates for the transition from the Bronze Age to the Iron Age if that transition is taken to mark the widespread introduction of iron technology. Only little iron waste and few iron artefacts have been preserved in the Netherlands. The date of 800 BC that we have adopted for this transition is based largely on evidence from Central Europe.[24] The exceptional early date of c. 1350 BC obtained for the – probably locally produced – wrought-iron pin that was found on a timber trackway in the peat near Barger-Oosterveld[25] is probably to be regarded as an exception.

The beginning of the Roman period – and the end of prehistory – has been fixed at 12 BC, the year in which Drusus used the rivers area in the central part of Netherlands as a base for his campaigns into the Elbe region. Although the campaigns that Caesar had previously led into the central part of the Netherlands around the middle of the first century BC had had devastating effects, there is no evidence to suggest that the territories covered in those campaigns were under Roman control before 12 BC.[26]

THE REPRESENTATIVITY OF THE EVIDENCE

A wide diversity of factors is responsible for the irregular distribution of sites across the Netherlands.[27] The numbers of finds per material also vary considerably. Particularly conspicuous is the small number of artefacts made from the metal that gives the Iron Age its name. In the next sections the most noteworthy gaps will be briefly discussed and explained where possible.

Geographical differentiation

In the Late Bronze Age and the Iron Age, mixed farming was the sole basis of existence. That implied reliance on arable land, pastures, timber and other resources. It is hence not surprising that settlements have been found mainly in zones that comprised a wide range of different types of landscapes and resources, such as the dunes and the edges of river and stream valleys.[28] But the less varied landscapes, like salt marshes and drained raised bogs, prove to have been well occupied, too. Until recently, the fertile loess region in the south of Limburg, on the contrary, seemed to have been surprisingly sparsely occupied.[29] However, a different picture has been emerging over the past few years, in which more surveys have been carried out in this region and find collections have been inventoried.[30]

The scarcity of sites in Zeeland is due to the poor preservation conditions of this area. Much evidence has disappeared in the sea. The same holds for the northern coastal region. We assume that the former salt marshes between Texel and northwest Friesland, where nowadays the Waddenzee lies, were as densely occupied as the adjacent *terpen* area of Friesland and Groningen.[31]

The distribution pattern of one of the settlement features characteristic of the sandy soils, i.e. the small fields marked out by low banks (Celtic fields), may also reflect differences in preservation conditions. It has been suggested that the scarcity of indications of Celtic fields to the south of the Rhine is due to the fact that the land reclamation activities in those regions had more drastic consequences than those further north, and were moreover carried out at an earlier date.[32] Much additional disturbance was caused in sod-cutting activities in the south. The fact that only very few hearths and no stall partitions whatsoever have been found in house plans unearthed in the south may again be attributed to poor preservation conditions.

The opposite situation is also encountered, namely there where occupation remains came to be buried beneath later deposits. This occurred in the coastal region (due to dune formation, sedimentation and peat growth) and in river valleys, but also on the higher sands. In the Middle Ages and later times the level of fields in some areas in the central and southern parts of the Netherlands, where the soil contains little loam, was raised with layers of sods, sand and litter. These layers, which are known as *Plaggen* soils or *es* covers and may be up to one metre thick, will have greatly improved the preservation conditions of any features buried beneath them, but at the same time they have reduced their chances of discovery.[33]

Chronological differentiation

Some regions show conspicuous absences of settlement sites from specific periods. In the peat and clay regions, in particular behind the coastal barriers, these gaps can be associated with the fact that wet conditions will from time to time have rendered these regions inaccessible, or at least economically unattractive. The peat lands of the western Netherlands, for example, show a hiatus in occupation in the 5th century BC (possibly also the 6th). Similar conditions appear to have affected the occupation of the rivers area in the central part of Netherlands, where the scarcity of both settlements and burials from the Late Bronze Age is associated with a period of sedimentation.[34]

In other regions our inability to set up chronological sequences is due to a lack of sufficient archaeological information. As the whole of the Netherlands has yielded only a few metal objects like ornaments and weapons, which usually prove to be of great chronological value elsewhere, we often have to rely on pottery, in

fig. 21.4

Distribution of the 55 sites with Middle Bronze Age barrows and the 210 urnfields from later periods found in the area between the Meuse, the Demer and the Scheldt. These numbers are unreliable indicators of the population density. Only a proportion of the deceased were buried in a barrow in the Middle Bronze Age, while the limited number of burials dating from the first half of the Middle Iron Age is more likely to be attributable to the poorer visibility of cremation burials from that period than to a decrease in population.

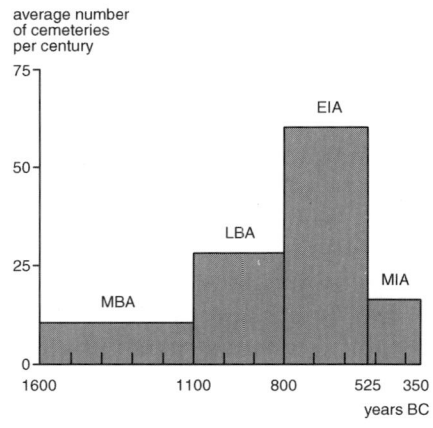

particular pottery found at settlements. And the fact that we actually know very little about the settlement pottery of the Late Bronze Age explains why such a remarkably small number of settlements from this period have so far been identified. It could well be that several of the sites that have been dated to the Iron Age are actually of Late Bronze Age date. The relatively large number of Late Bronze Age burials found in urnfields probably provides a better indication of the settlement density in this period.

In the south of the Netherlands in particular, settlements greatly outnumber burials from the Middle Iron Age onwards. This development must be attributed to changes in burial rites that reduced the archaeological visibility of the burials (fig. 21.4). After the Early Iron Age the custom of burying remains in urns, accompanied by grave goods, gradually died out, as did the practice of surrounding burials by peripheral structures.

That the southern and central parts of the Netherlands continued to be densely occupied in the Late Iron Age can be inferred not so much from occupation remains or burials, which are both fairly scarce, but from the large numbers of fragments of imperishable glass bracelets and rings that have come to light in these areas.

We still have no idea what burial rites were practised in the western and northern coastal regions in the last millennium of prehistory. Since hundreds of settlements have been found in those regions, the conspicuous absence of burial evidence probably means that the population of the coastal regions did not adopt the burial rites that started to be practised in other parts of the Netherlands after the Middle Bronze Age. The urnfield closest to the coast is that which was found on the Westerheide near Hilversum.[35]

Material differentiation

The different materials that were used in late prehistoric times have been preserved in greatly varying amounts, depending on their physical properties and the environments in which they were deposited. There where archaeological finds have been preserved beneath the water level, for example in peats, stream beds or wells, or have otherwise been sealed off from the atmosphere, for example because they were buried beneath clay deposits, we obtain a fuller picture of the material culture and the subsistence (thanks to preserved floral and faunal remains) than on the higher sandy soils. This makes it so regrettable that – due to the employed collection method – only few of the many organic remains recovered from the terpen can be dated to specific periods.[36] Only very little use can hence be made of this potentially informative category of archaeological finds in the discussion of the material culture (see chapter 27).

The fact that more bronze than iron objects are known from the Iron Age will be largely due to the latter metal's poorer resistance to corrosion. Apart from that, this scarcity must in part also be attributable to developments in cultural traditions. The custom of depositing metal objects (hoards) in watery environments died out when iron started to be used as a raw material. The evidence suggests that around the beginning of the Iron Age prestige objects started to be buried in graves instead,[37] but in those contexts the conditions for the preservation of iron were less favourable. Moreover, the archaeological visibility of these later graves is much poorer because the deceased were accompanied by increasingly fewer grave goods from the 6th century BC onwards.

fig. 21.5
The urnfield on the Boshoverheide near Weert is one of the exceptional sites where many of the barrows have remained visible. Several of the barrows have incidentally been restored to their original shape.

HISTORY OF THE RESEARCH

The earliest archaeological interest aroused in the Netherlands concerned the remains visible aboveground, which were believed to be ancient largely on account of the legends that revolved around them. The visible archaeological remains from the Late Bronze Age and the Iron Age comprise mounds, Celtic fields ('heathen camps'), which Johan Picardt, a minister from Coevorden, described as early as 1660, and *terpen*. It is hence not surprising that the northeastern part of the Netherlands, where many of these remains are to be found, have attracted the attention of scholars with a professional interest in late prehistory at an early date. This interest will have been greatly increased by the unusual finds that came to light in peat-cutting operations in those same areas (bog trackways, bog bodies, votive deposits), especially in the 19th and the first half of the 20th century.

When we consider the Netherlands as a whole, however, until about 1960 the great majority of the archaeological finds came from the many urnfields. For many centuries, the mounds that had been thrown up over the graves in late prehistoric times were poorly recognisable as many of those mounds, which were on average smaller than the barrows of the preceding periods, were overgrown, lying as they then did in forested areas. However, as the heaths expanded, they became increasingly conspicuous and in the nineteenth and early twentieth centuries many fell prey to treasure hunters or were destroyed through ignorance during the major heath reclamation projects before scientific interest gained the upper hand (fig. 21.5).[38] But even the archaeological excavations of barrows that were conducted in the nineteenth century were aimed at little more than the collection of urns and grave goods. Features – in particular of peripheral structures – escaped attention, find contexts were only rarely recorded and many of the unearthed remains were lost during the excavation or afterwards. Even the most sincere amateur archaeologists would sometimes investigate more than ten barrows in one day.

The introduction, in the first decades of the twentieth century, of systematic and better documented excavation of urnfields by J.H. Holwerda of the Leiden National Museum of Antiquities and A.E. van Giffen of the *Biologisch-Archaeologisch Instituut* of Groningen University marked the beginning of a period of major advances in urnfield research. The excavation of the urnfield of De Hamert, near Venlo, is a good example of the work that was done in that early period.[39] Urnfields continued to attract much attention until 1960-1970, when the emphasis shifted to settlement research. In the northern part of the Netherlands settlement research had got well under way relatively early – and on a large scale from the very start – thanks to the advanced excavation method developed by Van Giffen.[40] He had first used this method in his renowned excavation of the plans of farms on the *terpen* of Friesland and Groningen in the first decades of the twentieth century. In 1934 he excavated the fortified settlement of Zeijen on the sandy soils of Drenthe. Thanks to these efforts, H.T. Waterbolk was able to select from a wealth of settlement finds for his 1962 survey of the Iron Age occupation of the northern Netherlands. In 1948, in writing his survey of the *Niederrheinische Grabhügelkultur* further south, W. Kersten had still had to rely exclusively on burial evidence; even the more comprehensive study by Desittere, which was published in 1968, was, from sheer necessity, based solely on evidence from funerary contexts.

From the end of the 1950s onwards the gap in our knowledge of settlements, especially outside the northern part of the Netherlands, was gradually filled thanks to the efforts of the various archaeological departments and organisations of amateur archaeologists. The western Netherlands, which, due to the complete absence of burials, had hitherto been a blank space on the archaeological map of the first millennium BC, proved to have been densely occupied, even in the peat regions.[41]

Until in the 1970s research in the form of field surveys and the analysis of artefacts focused on the definition of typological sequences and the establishment of regional variations in burial rites, house plans and material objects. Research in the *terpen* area sparked off studies into the relations between prehistoric man and his changing environment at an early date. Grave goods and other material objects, such as votive deposits, led to conclusions regarding differences in status ('princely burials'), trade contacts and migrations. Distribution maps were used to distinguish different ethnic groups, in particular in the period just before the appearance of historical sources. The contents of those historical sources, especially those of Caesar and Tacitus, will certainly have contributed much to the tendency to interpret (assumed) cultural discontinuities in terms of invasions and conquests. Chronologically significant points such as the beginning of the Late Bronze Age and the beginning of the Iron Age were for example associated with 'Urnfield invasions' and an 'invasion of Hallstatt warriors', respectively.[42]

fig. 21.6
Harvesting grain with a replica of a flint sickle. After use the traces on the surface are microscopically compared with those on the prehistoric artefact.

As the available evidence increased – in particular that on settlements – a better chronological perspective emerged, field surveys were expanded to embrace entire regions, and previously untouched topics became objects of study. This development enabled Waterbolk to advance his thesis based on 'shifting settlements', relative to fixed urnfields.[43] By integrating evidence from burials and settlements (including botanical and zoological evidence) and reconstructing former environments, it proved possible to calculate demographic figures and to express aspects of the agricultural economy in quantitative terms.[44] Around the end of the 1970s the views of processual archaeology inspired a new research topic, namely the relations between the various settlements within a particular region.[45]

After the results of the aforementioned studies on regions in the northern and western parts of the Netherlands had been published, Roymans presented an integrated study of the macroregion between the Rhine and the Seine in the last five hundred years of prehistory, in which he also paid ample attention to the social and ideological aspects of the communities that inhabited that region.[46]

Over the years, the objectives of the study of material cultures changed only very little. In the analysis of the most extensive find category, i.e. pottery, the emphasis remained on the determination of typological sequences and distribution patterns. Only very little systematic research was carried out into the origins, technological aspects and functions of the vessels.[47] Experimental replication was found to be a useful aid in determining technical and economic functions and the life spans of other classes of artefacts (fig. 21.6).[48] In the case of flint sickles, experimental replication combined with microwear studies has even yielded unexpected results.[49] As for other aspects of material culture, reference should be made here to the increased efforts to place certain elements of material culture in their social, ritual and ideological contexts, whether or not in the tradition of contextual archaeology.[50] Of interest in this respect is that finds recovered in dredging operations – a poor category of finds from a methodical viewpoint – have in fact proven to be a source of extremely relevant information.

CURRENT RESEARCH TOPICS

The topics that determine the main course of current research projects or play major parts in those projects can be split into two main groups: first of all topics concerning relations between the environment, settlement and the subsistence economy and secondly topics relating to socio-political, ritual and cognitive aspects of societies.

The first field of study is directly connected with the research of the past. In geographical terms the emphasis of this study is on the coastal region, the most dynamic part of the Netherlands as far as this topic is concerned.[51] An important aspect of this research topic is the way in which a particular community exploited the different environments (exploitation zones), either in the context of the annual economic cycle,[52] or in successive occupation phases. A specific question in the latter case is whether the permanent settlement, at the end of the Early Iron Age, of the salt marshes that had recently emerged from the sea in the north of the Netherlands was preceded by a phase of transhumance.[53]

Thanks to the peculiar preservation conditions of the coastal zone we have sound evidence for the reconstruction of the former environment and the agricultural economy. Of crucial importance with respect to the evidence for the extensive occupation of the peat along the western coast is the question of the agricultural potential of this environmental zone, in particular its potential for crop cultivation.[54]

Large-scale research projects focusing on the same topics are now also being carried out in the less dynamic hinterland.[55] In view of this area's poorer opportunities for ecological research (little organic material has survived due to the poor preservation conditions) the emphasis of these projects is by sheer necessity on settlements and their dynamics. A separate study is being carried out into the question as to whether the settlements remained within the limits of specific territories over long periods of time, in spite of the fact that the farms were constantly rebuilt at different locations.[56] The void which until recently characterised our knowledge of Bronze Age and Early Iron Age settlements is now slowly being filled.[57]

The second major research topic relates to the socio-political, ritual and cognitive aspects of late prehistoric societies – aspects which until recently received only marginal and incidental attention in the Netherlands. The only possible exception concerns the efforts that have been made to reconstruct burial rites and to interpret votive deposits and other unusual finds recovered from the peat bogs in the northeastern part of the Netherlands in terms of sacrificial and other rites. The latter finds are still receiving a good deal of attention, only the emphasis has now shifted more towards social and demographic aspects.[58] An additional (socio-political) element in the interpretation of votive deposits is the prestige-enhancing effect of the deliberate destruction or removal from circulation of offerings.[59]

In the cognitive research that is currently being carried out specific attention is being paid to the domestic environment, too. This is for example apparent in the studies into the non-profane selection of types of timber for the construction of farms and the symbolic significance of hearths.[60] Prehistoric man's perception of his natural and domestic environments is a factor that is being considered in attempts to explain why certain choices were made, for example why new environments were colonised.[61]

Socio-political, ritual and cognitive aspects are closely interrelated in a recently launched comprehensive study into elites and their power networks in a long-term diachronic context.[62] This study is largely based on results of the analysis of deposits and grave goods; specific attention is being paid to the elite's economic basis.

Now that the possibilities of determining the sex and age of cremated remains have increased, we are finally in a position to infer demographic data from late prehistoric burials. The amount of urnfield research may have decreased considerably since the 1970s, but the remains that were excavated in the past – at least those which have been separately and carefully preserved – constitute an extensive source of additional information which is now being tapped.[63]

For practical reasons some of the topics that will be dealt with in the following chapters will cover the entire Bronze Age and the Iron Age and not just the Late Bronze Age and the Iron Age. In particular, this holds for cult practices (chapter 29) and the subsistence economy (chapter 22), which was dominated by integrated mixed farming from the beginning of the Bronze Age onwards.[64]

1   Janssen 1974; see also Groenman-van Waateringe 1988a.

2   Zagwijn 1986, 17.

3   Fokkens 1991a; Waterbolk 1988.

4   Bierma et al. 1988.

5   Van Heeringen 1988b and 1992.

6   Louwe Kooijmans 1985; Waterbolk 1988.

7   But see Bloemers 1978, 99; Van den Broeke 1987b, 111; Waterbolk 1985a, 70.

8   Verlinde 1987.

9   Kersten 1948; see also Verlinde 1987.

10 Kooi 1979; Waterbolk 1985.

11 For a summary see Ruppel 1985, note 2.

12 Krause 1989, 107, as opposed to Verlinde 1987, 292. The low mounds (Grabhügel), which Kersten incorporated in the culture's name, to distinguish them from both the large Hügelgräber of the preceding period and the mostly flat graves of the Urnfield culture, we also find in the north of the Netherlands. That is why the term 'Lower Rhine Urnfield groups' (Roymans 1991, fig. 9) is sometimes also used for the whole area between the Scheldt basin and the lower Weser.

13 Waterbolk 1962 and Waterbolk 1985a, respectively.

14 See on the contrary Verlinde 1987, 292 ff. and the comments in Brandt 1988a, 219.

15 Van Heeringen 1992.

16 Baillie/Pilcher 1983, 58.

17 Boersma 1988a; Taayke 1990a, 1990b.

18 Van den Broeke 1987a.

19 Van Heeringen 1992; Van Trierum et al. 1988.

20 Chronologie... 1986.

21 Verlinde 1987.

22 Van den Broeke 1991; Ruppel 1985.

23 Cf. Kooi 1979, 147; Verlinde 1987, 288-289.

24 A date of 800 BC has been assumed for the beginning of the Gündlingen phase distinguished by Pare (1991); its end has been fixed at 720/700 BC. In spite of the fact that this phase is characterised by bronze swords of the Gündlingen type and the transition to iron (Mindelheim) swords did not take place until in the 7th century BC, Pare classes the Gündlingen phase as part of the Central European Hallstatt period (Ha C/D, Early Iron Age).

25 Casparie 1984, 62.

26 Van Es 1981, 25 ff.; Willems 1986a, 24.

27 Cf. maps in Van Es et al. 1988, 81 ff.

28 Cf. Harsema 1982.

29 Van Es et al. 1988, 81 ff.

30 E.g. Dijkman 1989, 3; Van der Graaf 1989.

31 Van Es et al. 1988, 84.

32 Cf. Roymans 1990, 101.

33 Cf. Groenewoudt 1994.

34 Cf. Louwe Kooijmans 1993.

35 Wimmers 1988.

36 Cf. Miedema 1983.

37 Roymans 1991.

38 E.g. Addink-Samplonius 1983.

39 Holwerda n.d.

40 Survey in Waterbolk 1989, 1990b.

41 Wind 1973.

42 E.g. De Laet/Glasbergen 1959; De Laet 1979.

43 Waterbolk 1982 and Kooi 1979, respectively.

44 Brandt/IJzereef 1980; Brongers 1976a; Harsema 1980a, 1980b; Kooi 1979.

45 Brandt et al. 1986; see also Therkorn 1991.

46 Roymans 1990.

47 Van den Broeke 1986, 1987b; Franken/Kalsbeek 1984; Van der Leeuw et al. 1987.

48 Harsema 1979 and 1985.

49 Van Gijn 1988.

50 Garthoff-Zwaan 1987; Roymans 1990; Roymans/Van der Sanden 1980; Therkorn 1987b.

51 Cf. ROB 1990 Annual Report, 19; Abbink 1993a; Bierma et al. 1988; Bloemers 1988; Bosman/Therkorn 1993; Fokkens 1991a; Van Heeringen 1992; Van Trierum 1992; Woltering 1991b.

52 Cf. Brandt/Van Gijn 1986.

53 Van Gijn/Waterbolk 1984; Waterbolk 1988.

54 Brinkkemper 1993.

55 Fokkens 1991b; Kooi 1991-'92; Schinkel 1994.

56 Waterbolk 1987.

57 Fokkens/Roymans 1991.

58 Butler 1986; Van der Sanden 1990.

59 Fokkens 1991a, 87; Roymans 1991.

60 Garthoff-Zwaan 1987 and Therkorn 1987a and 1987b, respectively.

61 Brandt 1988b; Van der Waals 1987.

62 Roymans/Theuws 1991.

63 Cf. ROB 1990 Annual Report, 30.

64 Since this introduction was written, the view that the climate had only little influence on late prehistoric occupation has been disputed (Van Geel et al. 1997). In the meantime a (commercial) English edition (Fokkens 1998a) of the work on the drowning landscape at the periphery of the Frisian-Drentian plateau (Fokkens 1991a) has been published.

22 All-round farming
Food production in the Bronze Age
and the Iron Age

Otto Brinkkemper and Louise van Wijngaarden-Bakker

INTRODUCTION

A recurrent question in reconstructions of subsistence economies of the past concerns the ratio of crop cultivation and stock keeping. Conclusions regarding the relative importance of different crops, crop yields and consumption figures sometimes have to be drawn from evidence comprising little more than a few grams of carbonised cereal grain. Another complicating factor is that the chance of recovery of the different crops varies: oil-yielding seeds stand a smaller chance of being recovered than cereal grain, whereas the chances of legumes being found are virtually nil.[1]

Something similar also holds for animal remains: bones of small species are preserved less frequently because they are more easily crushed or erode more rapidly than large bones. The employed butchering methods and gnawing by dogs are examples of other taphonomic processes (*i.e.* processes that take place between an animal's death and the ultimate excavation of its preserved remains) that greatly influence the chances of preservation, and hence the possibility of quantifying animal remains. Due to such factors, the evidence available for the Netherlands is unequally distributed. For the fluvial and marine clay regions we have both archaeobotanical and zooarchaeological evidence. As for the latter category, however, unless they have come into contact with fire or are submerged beneath the groundwater, bones do not survive in peat, sand or decalcified loess. This means that very little evidence on stock keeping is available for the parts of the Netherlands outside the clay regions, and our reconstruction of the agricultural economy is consequently strongly biased. In the following discussion, the subsistence economy will therefore be dealt with per ecological zone.

RIVER AREAS

Environment

Today, the flood plains of the major Dutch rivers are covered with vast meadows. All riverine forests have disappeared in the Netherlands and adjacent areas. Elsewhere in Europe, in particular along the Danube and the Loire, the riverine forests show a marked similarity due to the dynamic nature of the floods (fig. 22.1). In areas that are flooded to some extent in the summer we find softwood forests of willows and poplars (fig. 22.2). Hardwood riverine forests cover the highest parts of the flood plains, which are flooded only briefly in the summer. They are dominated by oak, followed by elm and ash.[2] The relief of the flood plains ensures the survival of a varied mosaic of forest ecosystems with numerous different transitional forms at the margins of open grassland vegetations. We may assume that both types of riverine forests bordered the rivers in the Netherlands in prehistoric times. Due to frequent sedimentation during floods, the soils of the levees were

fig. 22.1
River bank forests along the Danube. The presence of gulleys alongside the main riverbed makes this landscape comparable with the drainage basin of the river Waal.

fig. 22.2
Model of a riverbank with a vegetation cover showing the high-water levels in summer (a) and winter (b). The water levels have a strong influence on the composition of riverine forests. Areas which are flooded for long periods in summer favour the development of softwood forests, with poplars and willows (c). Higher up the banks hardwood forests may develop, with oaks, ash and elms (d).

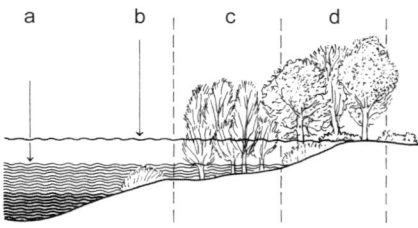

rich in minerals. As they were eminently suited to crop cultivation, they were already deforested on a large scale in prehistoric times.

The riverine forests constituted a favourable habitat for herbivores of all sizes, such as red deer, elks and beavers. For human communities whose economies were largely dependent on hunting, the wealth of natural resources to be found in the river areas made them very attractive for temporary settlement. Several of such temporarily occupied settlements, which are known as 'extraction camps', are known from the Bronze Age.

Bronze Age subsistence

Two sites have yielded evidence of the seasonal exploitation of the natural resources of the riverine forests. One of the two is the site P14 in the Noordoostpolder, situated in the former estuary of the Vecht river in Overijssel. Bones of game (mainly beaver and red deer) and large amounts of bones of freshwater fish (different cyprinid species, eel and pike) dating from the Early Bronze Age have been interpreted as the remains of a fishing camp (fig. 22.3, see also fig. 10.5).[3] The absence of indications of permanent occupation or of crop cultivation suggests that this settlement was a seasonal camp which was probably occupied in the summer only. The few bones of domestic animals encountered may be the remains of food that was brought along to the camp or of animals that were pastured in the flood plains in the summer. An unusual aspect of the cattle bones is that they show no signs of the decrease in size generally attested by faunal assemblages from the Middle and Late Bronze Age: apparently this process had not yet started (in this area).

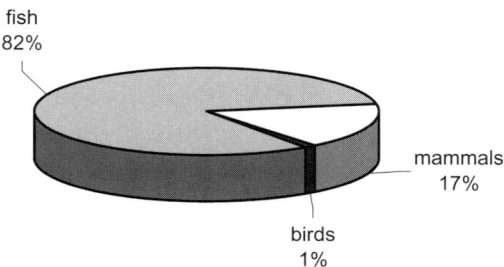

fish
82%

mammals
17%

birds
1%

The excavation of a settlement near Oldeboorn in Friesland also yielded indications of the seasonal exploitation of the wealth of resources of a river area.[4] The environmental conditions of this site were slightly different. The subsistence activities of the early Middle Bronze Age occupants of the site, which was situated on a small dune in the valley of the Boorne surrounded by peat, included both hunting and fishing. Hunting focused on beavers, while 84% of the recovered fish remains were of pike. This indicates that the camp was used in the early spring, when pike spawns, and often cluster in large groups close to the stream banks. A conspicuous aspect of these pike remains is the large proportion of parts of the heads. This could indicate that the fish were cleaned and preserved at the site.[5]

The extraction camps did not constitute the base of the subsistence economy, though. Agricultural settlements with a strong emphasis on cattle keeping, such as those at Zijderveld and Dodewaard in the central part of the Netherlands, are more representative of the Bronze Age subsistence economy of the fluvial area (fig. 22.4).

Iron Age subsistence

A somewhat different picture emerges for the subsistence economy of the Iron Age settlements in the river areas. Reconstructions of crop cultivation are still entirely based on the results of the analysis of samples from the surrounding peat regions. Pollen analysis of samples from Voorne-Putten revealed a decline in oak and elm in the Early Iron Age; the hardwood riverine forests on the levees bordering the Meuse were reduced by more than fifty percent. Although the levees in the Meuse estuary have disappeared completely due to later erosion (Dunkirk III), we know from the analysis of seeds from settlements on these levees that crops were most probably grown there. Their soils were very suitable for the cultivation of (summer) cereals and for horticulture. The grassland that was formed in the clearances in the flood plains was suitable for grazing.

Cattle dominate the bone spectra of the settlements in the river areas (fig. 22.4), always followed by sheep/goat remains. The second category will have been almost exclusively sheep, as the wet conditions were less favourable for goats.[6] Pigs ranked third in importance.

Noteworthy is the consistent presence of horse remains. What role horses played in the subsistence economy of this and the other ecological zones we do not know. Although there are indications that horse meat was eaten, horses seem to have had a different status from the other domestic animals. This is for example apparent from the lower degree of fragmentation of long bones among the remains and from the burials of (parts of) horses that have been found. The harness or breast collar, which made it possible to use horses for strenuous work, such as ploughing and pulling heavy carts, was not invented until about the 8th century AD.[7] Oxen were the main draught animals. Horses will have been used for riding

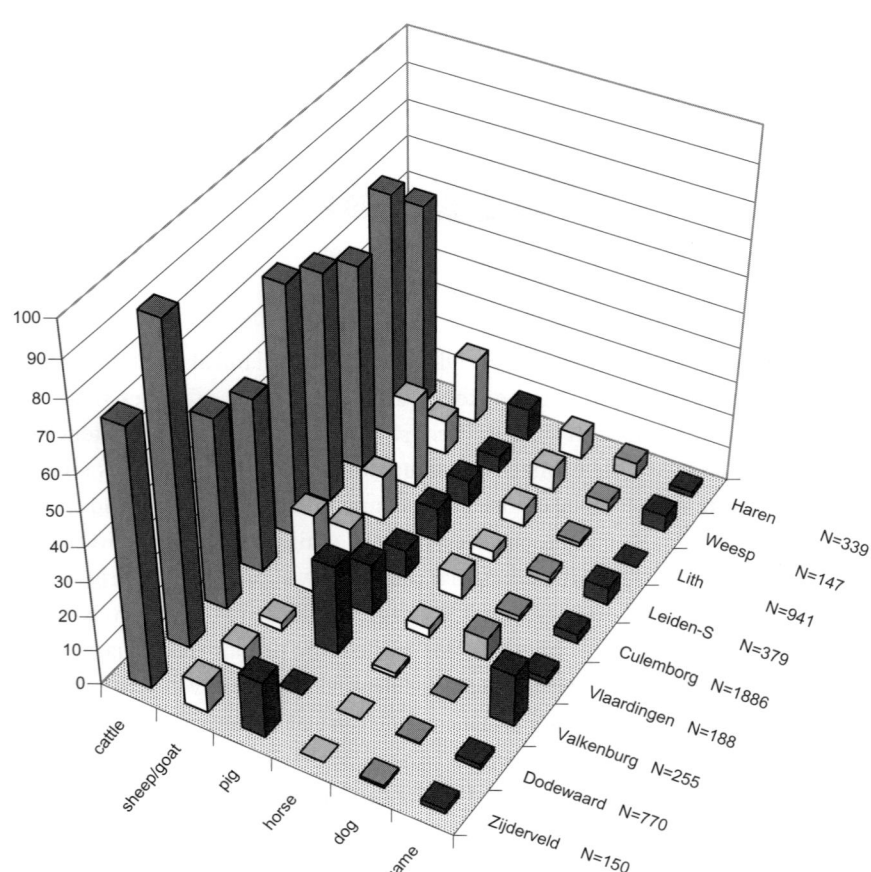

fig. 22.4

The ratios of the different domestic animals at various settlements in river areas in percentages of identified fragments. N = total number of identifications.

Iron Age	Haren
Late Iron Age	Weesp
	Lith
Middle Iron Age	Leiden-Stevenshof
	Culemborg
	Vlaardingen-De Wetering
Early Iron Age	Valkenburg
Middle Bronze Age	Dodewaard
	Zijderveld

and/or for bearing loads, but will certainly also have given their owners status.

Dog meat seems to have been consumed in exceptional cases only. The remains of uncommonly large dogs found at Iron Age settlements suggest that dogs were being kept specifically for guarding or defending property in late prehistoric times already.

The intensive occupation of the stream ridges and the expansion of grassland at the expense of the riverine forests will have led to a decrease in the density of game over the centuries. Nevertheless, all the Iron Age bone spectra of river areas have produced evidence for hunting, in particular of herbivores such as red and roe deer (fig. 22.4). Some sites have yielded information on fishing. The occupants of Lith for example, a site along the Meuse, caught freshwater fish, mainly pike and different kinds of cyprinids. Anadromous fish,[8] such as salmon, shad and twaite, were conspicuously absent at this site. Sturgeon was caught in river areas closest to the coast, for example at Valkenburg and Spijkenisse. Sturgeons making their way towards their spawning areas were being caught in this area in the Neolithic already, and were still caught there up to the beginning of the 20th century. Finds of sturgeon remains at Weesp and Baambrugge indicate that some sturgeons penetrated into the smaller channels further inland.[9]

THE WESTERN NETHERLANDS IN THE BRONZE AGE

The dune belt

In the coastal region, the importance of hunting already started to decline in the Early Bronze Age. This could indicate a considerable decrease in the density of

494

wild animals. The bone assemblage of a site in the dunes near Vogelenzang, for example, includes about a hundred bones of cattle, while wild animals were only represented by a few remains of grey seal.[10] Red deer is frequently encountered in Bronze Age bone spectra, but the remains in question are almost always fragments of antler, and they do not necessarily imply hunting in the vicinity: shed antler will have been a useful raw material. As for stock keeping, all the known domestic animals are represented: cattle, sheep/goat, pig and – from this period onwards – horse.

Ard marks have been recorded extensively in the dunes (fig. 22.5), in particular in the Velserbroekpolder, but the developments in the subsistence economy during the Middle and Late Bronze Age are best illustrated by the results of the thorough ecological research carried out at the settlement of Het Valkje at Bovenkarspel (Westfrisia). They have presented us with a detailed outline of the changes that took place in the agricultural system.

Farming at Bovenkarspel

The environment

At Bovenkarspel, crops were cultivated on the low stream ridges of fine-grained sand whose formation was completed in the first stage of the Dunkirk 0 transgression. At first, settlement concentrated mainly on the flanks of the ridges rising from the surrounding salt marshes. Archaeobotanical and zooarchaeological analyses have both yielded useful data for the reconstruction of the former environment. Four biotopes have been distinguished on the basis of the results of the identification of sieved remains of rodents (fig. 22.6):

 – extensively grazed pastures (root vole and water vole);

fig. 22.5
Intersecting *ard* marks preserved beneath drift sand in the dunes near Haarlem. The fields in question date from the Middle and Late Bronze Age.

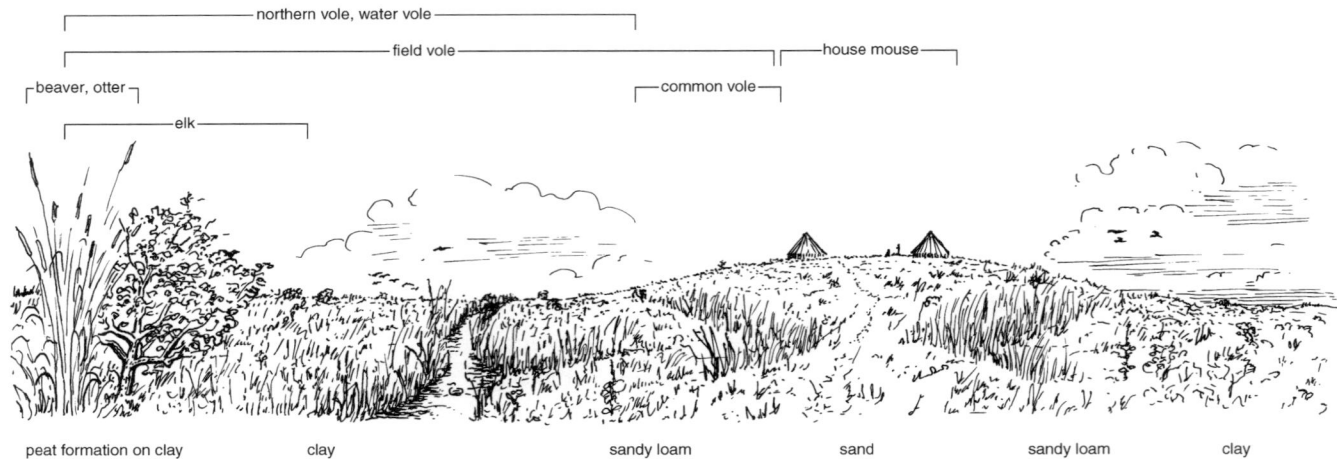

fig. 22.6

Schematic representation of the Bovenkarspel-Het Valkje settlement in the Middle Bronze Age showing the different soils (bottom) and the habitats of various animals (top).

– a transitional zone between clay and arable land (field vole);
– arable and fallow land (field mouse);
– houses and yards containing areas for grain storage (house mouse).

In the later part of this period these biotopes must have lain close together, because then water vole in particular was to be found near the houses.

The archaeobotanical evidence indicates that the landscape was open in the Middle Bronze Age, dotted with only a few willows or alders. The cereal remains found at the various sites were mixed with seeds of weeds characteristic of rich soils. The seeds of plants like nettle, members of the goosefoot family, common chickweed and black nightshade in particular are indicative of manuring. The splinters of bone and small sherds that have been found in furrows make it likely that manure (mixed with household refuse) was spread over the fields.

Crop cultivation

The first occupants of Het Valkje practised mixed farming. In the colonisation phase they grew only naked barley (*Hordeum vulgare* var. *nudum*), but they very soon started to grow the hulled variety (*Hordeum vulgare* var. *vulgare*) instead. Hulled barley presents the advantage that the grains, being hulled, are less susceptible to fungus infections and damage caused by pests. Hulled grain can also be stored better and larger yields can be obtained. All over the Netherlands the importance of naked barely decreased in the Bronze Age in favour of that of the hulled variety. By the beginning of the Iron Age naked barley had disappeared almost completely (tables 22.1 and 22.5). At Bovenkarspel emmer was also cultivated, besides hulled barley.

	upland				Westfrisia					river clay
	Son en Breugel	Oss - Ussen	Emmerhout	Elp	Twisk	Bovenkarspel	Opperdoes	Bovenkarspel	Opperdoes	Zijderveld
emmer	•	-	•	•	•	•	•	-	-	•
naked barley	-	-	•	•	•	•	•	•	-	-
hulled barley	•	•	-	•	-	•	•	-	•	•
millet	•	-	-	•	-	-	-	-	-	-
linseed	-	-	-	-	-	-	-	-	•	-
Bronze Age:	Middle		Middle/Late		Middle			Late		Middle

table 22.1

Cultivated crops in Bronze Age settlements.

496

The unthreshed grain was stored inside ring ditches, which ensured drainage.[11] The botanical contents of the fills of two such ring ditches have been investigated. They were found to consist of large amounts of carbonised grain (in one case 95% hulled barley, in the other 80% emmer), large amounts of chaff and straw fragments and seeds of both tall and low field weeds. Buurman concluded that the two different types of cereal were grown in separate fields.[12] The threshing and winnowing were probably both done near the houses, as large amounts of the waste produced in these processes were found in and around the house plans.

The analysis of the remains of amphibia and freshwater molluscs shows that conditions became much wetter in the Late Bronze Age,[13] making it impossible for the occupants to continue to grow emmer. All the cereal remains from this period are of hulled barley. Another crop that was cultivated in this period is flax.[14] The few seeds of oats and rape that have been found are more likely to have belonged to field weeds than to cultivated plants.[15]

Hulled barley, emmer and flax were also grown in other parts of this area. It has been argued on basis of samples with a mixed composition that the two types of cereal were cultivated together, in the same fields.[16] The great differences in the threshing processes of these cereals however make this rather unlikely.

Stock keeping

The simultaneous developments in stock keeping can be inferred from the zooarchaeological data obtained by IJzereef.[17] The number of bones that could be attributed to specific species and the minimum number of individuals in figure 22.7 both indicate a decrease, in the course of the Bronze Age, in the importance of cattle in favour of sheep (and probably also goats) and to a lesser extent pigs.[18] Horse bones are conspicuously absent among the Late Bronze Age remains.

The cattle were slaughtered at an early age. They were small animals, with withers heights f between 93 and 123 cm (figs. 22.8 and 22.9). The ratio of cows, bulls and oxen has been calculated on the basis of the differences in the shapes and sizes of the horn cores (fig. 22.10). Cows and oxen predominated in the Middle Bronze Age. The large proportion of cows indicates that they were kept for their meat. The oxen will have been used as draught animals, for example for the ploughs. The decrease in the proportion of oxen in the Late Bronze Age may hence suggest that crop cultivation became less important in the agricultural system. However, in view of the small absolute numbers of cattle bones from the period in question we must be careful not to jump to conclusions.

The farms of Bovenkarspel had large byres; part of the stock will have been stalled in the winter, at least at night. Due to a lack of uncarbonised botanical remains from the byres we do not know what the animals were fed in the wintertime. An added advantage of stalling, besides that of better control, was that manure could be collected, which could then be used to fertilise the soil of the fields.

On the basis of the age ratios in the bone assemblages it is assumed that cows were milked in the Late Bronze Age, but the bones provide no direct evidence, only an indication. Runia attempted to obtain such evidence by subjecting animal and human bones to chemical research.[19] The analyses concentrated mainly on the element strontium, which can be used as an indicator of diet. Bones of herbivores have relatively high strontium concentrations, whereas those of carnivores yield low values. The strontium values of omnivorous human beings lie somewhere between those of absolute herbivores and absolute carnivores.[20] The strontium is stored in the bones and its ultimate concentration remains virtually unaffected, even after long periods of burial in the soil.

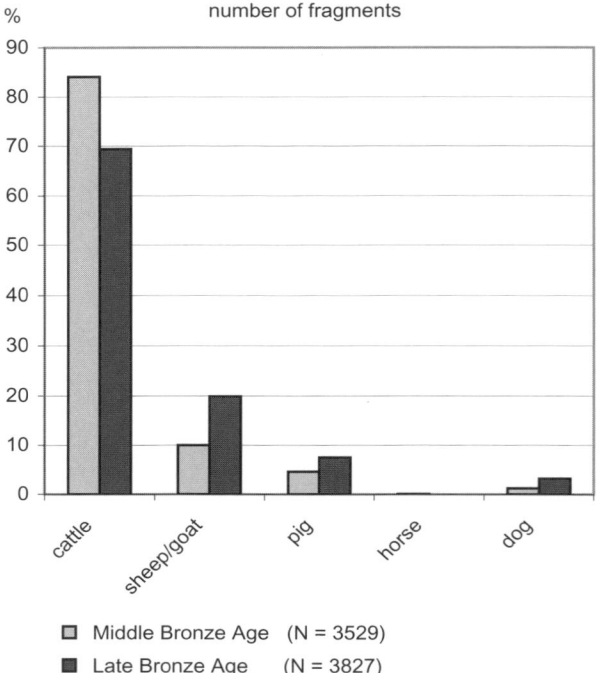

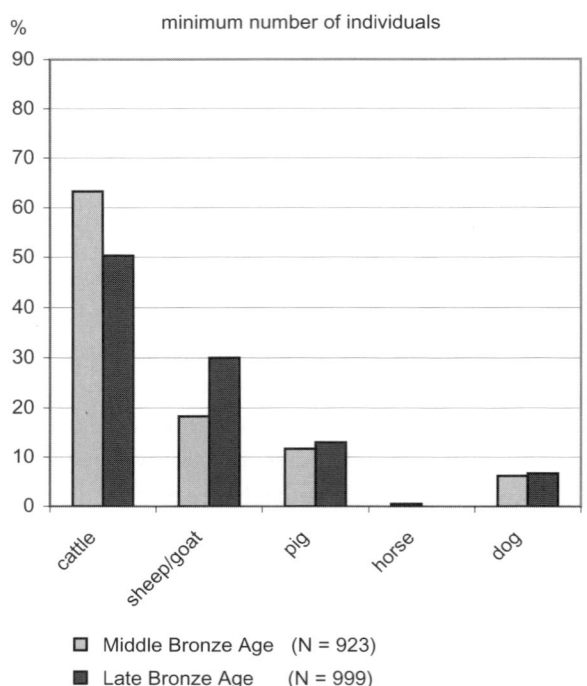

fig. 22.7

Domestic animals at Bovenkarspel-Het Valkje, numbers of identified fragments and minimum numbers of individuals. Middle Bronze Age N=80, Late Bronze Age N=20.

The analysis of the strontium contents of human and animal bones from Bovenkarspel yielded some unexpected results (table 22.2). Runia assumed that the observed differences between cattle and sheep/goat, both of which are herbivores, were due to the fact that the animals had been pastured in different areas. According to his model, the cattle were kept in the immediate vicinity of the settlement, whereas the sheep were pastured further away. As the landscape surrounding the settlement was virtually treeless, the pigs will have been kept in and around the farm and will have been fed exclusively plant food. This explains why their strontium contents correspond to those of herbivores. The bones of the dogs quite unexpectedly yielded high strontium values, possibly due to the gnawing of sheep bones.

Virtually no differences were observed between the Middle Bronze Age and Late Bronze Age values, except in the case of sheep/goat, whose strontium contents were found to increase. They may have been more frequently pastured closer to the sea, where the vegetation had higher strontium contents. According to Runia's model, however, the ratio of vegetal and animal food did not change. IJzereef's proposed increase in the amounts of milk consumed was neither confirmed nor denied by the chemical research, but the increased strontium contents of the hu-

fig. 22.8

Bovenkarspel-Het Valkje, burial of a complete cow.

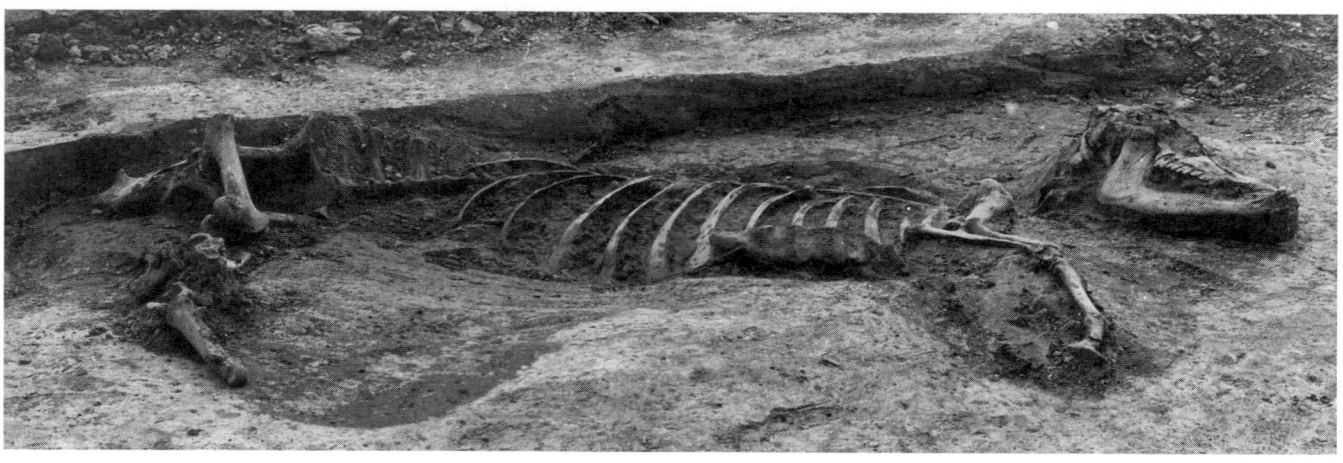

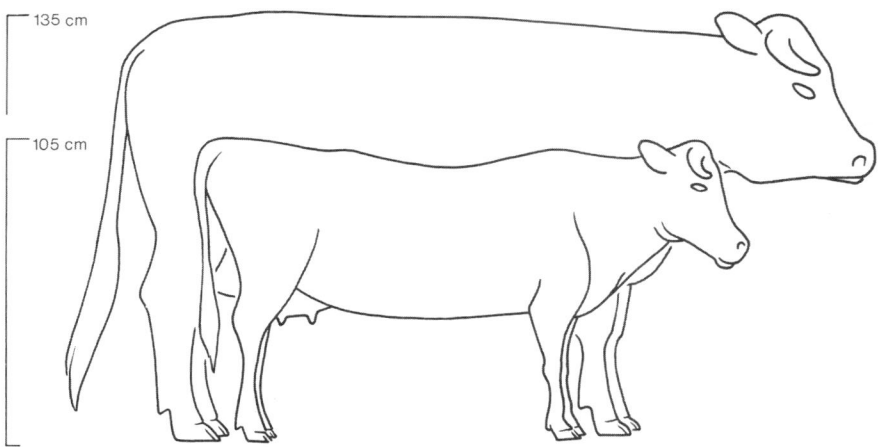

fig. 22.9
A Middle Bronze Age cow from Bovenkarspel compared with a modern cow. The Bronze Age animals were extraordinary small and had different proportions as well.

man bones provide some support for another of his hypotheses, namely that the proportion of beef in the diet decreased in favour of that of mutton.

Data obtained from other Bronze Age settlements in Westfrisia further confirm the above reconstruction based on the data from Bovenkarspel, of a mixed farming economy of which the relative importance of crop cultivation and stock keeping is difficult to quantify. Zooarchaeological data invariably show a strong predominance of cattle, a total absence of horses and only very few remains of wild animals.[21]

	Middle Bronze Age	Late Bronze Age
man	959 ± 94	987 ± 99
cattle	1112 ± 94	1101 ± 120
pig	1144 ± 100	1219 ± 166
dog	1235 ± 128	1280 ± 118
sheep/goat	1315 ± 122	1439 ± 257

table 22.2
The strontium content in human and animal bone at Bovenkarspel-Het Valkje: mean values and standard deviation in mg/kg cremated bone.

THE WESTERN NETHERLANDS IN THE IRON AGE

The dune belt

The animal remains found in the dunes differ very little from those of the regions discussed above (see fig. 22.11), except for the fact that the proportion of bones of sheep/goat is relatively high in the case of some of the assemblages, in particular those of Velsen-Hoogovens and Zandvoort. Unfortunately, no data are available

fig. 22.10
Bovenkarspel-Het Valkje, subdivision of Middle and Late Bronze Age cattle on the basis of horn-core characteristics.
Middle Bronze Age N=80; Late Bronze Age N=20.

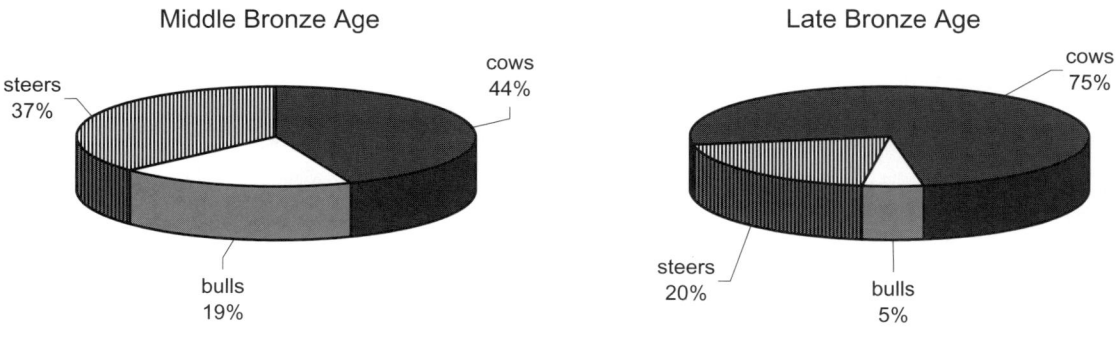

Middle Bronze Age

steers 37%
cows 44%
bulls 19%

Late Bronze Age

cows 75%
steers 20%
bulls 5%

for the ages at which the animals were killed in this region. Such data can provide an indication of the purpose for which the animals were kept. Animals that were killed at maturity were usually kept for their meat, whereas a large proportion of remains of older animals is an indication of dairying and/or wool production.

No botanical data are as yet available for the settlements in the dunes, so we have no evidence from the production side to support the proposed hypothesis that the occupants of the peat regions obtained their grain from the occupants of the dunes.

The peat regions

Improved natural drainage made the peat in the Holocene coastal zone behind the beach barriers of the western Netherlands suitable for occupation for several centuries. The drained peat was colonised in the 8th century BC, at the beginning of the Iron Age.[22]

The Meuse estuary

A relatively large number of settlements have been found in the peat regions on either side of the Meuse estuary, in particular in Midden-Delfland and on Voorne-Putten.[23] These areas were first occupied in the 7th or 6th century BC. The botanical analyses of samples from three of the earliest settlements on Voorne-Putten yielded a fairly heterogeneous picture (table 22.3). No remains of crops or field weeds were identified in the samples from the site Rotterdam-Hartelkanaal, but a few sherds showed impressions of grains of hulled barley (fig. 22.12). The timber structures had been built almost exclusively from alder wood, which is not very durable. This and other evidence suggest that this settlement was occupied for a short time only. The occupants of the farmstead probably relied on stock keeping

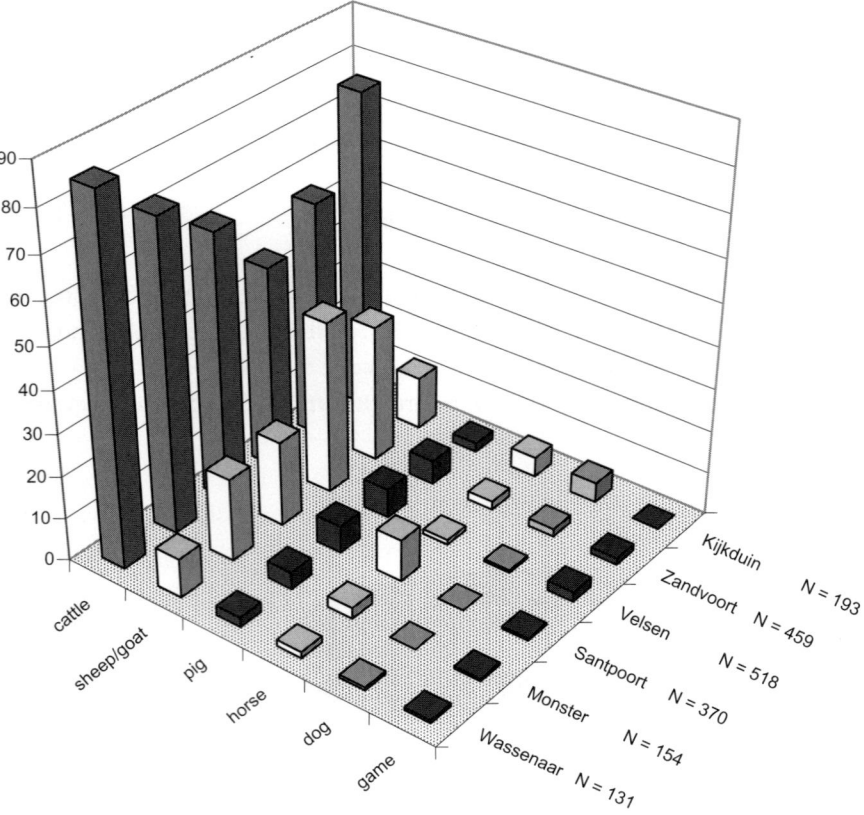

fig. 22.11
The ratios of the different domestic animals at various settlements in the dunes in the west of the Netherlands in percentages of identified fragments. N = total number of identifications.

Late Iron Age	Kijkduin
	Zandvoort
Middle Iron Age	Velsen
	Santpoort
	Monster
Early Iron Age	Wassenaar

only and obtained their grain via exchange with the occupants of the levees bordering the Meuse or the occupants of the dunes.

Spijkenisse site 17-30 yielded remains of wheat and millet. The occupants of this site also grew (or gathered) rape. No remains of the other oil-yielding crops known from the Iron Age, i.e. linseed and gold of pleasure, were found here (fig. 22.13). Palynological analyses of samples of a peat deposit a few metres away from the farm revealed no pollen of cereals, which means that cereals were not threshed on a large scale. The economy of this site was probably also (virtually) exclusively based on stock keeping.

The third Early Iron Age findspot did yield a little evidence for the cultivation of crops, i.e. hulled barley and linseed. But whether they were grown in drained peat, like the barley and rye that were cultivated in the western Netherlands in the Middle Ages, cannot be inferred from the present data.

The Middle Iron Age occupants of Voorne-Putten seem to have been more self-sufficient: they grew wheat, hulled barley, gold of pleasure and linseed (table 22.3). The threshing waste found at the site, i.e. rachis segments of hulled barley, proves that this cereal was grown at the site. The remains of field weeds that were encountered among the threshing waste were all of species associated with summer cereals. At Iron Age settlements on the Pleistocene sands, such as that of

	Assendelft Q	Hartelkanaal	Spijkenisse 17-30	Spijkenisse 17-35	Midden-Delfland 15.04	Midden-Delfland 11.17	Voorne-Putten	Voorne-Putten
emmer	•	-	•	-	•	•	•	•
hulled barley	•	•	-	•	•	•	•	•
millet	•	-	•	-	•	-	-	-
linseed	•	-	-	•	•	•	•	•
gold of pleasure	•	-	-	•	•	•	•	•
rape	-	-	•	-	•	•	•	•
oats	•	-	-	-	-	-	-	-
Iron Age:	Early				Middle			Late

table 22.3
Cultivated crops in Iron Age settlements in peat areas.

Oss-Ussen, field weeds associated with winter cereal have also been found, as well as those associated with summer cereal. They make it rather unlikely that the occupants of the peat imported cereal from those regions.

As already mentioned above, the levees bordering the Meuse were deforested on a large scale in this period. The soil of the cleared areas was very suitable for crop cultivation, but only in the summer, as the land was flooded in the winter. However, the disadvantages in terms of tillage and protection of crops implied by the distances of several kilometres between these levees and the investigated settlements make it likely that the occupants of the peat obtained their wheat via exchange with the occupants of the levees. Barley was probably cultivated in the peat region itself, too. The drainage of the peat may have been deliberately improved somewhat in this period by digging ditches of the kind encountered at Spijkenisse. We do not yet know to what extent the picture outlined above also applies to other Iron Age sites.

At most settlements in the peat areas only very few faunal remains have been

fig. 22.12

Impressions of a barley grain and mouse teeth in a sherd from an Iron Age settlement at Rotterdam-Hartelkanaal. A wood mouse tried to gnaw the grain out of the pot before it was fired. Length of the grain 0.8 cm.

fig. 22.13

Charred seeds of crops, which for the first time were cultivated in the Iron Age, all from Iron Age and native Roman settlements on the island of Voorne-Putten (cf. feature P).

1 rape (Brassica rapa)
Spijkenisse   10x enlarged

2 Celtic bean (Vicia faba)
Nieuwenhoorn   5x enlarged

3 silicles of gold of pleasure
(Camelina sativa)
Geervliet   5x enlarged

preserved due to the generally acid conditions of the soil. In the case of Voorne-Putten we must consider all the investigated Iron Age settlements together to obtain usable quantitative evidence (fig. 22.14). As in the areas discussed above, cattle were the main source of animal food. The animals were small, with withers heights of at most 1.15 m (fig. 22.15). In view of the fact that more than half of the animals were killed before they had reached the age of four, we may assume that they were not kept primarily for their milk. We know that the milk yields for human consumption were fairly small in the Bronze Age and Iron Age; estimates lie around 100 litres per cow per year.[24] In order to obtain an impression of the relative importance of crop cultivation and cattle keeping, the proportions of field weeds and grassland species have been compared for settlements on Voorne-Putten.[25] The results are in accordance with the picture outlined above. For the Early Iron Age an almost complete absence of field weeds was noted; the rare remains of field weeds that were encountered all came from the few settlements where the presence of chaff suggested that cereal was grown at the site itself. The proportion of field weeds increased in the course of the Iron Age. The calculated percentage of grassland species may however not be regarded as an absolute measure of the importance of stock keeping.

The relative importance of animal products in the subsistence economy has been calculated on the basis of the number of stalls observed in the excavated house plans.[26] It was found that the major part of the protein requirement of four to six individuals could have been covered with animal products from a farm with ten stalls. According to this model, the livestock comprised fourteen cattle, two horses, four sheep and two pigs. They will have covered about half of the occupants' caloric requirements. This stock will have required 18 ha of pastureland in the case of intensive grazing, or an area many times that size in the case of extensive grazing. An area of no more than 2.5 ha was required for cereal production to cover the remaining protein requirement.[27]

A large portion of the uncarbonised stem remains recovered from the stalls of Voorne-Putten were found to be reed stems. No cereal straw was identified. Present-day grazing experiments have shown that reeds can be used as cattle feed, provided that they are cut while still green. The fact that most of the Iron Age settlements of Voorne-Putten lay in reed marshes[28] makes it quite likely that reeds cut in the late summer were used as winter feed for the stalled cattle. Alternatively, the reeds may have been used as bedding. If the animals were only stalled for the night they will not have required any feed.

The Oer-IJ estuary

Another peat region that was occupied in the Iron Age is that of the Assendelver polders, which bordered the former Oer-IJ estuary. It is assumed that the region was exploited on a seasonal basis before it was permanently occupied.[29] Summer pastures enabling transhumance became available when drainage conditions improved. The entire region was – intermittently – occupied from the eighth century BC until in the second century AD. The farming system may well have been almost entirely based on stock keeping.

The most thoroughly investigated settlement is that of house Q, from the Early Iron Age.[30] The farm lay on a relatively dry, oligotrophic peat cushion in an otherwise practically impassable reed swamp. The economy was almost exclusively based on stock breeding, focusing on cattle, sheep and goats.[31] Some of the samples of the layers of manure in the byre of house Q were found to contain many small, round coprolites. Their shape and contents – virtually exclusively bog myrtle – suggest that goats were stalled in the byre.[32]

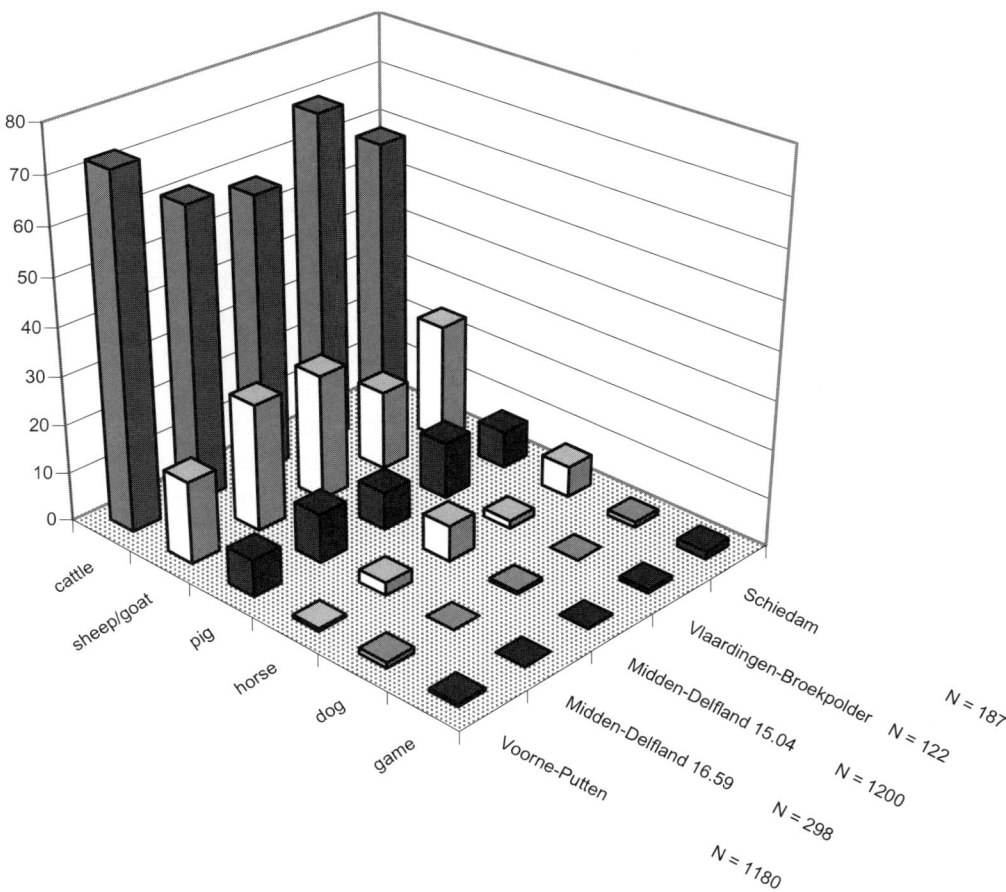

fig. 22.14

The ratios of the different domestic animals at various settlements in peat areas in percentages of identified fragments. N = total number of identifications.

Late Iron Age	Schiedam
Middle Iron Age	Vlaardingen-Broekpolder
	Midden-Delfland site 15.04
	Midden-Delfland site 16.59
Early-Late Iron Age	Voorne-Putten

fig. 22.15

Late prehistoric sheep, pigs, cows and horses were substantially smaller than contemporary animals (black).

Some stalls were also found to contain cattle manure. If cattle were stalled here in the wintertime, the occupants must have gathered and stored winter fodder. In this context it is interesting that gold of pleasure seems to have been the only crop cultivated in the immediate vicinity of the settlement. Gold of pleasure, a crop which demands little of the soil (cf. table 22.4, fig. 22.13), was first cultivated in the Netherlands in the Iron Age. It is quite possible that the cultivation of gold of pleasure was one of the factors that enabled people to settle in more marginal areas, such as peat regions, in the Iron Age. The seeds yield oil, but apart from that, the crop is known to be eminently suitable for feeding livestock; it may very well have been fed to cattle in the wintertime. The low frequencies of seeds in the samples suggest that in that case only the chaff was fed to the cattle.

The evidence for the stalling of goats and cattle may suggest that animals (with young) were stalled in the winter to protect them and to be able to use them for milk production. This is also suggested by the bones of calves and young bovines: in an economy based on dairying it was mainly young animals (between six months and one year) that were killed for consumption.[33]

The evidence for the later periods shows that changes took place in the subsistence economy of the Assendelver polders. After the Dunkirk Ib transgression, crops could be grown on a limited scale on the levees of the newly formed creeks, the most important being hulled barley. However, the presence of spike rush and bulrush among the field weeds implies that the fields were very moist.[34] Features observed at settlement sites indicate that the crops are likely to have been grown in areas that bore a closer resemblance to gardens than fields. The occupants of these settlements were probably still partly dependent on the import of grain from higher areas, in exchange for – presumably – their surplus from stock keeping.

It is assumed that the economy was still chiefly based on stock keeping, with an increasing degree of specialisation. The entire area has yielded indications of dairying, in the form of both slaughter patterns and sherds of pottery used in cheese production, in particular in the Roman period.

In the last occupation phase the settlements on the levees contained elevations without houses (known as platforms), onto which the herds may have been driven to be milked. From the distribution of earthenware cheese moulds we know that the cheese was produced at the farms themselves.[35]

Although the estuary is believed to have held a wealth of natural resources, hunting, fowling and fishing do not appear to have played important parts in the cattle farmers' subsistence system. The faunal samples contained very few remains of typical estuarine animals, such as otter, beaver, duck or goose.

THE SALT MARSHES IN THE NORTH OF THE NETHERLANDS

The agricultural economy of the salt marshes of Friesland and Groningen was based on mixed farming. The emphasis will undoubtedly have been on stock keeping. However, the granaries or platforms found in the settlements on the salt marshes suggest that the importance of crop cultivation must not be underestimated, although we may not exclude the possibility that these structures were used for the storage of goods other than crops.

Ideal pastures

The salt marshes were colonised in the 6th century BC. It has been suggested that the definitive colonisation was preceded by a period of transhumance, a consequence of increasing pressure on the arable of the Drenthe plateau further south.[36] The natural grassland of the salt marshes will have been very suitable for such seasonal grazing.

The earliest occupation remains found at the site of Middelstum-Boerdamsterweg were initially interpreted as the remains of a summer camp used in this transhumance phase. The zooarchaeological research[37] that has been carried out has however shown that the range of animals kept in the early occupation phase of Middelstum was no different from those in later periods (fig. 22.16). The evidence indicating that cattle were being killed in this earliest phase already makes it more likely that the site was occupied on a permanent basis than that it was a camp used for summer grazing. All the data point to a strong emphasis on cattle keeping; neither sheep nor pigs seem to have played an important part in the stock system. Most of the animals were killed at maturity, which suggests that they were kept mainly for their meat. The consistent presence of horses observed at Iron Age sites elsewhere holds for this area, the area of the *terpen*, too.

Game was caught only sporadically: out of a total of 2560 identified animal remains only seven were found to derive from hunted animals (red deer, grey seal, duck and white-tailed eagle).

Two other excavations of *terpen* yielded very much the same evidence as Middelstum. At Kimswerd, where the remains of a *terp* that was occupied between 350 BC and AD 50 were excavated, cattle and sheep/goat were also the principal stocks; no remains of pig whatsoever were found at this site.[38] An unusual discovery were two cat bones, which have been ascribed to a domestic cat. Cats were introduced into transalpine Europe by the Romans. In view of the time span obtained for the occupation of Kimswerd, which continues into the first century AD, these finds suggest direct or indirect contacts with the Romans.

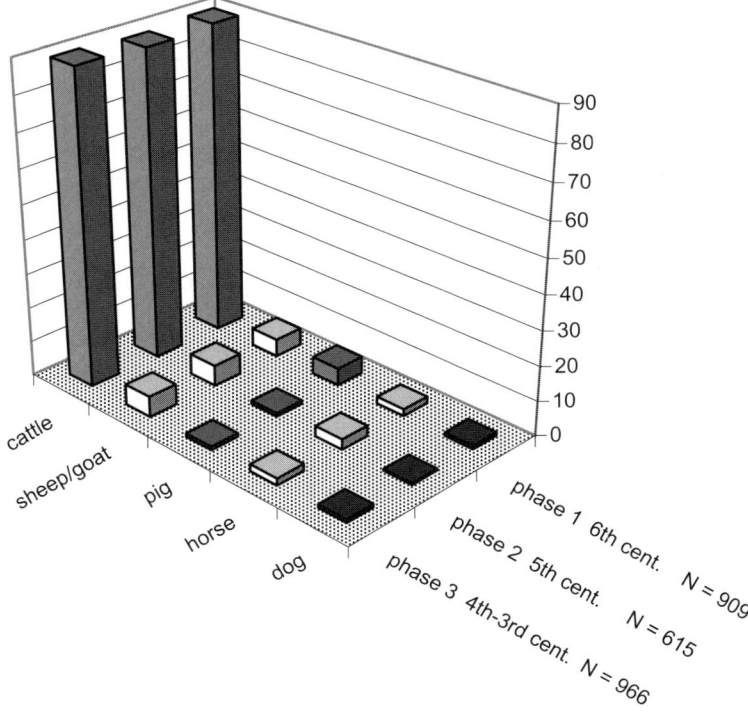

fig. 22.16

The ratios of the different domestic animals in the various phases of the Iron Age site of Middelstum-Boerdamsterweg. N = total number of identifications.

crop	year	sowing-seed grams	harvest grams	S : H
gold of pleasure	1975	20	1150	1 : 57.5
rape	1977	20	565	1 : 28.3
oats	1975	130	2850	1 : 21.9
Celtic bean	1975	180	3000	1 : 16.6
linseed	1975	60	890	1 : 14.5
hulled four-row barley	1977	125	1650	1 : 13.2
millet	1975	60	330	1 : 5.5
bread wheat	1977	130	305	1 : 2.4
two-row barley	1977	130	230	1 : 1.8
emmer	1976	60	37	1 : 0.6
spelt	1976	40	-	1 : 0.0

table 22.4

Maximum yields for various crops in the agricultural experiment on the Groningen salt marshes.

The range of animals represented at Paddepoel, a *terp* dated between 200 BC and AD 250, is also indicative of an economy based largely on stock breeding with the emphasis on cattle and sheep.[39] Unusual finds recovered at this site are the remains of domestic hen, which, like domestic cat, is considered to have been a typical Roman import.

A botanical experiment

A long-term agricultural experiment has provided much information on the possibilities of crop cultivation in the salt marshes. Between 1969 and 1978, different crops were grown on a salt marsh in Groningen.[40] It proved to be quite possible to grow crops in this area, but only on the high parts of the marshes (the marsh bars), which were not affected by summer storm floods. It was found that winter floods did not have an adverse effect on the harvests. The best results were obtained when the seed was sown late in the spring. The experimental fields that were fertilised with dried manure yielded slightly larger harvests than the unmanured fields. Several harvests were lost when the crops were insufficiently protected against grazing young cattle.

The largest harvests by far were obtained with gold of pleasure (table 22.4). Other oil-yielding crops, such as rape and linseed, along with oats, hulled barely and Celtic bean also fared well under experimental conditions. Several kinds of wheat and millet, however, did not grow at all or grew only very poorly.

These experimental results make it unlikely that the emmer that was found at Middelstum – along with gold of pleasure and barley – was cultivated locally,[41] although the possibility that it was may not be altogether excluded.

THE SANDY SOILS

Stock keeping and crop cultivation

As already mentioned above, virtually no bones have survived in the areas of the Pleistocene sands. The importance of animal products in the subsistence economy of the occupants of these areas is apparent mainly from the many stalls observed in the well-preserved plans of the longhouses.[42]

The range of crops cultivated in the sandy regions was the same as that in other areas. In the Bronze Age this range was still very limited: emmer, hulled and naked barley were the main cereals, the only other cereal so far encountered being millet (table 22.1). In the Iron Age a new type of cereal started to be grown here and there, too, namely spelt (table 22.5). We do not know for sure whether the encountered oats were of a wild or a cultivated variety. An oat impression in Iron Age pottery from Wijchen was found to derive from a cultivated variety.[43] Celtic bean (*Vicia faba* var. *minor*) was added to the range of crops cultivated in the Iron Age, and crops with oil-yielding seeds started to be grown on a larger scale. Linseed was already known. The cultivation of gold of pleasure is believed to have started in the Iron Age.

Several of the above crops may have been sown either in the autumn or in the spring (yielding winter and summer crops, respectively). The diet did not include any species that could only be sown in the autumn. Millet, barley and linseed will have been grown as summer crops only, as they are all very susceptible to frost. However, field weeds associated with winter cereal encountered in some Iron Age samples indicate that winter cereals were also grown on the Pleistocene sands. This makes it interesting to speculate whether the Iron Age farmers already used the three-course rotation system that is known to have been employed in the Netherlands in the Middle Ages. In this system, winter cereal was cultivated the first

	Angelslo	Colmschate	Oss - Ussen	Oss - Ussen	Son en Breugel	Ermelo	Dommelen	Gees	Noordbarge	Oss - Ussen
einkorn	-	-	●	●	-	-	-	-	-	-
emmer	●	●	●	●	●	●	●	●	-	●
spelt	-	●	●	●	-	-	-	-	-	●
naked barley	●	●	-	-	-	-	-	-	-	-
hulled barley	●	●	●	●	●	●	●	●	●	●
millet	●	●	●	●	●	●	●	-	●	●
rye	-	-	-	-	-	-	-	-	●	-
oats	o	o	o	o	o	o	-	o	-	o
Celtic bean	-	-	-	●	-	-	-	-	-	●
pie	-	o	-	-	●	-	-	-	-	-
linseed	-	●	●	●	●	-	●	-	-	●
gold of pleasure	-	●	●	●	●	●	-	-	-	●
rape	-	-	-	-	-	-	-	-	-	●
poppy	-	-	●	-	-	-	-	-	-	-
Iron Age:	Early			Middle				Late		

table 22.5

Cultivated crops in Iron Age settlements on the upland sands. Open symbol: uncertain identification.

year, followed by summer cereal the next, after which the land was left fallow for a year. It is far from certain that this system was already being used in the Bronze Age or the Iron Age. Fallow periods are particularly difficult to demonstrate; the evidence provided by ribwort plantain, which may be an indicator of fallow land, is rarely conclusive. Moreover, a small amount of a particular crop found mixed with a large stored supply of a different crop is not necessarily an indication of the type of crop cultivated the previous year. Unfortunately, therefore, crop rotation and fallowing remain matters of conjecture.

The importance of crop cultivation in the Iron Age is evident from the Celtic fields. *Ard* marks have been observed in some of the small plots of these fields, which measured about 30 x 30 m (fig. 22.17) and were marked out by low banks. It has been suggested that the size of the plots corresponded to the area that could be opened up in one day.[44] Experiments have shown that such an area could also be ploughed, and later harvested, within one day.[45] The employed sowing method and the crop yields are still matters of controversy. It is often assumed that the seed was scattered widely across the plot – what is known as 'broadcasting' – in amounts of about 200 kg per hectare. A fair amount of seed is lost in broadcasting, large quantities being consumed by birds. A crop yield ratio of 1:3 is often assumed for this form of sowing. Of the 600 kg of grain that could be harvested per hectare, 200 kg had to be stored for sowing the next year; the remaining 400 kg could be consumed.

In his calculations for the sandy Drenthe plateau, Fokkens[46] assumed that the seed was sown in rows (furrows), as was also done at the Butser experimental Iron Age farm in southern England. At this farm, the average yield ratio in a period of fifteen years was about 1:30. Low extreme values were 1:4 and 1:7.[47] Each sowing season 60 kg of seed per hectare were sown in the shallow furrows produced with the aid of an *ard*. Sowing in furrows is far more labour-intensive than broadcasting, but this method may quite conceivably have been used in the relatively small-scale crop cultivation practised in the Iron Age, especially if it was found to result in greater yields.

Depending on its size and the relative importance of crop cultivation, a household will have sown between about 1 and 5 hectares of arable land per year.[48] It will have taken about a month to harvest thirty plots (2.7 ha) of a Celtic field. If, on the basis of the aforementioned results, we assume a low yield ratio of 1:10, seed sown in furrows (60 kg/ha) will have yielded about 1460 kg of grain, after deduction of the seed required for the next harvest. If the seed was broadcast, the nett yield will have been 1080 kg.[49] According to present standards, the first quantity of grain will have been sufficient to cover almost the entire caloric requirement of a family of at least six persons. It will in principle also have covered their protein requirements, provided that they supplemented their diet with protein from a different source, as cereal does not contain the full range of essential amino acids. A small herd will have sufficed to cover the remaining caloric and protein requirements.

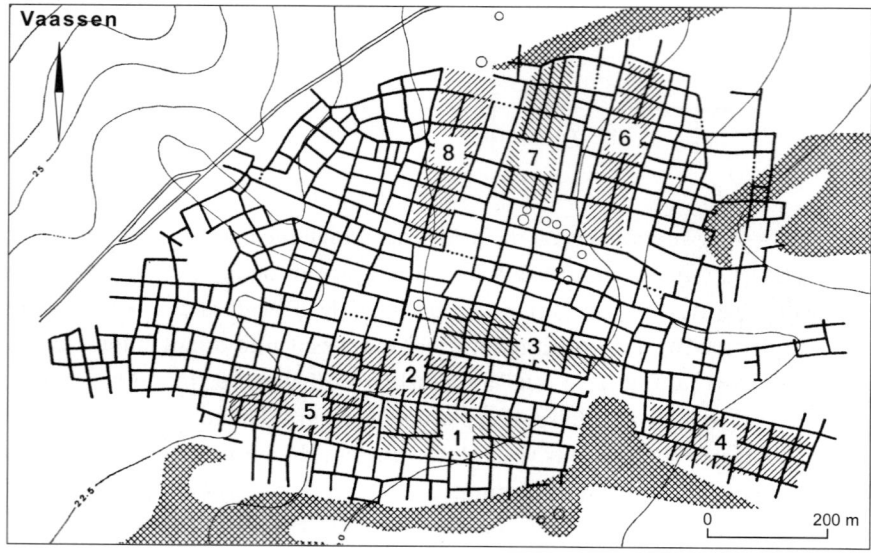

fig. 22.17
The 76-ha Celtic field of Vaassen divided into several hundred units by low banks. The light grey, numbered units are assumed to have been brought under cultivation first. The moist, low-lying edges of the field system are indicated in dark grey. The circles stand for barrows, which are all thought to predate the Celtic field.

Unlike the areas discussed above, the Pleistocene sands and the loess regions presented the possibility of storage underground. Experiments have shown that pits are eminently suitable for the storage of grain, provided that they are impermeably sealed and lie above groundwater level.[50]

Botanical analysis of samples from Iron Age storage pits at Colmschate (Overijssel) showed that the pits were used for the storage of emmer and barley, in varying proportions (fig. 22.18).[51] The grain was stored unthreshed, probably to ensure better preservation under moist conditions.

Their large volumes (often 3-4 m³) suggest that the pits were used mainly for the storage of seed grain: once opened, such a pit had to be completely emptied because otherwise the oxygen that was then admitted into the pit would cause any remaining grain to rot or germinate.[52] The grain intended for consumption was probably stored in granaries or in large storage vessels inside the house.

THE LOESS REGIONS

As hardly any Bronze Age occupation remains and no plant or animal remains whatsoever have been found in the loess regions we know very little about the farming practices of this period. We are somewhat better informed about the next period thanks to the results of the botanical analyses of samples from a few Iron Age settlements (table 22.6). As is usually the case with samples of carbonised matter, cereals, in this case emmer and hulled barley, predominate. Some of the samples were found to contain bread wheat, a kind of wheat that was hardly grown at all in prehistoric times, but became quite popular in the Roman period. It was to be grown on a large scale throughout the rest of history and is today the most important cultivated cereal in Western Europe. Because of its high nitrogen requirement, it could probably only be grown on very rich soils in prehistoric times.

A second remarkable crop encountered in the samples is poppy. Poppy was quite common in *Bandkeramik* times, but it then disappeared until the Iron Age, when it reappeared in very small quantities only. This oil-yielding crop was not to become fairly common again until in the Roman period. As elsewhere, naked barley disappeared after the Early Iron Age.[53]

fig. 22.18
Cross-section of a storage pit containing a layer of carbonised cereal in an Iron Age settlement at Deventer-Colmschate.

In the Bronze Age and the Iron Age a system of integrated mixed farming was practised throughout the whole of the Netherlands, with the possible exception of the peat regions in the western part of the country. The occupants of the latter regions, which were colonised from the 8th century BC onwards, seem to have specialised in stock keeping, at least in the Early Iron Age.

Cereals and oil-yielding crops were the mainstays of the crop-cultivation component of the mixed farming system. Barley was the main cereal; the naked variety that was grown first was gradually replaced by the hulled variety. Other cultivated crops were millet and, in areas of richer soils, emmer. The grain will have been ground and then consumed in the form of porridge or gruel and possibly also bread.[54] The straw may have been used as bedding or as fodder. The importance

	Geleen - Krawinkel	Geleen - Urmonderbaan	Heerlen - Welten	Heerlen - Vrank	Sittard - Hoogveld	Sittard - Haagsittard
einkorn	-	•	-	-	•	-
emmer	•	•	-	•	•	-
spelt	•	•	-	-	-	•
bread wheat	•	-	-	-	-	-
naked barley	•	-	-	-	-	-
hulled barley	•	•	•	•	•	•
millet	•	•	-	-	•	-
Celtic bean	•	-	-	-	•	-
pea	•	-	-	-	•	-
lentil	•	-	-	-	-	•
linseed	•	-	-	-	-	-
gold of pleasure	•	-	-	-	•	-
poppy	•	-	-	-	-	-
Iron Age:	Early	Ea / Mi	Early	Ea / Mi	(Ea) / Mi	Middle

table 22.6

Cultivated crops in Iron Age settlements in the loess district.

of horticulture is unknown because horticultural products, such as foliage plants and legumes, are underrepresented, as they are generally not (or unrecognisably) preserved. We know that Celtic bean, a kind of small broad bean, was grown in the Iron Age. We are much better informed about the cultivation of oil-yielding crops: linseed was grown from the (Late) Bronze Age onwards, rape and – in wet areas – large amounts of gold of pleasure from the Iron Age onwards. The oil that could be extracted from the seed may have been used for human consumption, but these crops may also have been used as fodder.

The picture that emerges for the Netherlands does not differ very much from that of the surrounding areas, with the exception of Germany.[55] In Germany, too, barley was the principal crop in the Bronze Age, but the naked variety was replaced by the hulled variety many centuries later than in the Netherlands, i.e. mainly in the Roman period. Another difference is that millet played a much greater part in the diet in Germany.

In the Bronze Age as well as the Iron Age cattle were the main stock. In this respect the Netherlands differed from its southern neighbours (Belgium, northern France). One of the causes of this difference will most certainly have been the vast stretches of natural pastures with their rich resources that were to be found in the western and northern Netherlands. In the mixed farming economy the cattle were kept for their meat, milk and hides on the one hand and for their manure and traction on the other. Horses, which were kept only incidentally in the Bronze Age, are consistently represented from the beginning of the Iron Age onwards. Horses, sheep, goats and pigs were of minor importance in the stock system. Only in the dunes has evidence for extensive sheep breeding been found. On the whole, the importance of the secondary products of stock breeding, i.e. the milk of cattle and/or sheep and sheep's wool, increased over the centuries.

The farms included byres from, at the latest, the beginning of the Middle Bronze Age onwards. It is however debatable whether the cattle were permanently stalled throughout the winter, the implied necessity of gathering large amounts of winter feed would have meant a lot of extra work. Cattle, as well as sheep and pigs, could perfectly well be kept outside all the year round in the Dutch climate. Only goats had to be stalled in the winter.

Stalling the domestic animals exclusively in the winter, and then only at night, will have implied few consequences for the farming system, compared with a situation in which the animals stayed outside throughout the year. What may have been a crucial advantage for the mixed farming system was the fact that manure could be collected in the byres, which could then be used to fertilise the fields.

Gathered fruit and nuts, such as hazelnuts, acorns, blackberries and sloes, were consumed in remarkably small amounts. Apparently there was no need to augment the diet with wild plants. However, at one site an exceptional concentration of several thousands of acorns has been found.[56]

Hunting and fishing do not seem to have been very important either. Only for the beginning of the Bronze Age do we have evidence of specialised fishing camps. From the Middle Bronze Age onwards the subsistence economy was based entirely on farming.

NOTES

1 Results of palynological research will play only a minor part in the following survey. This is mainly due to the fact that it is not possible to identify the species of most pollen. Moreover, as many crops are self-pollinated, their pollen is not spread very far from the plant. The chance of pollen of such crops being recovered is very small.

2 Overmars 1987.

3 Gehasse 1992.

4 Fokkens 1991a.

5 Kasteleijn 1982.

6 Van Wijngaarden-Bakker 1988.

7 Slicher van Bath 1987. The latest views are that horses were being used for riding around 4000 BC already, at least on the steppes of Russia (Anthony/Brown 1991). The much greater mobility permitted by the use of horses, which was a particular advantage in raids and other conflicts, may have been one of the main reasons why domestic horses were kept at all settlements from the Bronze Age onwards.

8 I.e. fish that swim upstream to spawn.

9 Van Wijngaarden-Bakker 1985, 1988.

10 Clason 1967.

11 Buurman 1979.

12 Buurman 1988.

13 Kuijper 1981.

14 Buurman/Pals 1974.

15 Buurman 1988, 277.

16 Pals in Bakker et al. 1977.

17 IJzereef 1981.

18 The ratios of the various domestic animals can be quantified in different ways. These ratios are to a great extent dependent on the excavation method used. If sieved samples are included in the quantification, the percentage of small domestic animals will be higher. Whether the figures then obtained have to be corrected is open to discussion. Sieving experiments have shown that the ratio based on the minimum number of individuals of the large domestic animals remains the same, whether the sieved samples are included or not (IJzereef 1981, 32). The ratio based on the minimum number of individuals is probably more reliable than that based on the total number of fragments in reconstructing the diet in a subsistence economy in which the killed stock was eaten at the site and parts of the carcass were not exported.

19 Runia 1987.

20 Van Wijngaarden-Bakker 1986; Runia 1985.

21 Prummel 1979.

22 Van Heeringen 1988b; 1992.

23 Abbink 1993a; Van den Broeke 1993; Van Heeringen 1992; Van Trierum 1992.

24 Prummel 1989.

25 Brinkkemper 1993.

26 Prummel 1989.

27 Brinkkemper 1993.

28 Brinkkemper 1993.

29 Brandt et al. 1984.

30 Therkorn et al. 1984.

31 Van Wijngaarden-Bakker 1988.

32 However, the possibility that the coprolites are of sheep cannot be altogether excluded (cf. Schelvis/Koot 1995).

33 McCormick 1987, 1992.

34 Pals 1988.

35 Therkorn/Abbink 1987; Van Wijngaarden-Bakker 1988.

36 Van Gijn/Waterbolk 1984.

37 Van Gelder-Ottway 1988.

38 Milojkovic/Brinkhuizen 1984.

39 Knol 1983.

40 Van Zeist et al. 1976; Bottema et al. 1980.

41 Van Zeist 1989.

42 Waterbolk 1975.

43 Van den Broeke 1984, 94.

44 Brongers 1976a, 60.

45 Cf. Brinkkemper 1993.

46 Fokkens 1991a.

47 Reynolds 1992.

48 Cf. Fokkens 1991, 157.

49 Based on an amount of 200 kg of seed per ha and a crop yield ratio of 1:3 (see Sigaut 1992).

50 Reynolds 1974; Meurers-Balke 1985.

51 Buurman 1986.

52 One way of cleaning the storage pits was by burning them. It is not yet clear whether the layers of carbonised grain that have occasionally been found at the bottom of storage pits were indeed formed in cleaning the walls of the pit by burning (Bakels 1991b, 288).

53 Gelissen 1992.

54 Cf. Währen 1987.

55 Knörzer 1991. Too few data are yet available for Belgium to allow sound comparison (cf. Bakels 1991b, 286).

56 Buurman 1990.

M   Salt makers along the North Sea coast
The production of salt for the hinterland

Peter van den Broeke

Salt production

As early as the Neolithic, salt was being produced in Continental Europe by causing water to evaporate from salt-containing sources, lakes and rivers.[1] The fired clay objects that were used for this purpose are referred to as *briquetage*. This term is sometimes also used for the method of salt production itself.

In the course of the Bronze Age, *briquetage* started to appear along the coasts of Western Europe too, first of all in Great Britain.[2] The oldest evidence for salt production found along the southern North Sea coast (at Assendelft, Velserbroek, Monster and Leiden[?]) dates from the Early Iron Age. The distribution area of the objects in question ends abruptly a short distance to the north of the Rhine estuary (fig. M1). The findspots are not limited to the coastline itself;

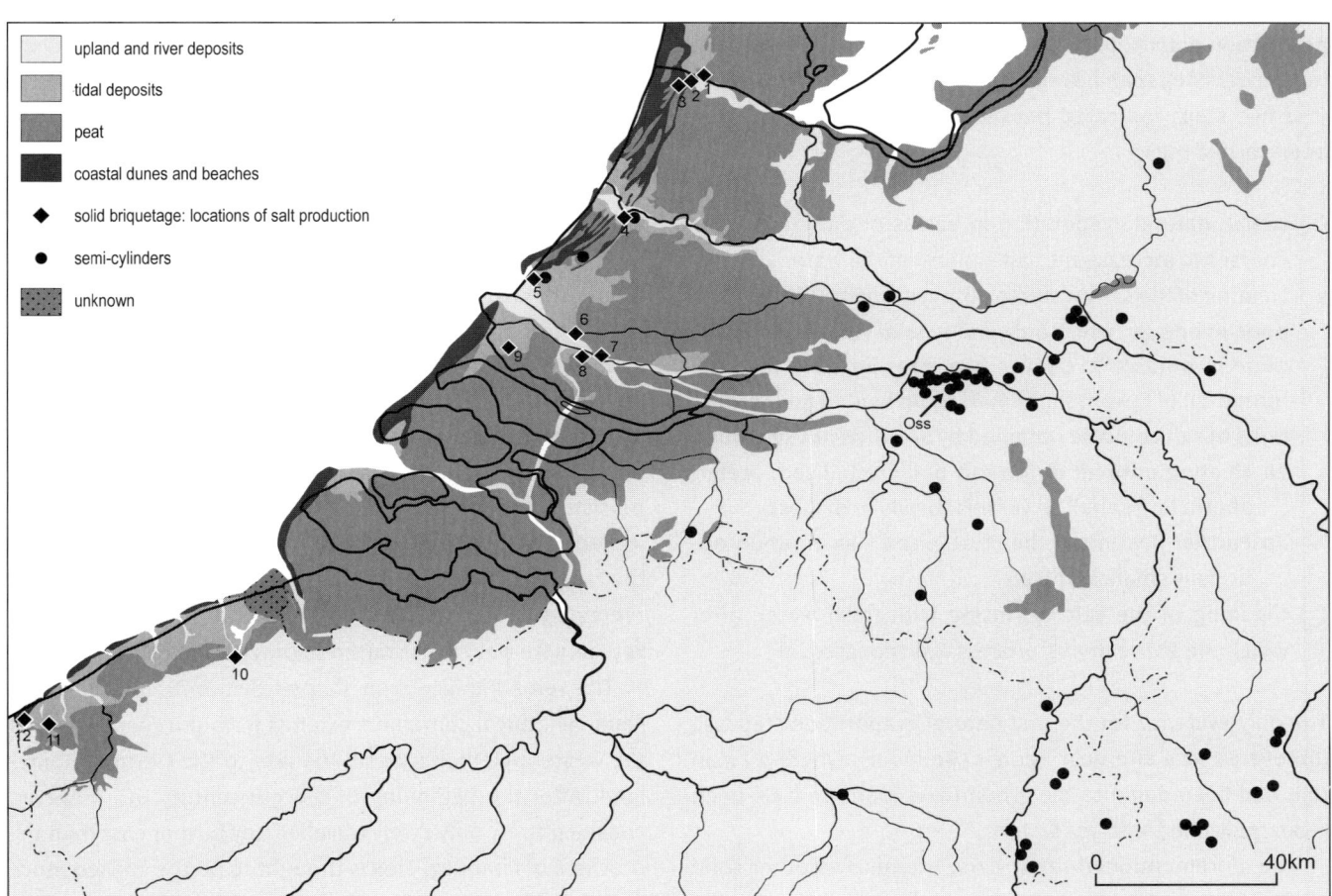

fig. M1

Findspots of Iron Age *briquetage*. Semi-cylinders are the sea-salt containers used in the second half of the Early Iron Age. Palaeogeographic situation of the Belgian coast and the Netherlands around the beginning of our era.

Locations of salt production

1 Assendelft (2x)	5 Monster (2x)	9 Rockanje (3x)
2 Velserbroek	6 Vlaardingen	10 Brugge
3 Santpoort	7 Poortugaal	11 Veurne
4 Leiden	8 Spijkenisse	12 De Panne

briquetage has also been found at inland sites in the coastal peat region, where salt could be produced from the water of the large estuaries and tidal creeks.[3]

The primary evidence for salt production consists of solid *briquetage*: reels, pedestals, tripods, clay nails and bars.[4] At several sites these objects have been found in association with vessels of the same specific fabric and sometimes also with thick layers of ash or large amounts of charcoal. Very interesting in this context are the several dozen tripods that were discovered among the remains of the living area of a Late Iron Age farm at Rockanje.[5]

At these and other locations it is however not always possible to say whether the finds are evidence for the production of salt, or simply for the production and storage of the implements required for salt production. This, and the fact that the remains are often found mixed with settlement waste, makes it very difficult for us to reconstruct the method of salt production practised along the North Sea coast. The following general steps can be inferred from the available evidence (the two steps indicated between brackets need not have been carried out):

(1) Initial, natural evaporation in basins or dammed water courses to increase the salt content of the water.

2 Heating of the salty water to obtain dry salt. This could be done in one go, using only one type of vessel, but it was more favourable to do it in two steps because then the formation of Epsom salts could be prevented and smaller units of salt could be obtained by an efficient use of fuel:

2a Heating until all of the salt had crystallized, preferably in large shallow vessels (bowls or dishes).

2b Further heating of the crystallized salt in other, optionally smaller, vessels.

(3) Cleaning of the salt by rinsing with fresh water, after which the above drying process was repeated.

The only evidence for the first natural evaporation step was discovered at a site near Veurne (Belgium), where a basin that had been dug into the ground was found to have been repeatedly filled with sea water.[6]

The aforementioned reels, bars, tripods and other solid objects presumably served to support the vessels used in the heating steps. We do not yet know what type of pottery was used for the evaporation of the sea water (step 2a). It may have been large, thick-walled dishes of the kind of which fragments have been found at De Panne, but it could also have been ordinary settlement pottery. The pottery that was used to dry the salt (step 2b and optionally step 3) is more easily identifiable, usually by its soft, porous, fabric (the pores being the result of the burning of the vegetable temper), its poor finish, and its light yellow to light red surface (plate 36A).

When the salt had been dried to a solid lump the container had to be broken. A unique feature of the method of salt production practised along the southern North Sea coast, which has otherwise only been observed in England, is that the containers were not usually broken until they had reached their destinations, some of which lay more than two hundred kilometres inland. Microscopic diatom analysis has shown that the salt containers found at these inland sites are indeed imports and not locally manufactured imitations of pottery types produced in the coastal region: they were found to have been made from clay from brackish or salty environments.

Coastal pottery in the hinterland

The thousands of fragments of coastal pottery that have been recovered from inland locations represent a millennium of continuous trade in sea salt from the 7th century BC onwards. Until about 500 BC the salt was transported in semi-cylindrical containers that were usually open at both ends (fig. M2: 1). These half cylinders (*gootjes* in Dutch) must have had a volume of about 0.1-0.2 litres.[7]

The semi-cylindrical containers were later replaced by differently shaped but equally small containers, mainly conical beakers (fig. M2: 2). In the 4th century BC there came an end to the uniformity that had prevailed until then, and containers of varying fabrics, shapes and sizes started to be used to transport the salt (fig. M2: 3-4). One of the containers even had a volume of more than ten litres. This diversity persisted throughout the Late Iron Age, during which thick-walled bowls, presumably with round bases, were added to the range of thick-walled dishes and pots (fig. M2: 5). Bowls remained in use until the Roman period, when cylindrical vessels with wavy rims started to prevail (fig. M2: 6).

The remarkable ribbon-shaped distribution area of the semi-cylindrical containers extends from the coastal area of the western Netherlands all the way to the German Rhineland. After the beginning of the 5th century BC, however, coastal pottery only rarely travelled any further east than the province of Limburg. This is thought to be the consequence of the development of a salt industry in Central Europe. Of particular significance in this context is the emergence of the production centre at Bad Nauheim (Hessen) in an early phase of the La Tène period. This meant that the occupants of the Lower Rhine area could obtain salt from a site that was much more nearby than the old salines at Halle, in the valley of the Saale, and those in the valley of the Seille, near Nancy, two salt-production centres about whose trading activities we know virtually nothing owing to the almost complete lack of containers.

In the settlements sea salt was undoubtedly used as a

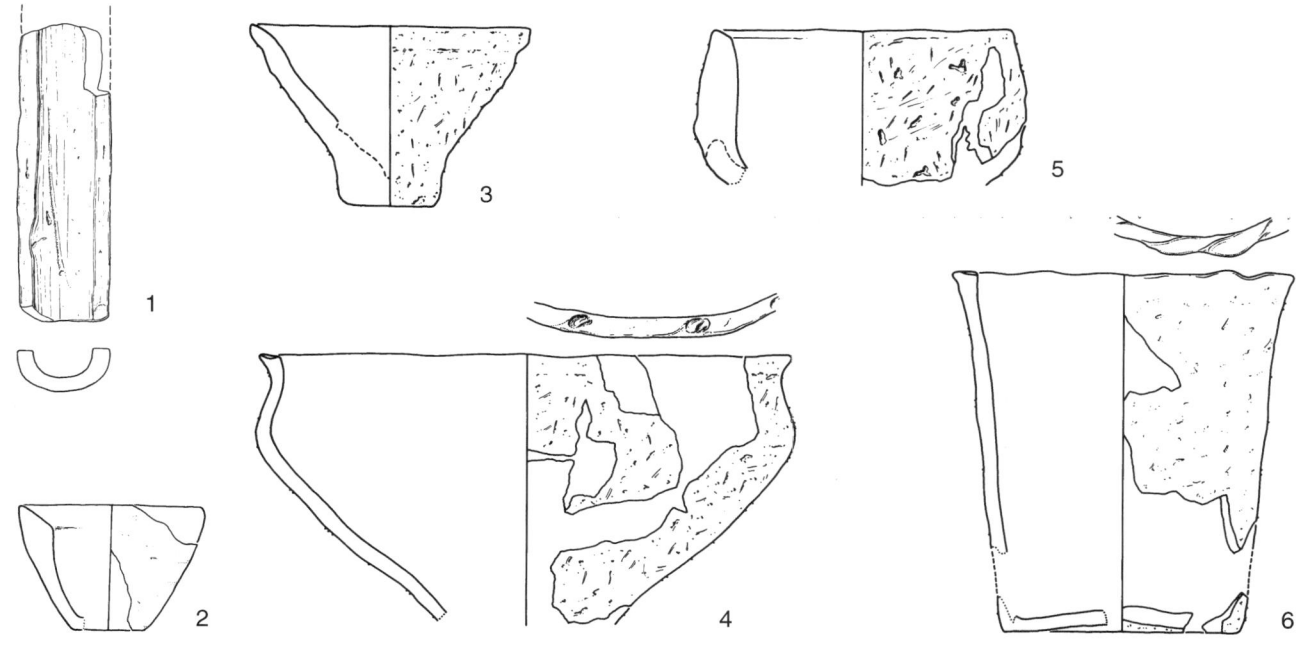

fig. M2

Some types of *briquetage* vessels from findspots in the hinterland. Scale 1:4.

1	Wijchen	Early Iron Age
2	Macharen	beginning of Middle Iron Age
3-6	Oss-Ussen	3-4 Middle Iron Age
		5 Late Iron Age
		6 Roman period

nutrient and as seasoning. Salt may also have been used as a tanning agent and as a preservative, in particular for dairy products and meat. Thanks to the information obtained at the site Oss-Ussen (North Brabant) we now know much more about the various applications of salt in prehistoric times.[8] The pottery found at this site showed that the previously observed increase in the size of the salt containers during the 4th century BC was accompanied by an increase

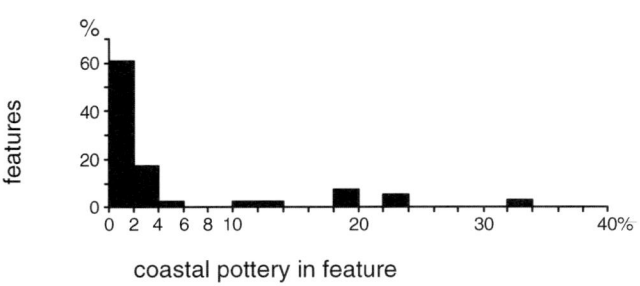

coastal pottery in feature

fig. M3

Frequency distribution of coastal pottery encountered in 41 Iron Age features at Oss-Ussen that yielded more than 100 pottery fragments from phases G and H (*c.* 4th century BC). Most of the pits yielded relatively little coastal pottery, whereas some contained concentrations.

in the number of containers. We may assume that after the beginning of the 4th century BC, sea salt started to be used for several purposes instead of consumption alone. The distribution pattern of the 4th-century containers within the settlement moreover suggests some form of specialisation in activities involving the use of salt (fig. M3). A number of pits spaced far apart across the settlement were found to contain large proportions of salt containers, some up to 33% of the pottery. Several of these same pits also contained fragments of a very rare, locally produced type of pottery that is thought to have been a cheese mould (fig. 27.17: 6). Around the 4th century BC, a number of households in the settlement of Oss-Ussen apparently specialised in cheese production, in which sea salt was used to preserve and season the cheese.

Sea salt as a means of power?

The concentration of prestige objects found near the salt mines of Hallstatt and Hallein in Austria shows to what great wealth – and hence also power – control of the salt trade could lead. It has been suggested that the wealth that is apparent from a number of unusual objects found in 7th-cen-

fig. M4

Impression of salt production along the North Sea coast in the Early Iron Age. Salt production was typically a summer activity, easily combined with herding livestock. In the depicted situation the forced evaporation of seawater has been completed. No archaeological evidence has yet been found for this phase in the production process. Recurrent finds of ceramic semi-cylinders in association with reels however suggest that the salt was dried in the semi-cylinders by heating the semi-cylinders on the reels above a fire pit. The salt cakes were subsequently transported in the semi-cylinders.

tury graves in the rivers area of the eastern Netherlands is likewise largely the result of the control of the trade in sea salt from the western Netherlands.[9] The remarkable early Hallstatt (period Ha C) prestige objects that have been found in this area, the finest of which is undoubtedly the ceremonial wagon from Wijchen, have been associated with the transit of sea salt to the Upper Rhine areas. In this context it has been suggested that the (small-scale) flow of sea salt that can be inferred from the known number of semi-cylindrical containers is only part of a larger flow that included salt that was traded in bulk or in perishable containers, for which we have no physical evidence. This would imply tremendous amounts of production waste at the coast. However, the coast of the western Netherlands has yielded no more than one cubic metre of *briquetage* from the entire Iron Age. Some salt production centres have undoubtedly vanished in the sea, but even so it is rather inconceivable that this single cubic metre of finds represents the waste of an industry comparable with that in the valley of the Seille in the north of France, which yielded at least one million cubic metres of *briquetage*.[10] It is more likely that the occupants of the Upper

Rhine areas obtained their salt from this site in France than from the North Sea coast. All in all, there is no reason to assume that the Early Iron Age sea-salt trade of the coastal area of the western Netherlands was any greater than can be inferred from the distribution of the semi-cylindrical containers.

It is quite conceivable that the elite in the rivers area controlled this fairly modest sea-salt trade on a local or a regional level and that this gave them political power. But this does not explain how they acquired the remarkable prestige goods from Central Europe.

The occupants of the coastal area do not seem to have benefited much from the salt trade. Salt boiling was a seasonal and labour-intensive activity (fig. M4) that was much less productive than salt mining. This, and the scarcity of luxury goods in the coastal area, suggests that the occupants of these areas used the salt primarily as a means for obtaining certain elementary goods. The fragments of tephrite querns from the Eifel that have been found at the coast could be interpreted in this context. The coastal area was devoid of coarse stone. The inhabitants of this area appear to have expediently availed themselves of the proximity of the North Sea – an inexhaustible source of salt – to secure querns and probably also other coveted exchange goods from the hinterland.[11]

Notes

1   Jodlowski 1976; Nenquin 1961. Large-scale mining of rock salt did not start until some time during the Late Bronze Age (Hallstatt), for example in the mines of Hallstatt and Hallein in Austria.

2   Bell 1990, 172.

3   The possibility that the prehistoric occupants of this area produced salt from peat, like their medieval successors, may be pretty much excluded. The relatively efficient procedure according to which peat is burned to a salty ash, which is then dried and leached to obtain a concentrated brine (*moernering, zelnering*), cannot have been practised on anything more than a regional scale until the end of the Dunkirk I transgression, around the beginning of our era. The known salt-production sites along the southern North Sea coast are all believed to have been producing salt before then. Moreover, research in the peaty coastal area of Belgium has shown that salt was extracted from tidal creeks not only in the Iron Age but also in the Roman period, when salt was already being traded on a large scale (Thoen 1987, 46 ff.; Thoen 1990). It is more likely that peat was used exclusively as fuel until the early Middle Ages.

4   Van den Broeke 1986; Van Heeringen 1992, 323-325; Thoen 1990.

5   Van Trierum 1992.

6   De Ceunynck/Termote 1987.

7   Van den Broeke 1986, 1987c; Simons 1987. The large half cylinders from Assendelft 60 (Van Heeringen 1992, 81) and Velserbroek are

not regarded as *gootjes* here. For possibly older and different coastal pottery at inland sites see Roymans/Hiddink 1991, 125.

8 Van den Broeke 1987b, 1995.

9 Pare 1992, 171; Roymans 1991. Van Doorselaer (1990) has suggested a similar relationship between the Celtic fortified site on the Kemmelberg (West Flanders) and the large amounts of salt produced near De Panne, forty kilometres from the fortified site. However, all of the objects that have so far been found among the remains of the aristocratic settlement of the Kemmelberg (Van Doorselaer *et al.* 1987) seem to date from the 5th century BC, whereas the greater part of the pottery found at De Panne is of a later date; only a very few fragments may date from the 5th century BC (*cf.* Thoen 1990, 189, but also Van Doorselaer 1990). The pottery of the nearby pro-duction sites at Bray-Dunes, Veurne and Zuydcoote is also of a later date.

10 The greater part is of Early Iron Age date (Bertaux 1977).

11 After this contribution was written an intriguing site with Early Iron Age *briquetage* was investigated in the Hoeksche Waard region (Van Heeringen *et al.* 1998). The inland position of this site, along a former course of the Meuse, suggests that the objects concerned were used for the purification rather than the production of salt. Another possibility is that salt was at this site recovered from the ash of halophytic plants in the same way that brackish peat was later to be exploited for salt production (Van den Broeke 1996a). It is thought that salt was also imported from the French Channel coast from the Roman period onwards (Van den Broeke 1996b).

23 Hamlets on the move
Settlements in the southern and central parts of the Netherlands

Kees Schinkel

THE LANDSCAPE

In the Late Bronze Age and the early part of the Iron Age there were only unfortified settlements in Northwest Europe. After *c.* 500 BC, however, a differentiation became apparent in the hilly region surrounding the Lower Rhine Basin: fortified sites started to appear, in particular at high points. Some of these were possibly no more than temporary refuges, others developed into economically and politically important centres.[1] An early example of the latter type of fortified site is the Kemmelberg in Western Flanders.[2] The majority of the defended sites are datable to the first century BC; many are to be identified as the *oppida* and *castella* from which Caesar encountered resistance in the Gallic war. No traces of fortified sites whatsoever are known in the area immediately to the north of the hills. Outside the loess zone only simple agrarian settlements have been found.

To the west the region discussed here is bordered by the peat of Zeeland and South and North Holland, which were still expansive in prehistoric times, and to the north by the IJsselmeer and the river IJssel. Coversand areas formed in the final glacial period are the largest landscape units. Clayey basins of the major rivers, loess deposits (Limburg) and raised bogs (the Peel region) occupy a much smaller area.

In comparison with the environment of the coastal provinces and the rivers area, the coversand landscape was stable; the changes that did take place in it, such as the formation of sand drifts, are virtually entirely attributable to man's activities instead of to natural causes. The landscape was suitable for long-term occupation. The light soils were greatly suited to agriculture, pastures were to be found in stream and river valleys and forests yielded timber and firewood and additional fodder for the cattle. However, the fields (and the settlements) did have to be shifted regularly to avoid exhaustion of the soil.

Many of the settlements are located in the very areas where we would expect them to be, assuming that the aim in late prehistoric times was to make maximum use of different ecological zones, *i.e.* at the edges of coversand ridges at the transition from wet to dry zones. In those areas the landscape offered unrestricted possibilities for suitable settlement sites. This was not the case in the rivers area in the central part of the Netherlands, where only the highest parts of stream ridges were fit for occupation. Examples of settlements in the latter areas are those at Beers, Wijk bij Duurstede and Zijderveld.[3]

For archaeologists the sands present more drawbacks than the river areas, namely problems concerning *preservation*. On the other hand, the sandy soils are pre-eminently suited to large-scale research. As a result of the research carried out on the sandy soils of North Brabant we are well-informed about settlements in this area, whereas settlements on the loess in Limburg, in the rivers area and on the sands of Gelderland and Overijssel are underrepresented.[4] The same holds for the adjacent parts of Belgium and Germany, with the exception of the intensively investigated Lower Rhine loess zone.[5]

fig. 23.1

Since 1976 archaeological excavations have
been and still are conducted in Oss-Ussen
and its environment prior to the scheduled
construction of new residential areas. The
large exposed areas yield a lot of information
on settlement sites from the Bronze Age, the
Iron Age and the Roman period.

fig. 23.2

One of the finds of organic material from
Oss-Ussen: a carved oak plank recovered
from a Late Iron Age well. The carving
bears a striking resemblance to the symbols
observable on the gables of recent Dutch
houses, but the object may well have had an
entirely different function. Scale 1:5.

In the following sections the research carried out at Oss-Ussen in North Brabant will be extensively discussed first, because the remains found at this site span
the greater part of the period discussed here, and the resulting picture may be considered representative of the entire region, with the exception of the many wells
and pits that were discovered at this site. Moreover, Oss-Ussen has yielded information on all levels, i.e. on the plans of individual structures, on the farmyard,
the settlement and the microregion. The more thematic sections further on in this
chapter discuss information obtained from the whole of the southern part of the
Netherlands.

THE OCCUPATION OF OSS-USSEN

Oss-Ussen lies at the transition from the valley of the Meuse to the higher coversand of North Brabant. Today the distance to the Meuse is about 5 km, but in late
prehistoric times it was probably less, at most 2.5 km. Prior to the construction
of new houses at Oss (fig. 23.1), the Institute of Prehistory of Leiden University
investigated a first part of some 40 ha (20%) of a microregion measuring 1.3 x
1.5 km (approx. 2 km²).[6] Many parts of the unexcavated area which are now built
over must also have contained occupation remains. Moreover, the limits of the
occupation remains were not found along any of the sides of the excavated area.
This means that the results of the calculations presented below for the number of
buildings, population density, etc., are minimum figures, and that shifts in the settlement pattern can only be indicated with reserve.

The first indications of human activity at Oss-Ussen date from the Late Neolithic, the earliest features of buildings being of Middle Bronze Age date. Oss-Ussen
was also occupied in the Late Bronze Age, as indicated by a small number of wells
and pits dating from this period, but no Late Bronze Age house plans have been

found. In the aforementioned periods occupation was virtually exclusively limited to an area in the northern part of Ussen, relatively close to the Meuse.

The history of the occupation after the end of the Late Bronze Age can be continuously followed until in the Roman period. From this whole time span, house plans, granaries, wells, pits and funerary structures are known; cult sites can be added to this list for the period after the Early Iron Age. Because of this, we are able to follow the development of the occupation in great detail, not in the last place thanks to the availability of a close-knit chronology based on pottery from closed contexts.[7]

Thanks to the wealth of deep pits and wells, the number of organic remains discovered – among which are unique wooden artefacts (fig. 23.2) – is unusually large for the sandy soils. This furthermore means that our knowledge of the occupants' farming practices is based on more than just settlement remains and artefacts. Seed research has shown that cereals, such as millet, barley and emmer, and oil-containing seeds, namely linseed and gold of pleasure, were cultivated here from the Early Iron Age onwards.[8] Cattle and remarkably large numbers of horses were the main stocks, but pigs, sheep and goats were also kept. Only few remains of game have been found and no remains whatsoever of fish.[9]

fig. 23.3
Schematic representation of the Early Iron Age elementary structures at Oss-Ussen. Scale 1:10,000.

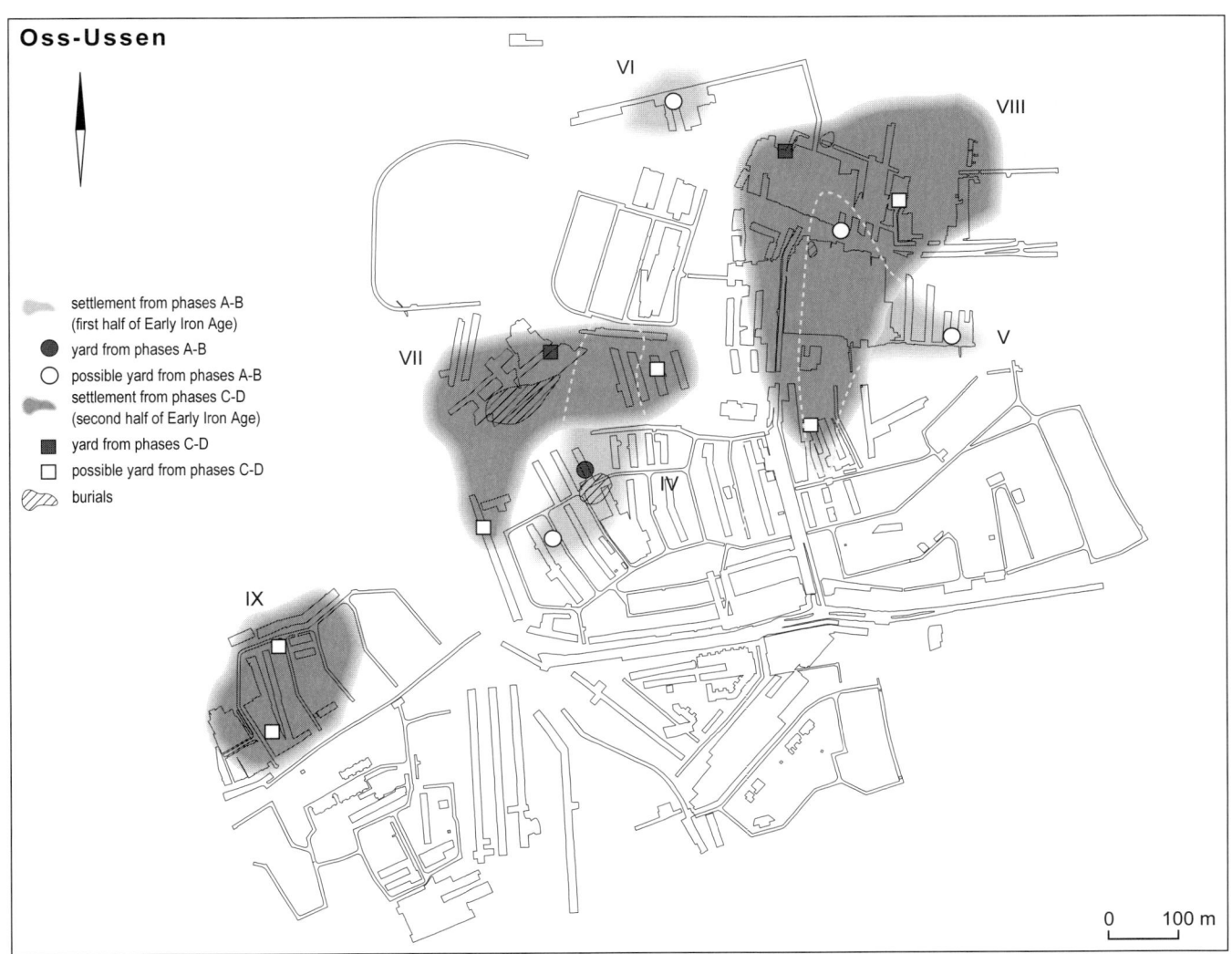

Oss-Ussen

settlement from phases A-B
(first half of Early Iron Age)
● yard from phases A-B
○ possible yard from phases A-B
settlement from phases C-D
(second half of Early Iron Age)
■ yard from phases C-D
□ possible yard from phases C-D
▨ burials

0   100 m

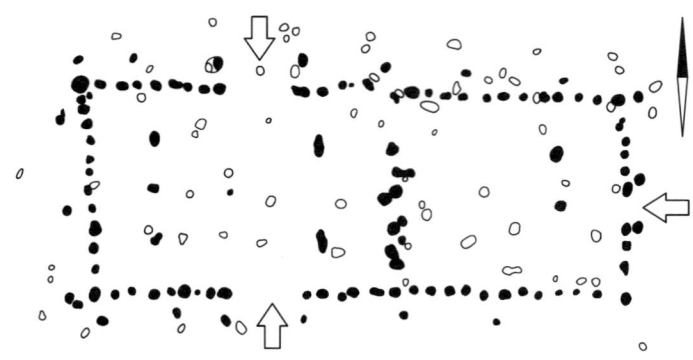

fig. 23.4

Oss-Ussen: house plan of type Oss 2A from the Early Iron Age. The plans of this type are partly four-aisled and comprise wall posts set close together and outer posts spaced far apart which supported the edge of the hipped roof. There were two entrances opposite one another off-centre in the long walls and a third entrance in one of the short walls. The latter is assumed to have provided access to the part of the house used for stalling cattle. Scale 1:200.

Early Iron Age

Four settlements are known from the Early Iron Age (fig. 23.3). Three of these lie at intervals of some 300 m along a line running from the northeast to the southwest. The fourth (not included in fig. 23.3) lies 400 m to the northwest of that line. The settlements measured between 150 x 150 m and 450 x 450 m. The house plans, which were recognised at three of the four settlements, belonged to longhouses of type Oss 2 and in one case of type Oss 3 (figs. 23.4-6). They have a partly four-aisled basic plan and are substantially shorter than the farms of the Middle Bronze Age (see chapter 18).

Not one house plan was discovered at the southernmost settlement, but we may assume that there were houses at this site, too, because of the granaries, wells and pits that were found and, moreover, the large amounts of settlement waste that they contained.

fig. 23.5

Oss-Ussen: reconstruction and plan of house type Oss 2B from the Early Iron Age. The house's basic structure and layout were the same as those of type Oss 2A, except that the edge of the hipped roof was supported by outer posts set close together and the wall was founded in a shallow bedding trench. Neither are there any indications of a separate entrance to the part used for stalling cattle. The hatched features may also form part of the house plan. Scale of plan 1:200.

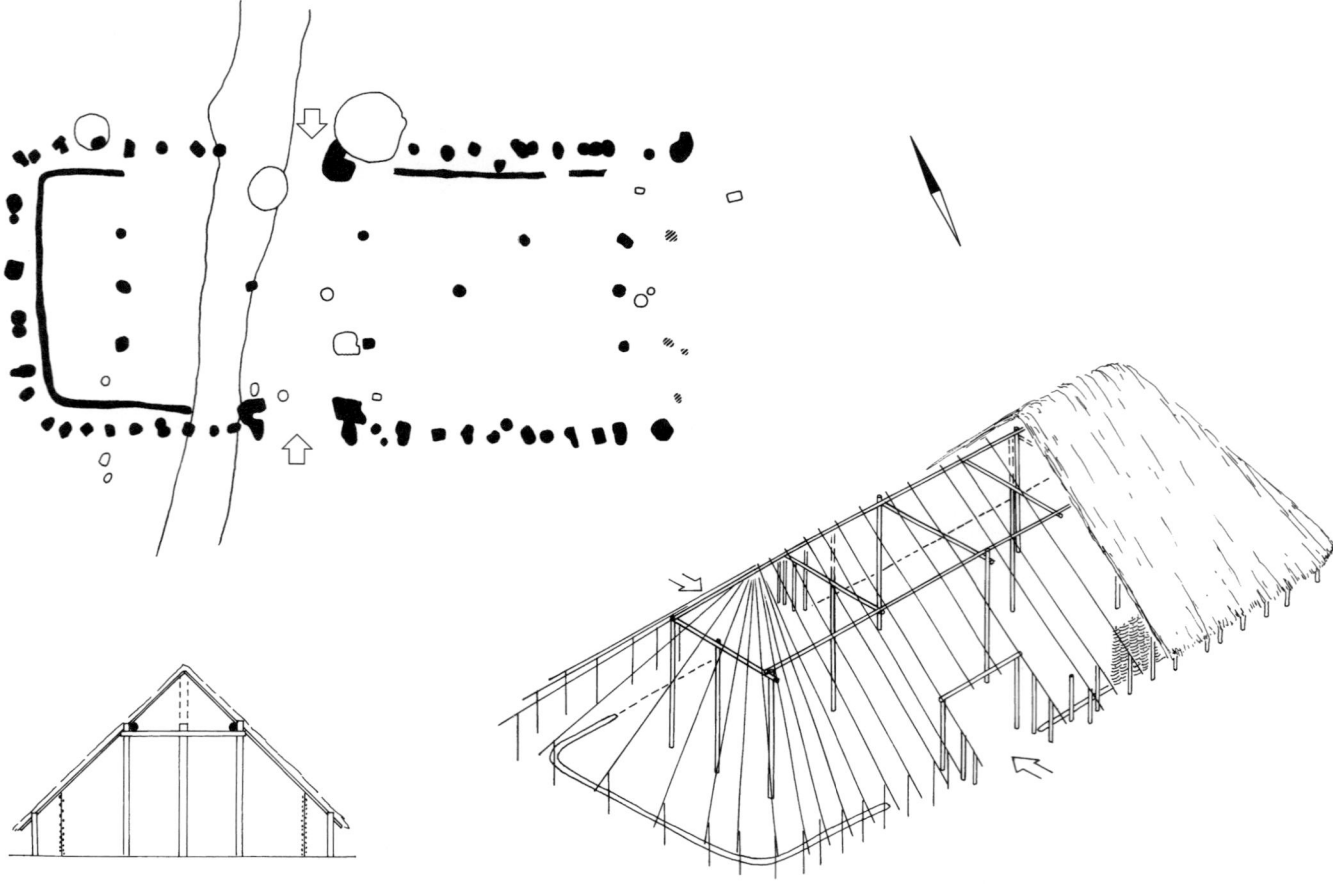

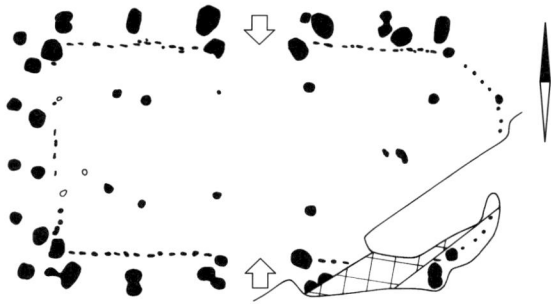

fig. 23.6
Oss-Ussen: house plan of type Oss 3 from
the Early Iron Age. The house had a three-
aisled layout, the edge of the hipped roof
was supported by sturdy double outer posts
spaced far apart and the wall by light thin
posts set close together alternating with
somewhat sturdier posts. The house had two
entrances lying opposite one another more or
less in the middle of the long walls.
Scale 1:200.

The layout of the area around the farms, the farmyard, is not clear. Fences and
ditches marking the limits of the yards were only found at the northwest settlement and they were only very fragmentary.[10] Because of this, it is often not clear
which features are to be associated with a particular farm. The most completely
excavated farmyard (fig. 23.7) clearly shows that there were areas for different activities around the farm, within a radius of 50 m. To the west of the house were
five granaries, to the southwest five shallow pits and to the east four wells and
three deep pits. The large number of wells and water pits suggests that they had

fig. 23.7
Oss-Ussen: Early Iron Age yard surrounding
the farm shown in figure 23.5. The grey
elements date from the Early Iron Age.
Scale 1:500.

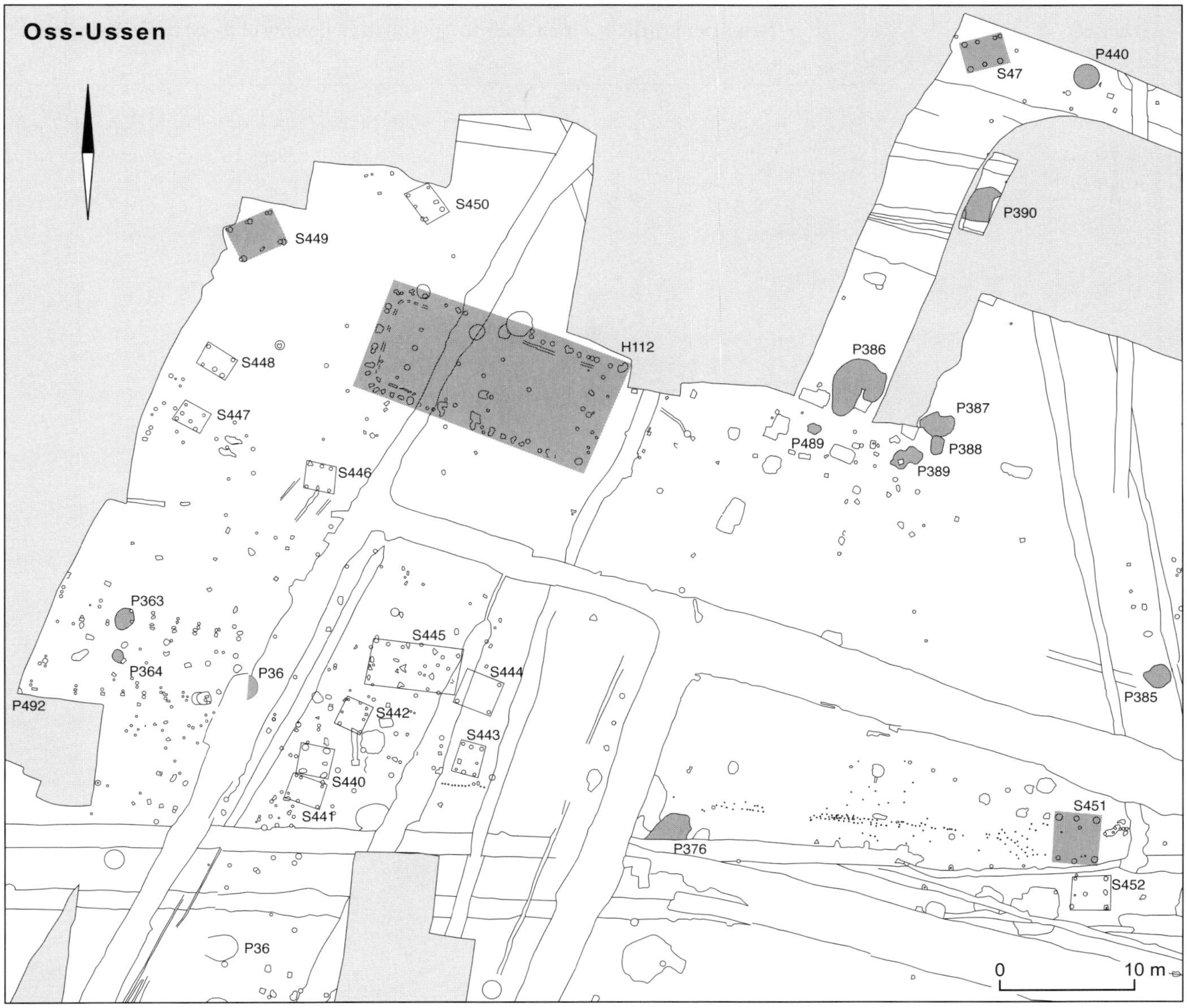

Oss-Ussen

S47
P440
S450
S449
P390
S448
H112
P386
S447
P489
P387
P388
P389
S446
P363
P364
P36
S445
S444
P492
S442
S443
P385
S440
S441
S451
P376
P36
S452

0   10 m

shorter lives than the farms and that new wells and pits had to be dug regularly.

The four settlements were not occupied simultaneously. If they had been, an assumed life of 25 years would imply a total of 48 farms for the period 800-500 BC, whereas not more than sixteen farmyards have been identified with varying degrees of certainty at Ussen. At the beginning of the Early Iron Age there was probably one, constantly shifting, farm at Ussen, to which a second was added later on in the Early Iron Age. So what we call 'a settlement' in actual fact represents the remains of a number of intermittent phases of occupation.

Because families in the Early Iron Age did not select a new occupation site at random, but returned to previously occupied sites, we may use the term 'shifting cycles'. Environmental – and also socio-cultural – factors will undoubtedly have played a role in these cycles. Remarkable in this context is the fact that the few known graves all lie inside the settlements and are often directly associated with settlement features (see fig. 23.3). In this respect Oss constitutes an exception in a period characterised by urnfields situated outside the settlements.[11] There may have been an urnfield outside the excavated area, though.

If we assume that on average six people lived in a farm, then the Early Iron Age population density of Ussen was three to six individuals per square kilometre. This figure agrees fairly well with population densities calculated on the basis of data from urnfields in North Brabant, Overijssel and Drenthe.[12] The figures obtained for the last two provinces are based on the assumption of two to three contemporary farms per urnfield, which leads to a population density of 3-4.5 individuals/km².

fig. 23.8

Schematic representation of the Middle Iron Age elementary structures at Oss-Ussen. Scale 1:10,000.

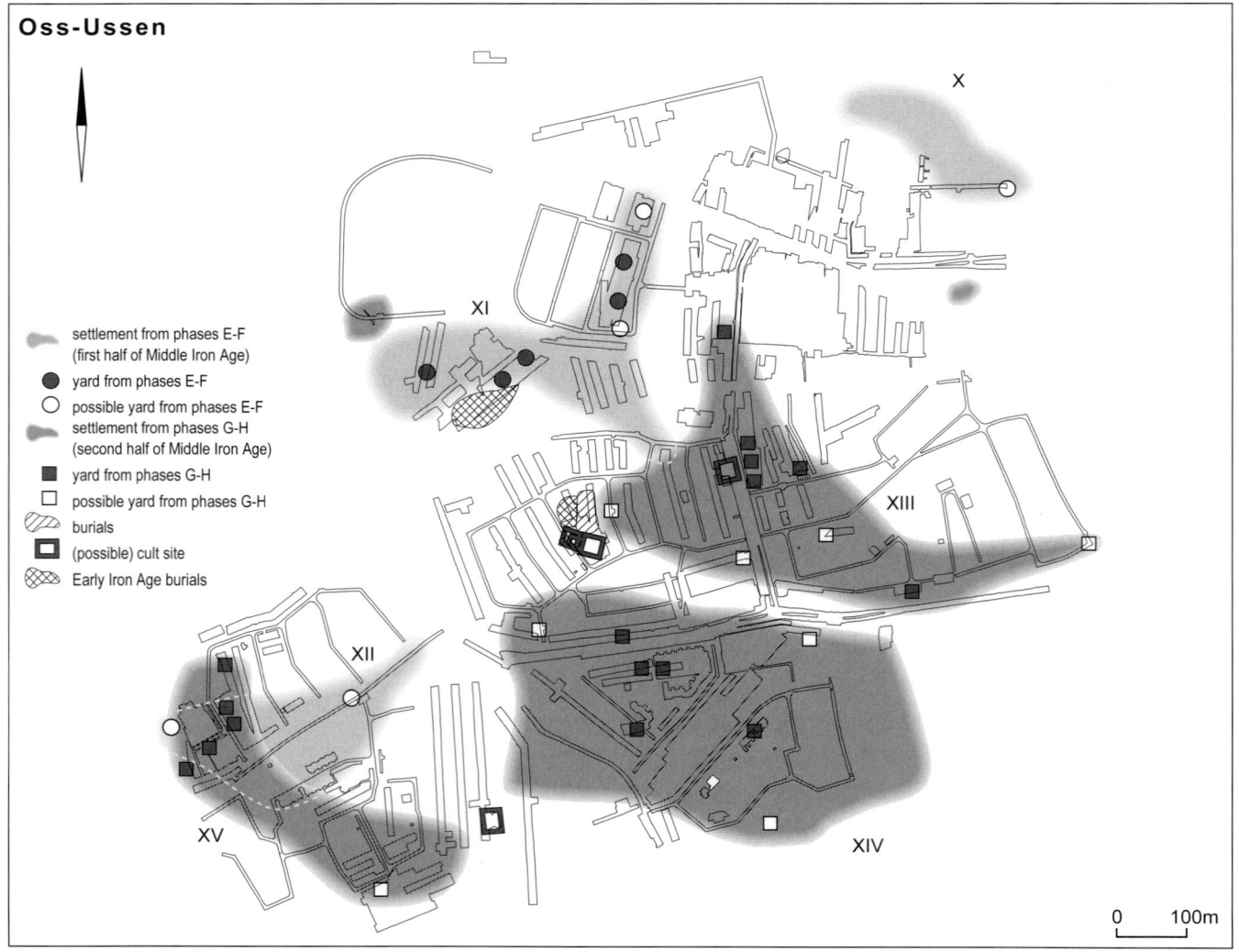

The exact locations of fields, pastures and wasteland are unknown. The cattle was probably grazed on pastures some distance to the north of the settlements, in the direction of the Meuse. In view of the quality of the soil, it is likely that the fields lay in the vicinity of the settlements. There was sufficient space for them around the settlements because a family of six needed at most six ha of arable, including fallow land.[13] This figure is based on a low estimated seed/yield ratio (1:3). Wasteland, where pigs could be herded and from where timber and firewood could be obtained, was probably found in the relatively high, feature and findless area to the south of the settlements. As no streams or other watercourses were observed in the excavated area we may assume that the occupants obtained their water from the many wells and water pits. In most places the groundwater was less than one metre below the surface.

Middle Iron Age

In the first half of the Middle Iron Age the occupants lived in more or less the same areas as those occupied in the Early Iron Age. In the course of this period settlement did shift slightly towards previously unoccupied land, but the basic settlement pattern was still three settlements lying on a northeast-southwest line (fig. 23.8) and one settlement to the north of that line. The most thoroughly excavated settlement, which measured 400 x 330 m, contained five plans of the two-aisled house type Oss 4A, better known as the Haps type (figs. 23.9 and 10). These houses were probably not contemporary, but succeeded one another. The distance between the plans varied from 30 to 140 m. The fact that the plans of the Haps type date from as early as the first half of the Middle Iron Age was inferred not from the finds, but from the positions of the plans in a complex of features dating from that period.

In spite of the lack of traces of the limits of the yards, it was apparent that gra-

fig. 23.9
Oss-Ussen: reconstruction and plan of an early example of house type Oss 4A from the Middle and Late Iron Age, also known as the *Haps* type. The longhouses of this type were two-aisled and had a hipped roof whose edge was supported by outer posts set far apart. The wall was supported by the inner row of widely spaced posts, which were alternately arranged with respect to the outer posts. The sturdily designed entrances lay opposite one another off-centre in the long walls. The entrances and central posts of the house whose plan is represented here were at some time replaced (hatched features). Scale of plan 1:200.

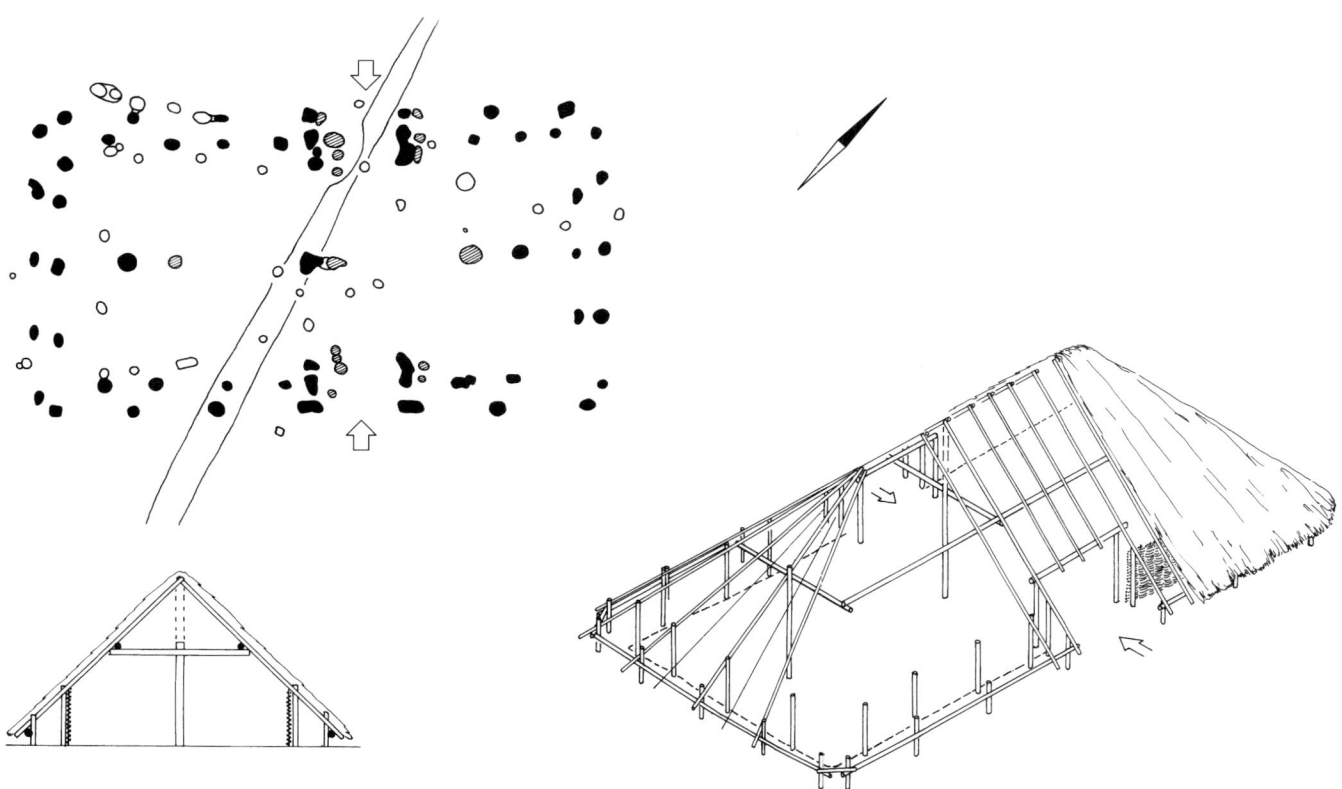

fig. 23.10

A full-size farm has been reconstructed at the site of the *Stichting Prehistorisch Huis* (Prehistoric House Foundation) in Eindhoven on the basis of the plan shown in figure 23.9.

naries, wells and water pits were recurrent elements in the surroundings of the farms. Watering places and shallow pits were less common.

The beginning of the second half of the Middle Iron Age saw a change in the fixed pattern: between 400 and 350 BC all of the settlements, with the exception of the southernmost, were abandoned. The fact that only the southernmost settlement, which was situated furthest inland, remained occupied could indicate increased influence of the Meuse. However, due to the lack of good palaeogeographic data for the area south of the Meuse this is not entirely certain. The occupants of the abandoned settlements built two new settlements 300-500 m away, on the higher and previously uninhabited grounds to the southeast of Ussen (see fig. 23.8). From *c.* 375 to 250 BC there were hence three settlements. Each of them comprised a total of five to six houses. The sizes of the settlements varied from 380 x 330 m to 750 x 450 m.

At the centres of these settlements were four houses spaced less than 100 m apart, which were surrounded by granaries, wells with wattlework linings and water pits. Due to the excavation strategy, it is not clear whether these elements were present around every farm. Wells in particular were found widely distributed outside the centres of the settlements.

The majority of the farms were still longhouses of type Oss 4A, but the first representatives of type Oss 5A had possibly started to appear, the house type characteristic of the Late Iron Age, which was also two-aisled (fig. 23.11). The number of plans per settlement and the period of occupation of about 125 years lead to the conclusion that there was one shifting farm in each settlement in the second half of the Middle Iron Age. However, this is a minimum option because it is likely that some house plans have remained undiscovered. This brings us to a population density of at least nine individuals/km^2.

Virtually no graves are known from the Middle Iron Age. Three, possibly four, cult sites have been excavated, though. Most of these date from the second half of the Middle Iron Age (figs. 23.8, 29.16).[14] The oldest was surrounded by rows of posts arranged in a square. The next, at the same location, measuring 32.5 x 33.5 m, was enclosed by a square ditch. The known graves were situated near this cult site. The distance to the closest settlement was more than 100 m. The same holds for what may have been a cult site surrounded by a trapezoid ditch. The smallest

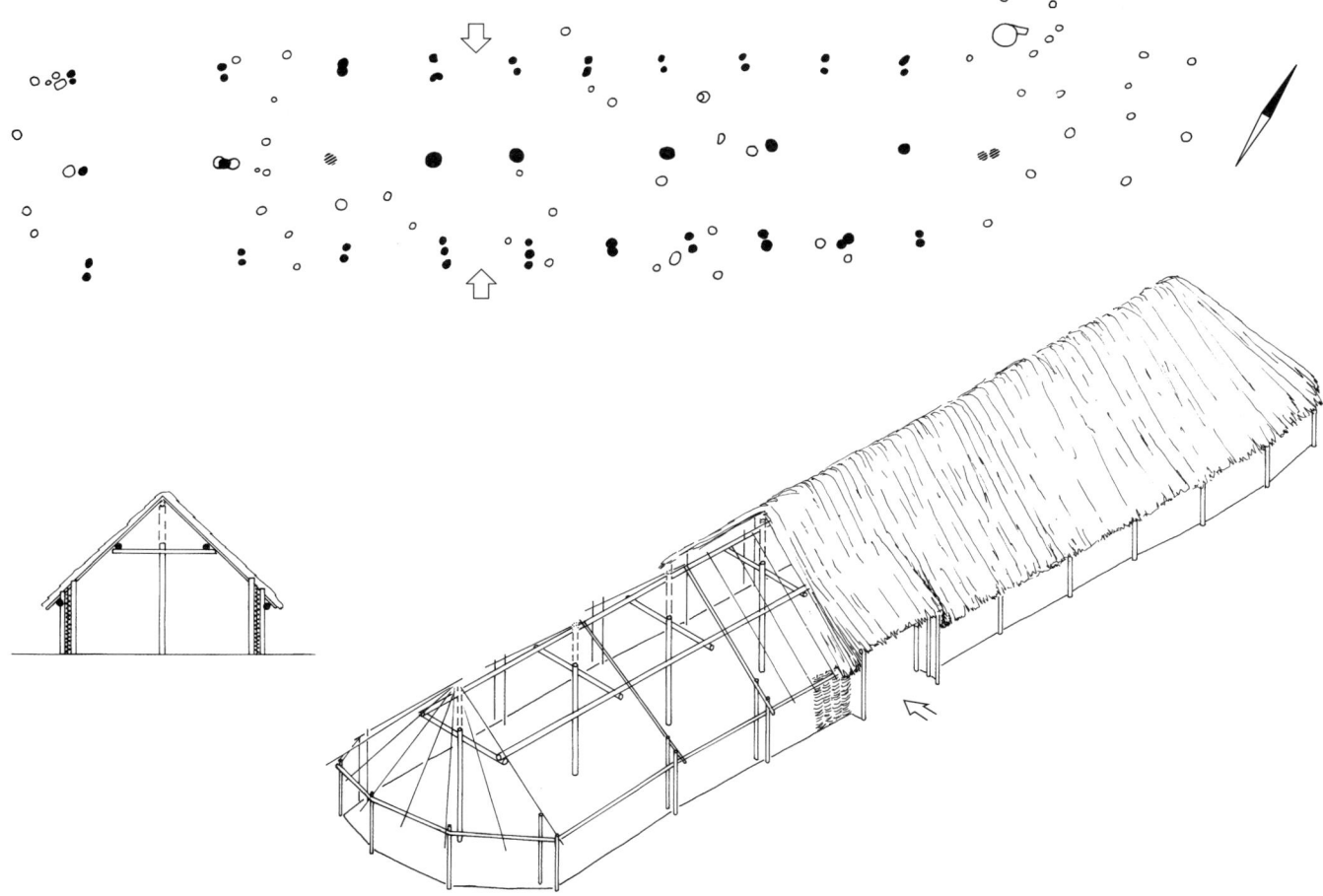

cult site, enclosed by a square ditch, is also the only one situated in the immediate vicinity of contemporary house plans. In view of the central positions of the first large cult sites mentioned above and the association with the graves, it is possible that they served as centres for ritual activities. Another remarkable point is that the layout of cult sites seems to be associated with the southward shift of the area of occupation. In the Late Iron Age, when settlement moved north again, the cult sites fell into disuse.

Late Iron Age

The history of the occupation in the Late Iron Age can be divided into phases in part only. The scarce remains that are datable to the first half of this period were found in the northern half of Ussen. On the basis of typological evidence a few house plans in the southwestern part have also been dated to this period of occupation.

In the second half of the Late Iron Age we again recognise the familiar pattern of the Early Iron Age and the first half of the Middle Iron Age, of three settlements lying along a northeast-southwest line (fig. 23.12). But that is as far as the resemblance between the two periods goes. The later settlements were far more densely populated, as appears from for example the house plans, which overlap one another or are set close together. At the settlement furthest southwest, where sixteen

fig. 23.11
Oss-Ussen: reconstruction and plan of the Late Iron Age house type Oss 5A. The house plans of this type are two-aisled. The houses are assumed to have had a hipped roof, borne by paired posts, which also supported the walls. Entrances are often indistinguishable in these plans. There was one entrance off-centre in the long wall of the plan illustrated here. The hatched features may have formed part of the plan, too. Scale of plan 1:200.

527

house plans were unearthed, two contemporary farms shifted from the west to the east. In the first half of the Late Iron Age these farms were of different types, *viz* Oss 4A/4B and Oss 5A. In the second half of this period both farms were of type Oss 5A.

At the middle settlement, where nine house plans were found, the movement of one farm, in the eastern part of the site, can be followed throughout the first half of the Late Iron Age. The evidence for a second shifting farm, in the southwest part of the site, goes back only as far as the second half of the Late Iron Age. The plans of the farms of the first group developed from that of type Oss 4A/B, via type Oss 5A to type Oss 7A, a house with walls founded in trenches with a partly one-aisled, partly two-aisled plan (fig. 23.13). The farms of the second group were of the one-aisled type Oss 6 with walls founded in trenches.

With what is thought to be a total of 27 house plans, the northeast settlement was the largest and most densely populated of the three. A remarkable fact is that the orientation of the house plans at this settlement changed after 200 BC from southwest-northeast to southeast-northwest. At the other settlements the orientation of the houses remained the same as in the Middle Iron Age, i.e. southwest-northeast. At the northeast settlement the development of three to four contemporary farms can be followed. Here, too, there were at first farms of type Oss 4A as well as type Oss 5A until about the middle of the Late Iron Age. And here, too, the plan of at least one farm developed into that of a building with walls founded in trenches in the 1st century BC. The latter, however, is not of type Oss 6 or 7A but

fig. 23.12
Schematic representation of the elementary structures from the Late Iron Age (phases I-L) at Oss-Ussen. Scale 1:10,000.

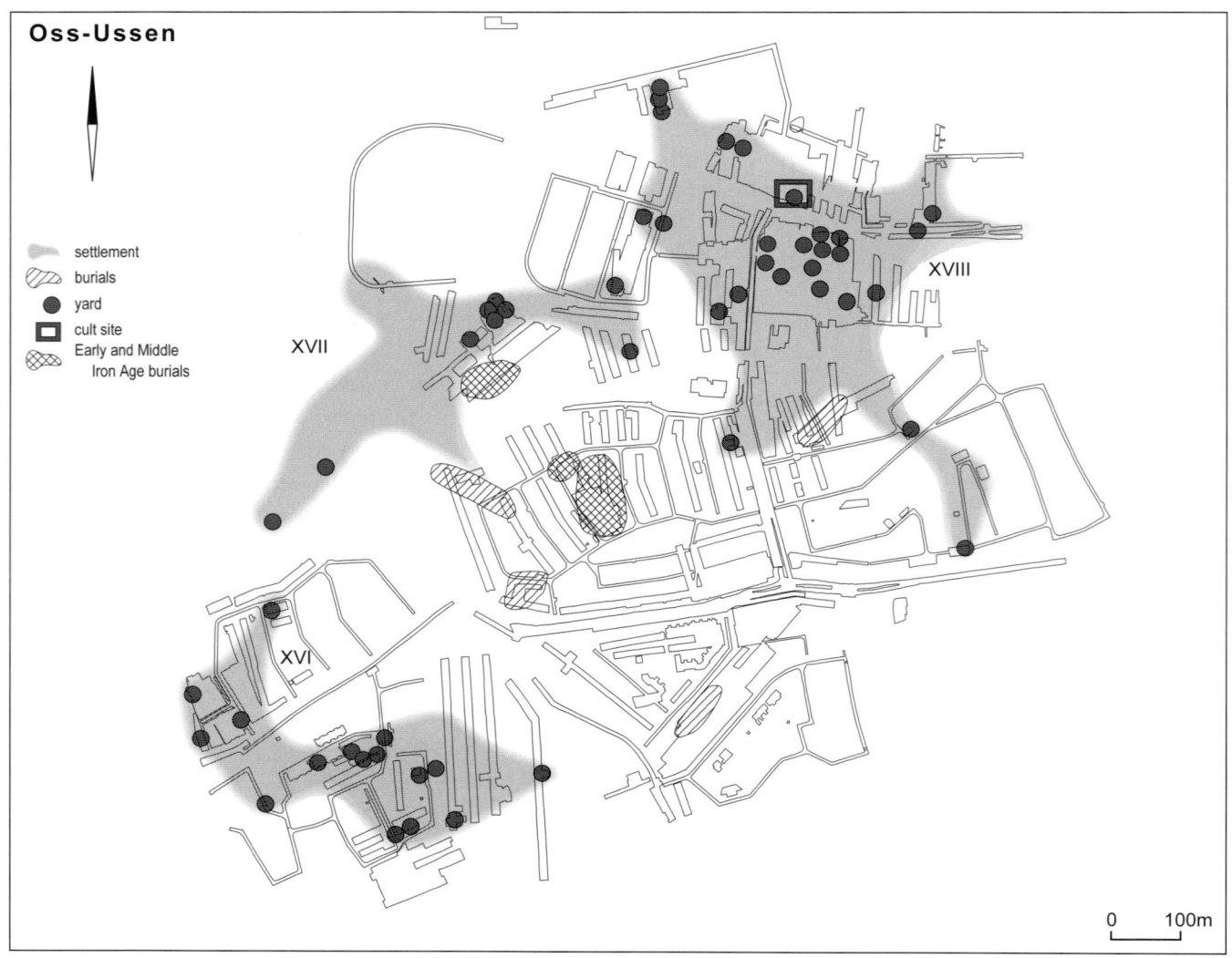

Oss-Ussen

settlement
burials
yard
cult site
Early and Middle
  Iron Age burials

XVII

XVIII

XVI

0   100m

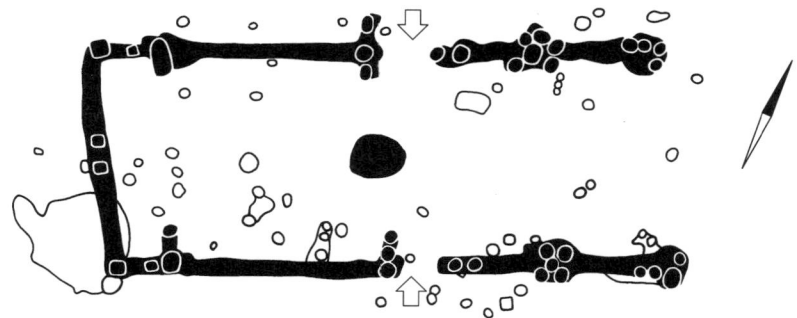

fig. 23.13
Oss-Ussen: plan of house type Oss 7A from the second half of the Late Iron Age. Houses of this type were characterised by a partly one-aisled, partly two-aisled layout and walls founded in a bedding trench, which also contained extra posts to help support the weight of the roof. The shape of the roof is not entirely clear: the house may have had a saddle roof at the end where the short wall was founded in a trench and a 'normal' hipped roof at the other end. The two entrances lay opposite one another, more or less in the middle of the long walls. Scale 1:200.

fig. 23.14
Oss-Ussen: reconstruction and plan of house type Oss 8C from the 1st century BC. The houses of this type were two-aisled, had heavy, deeply founded central posts, walls founded in a bedding trench and outer posts that supported the edge of a saddle roof. It is assumed that these houses had a saddle roof as the central posts at either end of the building were incorporated in the short walls. There were three entrances off-centre in the long walls, two of which lay opposite one another. The white blocks in the central holes represent the remains of oak posts. Scale of plan 1:200.

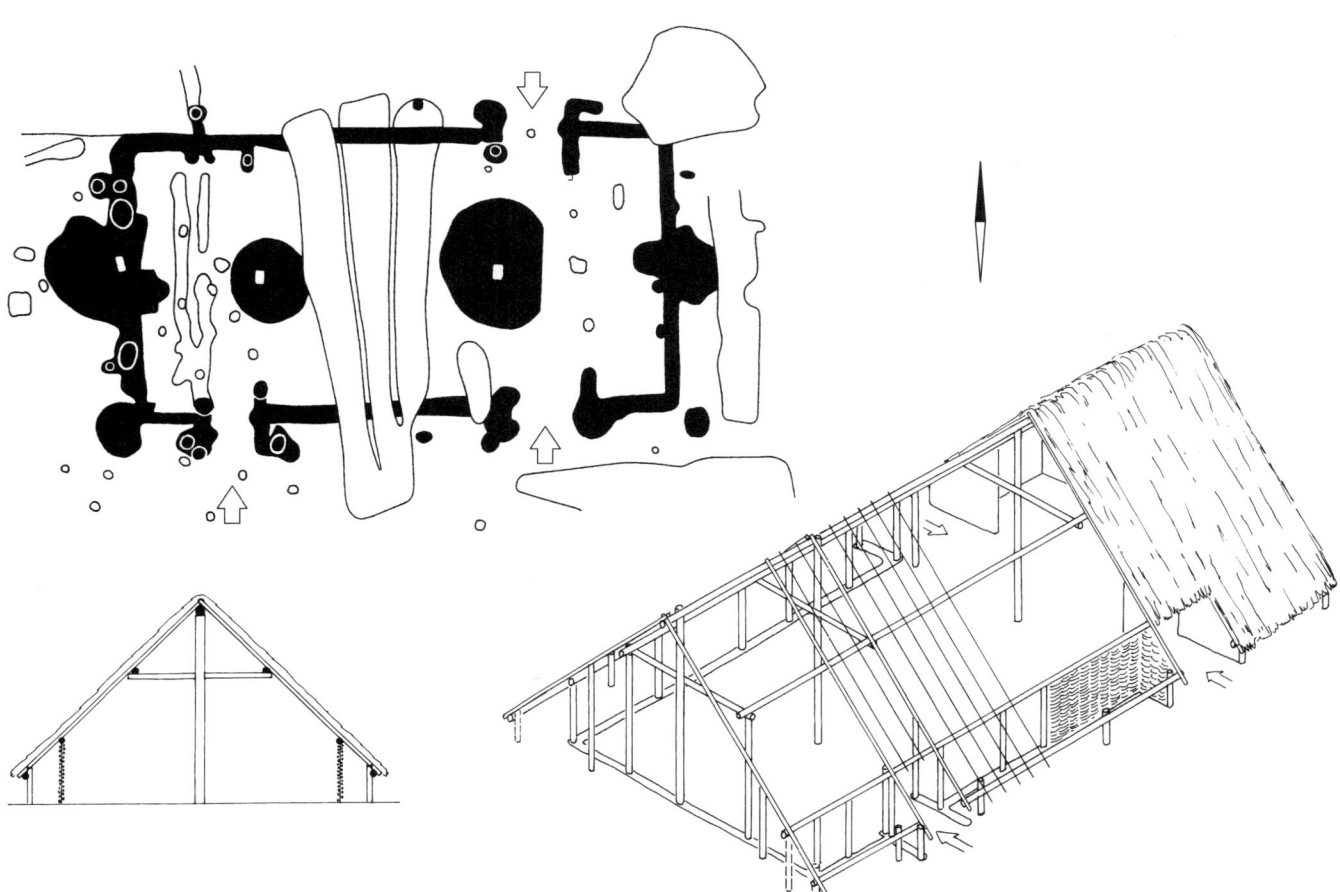

of the two-aisled type Oss 8C (fig. 23.14). With the introduction of this house type the orientation moreover changed to west-east.

What has been said above gives the impression that the introduction of houses with walls founded in trenches was a local development. There are arguments supporting as well as contradicting this supposition. Arguments in favour of a local development are the locations and the absence of qualitative differences in the material culture. However, the substantial innovations in building techniques, which are not logical developments from the techniques used to construct houses of type Oss 5A, and the absence of houses with walls founded in trenches at the southern settlement do suggest influences from outside. It is tempting to associate the new house types at Ussen, in particular type Oss 8C, with the historically attested arrival of the Batavians around the middle of the 1st century BC. Another possibility, besides that of the settlement of Batavians at this site, is the adoption of Batavian building traditions by the indigenous population. But as long as we have no information about the house plans in the area of origin of the Batavians the assumption of immigration remains hypothetical.

The large number of house plans bears no relation to the number of wells, water pits and other pits. It would seem that in the first half of the Late Iron Age in particular, people had a different way of obtaining water other than by digging wells. In the second half of the Late Iron Age the number of wells and pits increased again at the northern settlement. These wells and pits are not equally distributed across the area occupied but are instead all clustered in groups, with the odd exception. No such clusters are known from the other settlements. At all of the settlements there were virtually exclusively granaries in the immediate vicinity of farms, and only few wells and water pits (fig. 23.15).

It is estimated that the population needed about 36 ha of arable land, including fallow land, in the Ussen microregion in the Late Iron Age. This is slightly over one sixth of the overall area of the microregion. The population is assumed to have consisted of at least six families of six individuals each, which results in a population density of at least eighteen individuals/km².

Of only a few of these people do we know where they were buried. As far as this matter is concerned, however, Oss-Ussen has yielded more information than the other settlements in the south of the Netherlands, where we know absolutely nothing about the relationship between settlements and graves, neither for the Middle Iron Age nor for the Late Iron Age.

The majority of the graves were situated on the higher grounds south and east of the settlements (fig. 23.12). Four graves lay in the extensive cemetery from the Roman period found in this area and may possibly be interpreted as the first graves of that cemetery. A second group of graves constitutes an exception because of its situation to the north of the largest settlement. A common characteristic of the graves is that they were all situated at some distance from contemporary settlement remains. This does not hold for the one cult site from the end of the Late Iron Age or the beginning of the Roman period.[15] This square ritual site measuring 45 x 40 m or more, which was oriented towards the four points of the compass and was surrounded by a ditch, lay within the limits of the northern settlement (fig. 23.12). The date and the orientation of this cult site make it likely that it was laid out by the occupants of the houses with walls founded in trenches.

The settlements at Oss-Ussen were not abandoned when the southern part of the Netherlands came under Roman influence. Precisely in this period two settlements were founded, according to a plan; a third was added at the end of the 1st century AD. All three were founded in the same areas that had been occupied in the Late Iron Age.[16]

The only conclusion following from a survey of the entire period is that there were three more or less fixed territories at Ussen, within which occupation concentrated to an increasing extent in the course of the Iron Age. This brings to mind another region where settlements have been intensively investigated: the sands of Drenthe. There, too, evidence has been found for shifting farms within fixed territories occupied for long periods of time[17].

In the following sections various aspects of the settlements will be discussed once again, only now on the basis of the evidence obtained from the whole of the southern and central parts of the Netherlands.

SETTLEMENT ELEMENTS

Houses

The house plans from the Late Bronze Age and the Early Iron Age are in principle three-aisled. More than half of the plans also included one or more holes for posts at the centre of the house, giving the plan an entirely[18] or partly[19] four-aisled character. Two-aisled plans from the period discussed here have been found in Belgium in particular,[20] but also in the southern part of the Netherlands.[21] The only partly two-aisled, partly three-aisled, plan was unearthed at Elst in the province of Utrecht.[22]

fig. 23.15
Oss-Ussen: part of the Late Iron Age northeastern settlement. Many of the plans of farms from the Late Iron Age overlap one another. This is a direct consequence of the changing settlement structure. Only some of the plans can be chronologically ordered. It is however clear that several farms were occupied simultaneously. Scale 1:500.

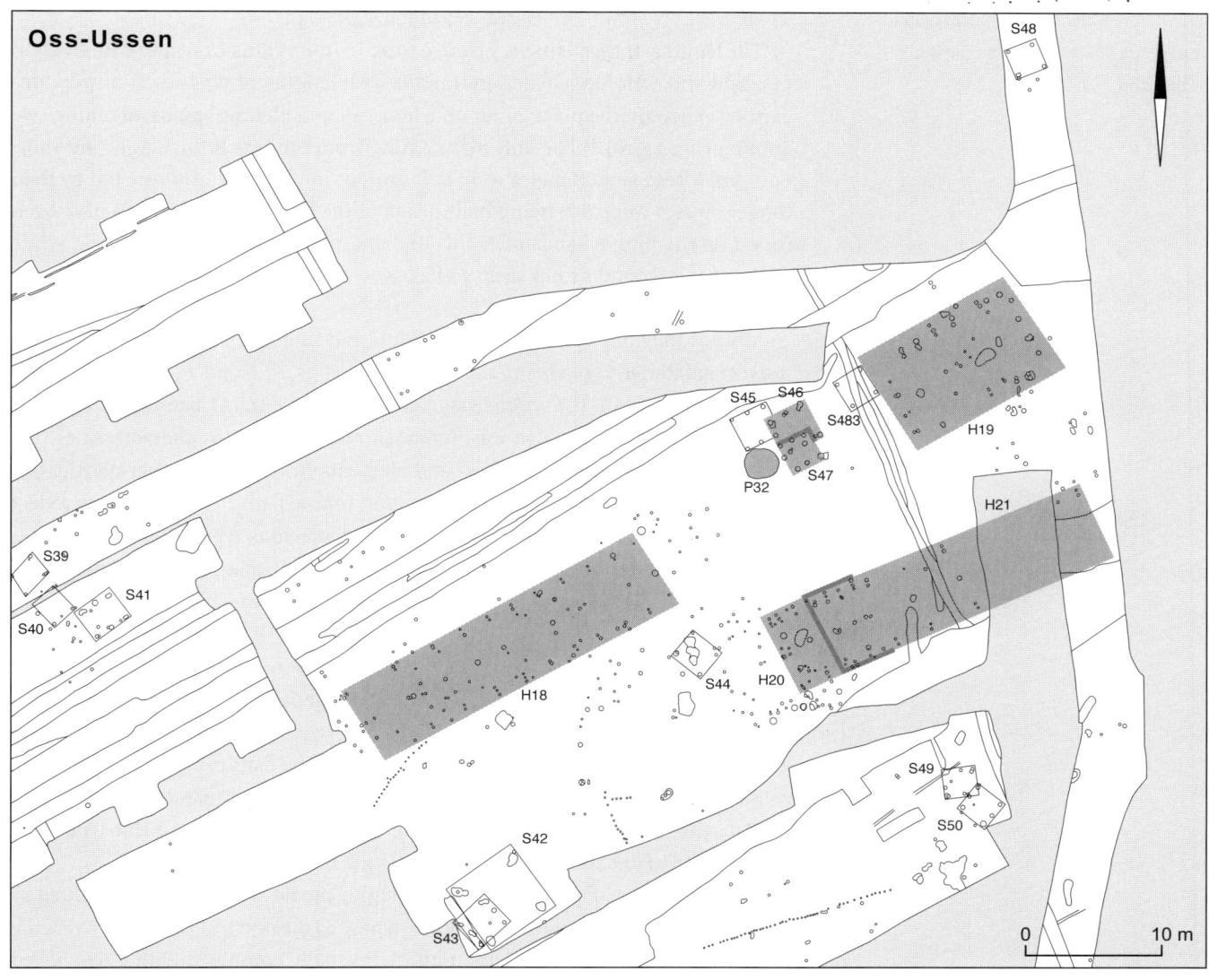

Oss-Ussen

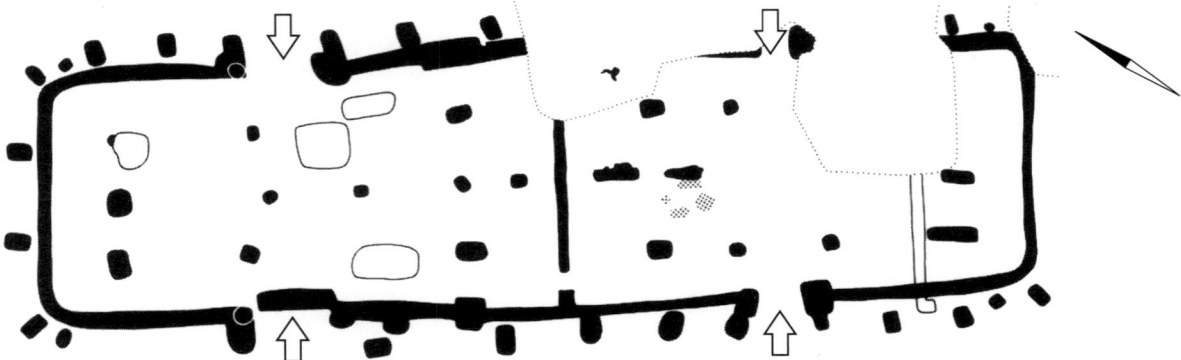

fig. 23.16

Silvolde: partly four-aisled house plan from the Early Iron Age with walls set in a bedding trench, outer supports spaced far apart and entrances lying opposite one another in the long walls. The central bedding trench divided the house into two parts of the same length. The hatched features represent a hearth. A few pits used for underground storage are observable along the walls.
Scale 1:200.

In most cases the walls were founded in shallow trenches. Where there are no trenches the course of the wall is indicated by rows of postholes, sometimes with small diameters. Posts set outside the walls intended to help support the weight of the roof are common elements of plans from the Early Iron Age onwards, but a plan discovered at Loon op Zand (North Brabant)[23] shows that this architectural feature must have been introduced already in the Late Bronze Age. The entrances were usually opposite one another in the long walls. According to their positions, they divided the houses into two equal parts or into one large and one smaller part. There were very few (byre) entrances in the short walls.

The lengths of the plans vary from 9 to 20 m, the widths from 5 to 8 m. At Loon op Zand and Silvolde (Gelderland) plans with lengths of 23 and 26 m were unearthed. They are the plans of 'double houses': two identical plans adjoining one another (fig. 23.16).[24] The only plans dating from the Late Bronze Age[25] are short (<15 m). These small houses were still present in the Early Iron Age but by then longer houses were also being built. Plans of the first group of houses have been found on the higher sands of North Brabant and Overijssel, in particular, while those of the second group seem to be associated with the major rivers, i.e. with lower-lying areas.

Most of the house plans from the Middle and Late Iron Age are two-aisled, the most characteristic type being the Haps house (figs.23.9 and 23.10). The lengths do not exceed 20 m, the widths vary between 5 and 8 m. At Bennekom (Gelderland) an unusual house plan was found, showing both Haps characteristics (the wall, outside posts and entrances) and elements from an earlier period (the layout of the interior, which was both two- and four-aisled).[26] This plan may reflect the continuous evolution of house types from previous types. Two other plans, found at Heijen (Limburg) and Lunteren (Gelderland), also show a possible rudiment from the Early Iron Age in the form of wall posts of which some are set in a trench.[27]

Farms of the Haps type were widely distributed across the entire southern part of the Netherlands in the Middle Iron Age in particular. Possibly already at the end of the Middle Iron Age in North Brabant a new two-aisled type started to be built alongside houses of the Haps type. The characteristic feature of this type is paired wall posts (fig. 23.11). The lengths of these houses vary considerably, from 6 to 29.5 m, the widths less, from 4 to 6.5 m. With the appearance of this type there came an end to the hitherto limited variation in length.

The final phase of the Late Iron Age, roughly the 1st century BC, was marked by a strong increase in the number of house types. To the north of the major rivers the three-aisled form of construction returned, usually combined with a two-aisled design, resulting in partly two-, partly three-aisled house plans[28] (fig. 23.17). In the south, too, more variations of the two-aisled type started to be built, the walls being more and more frequently founded in trenches. Two-aisled house plans with deep central postholes have been found at Oss (fig. 23.14) and at Neerharen (Belgium)[29] and partly two-, partly one-aisled plans at Oss (fig. 23.13). The variation in length and width increased again with these new house types.

Further south, for example at Beegden (Limburg) and Huise (Belgium), the typical longhouses are absent.[30] Here the houses bore a close resemblance to the buildings which had been built in the Lower Rhine loess region since the Early Iron Age at least[31]: simple two-aisled structures with lengths that did not exceed 10 m. It is possible that such structures are also responsible for the clusters of postholes encountered at many settlement sites in the eastern part of the Dutch rivers region; in none of these clusters have plans of the usual longhouses been recognised.[32] Except for the houses of the Haps type, all of the aforementioned house types continued to be built in (the early part of) the Roman period.

Most of the plans described above are assumed to be plans of longhouses. Direct evidence for this is scarce though. A structural division (combined one-/two-aisled or two-/three-aisled plans) points to a functional division, but which part was used for which purpose remains unclear. Hearths, which may be regarded as characteristic of the domestic part, were preserved in a few plans only (fig. 23.16). Where the entrances divided the house into two parts of unequal lengths, the hearth was usually situated in the smallest part. This part may hence be considered the living area. An entrance in a short wall is to be regarded as an indication of the position of the byre (figs. 23.4 and 23.17).

In the Netherlands, ditches marking partitions for cattle are known from the Roman period only. They have been found exclusively in the three-aisled parts of two-/three-aisled plans.[33] An Iron Age house plan (of the Haps type) found at Meppen in Germany, however, contained what are thought to be traces of stall partitions in the part of the house opposite that containing a hearth (fig. 23.18).[34]

fig. 23.17
Wijk bij Duurstede-De Horden: partly two-aisled, partly three-aisled house plan from the Late Iron Age. Some of the wall posts were set in a trench. There were two entrances lying opposite one another at the transition from the two-aisled part to the three-aisled part. The eastern short wall contained a third entrance, which is assumed to have provided access to the byre. At the centre of the house was a large pit for underground storage. The plan is surrounded by ditches. Scale 1:250.

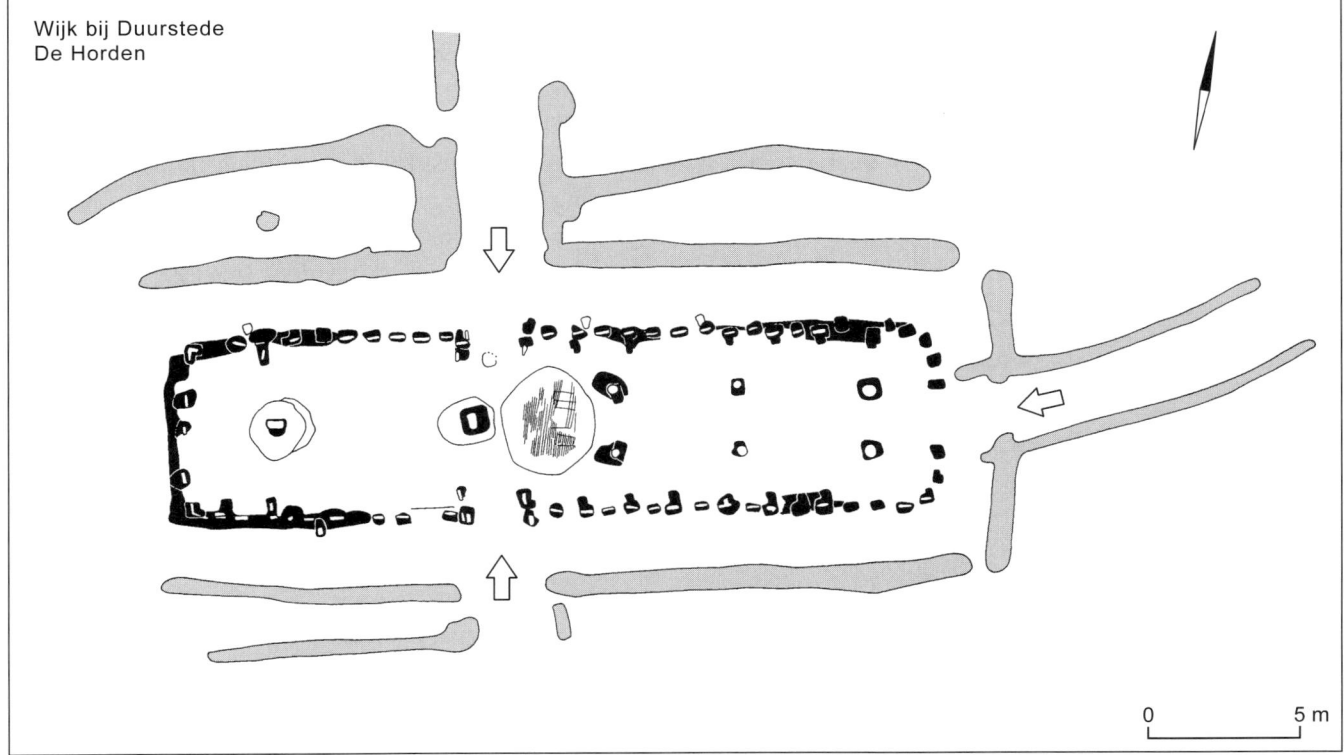

Wijk bij Duurstede
De Horden

0   5 m

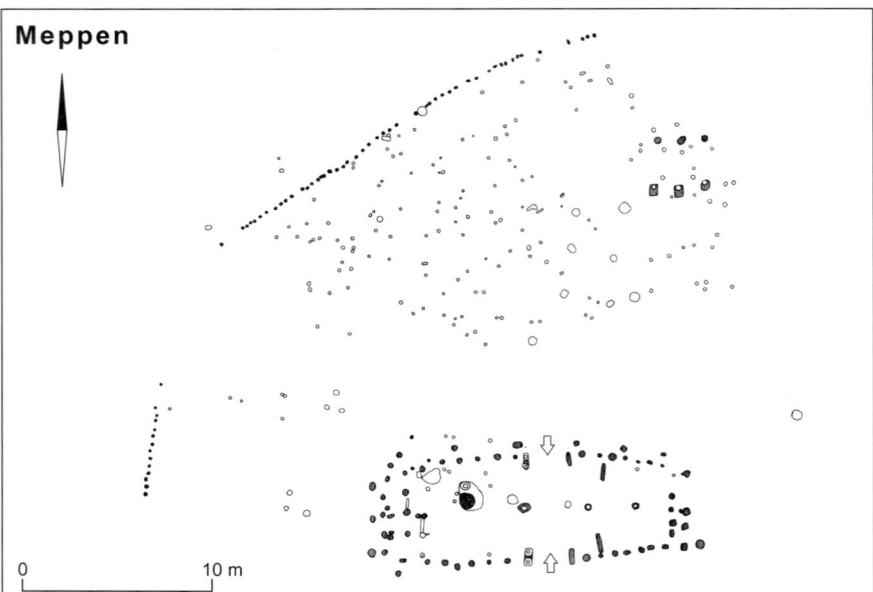

Meppen

0   10 m

fig. 23.18

Meppen (Germany): a palisade-enclosed yard from the Middle or Late Iron Age containing a house plan of the Haps type and a six-posted granary. Unusual of this plan is that both a hearth and ditches marking the partitions of the cattle stalls have survived. Scale 1:400.

In addition to hearths, some of the house plans contained pits that were probably used while the house was occupied. Such pits have however been found virtually exclusively in the relatively small plans from the Late Bronze Age and Early Iron Age on the higher grounds. Depending on their shapes, the pits have been interpreted as storage pits for cereal or other goods, or as cellar pits (see below). The cellar pits were usually immediately beside and parallel to the long walls (fig. 23.16). No such rule appears to hold for the storage pits.

Granaries and sheds

In addition to house plans, all kinds of plans of smaller, less complex buildings have been found at most sites. They are usually assumed to be the plans of structures intended for the storage of food, in particular, (commonly referred to as 'granaries') if they comprise at most twelve postholes and have small dimensions (fig. 23.19). Plans comprising more postholes and/or having larger dimensions are assumed to be plans of sheds (fig. 23.20). They are thought to have been used mainly for the storage of agricultural implements. The most common granaries had four, six, eight or nine posts, set in a square or rectangle. Their dimensions varied from 1.2 x 1.3 m to 3.5 x 4.5 m. Most of the postholes were deep, indicating that heavy loads of goods must have been stored in the structures. It is likely that harvest products were stored on raised floors.

Sheds are less common; none whatsoever are known from the Middle Iron Age. Perhaps some of the larger granaries were used as sheds at sites where no evidence for 'sheds proper' has been found. Sheds comprised two or three rows of posts enclosing an area ranging from 3 x 4 m to 4 x 9 m. Foundation trenches around two sheds at Sint-Oedenrode are the only indications of walls found so far;[35] whether the other sheds had walls cannot be inferred from their plans.

Palisades and ditches

Evidence for palisades or fences in the form of rows of postholes with very small diameters has been found at a small number of settlement sites only. They en-

fig. 23.19

Oss-Ussen: plans of Iron Age structures ('granaries') which were in all probability used for storing crops. Scale 1:200.

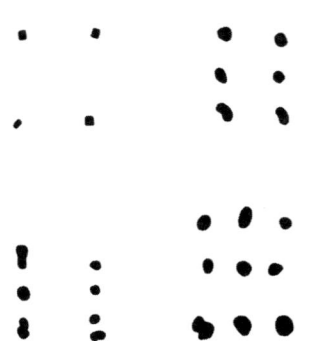

closed farmyards or areas within the yard. The most complete example of a palisade enclosing a house site was found at Meppen in Germany (fig. 23.18). Palisade ditches describing rectangles with rounded corners may possibly be interpreted as the remains of cattle pens. An example is the area of 1 ha enclosed by a ditch and having a funnel-shaped entrance which was found at Bladel-Kriekeschoor.[36] At Loon op Zand a ditch enclosed an area of 29.5 x 33.5 m with an entrance in the southwest.[37] Within this enclosure was a smaller, oval area enclosed by a ditch. Ditches marking the edges of fields and drainage ditches are known from the low-lying settlement of Wijk bij Duurstede.[38]

Pits and wells

Pits, of many different shapes and sizes, are virtually always found at settlement sites. They often contain occupation debris and are therefore commonly termed refuse pits. However, pits appear to have been only rarely or never dug specifically for the purpose of depositing refuse in them; their use as refuse pits was secondary. Of only a small number of pits can the original function be inferred from the shape, and sometimes also the contents, of the pit. Among these pits are in particular the aforementioned storage and cellar pits. Storage pits have round horizontal sections with diameters of 1.5-2 m, cylindrical or conical vertical sections and flat bottoms. At the bottom of several of these pits layers of carbonised cereal have been found, which are believed to be the remains of cleaning of the pits by burning. Cellar pits differ from storage pits in that they have rectangular plans measuring 1.8-3 x 0.9-2.2 m and are less deep. The goods that were stored in this type of pit were placed in, for example, earthenware or wooden containers.[39] Cellar pits are encountered exclusively inside house plans, whereas storage pits are found both inside and outside the house plans at settlements with low groundwater tables. Underground storage clearly declined after the Early Iron Age, when storage above ground began to be preferred. Other pits with specific functions are loam pits and oven pits.

Wells and deep pits that are to be associated with the supply of water (water pits) were found in large numbers at Oss-Ussen. At other settlement sites either no wells at all or only one or a small number of wells are usually found. Wells lined with hollow tree-trunks are known from the Bronze Age onwards (fig. 23.21:1). The uniformity in the form of lining used ended in the course of the Early Iron Age, when wells lined with wattlework (fig. 23.21:2), or thin posts, or planks arranged vertically alongside one another (fig. 23.21:3) started to appear. A few well linings consisting of horizontally arranged planks are also known from this period.[40] In the Middle and Late Iron Age wells lined with wattlework prevailed. Sometimes household objects, such as a churn or a bucket, found secondary use as well linings. Some wells from the Late Iron Age show combined forms of lining. At Colmschate and Haps wells were found that were lined with a plank structure encasing a hollow tree-trunk.[41] This type of lining was not used at Oss until in the Roman period.

Deep unlined water pits may have provided water for human beings and animals. If they were intended for animals, they are referred to as watering places. Watering places have diameters of over six m and a slope along at least one side, via which the cattle could gain access to the water. Several examples of such watering places are known from Oss-Ussen; another was found at Goirle (North Brabant).[42] Besides as sources of drinking water, the other water pits may have been used for all kinds of industrial activities, such as the retting of flax or the tanning of hides.

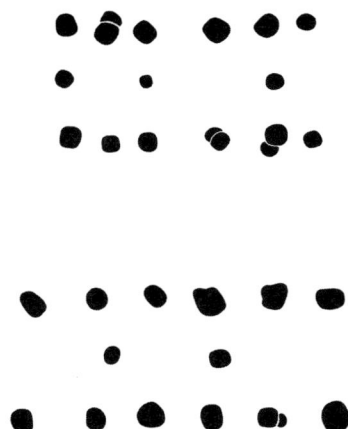

fig. 23.20
Den Dungen: plans of outbuildings or barns that are thought to date from the Early Iron Age. Scale 1:200.

1   2   3

fig. 23.21

Wells at Oss-Ussen.

1 An unusual form of lining is this 90-cm-
high lugged barrel dating from the first
half of the Middle Iron Age. The barrel was
made by hollowing out a tree-trunk.

2 Oval wattlework well lining from the Middle Iron Age. Pressed against the lining
was a loop of lighter wattlework whose
function is not clear.

3 Middle Iron Age well lining made by driv-
ing 11 planks into the well's floor. How the
well was dug is visible in the section; the
area between the sloping wall of the pit and
the well lining was later filled with dark
soil.

Information on the relationships between different elements, such as house plans,
granaries and wells, is scarce. Of many excavations only data on the most important structures have been published, *i.e.* on the house plans. And then there is the
problem of interpretation, in particular concerning the chronological relationship
of features found close together (which, if any, are contemporary?).

In general terms it can be said that houses, granaries and/or storage pits together constitute spatial unities: farmyards. The number of granaries per farm
varies from one to five. They were not necessarily all contemporary, but may have
succeeded one another. Granaries and storage pits do not exclude one another.[43]
This could mean that different storage strategies were used. At Son en Breugel
(North Brabant) an exceptional discovery was made of an entire area of storage
pits from the Middle Iron Age adjoining at least one farm.[44] Plans of sheds, wells,
watering places and other pits are less common. They are encountered near farms,
but at Oss-Ussen they were also found widely distributed outside the presumed
farmyards.

A farm with a yard may be considered the simplest form of settlement (plate
36B). Some settlements may also have consisted of several contemporary yards,
but this can rarely be irrefutably proved. At Wijk bij Duurstede, Colmschate, Riethoven and Sint-Denijs (Belgium) farms were found that lay at short distances
from one another (at most 50 m) but in none of these cases was it clear whether
the farms were contemporary or not.[45] At Colmschate the farms were grouped in
pairs, lying in line with one another, at distances of 25 and 40 m.

Much greater distances between individual farm plans dating from the Late
Bronze Age/Early Iron Age were observed at Den Dungen, Loon op Zand, Oss and
Sint-Oedenrode.[46] This pattern has been interpreted as the result of the constant
shifting of settlements consisting of one farmyard. Major assumptions in this interpretation are that a particular area was continuously occupied and that a farm
was not shifted over distances of several kilometres at a time.

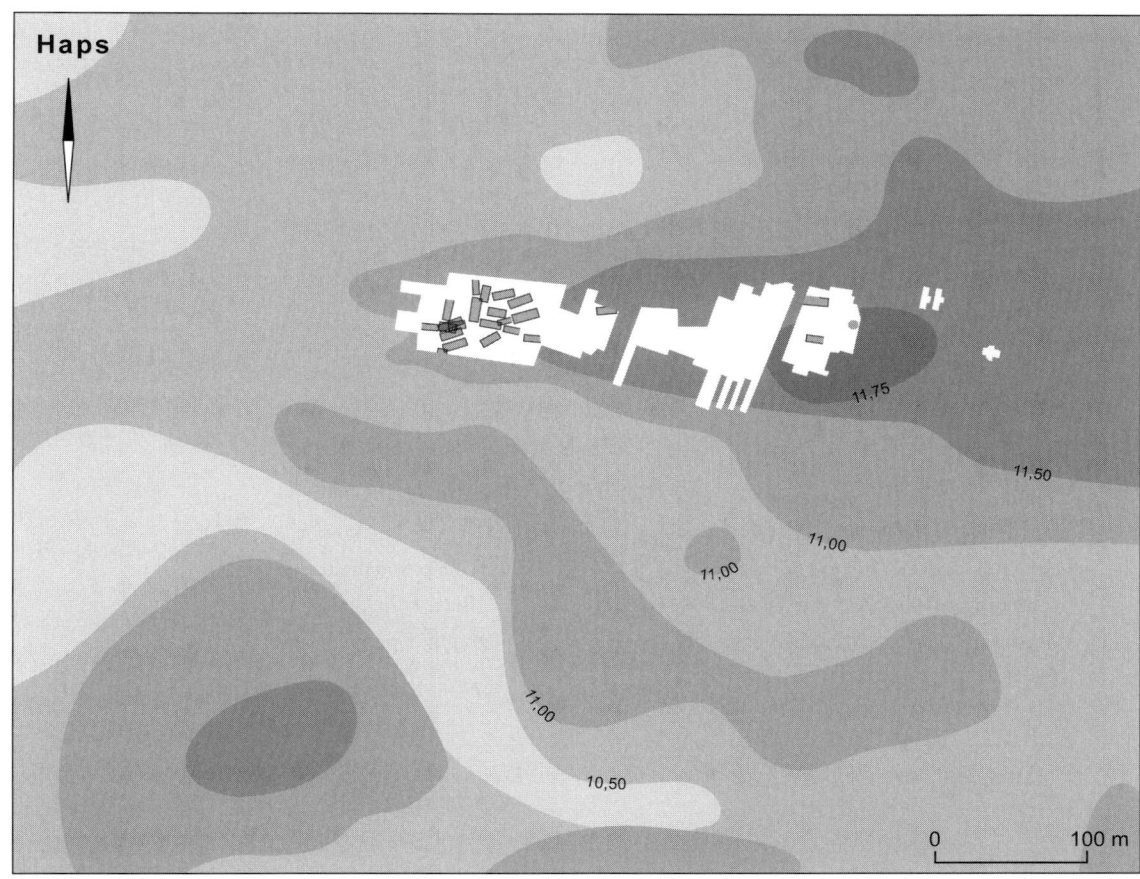

fig. 23.22
Most of the house plans of the Haps settlement dating from the Middle Iron Age and the early part of the Late Iron Age were concentrated on a narrow sand ridge. The many overlapping plans in the excavated area (white) indicate that this site was occupied in several phases, possibly seven, with on average three contemporary farms. The elevations are in metres above NAP (Normal Amsterdam Level). Scale 1:5000.

The settlements of the Middle and Late Iron Age consisted of at most a few contemporary farmyards, which usually lay far apart. They had the character of an open hamlet. The only exception is the settlement at Haps,[47] where very little space was available on the narrow coversand ridge. Because of this, the site plan appears quite full, crowded with house plans set close together or overlapping one another (fig. 23.22). In actual fact, however, the settlement of Haps is estimated to have consisted of not more than three farms at a time, in seven phases of occupation spanning a period from *c.* 400 to 200 BC.[48] At other settlements (Oss, Neerharen [Belgium]) the first overlapping plans are of later date, *i.e.* Late Iron Age.

The above leads to the conclusion that the distance across which farms were shifted gradually decreased in the course of the Iron Age, while the attachment to a specific site increased (fig. 23.23). In the Roman period this development culminated in the formation of hamlets or small villages, within which farms were constantly rebuilt in the same farmyard.

DIFFERENTIATION

The first settlements that had a different function from the unfortified agrarian settlements date from the Late Iron Age. They are the fortified sites of the southernmost, and most hilly, part of the area discussed in this chapter. The functions that are mentioned in the literature are those of temporary refuge, defended collective storage and the possible dwelling of an elite.

The only defended site that has been found in the Netherlands is that of Voerendaal.[49] This site can be classified in the category of small fortified sites, having areas of up to five hectares.[50] In the first building phase, at the end of the Late Iron Age, a 2.5-m deep and 3.5-m wide ditch with a V-shaped section was dug around a site of at least 90 x 74 m. In the second phase, around the beginning of our era, a ditch enclosed an area measuring 264 by more than 172 m. Features of small timber structures within the enclosed area are known from this second phase only.

fig. 23.23

Model showing how yards moved at Oss-Ussen in the Middle Bronze Age (top left), the second half of the Early Iron Age (top right), the second half of the Middle Iron Age (bottom left) and the second half of the Late Iron Age (bottom right). The settlement's limits and the actual movements are very hypothetical, but they do reveal various trends, such as a decrease in the distance across which the yards moved within the territory and increasing topographical permanence of the farms. Scale 1:20,000.

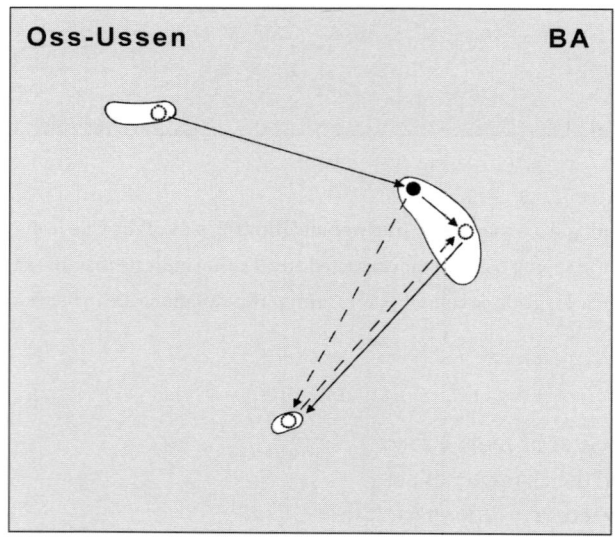
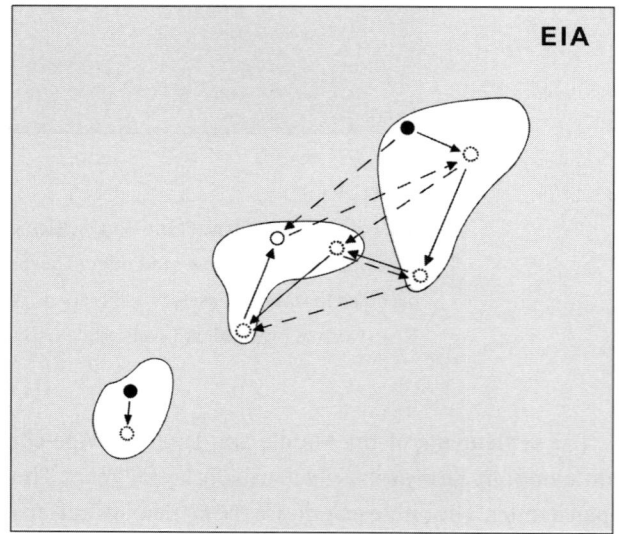
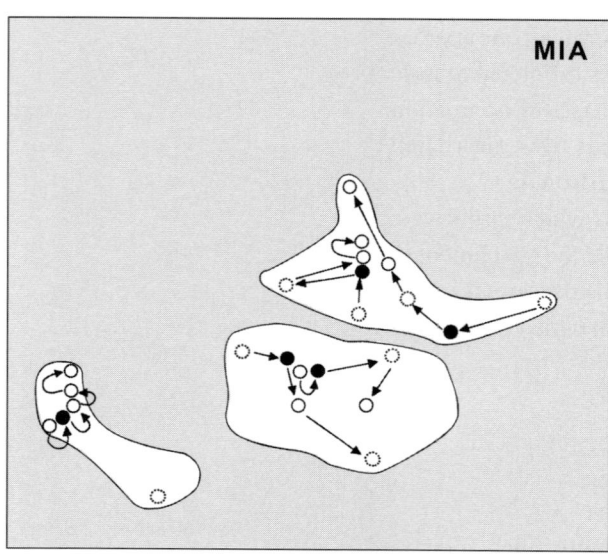
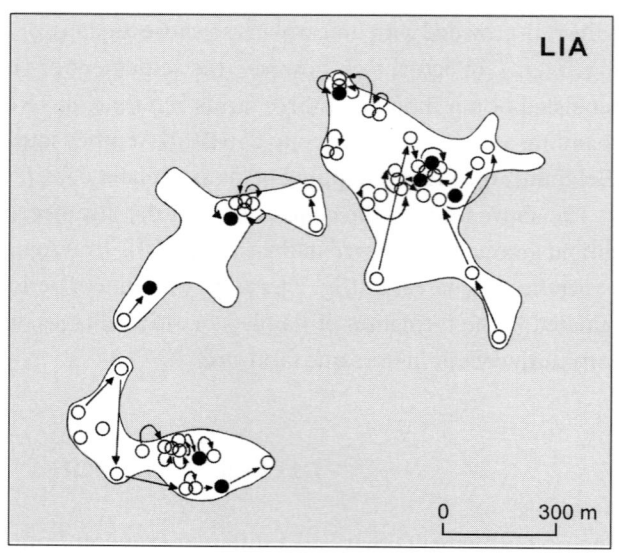

○ yard   ○ possible yard   ● contemporary yards   – → alternative to movement of yard   —→ movement of yard

With its area of twenty hectares the fortified site at Kanne-Caster (Belgium),[51] near Maastricht, has the size of an *oppidum*. A 4-m deep and 10-m wide ditch with a V-shaped section was dug along three sides of the site. Along the west and south sides of this ditch was a terrace, on which traces of a palisade were found, followed by a 5.5-m tall and 7.5-m wide rampart. Along the east side the steep bank of the Meuse valley constituted a natural defence. There were entrances in the northwest and southeast corners. So far only the defences have been investigated and not the interior, which means that we know nothing about the site's function. The date of (autumn) 31 BC obtained for the felling of some of the oak trees used in the rampart[52] excludes a connection between the construction of the fortification and Caesar's campaigns in Gaul around the middle of the 1st century BC.

The fortifications may be regarded as northern 'outposts' of the settlement system in the adjoining – Celtic – area, of which defended sites were a fixed component. In that area settlement differentiation already had a longer history, and included a clearly hierarchical element.[53]

THE AGRARIAN ECONOMY

The location of the settlements provides additional evidence, on top of that of the longhouses and the various storage facilities, for an economy based on mixed farming. We may assume that there were pastures and extraction points for drinking water in the low-lying zones and arable land in the higher areas, although we have no solid evidence for this, due to the poor archaeological visibility of fields and pastures. At Wijk bij Duurstede a plot measuring 24 x 50 m enclosed by a ditch has been tentatively interpreted as a field. At Riethoven the remains of a Celtic field were found, which are possibly datable to the Early Iron Age. A settlement from this period was discovered about one kilometre away.[54] Celtic fields from the Middle and Late Iron Age have been found at Lunteren and Vaassen, both in Gelderland (fig. 22.17).[55] They contained house plans and are therefore associated with similar field complexes found further north, for example at Hijken.

The settlement data can help us only a little way in reconstructing the economy of the Late Bronze Age and the Iron Age. There are no indications of agrarian specialisation whatsoever. All elements point to a largely self-sufficient subsistence economy based on mixed farming. It is remarkable that the Late Bronze Age and Early Iron Age farms of the rivers area and the adjacent coversand zones were longer than those in the uplands. This could mean that cattle keeping was more important in the wetter regions, where large areas of good pastureland were available. There is however no evidence for any specialisation in cattle keeping.

In some areas, for example at Beegden and in the eastern part of the river district, no Middle or Late Iron Age remains of the typical longhouses have been found, which could suggest that cattle breeding was less important in those areas in this period.[56] However, this may not be correct, because cattle may have been stalled in a different manner, or may not have been stalled at all. Bone assemblages, which provide information on the stock kept, have been found virtually exclusively in the settlements along the rivers in the central part of the Netherlands.

Although bone remains are very scarce in the sandy areas, large numbers of spindle whorls and loom weights have been found there, which will have been used substantially for processing sheep's wool. Roymans[57] has associated the increase in the numbers of these attributes after the Middle Bronze Age – together with the expansion of the heaths – with the observed decrease in the length of the farms. In his opinion, this is evidence that cattle were becoming less important than sheep, which did not have to be stalled inside the farm.

The settlement data provide as little information on crop cultivation as on stock keeping. In the first place, with the exception of the few Celtic fields mentioned above, no fields from this period have been preserved or have been recognised due to poor archaeological visibility. Secondly, granaries and storage pits cannot tell us whether the crops stored in them were produced locally or not. The questions regarding the place of production (local or not?) and the type of crops grown (wheat, barley, millet, *etc.*?) can only be answered by studying the botanical remains.

SOCIAL STRUCTURE

In agreement with the evidence for substantial economic independence all the settlement data point to a low degree of social differentiation. This is in contrast with the evidence obtained from graves, where the princely burials of the Early Iron Age in particular clearly reflect differences within the social organisation. However, no traces of settlements have been found near these graves. The settlements that have been excavated and those discussed above provided no evidence for social differentiation whatsoever. There is no hierarchy in the settlement structure because the settlements consisted of only a few farms at the most. There are differences in the lengths of the farms and in the number of granaries per farm, but these cannot be regarded as measures of any degree of social differentiation. The settlement pattern is likewise entirely devoid of indications of a non-egalitarian society. Each settlement was an independent production unit, consisting of one or more households, which formed part of a regional network without a clear centre of power.[58]

NOTES

1 Roymans 1990, 169 ff.

2 Van Doorselaer *et al.* 1987.

3 Heidinga/Vreenegoor 1990, Hessing 1991a and Hulst 1973, respectively.

4 Two recent publications give excellent general surveys of settlements from the Late Bronze Age and the Early Iron Age and settlements from the Iron Age: Fokkens/Roymans 1991 and Roymans 1990, respectively.

5 Simons 1989.

6 Fokkens 1991a; Van der Sanden/Van den Broeke 1987; Schinkel 1994.

7 Van den Broeke 1987a.

8 Bakels 1994.

9 Lauwerier/IJzereef 1994.

10 Fokkens 1991b.

11 Usually the distance between a settlement and an urnfield is between fifty and several hundred metres. This is the case at Beek and Donk (Huijbers 1990), Colmschate (Groenewoudt 1989), Donk (Belgium) (Van Impe 1991), Sint-Oedenrode (Van der Sanden 1981) and Wijk bij Duurstede (Hessing 1991a).

12 Slofstra 1991.

13 Slofstra 1991.

14 Slofstra/Van der Sanden 1987; Van der Sanden 1994b.

15 Slofstra/Van der Sanden 1987.

16 Van der Sanden 1987d.

17 Waterbolk 1982, 101.

18 Den Dungen: Verwers 1991; Nijnsel: Beex/Hulst 1968.

19 Besides Oss-Ussen for example Colmschate (Verlinde 1991); Sint-Oedenrode (Van Bodegraven 1991); Wijk bij Duurstede (Hessing 1991).

20 Sint-Denijs, Sint-Gillis (Bourgeois 1991a).

21 Sint-Oedenrode (Van Bodegraven 1991); Wijchen (Roymans 1990, 172).

22 Van Tent 1988.

23 Roymans/Hiddink 1991.

24 Roymans/Hiddink 1991; Hulst 1989.

25 Colmschate-Holterweg (Verlinde 1991, 34-35); Loon op Zand (Roymans/Hiddink 1991).

26 De Grood 1984.

27 Willems 1983b; Verwers 1972, 87.

28 For example Colmschate (Verlinde 1986); Ede (Willems 1986a, 224); Wijk bij Duurstede (Van Es 1982).

29 De Boe 1985.

30 Bourgeois 1984; Roymans 1988.

31 Simons 1989.

32 Roymans 1990, 177, 179; Willems 1986a, 223-230.

33 Van der Sanden 1987f, 86-87.

34 Zoller 1977.

35 Van Bodegraven 1991.

36 Roymans 1982.

37 Roymans/Hiddink 1991.

38 Hessing 1991a.

39 Bursch 1929; Roymans 1977.

40 Besides at Oss-Ussen also at Wehl in Gelderland (Hulst 1986).

41 Verlinde 1987; Verwers 1972, 94.

42 Hendriks/Van Nuenen 1989.

43 See for example Colmschate-Holterweg (Verlinde 1991); Loon op Zand (Roymans/Hiddink 1991).

44 Van den Broeke 1980a.

45 Hessing 1991a, Verlinde 1991, Slofstra 1991 and Bourgeois 1991a, respectively.

46 Verwers 1991, Roymans/Hiddink 1991 and Van Bodegraven 1991, respectively.

47 Verwers 1972, 63.

48 According to the excavator, Haps was occupied from 450 BC until AD 150, but recent reinterpretations based on the pottery and other evidence have led to a period of occupation of about 200 years, from 400 to 200 BC.

49 Willems/Kooistra 1988.

50 Roymans 1990, 190 ff.

51 Roosens 1975; 1976.

52 Hollstein 1980, 69-70; originally dated around 57 BC (Hollstein 1976).

53 Cahen-Delhaye et al. 1984; Roymans 1990, 190-211.

54 Milikowski 1985.

55 Brongers 1976a.

56 Roymans 1988; Willems 1986a, 225-226.

57 Roymans 1991, 68.

58 In the meantime, an English publication based on Schinkel's dissertation on the prehistoric occupation of Oss-Ussen (1994) has appeared (Schinkel 1998; for the subsequent native Roman occupation see Wesselingh 2000). Another work on the extensive Oss excavation has been published by Jansen/Fokkens (1999). In other parts of this region evidence has meanwhile been obtained to fill geographical or chronological gaps to some extent, or large occupation areas have been excavated: Boxmeer, where a Late Bronze Age house plan came to light (Van der Velde 1998); Breda (Van den Eynde/Berkvens 2001); Mierlo (Tol 1999); Someren (Kortlang 1999); Raalte (Groenewoudt et al. 1998); Weert, where, amongst other remains, a Late Iron Age defended site was found (Roymans 1995c, Roymans/Tol 1996, Roymans et al. 1998); Zutphen (Fontijn 1996a, 1996b). Complementary works with a regional scope have been published by Van den Broeke 2001b, Van Enckevort 2001, Fokkens/Jansen 2002, Verlinde 1999 and in particular Gerritsen 2001.

pl. 33A Section of a barrow of the Beaker cultures in Appense Veld, southeast of Apeldoorn. The fact that the barrow was built from soil that had not (yet) podzolised (*cf.* plate 34A) implies that it dates from the Beaker period. This barrow was probably built from sods from grassland or a forest soil. The mound was built in three phases or 'periods'.

pl. 33B Burial of a fifteen-year-old boy found at Molenaarsgraaf, dated to the end phase of the bell beaker culture. The rectangular violet feature shows that the pit was lined with wooden planks to create a burial chamber. The boy's body was placed in the chamber in the characteristic crouching position, oriented east-west, with his head facing south. A late type of bell beaker was placed at his knees. The burial dates from around 2000 BC.

pl. 34A Section of a Bronze Age sod barrow at Alphen (North Brabant). The original soil beneath the barrow has fossilised. Clearly visible in the ferriferous orange-yellow sand is a humus-iron podzol containing a black layer of organic matter and a white illuvial horizon. The sods were stacked upside down.

pl. 34B Two so-called tangential secondary interments in the Bronze Age barrow of Elp. To the left the soil mark of a wooden coffin in a large grave pit. One of the post holes of the primary post circle is visible to the left of this pit. To the right the foot-end of a second burial, intersected by the former one. Cf. fig. 18.4.

pl. 35A Restored Middle Bronze Age barrows surrounded by posts circles on the Rechte Heide near Goirle. The barrows were built on a coversand ridge between two streams, probably on or near a boundary between different territories. The mounds were built from sods with a well-developed podzol horizon, indicating that this area had been heathland for at least 300 years by the time the barrows were erected.

pl. 35B Exceptional simultaneous burial of twelve individuals at Wassenaar. The deceased were the victims of a violent conflict that occurred approximately 1700 BC, around the transition from the Early to the Middle Bronze Age. At the front right is an 18-months-old infant next to the skeleton of a young woman aged 18.

pl. 36A Fragments of Early Iron Age pottery semi-cylinders and bars that were found at a settlement site near Monster. The objects are thought to have been used in drying sea salt. The largest fragment is 22 cm long.

pl. 36B Impression of an Iron Age farmyard in the river district. The occupants selected the highest part of the land for their farm and granaries. This is also where the trees with better-quality wood (oak, ash and elm) were to be found and where the people grew their crops. The adjacent backswamp, with predominantly alder and willow trees, was particularly suitable for pasturing. Pigs will have been kept in the yards.

pl. 37A Aerial view of Celtic fields in Wekeromsche Zand near Lunteren. The low banks are visible as light coloured lines. They are hardly visible at the surface, especially not, where the terrain is wooded.

pl. 37B Artist's impression of the extensive Celtic field of Hijken. Some of the plots contain houses and granaries and were in use as a yard. On others some granaries are grouped together. Some of the fields are used for growing cereal (yellow) or flax (light blue), while yet others lie fallow. Cattle graze the stubble in the fallow fields and enrich the soil with their manure.

pl. 38A Section through salt marsh deposits and the margin of the *terp* of Heveskesklooster, during the excavation in 1985. To the left the fill of a small gulley, that had cut into the peat, that had started to grow on the Pleistocene coversand on this location in the early Subatlantic. The peat is covered by a tripartite Dunkirk I-clay (bluish grey), separated by a vegetation horizon from a Dunkirk II clay. On this clay to the left the *terp* layer. To the right the moat of a medieval cloister. The background is formed by Delfzijl.

pl. 38B Cross-section through a succession of floors of a farm built on the peat at Maasland (Midden-Delfland, site 11.17) in the Middle Iron Age. The farm's floor kept sinking into cracks in the peat and had to be raised each time. Thin layers of manure, reeds and rushes alternate with layers of domestic refuse.

pl. 39A Detail of the wattle wall of a native Roman-period farm, site 09-89 at Nieuwenhoorn, on the island of Voorne-Putten. Iron Age farms had identical wattle walls.

pl. 39B A Late Iron Age wattlework hurdle that was found washed away from its original position in tidal deposits in the Rhine estuary in the Stevenshofjespolder near Leiden. The wattlework is contained in an ash frame consisting of two vertical beams whose tops were connected to a rectangularly carved plank via very neat tenon and mortise joints. It consists of willow branches woven between five pickets inserted in holes in the plank. This wattlework constitutes unique evidence of how vertical structures were built at this time. The 150-cm-high structure may have been a stall partition in a byre. See also fig. 26.8.

pl. 40A Two Early Iron Age pots. On the left is a characteristic Harpstedt pot with a roughened (*besmeten*) surface and impressions on the shoulder and along the rim. Behind is a pot adorned with 'Kalenderberg' ornamentation: plastic decorations applied with a spatula or the fingertip arranged in blocks. Such pots were used for ordinary domestic purposes and are frequently encountered in settlement assemblages, but they were also used as urns, as in the case of these two specimens. The pots were found at Wijchen and Bergen, respectively, along the Meuse in north Limburg.

pl. 40B Example of Late Bronze Age pottery decorated with *Kerbschnitt* ornamentation found in an urnfield at Vlodrop. The decorative elements (triangles and grooves) of both the urn and the bowl used as a lid were cut into the clay before it had dried completely.

pl. 41A Fragments of glass bracelets and a single bead from find spots near Wijchen. It is assumed that this area contained one or more production centres of glass bracelets, especially bracelets of the types that have been found in this particular area in far greater numbers than elsewhere. Those types are the illustrated smooth bracelet decorated with raised yellow zig-zags and the two-, five- and seven-ribbed types. Parts of broken bracelets were often turned into pendants (top right).

pl. 41C Hoard of four flint sickles and one bronze specimen from Heiloo. Maximum length 17 cm. Most of these flint sickles date from the Late Bronze Age or Early Iron Age. The dating of the bronze sickle of this hoard to the Middle Bronze Age B is being disputed. A study of the intensive gloss on most of the 'sickles' points to their use in cutting sods.

pl. 41B Gold *stater* of the Celtic tribe of the Ambiani (northwest France) from the mid-1st century BC, found at Bladel. Diameter 1.7 cm.

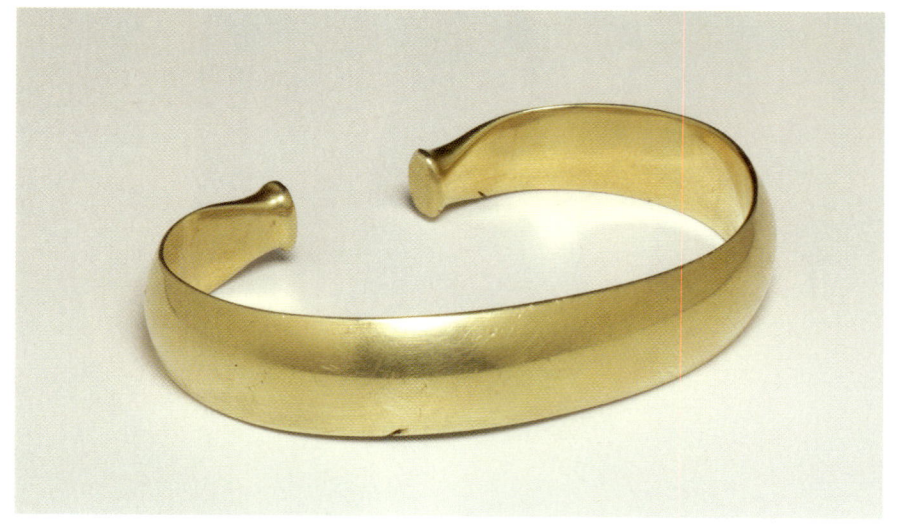

pl. 42A Early Iron Age bronze neckrings from a deposit found in the peat near Uddel. One of the rings is decorated with an amber bead. The largest has a diameter of 17.5 cm.

pl. 42B Solid gold Late Bronze Age bracelet, 76 gram, that was found during ploughing in a field near Lunteren. The source of the gold is unknown, but its typological affinities with the bronze so-called omega bracelets are more indicative for local production then for import.

pl. 43A A pair of shoes from the peat near Weerdinge, recovered during peat-cutting activities in 1851. They are of a simple type, known as a *Bundschuh* (litt.: 'farmers shoe'), cut from a single piece of leather. The leather of the upper part was cut into loops that were tied around the foot with a thong. This type of shoe is known in Denmark from the Iron Age onwards. This pair has been dated to the first centuries AD on the basis of the results of pollen analyses of peat adhering to the shoes.

pl. 43B Detail of the woollen undergarment of the Emmer-Erfscheidenveen bog body which a ^{14}C date has placed in the Middle Bronze Age, between 1380 and 1100 BC. The garment is adorned with a decorative border made up of three cords.

pl. 44A Highly podzolised ring ditch with annex, a so-called keyhole-shaped ditch, in the Buinen urnfield. Surrounding structures of this type are the oldest in this urnfield, dating from the Late Bronze Age.

pl. 44B Square ditched enclosures of two Late Iron Age cinerary barrows near Noordbarge, which were excavated in 1972-'74.

pl. 45A Contents of an exceptionally rich Early Iron Age burial found at Oss. The bronze bucket was used as an urn. Besides the cremated remains, the bucket also contained various grave goods. The iron sword with a hilt inlaid with gold leaf was bent so that it would fit in the bucket.

pl. 45B Four axle caps found among other objects in an Early Iron Age cremation burial that was discovered on Wezelsche Berg near Wijchen in 1897. The linchpins are decorated with the stylised heads of men. They may have been made in Etruria, but it is more likely that they derive from the south German Hallstatt culture.

pl. 46A Skull found in an inhumation burial from the beginning of the Middle Iron Age in a cemetery at Lent-Laauwikstraat. Near the skull of the man whose body was placed at the bottom of the double grave were three bronze ornaments; visible here are an earring and one of two rings that were worn around tresses or plaits of hair.

pl. 46B Impression of the man whose skull is shown in plate 46A, with his bronze earring and plait rings. The earring was not suspended from the lobe, but was worn inserted through the auricle or rolled in it.

pl. 47A Bronze neckring with slides and an amber bead that was recovered from the peat of Onstwedder Barlage. The find has been dated to the Early Iron Age.

pl. 47B One of the objects that are assumed to be votive gifts deposited at the cult site of Empel: a Late Iron Age bronze belt hook with rivets inlaid with red enamel.

pl. 48A Detail of the gilt silver ornamental disc that was found in the mid-19th century during peat-cutting activities near Helden: a hero wrestles with a lion (cf. fig. 29.9). The disc was produced in Thrace in the first century BC and found its way to the Netherlands, where it was deposited in a bog as a votive gift, either via the late Celtic contact networks or through early Roman troop movements.

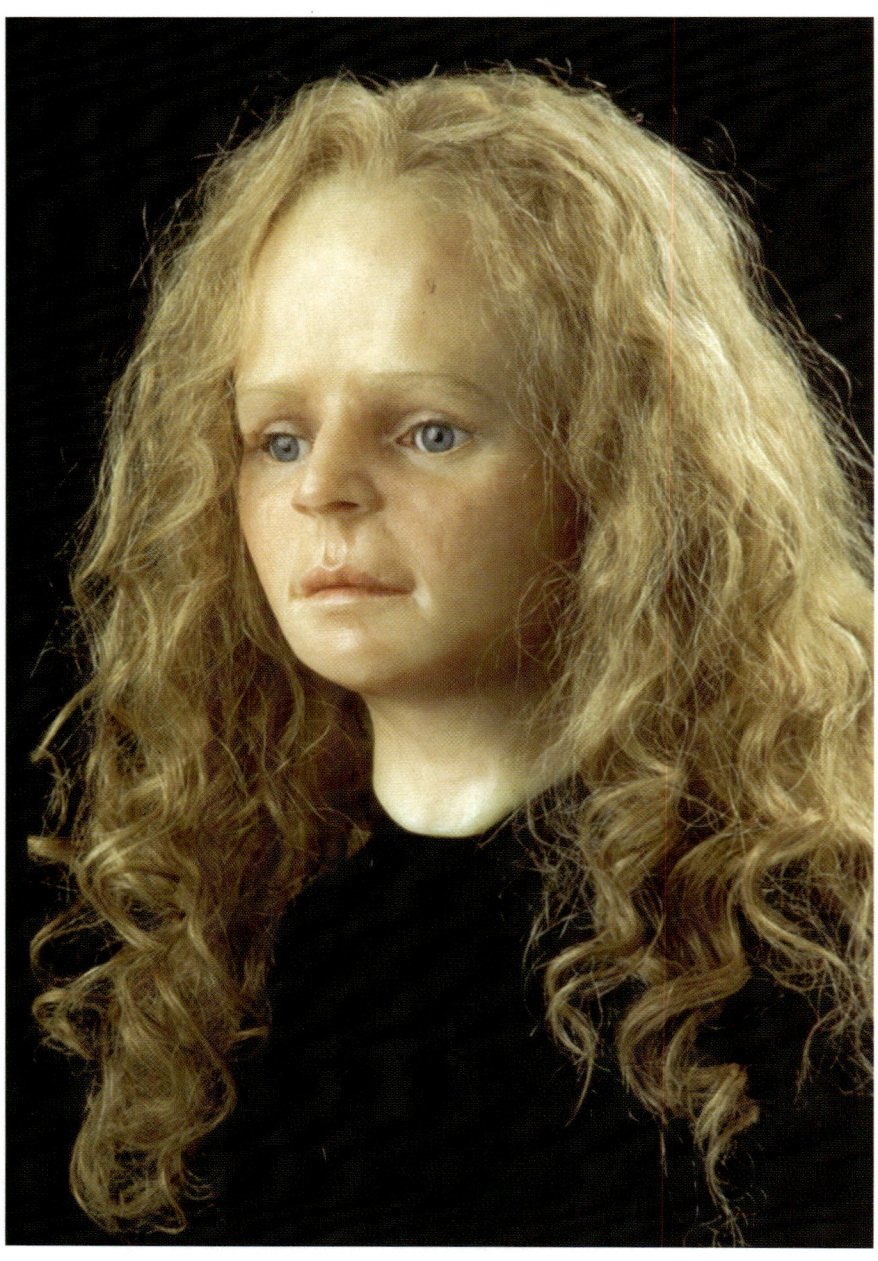

pl. 48B 'Yde Girl' lived some time in the last centuries BC or the first centuries AD and was 16 years old when she was sacrificed in a bog. The reconstruction, based on anatomical features of the girl's skull and remains of her hair, looks a good deal more attractive than the bog body itself. The body and the reconstruction evoke widely varying emotions which incidentally equally arouse a keen interest in prehistory. This way, 'Yde Girl' has unwittingly become an ambassador of Dutch archaeology.

24 Farms amongst Celtic fields
Settlements on the northern sands

Otto Harsema

THE LANDSCAPE

Secluded by the vast, uninhabited expanses of raised bogs, the Pleistocene land-scape to the north of the river IJssel consisted of uplands covered with mixed deciduous woodland and constantly expanding moors, intersected by wooded stream valleys. The uplands of this area, the Drenthe plateau, contained numer-ous small, largely overgrown depressions; these are the remains of pingos dating from the Weichselian. It is in these uplands that the small settlements were to be found. Many of these settlements were in gradient situations from which differ-ent soil types in the vicinity could be exploited.[1] Another factor that had clearly played a part in the selection of the settlement sites was good drainage. This is for example apparent from the preference for the Hondsrug, a low ridge, and for the fringes of valleys in flatter parts of the plateau.

New, man-made landscape features in this period are the field systems con-sisting of usually rectangular to square plots of arable land separated from one another by low banks. They are known as Celtic fields. Stratigraphic evidence has shown that the Celtic field system, which is typical of Northwest Europe, started to be used in this region in the Early Iron Age at the latest: two cinerary barrows proved to have been thrown up on a bank on the Noordse Veld near Zeijen in the Iron Age, while another bank of that same field was found to contain the burned remains of a house dated around the 4th century BC.[2]

The layers of drift sand that have been observed at many sites in this area[3] may to a certain extent have been a consequence of the Celtic field cultivation system if sods were cut from the waste land to increase the organic content of the topsoil of the fields.[4]

It is not clear to what extent sand drifts affected the area's suitability for oc-cupation. What we do know for sure is that the amount of area that was fit for occupation decreased in the Iron Age. The western margin of the plateau became increasingly wet due to the continuing rise in the sea level and the groundwater level and peat started to grow there. The adjacent salt marshes that became fit for occupation in the Early Iron Age will have appealed much to the occupants of this peripheral part of the sandy region in particular.[5]

THE LATE BRONZE AGE OCCUPATION

The classic example of a Bronze Age settlement on the northern sands is the one found at the edge of a wide stream valley near Elp in Drenthe. According to Water-bolk's later reinterpretation of the evidence, the site was occupied in ten phases (a-j), covering a total span of about seven centuries, from 1600 until 900 BC.[6] In each phase the settlement comprised a single longhouse and one or more out-buildings (fig. 24.1, compare fig. 18.4). In view of the short life of a timber-built farmhouse, the investigated site cannot have been occupied continuously through-out the aforementioned period. The occupation phases distinguished at this site

543

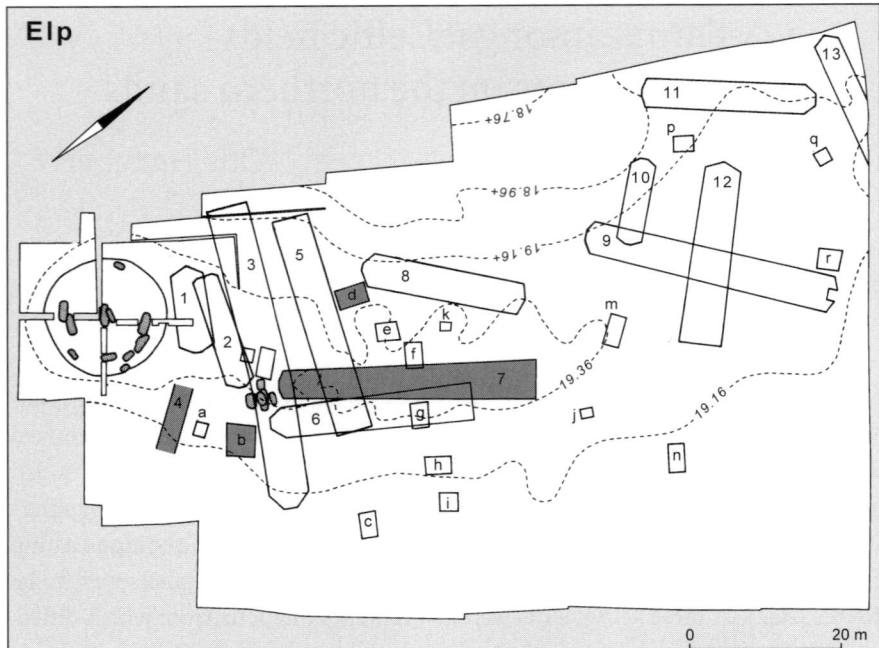

fig. 24.1

The Elp settlement. According to Waterbolk (1990a), the grey area was occupied in phase h (Late Bronze Age). In addition to the large farmstead (fig. 24.2), this area also included three outbuildings. The family barrow and the group of flat graves found near the farm date from the Middle Bronze Age, as do some of the buildings. Scale 1:1000. See also fig. 18.4.

were probably separated by periods of occupation in other areas along the edge of the valley. In the Late Bronze Age such an area may have been the surroundings of the Elp-Zuidveld urnfield, some 800 m further south.

Plans of several farms of the settlement at Elp are of the so-called Elp type, which is characteristic of the Late Bronze Age.[7] The exterior and interior postholes of the plans of these farms are less closely related than in the preceding period, but a more distinctive feature appears to be the way in which the plan is divided into two parts, with the interior postholes of one part being set much closer together than those of the other part (fig. 24.2). The part with the closely set interior postholes is believed to have been the byre. One cow could be stalled between each pair of successive posts.

Some of the plans with rounded byre ends that were also observed at Elp may be regarded as early representatives of this type.[8] Later farms of the Elp type had byres with straight ends, whose widths increased slightly towards the end (fig. 24.2). Houses of the Elp type were built from about 1200 BC until well into the Late Bronze Age (2750 BP, c. 900 BC).

The houses of the Elp type were typical longhouses. For the first time the farms seem to have been used for only two main purposes: habitation and stalling cattle. Cereal will have been stored mainly in smaller outbuildings in the period discussed here. In the Bronze Age use was made of granaries with four, six or eight posts. The four-post type started to prevail in the Iron Age. Evidence for cattle pens adjacent to farms has also been found at some sites.[9] Unlike the southern part of the Netherlands, no wells were dug in these settlements in prehistoric times. Ap-

fig. 24.2

Plan of a longhouse of the Elp type found at Elp, with a length of 33 m. Characteristic of this house type are the rows of posts set close together in the byre. Scale 1:200.

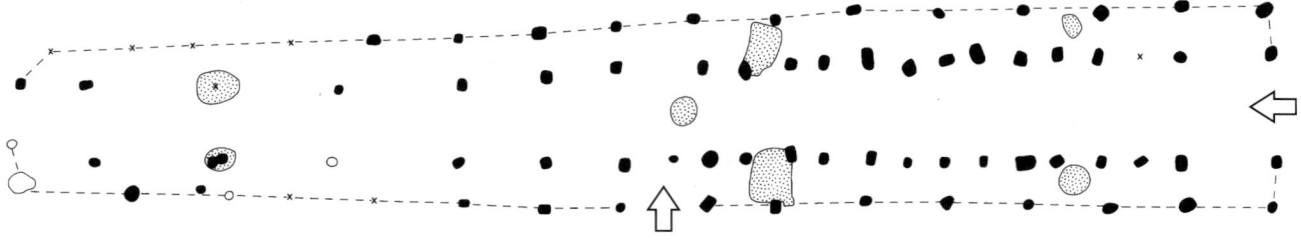

544

parently there were sufficient natural water sources (streams and pools).

In the case of Elp it is quite conceivable that the settlement comprised only one farmstead. Although the possibility of the existence of a second, contemporary farm at Elp cannot be altogether excluded, stronger evidence for a larger settlement in the Middle and Late Bronze Age comes from the surroundings of Emmen. Farms of the Elp type have been found both in the Angelslo part of Emmen and at Emmerhout. Outside Drenthe, farms of the Elp type are not widely known. One of the plans excavated on the Margijnen Enk near Deventer in 1954 may be of this type. The same holds for the plan discovered near Weener (Germany).[10]

Elp represents the settlement of a small group of people – an extended family – who chose to live at the edge of a valley. Their economy was based on mixed farming. The farms' large byres reflect the importance of cattle breeding in the Late Bronze Age. The specific location selected for the settlement, at the transition of two landscape features, could indicate economic diversity. Still, the emphasis, also as far as cattle breeding was concerned, will have been on the exploitation of the uplands. The podzolized layers observed beneath the burial mound found near the settlement indicate that the landscape around Elp was already partly open at the time of the arrival of the first settlers.

THE EARLY AND MIDDLE IRON AGE

House types

The next widely distributed characteristic house type of which many plans have been found in the northern part of the Netherlands – the Hijken type of the Middle Iron Age – was preceded by two others. The first of these two Early Iron Age house types was referred to as the 'transitional Hijken type', the precursor of the Hijken type proper, by Huijts.[11] This type will be referred to below as the 'Een type'.[12]

The houses of the Een type were shorter and wider than those of the Elp type. Whether part of the house was used as a byre cannot be inferred from the configuration of the interior postholes (fig. 24.3), but the plan does consist of two parts, separated by two entrances approximately in the middle of the long sides. A conspicuous feature of the plans are the large, closely set postholes marking the circumference of the house, which curved inwards a little at the entrances.

The actual wall of the house stood at a considerable distance (0.50 to 0.75 m) inside this circumference. In several plans no traces of the wall had survived. The walls varied considerably in structure and design: some consisted of rows of posts, others were made of wattlework; some were founded in bedding trenches, others were not. Another conspicuous feature of these three-aisled houses is that they

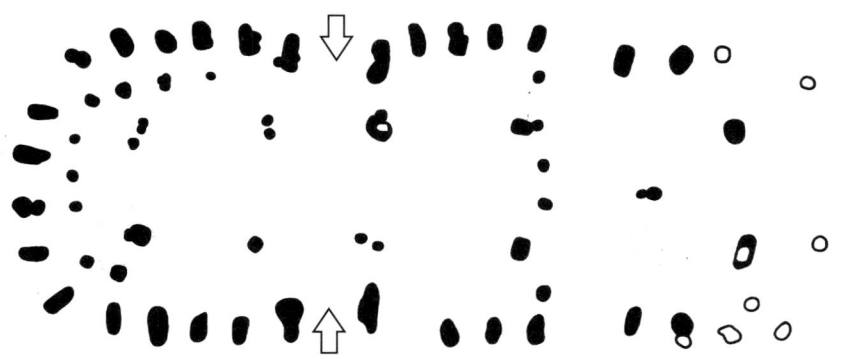

fig. 24.3
Plan of a farm of the Een type found at Zwolle-Ittersumerbroek. The postholes marking the outer circumference contained the posts that supported the edge of the roof. They were probably all at some point replaced by new posts that were set slightly further outwards, which would explain the elongated shape of the postholes. The wall, only the left side of which has survived, stood further inwards. No byre can be distinguished. Scale 1:200.

545

contained only few interior posts: often not more than six or eight, arranged in three or four pairs. The fact that many of the houses were about 20 m long means that the plates or 'purlins' that supported the rafters were sometimes more than 6 m long. The roof's span was also fairly large, up to 8 m, the wall-to-wall width of the house being 5-7 m.

Besides at Een, house plans of this type have been found in Drenthe at Peelo[13] and at Emmen-Angelslo.[14] Further south, a plan of this type came to light at Zwolle-Ittersumerbroek[15] and comparable plans are known from Deventer-Colmschate, Wijk bij Duurstede-De Horden and even from sites to the south of the Meuse, *e.g.* Oss-Ussen.

The second Early Iron Age house type that preceded the Hijken type, also classified as 'transitional Hijken', was smaller (10-15 m long) and often had a symmetrical layout. It usually had thick wall posts and often also posts outside the house, set fairly close to the wall. Groenewoudt and Verlinde called this type the 'Sint-Oedenrode type'.[16] As this name suggests, the greatest concentration of plans of this type was found in the southern and central parts of the Netherlands. In the northern part of the Netherlands this type has only been encountered at Emmerhout. A little further south plans of this type have been unearthed at Deventer-Colmschate and Enschede;[17] a double house plan of this type came to light at Silvolde in Gelderland (fig. 23.16).

In the Middle Iron Age, houses designed according to the southern tradition of this period were built at some sites in the northern sandy region, too, namely at Dalen and Noordbarge (Drenthe).[18] House plans of this type are also known from Wengsel (Germany), Lunteren and Putten (Gelderland). These two-aisled house plans differ from the plans of the Haps type proper in one respect only: at one point one of the central posts has been substituted by a pair of posts, marking the entrance into what is assumed to have been the byre.

The main stages in the development that resulted in the Hijken house type in the northern part of the Netherlands can be understood by assuming that indigenous elements – houses incorporating byres – were combined with building principles that may have been introduced from elsewhere. In the first place, a three-aisled byre is recognisable in one of the halves of the plans based on the new principles. Secondly, the large number of thick exterior posts arranged in a curved line were replaced by a smaller number of thinner, more widely spaced posts. This decrease in the number of exterior posts is apparent in plans II and III of Peelo-Kleuvenveld, from the Early Iron Age; Peelo III moreover shows the incorporation of the characteristic byre.[19]

By the end of the Early Iron Age or the beginning of the Middle Iron Age this development had resulted in the type known as the Hijken house (figs. 24.4 and 24.5). We may then speak of a 'northern tradition' again. Distinguishing features of this house type are the relatively large number of paired interior posts, the great regularity in the arrangement of the posts, the three-aisled layout of the entire

fig. 24.4

Plan of a farm of the Hijken type as found at Hijken. This plan suggests a less sturdy building than other house plans; the occupants tried to restrict the size of the postholes and probably used split trunks for the outermost posts. The left part, where the roof supports are set closer together with extra posts along the inside of the wall, was the byre. Scale 1:200.

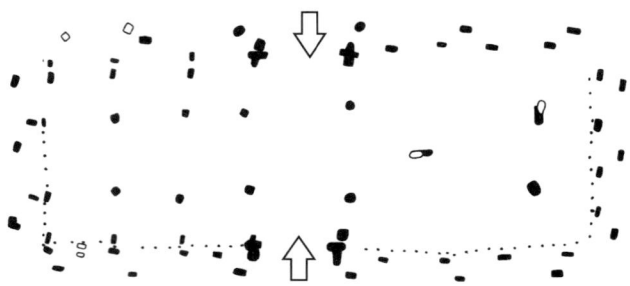

fig. 24.5
At Orvelte a farm of the Hijken type was
reconstructed in 1978 on the basis of the
plan shown in figure 24.4. Two four-post
granaries were built next to the farm.

plan, the virtually always well-recognisable byre and the characteristic design of
the entrances. Almost all of the plans comprise exterior posts. As they were connected lengthwise, only a small number of posts was required. Houses of this
type continued to be built throughout the entire Middle Iron Age and probably
for the greater part of the Late Iron Age, too. Examples of plans of this type have
been found at Hijken, Noordbarge, Peelo and also at Ezinge, in the Groningen salt
marshes.

At Hijken, however, there were also houses without exterior posts, in addition
to houses of the Hijken type.[20] They may be the oldest plans of this settlement.
The lengths of the houses vary from about 10 to 20 m, as can be concluded from
the entire set of houses from the Middle Iron Age. The arrangement of the interior
posts indicates that all of the houses incorporated byres. The widths between the
exterior posts that supported the edges of the roof varied from 6.5 to 8 m, but most
of the houses were relatively narrow inside, measuring 5-5.5 m from wall to wall.
The Hijken settlement has also yielded information on settlement form and land
use.

Hijken: a Middle Iron Age settlement in the northern part of the Netherlands

The excavations that were carried out on the Hijkerveld to the northwest of Hijken
from 1969 until 1974 yielded the remains of a concentrated Middle Iron Age settlement consisting of a few houses lying close together.[21] For many centuries this
settlement was repeatedly moved within a limited area showing clear characteristics of a Celtic field (fig. 24.6 and plate 37). The main difference between the
economy of this Middle Iron Age settlement and the Late Bronze Age economy lies
in a 'more intensive land use',[22] in the form of the long-term, intensive use of a series of plots of the Celtic field immediately surrounding the farm (what is known
as the 'infield') plus less intensive use of other parts of this Celtic field and of parts
of land lying further away from the farm (the so-called 'outfield'). The period of
use of the infield possibly coincided with the life of the farm, which is estimated to
have been about twenty years.

The individual plots of the Celtic field often measured about 30 x 30 m, but

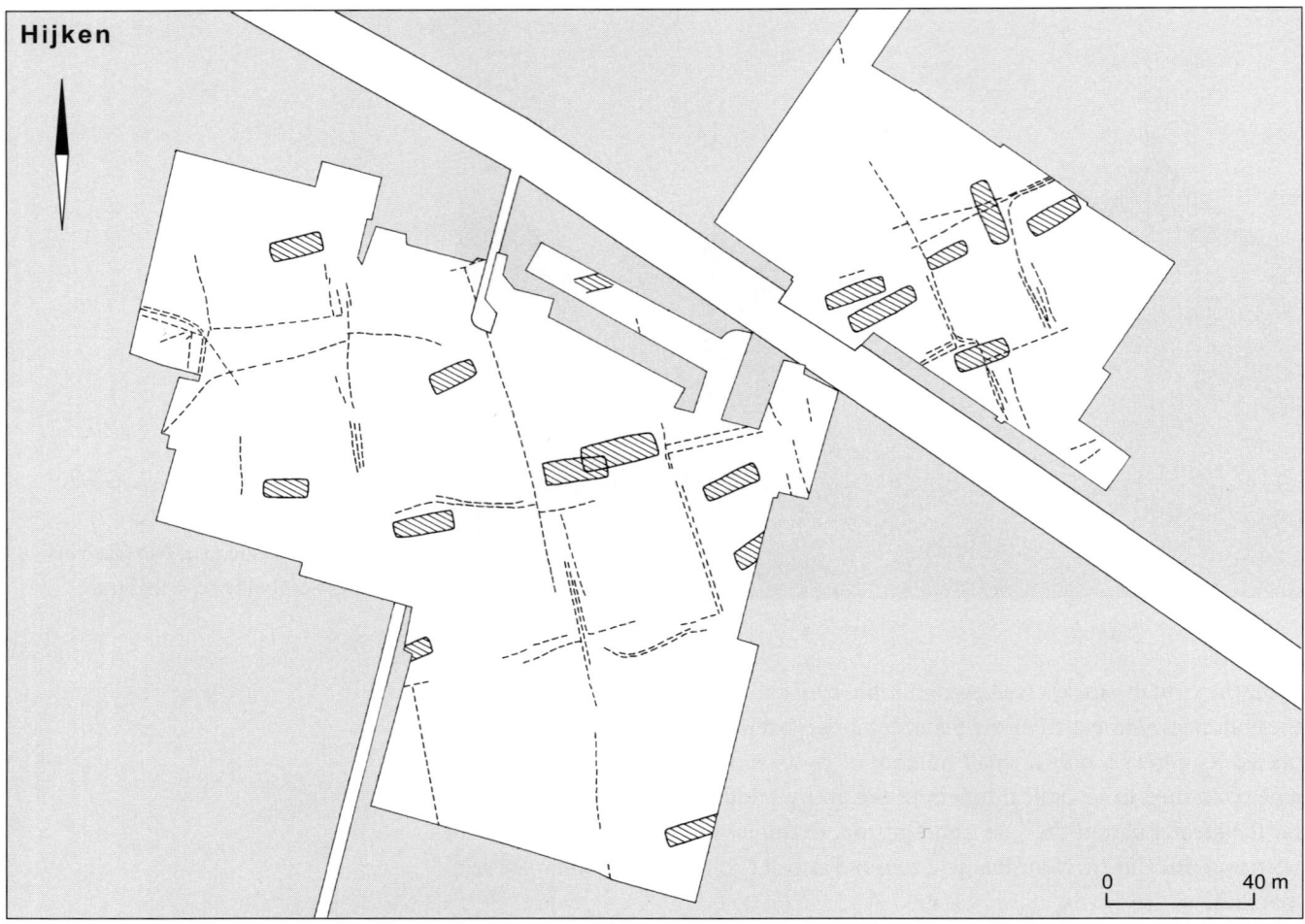

Hijken

0   40 m

fig. 24.6

The area excavated at Hijken showing the Iron Age houses and field system. Scale 1:2000.

there were also plots of very different sizes. The banks that separated the plots had gently sloping flanks; they are now up to 8 m wide and up to just over 0.5 m high. Strips of such plots, recognisable by banks extending in a straight line over a great distance, usually consisted of 10-20 plots. Brongers is of the opinion that units consisting of two or three such strips are distinguishable at Vaassen, in the province of Gelderland (fig. 22.17). In his opinion, these approximately 2-ha units were the first parts of the land around the settlement to have been brought into cultivation. These primary clearings may correspond to the aforementioned infields.

The infields and the farms that exploited them lay in different parts of the Celtic field in the three to four centuries that the Hijkerveld was occupied. If we interpret the excavation results in the light of an exploitation model,[23] we find that it is more likely that the settlement as a whole, i.e. all the farms together, was shifted around the Celtic field than that the farms were shifted individually. According to this model, three alternately used occupation sites would have been sufficient. This would mean that this Celtic field must contain three areas of infields and the associated concentrations of settlement remains. One of these occupation sites will have been situated in the excavated southwest part of the 75-ha large Hijkerveld. According to the model, this part will have been occupied for one-third of the overall period of occupation, but not continuously: an occupation phase of about twenty years will have been followed by a period of twice that length in which the other parts of the Celtic field were occupied.

On the basis of the results of a recalculation of the agrarian production and consumption figures we may assume four, or at most five, contemporary households for Hijken.[24] During the excavation, seventeen house sites were identified. They represent the use of the southern part of the Celtic field by some of the four or five households in between five and seven phases, depending on the length of the overall period of occupation (three to four centuries).

From dates obtained for some of the house plans we know that the area was definitely occupied around 400 BC, but the first settlers probably arrived here a century or more before then. The date obtained for the house plan that is assumed to be the youngest suggests that the area was abandoned in the first half of the 2nd century BC.

THE LATE IRON AGE

The evidence obtained in the excavation at Noordbarge gives us an impression of the further development of houses in the Late Iron Age.[25] The exterior posts were drawn closer to the wall and the wall itself was more solidly constructed (fig. 24.7). A few house plans at Noordbarge give the impression that in the later part of the Iron Age the wall consisted of closely set thin trunks,[26] or possibly of trunks split lengthwise and with squared ends. One plan suggesting this was found at Hijken (house 2) and a similar plan was observed at Peelo.[27] It was then only a small step to the next stage in the development, represented by the plans of Fochteloo[28] and the plans of Noordbarge incorporating bedding trenches. The houses of Fochteloo were still three-aisled; in those of Noordbarge the pairs of interior posts were combined or alternated with single posts along the central axis already before the phase of the houses with bedding trenches. As mentioned above, at a few sites in the southeastern part of Drenthe evidence has been found for early contacts with the world of the southern, two-aisled building tradition.

Around or shortly after the beginning of our era the Noordbarge site consisted of a compactly arranged enclosed settlement, with parallel houses with bedding trenches (fig. 24.8). The complex house plans, consisting of several linked parts, are probably the results of a series of building phases in which extensions were added to the original structures. There may never have been any buildings with the full lengths of the unearthed plans.

Such compact and enclosed settlements are (still) quite rare in the northern part of the Netherlands. We may wonder whether the structure, the location and the time of appearance of the enclosed settlement of Noordbarge reflect the unrest caused by the activities of the Roman army in these regions. It should in any case be added that similar developments were taking place further south, too.

Renewed pottery research has shed some doubt on the validity of the (Iron Age) dates which have for the past years been assumed for settlements like that of Fochteloo.[29] There are more reasons for reconsidering the dates of the settlement's house plans. One concerns the striking similarities shown by house plans

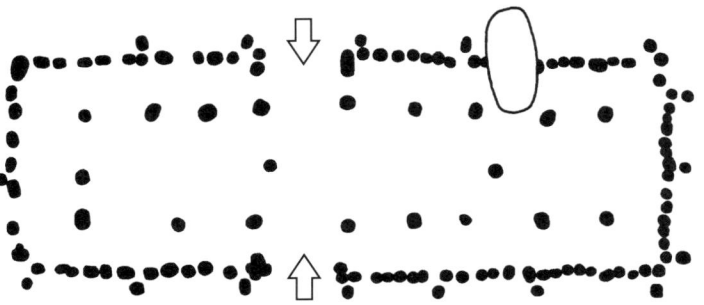

fig. 24.7
Plan of a house dating from the last part of the Iron Age found at Noordbarge. The house's wall consisted of posts spaced close together but still individually set in the ground. Scale 1:200.

549

fig. 24.8
The Noordbarge settlement in the first decades AD, characterised by regularly grouped farms with walls founded in trenches. The plan showing complexes of connected buildings represents successive building phases (expansion and replacement). The buildings will not have existed over their whole length at the same time. The depressions of sunken huts were found between the houses. The settlement was enclosed by a fence set in a bedding trench. Scale 1:2000.

unearthed in a very wide area, comprising the northern and eastern parts of the Netherlands and the adjacent parts of Lower Saxony and Westphalia. The dates proposed by archaeologists vary from the Middle Iron Age to the early part of the Roman period. Some of the house plans have already been mentioned above,[30] but there are several more examples of plans of this kind.[31] Conspicuous features of these plans are the large byres, which were always three-aisled – even when the living area had posts in the central axis – the rows of closely set postholes marking the position of the walls and the usually fairly wide entrances situated opposite one another. The time range previously assumed for this type of house may very well be too wide. The most likely time range for the majority of the plans of this type is from about 150 BC until AD 50.

FORTIFIED SETTLEMENTS

For several millennia the settlement system of the sandy region consisted of isolated single farmsteads of more or less the same kind, or at most hamlets of a few farmsteads. A settlement's importance and size will to some extent certainly have depended on its position in the road network linking the individual settlements. The walled enclosures of Rhee, Vries and Zeijen (I/II)[32] that made their appearance in the northern part of Drenthe are probably also to be regarded as elements within a spatial network, in this case including the nearby salt marshes, or rather: the occupants of the salt marshes. Of these sites, which were at most 0.5 ha large and were enclosed by different combinations of banks, palisades and ditches, only that of Rhee seems to have been an agrarian settlement. The other enclosed sites contained unusual main buildings (barns?) and granaries (figs. 24.9 and 24.10). For this reason they are generally assumed to have been storage and trade centres,

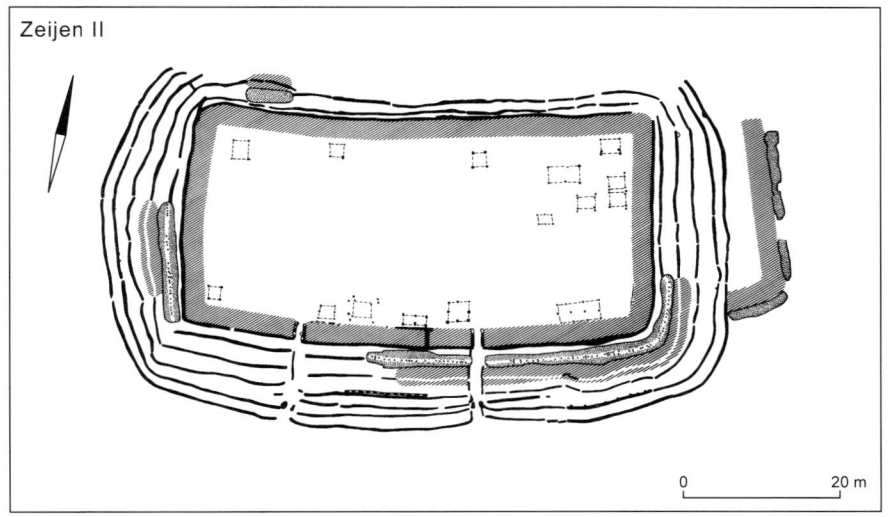

fig. 24.9
The walled enclosure Zeijen II in phase 2.
Several palisades, banks and ditches enclosed
an area, which in this phase possibly
contained only small structures with a
storage function. Scale 1:1000.

the products stored and traded most probably having been cereals.[33] Waterbolk
suggested that they may have been centres of power of local, rival leaders in the
last centuries BC, which may simultaneously have served a ritual function.[34] However, the results of the aforementioned pottery research also shed some doubt on
the pre-Roman dates proposed by Waterbolk.

CELTIC FIELDS: THE VISIBLE CORE OF THE ECONOMY

As far as the economy is concerned, there is virtually no evidence to suggest that
the settlements were inhabited by anything other than self-sufficient agrarian
communities throughout the entire period from c. 1400 BC until the beginning of
our era. It is assumed that the older settlement near Hijken, dating from the last
part of the Middle Bronze Age, at some time consisted of four farms and a shared
cattle pen.[35] All the house plans from the Late Bronze Age onwards indicate that
the cattle was stalled inside the main buildings. They also indicate many heads of
cattle per house. Houses Elp 12, 6, 7 and 9 contained stalls for 20, 20, 24 and 32

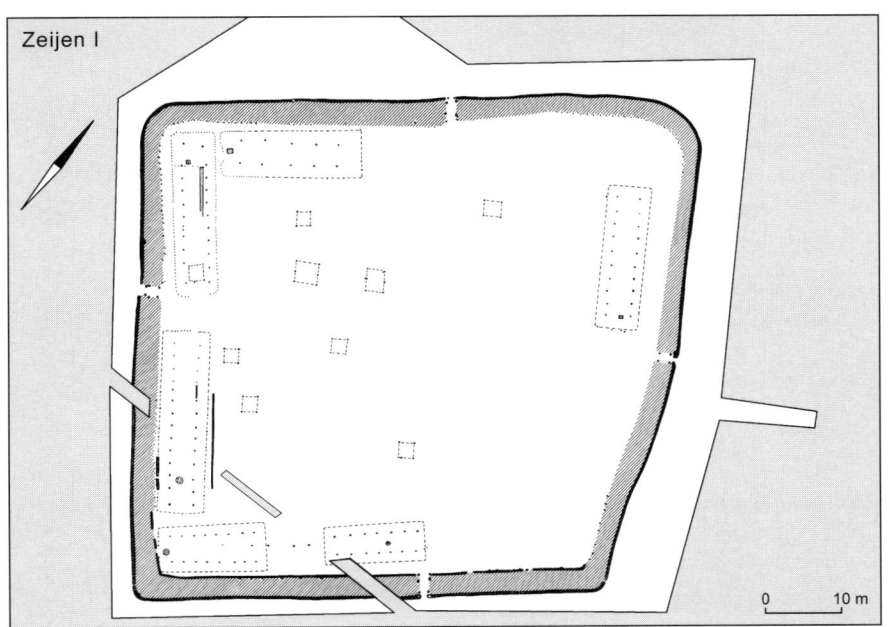

fig. 24.10
The walled enclosure Zeijen I in phase 3a.
The earthen bank supported with palisades
enclosed large buildings (byres and sheds?)
and granaries. Scale 1:1000.

heads of cattle, respectively; that of Rechteren also for 20-24. The largest building of the Angelslo 7 farm complex contained stalls for 20 heads of cattle originally, and for 36 after it had been extended. The figures for the houses of the Elp type at Emmerhout vary from 24 to 32 heads of cattle.

Cereal cultivation, with emmer and barley as the main crops, was also important. The relatively small number of granaries associated with the Middle Bronze Age houses of Hijken compared with the larger number in the younger part of Elp could imply that some, if not all, of the cereal was stored in the main building in the Middle Bronze Age.[36]

In the Bronze Age there may well have been a system of land use on the sandy soils according to which different areas were exploited alternately, as already indicated above for Elp. On the assumption that such areas lay about one kilometre apart, then, in the case of Emmen, the sites of Angelslo and Emmerhout and, in the case of Hijken, the site excavated along the Leemdijk and the surroundings of the barrows on the Hooghalen estate, may have been alternately used.

Such a system would then have been the precursor of the Celtic field system of the Iron Age. The latter system, characterised by the intensive use of small plots and constant reuse of the same areas after intervals in which the soil was allowed to regenerate, left behind clearly recognisable traces in the form of banks marking the limits of the plots (fig. 24.11, plate 36). These banks may have been formed and expanded when the infields were brought into cultivation in the successive phases of use. Many of the publications discussing the formation of these banks suggest that they are the results of the deposition of stumps, stones and uprooted weeds along the edges of the plots. Another frequently suggested interpretation is

fig. 24.11
Aerial photo from c. 1950 of the northern part of the Hijkerveld, the area to the northwest of Hijken; visible at the bottom left is the Oranjekanaal. In the Iron Age this area contained a Celtic field. The field system's banks were levelled when the heathland was brought under cultivation, shortly before this photo was taken. The white lines visible in the photo indicate the banks; the lighter subsoil has been exposed along these lines.

that they consist of exhausted soil dug from used plots.[37] Whatever the case, the aforementioned observation of a layer of burned house remains in such a bank on the Noordse Veld at Zeijen, indicating that a house was built on top of this bank between different stages in its formation, illustrates the phased and dynamic use of the Celtic field.

Manuring will have been very important for the success of the Celtic field system. The fact that the Middle Iron Age byres, which had stalls for 12 to 24 heads of cattle, were on the whole smaller than those of the Late Bronze Age possibly indicates that manure was collected and used in a more efficient manner in the Middle Iron Age. Cattle will have been the main suppliers of this manure, which may have been mixed with soil, in particular sods.[38]

Calculations have shown that the banks of the Dutch Celtic fields contained more soil than is likely to have come from the enclosed plots.[39] On basis of this information, and the high phosphate content obtained for the soil of the banks of some northern German examples, it was concluded in another study that the banks may have been composed from soil dug from the field itself, manure and possibly also sods from elsewhere.[40]

The substitution of naked barley by the hulled variety – a development that took place largely in the Iron Age – may have contributed towards the success of the more intensive system of land use. Hulled barley has less stringent soil requirements.[41] The assumed greater importance of beans in the range of crops cultivated may also have had a favourable effect, because beans increase the soil's nitrogen content.

In answering the question how long the Celtic field system remained in use reference is usually made to the adjacent part of Germany, especially the area around Flögeln. There the characteristic plots – with their exceptionally wide banks – are known to have remained in use until in the Roman period.[42]

As far as the non-agricultural component of the economy is concerned: we have virtually no evidence for the winning of iron ore or the production of iron in the northern part of the Netherlands in the Iron Age. In the later part of the Iron Age iron was however definitely produced in the adjoining parts of Westphalia and Lower Saxony.

It is difficult to estimate the economic relations between the occupants of the interior sandy regions and those of the northern coastal margins. Besides being the area of origin of (some of) the colonists of these areas, Drenthe was probably also a source of timber and possibly cereals.

DEMOGRAPHY AND SOCIAL STRUCTURE

The size of the population of a settlement depended on the number of farms it comprised, but it is not possible to give a fixed number of occupants per farm – that, in turn, depended on the number of neighbouring farms, or rather on the number of neighbours. If there were no neighbours to rely on in the agricultural peak periods then all the labour required had to be available at the farm itself. This is well illustrated by the figures relating to the purely agrarian settlements belonging to the jurisdiction (so-called *dingspel*) of Rolde in the 17th century: the smaller the number of farms per settlement, the greater the number of occupants per farm. Whereas the farms of the single-farm settlements were occupied by between twelve and sixteen persons, the households of the purely agrarian settlements consisting of six or more farms comprised no more than about seven persons.[43] Of course these 17th-century farms functioned partly in a market economy. We cannot simply adopt these figures for prehistoric times. The farms of the 17th century (and those of the Middle Ages, too) were moreover of a different size. Nevertheless, we may assume that a prehistoric single-farm settlement had about eight occupants, while the larger farms of the Elp type may have had eight to ten occupants. For hamlets of three to five farms we may assume an average of six persons per farm.

That there were indeed hamlets comprising three or more farms in Drenthe in the Late Bronze Age and the Early Iron Age, we can infer from the information obtained from urnfields. A few of the urnfields were in use continuously, irrespective of the positions of the settlements associated with them.[44] Only a few of the known urnfields are however suitable for calculations. The Late Bronze Age urnfields of Noordbarge, Wapse and Vledder and the Early Iron Age urnfield of Ruinen may presumably be regarded as continuously used cemeteries. Estimates (or re-estimates) of the total number of burials and of the period of use (re-estimated in the case of Ruinen) lead to average populations of 23 individuals for Noordbarge, 16 and 15 individuals for Vledder and Wapse, respectively, and 29 individuals for Ruinen. Expressed in the number of farms or households this implies three to four farms for Noordbarge, two for Vledder and Wapse and four to five for Ruinen.

The figures obtained for Ruinen correspond to those calculated for the Middle Iron Age settlement of Hijken on the basis of the size of the Celtic field. Both will have been relatively large settlements in their times. The Celtic field of Hijken measured about 75 ha. That of Vaassen was of a comparable size and the settlement associated with it may hence have had a comparable number of occupants, i.e. about 24. The Celtic fields of these two settlements are among the largest known in the Netherlands. Most of the others are much smaller. Even the well-known Celtic field of the Noordse Veld near Zeijen is only about half the size of that of Hijken.

On the basis of the distribution of the Celtic fields and historical demographic data a population density of three to four persons per square kilometre has been calculated for the part of Drenthe that was fit for occupation in the 5th century BC.[45]

The settlement data yield little information on the degree of social differentiation within the community. At Hijken, house no. 3, dating from the Middle Iron Age, differed from the others in size, in particular in width.[46] The great length of the house plan is largely due to the size of the byre, which contained stalls for 24 heads of cattle. This house plan stands out from the other Iron Age house plans of Drenthe. The head of the farm's household may have had a special status. The other settlements yielded virtually no indications of any social differentiation.

NOTES

1 Harsema 1982.

2 Waterbolk 1977a.

3 Van Gijn/Waterbolk 1984.

4 Cf. Brongers 1976a, 61 ff; Fokkens 1991a, 129.

5 Fokkens 1991a, 162.

6 Waterbolk 1986, 1987, 1990a.

7 Contrary to Waterbolk (1987), I believe that four rather than five main buildings were of this type, namely Nos 12, 9, 7 and 6 (in my opinion in this chronological order), dating from Waterbolk's phases f, e, h and i, respectively. Note that the plans numbered 7 and 12 in

Waterbolk 1987, fig. 9, have been switched.

8 Cf. Elp No. 12 (Waterbolk 1987, fig. 9) and Rechteren, Overijssel (Verlinde 1982b).

9 E.g. at Elp, which is in my opinion to be associated with house 12 (instead of with house 9, as Waterbolk assumed).

10 Deventer: Modderman 1955a, fig. 7; one of the two houses which were formerly dated to the Iron Age. Weener: Schwarz 1993, 86-87.

11 Huijts 1992.

12 The first extensively discussed characteristic example of this type was found at Een, municipality of Norg (Van der Waals 1963a; see

also Huijts 1992, figs. 61 and 62). This type is also known as type Peelo C.

13 Kooi/De Langen 1987, fig. 2; see also Huijts 1992, figs. 58 and 59.

14 Huijts 1992, fig. 63, and the results of the research carried out at Angelslo-Oost, 1963/64, unpublished.

15 For example plan 5 of unit 6 (Verlinde 1993b, fig. 5).

16 Groenewoudt/Verlinde 1989.

17 Verlinde 1991, fig. 6, and Verlinde 1993a, respectively.

18 Harsema 1987, fig. 5; 1994. The term 'Lunteren variant' of the Haps type was introduced for this type in the latter publication.

19 Kooi/De Langen 1987, figs. 3 and 4.

20 Harsema 1980a, 1980b.

21 Harsema 1980a, 1980b, 1982.

22 Brongers 1976a.

23 Harsema, in preparation.

24 Original calculation in Harsema 1980a, 1980b.

25 Harsema 1976; 1980a, 40-43.

26 For example Noordbarge 12, erroneously referred to as 'house 1' by Huijts (1992, fig. 71).

27 For example house 27 (Huijts 1992, fig. 74).

28 Nos 2 and 4 according to the numbering in Huijts 1992; his figs. 88 and 91, respectively.

29 Taayke 1991.

30 Peelo 27, Fochteloo 2 and Noordbarge 12.

31 Diphoorn, Vreden (Kr. Borken, Germany), Denekamp, Colmschate, Wijster (house 14), Ezinge (house 40) and in some respects also houses of Feddersen Wierde.

32 Waterbolk 1977b.

33 Harsema 1980a, 33.

34 Waterbolk 1985, 73.

35 Harsema 1991.

36 The obvious comparison between the early and the late phase of Elp has been omitted here on account of the uncertainty regarding

the nature of the 'outbuildings' (cf. Waterbolk 1964, and Waterbolk 1986, 1987).

37 For a survey, see Fokkens 1991a, 128-129.

38 That this was practised in Northwest Europe at an early date already was inferred from observations on the German island of Sylt. It is assumed that people on this island added organic material to the soil in the Middle Bronze Age already and it is believed that sods were used for this purpose in the Iron Age. This would have enabled a more intensive use of the land (Harck 1987; Kroll 1987). It has, however, not been taken into consideration that the main reason for the use of sods could have been to diminish or to prevent sand drifts, for which the area was vulnerable. The beginning of the formation of the 'classic' *Plaggenböden* or *esdekken* (the German and Dutch terms used for layers of soil mixed with dung and sods) is generally dated in (the final phase of) the early part of the Middle Ages at the earliest (*e.g.* Behre 1976).

39 Brongers 1976a, 61-62.

40 Fokkens (1991a, 129) assumes that the banks were in fact compost heaps, composed of soil from the field itself, manure and optionally sods from elsewhere. He does not explain why the contents of such heaps were not spread over the fields after the composting process.

41 W.A. van Zeist, personal communication.

42 Zimmermann 1984. The high phosphate content of the banks and their widths of up to 16 m has led to the belief that crops were actually cultivated on the banks themselves. It is possible that at Flögeln, in the last period of use of the arable land at that site, crops were cultivated almost exclusively on these banks, which may have been formed by piling up soil from former Celtic field plots.

43 Harsema 1980a.

44 Kooi 1979.

45 Harsema 1980a, 32. Brongers previously arrived at a density of one person per km^2 (Brongers 1976a, 66).

46 Harsema 1980a, 25, centre.

N Dwelling mounds on the salt marshes
The *terpen* of Friesland and Groningen

Jaap Boersma

Introduction

Terpen are artificial mounds that served mainly as dwelling places.[1] Large, high *terpen* are the result of the systematic raising and extension of the mounds over many centuries, in response to threats of floods and the growth of the population. The mounds were raised with turfs or sods dug from the surroundings of the *terpen*, combined with refuse produced by human beings and animals, in particular manure (plate 38A).

The *terpen* were built in areas which, before the construction of dikes, were periodically exposed to floods. The mounds' present environment hence differs considerably from that before the construction of the dikes. Nowadays, the distribution pattern of the *terpen* is associated with the types of soil on which they were constructed, i.e. marine clays in the coastal zone, fluviatile clay deposits along rivers, and some low-lying soils containing little clay. Most of the mounds that are known as *woerden* in the rivers area in the central part of the Netherlands are raised natural elevations and are therefore not *terpen* in the sense intended above.

The coastal region of the provinces of Friesland and Groningen is the *terp* area of the Netherlands. It forms part of a long belt dotted with *terpen* extending from the coast of the region known as Westfrisia in the province of North Holland to the southwest part of Denmark.

So the geological and geographical situations of the mounds differ, but so do their dates of construction. In the Netherlands, *terpen* started to be constructed in the 6th and 5th centuries BC. The widespread construction of raised dwelling mounds came to an end in the Middle Ages, around the 11th century. After that, only a few small *terpen* were built or raised in areas that were not protected from the sea by dikes or in areas where it was believed that the dikes provided insufficient protection. But there is one thing that all these *terpen* have in common, irrespective of their situation or age: they all bear formidable witness to man's ability to adapt to his natural environment.

The meaning of the word *terp*

The basic meaning of the word *terp* is 'an area surrounded by fences', more in particular 'arable land'. The same meaning underlies the Dutch secondary form *dorp* in the sense of 'hamlet'. As all the arable land lay on or around these mounds

before the construction of the dikes, the term *terp* started to be used for the mounds themselves. It replaced the originally used term *wierde*, at least in the Frisian language that was spoken in what is now the province of Friesland, and later also in the Dutch language. Only in the province of Groningen did the term *wierde* continue to be used. The meaning of the word *wierde*, 'yard surrounded by fences' or 'farm', is the same as the basic meaning of the word *terp*.[2]

Early archaeological interest

Archaeological interest in the *terpen* increased around 1840, when the fertile soil of the mounds, which had previously been used for private purposes on a small scale only, started to be exploited on a wider, commercial scale. This soil was

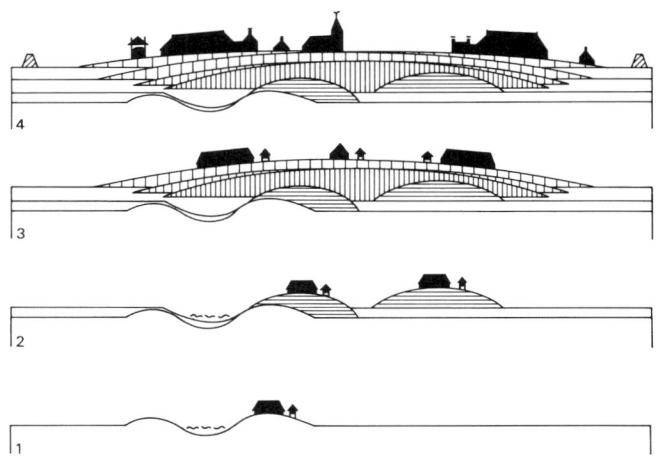

fig. N1

Schematic representation of the development of a *terp*.

1 First phase of occupation on a levee bordering a stream.

2 Accumulation of refuse and the raising of the surface level with sods cause the occupied area to grow in height and circumference (horizontally hatched area). This takes place in response to floods resulting in new deposits. A house *terp* is erected on such a new deposit (also horizontally hatched).

3 In the next phases the two *terpen* are raised and expanded jointly (vertically hatched). The gulley, which has meanwhile fallen dry, has disappeared beneath the *terp*.

4 The expansion of the *terp* comes to an end with the construction of dikes. Buildings are made of stone and become more varied. This marks the beginning of the development of the present-day *terp* village.

used to enrich poorer soils, for example the soils of newly reclaimed moors, reclaimed peatland, sandy and peaty soils and the soil of lowland pastures. The soil that was dug from the mounds was found to contain various kinds of ancient objects, which started to be collected and put on display in antiquities' rooms (*kabinetten van oudheden*). At the same time the first questions regarding the function, age and origins of the *terpen* began to be asked. All this led to small-scale trial excavations in two *wierden* in Groningen as early as 1827, an exhibition of finds from *terpen* and other objects in Leeuwarden (1877) and the supervision of the commercial levelling of the Hogebeintum *terp* (1905).

Generally speaking, *terpen* research was approached more scientifically in Groningen than in Friesland. The *Vereniging voor Terpenonderzoek* (Foundation for *terp* research), which was established in 1916, constituted a platform for systematic, scientific research into *terpen*. The first mound to be scientifically excavated was the *wierde* known as 'De Wierhuizen' near Appingedam (1916-1917). The excavation was supervised by the biologist A.E. van Giffen, who was later to be called the *Altmeister der Wurtenforschung* (grand champion of *terp* research). The foundation, in 1920, of the *Biologisch-Archaeologisch Instituut* at the State University of Groningen, which was led by Van Giffen, marked the beginning of a new stage in *terp* research.[3]

The excavation of the Ezinge *wierde* (mainly 1931-1934) is still classed as a milestone in Dutch *terp* research. The archaeological content of the mound had been beautifully preserved by thick layers of 'manure' and thanks to the excellent excavation methods employed in its investigation a great amount of useful information was obtained. The remains of the Middle and Late Iron Age farms in particular greatly impressed researchers and laymen alike; in some areas the aboveground parts of the farms had been preserved up to one metre. The research demonstrated continuity of occupation at this site, yielded essential information on prehistoric house construction and provided insight into the settlement's layout, economy and material culture of the period from c. 400 BC until AD 400.

Terpen of all kinds and all sizes

Large, high *terpen* are always based on a settlement. In elevated parts of salt marshes the original settlement will have been founded at ground level (fig. N1). The practice in low-lying parts was to build a raised podium, or several smaller podia, each intended for only one house (house *terpen*). Those podia were then gradually expanded, ultimately resulting in large mounds; sometimes several small *terpen* lying close together fused in the process of expansion and were subsequently expanded and raised as one mound. The primary

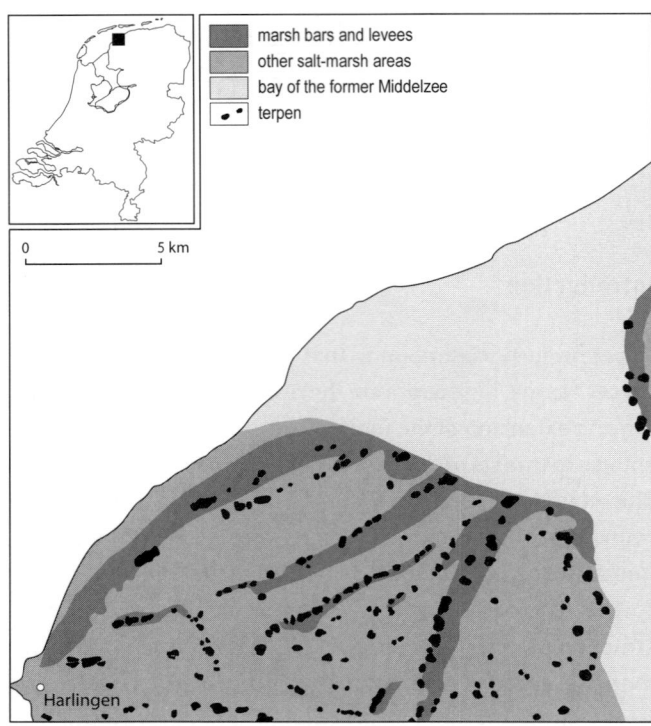

fig. N2

For reasons of safety, ease of drainage and tillage, the colonists of the salt marshes chose to settle on marsh bars and levees. This form of adaptation to environmental conditions is in some places clearly visible in the landscape in the distribution of *terpen* 'as a string of beads', as in the northern Westergo area.

terpen in such cases are called *kernterpen* (nuclear *terpen*). Archaeological research has revealed how some *terpen* originated. The no longer extant *wierde* of Middelstum-Boerdamsterweg, for example, was formed from a settlement founded at ground level. The Heveskesklooster *wierde* and the slightly younger *terp* of Wijnaldum-Tjitsma are the results of the raising and expansion of one or more nuclear *terpen*. A few *terpen* appear to have been built to serve solely as cemeteries in the early Middle Ages (*e.g.* Groningen-De Paddepoel IV). A related kind of *terp* is that which was intended exclusively as a podium for a church and a cemetery. That type of *terp* is known as a *kerkterp* (church *terp*, *e.g.* Dokkum, Oterdum).

Terpen differ in size and height. Their sizes vary from about 5 ares in the case of small house *terpen* to many hectares in the case of large village *wierden* like that of Ezinge, which has an area of 16 ha. Most *terpen* have much larger areas than required for the number of houses built on them. The majority will have borne only a few farms and will have been used mainly for crop cultivation. Some village *terpen* may be regarded as the most important centres of certain districts. Examples of such village *terpen* are those of Ezinge and Feddersen Wierde, to the north of Bremerhaven. The latter settlement comprised about 30 contemporary buildings, including 16 medium-sized and 10 small farms, in period 5 (3rd century AD).[4]

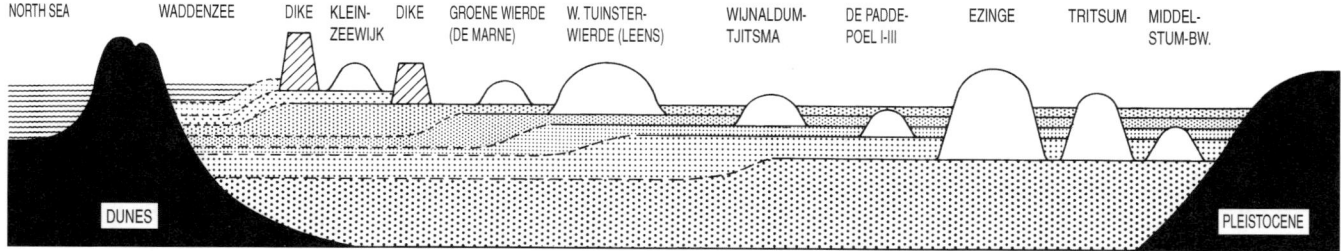

fig. N3

Schematic representation of the difference in the ages of *terpen* based on their position on deposits from different periods. To the right are the Pleistocene sands of the Drenthe plateau, to the left are the dunes of the Frisian islands.

Terpen that were no longer occupied will have been used for cultivation: the altitude of the fields precluded the risk of them being flooded and becoming brackish, which would have led to poor harvests. The heights of the mounds varied from less than 1 m in the case of a nuclear *terp* to almost 9 m to the top of the highest *terp* (Hogebeintum).

Due to changes in the surrounding environments, resulting from, for example, the construction of dikes or the settling of the land, the youngest *terpen*, from the middle and late parts of the Middle Ages, did not really evolve beyond the stage of house *terpen*. Such house *terpen* are to be found in widely varying regions: on the marine clays of South Holland and Zeeland, in certain areas around the former Zuiderzee (for example on Kampereiland and the former islands of Schokland and Marken,[5] where they are called *werven*), on some fluviatile clays and on the peats (which are here and there covered with clay deposits) to the south of the city of Groningen and to the north of Amsterdam. The centre of the latter city[6] and those of some other towns in North Holland are also founded on series of fused 13th-century house *terpen*. This category will be left out of consideration here.

The *terpen* landscape

The *terpen* in the coastal plain differ from one another, not only in origin, age, size and height, but also in altitude, shape and the pattern of the lots that were laid out on them. For a long time it was assumed that *terpen* were constructed mainly in periods of wetter conditions, which proved to have occurred in large parts of the Netherlands and were found to have coincided with transgressions. The wet periods were therefore associated with the transgressions. Current opinion, however, is that the changes to wetter conditions, also those to dryer conditions, are more likely to have been caused by variations in regional and local geological circumstances and, from the end of the early Middle Ages onwards, increasing human activities.[7] It has for example been found that the main reason why the Heveskesklooster *wierde* was expanded and raised after the 9th century is that the digging of drainage ditches had

caused the ground, which contained much peat, to subside, peat being extremely susceptible to drainage.

This new interpretation has made the former assumption of a relation between the construction and further development of *terpen* and the occurrence of transgressions (which was believed to have resulted in generations of *terpen*) no longer tenable. This is further confirmed by the results of research into pottery from Westergo, which show that the expansion of the population of that area – and hence the foundation of new settlements – was a continuous process.[8]

The microrelief played an important part in the colonisation of the salt marshes. For reasons of safety, drainage and tillage the colonists settled on the comparatively high sandy clay levees and marsh bars, some of which had silted up to about 2.50 m above the average sea level. This settlement pattern is clearly reflected by the rows of *terpen* that can still be observed in Friesland and Groningen today. They embody a cultural-historical phenomenon in due form (fig. N2). The altitude of the base of a *terp* gives a rough indication of the mound's age. Due to the constant rise in sea level, and hence in the level of the clay deposits, the altitude of the bases of the youngest *terpen*, lying closest to the sea, is the highest (fig. N3).

Different types of *terpen*

The type of *terp* that has always been considered the ideal type is the fully developed, round *terp* with a radial layout, surrounded by a ring road accompanied by a ring ditch at the foot of the mound. The living areas of the farms on such a *terp* are ideally oriented towards the centre, the byres towards the road. The centre is open or, quite frequently, contains a church and a cemetery. Some *terpen* have a pool of drinking water in the centre (figs. N4).

The surviving *terpen* vary in shape, some being more or less round, others square to rectangular (fig. N4: 3) or elongated. The pattern of the lots that were laid out on the mounds also varied, radial and rectangular layouts being representative. These two layouts were also combined on some *terpen*. How-

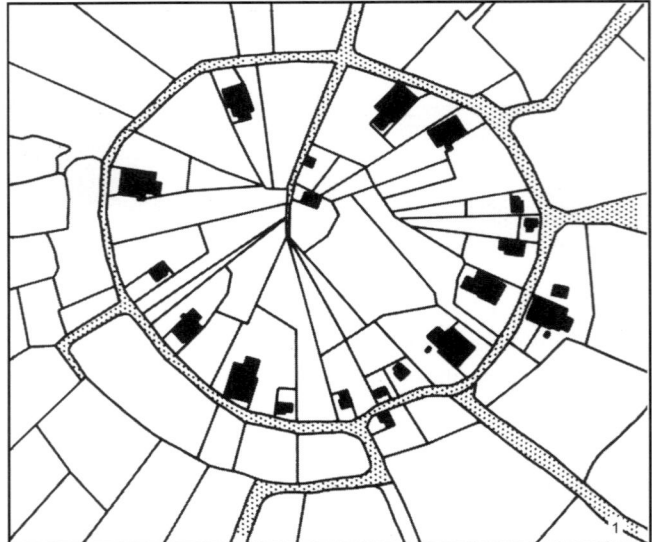

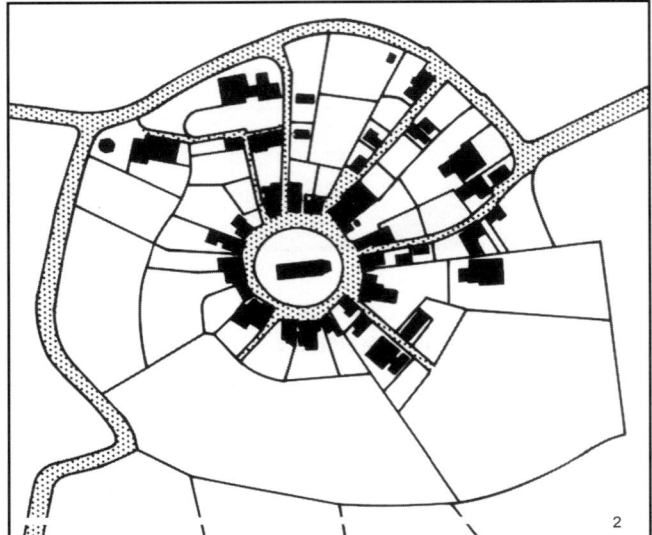

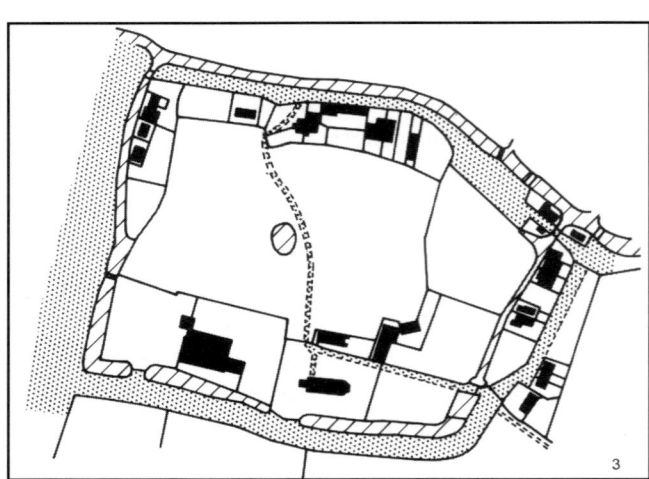

fig. N4

Different forms of subdivision of the land on various *terpen* according to the original cadastral maps of *c.* 1830. Grey: roads; hatched: water.

1 Biessum. *Terp* with a radial layout enclosed by a ring road. The farms are oriented with their living parts towards the centre and the byre towards the road. In former days there will have been a pool of drinking water at the centre.

2 Niehove, formerly called Suxwort. This *terp* also has a radial layout. At the centre are the church and the churchyard enclosed by a ring road. Part of the other ring road, circling the edge of the *terp*, has survived.

3 Achlum. *Terp* with a rectangular layout enclosed by ditches and a canal, the Achlumervaart (in the north). The church and churchyard lie on the southern flank. At the centre is a pool of drinking water.

ever, the layouts of most *terpen* cannot be properly classified. It is not correct to regard the round *terp* with a radial layout as the ideal type.

Besides round and rectangular *terpen*, which are typical of agrarian settlements, there were also elongated *terpen* with a street along the mound's longitudinal axis and buildings on either side of the street. *Terpen* of this type and its variants date from the 8th and 9th centuries and are archaeologically best-known from Ostfriesland (Germany). The economy of the occupants of these *terpen* was not based on agriculture, like that of the above *terpen*, but on trade and industry. These *terpen*, which are therefore known as 'trade *terpen*', are believed to have been centres of regional importance.[9]

The difference in the layout of the settlements appears to indicate a difference in the age of the *terpen*, but this is a matter of much controversy. It would be incorrect to date a *terp* on the basis of one characteristic only. Without further research, the possibility that one form of layout was gradually replaced by an entirely different form cannot be excluded.[10]

Notes

1 For some general literature on *terpen* see: Bierma *et al.* 1988; Boeles 1951; Boersma 1972; 1991; Van Es n.d.; 1965-'66; Jaarverslagen Vereniging voor Terpenonderzoek from 1917 onward; Taayke 1990; Waterbolk 1965-'66; Waterbolk/Boersma 1976.

2 Halbertsma 1963, 122-128; Van Berkel 1987, 6-7.

3 Halbertsma 1963, 11-85; Waterbolk 1970b.

4 Haarnagel 1979, 192-198; Schmid 1984, 208.

5 Vervloet 1974.

6 Baart 1990, 152-154.

7 Knol 1993, 15-24.

8 Taayke 1991, 113.

9 Brandt 1984, 100-113.

10 Since this contribution was written (summer of 1994) some works containing important additional information on this subject have been published, notably Besteman *et al.* 1999, Boersma 1999 and Taayke 1996.

25 Colonists on the clay
The occupation of the northern coastal region

Jaap Boersma

GEOGRAPHICAL SETTING AND LANDSCAPE

The clay region of Groningen and Friesland now constitutes a continuous belt with a varying width along the south coast of the Waddenzee and the east coast of the IJsselmeer. In the first millennium BC, however, the coastal strip was indented and formed part of the southeast coast of the North Sea because the Frisian islands either had not yet been formed or consisted of only narrow coastal barriers.[1] The clay deposited in this zone is all marine clay; there is no river clay in this area.

To the west, the prehistoric clay landscape extended up to the island of Texel. The former composition of this western area would have been the same as that of Groningen and Friesland: a strip of clay along the coast bordered by peat on its landward side. To the east the area discussed bordered on the coastal region of northwest Germany, which differed somewhat from the adjacent coastal region of the northern Netherlands. Whereas in the Netherlands the coastal plain was separated from the Pleistocene sands further inland by a wide strip of peat, in Germany clay and sand bordered one another and the peats were enclosed in the sand plateau. Another difference concerns the presence of large rivers: in the eastern part of the coastal region were the Weser and the Ems, in the western part was only the smaller Hunze. The other rivers in the north of the Netherlands were fairly modest.

The coastal plain consisted of a wide salt marsh controlled by the tides. At high tide the saltwater from the Waddenzee penetrated far inland via inlets, tidal channels and a maze of gulleys. The mud and sand deposited during floods led to the formation of marsh bars and levees. After physical ripening, these formations were ideally suited to human occupation because of their elevation and their soil structure (see feature N). A distinction can be made between settlements on marine clay and settlements on river clay.

THE COLONISATION PHASE (C. 600-350 BC)

The first settlements

The chronology of the period of colonisation of the clay regions is based primarily on the typology of settlement pottery. Cemeteries from this phase are still unknown in the clay district. Objects of bronze and iron, which usually serve as type fossils elsewhere and which can be dated more accurately than pottery, are extremely rare here. This is the reason why there is no consensus concerning the date of the arrival of the first settlers. This holds for the clay region of the northern Netherlands as well as for that of north Germany.

The river deposits of the Weser are assumed to have been colonised in the Late Bronze Age (Rodenkirchen-Hahnenknooper Mühle); the settlement of Huntebrück-Wührden dates from the Early Iron Age.[2] The oldest settlements on the river clay of the Ems are datable to the transition from the Early to the Middle Iron Age: Jemgum 1 and Boomborg-Hatzum date from periods Ia/Ib and Ib-IIb, respectively, according to Harck's chronology.[3] In absolute terms, period Ia is dated to the late 6th century BC; the 5th century BC is assumed as a working hypothesis for period Ib.[4]

In the coastal region of the northern Netherlands the settlement Middelstum-Boerdamsterweg represents the earliest occupation phase.[5] The site was colonised in the 6th century BC. Examples of other settlements in Groningen from around the same time are Feerwerd-Noord, Garnwerd, Brillerij and Joeswerd, all of which lie in the area known as Middag, on marsh bars and levees to the west of the Hunze. The excavated part of the Ezinge *wierde* (the term used for a *terp* in Groningen) dates from a later occupation phase.

A larger number of early settlements have been found in Friesland, especially in the southern part of the area known as Westergo. Settlements in this area include Walperd, Wommels, Hichtum, Schettens, Baarderburen and Pingjum. Fewer settlements from the colonisation phase have been found in the northern part of Friesland. A good example of such a settlement in the latter region is Hogebeintum, in the western part of Oostergo.

Characteristic finds from the period of the arrival of the first immigrants are flint 'sickles', Ruinen-Wommels I pottery and the less common pottery with older roots such as Harpstedt ware and pottery decorated with impressions made with the aid of a bracelet that was twisted once.

The colonisation of this region was not a massive event but is to be conceived as the successive arrivals of small groups of immigrants over a period which, in the area to the west of the Ems, is assumed to have lasted two and a half centuries, until around the middle of the 4th century BC. The marine clay of Ostfriesland to the east of the Ems became suitable for occupation only in the 1st century BC.[6]

The river clay of Ostfriesland, lying at a safe distance from the sea, was colonised already at the end of the Early Iron Age. The immigrants settled on the left bank of the Ems. Of the settlement sites discovered in this area Boomborg-Hatzum in particular has been investigated on a large scale.[7] Research into botanical remains showed that the settlement was founded in a freshwater environment, among groves dominated by ash and elm.[8] The environmental conditions differed fundamentally from those of the saltwater tidal landscape at the coast, where no trees could grow.

The first settlements of the colonisation phase were founded directly on the clay (unraised settlement). The construction of artificial occupation mounds, or *terpen*, is characteristic of a later occupation phase (see also fig. N1). The elevation of the earliest unraised settlements varies, depending on the distance to the shore. At Rodenkirchen-Hahnenknooper Mühle the occupation remains were found at a depth of 1.10 to 1.79 m below NAP (Normal Amsterdam Level), those of Boomborg-Hatzum at a depth of 0.40 to 0.90 m below NAP and those of Middelstum-Boerdamsterweg at 0 to 0.50 m below NAP. The average sea level at that time was about one and a half metre lower than it is today.

The origins of the first settlers of the marshes

In the past, all kinds of theories were put forward for the origins of the first occupants of the clay of Groningen and Friesland on account of their alleged Frisian identity. It was first thought that they came from the Middle Rhine region; next they were assumed to have arrived by ship from northwest Germany. The resemblance between the cultures of the colonists and the occupants of the Drenthe plateau was not recognised until later. It was then believed that the deteriorating natural conditions on the plateau, due to constantly expanding peat growth, exhaustion of the soil and increasing trouble caused by sand drifts, forced the occupants to move to the fertile salt marshes. As a result, the ethnic term for the occupants of the salt marshes was replaced by a cultural term: the Zeijen culture, which refers to the presumed area of origin, the province of Drenthe.[9] Fokkens presented a more nuanced view and suggested the western periphery of the Drenthe plateau as the most likely area of origin.[10]

Besides this view there is the hypothesis that the southern part of Westergo had already been occupied, for a long or a short period, before the arrival of the above immigrants. The adherents of this hypothesis regard the flint sickles found in this area as type fossils of this early colonisation phase. According to Waterbolk, North Holland, and in particular Westfrisia and Texel, is likely to have been the colonists' area of origin.[11] Van Heeringen is of the opinion that they came from the distribution area of the Assendelft pottery group.[12] However, Westergo has yielded no pottery that is indisputably older than the Ruinen-Wommels I ware; moreover, flint sickles have also been found elsewhere in the distribution area of the Zeijen culture. In view of these facts it seems unlikely that there was an earlier occupation phase.

Because of the absence of a difficultly negotiable intermediate peat barrier as in the Netherlands, migrations from *Geest* (sands) to *Marsch* (marshland) have always been taken for granted in northwest Germany. Recently, it has once again been argued that the first occupants of the salt marshes of the northern Netherlands came from northwest Germany, in particular from the deposits along the Ems and the Weser, and hence that they arrived along the shore.[13] If this is true, the immigrants from the Drenthe plateau must represent a later invasion wave. Whatever the case may be, we do know for sure that the first colonisation phase lasted for several generations.[14]

SETTLEMENTS

Middelstum-Boerdamsterweg

The situation of the unraised settlement of Middelstum-Boerdamsterweg, which has been completely excavated, is typical of the early occupation of the salt marshes, i.e. along a gulley which joined up with a channel which flowed into the sea, in this case the Fivelboezem, after a presumably short distance. The occupants inhabited two sites lying 70 m apart on the left bank of the gulley (fig. 25.1).[14]C dates cannot tell us which site was inhabited first.[15] Dates based on archaeological evidence point to the 6th century BC in both cases. The history of the occupation of both sites can be split up into several periods and phases.

In period 1a of the eastern site there were three elements: a platform supported by stout foundation posts set in a rectangle measuring approximately 15 x 5 m at the edge of the gulley, a house measuring approximately 13.4 x 6.4 m right next to it and a storage structure lying a few metres away, which was rebuilt twice on the same spot. Together these elements constituted a single farmstead (Gehöftsiedlung), which was enclosed by a crescent-shaped ditch, which joined up with the gulley at both ends. The building, a longhouse, was three-aisled and had a non-supporting wall of stakes held together by wattlework, beyond which was a row of posts set 1-1.5 m apart. Along the central axis were two – originally probably three – posts.

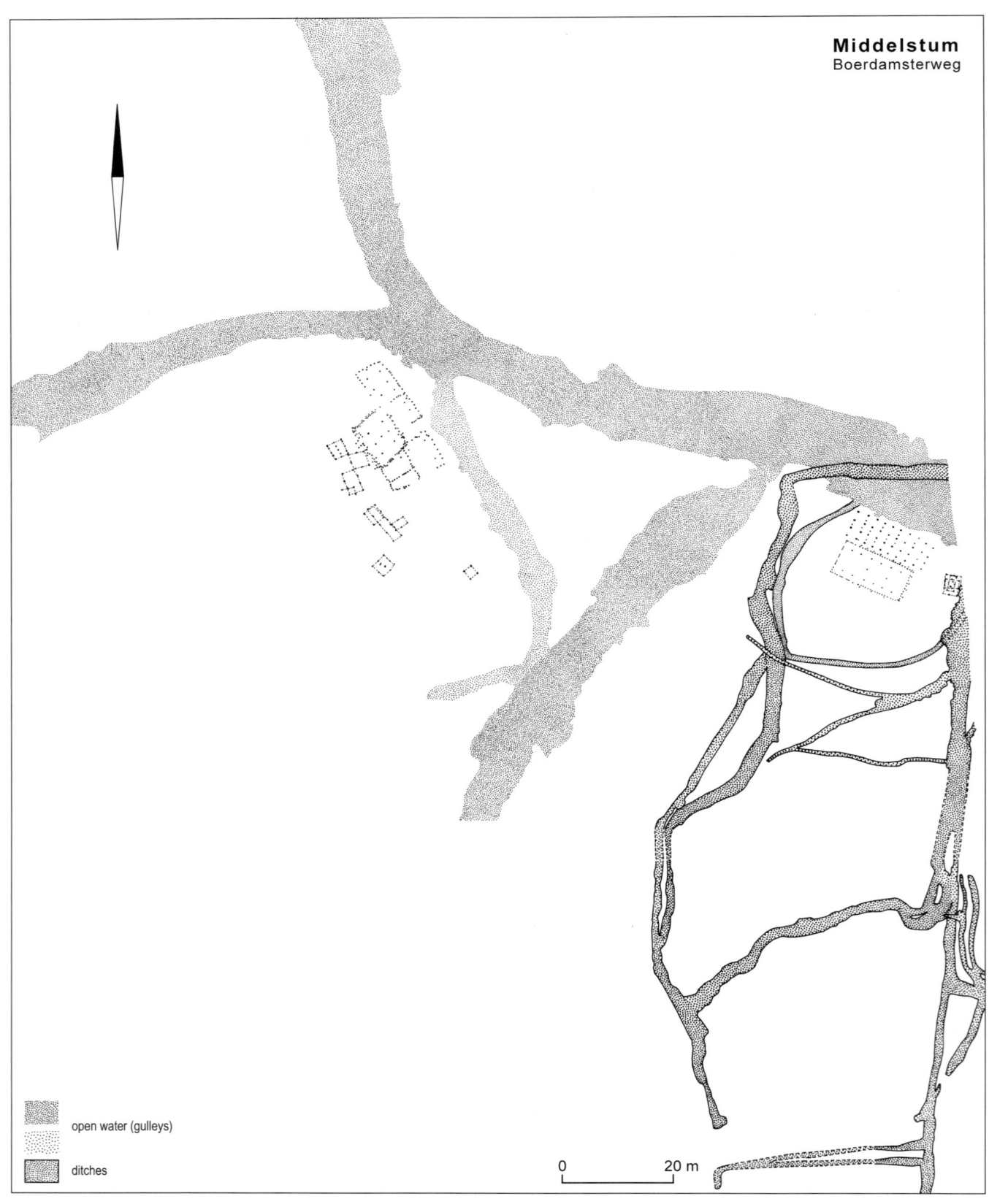

Middelstum
Boerdamsterweg

open water (gulleys)

ditches

0   20 m

fig. 25.1

The Middelstum-Boerdamsterweg unraised settlement along a main and a side gulley; period 1 (6th-5th century BC). In period 1b the eastern occupation centre formed part of a system of fields divided by ditches. The structures of period 1a will have disappeared by then. Scale 1:1000.

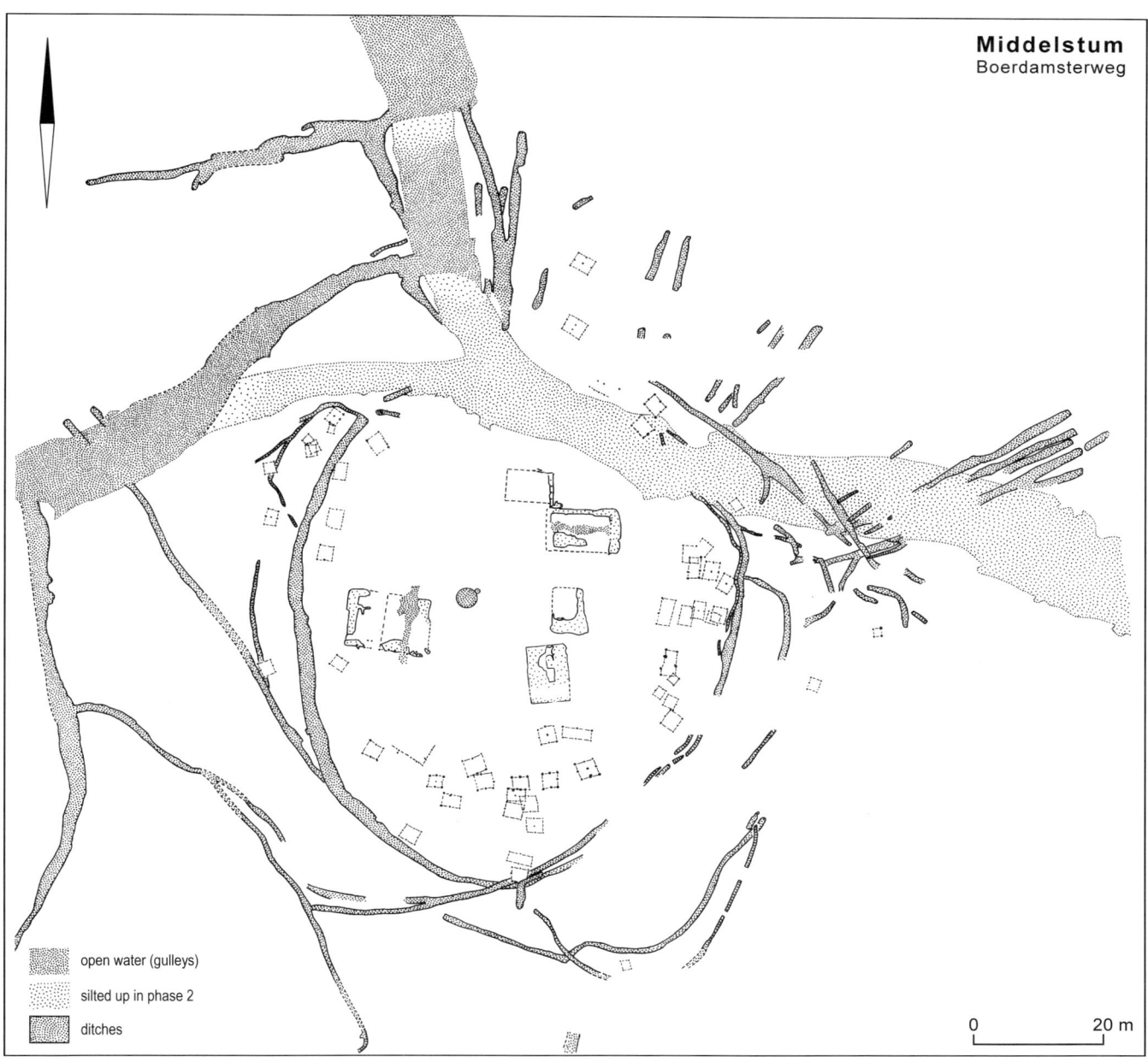

open water (gulleys)

silted up in phase 2

ditches

0   20 m

There were two entrances: one in a long side and another in a short side.

The distribution of platforms appears to be limited to the coastal strip (Middel-stum-Boerdamsterweg, Jemgum, Ezinge). No such structures have been found on the sandy soils. We can only guess their function, but it seems most likely that they were storage structures. It is possible that they were primarily intended not for the storage of cereal but for the storage of hay and reeds, to be used as fodder and as bedding 'straw' in the winter, and of meat and raw materials like hides and wool. Another possibility is that they originally also served as places where for example cattle herders could sleep. The small storage structure was of the type with more than four posts.

By the beginning of period 1b the gulley had partly silted up and the yard had expanded over it. The yard then formed part of a series of at least three adjacent plots of some sixteen ares each. The structures described above would have disappeared by then and the yard, like the other plots, would have been under cultivation.

The western site (period 1) lay at a point where a small gulley flowed into the main gulley. These two water courses constituted the limits of the settlement on

fig. 25.2
In period 2 (5th century BC), the western occupation centre of Middelstum-Boerdamsterweg was a *wierde* enclosed by a ditch. The enclosed area contains the plans of rectangular structures, the postholes of granaries and a round well in the centre. The settlement expanded in several stages with more buildings, including granaries. The gulleys of period 1 had meanwhile partly been filled with sediment. Scale 1:1000.

565

one side; the other side was open. The two largest structures, each of which had annexes, were structurally connected and measured 8 by 5.4 m and 8.6 by 6.8 m. The structures were flimsily built and lacked the regular layout typical of Middle Iron Age farms. The remains appear to represent a number of fenced enclosures, presumably cattle pens. Nearby were several granaries of different types. These structures may have formed part of the eastern farm complex. The discovery of half of an earthenware face mask (fig. 29.1) in one of the buildings moreover seems to suggest ceremonial activities.

By the beginning of period 2, which has been dated to the 5th century BC,[16] the western site had developed into a low mound surrounded by a ring ditch (fig. 25.2). The gulleys of the previous period had only partly silted up. There was a remarkably large number of granaries situated mainly along the periphery of the mound. Grouped around the centre, where there was a large well, were five rectangular patches of clay; they are assumed to be the remains of buildings with walls built of sods, which may have been byres. As both gulleys had silted up, period 2 at the western site may have been contemporary with period 1b at the eastern site, which was at that time under cultivation.

In period 2 the mound apparently served as a collective storage place for harvest products of a group of salt marsh occupants; it may also have served as a stock enclosure when necessary. The number of occupants must have been small. Most members of the group will have lived in farms that are presumed on the nearby levees.

In period 3 the mound expanded. No remains of buildings from this period have been preserved. Just outside the mound were ring ditches, as in for example Westfrisia in the Late Bronze Age. The latter are thought to have been dug around

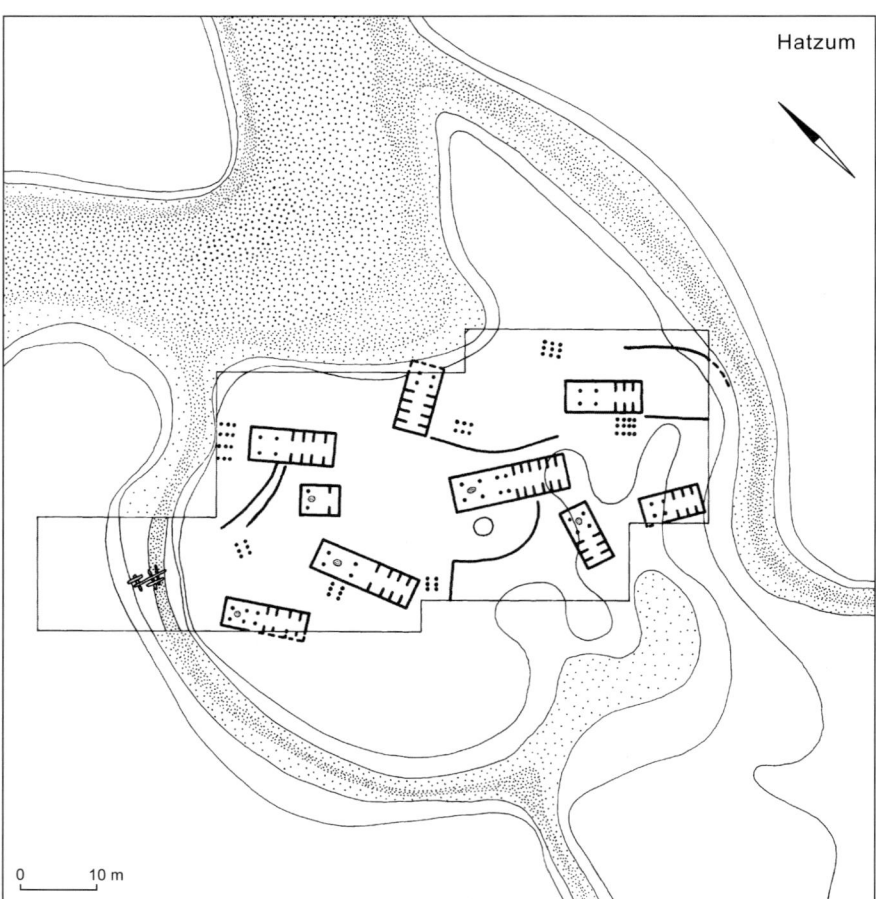

fig. 25.3
The Boomborg-Hatzum unraised settlement bordering a gulley in period 2 (5th century BC). The houses were arranged around an open area. Scale 1:1000.

cereal ricks or haystacks.[14]C analysis of three charcoal samples, obtained from a ring ditch and from pits inside and next to it, yielded a date in the 4th-3rd century BC.[17] The mound appears to have been abandoned after that. The presence of younger pottery suggests that the mound was occupied again in the early Roman period.

Occupation periods 1 and 2 were short. Houses were not rebuilt; granaries on the other hand were. The posts, which were made of beech, alder and elm, lasted for one or two generations at the most. Contrary to the opinion that Middelstum-Boerdamsterweg was a permanently occupied settlement already in period 1, it has been suggested[18] that in this period the site was a camp that was occupied in the summertime only, by transhumant shepherds. This hypothesis, however, is based partly on an incomplete representation and debatable interpretation of the longhouse at the eastern site.[19] The results of the analysis of the faunal remains do not suggest that the site was occupied in the summertime only.[20] Nor does the presence of *Triticum dicoccum* (emmer) necessarily indicate contacts with the occupants of the sands.[21]

Jemgum 1

Like the settlement at the eastern site of Middelstum-Boerdamsterweg in period 1a, the unraised settlement Jemgum 1 was a *Gehöftsiedlung*, of about the same date. The situation is exactly the same: they were situated on the levee of a gulley, which in this case flowed into the Ems. In each of its three occupation periods this settlement, which was not excavated in its entirety, probably comprised two houses with two or three granaries. A platform with a width of about 4 m whose length could not be determined is also assumed to have been a granary. In the first period there was one fenced house, one building which was not surrounded by a fence and which was probably also a house, and two nearby granaries. There were no byres.[22]

Boomborg-Hatzum

The remains of occupation periods 1-5 of the settlement of Boomborg-Hatzum date from the same period as those of Middelstum-Boerdamsterweg, but the medium-sized settlement is of a different character in that it consisted of groups of farms (*Gruppensiedlung*). It was located on a wooded levee, surrounded by gulleys, and was in contact with the sea via the Ems (fig. 25.3). Less than one-third of the settlement could be investigated and therefore no definitive statements can be made about its layout. At first, the settlement was unraised. Period 2 saw the beginning of the development of a *terp*: after floods, the low-lying parts of the site were filled with manure and clay, which led to the formation of a new, raised, occupation area. The houses of period 3, built after another flood, appear to have been erected on individual platforms as a kind of house *terpen* or nucleus *terpen*.

Throughout all the occupation periods the houses were grouped around a central area which provided direct access to the gulley and lay at more or less the same spot in each period. In some periods this central area was open, in others it contained a house or a longhouse. Whether these buildings had a special function or whether their occupants belonged to a social elite could not be determined.

The layout of the settlement was not dictated by this central area but by the relief. The remains of each period comprise the plans of about ten to fourteen farmsteads, which will however not all have been contemporary. Each farmstead consisted of a longhouse, a granary and sometimes a small house without a byre, which may have been a craftsman's house. There were also fences marking the limits of yards, fenced roads and ovens and/or kilns. No wells have been found, which means that the occupants and their animals must have obtained their water from the gulley. At the end of period 5, in the 3rd century BC, the settlement was abandoned as a result of storm floods. The site was reoccupied around the beginning of our era, but now in a marine environment.

fig. 25.4
Ezinge in periods 1b and 1c (5th century BC). In period 1b the western part of a *terp* enclosed by a fence was inhabited. In period 1c the *terp* was extended over the adjacent salt marsh, which was fenced in by wattlework and a palisade in front of it. Within the fence a platform was built as well as, on an artificial elevation, a house (No. 1). The branching gulley in the northwestern corner determined the settlement's orientation. Scale 1:200.

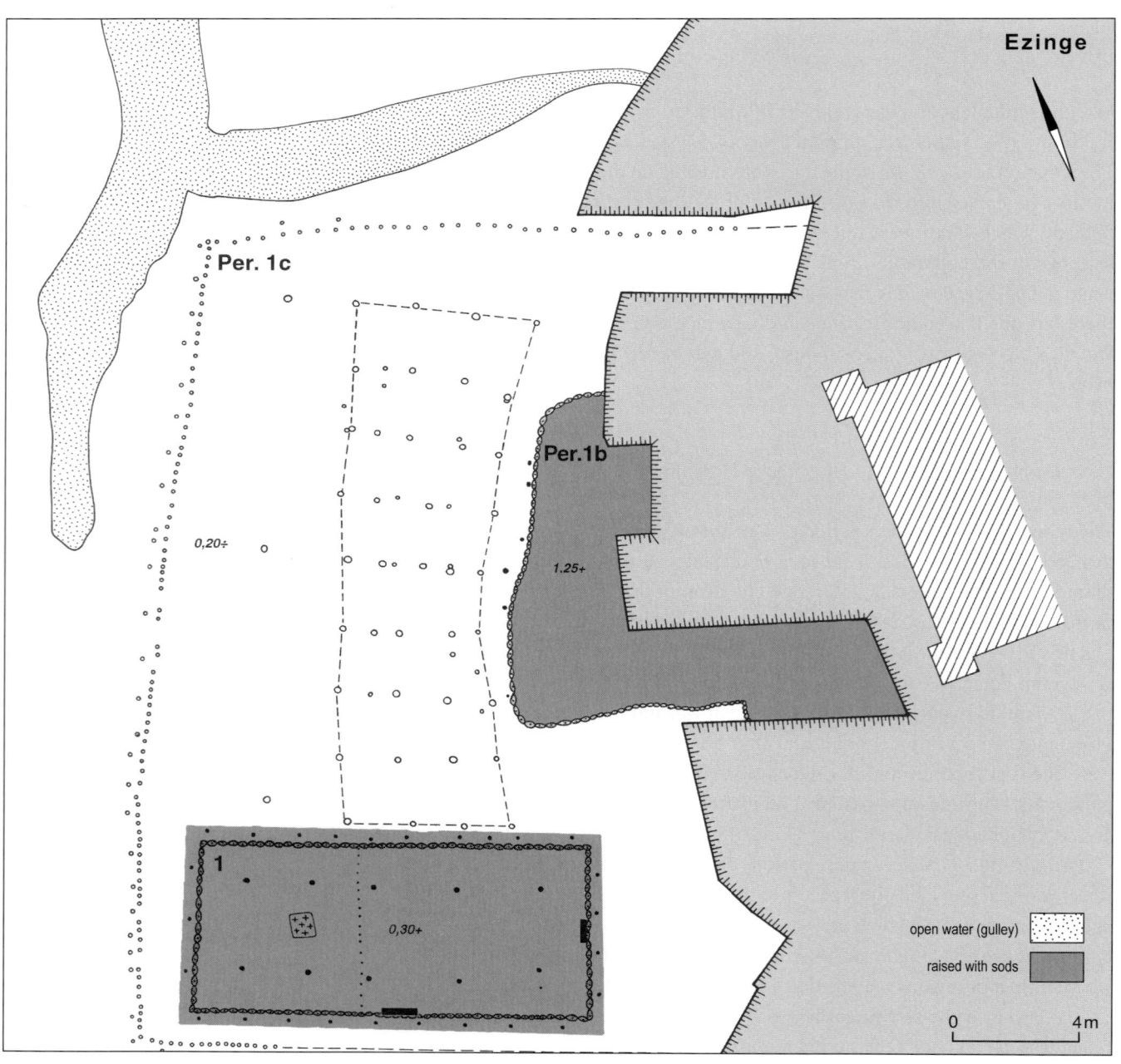

At Ezinge the cemetery on the *wierde* (*terp*) precluded research into the primary settlement form and the subsequent development of the settlement. On the basis of recently obtained evidence it is now assumed that the *terp* evolved as follows.

The oldest occupation remains consist of a wattlework wall with posts along the outside and a palisade in front. The old land surface was at salt marsh level (-0.2 m NAP). These remains lay at most 2 m from the front bank of the cemetery. They represent part of an enclosure surrounding the western side of an unraised settlement, the rest of which now lies buried beneath the *terp* (phase 1a). In a later phase there was a mound here, whose surface lay at least 1.25 m above NAP (phase 1b). Of this *terp*, too, only the remains of the western stretch of the enclosure could be recorded. They consisted of a wattlework wall with a few posts on the outside (fig. 25.4). This enclosure lay at the foot of the *terp* and served the double purpose of enclosing a farmyard and reinforcing the bank of the *terp*. The wall's course, curving in a southerly direction, indicates that the *terp* was larger than the primary settlement.

In the next phase (1c) the area of the *terp* was again expanded. And again only the western part of the *terp* could be exposed. It consisted of marshland that was not raised, but was surrounded by a rectangular wattlework enclosure with a palisade in front of it. The gulley which splits up to the northwest of the *terp* in the northwest dictated the course of this enclosure – and hence the orientation of the entire settlement. Within the enclosure was a platform that measured about 17 x 5 m, which would have been used for storing reeds, hay, crops and the like. The curvature of the eastern row of posts shows that the new structure was built in relation to the body of the *terp* of phase 1b. The house associated with the platform will presumably have stood on the *terp*.

The longhouse whose remains were found to the south of the platform is probably younger. This house, which measured 13 x 6 m (fig. 25.4 No. 1, *cf.* figs. 25.7 and 25.8) was built at salt marsh level, but the farm's floor and the land surrounding it were raised half a metre immediately after the farm's construction, so the occupants lived on a *terp* after all. This is an unusual development for a house *terp*. It could be related to the fact that little space was available around the farm. The usual custom was to raise the ground first and then build a house.

In the next phase the area with which the *terp* had been expanded in phase 1c was raised with sods, after which a large farm with outbuildings on both sides was built within an enclosure. The outbuildings were houses or living-working areas and byres (phase 2c). The rest of the settlement remains lie buried beneath the part of the *terp* that could not be excavated. In the following periods the mound continued to expand in size and height. In period 3 the settlement started to develop radially (fig. 25.5). In period 7b the radially arranged settlement was replaced by a single west-east oriented longhouse. There were sunken huts on either side of the building. The higher excavation levels could not be interpreted.

The development outlined above spans about eight hundred years. The remains of period 1 date from the 5th century BC at the earliest; the beginning of the radial layout is datable to the 2nd century BC and its end to the 4th/5th century AD.[23] During the radial phase Ezinge became a *terp* village. The development from a presumed unraised settlement to a village on a *terp*, its subsequent expansion and structural changes could be followed in outline only, due to the restrictive circumstances.

For a more detailed survey of the development of a *terp* settlement we can turn to the excavation of Feddersen Wierde, to the north of Bremerhaven.[24] This *terp* is smaller than that of Ezinge and was vacant at the time of the research; it has been excavated virtually completely. The occupation remains of this site date from

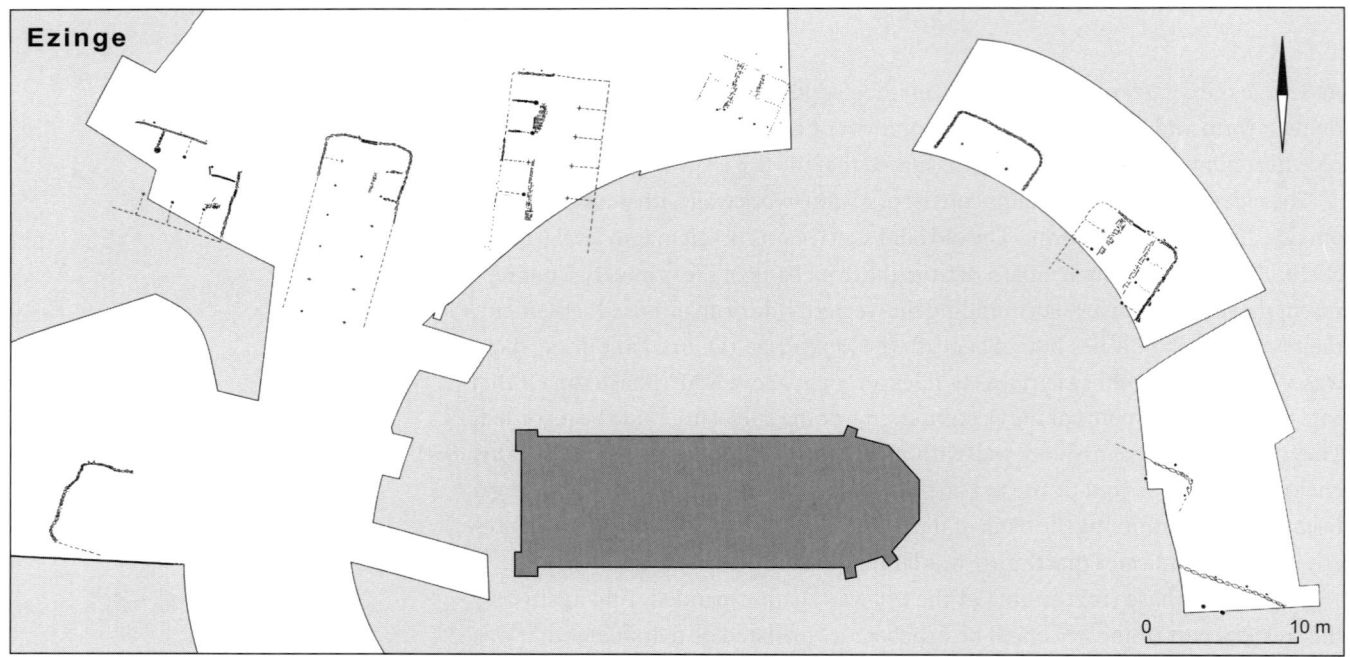

Ezinge

0   10 m

fig. 25.5

The Ezinge *wierde* in period 3b (2nd century BC). The plans of the farms, only parts of which could be exposed, are grouped radially around the centre. Scale 1:500.

a later period, from the second half of the 1st century to the beginning of the 5th century AD, but they can still give us a good impression of what must have taken place at Ezinge earlier on.

Groningen-De Paddepoel I-III and Heveskesklooster

The excavations of Groningen-De Paddepoel I-III and Heveskesklooster did yield evidence on the origin of a salt marsh settlement, the missing link in the evidence of Ezinge. The investigations at these sites showed that there were several different forms of primary settlements too.

The partly excavated settlements of Paddepoel I and III started as unraised settlements. The same probably holds for settlement II, which was also only partly investigated.[25] The earliest occupation remains of settlement III have recently been dated to c. 200 BC, those of settlement II to the 2nd/1st century BC and those of settlement I to the 1st century AD.[26] In phases, the unraised settlements, which had one or more centres, developed into a number of individual house *terpen* consisting of sods and refuse and enclosed by a ditch. In a following phase the mounds were expanded, sometimes over the ditches, and this expansion process went on for some time. The Dunkirk II transgression put an end to this development and the house platforms never fused to result in unified *terpen*. The radial layout of the house platforms of settlement III would have resulted in a round *terp*. The little house *terpen* of Paddepoel I-III are characteristic of the occupation of the inland peripheral zone of the old salt marsh.

The houses are all of the usual type. In one case the evidence suggests a longhouse with a dung gutter down the central axis. If this evidence is correct, the house in question is a unique exception. There were granaries in every phase. Plots of land marked out by ditches would have been fields.

The site of Heveskesklooster,[27] half of which has been excavated (fig. 25.6, plate 38A), was first occupied in the second half of the 1st century BC. The occupants lived on a house *terp* surrounded by a ditch at the foot of the mound. Instead of a granary there was a square patch of clay beside the farm, which is thought to

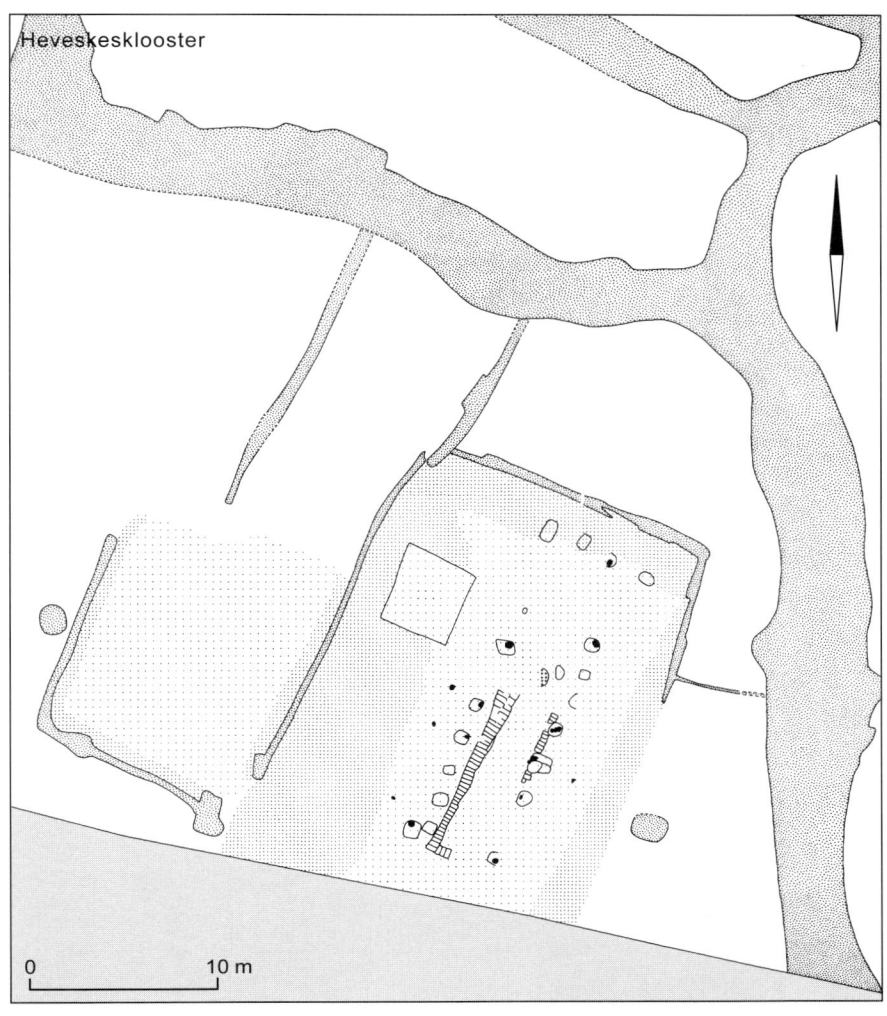

Heveskesklooster

0   10 m

fig. 25.6
The nuclear *wierde* of Heveskesklooster lies
at a knee bend in a gulley; period 1a, the first
decades AD. The eastern *wierde* was a house
terp, the western one was used for cultivation
or for stalling cattle. Scale 1:400.

have been the base of a haystack or a cereal rick. At the foot of the platform was
a well. There was probably a field or a stock enclosure on the adjacent *terp*, which
was also surrounded by a ditch.

The low ground level would have precluded an unraised settlement at Heveskesklooster. The available evidence suggests that the mound expanded in the traditional manner, *i.e.* both in circumference and in height.

HOUSES AND OTHER STRUCTURES

The houses common on the salt marsh are of the Hijken and the Fochteloo three-
aisled longhouse types (figs. 25.7 and 25.8), both in an adapted version (*cf.* chapter 24). They accommodated animals and human beings under the same roof; only
rarely was there a partition between the living area and the byre. The byre was situated lowest to ensure good drainage of the manure. No evidence of the Early Iron
Age 'Hijken transitional type' has been found in the clay regions.

The posts of the two rows inside the building were set closer together in the
byre than in the living area. There were transverse connections at the beginning
and end of the rows and sometimes, dependent on the length of the house, at a
few intermediate points too.[28] The hipped roof was supported by a row of posts
just outside the wall, which served mainly to relieve the wall. The wall itself had
a separating instead of a supporting function. It consisted of stakes held togeth-

fig. 25.7
Ezinge viewed from the southwest with in the foreground the three-aisled longhouse (No. 1) from period 1c (5th century BC). The living quarters containing the hearth were at the front of the house; behind them lay the byre. The enclosure marked by stakes is visible on the right. On the left are house remains from period 2c. The bank of the churchyard is visible in the background.

er by twigs. Such wattlework walls were often coated with manure or clay. A few houses had another row of posts, set further apart, beyond the wall. These posts supported the edge of the roof with the aid of a plate. In this way the wall was protected by eaves.

The stakes of the wattlework outer wall were set in a trench in one case at Boomborg-Hatzum. At a distance of some 0.3-0.4 m beyond this wall were the wall posts, which were spaced 0.70-1.05 m apart. At house no. 2 at Ezinge each stake was secured in a separate hole by means of a pin, which indicates that that part of the wattlework wall was made at the spot. The wall posts were set some 0.3 m in front of this wall, the distance between the posts being 1-1.8 m. A recent reinterpretation showed that the wall was freestanding and was not supported by a bank of sods on the outside, as previously assumed. The two oldest occupation horizons of Boomborg-Hatzum also contained the remains of walls consisting of planks or wattlework clamped between thick stakes.

Most of the longhouses of Boomborg-Hatzum were between 10-13 m and 15-17 m long and between 5.3 and 5.8 m wide. The largest were 20-21 m long and 6.3-

6.5 m wide. The central aisle had an average width of 2.5-3 m, the width of the side aisles being about 1.3-1.5 m. The houses at Ezinge had similar widths.

The byre was usually longer than the living area. At Boomborg-Hatzum there was a dung gutter on either side of the passage along the central axis to catch the manure. At Ezinge, on the other hand, there was a wicker mat. In front of the wicker mat was sometimes a wooden ledge, a wide thick plank, inside the stall for the cows' hind legs. The cattle were stalled two by two in stalls, which were separated by wattlework partitions. Sometimes there was a post near the outer wall, to which the stalled pairs of cows could be tied by the neck.[29] At Boomborg-Hatzum the number of (double) stalls varied from four to fourteen; at Ezinge some farms had more than twenty.

In the living area the hearth was always beneath the ridge, at varying distances from the transverse outer wall. Some of these hearths were paved with sherds and coated with clay, others were thick earthenware basins.

The large farms all had two entrances, one in one of the long sides, at the transition from the living area to the byre, the other in the middle of the short back side of the byre. Surviving thresholds indicate that the entrances were 0.8-1 m wide.

The houses of the Hijken type encountered on the sandy soils do not differ fundamentally from those on the clay, except for one aspect: the position of the entrances in the walls. Unlike the houses at the coast, they had two opposite entrances at the transition from house to byre and virtually never an entrance to the byre. Only one such a farm with opposite side entrances, and a separate working space in between, was found at Boomborg-Hatzum, dating from period 4. However, the cattle entered the byre of this farm in the same way as elsewhere on the salt marshes, via an entrance in the middle of the short byre wall.

An entirely different type of house, known only from Jemgum 1 and probably also from the earliest periods of Boomborg-Hatzum, is the small *Bohlenpfostenhaus*. At Jemgum this was a dwelling with four inside posts arranged in a rectangle measuring 7.25 x 4.75 m. The central aisle was 2.25 m wide, the side aisles 1.25 m each. As the German term implies, the house did not have wattlework walls but walls consisting of planks placed with their narrow sides horizontally, which were clamped between double wall posts. The planks, which would have been joined together at the corners, were set in grooves with triangular cross-sections in the door posts. There was a shelter over the door. The interior layout comprised an area with a hearth and an area that is assumed to have been a sleeping or working

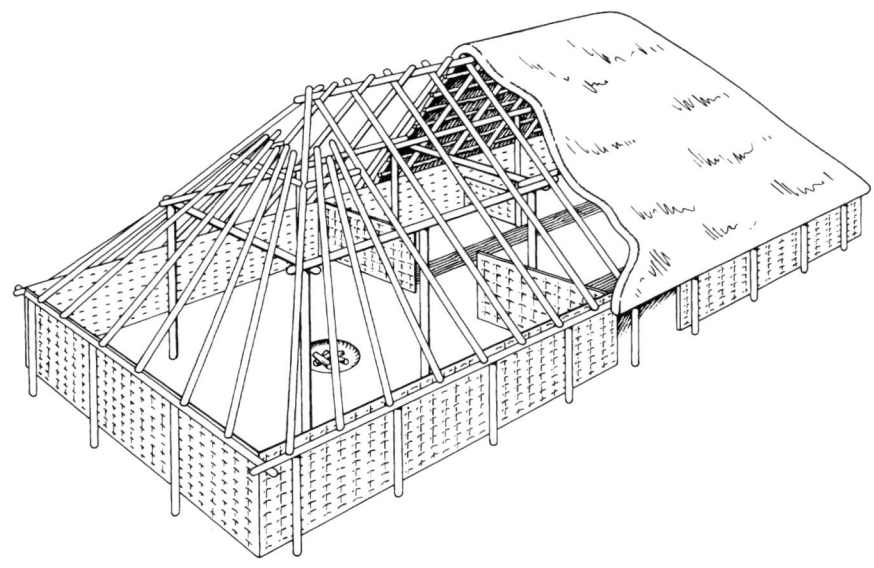

fig. 25.8
Reconstruction of the oldest fully excavated longhouse of Ezinge (No. 1), dating from period 1c (5th century BC). The wall is 1.60 m high.

573

space. The latter area had a wooden floor.

Besides longhouses there were also smaller rectangular buildings with lengths of 6-8.5 m and widths of 5-6.5 m at Boomborg-Hatzum. All of these buildings had two pairs of inside posts and an entrance in one of the short sides. As they lacked a byre and contained a hearth they are regarded as dwellings or living/working areas. Buildings without hearths are assumed to have been barns. This house type has not (yet) been found in the Netherlands.

The granaries of both Ems settlements were of the type with four, six or nine posts. There were three storage structures with twelve posts at Boomborg-Hatzum. The sturdy design of these structures suggests that some had several floors. Strangely enough, there were no such storage facilities at Ezinge. In phase 1c there was a raised storage structure instead.

SUBSISTENCE AND TRADE CONTACTS

The occupants of the *terpen* were farmers whose economy was based on crop cultivation and cattle keeping. Evidence for cattle keeping are the farms, whose byres were in some cases large enough for over forty heads of cattle, the numerous bones, the bone objects and the layers of manure in the *terpen*. Cattle, which were smaller than the present breed, were the main domestic animals. Next came sheep. Cattle were kept mainly for their meat and milk, but also for their traction, hides and manure (which was used as fuel). The sheep would have been kept mainly for their wool. The cattle were pastured on the elevated salt marshes.

Fresh water, essential for both human beings and animals, was obtained from wells. In addition, reservoirs were built to collect rain water. Further inland, the water of the gulleys, supplied by streams from the hinterland, was also drinkable.

Crop cultivation is less spectacularly evident in the archaeological record but in view of the composition of the diet it must likewise have played a prominent part. The main crops were barley, flax (for fibres and also for linseed), oil-containing gold of pleasure and Celtic bean. The conditions in the coastal region were less favourable for the cultivation of emmer, but this crop may nevertheless have been grown there.

Objects like querns, hammer stones, winnows, loom weights, spindle whorls, cheese moulds, *etc.* recovered from the *terpen* represent the processing of the products. Of many of these objects the exact dates are unknown. No irrefutable evidence for the production of salt, for example from peat impregnated with saltwater, has been found in this area. Hunting and fishing were also practised, but it is difficult to determine their relative importance in the economy.

The occupants of the *terpen* would have exchanged goods with the inhabitants of the nearby sands, in particular structural timber and wood for the manufacture of implements, of which there must have been a shortage at the coast. The flint sickles, bronze *fibulae* and jewels like glass beads indicate contacts over greater distances. Products that may have been given in exchange for these goods were cattle, meat, hides and amber, which could be collected along the shore and the gulleys.

Only with the aid of models can we obtain an impression of the population density of the coastal area. Such models, based on evidence from settlements that can be dated and arranged in chronological order on the basis of pottery, show a continuous growth in population and contraction in settlement, at least in the central part of Westergo and Middag, from the colonisation phase (c. 600-350 BC) until in the Roman period.[30] An alternative view is that the process of colonisation is to be regarded in terms of planned expansion from primary to secondary *terpen*, resulting in the formation of territories of some 7-10 km².[31] The size of the settlement determined the size of the territory: in the Late Iron Age it was 3 km² for a large village *terp* with eight medium-sized farms plus two craftsman's houses, and 1 km² for a medium-sized village *terp* with three medium-sized farms. A house *terp* must hence have had a catchment area of some 35 ha, of which some 5 ha was under cultivation. A farm household is assumed to have consisted of seven to eight individuals, who would have required food equivalent to six adults. It would seem that there were only one to three farms on most *terpen* in the Late Iron Age. Large village *terpen* like Ezinge were exceptions. The same holds for Feddersen Wierde, whose population in the 3rd century AD is estimated to have amounted to 300.[32] In certain areas the population density can also be inferred from the number of *terpen*, at least on the basis of models.[33] In the Early Iron Age the area to the west of the Hunze, which then measured some 90 km², is assumed to have been inhabited by at least 250 and at most 400 individuals, distributed among twelve *terpen* and unraised settlements with three or four farms each. In the Late Iron Age, when the area in question is assumed to have measured 130 km², the population figure was substantially greater. Calculations for that period are based on ten house *terpen*, thirty small village *terpen* with three medium-sized farms each, and fifteen large village *terpen* with eight medium-sized farms and two smaller farms each. The population figure was greatest in the Roman period.

In the Iron Age there were already more *terpen* in Friesland than in Groningen. It is estimated that there were 300 *terpen* in a part of Westergo measuring 200 km² in the Roman period. Such estimates must however be treated with due caution.

SOCIAL STRUCTURE

Because of the lack of cemeteries and completely excavated settlements we know nothing about the social structure of the population of the clay regions in the Iron Age. The radial layout on the *terp* of Ezinge in the Late Iron Age and the indications suggesting expansion from primary to secondary *terpen* indicate that there must have been some organising powers within the community, but where these powers lay remains unclear. The only evidence providing some insight into this matter is the *Herrenhof* or *Häuptlingshof* enclosed by a wattlework palisade that stood at Feddersen Wierde in the 3rd century AD. Inside this palisade were a separately enclosed house with its own access road, several farms with small craftsman's houses, an area with a large number of granaries and a metal-working site. The *Hof* also included a *Gemeinschaftshalle* with a stock enclosure with a watering place at the centre. The prominent person who resided in the *Hof* would have been a *primus inter pares*, the *pares* in this case being the owners of the large farms. He apparently controlled local artisanal production and also trade, as suggested by the imported goods found. This means that he had considerable economic power.

The rest of the population would have consisted of independent farmers and their client tenants and craftsmen.

No Iron Age or Roman-period settlement has been excavated in the coastal region of the northern Netherlands that is comparable with Feddersen Wierde in size and internal differentiation. Maybe the research at Ezinge would have yielded something similar under more favourable excavation conditions.[34]

NOTES

1 Zagwijn 1986.
2 Först 1991.
3 Löbert 1982.
4 Harck 1972, 36.
5 Boersma 1983, 1988a.
6 Schwarz 1990.
7 Haarnagel 1969.
8 Behre 1970.
9 Waterbolk 1959b, 1965-'66.
10 Fokkens 1991a, 162.
11 Waterbolk 1988, 12-15.
12 Van Heeringen 1992, note 119 and proposition 8.
13 Boersma 1991; Taayke 1991.
14 Taayke 1991.
15 2495 ± 35 and 2480 ± 35 BP for the eastern site; 2555 ± 35, 2510 ± 35 and 2415 ± 35 BP for the western site.
16 The ^{14}C dates are 2420 ± 35, 2400 ± 35 and 2360 ± 35 BP.
17 The ^{14}C dates are 2175 ± 35, 2205 ± 35 and 2205 ± 50 BP.
18 Van Gijn/Waterbolk 1984; Waterbolk 1988.
19 In Van Gijn/Waterbolk 1984, 115 and fig. 11, and in Waterbolk 1988, fig. 8, the entrance in the long side was erroneously left out and the structure was not interpreted as a longhouse.

20 Van Gelder-Ottway 1988.
21 Van Zeist 1989.
22 Schmid 1984.
23 De Langen/Waterbolk 1982-'88.
24 Haarnagel 1979.
25 Van Es 1968.
26 Streurman/Taayke 1989.
27 Boersma 1988b.
28 Huijts 1992.
29 Van Giffen 1973.
30 Miedema 1983; Taayke 1991.
31 Miedema 1983.
32 Haarnagel 1979.
33 Miedema 1983; Taayke 1991.
34 Since this contribution was written, in 1994, some essential works have been published on the earliest occupation of the northern coastal area. Besides a survey of the pottery, the dissertation by Taayke (1996) also contains a short synthesis of the history of occupation. The development of Ezinge is discussed in greater detail in Boersma 1999. Strahl has published a work (2001) on the earliest occupation of the adjacent coastal area of north Germany (Late Bronze Age).

O   Oak or alder?
The use of wood in Iron Age farms

Caroline Vermeeren and Otto Brinkkemper

In the past, wood was an even more important raw material than it is today. Until the Roman period houses were built exclusively of wood, numerous tools were made of wood and wood was also often used as fuel. Wood that became buried in carbonised condition, for example after it had been used in a hearth or after a building had burned down, has in most cases been preserved. Uncarbonised wood, on the other hand, only survives in damp, anaerobic conditions. Such conditions are to be found in the western Netherlands in particular, in layers of peat and clay deposits below the water table. Here remains of wood have been found which, even after thousands of years, still show clear tool marks.

Tool marks

The tool marks on prehistoric wood that have so far been investigated were left by different types of axes, adzes and gouging tools (figs. O1 and O2).[1] Sometimes chips are found intact on some of the best preserved facets. If they are carefully removed the shape of the edge of the axe can be determined (fig. O2). At sites where such marks are preserved on a large number of posts it is possible to obtain a picture of the different types of tools that were used. Tool marks observable on the Early Iron Age remains of house Q in the Assendelver polders[2] were found to have been produced by two or three different gouges and between eight and eleven axes and/or adzes. Some of these tools were used only during the demolition of the house.

Wood selection

At sites where remains of wood are found in structural contexts ever more research is being done to determine whether prehistoric builders used different types of wood for different structural elements. What types of wood were used for construction purposes will have depended on at least two factors: quality and availability. Considerations of a more ideological nature may have played a part too.

Today, the quality of wood is expressed in durability, flexibility and cleavability in particular. We must bear in mind that wood that is to be used for wattlework may have to meet completely different quality requirements than wood that is to be used for, say, load-bearing posts. Moreover, Iron Age

fig. O1 (left)
Point of a heavy wooden post from the eponymous site of the Late Neolithic Vlaardingen group. The post is worked all around with a (convex) flint axe with a curved cutting edge. The length of the stump is 47 cm.

fig. O2 (right)
Wooden post of an Iron Age farm, also near Vlaardingen. The post has been worked with a flat (metal) axe with a seriously damaged cutting edge. The marks left by the straight edge have been made visible by the removal of some chips (arrows). Scale 1:2.

requirements with respect to wood may have differed considerably from modern requirements. In the quality table to which reference is made below (table O1) the various wood types have been arranged according to their durability.

Did prehistoric builders consider the quality of the wood they used? This question can only be answered if we know what types of wood were available for use. For reasons of quality it may be preferable to build a house of oak, but if the

species	durability
oak	10-25 year
maple, elm	5-10 year
alder, ash, willow	<5 year

table O1

The durability of some important wood species in a moist subsoil.

only type of wood available for miles around the site is alder, then the house may be built from alder instead. In that case it is more effective to build a house from alder wood that may last for, say, five to ten years than to go to a good deal more trouble and build a house from oak that would be suitable for occupation for ten to twenty-five years.

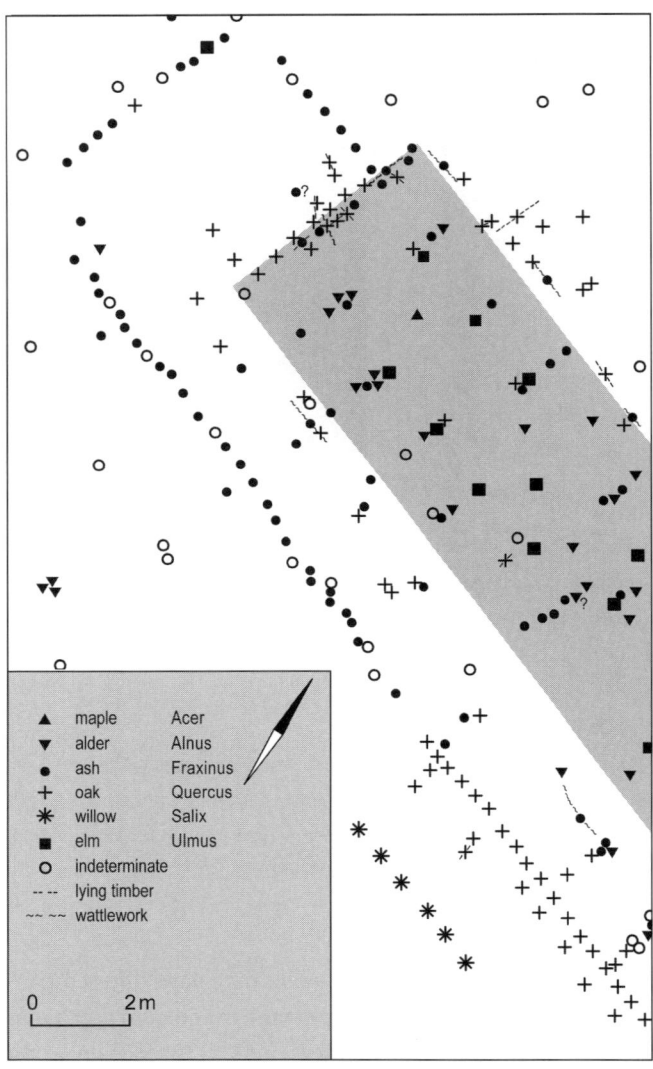

▲	maple	Acer
▼	alder	Alnus
●	ash	Fraxinus
+	oak	Quercus
✳	willow	Salix
■	elm	Ulmus
○	indeterminate	
---	lying timber	
~~ ~~	wattlework	

0   2m

fig. O3

Part of an Iron Age farm (grey) at Spijkenisse, site 17-35.
Determination of the employed wood showed that the occupants selected durable species for their dwelling.

In order to get an idea of the types of wood that were available to prehistoric builders we must study the environment around a settlement. By studying the geology of the surroundings of a site we can to some extent determine what kind of vegetation and what trees grew there. Pollen samples from the period of occupation constitute a second source of information. They enable us to arrange the various wood types according to their availability. However, some corrections have to be made in interpreting pollen diagrams because trees do not all produce the same amounts of pollen.[3]

The quality and availability tables thus obtained can be compared with the recovered wood remains. It is useful to correct lists of analysed wood remains to obtain an impression of the minimum number of trees used.[4] In view of the fact that identified remains only rarely represent entire trunks (load-bearing posts), a correction factor is used for branches, cleft wood and short structural elements.

The corrected data do not tell us the total number of trees that were required to build a house, because very few remains of elements above the ground, such as rafters and boards, are recovered in excavations. The report of the reconstruction of an aisled Iron Age farm[5] shows that more than forty trees with a usable length of eight metres were required to build the structure. Of these posts about half (just over twenty) stood partly in the ground. It is on such elements that most of our information on prehistoric structural timber is based.

Spijkenisse site 17-35: selection of durable wood

An Early Iron Age farm whose remains were found at Spijkenisse, on the island of Voorne-Putten, is a good example of a structure that was deliberately built from durable wood. After correction of the data, the partly enclosed aisled farm with byres[6] (fig. O3) was found to have been built largely from elm wood (see table O2). This was rather surprising because although elm wood ranks high in the quality table (table O1), on account of its durability it ranks very low in the availability table drawn up for this site (table O3). This elm wood had been used almost exclusively for the posts of the house, which, we may assume, had to bear the greatest loads. The walls were built mainly from ash and oak. Alder and maple wood was used for some other parts of the house. The wattlework was found to have comprised exclusively ash branches: presumably what was left after the wood for the posts had been stripped. Willow branches, which were used for the wattlework of many other Iron Age houses whose remains have been found on Voorne-Putten, had not been used in this house at Spijkenisse 17-35.

The palisade that enclosed part of the house was built from ash and oak. Strangely enough, the oak came from very

	percentage of identifications	percentage of trees
elm	9%	37%
ash	32%	26%
alder	19%	19%
oak	36%	11%
other	4%	7%
total	100%	100%
N =	121	27

table O2

Wood identifications and corrected numbers of the Early Iron Age farm at Spijkenisse, site 17-35 (palisade excluded). See the text for the calculation of the number of trees used.

large trees. Why these large oaks were not used for the posts of the farm we do not know.

The types of wood that were used for the farm would be classified as reasonably durable today. Durability was clearly a more important consideration than availability in the case of the main load-bearing elements and some of the wall posts and palisade elements, because pollen research has shown that the oak and elm wood that was used for these elements was obtained from the levees along the Meuse, several kilometres away from the settlement. Alder and willow will have been the dominant tree types in the reedy fen peat that surrounded the settlement.[7] The occupants of the site hence went out of their way to obtain the elm and oak wood. The gully that ran near the site will have made it possible for them to transport the wood from its distant source to their settlement.

Analysis of charcoal samples from the same site has shown that, as firewood, the occupants used wood that was available in the immediate surroundings: samples of alder clearly predominated.

A similar preference for durable types of wood is apparent from the load-bearing elements of house Q in the Assendelver polders: the supporting posts were all made of oak and ash, whereas oak ranks lower than willow and alder in the availability table for this findspot.[8]

Use of available wood

An Early Iron Age farm whose remains were found at Rotterdam-Hartelkanaal, as well as on the island of Voorne-Putten, shows us quite the opposite of what we have seen in the case

of the farm at Spijkenisse. The Rotterdam-Hartelkanaal farm was built from almost exclusively poorly durable alder wood; it contained one willow post. Very few occupation remains were found at this site;[9] apparently it was occupied for a short time only. An intriguing question is whether the occupants had foreseen that they would not be staying at this site for very long and were therefore satisfied with a less durable, but locally available, type of wood.

At another site, Spijkenisse 17-34 (Middle Iron Age), the occupants also used wood of poor durability, in particular alder, ash and willow. The thickest trunks were reserved for the supporting posts, though.

Ideological factors

From ethnohistorical sources we know that in the Middle Ages many non-economic factors played a part in the selection of building materials.[10] Similar factors may have been considered in prehistoric times, too. An example is the use of buckthorn wood in house Q in the Assendelver polders. This species, whose wood presents no particular advantages for construction purposes, prefers sandy soils and will not have been abundant in the peaty surroundings of the settlement. In the Middle Ages it was believed that buckthorn had the power to ward off demons, vermin and sickness. In the house at findspot Q buckthorn wood was used in four places, three of which are the corners of what is assumed to have been the sleeping area.

Also interesting is the use of willow wood in this house:

	number of identifications	correction-factor	corrected number	proportion aftea correction
alder	117	0,25	29,25	22,3%
oak	115	0,25	28,75	21,9%
hazel	92	0,25	23	17,6%
ash	18	1	18	13,7%
beech	12	1	12	9,2%
pine	25	0,25	6,25	4,8%
lime	3	2	6	4,6%
birch	19	0,25	4,75	3,6%
elm	4	0,5	2	1,5%
maple	1	1	1	0,8%
total	406		131	100,0%

table O3

The availability of various wood species on the present island of Voorne-Putten during the Iron Age, as based on a pollen diagram.

large amounts of willow wood were found in the former living area, but no willow whatsoever was recovered from the area of the byres. It has been suggested that nibbling willow was believed to adversely affect a cow's fertility. The fact that willow has been encountered in the byres of a number of other Iron Age houses whose remains have been found on Voorne-Putten, however, makes the above suggestion less likely, unless beliefs differed from one region to another.

Conclusion

Only when we have a clearer picture of the use of wood in the Iron Age will we be able to compare it with what is known for the Roman period. Right now it would seem that the types of wood that were selected for specific purposes changed, and that oak started to be transported across increasingly larger distances for use for military purposes in particular. There are indications that the oak that was required for a road that was constructed around AD 124 at the Roman *castellum* near Valkenburg came all the way from Germany.[11]

Notes

1 In the Late Bronze Age already (small) saws were being used in Northwest Europe (*e.g.* Borman 1980, fig. 128, Han-sur-Lesse, Belgium). It is not certain whether they were used for working wood though.
2 Therkorn *et al.* 1984, 363-367.
3 See Groenman-van Waateringe 1988.
4 Brinkkemper/Vermeeren 1992.
5 Harsema 1980c.
6 Van Trierum 1992, 49 ff.; Brinkkemper/Vermeeren 1992.
7 Brinkkemper 1993, 17 ff.
8 Groenman-van Waateringe 1988, 142; Therkorn *et al.* 1984. See also Van Rijn 2001 for a striking example of the use of durable wood.
9 Van Trierum 1992, 36 ff.
10 Garthoff-Zwaan 1987; Therkorn *et al.* 1984, 362.
11 Bult *et al.* 1989.

26 On unsteady ground
Settlements in the western Netherlands

Robert van Heeringen

LANDSCAPE AND HISTORY OF DISCOVERY

The coastal plain of the western Netherlands in the first millennium BC can be regarded as the delta of four rivers that flowed into the North Sea. From the south to the north they were the Scheldt, the Meuse, the Rhine and the so-called Oer-IJ (fig. 26.1). This coastal plain comprised four landscape features. A peat zone with a width of 30 km bordered the Pleistocene sands of the eastern Netherlands. Between this peat and the North Sea in the west was a narrow strip of elevated sands: the coastal barriers covered with Older Dunes. To the north, the coastal barriers and Older Dunes were bordered by outcrops of Pleistocene sand (the island of Texel and the former island of Wieringen). And the estuaries, finally, contained tidal flats and salt marshes near the coast and fluviatile deposits further upstream. These different landscape features were all occupied for varying lengths of time in the Iron Age. Occupation remains from the Late Bronze Age are virtually exclusively limited to the Older Dunes and the Pleistocene sand. The occupation of the salt marshes of Westfrisia came to an end around the beginning of the Iron Age.[1]

After the soil surveys that were carried out in the Westland region around 1950, and several small-scale rescue excavations had revealed the archaeological potential of the coastal region,[2] projects were launched to investigate the Older Dunes and the Pleistocene sands of Texel in the 1960s and 1970s.[3] The peat regions began to arouse professional archaeological interest in the 1970s and 1980s in particular.[4]

In less than fifty years the number of sites in the western Netherlands dating from the period dealt with in this chapter increased from 17 in 1945 to almost 400 in 1992.[5] This large number of sites has provided some insight into the distribution of the settlements over the different landscape features and the changes that took place in the distribution pattern (fig. 26.2). Thanks to the often excellent preservation conditions we are also well-informed about such factors as the types of crops cultivated, the stocks that were kept and the types of structural timber used.

A DYNAMIC SETTLEMENT PATTERN

The dynamic conditions of the coastal environment caused by the varying influence of the sea hampered or even precluded settlement in some periods but encouraged it in others. A major decisive factor in the selection of occupation sites was the groundwater level. But of course other factors, besides a particular site's suitability for occupation, played a part in determining the distribution pattern that has now emerged, such as economic considerations and – something that is even more difficult for us to ascertain – prehistoric perception of the appeal of a particular environment, such as that of peat regions.[6] What must also be borne in mind is that the distribution pattern has been greatly distorted by the effects of later erosion and sedimentation.

fig. 26.1

The western Netherlands in the Late Bronze Age and the Iron Age. Separately indicated are Pleistocene deposits (dark grey) and Older Dunes and sandy beaches (light grey). The black lines indicate the known limits of these sandy areas. The intermediate white area consisted of marine deposits, fluviatile deposits and peat. The areas that were occupied in the period covered in this chapter are indicated with numbers and letters.

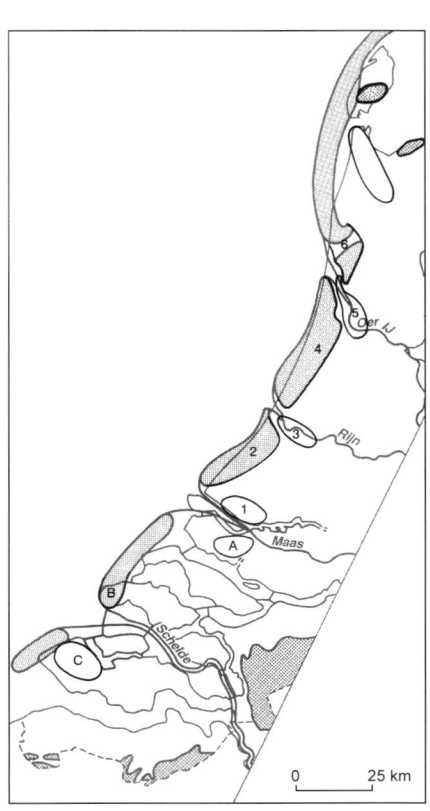

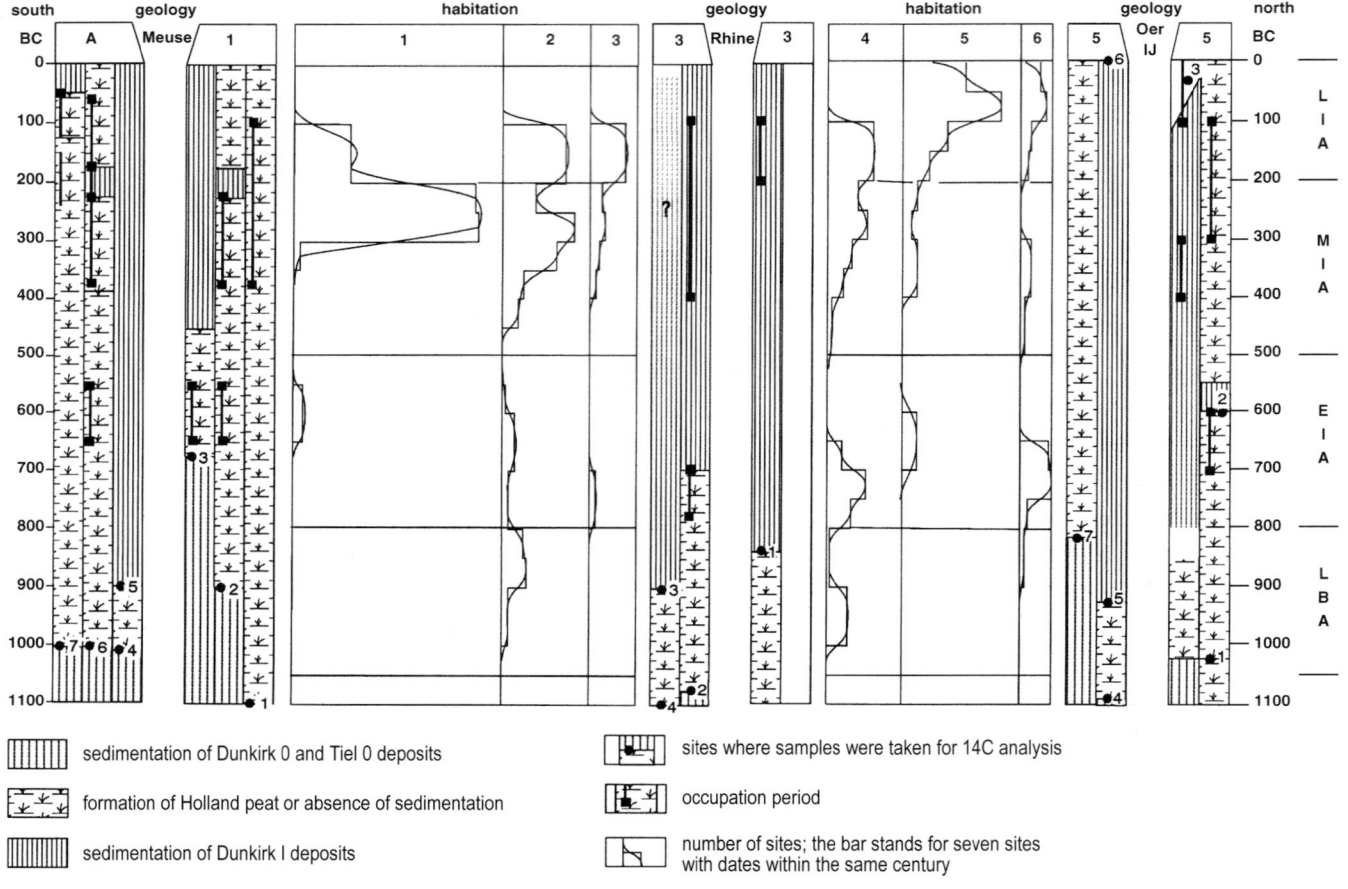

fig. 26.2

Geological developments in the estuaries and site densities in the numbered areas of figure 26.1. Each of the two or three columns on either side of the estuaries is based on a locally identified stratification. The numbers of sites from different periods in the various regions show pronounced fluctuations. Noteworthy is the high density of sites from around the 3rd century BC in the peat area to the north of the Meuse estuary (area 1) and the almost complete absence of sites from around 500 BC in all the areas. Sites from the 1st century BC are also absent in the areas to the south of the former river Oer-IJ (1-4).

The zone containing the coastal barriers and the Older Dunes can be said to have been continuously occupied until the first century BC, although the intensity of occupation varied considerably, with a conspicuous low point around 500 BC (fig. 26.2). Because of later erosion we are poorly informed about the occupation of the levees in the tidal delta systems. From a series of finds recovered from the levees of the Oude Rijn near Leiden we know that they must have been densely populated in the Middle and Late Iron Age.

A prerequisite for occupation in the peat regions was good drainage. In the 8th and 7th centuries BC the area of the Oer-IJ and the Meuse estuary, respectively, were well drained for a short period of time at the beginning of the Dunkirk Ia transgression. Detailed surveys have shown that the houses stood on small peat cushions (fig. 26.3). The same pattern of occupation has emerged for the second period of settlement in the peat regions, between c. 400 and 100 BC, before and during the Dunkirk Ib transgression. In that period the peat regions were far more densely populated than in the first occupation period. Besides the areas on either side of the deltas of the Meuse and the Oer-IJ, the peat bordering the Scheldt,[7]

582

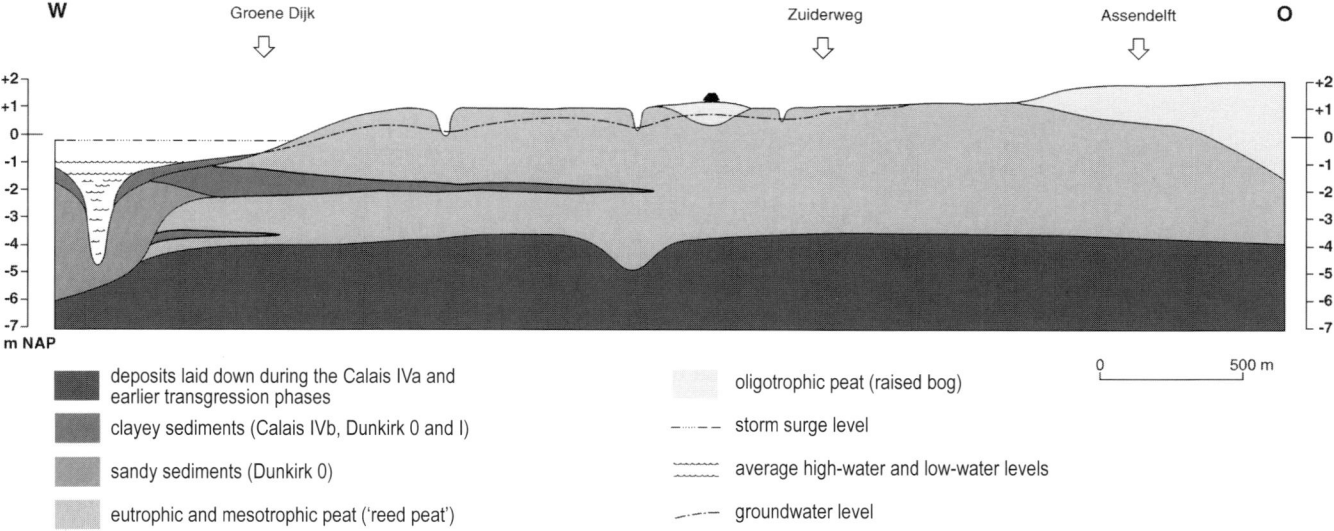

deposits laid down during the Calais IVa and earlier transgression phases

clayey sediments (Calais IVb, Dunkirk 0 and I)

sandy sediments (Dunkirk 0)

eutrophic and mesotrophic peat ('reed peat')

oligotrophic peat (raised bog)

storm surge level

average high-water and low-water levels

groundwater level

whose course then still coincided with that of the present Oosterschelde, was also occupied. We still do not know exactly what drew the colonists to the peat regions (see also feature P). It is remarkable that they made only little use of natural resources such as fish, waterfowl and larger game. The colonists must have wanted to continue their mixed farming practices and – after some modifications – they apparently succeeded in doing so.[8]

The creeks and tidal channels in the peat regions constituted ideal traffic routes in a period in which most transport will have taken place via waterways. With their mineral soils and dryer conditions, the levees bordering many of these waterways could be used for the cultivation of crops that could not be grown in peat soils. They also yielded different types of timber from those available in the peat regions. Several levees seem to have been occupied too.[9]

Around the transition from the Middle to the Late Iron Age, c. 250-200 BC, major floods made life difficult for the occupants of the peat surrounding the Meuse delta, but they had apparently come to appreciate the specific conditions of this environment too much to allow themselves to be driven away. The altered ecological conditions did lead to a contraction in settlement in the area to the east of the flooded land, near Schiedam. The number of sites in the Older Dunes also increased in the second century BC. The clay deposits that were then formed to the south of the Meuse were colonised, but those to the north of the river were not.

In the first century BC the coastal region was almost entirely abandoned. The occupation of the peat regions, the clay deposits and the dunes came to an end. Only the area to the north of the Oer-IJ showed a different picture. The settlements in the peat regions seem to have been abandoned around the beginning of the first century BC. In that same century, however, the Dunkirk I deposits newly formed in this area were occupied. It would seem that this area was considered so attractive that the occupants of the northern part of the dunes between the Rhine and the Oer-IJ decided to move here, too, because no sites from around the end of the Late Iron Age have been found in the latter area.

Around the beginning of our era, in the Roman period, the area to the south of the Rhine was recolonised. The hand-made pottery of the occupants of an area roughly between the Rhine and the Meuse, the *Cananefates*, betrays strong influences of that of the northern coastal region of Friesland. The peat region to the south of the Scheldt was not recolonised until some time around the middle of the first century AD, when an indigenous people moved there; they can be

fig. 26.3
Cross-section of the Assendelver polders around 600 BC. A small farm has been built on a small raised bog mound surrounded by fen peat.

identified as the tribe of the *Marsaci* or the *Menapii* known from written sources.

HOUSES AND SETTLEMENT LAYOUT

The remains

Chapter 18 described how the originally dense population of the area of buried stream ridges and clay zones of Westfrisia decreased. Before the occupants of this area were forced to abandon it for good, some time around the beginning of the Iron Age, *c.* 800 BC, they erected small *terpen*. Because of erosion in later times we do not know what the houses that were built on these *terpen* looked like.

The plans of the houses whose remains have been found in the coastal zone are almost all three-aisled. This holds for the plans found in the sandy and clayey parts as well as for those found in the peat regions. The remains of the settlements found in the different regions, however, differ considerably. Those in the peat regions consist of little more than the remains of the farms themselves, whereas in the sandy and clayey parts several hectares of the infrastructures surrounding the settlements have in some cases been preserved. The nature of the remains also differs. The preservation conditions of the peat regions are in many cases comparable with those of the *terpen*. At several sites the entire bottom parts of farms have been preserved, including the floor layers consisting of plant matter and manure, whereas often nothing more than postholes has survived in the sandy soil (plate 38B). Because of these marked differences, the two zones will be dealt with separately below.

The settlements with their average number of three farms that were to be found at Bovenkarspel-Het Valkje in the Late Bronze Age[10] were probably the largest settlements in the western Netherlands in the first millennium BC. The distribution of the sites in clusters across an area with a length of at most 500 m was largely determined by the presence of a stream ridge in the otherwise relatively flat salt marshes. Most of the other settlements that have so far been found in the western Netherlands consisted of one or at most two or three farms.

The sands and clay deposits

For an impression of the layout of the settlements in the Older Dunes from the Bronze Age until in the Middle Iron Age we must turn to the results of the investigation of the outcrops of Pleistocene sand on the island of Texel.[11] At a site near Den Burg occupation remains spanning the period from the Middle Bronze Age until the end of the Middle Iron Age have been investigated. The house plans show

fig. 26.4
Den Burg. Plan of an Early Iron Age longhouse. At the straight end of the house was a round hearth with a storage pit close by. Animals are thought to have been stalled in the part with the rounded end. Scale 1:200.

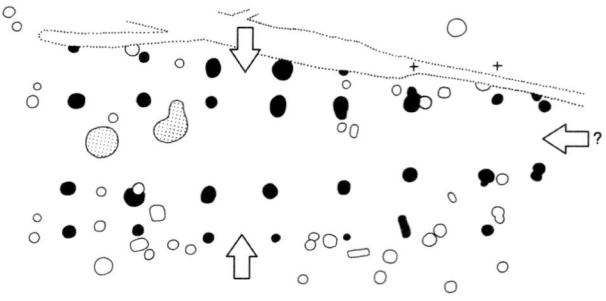

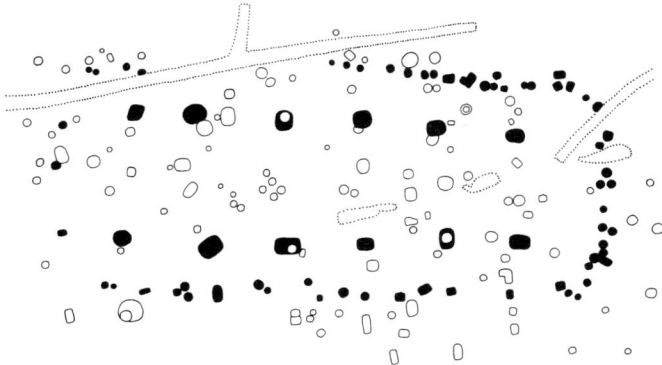

fig. 26.5
Den Burg. Plan of a longhouse dating from
the end of the Early Iron Age. The entrances
are poorly distinguishable. Scale 1:200..

the same reduction in length as observed in the houses of Westfrisia from the beginning of the Late Bronze Age onwards. The 5-m wide three-aisled plan J, from the Early Iron Age, is only 12 m long (fig. 26.4). The northwest end of the longhouse, which contained the living area, had a straight end. Besides a hearth, the living area also contained a storage pit with steep walls. The southeast part, which contained the byre, had a rounded end.

Plan O (fig. 26.5) represents a house type from the end of the Early Iron Age.[12] This house type was slightly larger, measuring 15 by 6 m. The greater distance between the paired roof supports suggests that the living area of this house was also in the northwest part of the building. The house had rounded ends and was probably covered by a hipped roof.

fig. 26.6
The longhouse of figure 26.4 surrounded
by granaries that are assumed to date from
the period when the house was occupied.
The eight granaries will not all have been
contemporary. Scale 1:400.

Outbuildings were quite common in the settlements of Den Burg from the Late Bronze Age onwards. The first outbuildings were granaries supported by four or six posts. In the Middle Iron Age there were also granaries supported by nine posts. The remains of eight granaries were found in the immediate vicinity of house J (fig. 26.6). At a different settlement, dating from the Early Iron Age, other forms of storage were also used besides granaries: pits with rectangular or round cross-sections and steep walls. One of these pits contained a large amount of carbonised threshed cereal mixed with fragments of a clay plate. The plate had probably served to cover the storage pit.

The limits of the small, rectangular fields were defined by shallow ditches, traces of which have only been found in a few low-lying areas. Although the dimensions of these fields are the same as those of the plots of Celtic fields, no remains of the low banks characteristic of the latter field system have been found. The relation between the observed *ard* marks and cart tracks indicates that the layout of the fields was determined less by the local microrelief than by the routes marked by the cart tracks. Whether other Iron Age features, *i.e.* ring ditches and rows of pits (with lengths of over 100 m), are also to be interpreted in an agricultural context is still not clear.

With the exception of the latter features, the above settlements closely resemble the contemporary settlements on the Pleistocene sands elsewhere in the Netherlands, in particular in the northern and eastern parts, in terms of the elements of their layout (dual-function longhouses, storage pits and granaries). As far as the period after the Early Iron Age is concerned, our information on the sandy parts of the coastal region is too scanty to allow such statements to be made.

The earliest plans found in the Older Dunes date from the Middle Iron Age. Plans of barn-like structures (fig. 26.7) were unearthed on the Spanjaardsberg near Santpoort. The plan of a structure of comparably small dimensions (6 x 3 m) came to light in The Hague.[13] The authors who mention this site suggest that it was occupied on a seasonal basis. Small-scale excavations in the dunes have also

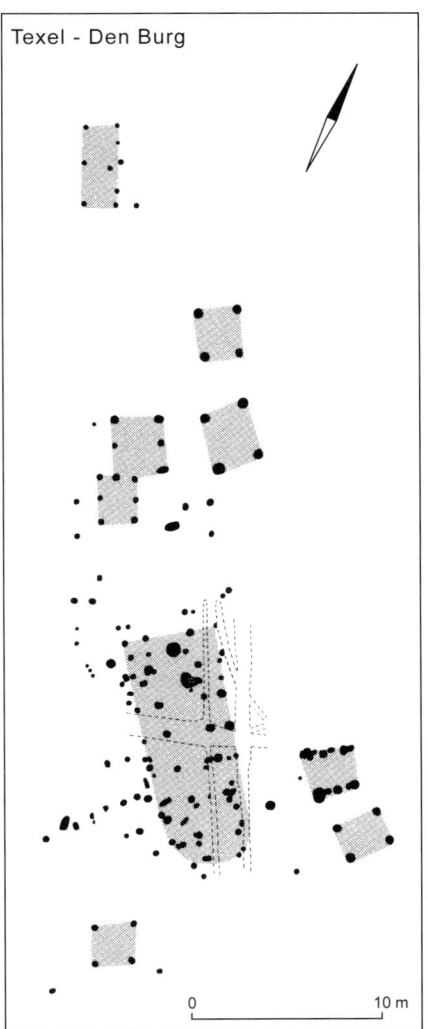

Texel - Den Burg

0   10 m

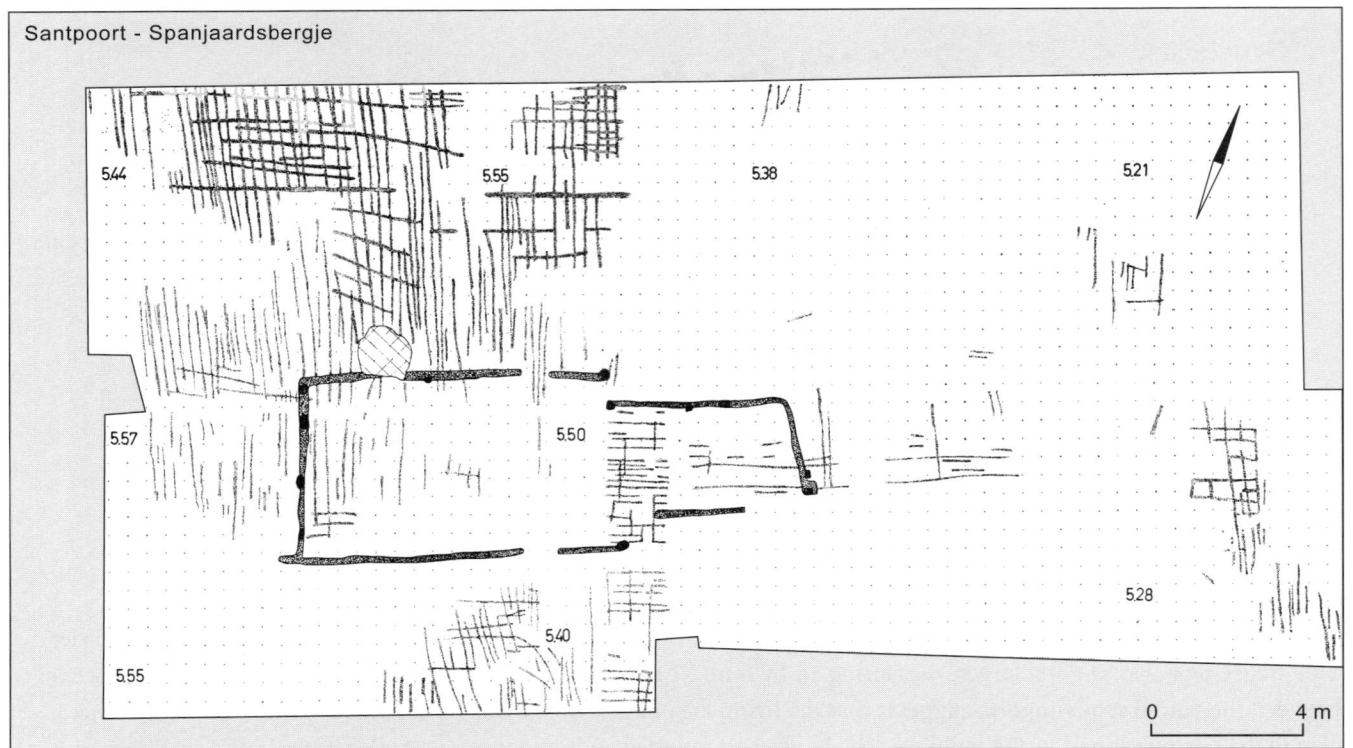

Santpoort - Spanjaardsbergje

5.44   5.55   5.38   5.21

5.57   5.50

5.40

5.55

5.28

0   4 m

fig. 26.7

Plan of a barn-like building unearthed in the Older Dunes at Santpoort. The structure was built in the Middle Iron Age on top of old *ard* marks, so on land that was formerly under cultivation. Scale 1:200.

revealed the features of ditches marking the limits of fields, wells (without wooden linings) and granaries dating from the Middle Iron Age.[14]

A few settlement sites have also been found on the clay deposits; they date mostly from the Middle and Late Iron Age. At Uitgeest, along the Oer-IJ, the features of irregular enclosures were found. They have been interpreted as cattle pens (fig. 26.9).[15] The salt marshes that had been formed in this area had already been used in a previous period, probably for summer grazing. The ditches marking the limits of fields and the *ard* marks observed near a farm indicate that this same land was under cultivation at the end of the Iron Age. From a rectangular enclosure surrounding a nine-post granary and other evidence we may infer that conditions in this occupation area had become wetter.

fig. 26.8

A Late Iron Age hurdle washed away from its original position was found in the Stevenshofjespolder near Leiden. The hurdle, which is about 150 cm high, may have served as a stall partition. See also plate 39B.

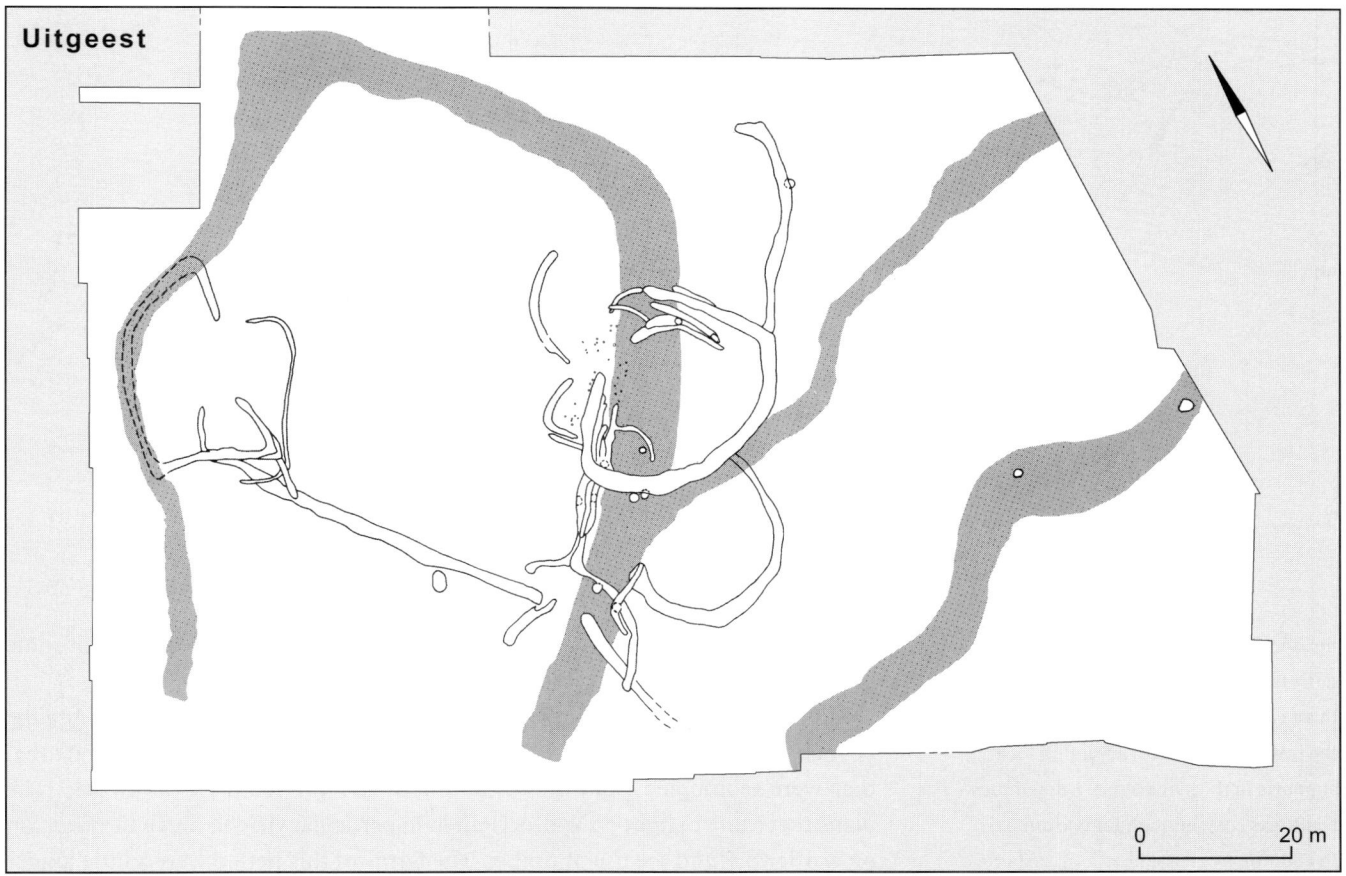

Uitgeest

0   20 m

The peat regions

The plans of Early Iron Age houses that have been found in the peat regions bordering the Oer-IJ and the Meuse do not differ much from those on Texel in size and layout. But thanks to the often exceptionally good preservation conditions we have more detailed information on the former plans. A good example is the plan of site 17-30 at Spijkenisse, to the south of the Meuse (fig. 26.10).[16] The longhouse, which measured 15 by 5 m, contained a byre in the east, a large hearth and, in the west, the living area. The house seems to have had only one entrance, at the end of the byre.

The byre was three-aisled (fig. 26.11). Together with less sturdy posts, the three pairs of roof supports constituted the partitions of six stalls. The part of the house intended for habitation was originally partly two-aisled. The nature of the preserved timber elements suggests that extra posts were added at a later stage to make the structure more substantial. Some of the new posts were founded on shoes (see feature P), which were in turn secured with the aid of thin posts that were driven into the peat.

The results of analyses of tool marks and the types of wood used can tell us something about the types of tool used and the availability of timber and its use in construction (feature O). On Voorne-Putten and in other peat regions, too, parts of wattlework walls, wooden thresholds and other structural elements have been preserved, which have yielded a wealth of information on structural details (plate 39).

So far, too few complete plans have been found to allow any conclusions to be drawn regarding cultural traditions. It is for example not certain whether the double wall of house Q (fig. 26.12) is a characteristic of a building tradition specific to

fig. 26.9
Irregularly shaped ditches dug in the clay area around Uitgeest in the Late Iron Age may mark cattle enclosures. In a later phase this area was used for cultivation and contained a farmyard. In the meantime gulleys (grey) had incised the plot and later silted up. Scale 1:1000.

587

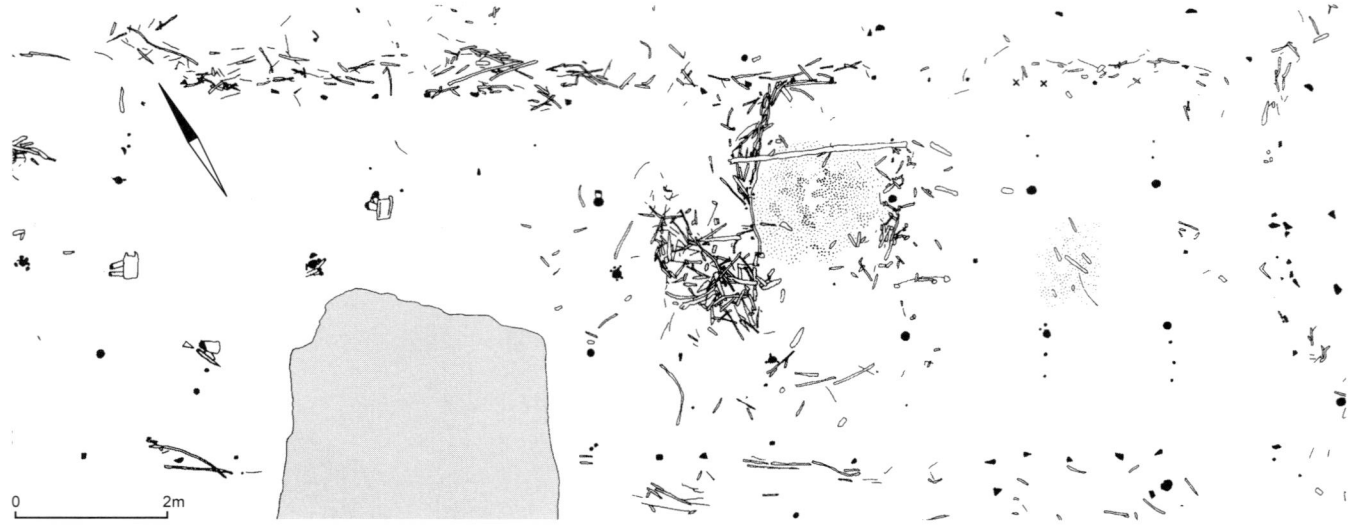

fig. 26.10

Early Iron Age farm at Spijkenisse. At least three cattle stalls can be inferred from the rows of thin stakes adjoining the roof supports in the byre (right). Each of these stalls was large enough for two animals. In addition to a large hearth (mixed grey) between the byre and the living parts there was another hearth (light grey dotted area) at the centre of the byre. Scale 1:100.

the area of the Assendelver polders. The space between the two walls was in some parts filled with peat.[17]

In the period around the transition from the Early to the Middle Iron Age the peat regions were uninhabited. House plans found in these regions indicate that they were reoccupied from the beginning of the 4th century BC onwards. The plans that came to light on Voorne-Putten in particular yielded much information on wattlework and the use of timber. The farms of this period were a little longer than their Early Iron Age predecessors. They had 7-8 pairs of roof supports, which together bore the weight of a roof with a length of about 20 m. In some of these essentially three-aisled dual-purpose longhouses extra posts were at a later stage inserted along the central axis, too. A new architectural feature is observable in one of the Late Iron Age plans of Rockanje-Oudeweg, which included two entrances set a good distance back from the wall, opposite one another between the byre and the living area (fig. 26.13). With its twelve stalls, the byre was quite spacious, but not exceptionally large for this period.

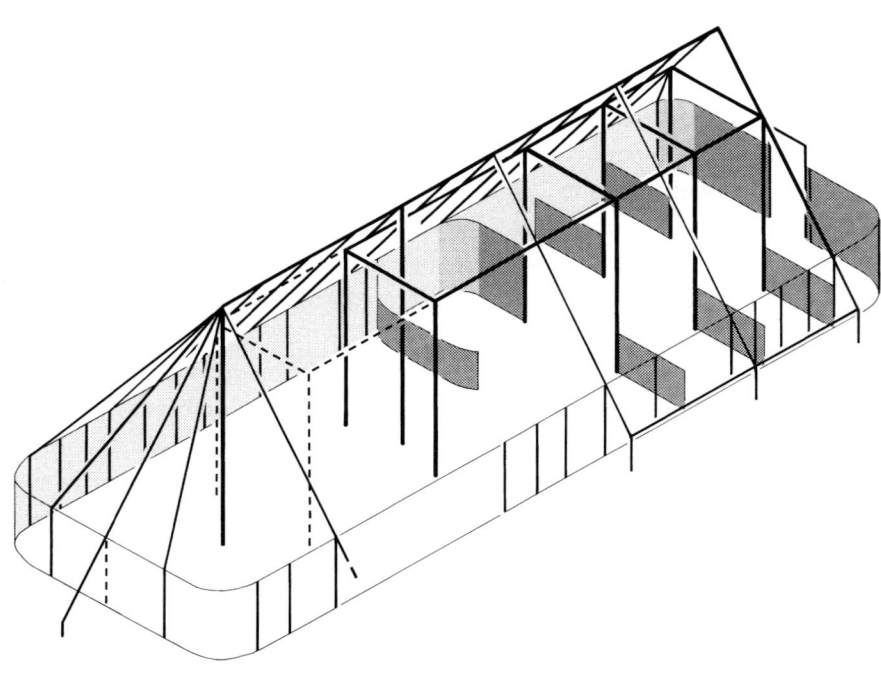

fig. 26.11

Reconstruction of the farm whose plan is shown in figure 26.10. The dashed line indicates the situation after renovations in the living parts.

588

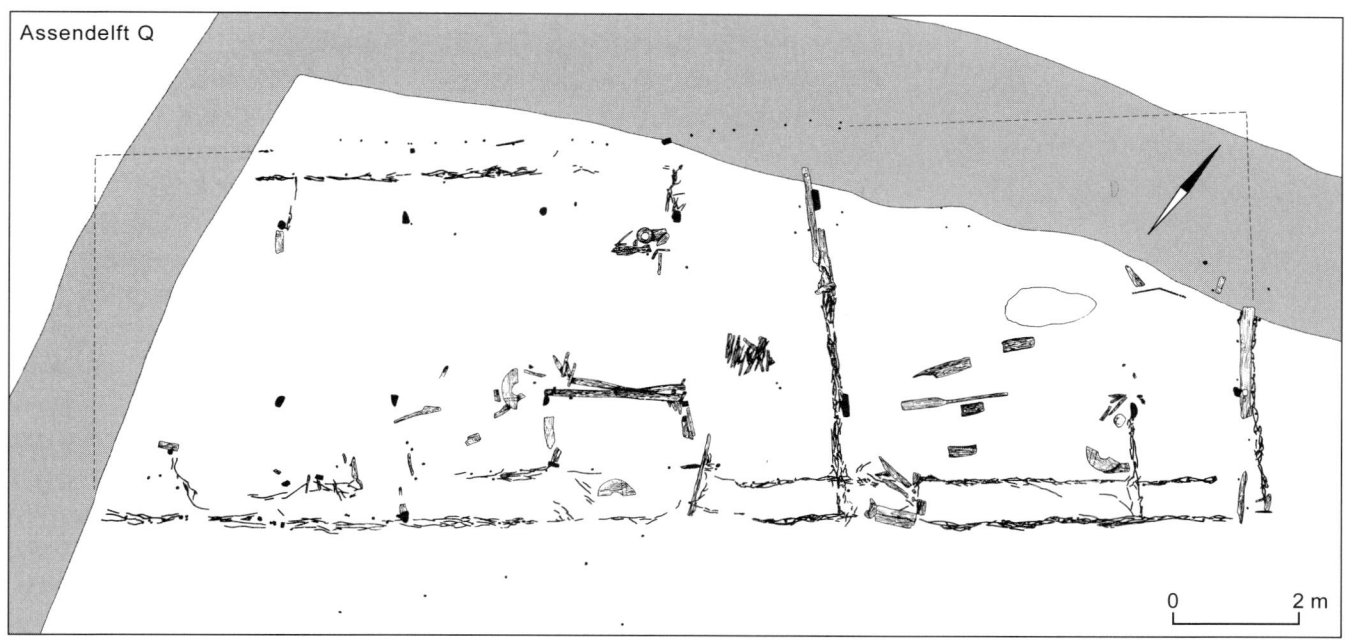

Assendelft Q

0   2 m

fig. 26.12

Early Iron Age house plan found at site Q in the Assendelver polders. An unusual structural detail is de wattle wall, which is double in parts. The living part (right) and the byre (left) were clearly separated by a partition. There was a wooden threshold in the entrance to the living parts. An intact paddle was found close to the elongated hearth in the living parts. Other noteworthy wooden finds are four parts of wagon wheels, which were found in different areas within the farm.

The plans unearthed in the peat regions have also yielded detailed information on the layouts of the farms. The hearths have survived intact far more frequently than in the sandy regions. They were fairly carelessly constructed in the Early Iron Age; however, the custom of paving the floors of the hearths with fragments of broken pots seems to have been fairly widespread in this period already (fig. 26.14). In most cases clay was used for the base of the hearth; that prevented the risk of smouldering of the floors. In some of the houses there seems to have been a hearth in the byre as well as in the living area.[18]

The floors of the houses had to be raised and new hearths had to be constructed from time to time, when the ground beneath the house subsided or cracked. At least four separate floor levels were distinguished at site Q in the Assendelver polders.[19] The floor of a farm from the Middle or Late Iron Age at Maasland (Midden-Delfland) was raised in phases, which ultimately resulted in a thickness of more than 50 cm (plate 38B). Manure and bundles of reeds or similar plants were used to raise the floor. The layers of domestic refuse formed on these floor layers con-

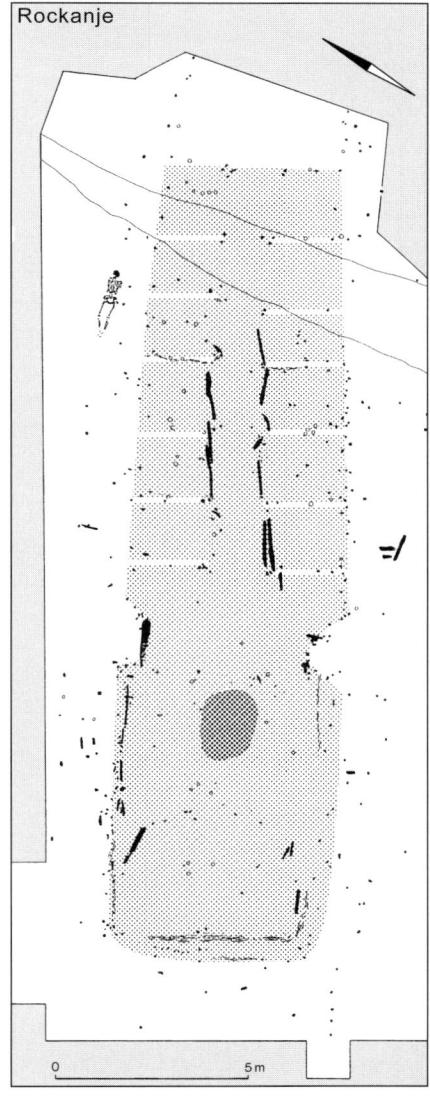

Rockanje

0   5 m

fig. 26.13

Late Iron Age house plan unearthed at Rockanje (site 08-52). The grey area is the floor, the dark grey patch in the living parts is the hearth. The recesses indicate the assumed partitions of the cattle stalls, which will have been large enough to accommodate at least 24 animals. Next to the byre was the skeleton of a man aged between 25 and 35. The skeleton was a surprising discovery as virtually no human remains dating from the Iron Age have been found in the western Netherlands. Scale 1:200.

fig. 26.14

Hearth paved with sherds in a farm dating from the 3rd century BC near Maasland (Midden-Delfland area).

tained ashes, sherds, bones and manure.[20] The custom of depositing most refuse inside the house, or in the yard just outside the door, was quite common in all of the peat regions (see also feature P).[21]

From the Middle Iron Age onwards, greater attention seems to have been paid to the living areas. In the Meuse delta the floors of the living areas were for example frequently covered with wood. And more attention seems to have been paid to the hearths, too: many proved to have been constructed on foundations of tree-trunks or branches.

It is not surprising that no wells or granaries have so far been encountered in the yards of the farms in the peat regions, considering the abundance of fresh water in the surroundings and the nature of the subsoil. On top of this, the chance of traces of any pits or ditches dug into the peat being discovered is very small; only those whose fills happen to contain many finds or those that were filled up with clay, such as the ditches of a settlement at Spijkenisse,[22] are occasionally recognised. The scarcity of traces of fields in the peat regions is understandable for the same reason. The consistent absence of traces of granaries, on the contrary, is conspicuous, considering the good preservation conditions for timber.[23] Did the occupants of the peat regions have fewer agricultural products to store or did they store their products inside the houses? Remains of structures other than farms are exceptional in the peat regions. This also holds for the two rectangular wooden fences that surrounded an Early Iron Age farm at Spijkenisse.[24]

The results of recent research, especially in Midden-Delfland, have made the former assumption of a distribution pattern composed of isolated farms no longer tenable.[25] In Midden-Delfland, clusters of house plans from the 4th-2nd century BC were found at several sites, in one case even six or more on a peat cushion at Maasland-Foppenpolder. However, as some of these plans overlapped one another, they cannot all be contemporary.

SETTLEMENT PATTERN

The possibilities of identifying patterns in the locations of the settlements in the western Netherlands differ from one environment to another. On the basis of the results of intensive field surveys and excavations at Den Burg it has been calculated that not more than about 5% of the original number of settlements dating from the period from the Middle Bronze Age until the beginning of the Late Iron Age has been discovered.[26] The uneven distribution of settlements is due to local geological conditions or the present use of the land. The results of the research at Den Burg led to the assumption of a settlement pattern composed of isolated farmsteads, which were constantly rebuilt in a different part of the field system used by the occupants of the settlement in question, in our opinion every 25-30 years.

It is more difficult to carry out such research in the Older Dunes. In many places deposits of Younger Dune sand with thicknesses of several metres and pits formed in sand-winning activities preclude the possibility of discovering sites in field surveys. Stratigraphic sequences observed at some sites suggest that the occupants of settlements that had been covered with drift sand often returned to their former occupation sites to continue their farming practices there. Evidence for five separate occupation phases between 400 and 200 BC was obtained on the Spanjaardsberg near Santpoort. Five Iron Age occupation phases were also distinguished in the dune stratification at Het Geestje near Monster, to the south of The Hague.[27] Small-scale research in the Older Dunes has shown that the settlement pattern of those areas also consisted of single farmsteads surrounded by arable land, which were probably rebuilt at different sites every 25-30 years.

There are no reasons to assume that the settlement pattern of the peat region was any different from that outlined above. The only difference may have been that the wetter conditions forced the occupants to return to a previously occupied site, on a peat cushion, more frequently.

POPULATION DENSITIES

It seems that areas comprising a variety of environments were relatively densely populated. The area bordering the southwest bank of the Oer-IJ is a good example as far as the Late Bronze Age and the beginning of the Early Iron Age are concerned. It is even more difficult to determine absolute population figures for the western Netherlands than it is for the Pleistocene sands. This is due to the absence of cemeteries. Estimates have to be based mainly on extrapolations of the numbers of sites in particular areas. Data obtained for Bovenkarspel-Het Valkje, for example, suggest that an area of 10 km² of the sandy clay ridge around the site may have been as densely populated as the settlement itself. Excavations will have to ascertain whether this area was indeed populated by some 600 individuals in the Late Bronze Age.[28]

The peat regions appear to have been as densely populated as the sands and clay deposits, at least in the second occupation period. A zone of 19 km² bordering the northern bank of the Meuse delta, coinciding roughly with the southern part of Midden-Delfland, seems to have been the most densely populated peat region. An average of 2-3 farms, or about 10-20 persons, per km² has been calculated for this region for the third and second centuries BC. Microregions within this region may have had population densities of up to twice this size, but it is estimated that the population of the region as a whole did not exceed on average 200-400 individuals.[29] The population densities of most of the other regions distinguished in figure 26.15 are also more likely to have been several hundred than several thousand.[30]

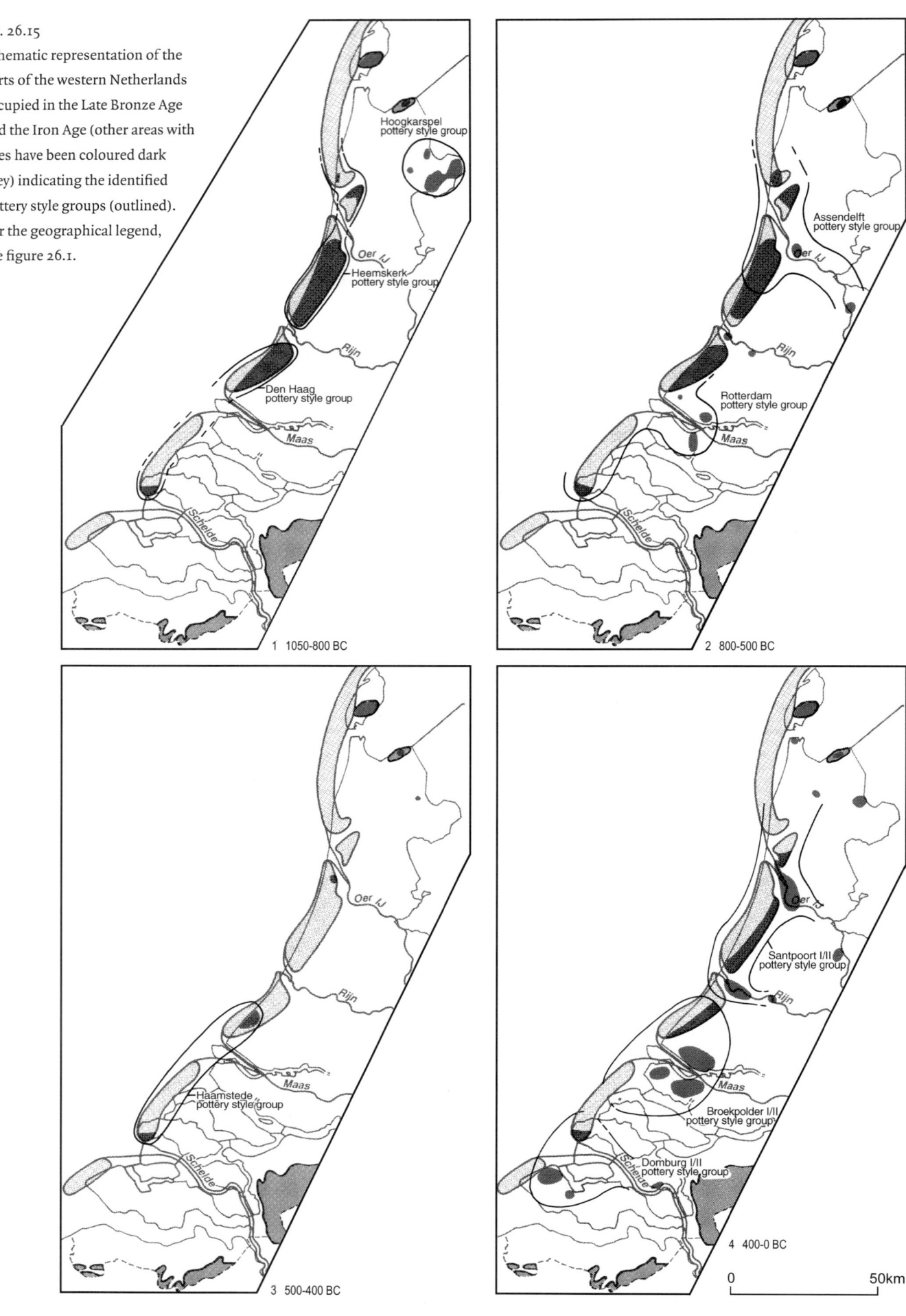

fig. 26.15
Schematic representation of the parts of the western Netherlands occupied in the Late Bronze Age and the Iron Age (other areas with sites have been coloured dark grey) indicating the identified pottery style groups (outlined). For the geographical legend, see figure 26.1.

Hoogkarspel pottery style group

Heemskerk pottery style group

Den Haag pottery style group

1 1050-800 BC

Assendelft pottery style group

Rotterdam pottery style group

2 800-500 BC

Haamstede pottery style group

3 500-400 BC

Santpoort I/II pottery style group

Broekpolder I/II pottery style group

Domburg I/II pottery style group

4 400-0 BC

0   50km

SOCIAL ASPECTS

The absolute lack of signs of differentiation in the nature or rank of the various settlements is balanced by a lack of differences in personal status or of hierarchic organisation. It is even assumed that the communities of Bovenkarspel and Andijk were hierarchically organised in the Middle Bronze Age, but that all differences in status vanished in the Late Bronze Age.[31]

The almost complete lack of burials dating from the period after the Middle Bronze Age in the western Netherlands is a great disadvantage for the study of the social structure of the communities that inhabited this area. A thorough study of the settlement pottery has provided at least some idea of the social relations between the various communities.[32] This study resulted in descriptions of a number of separate Late Bronze Age and Iron Age pottery groups, characterised by distinctive stylistic features: these have been called 'pottery style groups' (fig. 26.15). The main differences between contemporary groups concern the range of types and the nature and amount of decoration. The principal characteristic of the pottery of the Broekpolder II style group, for example, is the high percentage of pottery with decorated walls (almost 70%). That makes this pottery of the occupants of the peat surrounding the Meuse delta and the adjacent dunes the most conspicuous style group of the Late Iron Age. The style groups may not simply be interpreted in ethnic terms, but they do form a good basis for the analysis of the varying cultural influences in the coastal region itself or of the relations between the occupants of this region and those of the uplands.

There is no relation whatsoever between the distribution areas of the pottery style groups and the different landscape features distinguished in the coastal region. The distribution area of the Santpoort style group, for example, covers the clay deposits of the Rhine delta as well as parts of the Older Dunes and the adjacent peat regions. The resemblances between the pottery of the people who colonised the peat regions and that of the areas originally occupied, in particular the Older Dunes, are so great that we may assume that they represent contacts between the two regions. In view of the dissimilarity in agrarian potential between the two ecologically different regions, it is not very likely that contacts between the occupants of these regions will have been broken. The exchange of (pottery-making) marriage partners, besides the products themselves, could also be considered in this context.

ECONOMY

All the available evidence indicates that the western part of the Netherlands was inhabited by farming communities that may have been self-sufficient as far as food is concerned. The only possible exception concerns the occupants of the peat regions. If they themselves did not cultivate the wheat encountered at some of their sites on the mineral soils that were to be found at some distance from their settlements, they must have obtained it from the occupants of the dunes or of the levees bordering the deltas. Besides wheat, hulled barley, millet, gold of pleasure and linseed were widely cultivated in the Iron Age. Indications of crop cultivation in the form of the characteristic perpendicularly intersecting *ard* marks have been observed all over the coastal region, especially on the sandy soils, and here and there also the first furrows made with a plough fitted with a mouldboard[33].

The stalls in the farms, which are known virtually exclusively from the peat regions and the island of Texel, were of the same size as those of the contemporary dual-purpose longhouses of the sandy areas. Plans of farms containing a considerably larger number than the maximum of twelve cattle stalls have only been found in the *terpen* area (at Ezinge). Each stall was large enough for two cows or horses or three heads of small stock.[34]

It has frequently been suggested that cattle may have been taken to areas far away from the settlements for part of the year. The farmers of the dunes may have seasonally pastured their cattle in the peat regions,[35] or possibly on the salt marshes bordering the coast, which will also have had excellent pastureland.

As elsewhere in the Netherlands, cattle dominate the bone spectra. At several findspots, in particular in the dunes, sheep/goat[36] were relatively important as well. This is also apparent from the numerous loom weights and spindle whorls, attesting to the manufacture of woollen fabrics. In the peat regions, cattle will not only have been the primary means of subsistence, but will also have yielded the principal means of exchange, *i.e.* calves, hides, leather and dairy products.

Another relatively important product of the coastal region was sea salt. Attributes used in the production of salt have been found at sites in the dunes and along the estuaries, including the margins of the peat. That salt was used for consumption and as a preservative on more than a regional scale alone is apparent from the fact that the pottery containers in which this salt was produced and transported have been found at sites up to some hundreds of kilometres inland (feature M). The salt must have been a major trump card in obtaining articles that were scarce in the coastal region, such as objects of stone. Tephrite querns from the Eifel[37] belong to one of the few categories of articles that were introduced into the western Netherlands via exchange. Evidence of iron processing and crucibles for smelting bronze ore[38] indicate that metal was produced and worked locally on a small scale at least.[39]

NOTES

1 Only the odd stream ridge remained occupied or was recolonised in the Iron Age, after peat had grown over the former salt marshes. This proved to have been the case at the findspot Opperdoes (Woltering 1981 and 1985).

2 Van Liere 1948; Modderman 1949.

3 Van Regteren Altena 1970, 1980; Woltering 1975, 1979, 1991.

4 Assendelver polders project (in particular Brandt *et al.* 1983; Brandt *et al.* 1987; Therkorn 1991; Therkorn *et al.* 1984); Voorne-Putten project (in particular Van Trierum 1986, 1992; Van Trierum *et al.* 1988, 23-38); Midden-Delfland project (in particular Abbink 1989, 1993a and 1993b; Van den Broeke 1993; Koot/Vermeeren 1993); Oer-IJ Estuary project (see the annual archaeological reports that have been published in the journal *Holland* since 1987).

5 The majority were included in Van Heeringen 1992.

6 Brandt 1988b.

7 Van Heeringen 1988a, 1988b.

8 *Cf.* Brandt *et al.* 1986, 59.

9 For example on Walcheren (Van Heeringen 1988a) and at site N in the Assendelver polders (Van Heeringen 1988b, 1992; on the other hand see Van Gijn 1987). The levees of the Assendelver polders seem to have been more densely populated, in various types of settlements, in the Roman period in particular (see also Therkorn/Abbink 1987).

10 IJzereef 1981, 180.

11 Woltering 1991b. The results of the research at Velserbroek, which has not yet been concluded, may in the near future help to fill the gap concerning the occupation of the Older Dunes to some extent; for some preliminary results see in particular Perger/Hendrichs 1991.

12 Woltering also suggests the beginning of the Middle Iron Age, for which he assumes a date of around 600 BC, as a departure from the more commonly assumed date of 500 BC.

13 Waasdorp/Stuurman 1992.

14 Van Heeringen 1992, 314.

15 Therkorn 1989.

16 Van Trierum 1992, 42 ff.

17 Brandt *et al.* 1984.

18 For details on hearths see in particular Therkorn 1987a, 210 ff.

19 Therkorn *et al.* 1984.

20 Abbink 1989.

21 Therkorn 1987a, 209 ff; Van Trierum 1992.

22 Van Trierum 1992, in particular fig. 35.

23 It should be added that the immediate surroundings of the farms have only rarely been adequately investigated.

24 Van Trierum 1992, 49 ff (findspot 17-35).

25 Abbink 1993a; Van den Broeke 1993; Koot 1993.

594

26 Woltering 1979, 72.

27 Van Heeringen 1992, 94-98 (sites 30-West-11 and 30-West-14).

28 IJzereef 1981, 180 (100 contemporary farms with an average of six persons per farm). For the region as a whole (which is known as 'Het Grootslag') we must assume a density of less than the potential density of about eleven persons per km² that has been calculated for the Middle Bronze Age (Brandt/IJzereef 1980).

29 Van den Broeke 1993.

30 Van Heeringen 1992, 311 ff.

31 IJzereef/Van Regteren Altena 1991, 78.

32 Van Heeringen 1992.

33 Van Heeringen 1992, 329-330.

34 Prummel 1989.

35 Brandt/Van Gijn 1986; Brinkkemper 1993, 139-140.

36 IJzereef *et al.* 1992.

37 Van Heeringen 1985 and 1992, 320-321.

38 Van Heeringen 1992, 321.

39 Since this contribution was written two important works have been published that greatly enhance our understanding of the landscape and occupation of the western Netherlands, notably a collection of surveys focusing on various topics by Hallewas *et al.* (1997), the palaeogeography of the province of Zeeland (Vos/Van Heeringen 1997), the occupation of the levees of the Meuse in the Hoeksche Waard (Van Heeringen *et al.* 1998), and a dissertation on the history of occupation of the island of Texel by Woltering (2000). The models for the Bronze Age and Iron Age subsistence concluding the latter work are of more than only local relevance.

P   Peat farmers
Settlements on the peat to the south of the Meuse estuary

Marco van Trierum

The people who colonised the coastal region of the western Netherlands in the Iron Age built their settlements in the Older Dunes and in the clay and peat regions on either side of the estuaries of the rivers Scheldt, Meuse, Rhine and Oer-

IJ behind the dunes. Under the varying influence of the sea, periods of desiccation – and occupation – alternated with periods of sedimentation and peat growth in the latter areas. The results of intensive research on Voorne-Putten, to the south of the Meuse estuary, have revealed some specific characteristics of life in the peat district and the relationship between environmental conditions and farming practices, which will be discussed below.

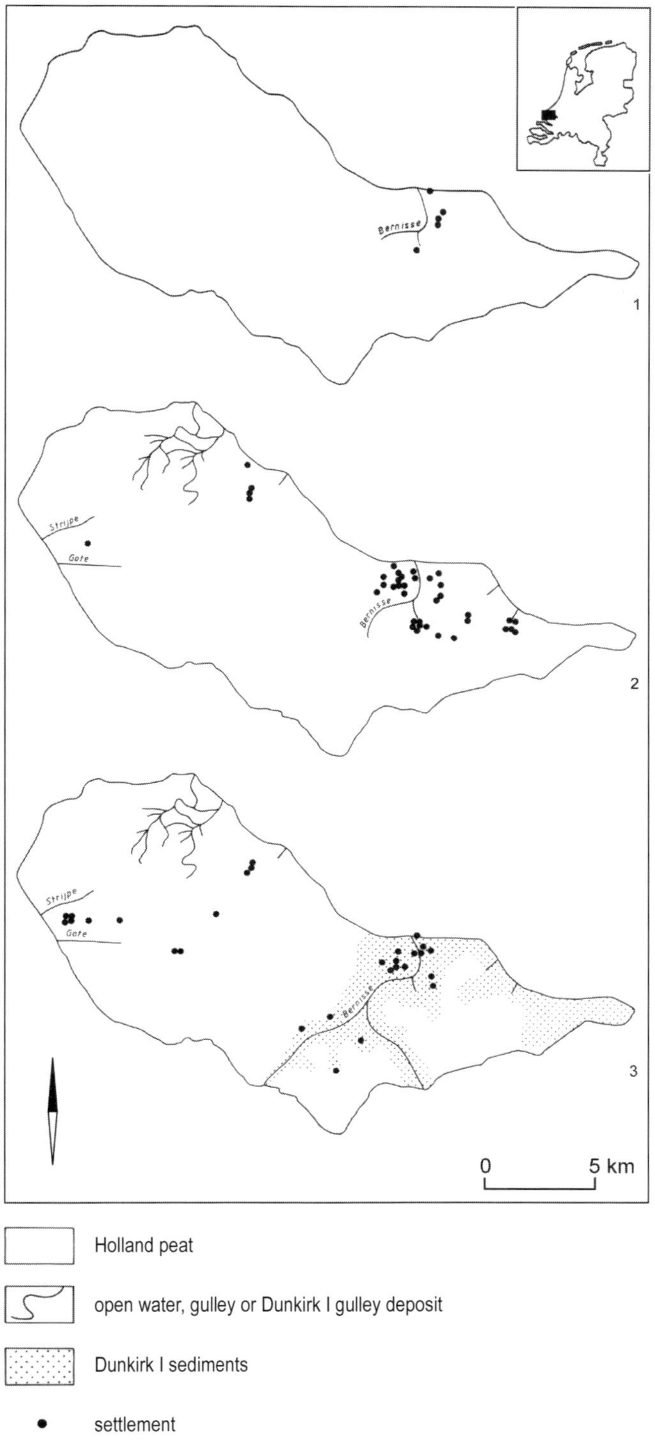

Drainage and colonisation

In the Iron Age Voorne-Putten formed part of a vast peat district between the Meuse and the Scheldt. To the north, the peat marshes were separated from the Meuse estuary by levees and other clay deposits. The dunes and coastal barriers, which lay a few kilometres to the west of the present coastline, provided protection from the sea. Originally, the area was a large bog, which was unfit for occupation, but when the influence of the sea began to increase in the Early Iron Age, new tidal channels and creeks penetrated the swampy area. They drained the bogs and made the peat fit for human occupation. The first settlers arrived at the beginning of the Iron Age, in the area around the creek system of the Bernisse (fig. P1: 1).

It is assumed that the people who colonised the peat district came from the dunes.[1] Population pressure, exhaustion of the poor dune soils, sand drifts or deterioration of the economic value of the occupation areas in the dunes due to some other cause may have induced the occupants of those areas to move to the peat region as soon as the opportunity arose. But it is equally possible that the peat had become so *attractive* that people moved there as soon as and for as long as the environmental conditions permitted it. The landscape of the drained peat appears to have been of great agricultural value, especially for cattle breeding. A richly varied vegeta-

Holland peat

open water, gulley or Dunkirk I gulley deposit

Dunkirk I sediments

• settlement

fig. P1

Voorne-Putten. The sites are from the Early Iron Age (a), the Middle Iron Age (b) and the Late Iron Age (c). The period of occupation of the peat around the Bernisse, which started in the Early Iron Age, came to an end after only about a century. The area was recolonised in the course of the Middle Iron Age, not only the parts bordering the Bernisse, but also areas further west.

597

fig. P2

Reconstruction of a farmyard on the island of Voorne-Putten in the Iron Age. The farm lies isolated in the peatland surrounded by groves and streams. The cattle graze on the wasteland around the yard. One of the fields lies on the other side of the stream.

tion guaranteed fodder throughout the year: moist pastures, wet moors with sweet gale shrubs, reed marshes in different stages of warping and willow and alder carr with dense undergrowth along the banks of streamlets. Reed in particular yielded high-quality fodder.

Peat cushions as occupation sites

Iron Age settlements have been found at dozens of sites in the peat areas of Voorne-Putten.[2] The colonists settled on the higher parts of the landscape, near tidal channels or peat gulleys. Each settlement consisted of only one farm with a yard; there was no room for anything else on the small peat cushions. This resulted in a scattered distribution of isolated farmsteads (fig. P2). A few clusters of settlements have also been found, but in these cases, too, the yards of the individual farms lay at some distance from one another, on different peat cushions. It is possible that these farms were not all in use at the same time.

The occupation sites appear to have been selected on the basis of the availability of fresh water – for both the colo-nists and the cattle – and the chance of surviving floods with dry feet. Apparently the peat cushions were high enough to remain dry during floods, because so far no indisputable evidence for the deliberate raising of the ground has been found.

The houses were 5-5.5 m wide and 10-24 m long. Their plans, which comprised at least a living area with a hearth and a byre with 6-12 stall boxes were three and/or four-aisled. An exception is the 5 x 10 m farm whose remains were found at the site of Rotterdam-Hartelkanaal: this is the only two-aisled house plan found in this area.[3] This different de-sign may indicate a different use of the building: it may have been occupied on a seasonal rather than a permanent basis. The absence of remains of cultivated crops and field weeds emphasises the exceptional position of this house site. The fact that alder wood was used to build the structure implies that the residents lived here for only a restricted number of years (feature O).

The farms that were built in peat regions elsewhere – to the north of the Meuse estuary and in the Assendelver pol-ders – were also three-aisled. It was probably safer to support the roofs of houses built on such a soft ground with paired posts rather than with single posts; the resultant structure will have been more sturdy. Both availability and durability prove to have been considered in the selection of the types of wood to be used to build the farms.

Building on a soft ground

A conspicuous feature of the plans of these farms, contrasting with the evidence obtained on, for example, the sands, is that none of the posts was founded in pits dug into the peat. This is understandable, because vertical timber would have found very little or no lateral support in a pit filled with lumps of peat. Single and paired roof supports and wall posts will have been lashed or hammered into the peat. Sometimes extra measures had to be taken after a house had been built; for example, pieces of wood were occasionally driven into the peat to secure posts that had come loose. Usually split, fairly flat pieces of wood were used for this purpose.[4]

On several occasions indications have been found that measures were taken to ensure that vertical posts would not sink into the peat. Structural elements designed to support large parts of the weight of the roof, such as single or paired roof supports and some wall posts, were given flat or truncated bases. In one case it was found that a roof support placed along the central axis had been doubly secured against movement in a vertical direction: the bottom end of the post had been truncated and a hole had moreover been made through it, through which a thick cross-beam had been inserted. This cross-beam, which rested on the old peat surface, increased the post's load capacity.[5]

A different method involved the use of shoes (fig. P3),

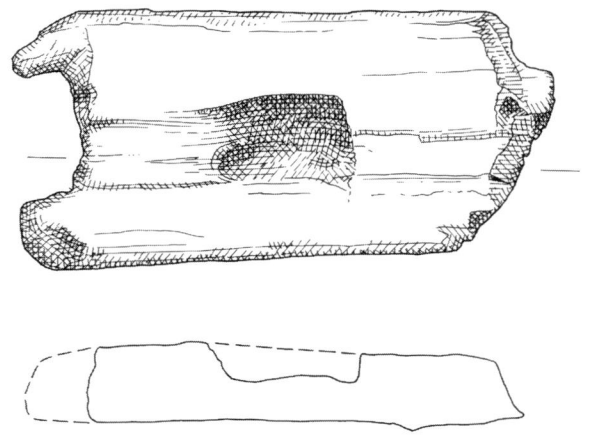

fig. P3
An alder shoe from farm 17-30 at Spijkenisse, viewed from above and in cross-section. The hole in the shoe held one of the building's supports in an attempt to prevent the risk of the support sinking into the peat. Scale 1:5.

as attested in a farm from the Early Iron Age, where it had proved necessary to install an extra wall post and roof support after the house had been constructed. These new structural elements could not be founded in the usual manner, by means of lashing or hammering. The use of shoes made it possible to install the posts exactly where they were needed, without the risk of them sinking into the peat.[6]

On the whole, building on peat involved no serious problems; the soft ground necessitated only minor modifications in some structural parts. The composition and thickness of the floors of the houses of Voorne-Putten show that the risk of sinking into the peat cannot have been a source of great anxiety to the Iron Age occupants of this area. The people who lived on the other side of the Meuse estuary seem to have had more problems in this respect.[7]

Usually manure was used for the floors in the living areas; in one case the manure was combined with plant matter, wooden beams and a mat of woven alder twigs and osiers.[8] The thickness of the manure floors varied from 8 to 15 cm. The floor of one of the farms probably consisted of two layers, which were each 10 cm thick.[9] The second layer was probably added to compensate for the consequences of the settling of the peat, indications of which were in some places observed beneath both the byre and the living area (8-12 cm). The floors of the byres also consisted of manure, but that is not surprising. The layers of manure, which sometimes rested on a thin layer of plant matter, varied in thickness from 10 to 20 cm. Only one farm had a different floor: the floor of the living area of the Early Iron Age farm whose remains were found at Spijkenisse consisted of a 1-2 cm thick compact layer of plant matter without manure; there was no manure in the byre either. This farm may have been used for only a short period of time, as also suggested by the small amount of settlement refuse found.[10]

Environment and farming practices

After the Middle Iron Age there were two concentrations of settlements in the peat areas of Voorne-Putten (fig. P1: 2-3). In the east was a cluster of settlements that were largely dependent on the prehistoric creek system of the Bernisse, a freshwater tidal area. The other cluster lay in the north-west of Voorne. As far as this last cluster is concerned, we are only well-informed about the settlements between the Gote and the Strijpe, branches of the former tidal inlet at Goeree. In this area the 'freshwater' peat lay in the vicinity of salt marshes. There were a few conspicuous differences in the economies of the occupants of the two areas.

In the Bernisse area the emphasis was on cattle keeping; sheep were much less important.[11] The relatively small numbers of calves and juvenile cattle that were butchered indi-

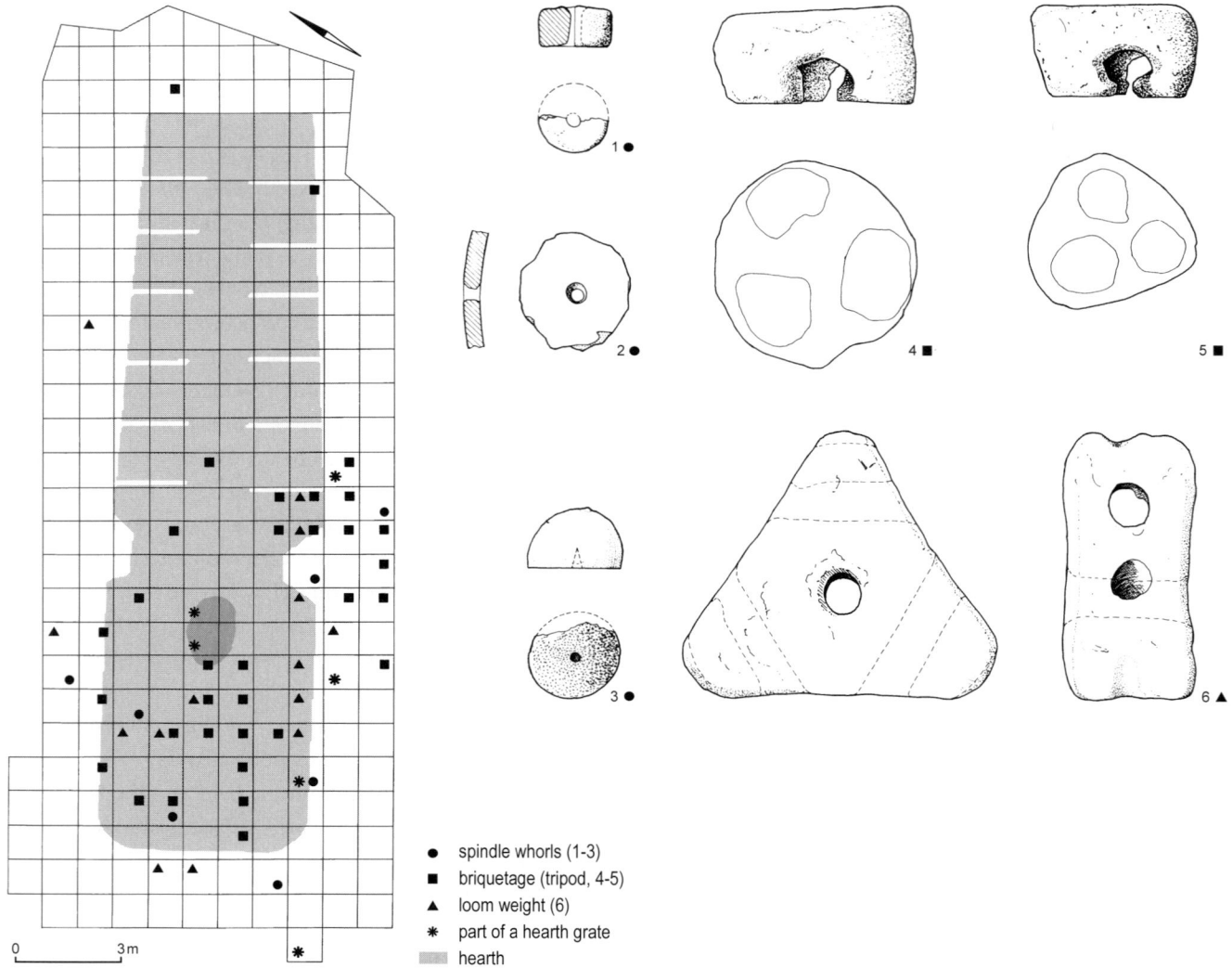

fig. P4

Distribution of various categories of finds recovered inside and around a Late Iron Age farm at Rockanje.
The objects are all of earthenware, except for a few bone spindle whorls (3). The thin spindle whorl (2)
was made from a sherd. Spinning and weaving evidently took place in the living area. Compare fig.
27.11. The tripods (4-5) are known as attributes used in the extraction of salt from seawater. House plan
scale 1:200, objects scale 1:3.

- ● spindle whorls (1-3)
- ■ briquetage (tripod, 4-5)
- ▲ loom weight (6)
- ＊ part of a hearth grate
- ▨ hearth

0 ⊢——⊣ 3m

cate that the animals were kept primarily for their meat and only secondarily for their milk. Juvenile cattle or hides and leather may have served as means of exchange for obtaining scarce or lacking goods. The sheep will have been kept primarily for their milk (and their wool). No less than 35% of the lambs were killed in their first year, which is indicative of dairying.

The peats were also suitable for crop cultivation. In the summer barley and millet may have been grown, possibly also gold of pleasure. It is assumed that crops like linseed and emmer, which were also encountered at the settlements, had to be grown in a mineral soil. They were probably cultivated on the levees bordering the Meuse to the north and east of the area[12] and possibly also on those of the adjacent island of IJsselmonde. Crops may also have been cultivated on the clay deposits bordering the creeks and gulleys which traversed the peat, on which the features of ditches have been found. By the beginning of the Late Iron Age a large part of the Bernisse area was covered with clay deposits (fig. P1: 3).

In the northern part of Voorne sheep were more important than in the Bernisse area. That is probably due to the presence of the salt marshes, which were environmentally more attractive for sheep than the damp peats. The age at which the animals were slaughtered suggests that they were kept for their meat rather than for their milk; their wool was certainly used.[13] The importance of wool and wool products is also apparent from the relatively large proportion of finds like carding combs, spindle whorls and loom weights in the settlements.

Another difference between the settlements in the northern part of Voorne and those of the Bernisse area concerns the frequent occurrence of *briquetage* at the former sites. The production of salt through the evaporation of sea water was probably an important activity. Like wool, this salt will have been exchanged for lacking goods, such as querns and certain metal implements.

The production of salt (or certain steps in the process) may also have been an indoor activity, like wool processing. This may be inferred from the distribution of various types of objects that were used in the above production processes at a house site at Rockanje (fig. P4). The concentration at the farm's southern exit represents a refuse dump. Whether the concentration found in the living area indicates that the objects were actually used in that area is not certain. It is possible that the *briquetage*, for example, was only fired in the hearth.

As far as crop cultivation is concerned, the differences between the two areas were definitely less pronounced. In the western part of Voorne the mineral soils required for the cultivation of linseed were to be found in the salt marshes instead of on levees; the peat soils themselves were also suitable for the cultivation of gold of pleasure and barley. Emmer does not grow on peat or in salt marshes. This crop must have been obtained from the dunes or from clayey soils elsewhere. It is not known whether the occupants of the western part of Voorne grew the emmer themselves or obtained it via exchange. Although these questions still remain unanswered, we may conclude that the occupants of the peat areas managed to support themselves quite well; their life was in no way inferior to that of the occupants of the surrounding environments.

Notes

1 Van Heeringen 1992, 197 and 218.

2 Van Trierum 1992.

3 Findspot 10-69 (Van Trierum 1992, 36 ff.).

4 Van Trierum 1992, figs. 25, 27, 37 and 48 (post 8).

5 Van Trierum 1992, fig. 37, post 8, and fig. 41.

6 Van Trierum 1992, 44, figs. 25 and 28.

7 Abbink 1993b. On Voorne-Putten the remains have been found of a settlement dating from the Roman period whose occupants did have difficulties. The farm that was constructed at the findspot Nieuwenhoorn had to be rebuilt three times when fissures formed in the peat at the site. Dendrochronological research has shown that the first three occupation phases lasted 6, 21 and 23 years, respectively. Although the activity of the subsoil will have limited the length of the occupation phases, it is noteworthy that the difference in length between the first and the later occupation phases corresponds to a difference in durability between the different types of wood that were successively used for the roof supports: in the first occupation phase the posts (with an average thickness of 13.9 cm) were of maple and elm, whereas mainly oak was used later. Various kinds of wood were each time used for the walls (Brinkkemper/Vermeeren 1992, 112; Van Trierum 1992, 88).

8 Van Trierum 1992, 61 ff. and fig. 56.

9 Rockanje 08-52 (Van Trierum 1992, 75 ff.; the floors are not discussed in this publication).

10 Spijkenisse 17-30 (Van Trierum 1992, 38 ff.). In the aforementioned publication it is suggested that the reason why so little settlement refuse was found may be that the refuse was used to improve the soil of the fields (p. 56). Van Heeringen (1992, 230) suggested that the site may have been used on a seasonal basis. Another possibility, suggested by the many structural modifications, is that the building was unsatisfactory from the very start and was therefore abandoned fairly soon.

11 Prummel 1989, 261; 1992, 132.

12 Brinkkemper 1993, 140 ff., 148 ff.

13 Verhagen/Esser 1992, 11.

27 Blacksmiths and potters
Material culture and technology

Peter van den Broeke

Like that of the preceding periods, the material culture of the Late Bronze Age and the Iron Age is characterised as 'poor'. This is mainly due to the scarcity of metal ornaments. Pottery constitutes the largest find category; other non-perishable materials, such as stone and glass, are less well represented. With due allowance for the distorting factor of preservation, wood, plant fibres, bone, antler, leather, wool, bronze and iron must have been used on a greater scale than the finds suggest. Objects of iron and glass featured prominently in the period discussed in this chapter, whereas flint gradually disappeared from the scene.

The production technologies will be discussed first, notably those of the categories of materials for which we have sound evidence that they were actually produced in the Lower Rhine area, *i.e.* metals, pottery, glass, textile and leather. The distribution patterns of these materials provide insight into production specialization, trade and cultural affinities. Next, a number of objects will be discussed in the contexts of their use, for example farm work and warfare.

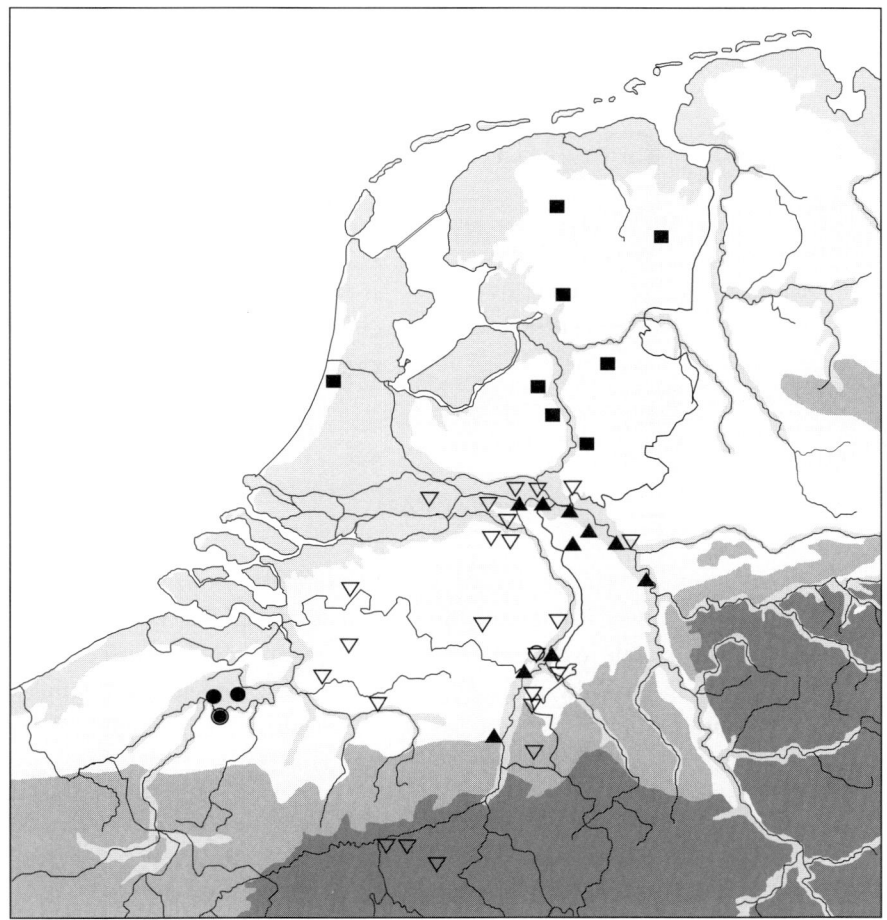

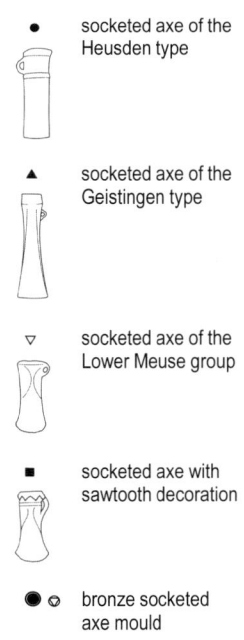

- ● socketed axe of the Heusden type
- ▲ socketed axe of the Geistingen type
- ▽ socketed axe of the Lower Meuse group
- ■ socketed axe with sawtooth decoration
- ● ◐ bronze socketed axe mould

fig. 27.1

The regionally restricted distribution of certain types of bronze socketed axes in the Lower Rhine area implies local production, in spite of the absence of the necessary ores. See also fig. 17.10.

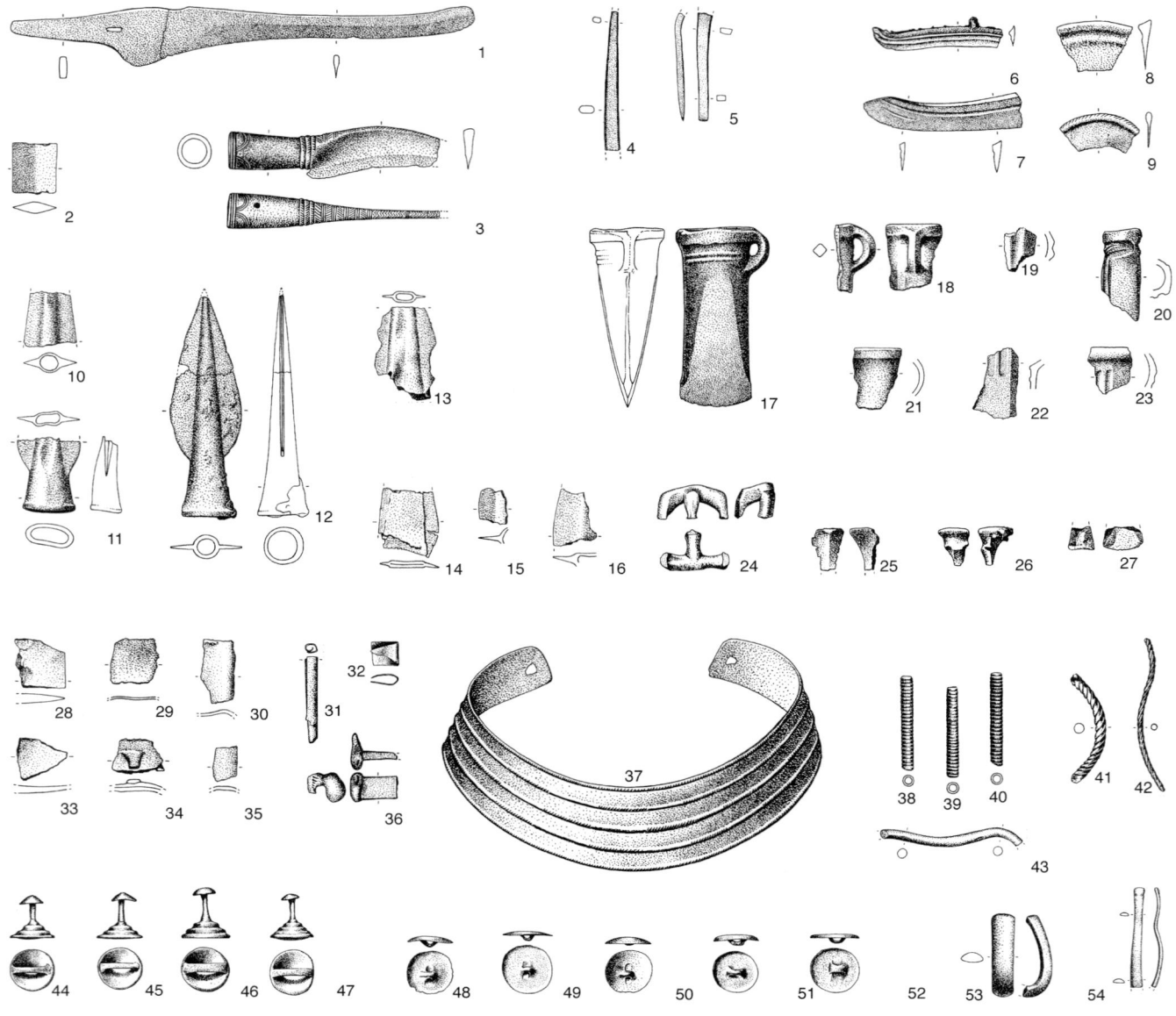

fig. 27.2

The greater part of a bronze hoard from Drouwenerveld. The bronze objects were contained in a pot. They were probably scrap metal as only some of the objects were in reasonable condition even before the pot and its contents were damaged by ploughing. Scale 1:3.

1-3	knives	17-23	socketed axes	38-40	ribbed tubes
4-5	punches	24-27	casting jets	41-43	bronze wire
6-9	sickles	28-36	indeterminable	44-52	buttons, including *tutuli* (44-47)
10-16	spearheads	37	collar	53-54	bracelets

BRONZE

As already mentioned in chapter 17, very few indications of bronze working have been found in the Lower Rhine area. End products of regional workmanship, most of which are datable to the Late Bronze Age, constitute indirect evidence for local production. The majority of these products are axes. Characteristic examples are the saw-tooth-decorated socketed axes of the northern Netherlands and the slender socketed axes of the southern Geistingen type (fig. 27.1). Certain types of 'urnfield knives' and omega-shaped bracelets are also believed to have been manufactured locally.[1]

The scarce direct evidence for local production consists of a few stray shaft axe moulds and one bronze casting-jet. A hoard discovered near Drouwen is also to be considered in the context of bronze production, although the hoard itself may actually have been produced elsewhere. It consisted of a vessel full of bronze objects and fragments of bronze that had been relegated to scrap (fig. 27.2). The range of types suggests a date around 850 BC and indicates a northern German origin.[2] This means that we know little more about the organisation of the supply of bronze in the Late Bronze Age and Iron Age than we do about that in earlier stages of the Bronze Age. Apparently bronze was produced locally as well as traded over long distances.

The various contacts with adjacent areas were maintained until the end of the Late Bronze Age,[3] but in the Early Iron Age the trade contacts between the northern Netherlands and northern Germany, Scandinavia and the Atlantic coast, which appear to have been so important until then, disappeared almost completely. Bronze products appear to have been imported from Central Europe in the wake of iron objects.

The local bronze industry was not abandoned when iron started to be used more widely. This is quite clear from the crucibles that have been found: these small vessels, which must have been used for bronze casting, all date from the Iron Age. Examples from the Middle and Late Iron Age (fig. 27.3) were almost certainly used for the local manufacture of ornaments and possibly also harness fittings. With the possible exception of those from the Caberg near Maastricht, these crucibles were all recovered from ordinary rural settlements, from the loess district in the southeast to the peat district in the western coastal zone.[4]

IRON

A stubborn material

Iron production called for completely different methods and tools than bronze production. For a long time it was technically impossible to cast iron because of its high melting temperature (1537 °C in the case of pure iron). In Europe wrought iron was the only type of iron produced until in the late Middle Ages. It was obtained by stacking iron ore and charcoal in a furnace, after which, at a temperature of around 1100 °C, slag separated from the raw iron to leave what is known as 'raw bloom'. This intermediate was then forged, to remove impurities (slag, charcoal) and to shape and harden the iron.

In view of the great difference in the production techniques of bronze and iron it is no coincidence that the bronze socketed axes with a loop for a securing thong were succeeded by iron specimens without that useful attribute. It is in fact remarkable that sockets continued to be produced at all. An iron socketed axe with such a loop from Kessel[5] (fig. 27.4) is to be regarded as a masterpiece.

Most other bronze objects could be reproduced in iron in exactly the same shape. The best known category of such objects is that of swords. An early iron sickle from Huissen (fig. 27.14:7) is a rarer example.[6]

Although relatively few iron objects have been recovered, metal weapons and tools must have been made chiefly from iron after the 8th century BC because we know of virtually no counterparts of the more corrosion-resistant bronze from after that time.[7] The latter metal was then used only for harness fittings and ornaments. Horse bits, fibulae, torques and the like were occasionally also made from iron.

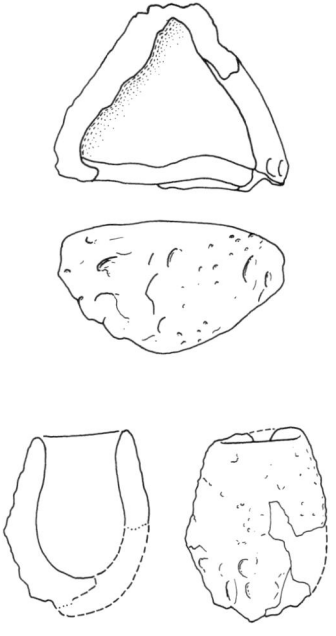

fig. 27.3
Middle Iron Age ceramic crucibles from the Maasland region (above) and Oss-Ussen (below). They were probably used for casting bronze. The pottery was affected by the high temperatures. Scale 1:3.

fig. 27.4
Wrought iron Early Iron Age socketed axe found during dredging operations near Kessel. The addition of an ear continued a Bronze Age tradition, but implied a more complex technique: the ear had to be attached by forging as iron casting was still an unknown technique in prehistoric times. Actual size.

As iron ore was fairly common in Europe, the supply of raw materials will have changed in the Iron Age. This certainly holds for the Lower Rhine area. Whereas this area lacked ore for the production of bronze, the soil contained much limonite (bog iron ore), adding to the economic value of swamps, stream valleys and possibly also the coastal plains. However, it seems to have been exploited on a very limited scale only, in spite of the enthusiasm with which the first experiments with this new source of raw materials were carried out.

Experiments in the processing of bog iron ore started already in the Middle Bronze Age, which is exceptionally early for the northern parts of Europe outside the Balkans. The oldest find in this context is an iron pin, discovered on a timber trackway leading into the bogs near Barger-Oosterveld (Drenthe). The shape and hardness of the pin were such that it could have been used for engraving bronze.[8] Dendrochronological analysis yielded a date between 1350 and 1345 BC for the construction of the trackway (see feature I). Presumed iron slag in the nearby Bronze Age settlement at Emmerhout appeared to be misinterpreted.[9]

The great iron ore resources of the northeast peat district are even regarded as a motive for the construction of the trackways. Some of these trackways end near small concentrations of siderite, a softer variety of iron ore. The many stone hammer axes (nackengebogene Äxte; fig. 29.8) from the Bronze Age and the Iron Age which have been found in this peat district, among other areas, are assumed to have played a part in the winning of iron ore, too, in particular in that of the hard limonite. The sites where the axes were found, but also the narrow shaft-holes and the many traces of use (wear, fracture), suggest a primary function as a cold chisel, for hacking and crushing iron ore.[10] It is however remarkable that these hammer axes are virtually exclusively limited to the cultural area of northern Europe. In that region the bogs were the ritual landscape par excellence. For other reasons, too, a ritual context is arguable for this type of artefact.[11]

Limited production

The highly corrosion-resistant iron slags that are known from scattered sites indicate that iron was worked in several places in the Netherlands after the Middle Bronze Age. Other indications are scarcer and are all of Iron Age date: a supposed furnace pit (containing slags of bog iron), the base of a pot into which slag was poured and the nozzle of a bellows (fig. 27.5).[12] Hardly any examples of the forging tools known from elsewhere, such as anvils, hammers, tongues and files, have been found in the Netherlands.[13] If we moreover compare the small number of iron objects found in Northwest Europe with the large quantities found in Central Europe and Great Britain, we get the impression that iron production in this area was not proportional to the great amount of ore available. The gap is particularly apparent in the case of the evidence from the Late Iron Age. A number of assemblages including large numbers of iron artefacts found in Eschweiler and Ochtrup (Germany) are the northwesternmost exponents of the vast Celtic iron industry.[14] The characteristically shaped iron ingots are rarely found beyond the lowland boundary.

The impression of a limited iron production is further strengthened by the proportion of specific imported objects. Although no research has yet been done into types that may have been produced regionally, it is to be assumed that many objects originated in Central Europe. This holds in particular for the Early Iron Age iron swords. The specimen of the Mindelheim type from Oss (plate 45A), whose hilt is inlaid with gold leaf, is the only clear example of a product of the Central European Hallstatt culture, but dozens of iron swords found in the Lower Rhine area probably came from the same area; other swords are more likely to have come from the Atlantic coast.[15]

There appear to have more contacts between the northern Netherlands and regions further south in the Iron Age than in preceding periods. The bronze and iron objects from the rich graves dating from the 6th century BC that have been found in Drenthe are associated with the Hunsrück-Eifel district in particular.[16] The bronze and iron dagger from Havelte, from the first half of the 5th century BC, is a product of the Marne culture of northern France.[17]

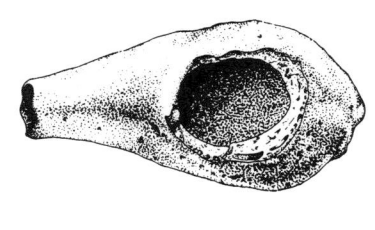

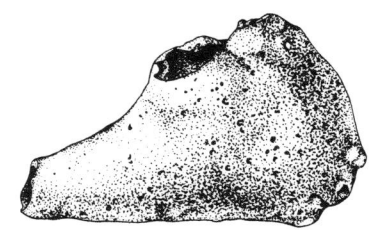

fig. 27.5
Ceramic tip of a pair of bellows, presumably used in the production of iron. The earthenware object has been deformed by heat. The same Santpoort-Spanjaardsberg settlement also yielded iron slag. Scale 1:2.

Organisation

Like bronze working, iron forging may very well have been a part-time activity of a farmer-smith who served one region.[18] The smelting of iron ore was probably a more specialist activity. Iron slags, the most common production remains, are a virtually untouched source of information on the actual organisation of the processing of iron. The study of the spatial distribution of slag separated during reduction and forging may lead to conclusions similar to those obtained for the north German salt marshes in the Roman period. The many remains of iron production found at the settlement of Feddersen Wierde proved to have been formed during the activities carried out after the slag had been separated from the raw bloom. The raw bloom had been transported from the sandy area, where the ore had been smelted.[19] The availability of fuel will have played a part here: the bare salt marshes lacked the wood for producing the charcoal required in the smelting process. Fifty to one hundred kilograms of wood were required for a furnace yield of one kilogram of forgeable iron, which gives an impression of the great extra amounts of wood that had to be obtained from the forests of the higher grounds for the local iron industry.

POTTERY

Production

Pottery underwent a true metamorphosis at the beginning of the Late Bronze Age. Although a certain amount of fairly coarse ware (*Grobkeramik*) continued to be produced, the greater part of the pottery of the Late Bronze Age had thin walls, was well finished and showed a great diversity of (new) types, decorative techniques and motifs. It is quite conceivable that this revival of pottery production inspired by developments in Central Europe was associated with the introduction of an advanced type of potter's kiln from the same area: the kiln in which the area in which the fuel was burned was separated from the firing chamber by an earthenware grate.[20] The oldest remains of grates so far found in the Lower Rhine region however date from the end of the Early Iron Age.[21] With the exception of the fairly small dimensions of the presumed kilns, *i.e.* diameters of about 1.25 m at the most, no details of the design can yet be given.[22]

The simpler kilns in pits continued to be used alongside the kilns above the ground. It is even possible that pottery also continued to be fired beneath stacks of burning twigs above the ground or in very shallow pits.[23]

In the western peat district pottery had to be fired above the ground because of the high groundwater level. Whether the many grates that have been found there and elsewhere in the coastal zone formed part of potter's kilns is however doubtful. The majority of the predominantly stray round grates were found inside houses, in or near hearths.[24] In only one case were there indications suggesting that a grate had formed part of an oven or a kiln (fig. 27.6). The find in question, which was discovered in Maasland-Foppenpolder and dates from the 3rd century BC, clearly had a shaft.[25]

In spite of the introduction of an advanced type of kiln, simple aids continued to be used in shaping the pots. At most a small pit in the ground or a support (for example a sherd) was used in shaping coils of clay into pots.[26] The wheel had not yet been introduced into the Low Countries. In the area north of Flanders the wheel was not used in the native tradition until after the Roman period.

If a pot was finished it was burnished and/or, from the Iron Age onwards, a clay roughcast was applied to create a rough or even lumpy ('besmeten') surface. Why this was done is not clear. Some believe it served a special function (to ensure a better grip or thermal advantage) whereas others stress the decorative effect. Only a small portion of the pottery was indisputably decorated, usually with patterns drawn in the clay while it was still soft with the aid of a spatula or a comb, or with impressions made with the aid of a spatula, the finger tips, *etc* (plate 40A). The technique of cutting out decorative elements (*Kerbschnitt*; plate 40B) was practised only in the Late Bronze Age. Some finds still show traces of a white paste of ground burned bone in the cut triangles and grooves. The small amount of painted pottery, dating from the beginning of the Middle Iron Age, will have been imported from the south.

Both wasters and pottery worn through use were sometimes reused for other purposes, for example for paving hearths or for tempering clay for new pots. Large sherds will have been used as lids more frequently than the finds from graves and other contexts suggest. In the western coastal region sherds were shaped into

fig. 27.6
An Iron Age settlement on the peat in the Maasland area was found to contain a concentration of remains of one or more (pottery?) kilns that could be dismantled. Illustrated are part of a grid (bottom) and part of a wall with a ring for supporting such a grid (top). The reconstruction shows what such a kiln may have looked like. The surviving parts are indicated in black. A layer of clay covered with sherds found among the remains will have served as the fire-resistant base. Scale 1:12.

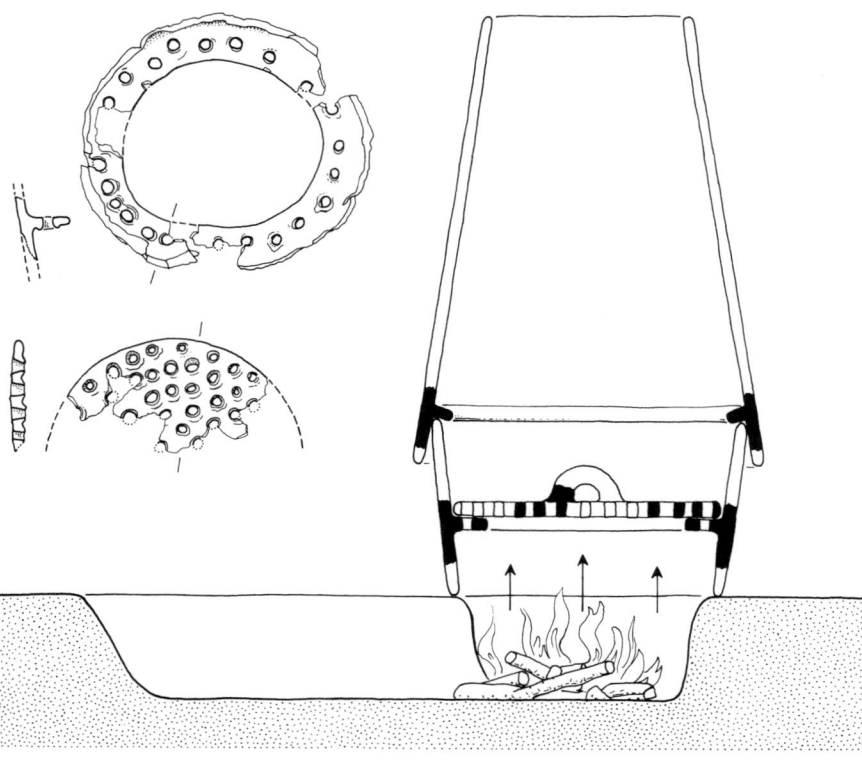

discs (counters?) and spindle whorls on a markedly greater scale than in the interior.[27]

Most spindle whorls, however, were produced specially and were usually of the same quality as the vessels. Other objects of fired clay or loam were generally of a poorer quality. Sling shots and loom weights were probably sometimes fired in smouldering hearths or were even used unfired. Other solid clay objects, such as possible spit supports (fig. 27.7), *briquetage* and grates, are of a similar soft fabric. Earthenware masks from Middelstum-Boerdamsterweg (fig. 29.1) and Maastricht-Klinkers further illustrate the diversity of the range of ceramic objects produced.[28]

Organisation

Very little research has so far been carried out into the organisation of pottery production in the Late Bronze Age and Iron Age. A crucial aspect, however, in view of the anthropological model according to which the potter's wheel is used only in societies in which (female) handwork has become a (male) specialisation, is the absence of the wheel.

The wheel was introduced into several parts of Central Europe, probably from the Mediterranean, in the 6th century BC. It was then used almost exclusively in hill forts, where the political elite attracted craftsmen.[29] The high-quality pottery of the northernmost fortified site of the first centuries of the Iron Age, on the Kemmelberg in West Flanders, was still produced by hand around the 5th century BC. However, the high quality and the local stylistic features betray craft specialisation.[30]

In the rural settlements of the Low Countries pottery production must have been a household activity.[31] The only question is: did each household produce its own pottery or was there some degree of specialisation, *i.e.* did some households produce pottery in somewhat larger quantities so as to be able to provide neighbouring farms or relatives elsewhere with pots, too?

That pottery sometimes travelled long distances we know from finds of high-quality hand-made pots, many adorned with an unusual decoration, which were produced in the area of the Marne culture or possibly on the Kemmelberg. Most of these are angular vases (*vases carénés*), dating from around 400 BC. Some were decorated with red paint. Their distribution area extends to the Rhine in the north.[32] These pots will have been coveted objects. An entirely different type of pottery that also travelled great distances, *i.e.* from the coast of the western Netherlands to the Lower Rhine loess district, was without doubt transported because of its contents, notably sea salt (see feature M).

Style

The fact that most of the pottery was produced locally would suggest considerable geographical stylistic variance. The opposite is true, however. On the whole, clear differences between contemporary pottery assemblages have only been observed in the case of assemblages recovered from sites lying several dozens of kilometres apart. This is best illustrated with reference to the heavily debated question regarding the origins of the colonists of the salt marshes in the north of the Netherlands: is their pottery characteristic of the province of North Holland, the northern German coastal area or possibly a region between the two?

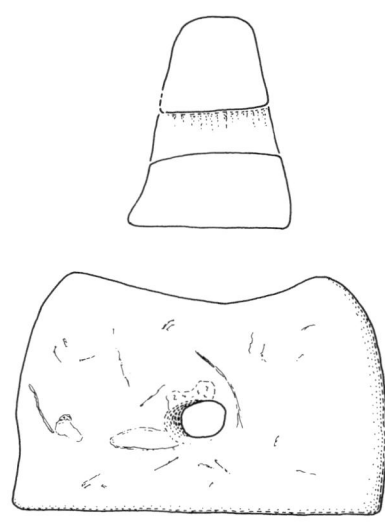

fig. 27.7

This coarse ceramic product was found in a settlement near Vlaardingen. It is thought that two such objects were used as spit supports. Artefacts of this type, dating from the 4th and 3rd centuries BC, have interestingly only been found in the area to the north of the Meuse estuary. Scale 1:3.

609

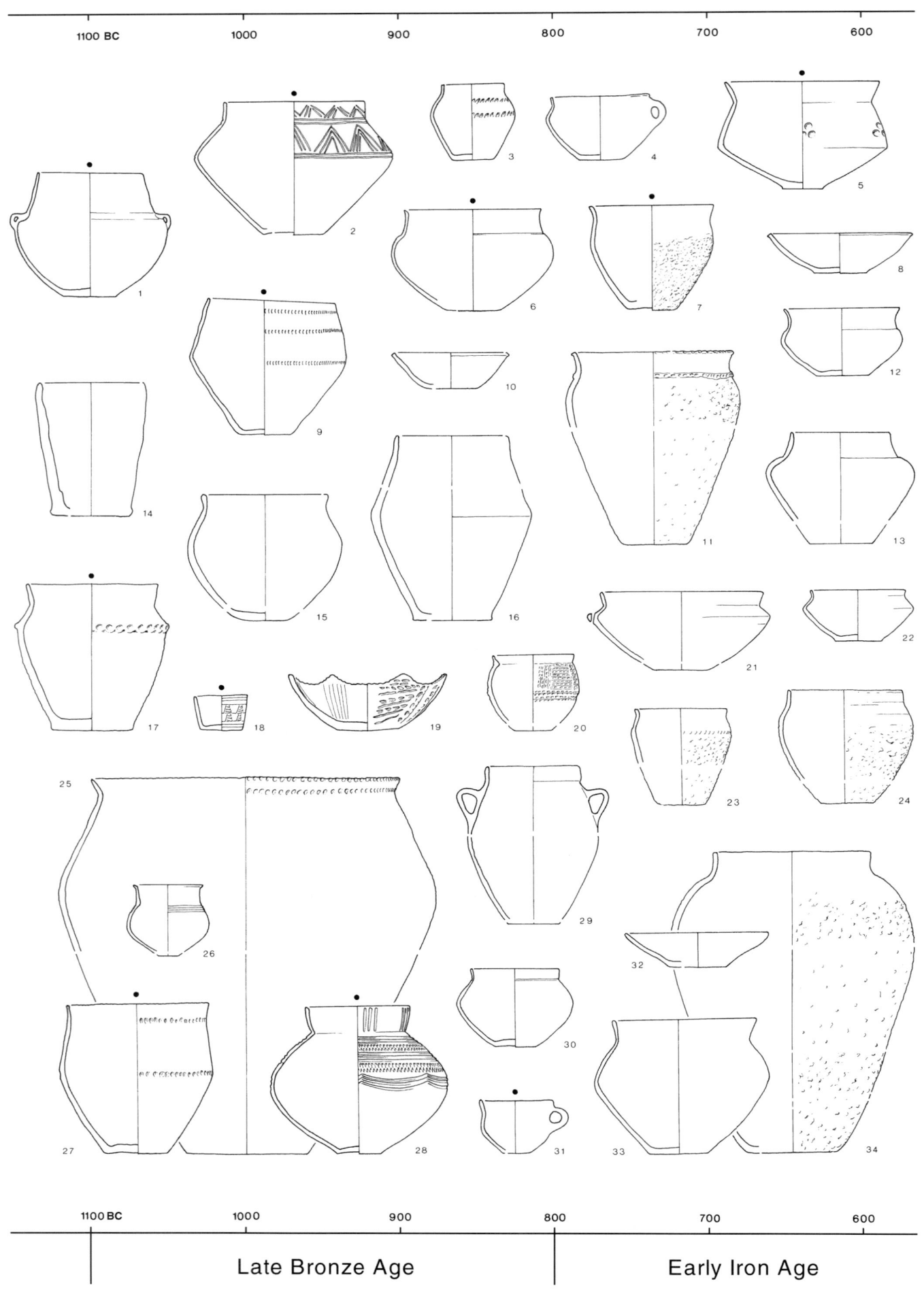

1100 BC   1000   900   800   700   600

1100 BC   1000   900   800   700   600

Late Bronze Age   Early Iron Age

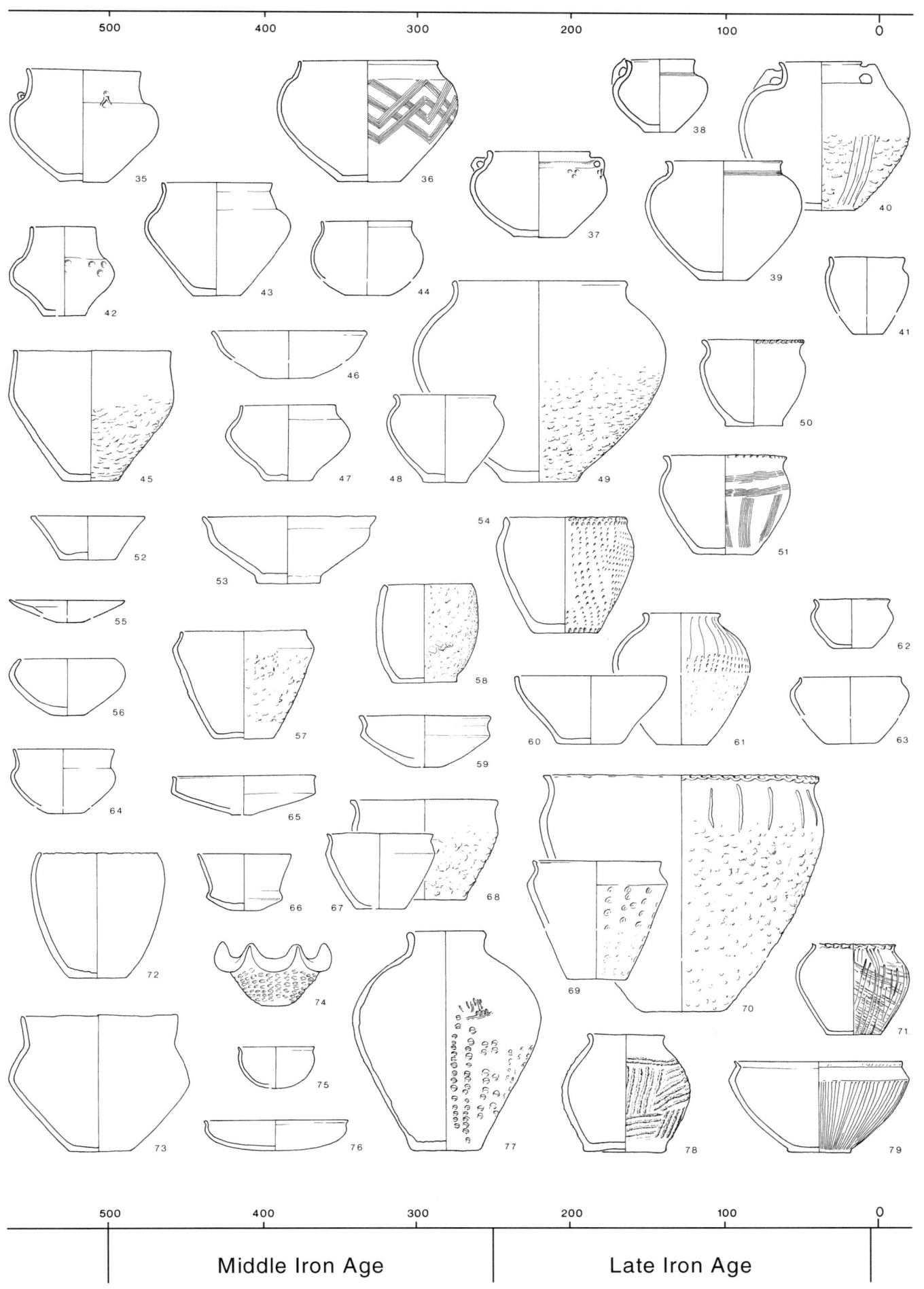

| 500 | 400 | 300 | 200 | 100 | 0 |

Middle Iron Age   Late Iron Age

In the past, pottery sequences tended to be based primarily on certain common characteristic types, mainly – in particular in the south of the Netherlands – of funeral pottery. Examples are the widely distributed *Schräghals* pots (fig. 27.8: 5, 30 and 33), the Harpstedt pottery[33] (fig. 27.8: 7 and 23) and the specifically northern Ruinen-Wommels I-IV types (fig. 27.8: 35 and 42 (I), 43 (II), 36-37 (III) and 38-40 (IV)).[34] Only in recent years has research into settlement pottery shown that the pottery of the last millennium BC in fact varied substantially in shape and decoration and that major changes took place in the range of earthenware products.[35]

In geographical terms, more pronounced stylistic differences are observable between the north and the south than between the east and the west, with the rivers area of the central part of the Netherlands constituting a diffuse border zone, without the Meuse and the Rhine being actual boundaries. This is illustrated by the distribution patterns of the Ruinen-Wommels ware, which was popular for the greater part of the Iron Age. This type of pottery is rarely encountered south of the Rhine. This same river roughly marks the northern limit of the distribution area of the angular Marne pottery.

The cultural affinities reflected by the shapes and decoration of the pottery changed over the centuries. In the Late Bronze Age there were clear links between the southern half of the Netherlands and the Urnfield culture in the western part of Central Europe. The pottery of the 5th century BC however shows influences from northern France. This is for example apparent in the imitation of several types of Marne pottery as far north as the northern bank of the Rhine. The northern half of the Netherlands maintained more enduring contacts with the adjacent part of Germany (the area of the Ems and the Münster Basin).

In the last four centuries BC the pottery of the entire area under consideration began to show signs of increasing regionalisation. This is most apparent from the development of a native pottery style in the salt marshes in the north of the Netherlands, known as 'terp pottery', which is best represented by the geometrically decorated pots of Ruinen-Wommels type III (fig. 27.8: 36).

GLASS

The means required for the production of the glass beads and bracelets known from the Iron Age (plate 41A) were not all available in the Lower Rhine area. If these objects were not obtained from elsewhere as end products, at least some of their raw materials (such as chalk and certain pigments) or semi-manufactured products (lumps or bars of glass) must have been imported.

A high density of finds, possibly indicating local production in the rivers area in the eastern part of the Netherlands, was noted already in the first study of the glass bracelets found in the Netherlands.[36] Since then, the number of finds has increased to over two thousand and more insight into various aspects of their pro-

fig. 27.8 (see previous pages)
Late Bronze Age and Iron Age pottery in the Netherlands, from north (top) to south (bottom).
The survey gives an impression of the variation in settlement pottery through the ages. Pottery
from burials has been included – out of necessity – mainly for the Late Bronze Age (marked
with a dot). Pottery from the final phase of the Iron Age is still very poorly known. Most
types and forms of decoration remained popular for more than a century in large parts of the
Netherlands. Scale 1:8.

duction has been gained.[37] The concentration of finds on either side of the Meuse in the east of the Netherlands (fig. 27.9) includes several sites, lying far apart, which yielded more than one hundred fragments of bracelets each, the maximum number being 379 (Beuningen-De Heuve). This indicates regional production, in several workshops, at least of the types which are far better represented in these areas than in other parts of Europe. They are the single-ribbed bracelet decorated with a thread of glass paste, the two-ribbed, the undecorated five-ribbed and the blue seven-ribbed bracelets. It is believed that there was also a workshop in the vicinity of Roermond, in addition to those in the eastern rivers area. Concentrations of seven-ribbed bracelets have been found in both areas, but virtually nowhere else.

This regional glass production appears to have started in the first century BC, after a period of about one century in which glass bracelets were imported from their original provenance, the area of the La Tène culture in Central Europe.

No other artefact type that was distributed from production centres has a distribution area within the Netherlands with such clearly marked limits as the glass bracelets; that is, the northern and western limits are clearly marked. In the western Netherlands glass bracelets were virtually the only luxury products in the Late Iron Age.[38] Nevertheless, fewer than ten fragments have been found in that densely populated area, whereas we know that there was a constant flow of sea salt in the opposite direction. When we compare the small number of examples from the coastal area with the more than two thousand specimens found in the rivers area further east we must conclude that glass bracelets had a special meaning in the

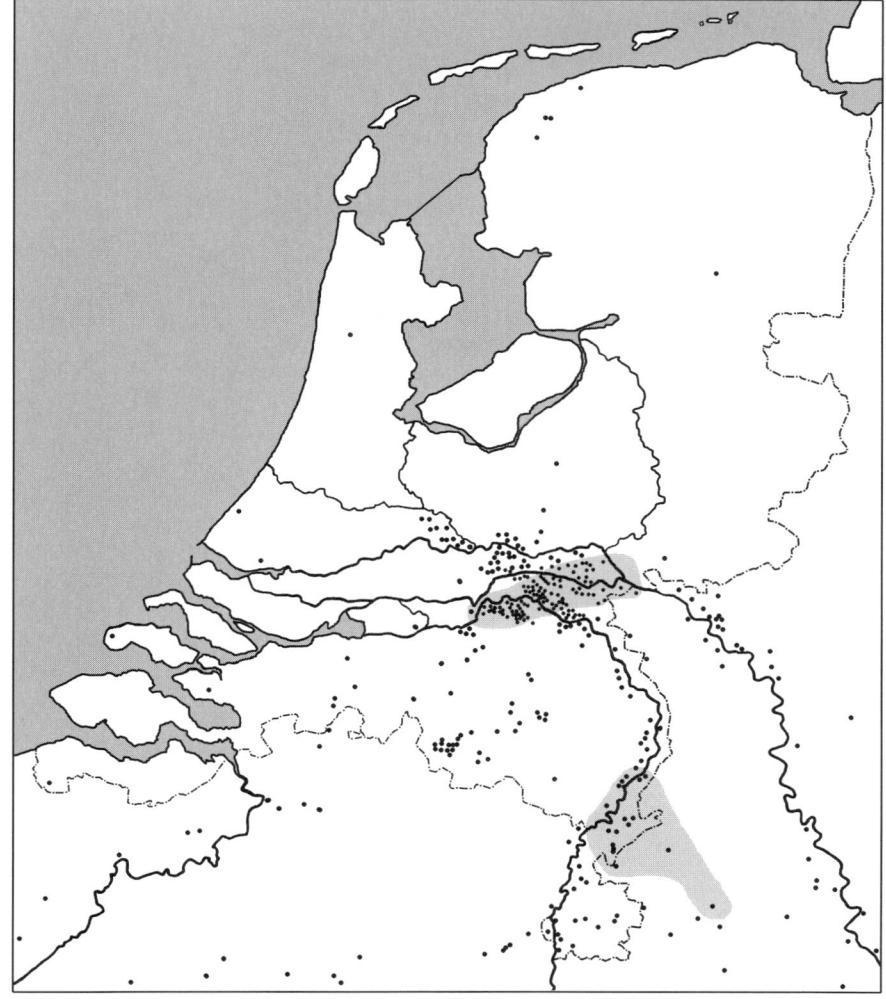

fig. 27.9
Findspots of glass La Tène bracelets in the Lower Rhine area. Dozens of bracelets of the blue seven-ribbed type have been found in the two grey areas. Only very few bracelets of this type have come to light elsewhere in Europe.

613

south of the Netherlands, in particular as expressions of communal identity or possibly also as standards in regional exchange.

TEXTILE AND LEATHER

Numerous human bodies and all kinds of objects have been preserved in the bogs of Northwest Europe. Whether they were buried or offered or ended up there in some other way, they have provided us with at least some knowledge of prehistoric clothing and footwear. For example, they have enabled us to reconstruct different weaving techniques, some of which are no longer in use today, such as the so-called sprang technique. The bogs of Drenthe are the westernmost source of information on the continent (see feature Q). Where and how the textile was made can be inferred from settlement finds. At sites where other craft activities besides pottery production were practised on a general, household basis it was usually spinning (of wool and flax) and weaving. Earthenware spindle whorls of many different shapes (fig. 27.10: 1-9) were widely used all over the Netherlands, especially after the Bronze Age. Loom weights were also fairly common, though in smaller numbers. These weights, weighing from several hundreds of grams to over a kilogram (fig. 27.10: 10-12), served to keep the bundles of warps of a vertical loom taut. The oldest type of weight, with a single hole at the top, may in principle have served as a net weight, too. This alternative use is less likely in the case of the flat triangular type with a hole at each of the three corners and sometimes a fourth at the centre. It is believed that it was easier to manipulate the weight and the fabric with this type.[39] Evidence for the implied technical innovation goes back to the 5th century BC.

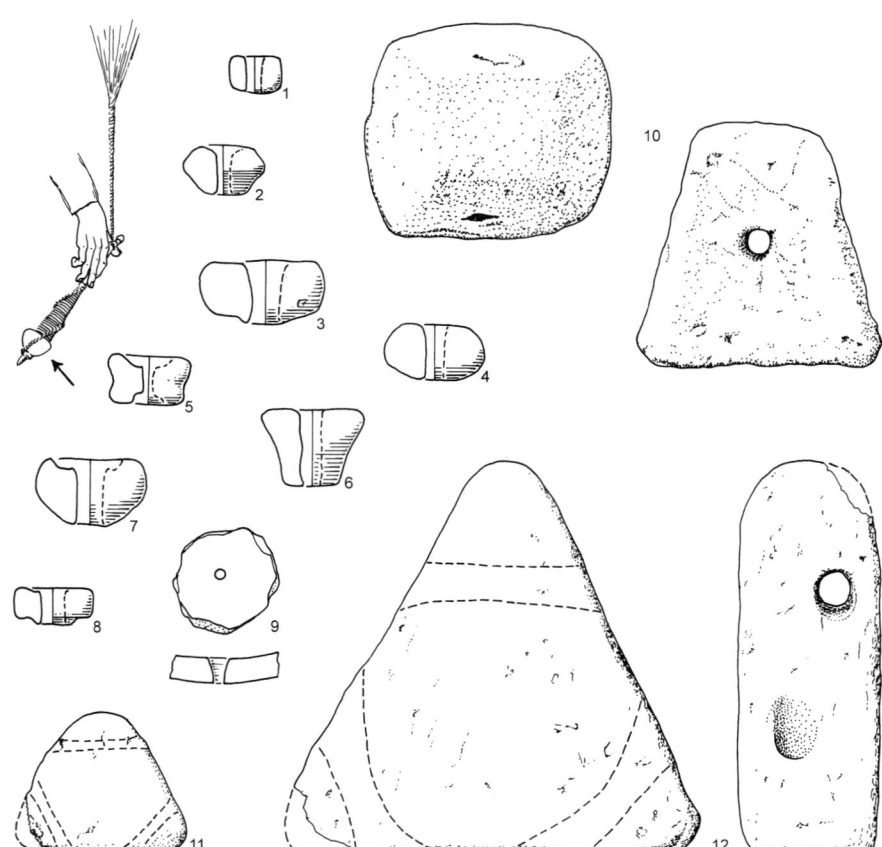

fig. 27.10
Ceramic spindle whorls (1-9) and loom weights (10-12). Spindle whorl No. 9 was made from a sherd. Scale 1:3.

1-8	Oss-Ussen	Middle Iron Age
9	Assendelft	Late Iron Age
10	Oss-Ussen	Early Iron Age
11	Oss-Ussen	Late Iron Age
12	Vlaardingen	Middle or Late Iron Age

Another implement that is to be considered in this context is the comb, which was probably used for carding or weaving (fig. 27.11). A small number of such combs – all made of deer antler – have been preserved in Iron Age settlements on the peats of the western Netherlands and in the rivers area in the east.

In view of the local character of the textile industry it is remarkable that triangular loom weights and combs of deer antler with comparable line decorations have been found in Great Britain, too.[40] There are no other indications of Iron Age contacts with Britain. Hence there is no reason to assume that the aforementioned attributes were distributed on anything more than a local scale. Historical and ethnographic data suggest that it is more likely that the products of textile manufacture, in particular fine fabrics, were widely distributed, as gifts or objects of exchange.

The processing of hides into leather bags, clothing, shoes, belts, horse gear and the like must also have been a common activity. Still, far fewer traces of this activity have been found than of textile production. This must be due entirely to the materials involved. Flint scrapers went out of use almost completely after the Neolithic. Only the odd scraper can be dated to the period discussed here with a reasonable degree of certainty, such as the examples in the Bourtangersluis hoard, which were accompanied by flint sickles.[41] The rare bronze and iron tools with sickle-shaped ends (fig. 27.12) may have been the more common counterparts of flint scrapers.

fig. 27.11
Middle Iron Age antler comb. The comb, which will have been used for carding or weaving, was found in a settlement near Vlaardingen. Scale 1:2.

DISTRIBUTION

Objects that changed hands will often have done so in social intercourse, as gifts and objects of exchange at seasonal feasts, weddings and the like. The prestigious imported Hallstatt objects (found at Oss, Wijchen) are also associated with exchange between elites living far apart, who later distributed the imports among their faithful followers within their own regions.[42] The intervention of professional traders may be suspected at the most, in particular in the case of metalwork. The transactions did not yet involve coins. The Celtic coins which were sporadically to be found in the southern part of the Netherlands in the 1st century BC (plate 41B) are thought to have been chiefly gifts presented to clientele, offerings and the like.[43]

Unlike several decennia ago, the appearance of new or different types of objects in an area is nowadays only rarely attributed to the arrival of individual settlers or groups of settlers. In this respect the finds recovered in dredging activities or otherwise from the Meuse/Waal basin between Rossum and Lith constitute an exception. These objects from the first century BC consist mainly of bronze bracelets, fibulae, iron broadswords with hilts composed of small discs and silver Celtic coins. The exclusive concentration of silver *triquetrum* coins of the Lith group (fig. 27.13) is the key to the hypothesis that Batavians settled here between 50 and 30 BC.[44] Clear precursors of these coins have only been found in Hessen, which, according to historical sources, is where this tribe came from.

fig. 27.12
Iron knife from Beegden which is thought to have been used for processing or cutting skins and leather in the Late Iron Age. Scale 1:3.

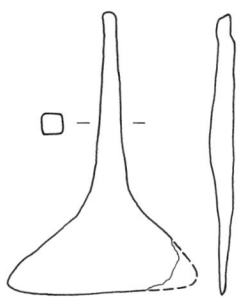

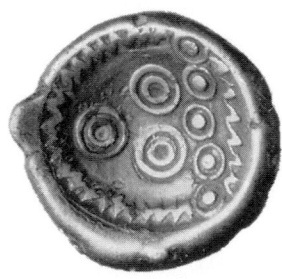

fig. 27.13

Silver Celtic coin of the *triquetrum* type recovered during dredging operations near Megen. *Triquetrum* coins of the Lith group, such as this, are thought to have been issued by the Batavi. Scale 2:1.

Transport

In view of the fact that in historical times most transport took place across water, the many – calm – watercourses in the lowlands must have been the main trade arteries in prehistoric times, too. In the Bronze Age already there were frequent trade contacts between England and France, which of course involved seaworthy ships. Simpler types of boats were used on inland waterways. The five boats known from Dutch prehistory are all canoes made from hollowed tree-trunks.[14]C dates have shown that three of these canoes, from Nigtevegt, Nijeveen and Rotterdam-Terbregge, were made in the Early Iron Age.[45]

Wagons and carts were used for transport by land. They differed in design and in the kind of draught animals used. The rich grave of Wijchen yielded evidence for the use of a wagon with four spoked wheels that was drawn by two yoked horses.[46] This type of wagon, however, was not used for transporting loads but was a showpiece for ceremonial purposes, reserved for the elite. A similar prestigious vehicle is a two-wheeled chariot with iron rims which was found in Nijmegen, also in a grave (dating from around 400 BC).[47]

Composite wooden disc wheels are also known from the Iron Age (fig. 27.14: 5). Those recovered from settlements (Assendelft, Ezinge, Oss) will have formed part of two- or four-wheeled carts used for transporting loads at farms. Horses could not be used to draw these carts until in the early Middle Ages, when the horse-collar was invented. Until then, oxen must have provided the traction for heavy loads. The use of a double yoke, an intact example of which was found in the Ezinge *terp* (fig. 27.14: 1), made it easier to draw both carts and ploughs.

Farm work (fig. 27.14-15)

From the shallow furrows with V-shaped cross-sections that have been observed in many places in the Netherlands we know that simple ploughs or *ards* were used to prepare seedbeds from the Neolithic onwards. However, the earliest indications of what these implements actually looked like date from the Early Iron Age. Arrow-shaped wooden objects with a length of about half a metre were probably the shares of bow *ards*.[48] From the Iron Age onwards the vulnerable wooden tip was protected with an iron point. The only Dutch prehistoric find of such a protective part, from Santpoort, is thought to date from the 3rd century BC.[49]

In recent years more and more indications that the plough proper was introduced into Northwest Europe already before the Roman period are being found in the coastal regions of the western Netherlands and northern Germany in particular.[50] Deep, obliquely dug furrows indicate the use of a mouldboard with which the soil could be turned. However, *ards* continued to be used alongside this simple precursor of the modern plough until in the Middle Ages.

As far as the harvesting implements from before the Roman period are concerned, we only have evidence for short metal sickles with wooden handles, which may also have been used as reaping or pruning hooks. The well-known bronze sickle of the Middle and Late Bronze Age (plate 41C) was fairly quickly succeeded by an iron version.

It is doubtful whether the hundreds of sickle-shaped objects of flint that have been found were actually used for harvesting.[51] Analysis of use-wear traces on some examples has shown that they were indeed also used for cutting silicon-con-

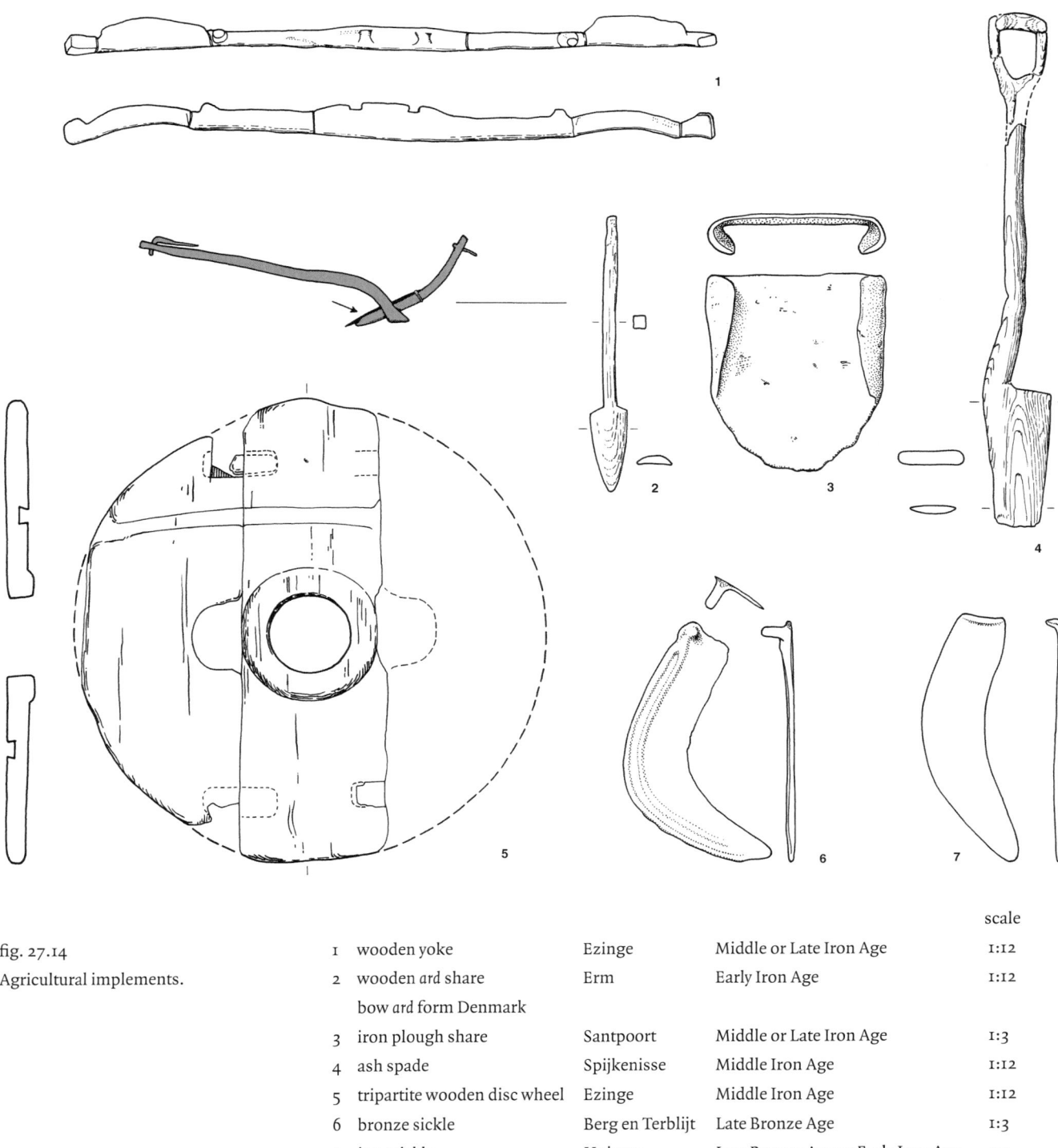

fig. 27.14	1	wooden yoke	Ezinge	Middle or Late Iron Age	scale 1:12
Agricultural implements.	2	wooden *ard* share bow *ard* form Denmark	Erm	Early Iron Age	1:12
	3	iron plough share	Santpoort	Middle or Late Iron Age	1:3
	4	ash spade	Spijkenisse	Middle Iron Age	1:12
	5	tripartite wooden disc wheel	Ezinge	Middle Iron Age	1:12
	6	bronze sickle	Berg en Terblijt	Late Bronze Age	1:3
	7	iron sickle	Huissen	Late Bronze Age or Early Iron Age	1:3

taining plants, but the characteristic gloss is attributable mainly to contact with the ground. In particular this is to be associated with the cutting of sods, to be used for constructing burial mounds or walls of houses, or for covering stable floors.

Materials readily available, such as shoulder blades of large animals, were also used for cutting sods, digging pits and ditches, cutting peat and similar activities.[52] In addition, carefully shaped wooden spades designed for heavy use were also manufactured, as indicated by a few examples of such implements preserved in the peat.

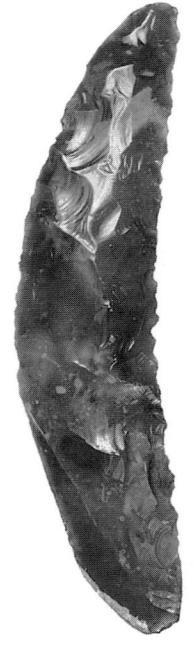

fig. 27.15
Flint sickle from Andijk showing the gloss
characteristic of this implement. Bronze Age.
Scale 1:2.

Of the attributes used for the processing, storage and consumption of the agricultural products, the earthenware pots are virtually all that has survived. A few wicker baskets have been preserved under favourable conditions. A basket woven from differently coloured twigs (fig. 27.16) was recovered from the ditch of an Early Iron Age settlement at Velserbroek. The shape of the basket suggests that it was used as a winnow for separating chaff from grain.

From the Neolithic until in the Late Iron Age cereal was invariably ground by moving a rubbing stone to and fro over a quern. The types of stone used for this purpose did change though. Around the beginning of the Late Bronze Age the granite commonly used until then started to be replaced by tephrite (basalt lava), a volcanic rock. The coarse, porous structure of the stone obviated the need to roughen the querns time and time again. The querns were distributed across a large part of the Netherlands from the quarries near Mayen in the Eifel.

The originally loaf-shaped grinding stone evolved into a type with a pronounced keel (known as 'Napoleon's hat'), which could be secured in the ground (fig. 27.17: 1). The revolutionary introduction of the rotary quern took place around 200 BC (fig. 27.17: 2).[53] With this type of quern one stone was rotated on another by hand. This improved form of grinding apparently led to a demand for tephrite querns among the occupants of the northeastern part of the Netherlands, too, where no examples of the older types have been found. In this area, where many moraines were to be found, rotary querns were also imitated in granite.

Settlement finds will undoubtedly also include stones that were used to crush herbs and oil-containing seeds. However, they are difficult to identify as such among other stones showing traces of grinding and tapping, which may have been used for shaping bone artefacts, polishing knives and axes, roughening querns and similar operations (fig. 27.17: 3-4).[54]

The vessels in which the products of the land were stored, cooked and served represent the largest group of finds recovered from the settlements, but our knowledge of the specific uses of the different types is inversely proportional to the number of finds. This is mainly due to the fact that the earthenware is usually found in secondary contexts, as sherds mixed with domestic waste. Exceptions are mainly pots that were lost or placed in wells[55] or that were deposited in (cellar) pits. The largest examples of these pots, with volumes of over 100 litres, were undoubtedly used for storage, in particular of products of the field, such as cereals.[56] Most of the vessels will have been used for cooking and serving food and drink. The recently begun technical analysis of residues in and on the pottery[57]

fig. 27.16
Wicker basket from Velserbroek. The basket
was woven from rows of differently coloured
twigs. Length c. 67 cm.

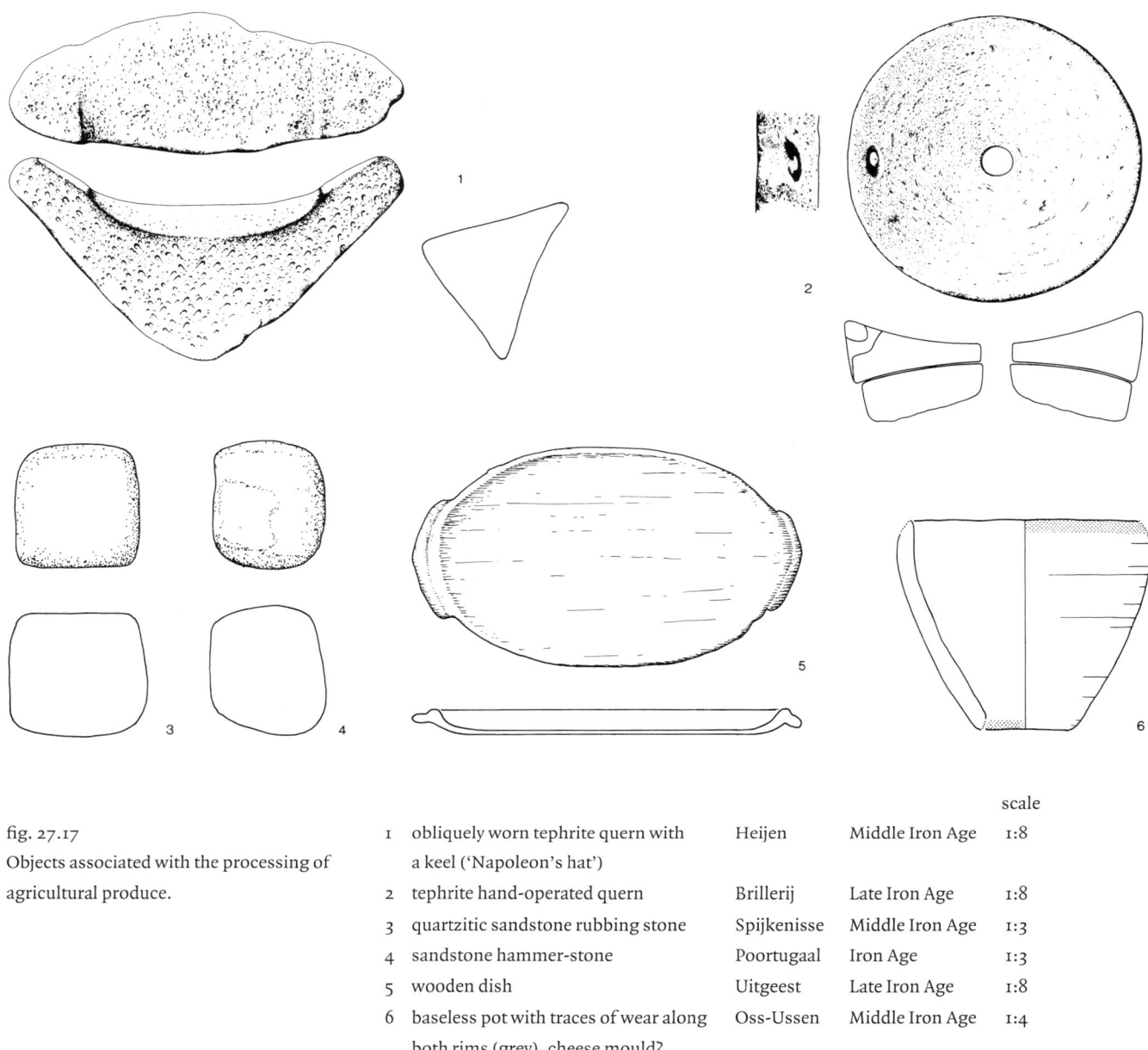

fig. 27.17
Objects associated with the processing of
agricultural produce.

				scale
1	obliquely worn tephrite quern with a keel ('Napoleon's hat')	Heijen	Middle Iron Age	1:8
2	tephrite hand-operated quern	Brillerij	Late Iron Age	1:8
3	quartzitic sandstone rubbing stone	Spijkenisse	Middle Iron Age	1:3
4	sandstone hammer-stone	Poortugaal	Iron Age	1:3
5	wooden dish	Uitgeest	Late Iron Age	1:8
6	baseless pot with traces of wear along both rims (grey), cheese mould?	Oss-Ussen	Middle Iron Age	1:4

may throw more light on the question of the specific functions of the various vessels.

We may assume that unusual types had a special function. In the case of the *Lappenschale* (fig. 27.8: 19) and the parasol bowl that evolved from it (fig. 27.8: 74) the shape, but also the frequent and lavish decoration, indicates that the vessels in question served a special function. This is also suggested by the wide distribution area, covering large parts of Europe, of the early variant in particular.[58] The contexts of use, *i.e.* in graves, settlements and caves (Belgium), and indications of the use of fire make it more likely that the vessels were used as 'coal' pans or oil lamps than that they played a part in dairying, as has been suggested for these vessels.

On account of their resemblance to present-day (wooden) cheese moulds, vessels with perforated bases and/or walls are often assumed to have been used in prehistoric cheese production. However, the vessels in question, which were rare until the Middle Iron Age, may in many cases also have been used as colanders or

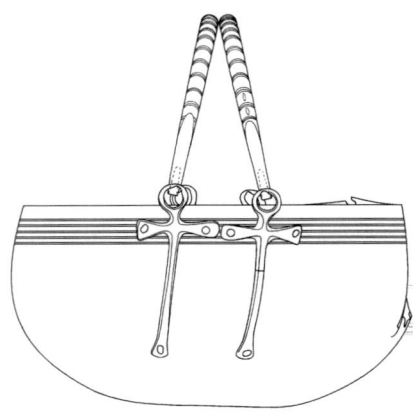

fig. 27.18
Bronze cauldron from the vicinity of Venlo.
Only the elite possessed metal vessels. This
specimen from the 7th(/6th) century BC
– a very rare find in northwestern Europe –
will most certainly have belonged to a local
elite. Such vessels are assumed to have been
produced south of the Alps. Scale 1:5.

– lined with cloth – as sieves. Only types without shoulders and necks may have
served as cheese moulds. An unusual type in this context is that of the funnel-
shaped vessels without bases which all show distinct signs of wear along their
edges (fig. 27.17: 6).[59] At least ten examples of this type have been recovered from
settlements in the rivers area in the central part of the Netherlands. Most of these
date from the Middle Iron Age. The recurrent association with earthenware which
most probably contained sea salt (see feature M) makes it even more likely that
they were cheese moulds.

With such a wide variety of earthenware vessels of different types and sizes we
may wonder what part was played by wooden vessels, leather bags and the like.
With the exception of the Late Iron Age dishes found at Uitgeest (fig. 27.17: 5)
and at Jipsinghuizen,[60] remarkably few wooden vessels have survived from prehistoric times. The scarcity of wooden vessels is particularly conspicuous in the peat
district of the western Netherlands, where many organic settlement remains have
been preserved.

Metal vessels are known mostly from graves; a few late cauldrons have been
found in rivers.[61] The earliest finds are bronze buckets (situlae) and a bronze cauldron (fig. 27.18). Most date from the 7th century BC (period Hallstatt C). Only a
few specimens date from later centuries, as do the metal vessels found in the Belgian province of Limburg (Eigenbilzen, Wijshagen).[62] There is no doubt that these
exotic imported goods belonged to members of the local elite, but whether they
used them for the same purposes as the elite in the imports' area of origin is highly
questionable. In the area of origin, essentially the northern part of the Alps and
its surroundings, they were used at (ritual) drinking feasts. Situlae were usually
placed in graves as parts of drinking services. This was not the case in the Lower
Rhine area, where they were usually used as urns.

Clothing, ornamentation and personal care (fig. 27.19, plate 42A)

Thanks to the good preservation conditions of the bogs in the northeastern part
of the Netherlands we have some impression of prehistoric clothing and footwear
(intermezzo Q). The bogs have even granted us a glimpse of hair styles, an example of which are the Iron Age plaits from Odoorn (fig. 1.8).[63] Most of the prehistoric combs that have been recovered will have been used for carding and weaving.
The decorated, probably fine-toothed bone comb from the Bronze Age settlement
of Bovenkarspel (fig. 27.19: 1), on the other hand, may have been used for hair
care.

The clothing of the bog bodies lacks cloak pins (fibulae) and buttons. It is indeed doubtful whether ordinary individuals could afford, or were allowed to wear,
such forms of fastening: metal ornaments were scarce in Northwest Europe in
prehistoric times. Some large Late Bronze Age spectacle fibulae have been found,
for example at Drouwen and Noordwijkerhout.[64] The much smaller and simpler
later fibulae remained extremely scarce until the Late Iron Age. The – equally
rare – long pins (*e.g. Bombenkopfnadel, Kropfnadel, Rollenkopfnadel, Keulenkopfnadel*)
may also have been used to fasten cloaks or they may have served as hair pins.
They were also used to fasten the pieces of cloth in which cremation remains were
bundled. The relatively large number of fibulae of middle and late La Tène types
that have been found is mainly attributable to the fact that these objects were deposited in the rivers in the eastern part of the Netherlands, probably in a ritual
context.[65]

Very rarely does the context from which these and other ornaments are recov-

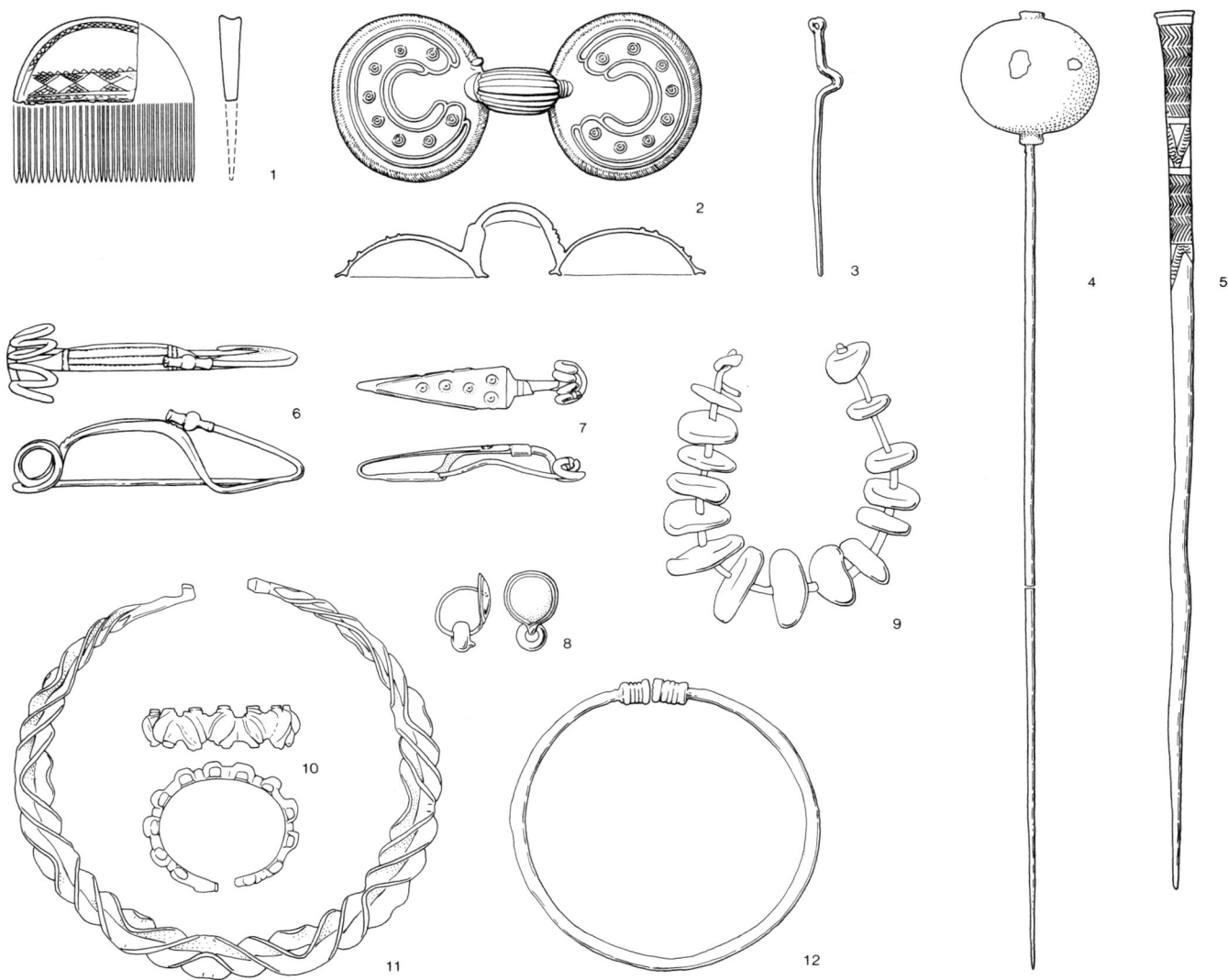

fig. 27.19
Comb and ornaments. Scale 1:3.

1	bone comb	Bovenkarspel	Late Bronze Age
2	bronze spectacle fibula, the pin is missing	Noordwijkerhout	Late Bronze Age
3	iron *Kropfnadel*	Colmschate	Early Iron Age
4	bronze *Bombenkopfnade*	Heerde	Late Bronze Age
5	bronze *Keulenkopfnadel*	Leidschendam	Late Bronze Age
6	bronze *Vasenkopfnadel*	Roden	Middle Iron Age
7	bronze *fibula*	Heemstede	Late Iron Age
8	bronze *Segelohrring* with a blue glass bead	Barger-Oosterveld	Middle Iron Age
9	leather thong with amber beads	Nieuw-Weerdinge	Early Iron Age
10	bronze bracelet	Wessem	Late Iron Age
11	bronze neckring	Uddel	Early Iron Age
12	iron neckring	Oss-IJsselstraat	Middle Iron Age

ered provide any information on the way in which they were worn. This also holds for ornaments found in graves: as the standard rite consisted in burying the cremation remains collected from the extinguished pyre, we do not know for certain how the deceased had worn the ornaments with which they were incidentally buried. In surrounding areas, for example the central Rhine region and the Ardennes, where inhumation started to prevail again in the Iron Age, close study of the positions of the ornaments in relation to the different parts of the skeletons has revealed general patterns. For example, at the end of the Early Iron Age (Hallstatt D) only women were buried accompanied by numerous metal ornaments in the central Rhine region. Identified ornaments include earrings, hair rings, neckrings, bracelets and belt ornaments. The combinations of ornaments differed according to age and social rank, while regional differences are also observable.[66] Several metal ornaments have been found in the Lower Rhine area, but we do not know how they were worn. There are indications suggesting that neckrings and bracelets were worn by both women and men.[67]

As for the types of metals used, gold and silver are conspicuously rare. Bronze was most frequently used for ornaments. The fact that iron was also used to manufacture ornaments from the beginning of the Iron Age onwards is in our eyes remarkable. From this we may infer that this new, stubborn material had a special value. That it was also associated with masculinity, in Central Europe at least, can be inferred from the frequent use of iron for male ornaments and for articles for grooming beards, such as depilating pincers and razors.[68] The iron pins found in the male elite graves of Oss and Haps justify the assumption that iron was associated with masculinity in the Lower Rhine area, too.

Amber was used in jewellery throughout the entire period dealt with here. It was used for pendants and beads, but it was also incorporated in metal neckrings. Bracelets made from stone are a new, but rare, phenomenon in this period.[69]

Until the Late Iron Age glass was used exclusively for beads, sometimes of many colours. Glass bracelets were introduced around 200 BC. Manufactured in different colours and designs (one- to seven-ribbed), they remained exceptionally popular (female) ornaments until in the early part of the Roman period, at least in the rivers area in the east of the Netherlands. Some of these glass ornaments are not round and closed; they are probably fragments of bracelets that were secondarily bent into a more or less round shape (plate 41A). They could have been used as pendants at the most. This has led to the hypothesis that the bracelets were objects of a standardised value ('primitive money'), which were divided into halves and parts like coins.[70] However, the lack of hoards and the large number of fragments found mixed with settlement waste make this hypothesis rather unconvincing.

From grave finds we may infer that horses were also adorned. The rich Early Iron Age graves of Oss, Wijchen and Havelte have yielded harness and/or yoke decorations. The most beautiful examples of what are thought to have been harness decorations are those from Anloo and Helden, dating from the first half of the Middle Iron Age and around the beginning of our era, respectively.[71] The treasure from Anloo includes nine objects of bronze, among which are two skilfully executed openwork discs showing a multitude of wheel motifs. The gold-plated silver ornamental disc from Helden (fig. 29.9 and plate 48A) is decorated with a scene dominated by animals executed in relief suggestive of Thracian origins.

Warrior equipment

In the graves male identity is expressed chiefly in the form of warrior equipment. There are reasons for assuming that metal weapons were not common property, but were reserved for a social elite. The nature of the weapons changed in the

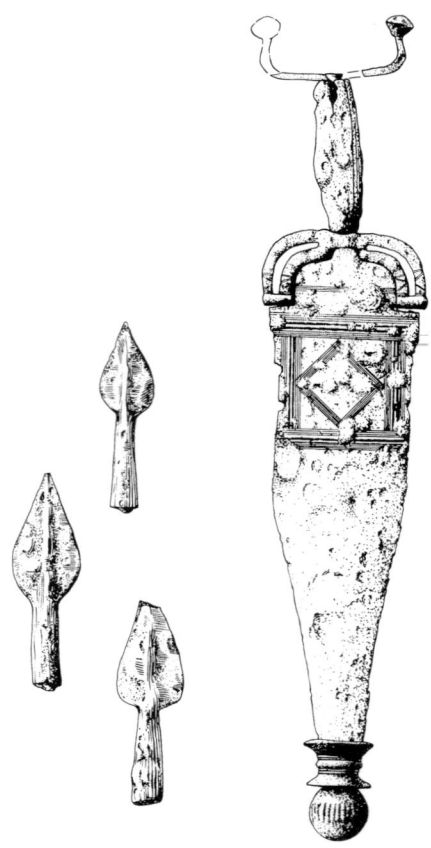

fig. 27.20

The weapons from the richest burial of Haps: three arrowheads and a dagger in its decorated scabbard. The objects are all of iron. Scale 1:3.

course of the last millennium BC, in line with new customs developing in Central Europe. Swords, which, along with spears, had prevailed in the period after the Middle Bronze Age, disappeared in the 6th century BC, when they were replaced by daggers, bows and arrows and (later?) spears (fig. 27.20).[72]

The unique discovery of a chariot in a grave at Nijmegen is insufficient evidence that chariots were actually used in warfare. In areas so far north of the region where chariots were fairly common attributes of the elite, i.e. southern Belgium, northern France and the Middle Rhine area, they are more likely to have been status symbols. The same holds for the weapons in general: in the Early Iron Age in particular they formed the basis of a warrior ideology, which will also have found ritual and ceremonial expression.[73]

An object less obviously associated with weapons, but which will certainly have been used as such, is the axe. Although axes were also used as tools, elite burials such as those of Oss, Rhenen and Wijchen suggest that they had a martial function, too.

In the course of the Middle Iron Age the deceased started to be disposed of in archaeologically less visible ways, which means that we know very little about warrior equipment from then onwards until the end of the Iron Age, when the slim iron long swords made their appearance. With their great lengths, sometimes more than 90 cm, these swords were extremely suitable weapons for horsemen (fig. 27.21).[74] The iron and bronze sheet scabbards in which some of these swords have been found must have been suspended from belts with metal belt-hooks (plate 47B).

From Caesar's *De Bello Gallico* we know what weapons the tribe of the Eburones, who lived in the region now known as the Campine, used in their first clashes with the Romans (54 BC). The passages that appear to refer to foot soldiers mention javelins. The conspiring Eburones, Nervii and Atuatuci later attacked a Roman camp with burning arrows and red-hot sling shots of fired clay. The latter can be identified as the roughly egg-shaped objects of fired clay which have been found virtually exclusively to the south of the Rhine, outside the coastal region (fig. 27.22). Such objects have been found among settlement remains from the beginning of the Middle Iron Age onwards, but the greatest number date from

fig. 27.21
Iron long sword recovered from the Meuse near Lith. The hilt consists of bronze discs, which will have covered some perishable material originally. Swords of this design have been found predominantly in the rivers area in the eastern part of the Netherlands. They are assumed to date from the 1st century BC. Scale 1:6.

fig. 27.22
Fired clay sling shots were used from the Middle Iron Age until in the Roman period. They were incidentally buried as grave goods, but most are known from settlements. A concentration like this one, from a Late Iron Age settlement ditch in Oss, is however rare.

around the beginning of our era. The subsequent disappearance of this weapon is to be ascribed to the impact of the Romans, who did not tolerate skirmishes between the native populations they subdued.[75]

NOTES

1 Butler 1973, 1979b.

2 Butler 1986.

3 See also O'Connor 1980, besides the aforementioned publications by Butler.

4 For example Dijkman 1989, 39; Van Heeringen 1992, Pl. XLV; Van der Sanden 1987g, 93; see also Simons 1989, Taf. 15:17-19.

5 This is probably an early specimen, which was still shaped according to the preceding tradition. Remains of the wooden haft yielded a ^{14}C date of 2540 ± 50 BP (Verwers 1988, 30-31).

6 Unpublished find, discovered beneath an occupation layer containing pottery from the 7th century BC. For the findspot see Neijenhuis 1983.

7 The few metal finds from the Early and Middle Iron Age may moreover reflect an actual scarcity of metal objects in this period (N. Roymans, pers. com.).

8 Charles 1984.

9 Van der Waals/Butler 1976; Van der Waals 2001.

10 Achterop/Brongers 1979. For dates see Fokkens 1991a, 137, and Groenendijk 1993, 104.

11 Groenendijk 1993, 104-105.

12 Dijkman 1989, 39 and 78 ff, Willems 1986b, 218, and Modderman 1960-'61a, 244 ff, respectively.

13 What is believed to have been a (metal) file dating from the Middle Iron Age was found at Son en Breugel (North Brabant) (Van den Broeke 1980a, 59).

14 Joachim 1980; Wilhelmi 1982.

15 Roymans 1991, 34 ff; Warmenbol 1988.

16 Kooi 1983a; Van der Sanden 1992b.

17 Jope 1961, 333, no 15.

18 Cf. Rowlands 1973.

19 Haarnagel 1984, 301.

20 Cf. Pressmar 1979.

21 Horst (Limburg): Schatorjé 1986; Willems 1984, 372-374; 1985, 163-164.

22 The reconstruction of a (domed) kiln found at Bemmel (Bloemers/ Hulst 1983, 111) is highly hypothetical in view of the nature of the remains recovered. The rare remains of kilns above ground that have been found in the Lower Rhine area are more indicative of an open-top updraft kiln (cf. e.g. Hinz 1964, Abb. 2:17; Knippels 1991, fig. 8.2; Willems 1984, fig. 14; for the similar hearth collars see Boersma 1976). A removable dome with a lid (and a flue hole) may have rested on the rim, or the load in the kiln may have been covered with for example sherds.

23 Cf. Van den Broeke 1987b, 102.

24 E.g. Stolp 1983; Van Trierum 1992, 81.

25 Flamman 1993; see also Harck 1984a, 296.

26 Van der Leeuw et al. 1987; Franken/Kalsbeek 1984. The use of a leather mould, which the aforementioned authors considered essential in the manufacture of a certain type of Marne pottery, is less likely.

27 Various secondary uses are suggested in Van Heeringen 1992 and Stolp 1983.

28 Bloemers et al. 1981, 71, and Theunissen 1990, respectively.

29 Collis 1984, 15.

30 Van Doorselaer et al. 1987, 40 ff.

31 Van der Leeuw et al. 1987; Van den Broeke 1987b.

32 Especially Van den Broeke 1980a 1984, 1987b; Dehn 1950; probably also several cases in Dijkman 1989, especially plate 1; see also Modderman 1960-'61b.

33 Waterbolk 1962; Verwers 1972. For grave pottery see also Desittere 1968; Kooi 1979; Ruppel 1990; Schoenfelder 1992; Verlinde 1987.

34 Waterbolk 1962, 1977b; see also Taayke 1988.

35 Especially Van den Broeke 1987a, 1987b, 1991; Van Heeringen 1992; Taayke 1988.

36 Peddemors 1975.

37 Roymans/Van Rooijen 1993.

38 Cf. Van Heeringen 1992, tables 57 and 59.

39 Loewe 1971, 35; Wilhelmi 1977b. However, a few triangular weights with three holes through the flat side, which were common in the Roman period, have been found in contexts suggesting that they were (secondarily?) used as net weights. Three such triangular weights were found together with eleven round ones, with only one hole, at the bottom of a tributary of the Rhine near Valkenburg (South Holland) (Bult/Hallewas 1987, 14).

40 Cf. Wilhelmi 1977b, Abb. 1 and Tuohy 1992, respectively. For similarities in decoration compare Van Trierum 1992, fig. 71:5, with Coles 1987a, figs. 3.37-3.46. For the applications see also Ryder 1993.

41 Groenendijk 1993, 119.

42 Roymans 1991, 51.

43 Roymans/Van der Sanden 1980; Roymans 1990, 131-134.

44 Roymans/Van der Sanden 1980.

45 J.N. Lanting, pers. com.; see also Van Heeringen 1992, 29 and 268; Van Trierum 1992, 30.

46 Pare 1987; Roymans 1991, 43 ff.

47 Bloemers 1986.

48 Van der Poel 1960-'61, 159. A ^{14}C date recently obtained for one of the two ard shares from Echten (Drenthe) has solved some of the uncertainty regarding the age of the Dutch finds. The ard share in question was found to date from the Early Iron Age (Van der Sanden 1993-'94).

49 Van Heeringen 1992, 25-West-9, period 5.

50 Van Heeringen 1992, 329; see also Zimmermann 1984, 256.

51 Van Gijn 1988, 1992. The majority of the flint sickles date from the Late Bronze Age and the Early Iron Age (Van Heeringen 1992, 320), but the oldest appear to have been produced in the Middle Bronze Age (B) already (Butler 1990, 94).

52 Cf. IJzereef 1981, 133 ff.

53 Harsema 1979a; Van Heeringen 1985.

54 For such material see e.g. Kars/Kars 1992 and Miedema 1983, 279-282.

55 Van den Broeke 1987b, 103; Taayke 1990b, 117.

56 This function could however not be confirmed in the case of the only example that has so far yielded information on its contents (that from Riethoven, North Brabant), probably because of its assumed secondary use for a different purpose (Vanderhoeven 1991, 153 ff). See also Roymans 1977.

57 Oudemans/Boon 1993.

58 Horst 1985, 98 ff; Lambot 1988. For dates see also Van den Broeke 1991, 206; Hutrelle et al. 1989, 204 ff.

59 Van den Broeke 1987b. For open types with perforated bases see also e.g. Van den Broeke 1984, fig. 10:1; Taayke 1990, 186-187. And for the Roman period: Van der Leeuw et al. 1987, fig. 11.22:13; Schatorjé 1985.

60 Groenendijk 1993, especially fig. 72. A few other types of wooden vessels have been recovered from Iron Age wells at Oss-Ussen, viz a bucket and a 90-cm-tall tub with lugs (Schinkel 1994, 116 and 176).

61 Roymans 1990, 85 (Rossum/Lith); 1991, 37 ff.

62 Mariën 1987 and Van Impe/Creemers 1991, respectively.

63 Van der Sanden 1990, 216.

64 Butler 1965, 1986 and Van Heeringen 1992, 104, respectively.

65 Roymans/Van der Sanden 1980; Roymans/Derks 1990, 1994b.

66 Joachim 1970, 1994b, 1985; Haffner 1976. See also Heynowski 1992.

67 Heynowski (1992) and others have pointed out the possibility of certain ornaments later becoming characteristic of the opposite sex.

68 Spindler 1983, 228-229.

69 Brongers/Woltering 1978, 104 ff., and Van Heeringen 1986a, respectively.

70 Willems 1983a, 110-112.

71 Beuker et al. 1991, 42, and De Grooth 1987a, respectively.

72 A survey is to be found in Roymans 1991, 38.

73 Roymans 1991, 56 ff.

74 Roymans 1991; Verwers/Ypey 1975.

75 Our understanding of the material culture has increased substantially since this contribution was written. Dissertations on the (northern) pottery have been published by Taayke (1996) and Woltering (2000). The contents of the rich Iron Age burials of Drenthe have been systematically inventoried by De Wit (1997-'98); none of those burial contents are however comparable with those of Rhenen, where a counterpart of the chariot burial of Wijchen has been found (Van Heeringen 1998-'99). Grave goods have moreover shown that glass bracelets were specifically female ornaments in the Lower Rhine area, too (Roymans 1996c). Thanks to the unexpected discovery of dozens of Iron Age inhumation burials (see feature R) we also know more about how metal ornaments were worn. And the results of a detailed study of triquetrum coins enable us to follow the movements of the Batavi (Roymans 2001).

Q Ancient attire
Remains of prehistoric clothing

Willy Groenman-van Waateringe

The oldest remains of clothing that have been found in Europe are fragments of a fabric woven from linen and other plant fibres datable to the Neolithic. Some parts of the equipment required to make such fabrics, such as spindle whorls and parts of looms, have also survived from this period. But what Neolithic clothing actually looked like we do not really know. All that has survived to give us some impression of what people wore in those days are a few pointed caps and a shoe made of some plant matter, which were found in Switzerland and southern Germany, respectively. For the rest we have to rely on representations of human figures in the form of figurines and illustrations scratched in bone, antler or stone. That is why the discovery made in 1991 in the Hauslabjoch, at the Austrian/Italian border, is so very important. The man who had been frozen in the glacier ice along with his clothing and other belongings for more than five thousand years has already yielded a wealth of information.[1]

For more information on prehistoric clothing we must skip several centuries and turn to the Middle Bronze Age. Thanks to the specific conditions of raised bogs, especially those in Northwest Europe, which favour the preservation of textile, fur and leather, the topic of 'prehistoric clothing' is not a complete mystery to us. In the Netherlands, too, many exceptional finds have come to light in the recent past, especially in the nineteenth and early-twentieth centuries, when vast expanses of peat were dug away in the

province of Drenthe. Most of these finds were discovered by chance; proper scientific surveys and excavations were never really carried out in those days. Because of this we know very little about the contexts from which the finds were recovered.

Most of the shoes have originally been dated via pollen analysis of adhering peat remains.[2] Recently, ^{14}C dates have however been obtained for almost all the shoes recovered from bogs. Those dates show that the chronological order is correct, but that the shoes are all younger than previously assumed on the basis of palynological evidence.[3]

Leather and fur

The earliest item of prehistoric clothing found in the Netherlands is a single shoe datable to the Middle Bronze Age B, *i.e.* between 1500 and 1100 BC (fig. Q1). This shoe, which was found in the Buinerveen around 1874, consists of an oval piece of leather with approximately 2-cm-long slits along the edge (fig. Q2: 1). A thong threaded through the slits served to fasten the shoe around the ankle. Impressions visible in the leather indicate that the shoe was also held in place by thongs tied around the foot. As regards both shape and thonging, the shoe bears a close resemblance to a Neolithic shoe of bark found in southern Germany[4] and to the shoes of the man from the Hauslabjoch.[5]

Other Middle Bronze Age shoes were likewise made from what were essentially oval pieces of leather, only the oval was cut somewhat straighter at the heel, where it was sewn together (fig. Q2: 2-4). The next step was to cut two small notches in the right edge of the oval so that the heel of the shoe fitted more closely around the foot (fig. Q2: 5-6). Only later were attempts made to fit the shoe more closely around the front part of the foot, too, by cutting deep incisions at the front and along the sides (plate 43A).

Even rarer than shoes are other garments of leather or fur. Although some of the old reports discussing the discoveries made in the peat mention fur cloaks, all that has been preserved are one fur cap and one fur cape. These two garments and a leather shoe were found with the Emmer-Erfscheidenveen bog body, which has been dated to the second half of the Middle Bronze Age.[6]

The cap (fig. Q3) was made of sheepskin. The animal's tail had been stripped off with the hide and formed a kind of tas-

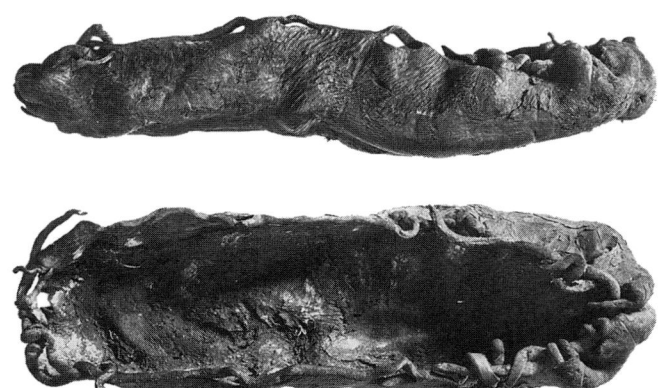

fig. Q1
Side and top views of a Bronze Age shoe recovered from the Buinerveen peat. Length 26.8 cm.

weaving technique employed is the clothing of the Emmer-Erfscheidenveen bog body and that of the 'Yde girl'.[7]

The woollen remains that were recovered from the Emmen-Erfscheidenveen consist of four fragments of a woven garment and a braided band. The woollen garment was made from a coarse plain-weave fabric (fig. Q4: 4). 'Plain weave' means that one weft thread passes alternately over and under one warp thread. The warp and weft threads were both made from 0.8-1.3-mm thick S-spun yarns (fig. Q4: 1). The wool itself was of a very fine quality and may have been of a light colour originally, before the many centuries in the peat turned it the brown colour it has today. The hems of the woollen garment were all decorated with a border of single S-spun yarns that had been twisted round one another in a Z direction so as to form a smooth plied thread (fig. Q4: 3). These threads were woven – two up, one down – through a loose structure of rows of whip stitches, the first row of which was used to fasten the garment's turned-back hem (plate 43B).

The shape of the fragments leads to a reconstruction of an undergarment (fig. Q5) that is reminiscent of men's clothing

fig.Q2

Typological sequence of prehistoric footwear from Drenthe. Scale 1:6.

Date:		Findspots:	
1-4	Middle Bronze Age B	1	Buinerveen
5-6	Iron Age	2, 5	Barger-Compascuum
		3, 4	Emmer-Erfscheidenveen
		6	Klazienaveen

sel worn with the furry side inside. The cape consisted of at least five pieces of skin, presumably of a calf. The cape was probably also worn with the fur inside, just like the cap.

Woollen clothing

Old find reports mention breeches, a smock, a tunic, a cloak and a mitten of wool, but very little of all this has been preserved. All that remains for analysis of the design and the

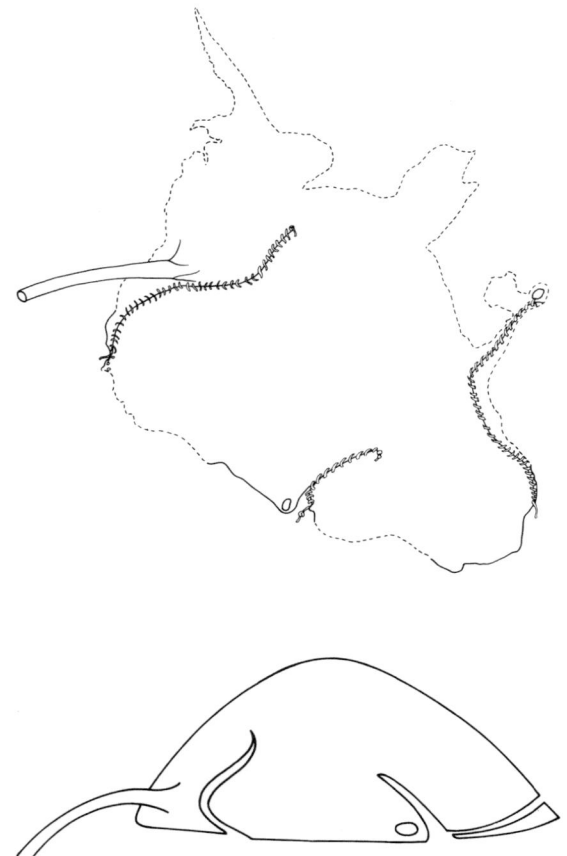

fig. Q3

Emmer-Erfscheidenveen: sheepskin cap (top) and reconstruction (bottom). Scale 1:5.

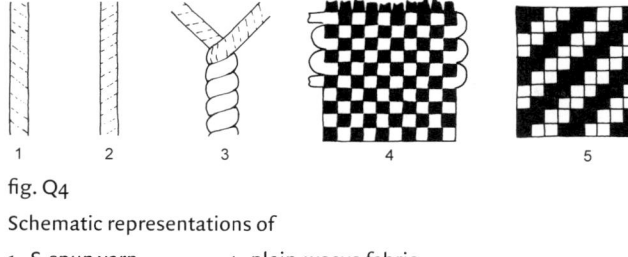

fig. Q4

Schematic representations of

1 S-spun yarn	4 plain-weave fabric
2 Z-spun yarn	5 two-over-two twill
3 twisted yarn	

found in Denmark: a more or less rectangular piece of cloth with what look like shoulder straps projecting at the top corners. The garment was wrapped around the body beneath the armpits so that the projecting flaps stuck up at the front, near the shoulders. The garment was held together by a belt or a band around the middle. The remains of seams indicate that the garment from the Emmer-Erfscheidenveen must have been composed of several smaller pieces. A loop was attached to one of the top corners of one of the fragments.

Besides this garment a braided band finished with whip stitches was found. The band was ten centimetres long and between one and two centimetres wide. Like the aforementioned loop, it may have formed part of the fastening of the woollen garment.

The 'Yde girl' (plate 48B) has been dated to the beginning of our era. This bog body was accompanied by a 'cloak' and a woollen band, with which she was strangled. The band was made according to the so-called *sprang* technique, which means that it was not woven but braided. Originally, it must have been about 215 centimetres long and four centimetres wide.

Six fragments remained of the 'cloak'. Together they constitute a garment of either 114 x 132 cm or 192 x 90 cm. The fabric was woven from irregularly spun yarn in a two-over-two twill weave (fig. Q4:5), which means that the weft threads were first passed over and then under two warp threads in a staggered pattern. Dark brown bands of varying width were woven into the light brown garment. The fabric was slovenly woven; it shows several weaving faults. Nevertheless, various worn patches had been repaired, if also in

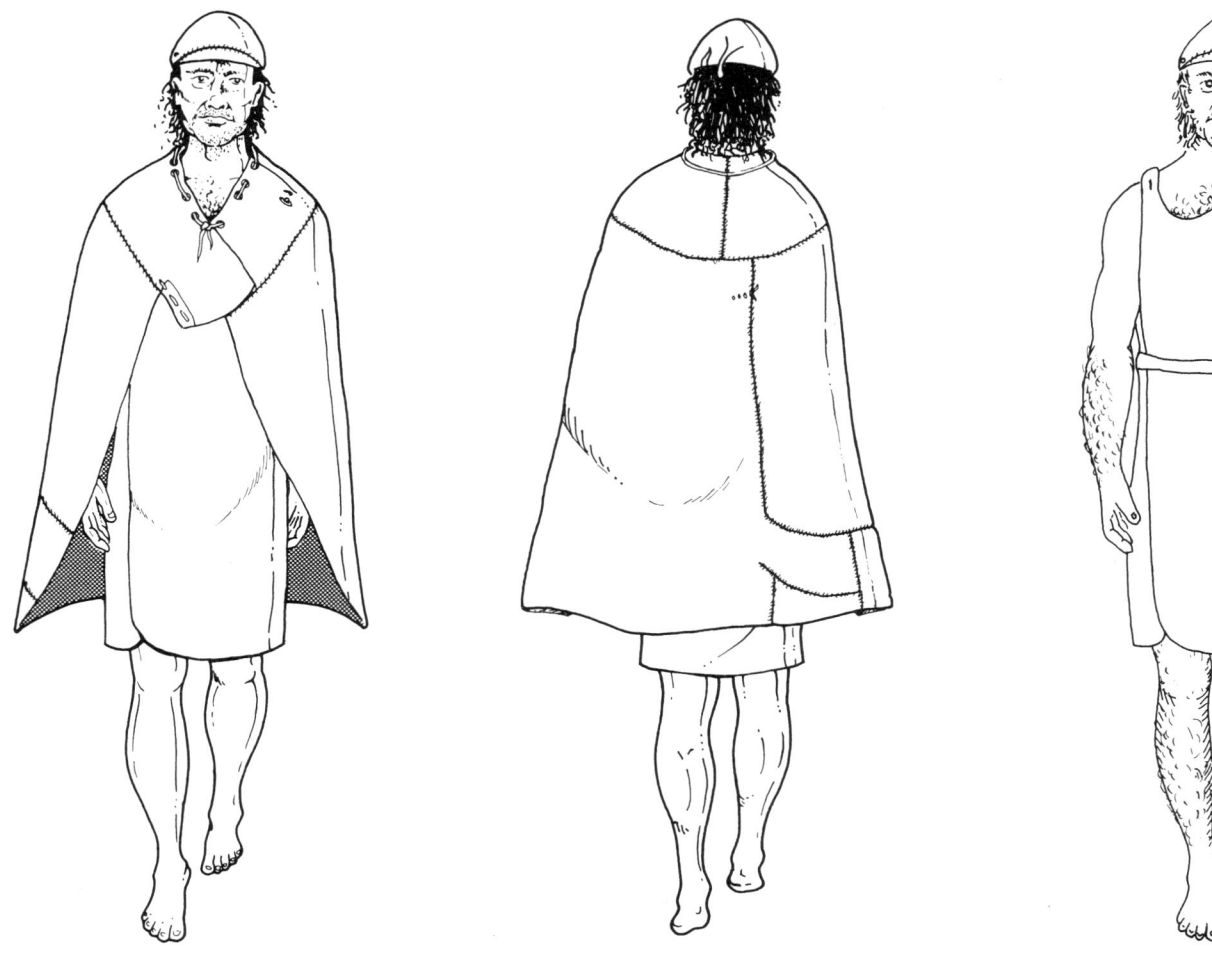

fig. Q5

Emmer-Erfscheidenveen Man wearing a fur cap, a cape and a woollen undergarment.

an extremely slovenly manner. Worn edges that had started to fray had been turned back and fastened to the inside of the garment.

In spite of their marked local character, the remains of clothing from the Middle Bronze Age phase B and from around the beginning of our era that have come to light in the Netherlands clearly belong in the technological and clothing traditions of Northwest Europe. Breeches, which are so conspicuously absent above, were not introduced until in the Iron Age, as we know from finds recovered from bogs in northwest Germany.

Notes

1   Höpfel *et al.* 1992.
2   Groenman-van Waateringe 1970, 1991, 2001.
3   This implies that the shoes were deliberately deposited beneath the surface of the peat. See also Lanting/Van der Plicht 2001-'02, 228-229.
4   Feldtkeller/Schlichtherle 1987.
5   Groenman-van Waateringe/Goedecker-Ciolek 1992.
6   Groenman-van Waateringe 1990, 2001; Van der Sanden 1990. An artist's impression of a reconstruction of this cape revised by S. Thijssen is to be found in Van der Sanden 1996, 148.
7   Vons-Comis 1990.

28 Urnfields and cinerary barrows Funerary and burial ritual in the Late Bronze and Iron Ages

Wilfried Hessing and Piet Kooi

THE CONTINUOUSLY CHANGING BURIAL RITES

In the Late Bronze Age fundamental changes took place in the burial rite practised in the Netherlands. In the Middle Bronze Age the burial of a small, select portion of the population beneath individual barrows had already started to give way to a more commonly adopted custom of burial beneath 'family barrows'. The next development involved the replacement of collective burials beneath a single, large barrow by individual burials in smaller funerary monuments erected close to one another. From this period onwards, almost the entire population was buried in a recognisable manner, at a fixed location. Over the ages, this led to the formation of extensive cemeteries in many places. These are now generally referred to as 'urnfields' – the term that was in the past used to describe such cemeteries in popular speech. In the Netherlands, about 500 cemeteries of this kind are known from archaeological excavation reports, surveys and records of discoveries made in the past.

In the southern Netherlands the gradual shift from inhumation to cremation was completed in the Middle Bronze Age period B, but in the central, western and northern parts of the country it was not to be generally adopted until later. This difference in the rate at which the new rite was adopted may explain why the burials from the early phase of the urnfield period in the northern part of the Netherlands show a greater degree of variation than those in the south. The earliest urnfields in the north were for example found to contain a few inhumation burials and *Brandskelettgräber* besides cremation burials (fig. 28.1). Little is still known about how the deceased were cremated in the Late Bronze Age and the Early Iron Age.

fig. 28.1
This burial monument near Vledder is typical of the early phase of the northern urnfields. The postholes of a mortuary house are visible inside an elongated ditched enclosure. At the centre is a burial containing cremated remains. The pit is large enough to have accommodated an uncremated body, as was common practice in the preceding period.

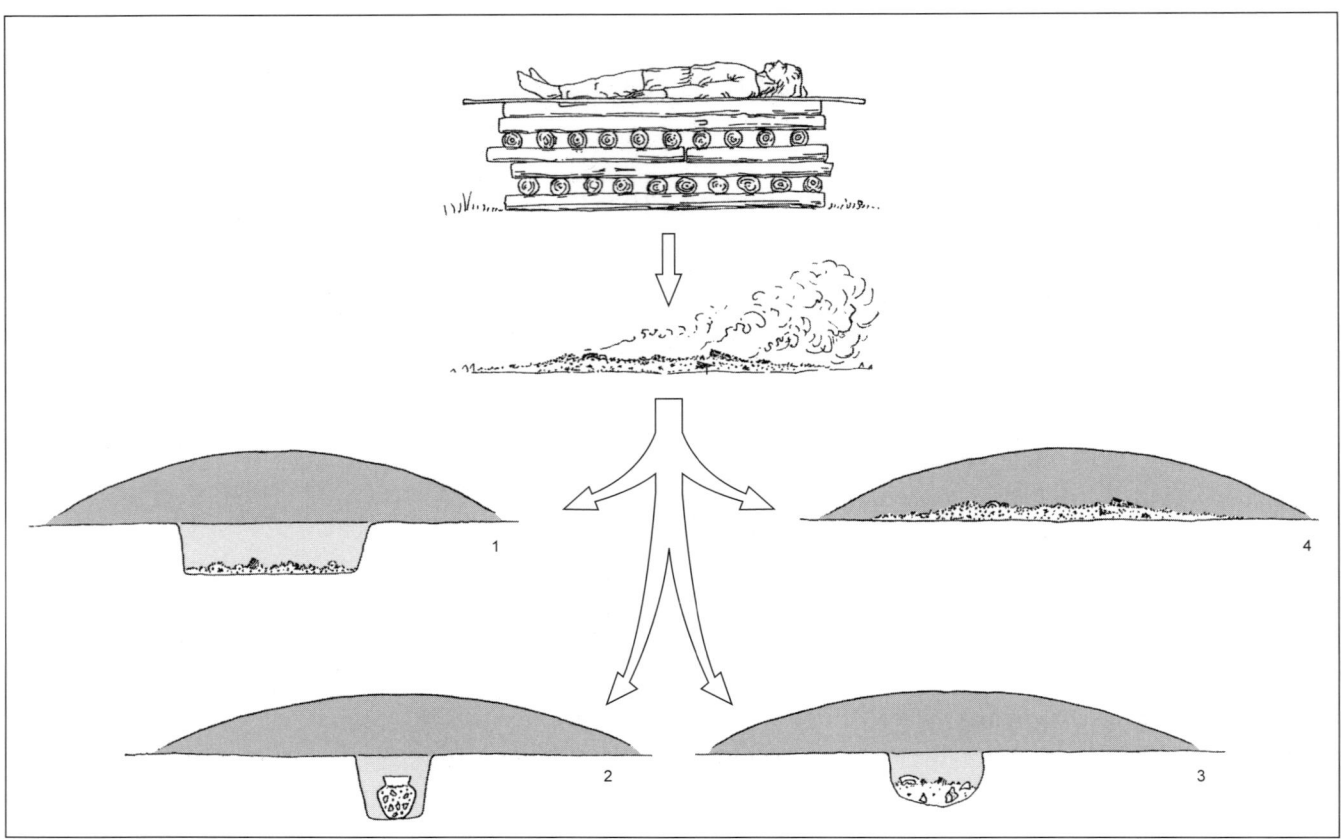

fig. 28.2

After a body had been cremated on top of or beneath a pyre the remains could be buried in various ways. Different forms of burial prevailed in different periods, among which were:

1 *Brandskelettgrab*: the bone remains were retrieved from the ashes and scattered in a pit having the size of a human body;

2 urn burial: the retrieved bone remains were deposited in an urn and buried in a small pit;

3 *Brandgrube*: the gathered remains of the pyre were deposited in a small pit. Such pits dating from the Iron Age often also contain burned pottery; apparently pottery was not burned along with the deceased in earlier periods;

4 cinerary barrow: a barrow was erected over the remains of the pyre.

The pyres themselves have been preserved only in exceptional cases.[1] The four-post structures that are sometimes encountered in the vicinity of burials cannot be unambiguously associated with pyres.[2]

Palynological research and the analysis of charcoal found among the cremated remains have shown that the pyres were constructed from wood that was available in the immediate surroundings.[3] We do not know how common it was to burn goods like foodstuffs, pottery or implements along with the deceased in the earliest phases of the urnfield period (fig. 28.2). In the Late Bronze Age the human remains were usually carefully collected from amongst the remains of the pyre and were then buried in a pit. From the Early Iron Age onwards increasingly more pyre remains and fewer human remains were buried in the pits. Around the end of the urnfield period this development culminated in the custom of covering the pyres themselves with a mound (cinerary barrows); many such buried pyres have been found in the northern part of the Netherlands in particular. Thanks to this development there is increasing evidence of pottery (containing foodstuffs) and clothing being burned along with the deceased within the last phases of this period.

REGIONAL DEVELOPMENTS

Traditionally, a distinction is made in Dutch archaeology between the urnfields in the northern part of the country and those in the south (fig. 28.3). This distinction is based partly on the aforementioned somewhat asynchronous developments in the two regions, especially in the early phase, but above all on the more general cultural difference between the north and the south, which is in part connected with the different origins of the new burial and pottery traditions in the two regions. The northern part of the country appears to have been influenced most by the traditions of the adjacent part of the North German Plain around Hanover (Ems culture) and to a lesser extent by those of the Münsterland, whereas the southern part formed part of the distribution area of the *Niederrheinische Grabhügelkultur*. Apart from this general distinction, a number of regional groups can be distinguished, most of which reveal close links with the middle Rhine region. In a wider context, the northern and the southern group are primarily to be regarded as two regional – northwestern – variants of the Central European Urnfield culture of the last centuries of the Bronze Age. The main characteristics of these variants are the low barrows surrounded by circular or elongated ditches that mark the cremation burials and the continuity of the new burial rite until well into the Iron Age. Most of the urnfields fell into disuse in the 5th century BC, but certain elements of the burial rite lived on until in the Roman period. In the Netherlands and the adjacent parts of Germany and Belgium the term 'urnfields' therefore does not refer to the Late Bronze Age alone.

The problem with such a north/south distinction is where to draw the line. This is particularly difficult when, as is the case in the Netherlands, the distinction is to some extent blurred by mutual influences and exchange. It may in fact be more correct to speak of two different geographical zones with overlapping networks of social relations and with unclear borders, which underwent various changes over the ages. Within this framework the central part of the Netherlands is then to be regarded as a transitional zone between the two core areas, comprising, roughly speaking, Drenthe and North Brabant/Limburg. The urnfields of this transitional zone show both typically 'northern' and typically 'southern' traits. It has been suggested that the term 'Gelderland group' should be used for this intermediate zone,[4] which is also classed as part of the distribution area of the *Niederrheinische Grabhügelkultur*. Future research will have to show whether it is justified to distinguish such a new, separate regional group.

An additional problem is that no Late Bronze Age or Iron Age cemeteries have so far been found in the western and northern coastal zone.[5] In this zone, cultural distinctions can be made only on the basis of stylistic differences in the (settlement) pottery, and not on the basis of the burial ritual.

THE SCARCITY OF BURIALS IN THE COASTAL ZONES

The few burials that have so far been recorded in the western and northern lowlands of the Netherlands consist of isolated inhumations within settlements.[6] In the whole of the coastal zone the remains of no more than a few dozen individuals from the entire Late Bronze Age and Iron Age have been found. Most of the burials were found immediately alongside or near a house or along the boundary of a farmyard. The positions of these burials and the evident care with which some of the remains were buried suggest that this form of disposal was not the general form of burial in the coastal area; it may have had a religious-ritual background and may have been some form of offering, for example. The small number of the burials further strengthens the conclusion that they are not ordinary burials, as was suggested for the human remains buried in Late Bronze Age settlements in Westfrisia.[7] In addition to these burials, small numbers of disarticulated human bones have frequently been found within settlements. Some of the bones themselves showed indications of ritual activities.[8] But even if we regard these disarticulated bones as the remains of disturbed inhumation burials, the total number of inhumations is still much smaller than would be expected if inhumation had been the common form of burial. Perhaps these groups of bones are more comparable

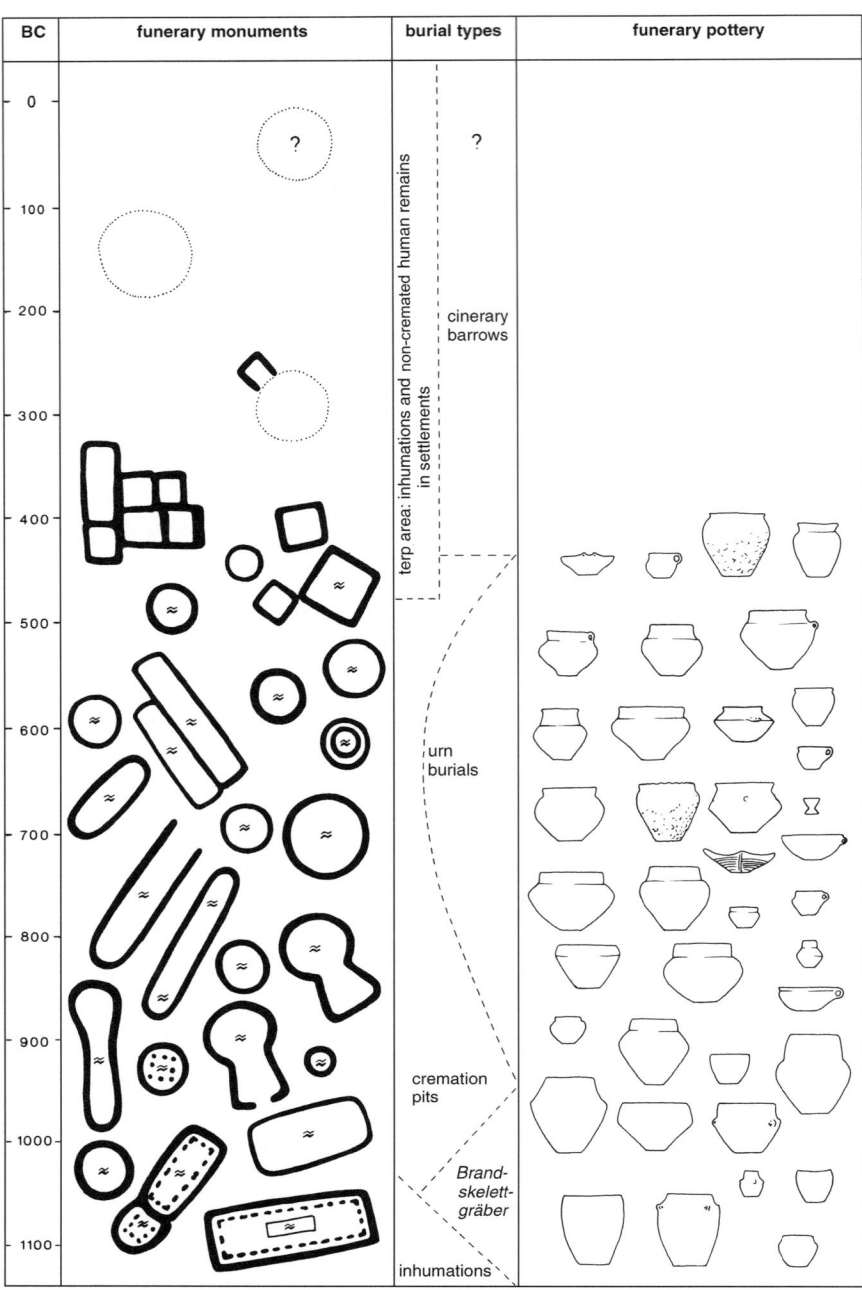

fig. 28.3a

Survey of burial monuments, different forms of burial and funerary pottery from the Late Bronze Age and the Iron Age in the northern part of the Netherlands.

with the bog bodies of Drenthe (see feature S). Unless the dead were disposed of in an entirely different manner, for example by means of aboveground exposure or excarnation, as has recently been suggested for large parts of Iron Age England,[9] we must assume that cremation was also the common custom in the western and northern parts of the Netherlands.

A more plausible explanation for the absence of cremation burials and urnfields in the coastal region concerns this region's specific environmental conditions. It is possible that the dynamic development of the landscape precluded the formation of occupation areas containing fixed cemeteries that could be used for a long period of time. We know for sure that the coastal zone was much less densely populated than the rest of the Netherlands in the Late Bronze Age and the Early Iron Age. Small cemeteries that were used for only a short period of time have poorer archaeological visibility. The chance of such cemeteries being discovered is even smaller when the employed burial rite leaves fewer archaeologically recoverable

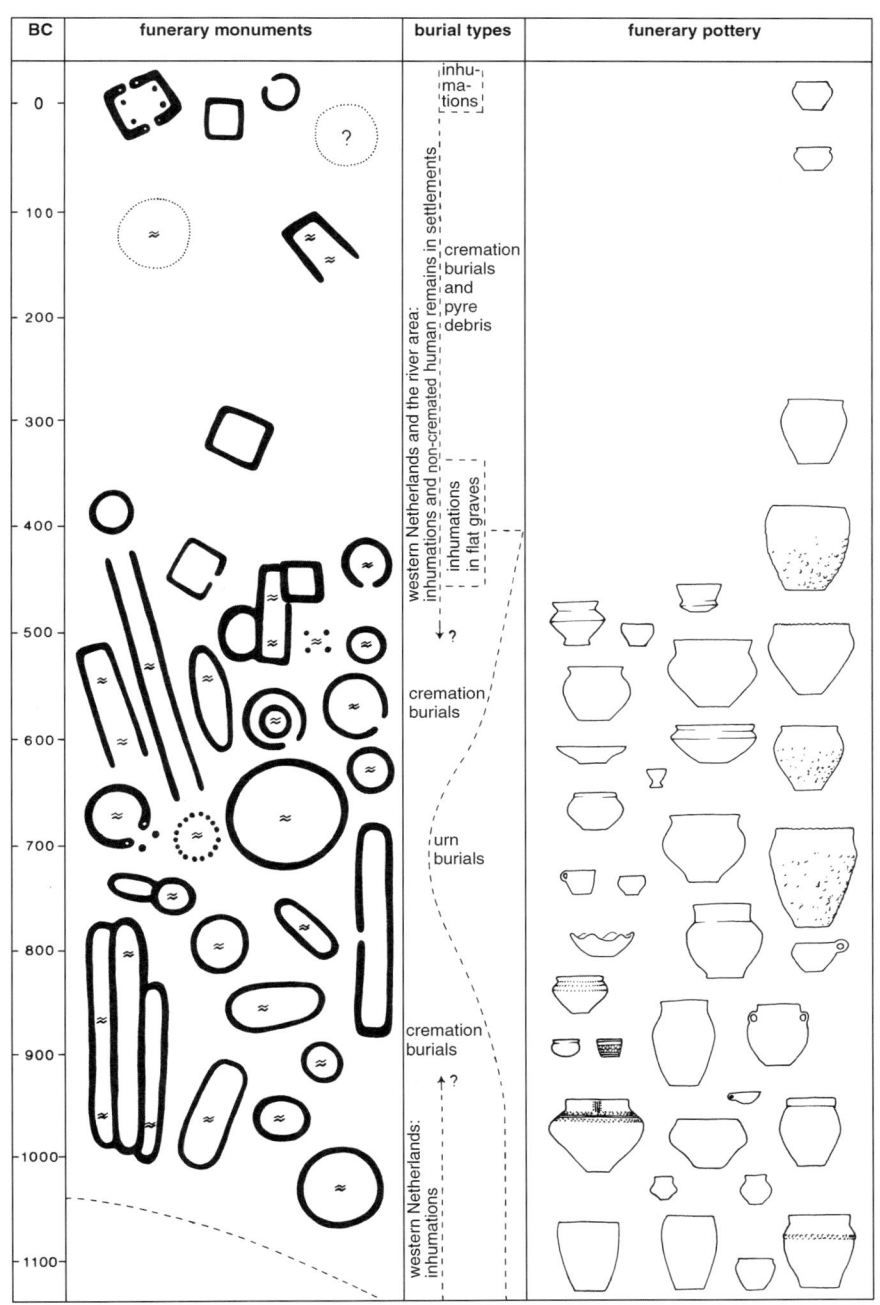

fig. 28.3b

Survey of burial monuments, different forms of burial and funerary pottery from the Late Bronze Age and the Iron Age in the southern part of the Netherlands.

traces than the rites that were commonly practised in the east and the south of the country in that period.[10] Moreover if, due to a shortage of suitable arable land, the deceased were buried in areas of marginal soils that were exposed to erosion and sedimentation or that have been dug away in later times (large parts of the inland dunes in the west of the Netherlands have for example disappeared in large-scale reclamation projects) the chances of discovering burials are very small.

BURIAL RITES UNTIL IN THE MIDDLE IRON AGE

The northern part of the Netherlands

In the north of the Netherlands the oldest funerary monuments containing the remains of deceased who were cremated according to the new custom are those with postholes that are assumed to be the remains of so-called mortuary houses (figs. 28.1 and 28.3). The mortuary houses whose postholes have been found in the urnfields of, for example, Gasteren, Vledder, Losser and Laudermarke[11] consisted of rectangular structures that comprised parallel pairs of posts along their long sides and one or two posts along their short sides. The regular distances between the postholes show that the structures must have been roofed. The sizes of the structures varied from 1.5 x 3 m (Zuidwolde) to 3 x 20 m (Gasteren). The central burial was covered with a low mound, which was surrounded by a rectangular ditch. These early burials still differ considerably in nature. At Gasteren a late inhumation burial was even found in one of the mortuary houses. Some of the burials are known as *Brandskelettgräber* – graves in which the cremated remains were scattered across the floor of a pit with the dimensions of a normal inhumation grave. In other cases the cremated human remains were carefully collected and then buried in a pit, sometimes contained in an urn. Eight ^{14}C dates have been obtained for barrows containing mortuary houses. These dates, from Vledder, Anloo and Holsloot, range from 3080 ± 45 BP to 2860 ± 35 BP,[12] which means that this type of monument started to be constructed in the Netherlands in the 12th century BC or even a little earlier. Postholes observed at the corners of earlier (inhumation) graves beneath barrows, for example beneath barrow 75 on the Noordse Veld near Zeijen (fig. 19.4),[13] and in groups of flat graves, show that the mortuary houses may represent the continuation of an older native tradition.

Another early, but simpler, variant of this type of funerary monument consists of a low mound surrounded by a rectangular ditch without a mortuary house. Such barrows have been found at, for example, Emmerhout, Noordbarge and Sleen. A ^{14}C date of 2935 ± 35 BP has been obtained for the central burial beneath one of these mounds, i.e. in the 12th/11th century BC.

A slightly younger type of monument, with an enclosure in the shape of a keyhole, seems to have originated in Westphalia. These monuments comprise a central burial beneath a small round mound, surrounded by a ditch enclosing a forecourt. The forecourt is generally oriented towards the southeast; some of the ditches were associated with causeways indicating that the forecourt may be regarded as an entrance.[14] The small circles of postholes that were found to surround some of the burials at Mander, Erica and Emmerhout may be relics of an older type of monument. The diameters of the surrounding ditches vary from 4 m at Sleen to 22 m at Noordbarge (plate 44A). Urnfields containing several barrows surrounded by keyhole enclosures have been found at Wessinghuizen, Buinen, Sleen and Noordbarge. Four ^{14}C dates have been obtained for the keyhole-shaped monuments in the northern part of the Netherlands; they range from 2990 ± 35 to 2810 ± 35 BP (approx. 12th-10th century BC).[15] This same period saw the appearance of the round barrows surrounded by circular ditched enclosures that were to remain the most common monuments throughout the rest of the urnfield period.

After this early phase the funerary monuments became more uniform in construction but varied in size. The round barrows surrounded by circular ditches vary in diameter from less than 1 m to over 13 m.[16] In some cases it was found that no ditch had been dug around a round barrow. As most of the urnfields have been completely levelled over the ages, monuments of this kind usually pass unobserved, the burials being recorded as unmarked graves.

Elongated mounds flanked by parallel ditches extending around one or both ends of the mound started to be constructed at the end of the Bronze Age. In Dutch archaeology the term *lange bedden* (literally: 'long beds') is usually used for these monuments. They are divided into different types on the basis of their shape and dimensions.[17] The burial is often situated in the middle of the central axis, as observed in the urnfields of Noordbarge and Havelte. Sometimes, however, it lies off-centre, occasionally even at one of the ends, as at Wapse. At Dwingeloo and Norg postholes were observed on either side of the burial; the posts apparently served to mark the position of the burial.

Around the 6th century BC rectangular and square ditched enclosures made their appearance. Small groups of large enclosures have been found at, for example, Den Hool, Eext and Noordbarge (7 x 7 m and 7 x 20 m, plate 44B). Larger complexes, as observed at Ruinen, Het Hunnenkerkhof near Oosterhesselen and Raalte,[18] consist largely of sets of linked smaller enclosures. In this same period it became increasingly common to bury the whole pyre beneath a mound instead of only the human remains collected from amongst the pyre remains. Such mounds are known as 'cinerary barrows'. They often lie within square ditched enclosures. Large groups of cinerary barrows have been found on the Noordse Veld near Zeijen, in the Tumulibos near Balloo, near the Galgenberg to the north of Sleen, and in Raalte. The earliest ^{14}C date obtained for a cinerary barrow (at Ruinen) is 2510 ± 50 BP. The youngest date so far is 2300 ± 35 BP (4th century BC), which was obtained for a barrow on the Hijkerveld.

Throughout the entire Late Bronze Age and Early Iron Age, existing monuments were used to accommodate new burials. This custom reached its height in the Early Iron Age. The secondary burials found in the northern part of the Netherlands show strong influences from the Hanover region in Germany, associated with the use of specific types of urns, namely vessels with fairly straight walls with partly roughened surfaces (Harpstedt ware, plate 40A). It was mostly older monuments that were used for these secondary burials, for example Bronze Age barrows, as at Diever and Eext, but sometimes mounds surrounded by circular ditches were used, as for example at Noordbarge and Wapse.[19] Many of the later cinerary barrows also contain secondary burials. The large groups of urn burials found in a drift sand dune between Emmen and Weerdinge and in a barrow at Noordbarge are exceptions to the rule of secondary use of barrows in the Iron Age.

The southern part of the Netherlands

The rectangular enclosures surrounding a mortuary house and usually a *Brandskelettgrab* that mark the transition to the urnfield period in the northern part of the Netherlands have not been found south of Twente. The records describing the only monument that shows any affinities with this type to the south of the Rhine, in the urnfield of Knegsel,[20] are too incomplete to allow any sound statements to be made. The keyhole-shaped enclosures also seem to be a northern phenomenon. Features bearing some resemblance to this type of enclosure have been found at Valkenswaard, Achel-Pastoorsbos (Belgium), Haps and Knegsel,[21] but it is not certain whether they are datable to the urnfield period and, even if they are, they are nowadays usually interpreted as combinations of a circular enclosure and a long bed.[22]

As in the northern part of the Netherlands, a – small – number of features have been found that recall the circular settings of postholes within Bronze Age barrows (fig. 28.3). However, they appear to date from both the early and the later phases of the southern urnfields and can hence not simply be regarded as indications of a transitional form of barrow. Several round and elongated variants are known.[23] From their very beginnings, in the 11th century BC,[24] the urnfields of the southern Netherlands are essentially characterised by two types of funerary monuments: low mounds surrounded by a round ditch without an entrance and elon-

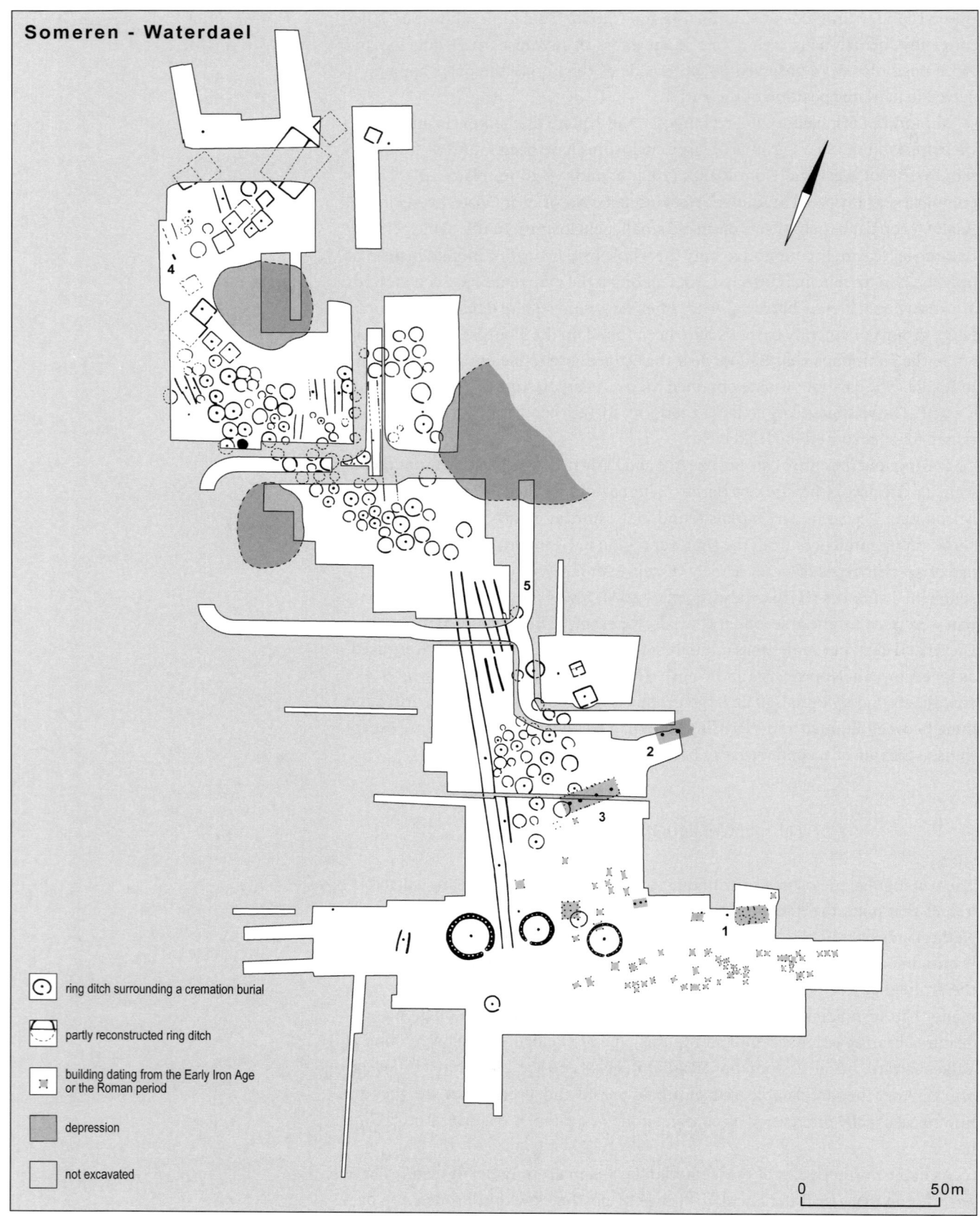

Someren - Waterdael

ring ditch surrounding a cremation burial

partly reconstructed ring ditch

building dating from the Early Iron Age
or the Roman period

depression

not excavated

0   50m

fig. 28.4
Survey of the urnfield and other features at Someren-Waterdael. Scale 1:2000.

Legend:
1   Early Iron Age farm
2/3 farms from the early Roman period
4   Middle Iron Age inhumation burial
5   inhumation burial dating from the Roman period

gated mounds ('long beds') surrounded by a ditched enclosure with or without entrances. In addition, many burials without recognisable peripheral structures or other markings are known from both the Late Bronze Age and the Early Iron Age.

The most common form of marking is the circular ditched enclosure, whose diameter is usually between 2 and 13 m. Unlike in the northern urnfields, very small enclosures, with diameters of less than 2 m, are very rare in the south; enclosures with diameters exceeding 13 m are on the contrary more common, although they occur in only small numbers per urnfield. A few exceptionally large enclosures are associated with unusual burials. The best-known example is the enclosure that surrounded the 'princely burial' of Oss. This enclosure had a diameter of no less than 52 metres.

An increasing number of enclosures from the Early Iron Age onwards have an entrance. Enclosures with entrances are not entirely unknown in the northern part of the Netherlands, but in the south they are often in the majority in an urnfield. Most of the entrances are oriented towards the southeast. Some were found to be flanked by postholes.

The earliest date obtained for a long bed in the southern Netherlands lies around the 11th century BC (2855 ± 35 BP; Goirle).[25] As in the north, many variants have been observed. In the Late Bronze Age the – mostly parallel – ditches[26] flanking the mound usually curved around the ends of it. Later on, the ditches became more rectangular. An exceptionally long mound was found at Berghem; its ditch had a setting of postholes in it. In some southern urnfields the long barrows were connected along their longitudinal sides, resulting in a complex of linked monuments.

Many of the ditches surrounding the long beds have entrances, usually in the short side or sides, but in a few cases also in one of the long sides.[27] A few long beds flanked by parallel ditches and with open ends were found in the urnfield of Someren-Waterdael, which was excavated between 1990 and 1992 (fig. 28.4).[28] The dimensions of most of the long beds vary from 2.5 x 8 m to 6 x 70 m. One of the long beds with unlinked parallel ditches in the Someren-Waterdael urnfield was even larger: approximately 4.5 x 145 m. It is not possible to divide the long beds into different functional types solely on the basis of their dimensions, as was suggested in the past.[29] As in the north, the primary burial was usually along the monument's longitudinal axis. Several long beds have been found to contain secondary burials in other places within the enclosure. It is less clear whether there is any connection between these secondary burials and the appearance of Harpstedt urns in the southern part of the Netherlands: primary burials with Harpstedt urns may be in the minority, but they are certainly not exceptional.[30]

In the south, too, rectangular enclosures followed by square enclosures mark the end of the development of the burial monuments encountered in the urnfields. Such enclosures have been found in, for example, the urnfields of Someren-Waterdael, Mierlo-Hout, Wijk bij Duurstede-De Horden and Oss-IJsselstraat.[31] As in the north, their appearance, probably in the 6th century BC, coincides with a marked decrease in the number of urned cremation burials. It would seem that here, too, the burial of carefully selected human remains gradually gave way to the construction of a mound over the funeral pyre. This and other changes in burial rites heralded the end of the urnfield tradition.

fig. 28.5

Late Bronze Age urn burial in the urnfield at Noordbarge.

Funerary pottery

The finds recovered from the urnfields consist largely of pottery. Different groups of pottery can be distinguished on the basis of the vessels' functions in the burial rite. The largest group is that of the urns themselves (fig. 28.5). It should be added that the percentage of urned burials may vary considerably per urnfield, partly depending on the period. Some urnfields in both the north and the south were found to contain very small proportions of urn burials (sometimes fewer than one-third of the burials). The quality of the vessels that were used as urns also varies, from simple – sometimes even damaged – vessels to lavishly decorated and well-finished ones. There is no real evidence to suggest that special funerary pottery was produced (although very few sound comparisons have yet been made between settlement pottery and pottery from funerary contexts),[32] but we may assume that the remains were preferably placed in specific types of domestic pottery.[33]

Many of the urns were sealed. There are indications that some organic matter, such as wood, was often used for this purpose.[34] Sometimes the urns were covered with a flat stone or a large sherd. Smaller, intact pots or dishes are frequently found lying on top of urns. It is assumed that most of those vessels had originally been placed on top of the organic lid and later slipped onto or over the urn when the lid decayed. They are hence primarily to be regarded as grave goods. Miniature vessels are also classed as grave goods. These vessels, similar in shape to the urns, only much smaller, are usually found inside the urn, on top of or among the cremated remains. Whether they served some special purpose we do not know. Sometimes other accessory vessels were placed in the grave along with the urn or in the ditch surrounding the burial. The grave goods found in the ditches need not all have been deposited there during the burial ceremony; people may have returned to the grave to commemorate their deceased relatives at set intervals.

There is a marked increase in the number of secondarily burned sherds from the Early Iron Age onwards. This may be due to the fact that the human remains were then less carefully selected from among the remains of the pyre. Apparently, vessels were burned along with the deceased. Unlike for the Roman period, we have very little direct evidence that those vessels contained foodstuffs. Burned animal bones, for example, have only very rarely been found among remains from the urnfield period.[35] But as boned meat, plant food and beverages will under normal conditions have left no archaeologically recoverable traces, we cannot exclude the possibility that the deceased were burned accompanied by goods of that kind. This is indeed supported by a find from the urnfield of Wijk bij Duurstede, namely a fragment of a ceramic salt container.[36]

Pottery types and decoration

The development of the types of pottery encountered in the cemeteries of the two different regions can serve as a useful basis for dating the individual burials (cf. fig. 28.3).

The urns found in the barrows containing mortuary houses in the north of the Netherlands were clearly derived from the coarsely tempered bucket-shaped earthenware of the Middle Bronze Age. The barrows surrounded by keyhole-shaped ditches yielded predominantly finely tempered biconical urns as well as vessels described as 'tureens', characterised by a sharp transition from the curved body to the tall, straight to conical neck. In the Early Iron Age the types became rounder and all kinds of hybrid types appeared. In the course of the 7th or the 6th century BC the tureen evolved into the Ruinen-Wommels ware that is characteristic of the northern half of the Netherlands. From the 8th century BC onwards the fairly straight, partly rusticated Harpstedt pot and the *Schrägrand* or *Schräghals* pot were used all over the Netherlands and over wide parts of the adjacent areas.

In the south, too, the oldest urnfield pottery includes a high proportion of coarsely tempered vessels, which appear to represent a logical continuation of the local Middle Bronze Age pottery. The later variants show a trend towards the Harpstedt ware. Besides this kind of local types, the pottery of the southern urnfields, especially that of the Late Bronze Age, is characterised by types with close parallels among the contemporary earthenware of the Middle and Upper Rhine area, where the Urnfield culture was then flourishing. The main types of this period are boxes with lids (*Deckeldosen*), handled vessels, cylinder-necked, funnel-necked and conically-necked urns and conical dishes. These types show a form of decoration characteristic of the south, consisting of patterns executed in the so-called *Kerbschnitt* ('chip-carving', plate 40B) technique.

The pottery of the Early Iron Age is more uniform. The most common types of this period are the *Schräghals* pot, the rusticated pots of the Harpstedt type and – still – conical dishes. The youngest pottery from the southern urnfields includes vessels of so-called Marne pottery (usually local imitations of Marne types). Marne pottery ware is represented in fairly small numbers, but it should be borne in mind that the number of urn burials rapidly decreased in this period. This Marne pottery indicates changes in the interregional contacts in the 5th century BC, characterised by increasing influences of northern French burial rites and less influence from the middle Rhine region, with which contacts had certainly been maintained in the 7th century BC.

Other grave goods

Other grave goods besides pottery are on the whole very rare. In both the southern and the northern urnfields the proportion of burials containing metal objects is almost always less than 5%. The majority of those metal objects are small ornaments like bracelets, neck rings and earrings and objects associated with personal care, such as pins, razors and tweezers. Only very rarely are rings and bracelets of bone or stone found and the same holds for amber beads. The majority of these objects had been burned along with the deceased.

A small number of burials in the north, and especially in the south, of the Netherlands contained different, more prestigious objects forming a conspicuous contrast with the poor grave goods of most of the other burials. They indicate the existence of a social elite and of long-distance exchange networks, and for this reason they deserve to be discussed in a separate section.

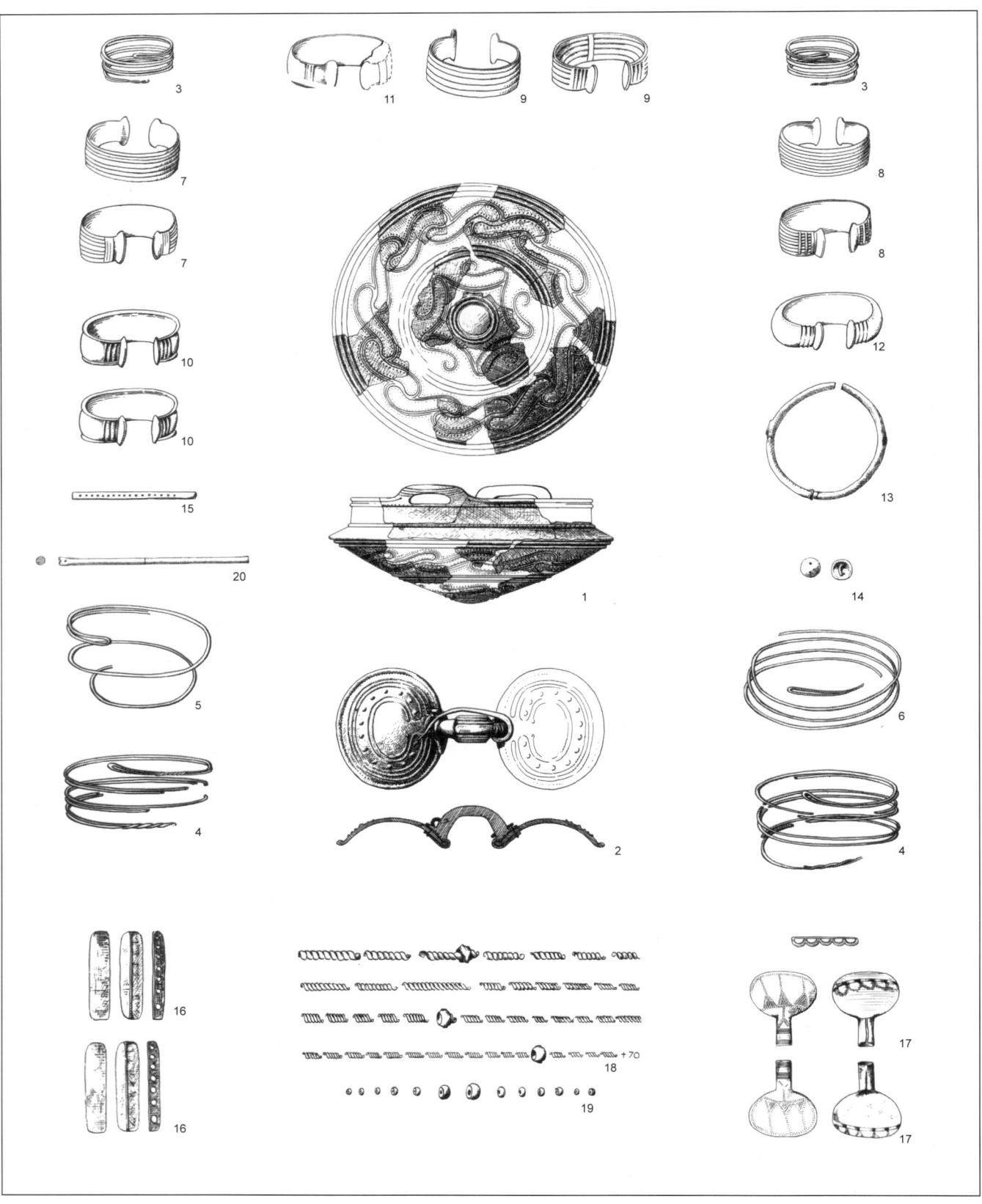

fig. 28.6

The contents of the rich grave of Drouwen. The bronze cauldron contained predominantly bronze ornaments, including a spectacle fibula (2). A noteworthy find is a bronze compass (15 and 20). Scale 1:4.

1	cauldron
2	spectacle *fibula*
3-6	spirals
7-12	omega arm rings
13	arm ring

14	buttons
15, 20	compass
16-18	elements of a neck ornament
19	beads, bluish green glass and jet

RICH BURIALS

Late Bronze Age

Throughout the entire urnfield period the burial rite – and the associated grave goods – is fairly uniform. Funerary monuments of an unusual design or of extreme dimensions were as rare as burials containing very rich grave goods. Apparently people did not feel a strong desire to express the deceased's individuality, rank or status in the burial rite. This distinguishes the earliest phase of the urnfield period from the preceding Early and Middle Bronze Age. Most of the valuable objects known from the Late Bronze Age come from (votive) deposits.

In fact, only one of the Late Bronze Age cemeteries known in the Netherlands has yielded prestige items, namely the large urnfield near Drouwen (Drenthe), where an exceptionally large number of objects were found lying close together. This 'treasure' had originally been buried in a hanging bowl of Scandinavian origin and comprised a large number of ornaments, including a spectacle *fibula*, seven flat bracelets (cast after Central European models), some bronze wire bracelets, two spacer plates and bronze, glass and jet beads. The bronze compass suitable for engraving bronze that was found among these objects indicates connections with a bronze smith (fig. 28.6). Closer research has shown that these finds came from the disturbed fill of a circular ditch.[37] The objects will have been intended for the deceased, like the simpler earthenware accessory vessels that were sometimes deposited in circular ditches. From the composition of the finds we may infer that in this case the deceased was a woman. The objects will have been her personal possessions. This is unusual in itself because most of the few burials from the urnfield period that have yielded prestigious grave goods contained traditionally male objects. This notable lady – who was in the past sometimes called 'the princess of Drouwen' – undoubtedly belonged to the elite of the community that lived on the plateau of Drenthe. The origins of her ornaments show us in what directions and over what distances contacts were maintained and objects were exchanged.

Elite burials from the 7th century BC

A larger number of rich burials are known from the Early Iron Age, the majority of which are datable to the 7th century BC. Of particular interest are the seven or eight burials in the southern part of the Netherlands and the river district that have yielded different combinations of swords, axes, knives, harness fittings, parts of wagons and bronze ware. In addition, we also know of a number of burials which contained only a single sword.[38] On the assumption that these grave goods to some extent reflect the deceased's social position, these burials reveal the existence of a social elite that seems to have been stratified itself. The composition of the richest burials and their distribution across Europe suggest that the highest-ranking members of this elite maintained direct contacts with elites in the core area of the Hallstatt culture.

At the top of the hierarchical system was the chieftain who was buried on the Wezelsche Berg near Wijchen. His grave, which was discovered in 1897, probably contained an entire four-wheeled wagon and the remains of a pair of horses (fig. 28.7). Parts of the decoration of this wagon may have been made in Etruria (fig. 28.8 and plate 45B). The decorated bronze *situla* (bucket) is certainly an Italian import.[39] The chieftain's personal armour included a long sword and an axe. The

fig. 28.7
Reconstruction of the four-wheeled ceremonial wagon of which parts were found in a cremation burial at Wijchen.

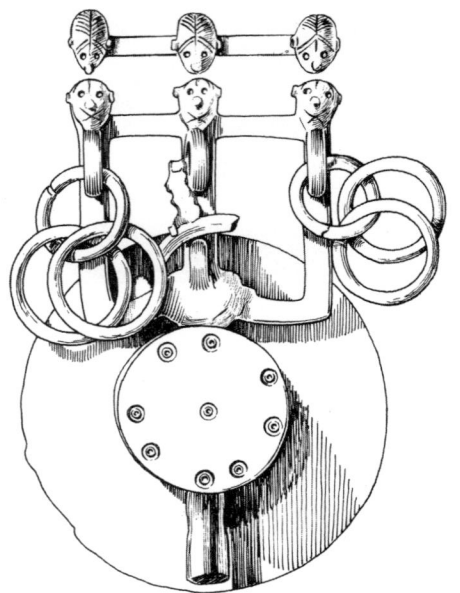
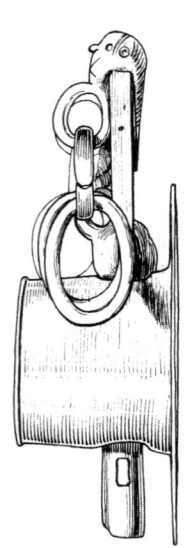
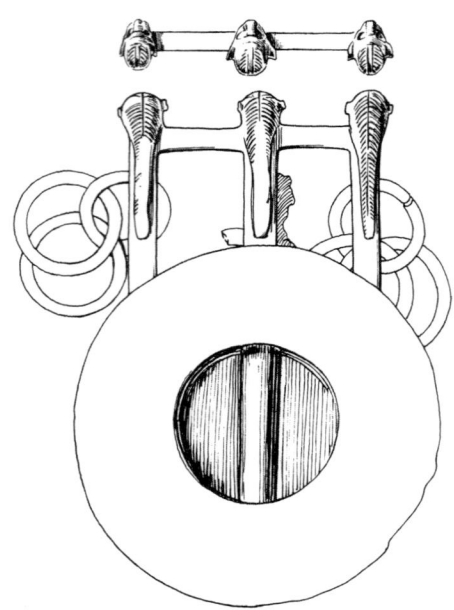

fig. 28.8

Bronze axle cap with linchpin and jingling rings from Wijchen. The ends of the linchpins of the bronze axle caps of which four were found in the rich grave are decorated with stylised human heads. Their design suggests that they were inspired by Etruscan originals. Scale 1:2.

comparably rich grave that was discovered at Oss (plate 45A) did not contain a complete vehicle,[40] but the bridle bits and parts of a yoke that were found in it may represent a *pars pro toto* form of wagon burial. The armour of the man who was buried here included a sword decorated with gold leaf, a dagger, an axe and a few knives. The bronze *situla* in which his cremated remains had been placed came from the eastern Alps. Unfortunately, the grave goods of most of the other contemporary burials containing bronze vessels that have been found in the Netherlands (Baarlo, Ede, Venlo and Rhenen) have survived only in part, but on the basis of evidence from burials just across the Belgian and German borders we may assume that they were originally comparable to those of Oss and Wijchen. The burials without a bronze vessel, but containing a sword, like those found at Meerlo, Horst, Someren (2x) and Heythuysen,[41] are much simpler. The cremated remains had in most cases been placed in an earthenware urn. The urn that was found at Meerlo also contained two bridle bits.

Whether we may infer from this somewhat greater degree of differentiation in rich burials that the social organisation and the structure of the elite of the 7th century were fundamentally different from those of the preceding period we do not know.[42] The few rich burials that have survived have provided insufficient reliable quantitative information for us to be able to answer this question. The fact that only one rich burial occurs per cemetery or per findspot seems to imply that the acquisition or establishment of power and prestige were still predominantly dependent on personal qualities. Apparently the elite was not yet in a position to pass its prestige and power on to later generations via kinship ties. The leader of a particular region was succeeded by a tribe member living elsewhere within that region, who may or may not have been related to him.[43]

Later elites

A few burials from the last phase of the urnfield period also seem to represent such local 'big men'. Among the uncontained cremated remains that formed the central burial within a circular ditched enclosure with a diameter of 7 m at Haps were an iron dagger with an antenna-shaped hilt, three iron arrowheads and an iron pin. The dagger, a Central European import, dates the burial to the 6th century BC. From around that same time are the two comparably rich burials that were found on the Bisschopsberg near Havelte. The first contained a set of bridle bits, bronze *phalerae* (decorative discs) and three iron spearheads,[44] the second contained a dagger imported from northern France and a bracelet for which clear parallels are known from the area of the Hunsrück-Eifel culture.[45] Bronze bracelets and other ornaments of the Hunsrück-Eifel culture dating from the 6th century BC have been found elsewhere on the plateau of Drenthe, too, for example in the urnfields of Balloo and Gasteren.[46] Probably only one *situla* burial is datable to the 6th century BC.[47] This *situla* was also found in a northern urnfield, namely that of Meppen near Zweeloo. It had been buried within a large circular ditched enclosure (diameter 16 m) and contained only cremated remains, no grave goods.[48]

Elites compared

The burials associated with bronze imports, harness fittings, parts of wagons and weapons that have been found in the Netherlands and the adjacent parts of Belgium and Germany show many affinities with the sometimes equally rich – but often far richer – elite burials of Central Europe, the core area of the Hallstatt culture. However, there are also clear differences, the most conspicuous being the function that the bronze *situlae* appear to have fulfilled in the burial rite. In the core area of the Hallstatt culture they usually formed part of a wine service, by which the deceased was accompanied in the burial chamber. However, these objects seem to have lost their original function in the Lower Rhine region, where they were usually used as luxurious urns – a use that was virtually unknown in the core area of the Hallstatt culture.[49] This adaptation of the foreign *situla*'s function to the native burial tradition may be regarded as an extra argument for assuming that the social elite of the Lower Rhine region was of local origins.

SITUATION AND INTERNAL STRUCTURE OF THE CEMETERIES

Various factors appear to have played a part in the selection of a location for an urnfield. A first important factor seems to have been the presence of older burials. In many urnfields the burials were found to be grouped around or near one or more Bronze Age barrows. This further supports the conclusion that the urnfields represent a continuation of the older Bronze Age traditions. The local relief seems to have played a part, too. Many urnfields lie on small coversand ridges or on pronounced slopes, with the long barrows often oriented parallel to their contours. That way, the natural relief helped to accentuate these monuments.

Some urnfields were found to contain strips of ground that were entirely devoid of burials, suggesting that a road ran through the cemetery. This has been observed at, for example, Gasteren, Noordbarge and Sleen in Drenthe, Noord-Elsen in Overijssel and Beegden and Venlo-De Hamert in Limburg.[50] In areas containing many urnfields part of the regional road system can be reconstructed on the basis of this evidence. Many of the urnfields lay along routes across large ranges of hills or along the side roads connecting those main routes.

Various questions still remain unanswered as far as the urnfields' internal structure is concerned. Some urnfields were found to contain separate clusters of barrows, indicating that the cemetery was used by several individual (kinship) groups. In the northern Netherlands those clusters were often grouped around

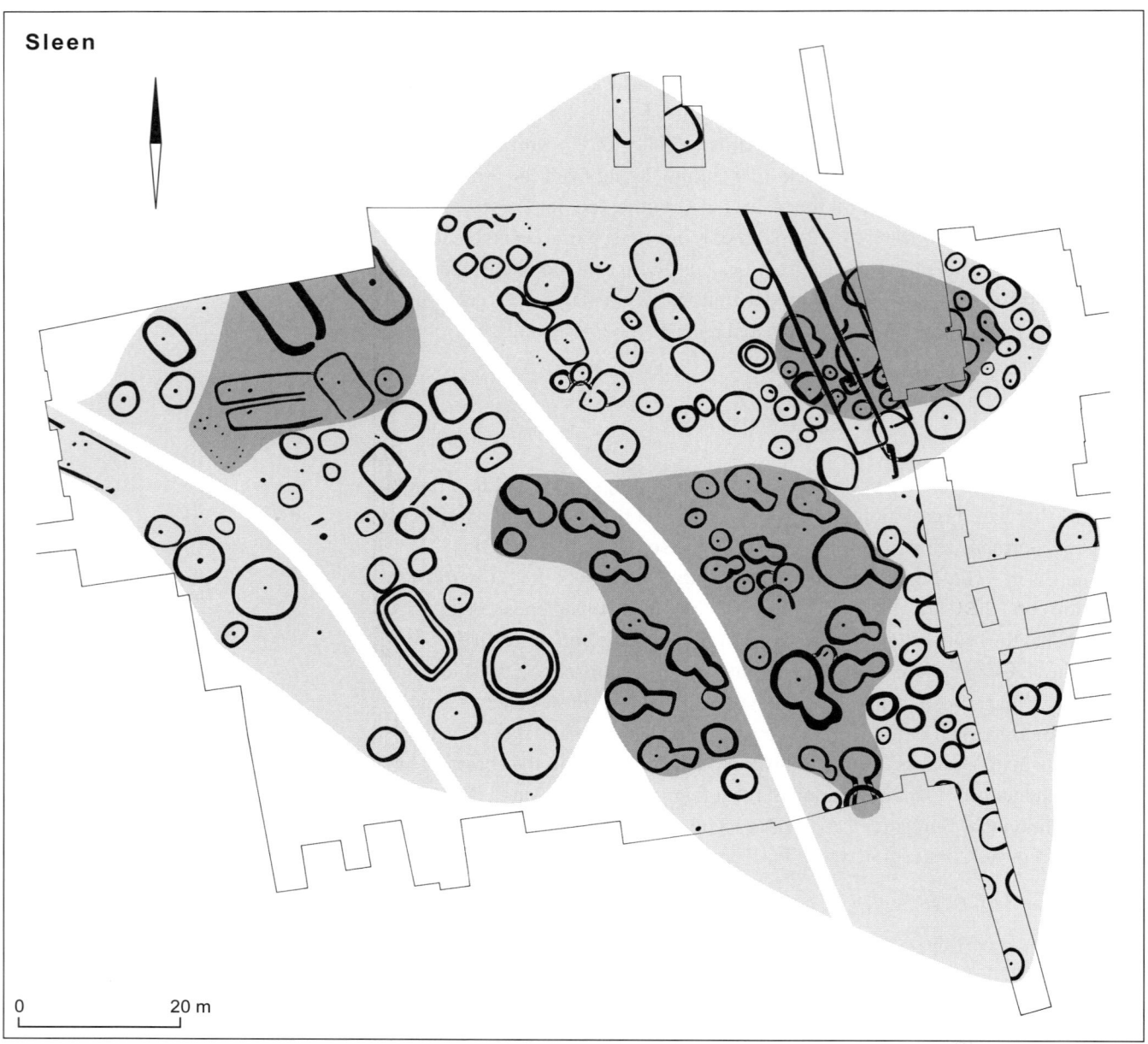

Sleen

0   20 m

fig. 28.9

The Sleen urnfield. The ages of the individual monuments indicate that this urnfield developed from three centres (dark grey) in the Late Bronze Age. The two strips of land devoid of graves suggest that roads ran between the burials. Scale 1:800.

barrows associated with mortuary houses or with keyhole-shaped enclosures. Besides these cemeteries that expanded from several individual centres or clusters, there are also cemeteries that show a more linear or radial development from a single centre. In the southern Netherlands the core structure of the latter kind of cemeteries is often a large long barrow, as for example at Someren-Waterdael. The lack of physical-anthropological data for most of the Dutch urnfields is a great handicap in their spatial analysis. We do not yet have sufficient evidence to demonstrate that groups of individuals of different sexes and ages (families) were buried close together. Nor are we able to answer the question whether certain monuments, for example long barrows, were reserved for a particular sex and/or age group.

The urnfield of Sleen (fig. 28.9) presents a fine example of the formation and expansion of a large, complex urnfield. Two roads were found to have run across this urnfield. The eastern road had the same orientation as the coversand ridge on which the cemetery was laid out, while the western road branched off towards the northwest. The oldest monuments seem to form three separate groups. Along the western road lay a barrow containing a mortuary house (without a ditch) and two early rectangular enclosures (without mortuary houses), one of which comprised a double ditch. In the south of the urnfield, along the eastern road, lay a group of keyhole-shaped enclosures, one of which was exceptionally wide. The unusual, distorted shape of two of the latter monuments suggests that the road proved an obstacle during their construction. A second group lay further north, to the east of that same road, to which it was connected by a path. Unfortunately, only a small area of the northern part of the urnfield has been excavated, but there are indications that this part contained a fourth concentration of barrows. The construction of mounds surrounded by circular ditches in the open areas between these monuments eventually led to the formation of a large complex, containing the buried remains of three or four different (kinship) groups.

The plan of the urnfield of Beegden can be regarded as a southern contrast to that of the Sleen cemetery (fig. 28.10).[51] It is a typical example of a small urnfield that was possibly used by only one, or at most two families. The barrows were spaced very far apart and the areas between them had not (yet) been filled up. The small number of burials suggests that this urnfield was used for a few generations only.

URNFIELDS AND DEMOGRAPHIC INFORMATION

The size of the urnfields and their distribution within certain areas can be used as bases for estimating population densities and the size of settlement territories. First of all, the average population figure has to be calculated for each individual urnfield. This can be done once the total number of burials in that urnfield, the population's average life expectancy and the urnfield's period of use are known.[52] An important assumption made in such calculations is that the entire population was buried in the urnfield. However, the results of the physical-anthropological research to which cremated remains from urnfields have been subjected recommend caution. Time and time again it is found that the youngest age group, of infants younger than two years, is substantially underrepresented in the urnfields. We must therefore allow for the possibility that this group was disposed of in a

fig. 28.10
Small Early Iron Age urnfield at Beegden.
Scale 1:1000.

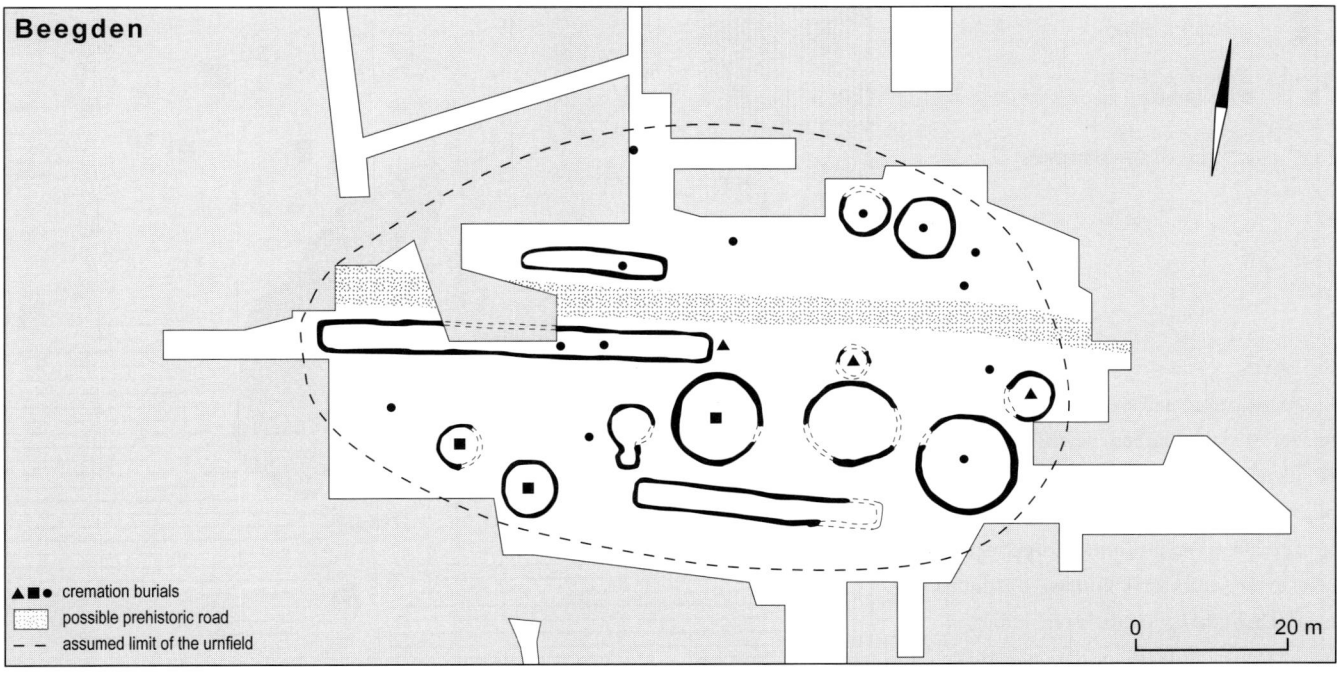

Beegden

▲■● cremation burials
░ possible prehistoric road
– – assumed limit of the urnfield

0   20 m

different way.[53] If this was indeed the case, then an extra correction factor has to be used in calculating the average life expectancy.

In the case of most urnfields the results of such calculations fall within a fairly narrow range. Kooi calculated that populations of 4 to 23 individuals buried their dead in the urnfields in Drenthe.[54] Verlinde's figures for the urnfields of Overijssel fall within this same range: 10-20 individuals.[55] The figures obtained for a few urnfields in the southern Netherlands are not much different: Wijk bij Duurstede 11-25, Someren 20-25, Beegden 4-8, Haps 8-15, Sint-Oedenrode 5-6. If we assume that the average family in this period comprised at least six individuals, then we find that most urnfields served as the cemeteries of very small communities, of one to at most four families. The impressive size of some urnfields, such as those of Noordbarge and Vledder with their 390 and 318 barrows, respectively, is primarily due to the fact that they were used for such a long period of time, often for over five centuries. The only real exception is the large urnfield from the Late Bronze Age and the Early Iron Age on the Boshoverheide near Weert. The figures calculated for the average size of the group of people who buried their dead in this urnfield amount to 37-79 individuals.[56]

The above figures are in accordance with the picture that has emerged for the settlement form in this period. Most settlements consisted of isolated farms or

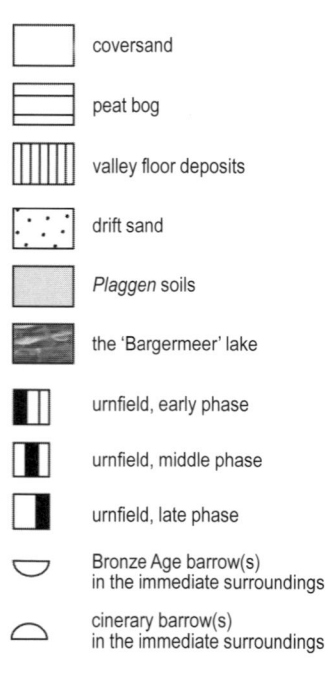

	coversand
	peat bog
	valley floor deposits
	drift sand
	Plaggen soils
	the 'Bargermeer' lake
	urnfield, early phase
	urnfield, middle phase
	urnfield, late phase
	Bronze Age barrow(s) in the immediate surroundings
	cinerary barrow(s) in the immediate surroundings

fig. 28.11

Rough situations and sizes of settlement territories in the southern part of the low Hondsrug boulder clay ridge in the course of the Late Bronze Age. The raised bogs, the stream valleys and the former Bargermeer (a lake) to the southeast of Emmen constituted natural boundaries. Urnfields are indicated on the map by a square and a serial number.

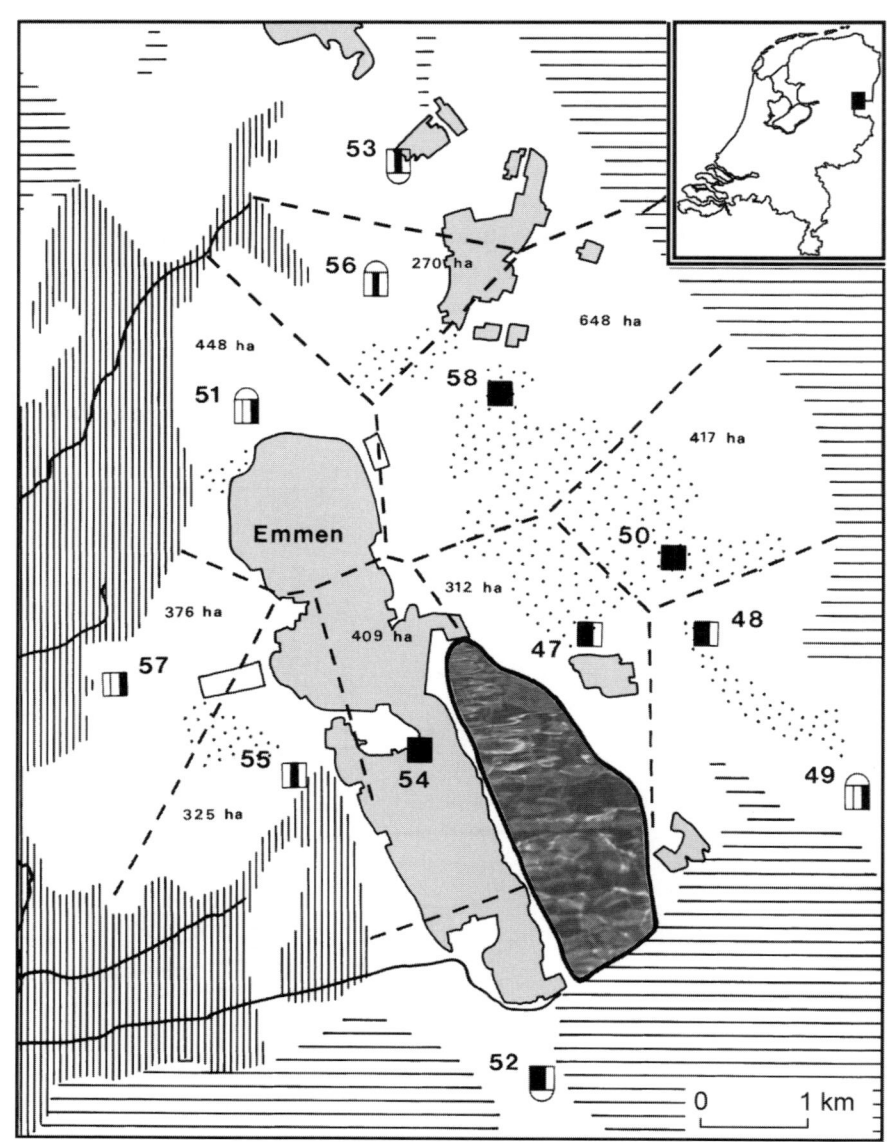

of complexes comprising not more than two to four main buildings. The largest urnfields, such as the one near Weert, may have served as communal cemeteries for several of such settlements. Assuming that most urnfields lay at a relatively short distance from the settlement or settlements associated with them,[57] we can reconstruct the size of the territories of those settlements on the basis of the distribution of the cemeteries. So-called 'Thiessen polygons' are obtained by drawing lines halfway between each pair of neighbouring urnfields (fig. 28.11). This has been done for the microregions of southeast Drenthe, Overijssel and part of the Kempen region of North Brabant.[58] The results were again remarkably similar. The average size of the territories was found to have varied from 2.7 to 6.5 km², with an average of between 3.5 and 4.5 km² for more or less the same exploitation possibilities. The corresponding population density varies from about 2 to 5 individuals per km².

The use of so many average values makes this a rather rigid, model-like approach, which almost completely obscures any demographic developments that may have taken place. Apart from that, it is not certain whether the individual territories were all equal. In view of the degree of social differentiation that has been found to have existed in this period there may well have been a certain form of settlement hierarchy, too. Moreover, the personal element in the organisation and the balance of power will from time to time have led to shifts in the boundaries of the individual settlement territories. But that is not to say that such basic models are not useful starting points for studying settlement systems. If there is anything that we can learn from the figures indicated above for the sizes of the settlements and the population densities it is that overexploitation of the traditional Late Bronze Age and Early Iron Age occupation areas cannot possibly have been the ultimate cause of any decreases that may have occurred in population figures or of the emigration to other regions that took place in the subsequent period. The contrast between the large numbers of urnfields and the much smaller number of burials and cemeteries known from the last part of prehistory has given rise to demographic crisis hypotheses for the plateau of Drenthe in the Middle Iron Age; similar hypotheses have been put forward for North Brabant, too.[59] However, according to the population figures, the pressure on the environment cannot have led to overexploitation on anything more than a local scale. The possibilities of reconstructing the size of the population in the last part of the Iron Age are seriously limited by other factors, not in the last place by the changes that took place in the burial rite itself.

BURIAL TRADITIONS FROM THE
MIDDLE IRON AGE ONWARDS

Gradual changes

In most of the urnfields in the Netherlands no burials or finds dating from after the middle of the 5th century BC have been found. As we have already seen above, changes took place in the burial rite after the 7th century, which in most cases had an adverse effect on the archaeological visibility of the burials. The most important of these changes are:
- the decrease in the number of burials in which the remains were placed in containers of durable material (pottery);
- the less careful selection of the cremated remains that were to be buried in the grave;

- the trend away from the separate burial of the collected cremated remains towards the erection of a mound over the pyre, resulting in the so-called cinerary barrows;
- the decrease in the number of burials in or beneath barrows surrounded by pronounced peripheral structures.

Therefore we cannot entirely exclude the possibility that remains were still buried in some of the urnfields after the mid-5th century, in graves that we are unable to recognise as such. On the other hand, there is clear evidence that people started to bury their dead in new cemeteries after the middle of the 5th century, in the same areas as the urnfields of the previous period, which were apparently no longer considered important.

The number of Middle and Late Iron Age cemeteries known in the Netherlands is still relatively small: only a few dozen, which forms a marked contrast with the hundreds of known urnfields. However, in areas where large-scale archaeological research is carried out and the peripheral zones of settlement territories are also investigated, new discoveries are frequently made. Good examples are the cemeteries recently found at Oss-Ussen[60] and Wijk bij Duurstede-De Horden.[61] But this does not alter the fact that, with their unspectacular contents and modest sizes, Middle and Late Iron Age cemeteries will have escaped notice far more frequently than urnfields during reclamation and building activities in the recent past.

It is for this same reason that no general demographic conclusions may be drawn from the different numbers of cemeteries from successive archaeological periods. The only possible way of arriving at sound statements is by viewing the limited funerary evidence in relation to the results of systematic settlement surveys. But no such results are as yet available for either the southern or the northern urnfield area. There are at most two microregions in northern Drenthe where the consequences of emigration to the salt marshes of Friesland and Groningen appear to be archaeologically detectable. Those regions are the Noordse Veld near Zeijen and the Ballooërveld, both of which have yielded a wealth of prehistoric evidence from various periods. Although cinerary barrows have been found in both regions, it would seem that the settlements were abandoned in the course of the Iron Age. The Noordse Veld and the Ballooërveld remained unoccupied in historical times, too. The land was not used at all, or at most very extensively, for a long period of time and consequently barrows, Celtic fields and other remains of prehistoric occupation have been relatively well preserved in those regions.

The end of the use of the urnfields and the formation of new cemeteries imply a break in the burial tradition. However, the aspects of the burial rite practised in the new cemeteries that are archaeologically detectable bear such a close resemblance to the customs of the last part of the urnfield period that this cannot have been a very radical break. The transition from the urnfields to the new cemeteries may have taken place at different times in different regions; in some areas it may even have been a very gradual process, spanning several generations. We have too little chronological evidence to be able to follow this process in detail. Why the custom of burial in urnfields came to an end is still a matter of speculation. Did the urnfields gradually lose their function as territory markers? Did people start to feel the need to bury their dead in a more personal, family-oriented manner, closer to the homestead? What we do know is that the observed changes in burial rites were not restricted to the northeast and southern parts of the Netherlands, but that the same changes were taking place over the whole of temperate Europe in the Middle Iron Age. It is possible – or even likely – that these changes in some way reflect more general social or cultural tensions within the Iron Age communities.

Cinerary barrows and cremation cemeteries

In the northern Netherlands, Middle and Late Iron Age cemeteries and burials have been found at, for example, Ruinen, Barger-Oosterveld, Zeijen, Balloo, Sleen, Hijken (Hijkerveld) and Vaassen.[62] Good examples in the south are Nijnsel, Wijk bij Duurstede-De Horden, Oss-Ussen, Oss-IJsselstraat, Grubbenvorst, Geldermalsen, Nijmegen, Valkenburg and Wessem.[63] On the whole, these cemeteries are small, comprising between fewer than ten and at most a hundred burials. Cremation was still the common form of burial, although inhumation appears to have been practised temporarily in some places in the south of the country in the 5th century BC. At Someren-Waterdael and Geldermalsen, for example, a few inhumation burials have come to light that have been dated to around the 5th century BC on the basis of the pottery found in them.[64] Around that same time a similar temporary break in burial customs occurred in the Middle Rhine region and in northern France. This shows that supra-regional contacts continued to exist in the southern part of the Netherlands. Otherwise the burial customs and grave goods are little different from those of the preceding period. Illustrative is the elite burial from between 450 and 350 BC that was found in Nijmegen. Besides one large and two small spearheads, this burial yielded the unburned remains of a harness for a pair of horses and of the fittings of a two-wheeled war chariot (fig. 28.12).[65] The closest known parallels are burials found in the core area of the La Tène culture in the Ardennes, northeast France and the Middle Rhine region. The northeastern part of the Netherlands, on the contrary, remained primarily oriented towards northern Germany, as is attested by imports like the eight *Segelohrringe* ('sail earrings') from a cinerary barrow from the 4th or the 3rd century BC near Barger-Oosterveld.[66]

Fewer recognisable funerary monuments are known from this period than from the preceding period. In the Middle Iron Age (cinerary) barrows were still constructed in the northern Netherlands, but after some time they were no longer surrounded by ditched enclosures. In the south, the ditched enclosures are the only recognisable parts of the monument. Here, unlike in the north, these peripheral structures continued to be dug after the Middle Iron Age, too. The enclosed burials seem to have acquired a more central function with time. Most cemeteries contain one or a few of these monuments, the majority having rectangular or square enclosures, but circular and oval ditched enclosures have also been found. Many of the Late Iron Age enclosures contained postholes inside the ditches, usually at the corners and on either side of the entrances in the case of the square enclosures (fig. 28.13). In addition, several individual barrows, some containing secondary burials, have been found in the peripheries of settlements. The dimensions of the late barrows are comparable with those of the barrows from the urnfield period, except that very large, isolated barrows with diameters of 15-20 m are relatively more common.

At De Horden near Wijk bij Duurstede a rectangular enclosure with an entrance in the southeast side was found to have fulfilled a special function within a cemetery that has provisionally been dated between 400 and 200 BC. At the centre of this rectangle was an elongated pit that bore the closest resemblance to a Roman *bustum* grave. This pit contained the completely cremated skeleton of a sturdy man of about 35 and a number of vessels and lumps of melted bronze that had been burned along with him. In line with the monument's entrance were the remains of a covered, central pyre and to the south of these two structures were some twenty cremation burials of men, woman and children. There were no burials of babies. Two more square ditches were found a few dozen metres further east. The rectan-

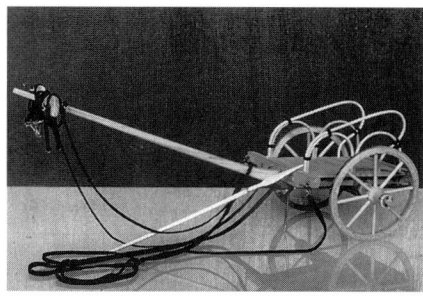

fig. 28.12

Reconstruction of the chariot of which parts were found in a cremation burial at Nijmegen.

fig. 28.13
Square burial monument from the Late Iron Age on De Horden near Wijk bij Duurstede. A post stood at each of the four corners of the ditched enclosure. The interruption in the ditch was also marked by posts.

gular monument seems to have served as a landmark for only a few generations of occupants at the most. After the end of the 3rd century BC the dead were buried on other locations within the excavated area of De Horden. A fixed location had apparently become less important.

Some funerary monuments or cemeteries may have continued to play a central part among the Iron Age communities in a different, more long-term manner, namely as cult sites. The clearest example of this has been found at Oss-Ussen (see chapter 29).

Owing to the poor archaeological visibility of the Middle and Late Iron Age burials, many questions concerning the development of burial rites during the last four centuries BC must remain unanswered. The burials from the beginning of the Roman period, which, thanks mainly to the larger number of grave goods and the trend towards burial at a fixed location, are more easily recognisable, show that very little had in fact changed in the rural cemeteries.[67] We may hence reasonably safely assume that there was a high degree of continuity in the burial tradition from the urnfield period until in the 3rd century AD, at least in the southern part of the Netherlands.[68]

NOTES

1 The remains of some pyres have been excavated on the Boshover-heide near Weert (Bloemers 1993, 16-17).

2 Van Vilsteren (1989) has suggested that structures of this kind, which are usually referred to as 'mortuary houses', formed part of the actual pyre. There are however no convincing arguments to prove that anything like this was the case in the urnfield period.

3 See *e.g.* Groenman-van Waateringe 1988; Hessing 1989a, 313; Kooistra 1990; Verlinde 1987, 212-213.

4 Verlinde 1987.

5 It is difficult to assess the soundness of older sightings of circular ditches and reports of urn finds at for example Driehuis (North Holland), Noordwijk, Maasland and The Hague (South Holland). Sources: Van Heeringen 1992, 317; ROB archives.

6 For a recent survey see: Hessing 1993b.

7 IJzereef 1981, 209-212.

8 Examples are the various crania showing trepanations and the related round pieces of crania bones that have been found in the *terpen* region and the apparent overrepresentation of skulls and skull and jaw fragments among the human remains found in settlements. Some of these skeletal parts showed clear signs of wear or of carving. See also Hessing 1993b. An unusual find is the human femur that was found in the posthole that had contained one of the roof supports of a house in the Assendelver polders (North Holland), which dated from around the beginning of the Christian era (Van Gijn 1987, 101).

9 Cunliffe 1993.

10 Illustrative is the fact that in Flanders, too, the evidence suggesting that cremation was practised in the Middle and Late Iron Age has only very recently been obtained (Bourgeois 1990a, 1990b), whereas the far more recognisable urnfields have been known for much longer.

11 See *e.g.* Kooi 1982, 8.

12 Vledder: *Brandskelettgrab* 185: 3080 ± 45 BP; peripheral burial 185: 2960 ± 35 BP; grave 230: 2860 ± 35 BP; Anloo: grave 156: 2965 ± 60 BP; grave 180: 2920 ± 55 BP; grave 155: 2860 ± 35 BP; Holsloot: grave 13: 2890 ± 50 BP and peripheral burial 10: 2880 ± 70 BP.

13 Waterbolk 1962.

14 See for example Buinen (Kooi 1979, fig. 60).

15 Buinen (2x), Noordbarge and Vasse (Kooi 1979, 131; Verlinde 1987, 196-197).

16 Circular ditches with diameters exceeding 13 m are extremely rare in the north. One of the few known examples is the ditch with a diameter of 16 m that was found in an urnfield near Meppen (Emmen). This monument's primary burial was also of an exceptional nature (see Van Giffen 1938a and below in this chapter).

17 See for example Kooi 1979, 130-134; Verlinde 1987, 170-190.

18 Kooi 1979, 118 ff and fig. 123; ROB 1993 Annual Report and Verlinde 1994; Waterbolk 1965, respectively.

19 Kooi 1979; Waterbolk 1962.

20 Braat 1936.

21 Beex/Roosens 1967, Brunsting/Verwers 1975, Hijszeler 1952 and Verwers 1972, respectively.

22 The keyhole-shaped enclosures marked out by postholes that were found at Haps and Knegsel could also date from the Middle Bronze Age. Several interpretations are conceivable for the ditches of Valkenswaard and Achel-Pastoorsbos.

23 For example Wijk bij Duurstede (Hessing 1989), Someren-Philips camping site (Modderman 1962-'63), Eersel-De Heibloem (Modderman/Louwe Kooijmans 1966), Zevenbergen-Berghem (Verwers 1966b) and Mierlo-Hout (Roymans/Tol 1993, 47).

24 Van den Broeke 1991, 193-194. The evidence suggests that the formation of urnfields with their characteristic funerary monuments started one to two centuries earlier in the north of the Netherlands than in the south. In the north, the two types of monuments described above went out of use before or in the 11th century BC already. That may explain why these types are so rare in the south of the Netherlands.

25 Lanting/Mook 1977, 137.

26 A boat-shaped ditched enclosure was found at Mierlo-Hout (Roymans/Tol 1993).

27 See for example Wijk by Duurstede (Hessing 1989).

28 Roymans/Kortlang 1993.

29 See Verlinde 1987, 286; Verwers 1966b, 54.

30 See *e.g.* Verlinde 1987, 277.

31 For this last urnfield see Fokkens 1993, especially fig. 18, and also Wesselingh 1993.

32 For a discussion of the settlement and cemetery pottery of Wijk bij Duurstede-De Horden see Hessing 1989, 320-321.

33 See Kooi 1979, 134-135; Verlinde 1987, 284.

34 Kooi 1979, 135 ff.

35 On average 20-30% of the cremation burials from the Middle Roman period contain animal bones. During the recent investigation of the cremated remains from the urnfields of Wijk bij Duurstede-De Horden and Deventer-'t Bramelt (Colmschate) one out of the 43 investigated cremation burials of the former urnfield and two out of the 61 investigated burials of the latter were found to contain animal bones (Cuijpers 1990; Hessing 1989).

36 Hessing 1989, 317-320.

37 See Butler 1979b, 128 and 1986; Van Giffen 1943; Kooi 1979, 91 ff.

38 For a recent survey of this kind of elite burials see Roymans 1991, especially table 4. As far as the 7th century BC is concerned, a burial containing a *situla*, a socketed bronze axe and a few other objects that was discovered in 1993 in a disturbed urnfield near Rhenen (Van Heeringen 1998-'99) and a burial containing parts of harness fittings found at Weert-Boshoverheide (Bloemers 1990, 10) can be added to that survey.

39 Pare 1992; Roymans 1991.

40 Modderman 1964b.

41 The burials containing swords that were found in the urnfield of Weert-Boshoverheide are of an earlier, 8th-century date (Roymans 1991, table 4).

42 Roymans (1991) has suggested that the 7th century saw the emergence of a trend towards increasing competition between regional leaders, which may ultimately have culminated in the dependence of some regional leaders on others. The most prominent leaders will then have maintained the contacts with the Hallstatt communities in southern Germany who provided them with prestige items.

43 In this context we assume that the common custom implied patrilocality.

44 Kooi 1983a.

45 Beuker *et al.* 1991.

46 Kooi 1983a.

47 For the arguments see Roymans 1991, 62. The aforementioned cauldron from Venlo may still have been in circulation in this period, too.

48 Van Giffen 1938a.

49 It would seem that only the *situla* of Wijchen did not serve as an urn, but was placed on the pyre. See also Roymans 1991, 60-61.

50 Holwerda n.d., Kooi 1979, 152-166, Roymans 1988, 354-355, and Verlinde 1987, 318-319, respectively.

51 Roymans 1988b.

52 Usually Acsádi and Nemeskéri's formula (1970) is used for this purpose: P(opulation) = k + (D x e)/ t (where D = total number of burials, e = average life expectancy, t = length of time for which the cemetery was used, k = a correction factor corresponding to 1/10 of the outcome of the fraction).

53 For recent physical-anthropological research see for example Cuijpers 1990; Hoogland in Hessing 1989; Van der Sanden 1981.

54 Kooi 1979, 167 ff.

55 Verlinde 1987, 322 ff.

56 Bloemers 1993, 19.

57 This assumption is supported by the results of recent research. For combinations of an urnfield and one or more settlements see *e.g.* various contributions in Fokkens/Roymans 1991; Roymans/Kortlang 1993.

58 See Kooi 1979, 173, Verlinde 1987, 324, and Slofstra 1991, 147-150, respectively.

59 For the discussion on Drenthe see: Fokkens 1991a; Van Gijn/Waterbolk 1984; for North Brabant see: Roymans 1991, 62-74.

60 See *e.g.* Fokkens 1993; Van der Sanden/Van den Broeke 1987.

61 Hessing/Steenbeek 1990.

62 See especially Kooi 1979.

63 Successively: Hulst 1964; Hessing/Steenbeek 1990; Hessing 1993a; Van der Sanden/Van den Broeke 1987; Fokkens 1993; Willems 1983, 241-242; R.S. Hulst/H.W. van Klaveren (pers. com.); Bloemers 1986; Bloemers 1975, 40-41; Louwe Kooijmans/Smits 1985.

64 R.S. Hulst/H.W. van Klaveren (pers. com.); Roymans/Kortlang 1993.

65 Bloemers 1986. A cemetery elsewhere in Nijmegen, on the Kops Plateau, was found to include a few more Middle Iron Age graves containing armour. The richest contained five iron arrowheads and a spearhead (ROB 1975 Annual Report, 20; 1992, 33). A *situla* (which was used as an urn) from the beginning of the Middle Iron Age was for a long time known from Overasselt, near Nijmegen. The recent restoration of the accompanying finds has shown that the finds in question included, amongst others, five iron arrowheads or spearheads, plus iron and bronze horse gear (*Verslag Provinciaal Museum Kam over de periode juli 1987-juli 1994*).

66 Kooi 1979, 122-123.

67 Hessing 1993a.

68 Since this chapter was written some important works have been published on the subject discussed here. Many of the results of recent research into the urnfields in the southern part of the Netherlands are presented in Theuws/Roymans 1999 (Beegden, Mierlo-Hout, Someren-Waterdael). This work also discusses the results of previous and recent urnfield research in the southern part of the Netherlands in relation to regional occupation, occupants' perceptions and landscape in a long chronological perspective. Related subjects are discussed in a study by Gerritsen (2001). This work also contains the first survey of sources on the urnfields in the area between the Meuse, the Demer and the Scheldt. Our understanding of the hitherto fairly unknown urnfields of Limburg has been expanded by the works of Dijkman/Hulst 2000 (Maastricht-Vroendael) and Tol *et al.* 2000 (Roermond-Musschenberg, Sittard-Hoogveld).

R   An alternative to the pyre
Iron Age inhumation burials

Peter van den Broeke and Wilfried Hessing

Coastal region *versus* the hinterland

The many urnfields and cremation cemeteries in the higher parts of the Netherlands form a marked contrast with the scanty evidence of burials from the 1st millennium BC in the coastal region. No cemeteries have yet been found in the latter area. Where graves have come to light they are not cremation burials, but individual inhumations in settlement contexts.[1] Besides more or less complete inhumations, stray finds of non-cremated human bones have also been made in settlements. In spite of their small numbers, these burials in settlements may well reflect the funerary custom that prevailed in the coastal region in this period (see also chapter 28).

The rest of the Netherlands presents an entirely different picture. There, after a period of varying preference for inhumation and cremation in the Middle Bronze Age, the pyre appears to have invariably awaited the deceased from the beginning of the Late Bronze Age onwards. Evidence found from the 1990s onwards however shows that in the river district, and in particular the Betuwe region, inhumation was for a short time an accepted alternative to cremation.

The Betuwe burial culture in the Middle Iron Age

The first cemetery containing both cremation and inhumation burials were found in 1992, at Geldermalsen. This discovery was all the more surprising because virtually no burial evidence whatsoever from either the Bronze Age or the Iron Age had hitherto been found in the entire Betuwe region. Randomly distributed among sixteen cremation burials were

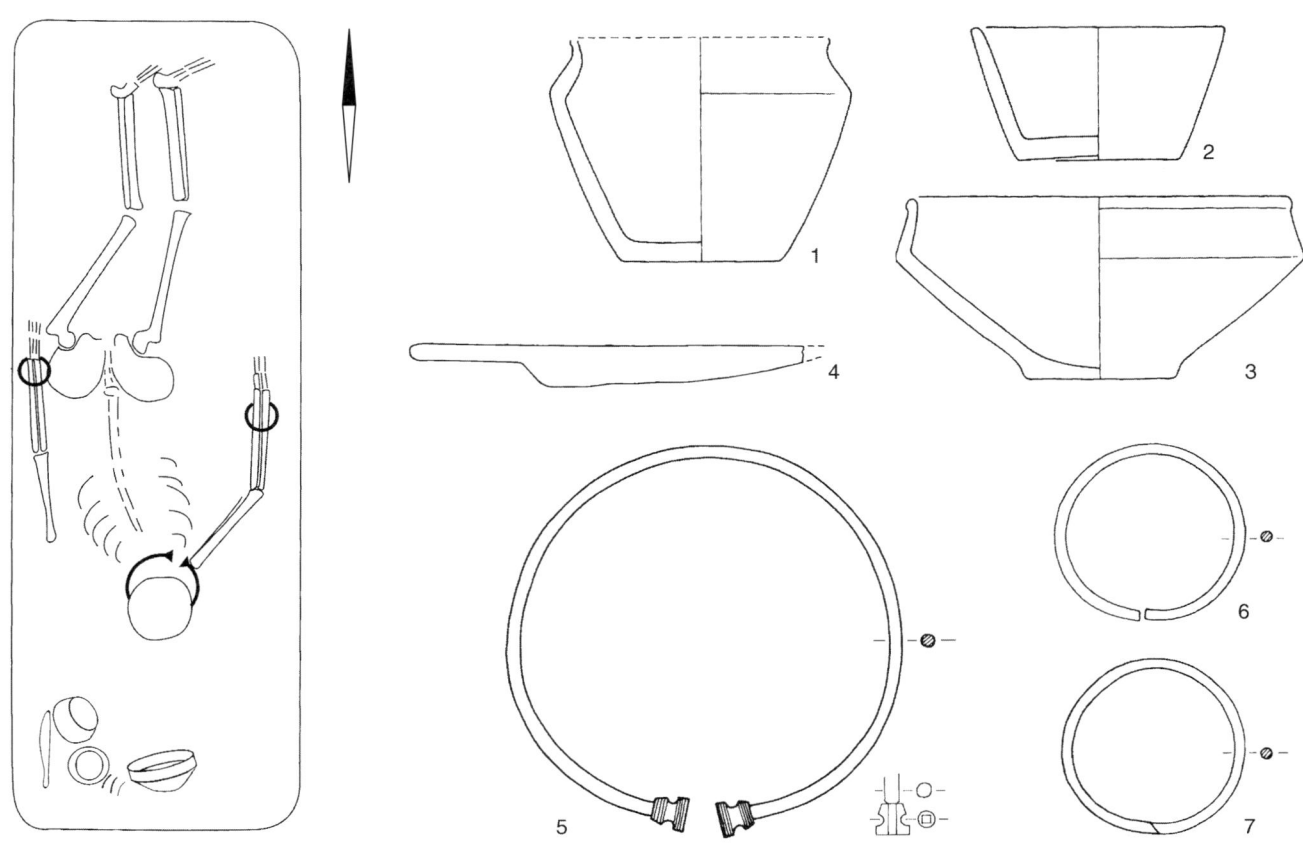

fig. R1

Geldermalsen, burial 1 containing the skeleton of a woman accompanied by various grave goods. Grave: 1-3   pottery
scale 1:20, grave goods: scale 1:3.   4   iron knife
5-7   bronze torque and bracelets

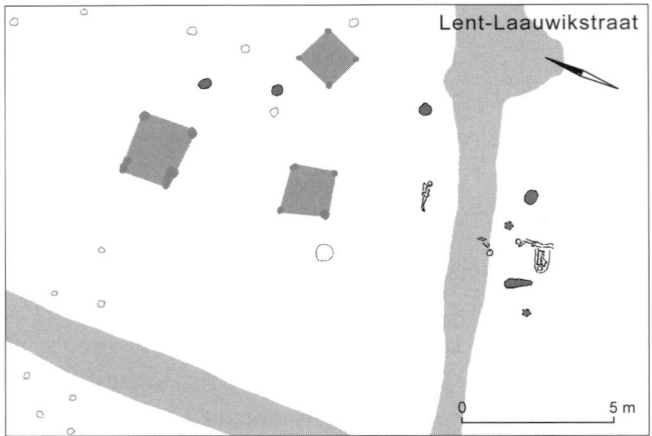

fig. R2

Lent-Laauwikstraat. Plan of the small cemetery containing cremation burials (dark grey) and inhumation burials among the features of older granaries. In the Roman period one of the inhumation graves was disturbed during the digging of a ditch. Scale 1:250.

seven graves containing skeletons, all of which are thought to date from the first half of the Middle Iron Age.[2] The remains are of adults of both sexes and also children. The individuals were deposited in the grave pits in varying postures. The most remarkable burial is that of a woman of about 34-40 who was accompanied by an unusual large number of grave goods (fig. R1). This burial and its contents are in every respect reminiscent of the most common form of burial practised in the Marne-Aisne region in northern France in the period 450-375 BC: the woman lies prostrate on her back and wears a bronze neckring and a bronze bracelet round each wrist. In accordance with the same – Celtic – tradition, her relatives placed three ceramic vessels, an iron knife and a pig's rib near the woman's head. The pottery shows the strong northern French influences characteristic of the ceramic tradition of the southern part of the Netherlands around the 5th century BC, which is known as Marne pottery.

A smaller mixed cemetery was excavated at Lent in 1998. Among at least five cremation burials were four skeletons, two of which were lying in an unusual position, one crosswise on top of the other (fig. R2). The man in the bottom grave was adorned with three bronze ornaments: an earring and what are thought to have been two plait-rings (plate 46), an ornament hitherto unknown in this region. In this case the inhumation burials have been dated to the first half of the Middle Iron Age on the basis of a ^{14}C determination.[3] Radiocarbon analysis also yielded the dates of the remains of two young individuals that were discovered near Meteren in 1999 in the context of the archaeological research conducted along the scheduled track of the *Betuweroute*, a new railway line that will intersect the Betuwe region. They were the last individuals to be buried in a repeatedly reused barrow.[4]

These surprising new discoveries are incidentally not restricted to the Betuwe. An inhumation burial has also come to light in the large urnfield of Someren-Waterdael (province of North Brabant). Although little more than a vague silhouette of the deceased had survived in the urnfield's sandy soil, the burial could nevertheless be dated to the first half of the Middle Iron Age on the basis of the Marne-style bowl that was placed in the grave.[5]

It is especially the cemetery of Geldermalsen that creates the impression that the adoption of northern French elements in the 5th century BC was not restricted to the material culture alone. Southern influences apparently also extended to the burial rite, with the most conspicuous aspect being the (re)introduction of inhumation.

Older roots

More recent discoveries, made in 2000 and 2001 in – again – Lent and its environs, have however raised doubts concerning the latter assumption. Some 250 m from the aforementioned small cemetery was a larger cemetery which may have been its predecessor.[6] The thirty burials that have been excavated in this cemetery comprise more or less equal numbers of randomly distributed cremation pits and inhumations. Particularly conspicuous are a double inhumation (fig. R3) and graves in which the deceased were deposited face downwards.

The shape of the urns in which the cremation remains were buried and ^{14}C dates obtained for some of the skeletons and cremated bone point to the Early Iron Age, with the 6th century BC being well represented, as can be inferred from bronze hair rings found in association with two female skeletons (figs. R3 and R4). In the only other area in which this

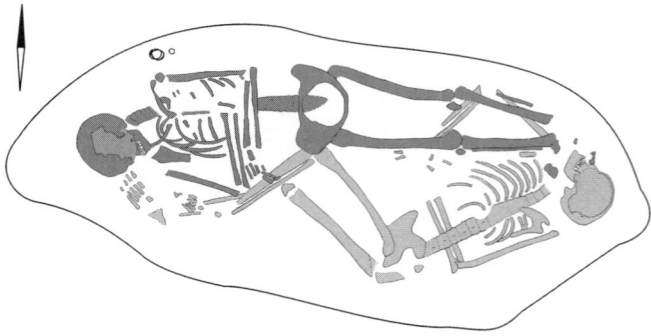

fig. R3

Lent-Steltsestraat. Burial of a man and a woman aged 25-35, measuring 1.65 m and 1.55 m, respectively. The woman (dark grey) lies on her back, the man (light grey) face downwards. The woman was accompanied by three ornaments of twisted bronze wire, placed near her left shoulder. They are thought to be two hair rings and a finger ring.

form of ornamentation is known, the Middle Rhine region, hair rings worn at the temples were in fashion in that century only.

Possibly even a little older are a few inhumation burials that have come to light at the periphery of a cemetery near Oosterhout, 3 km from the aforementioned cemetery. At the present stage of research the urns in the dozens of cremation burials suggest dates in the 8th-7th centuries BC.[7] The unburned remains of three individuals, two of which were buried in the same grave, were unearthed near the urnfield's limit. This peripheral position could imply that inhumation was an exceptional form of burial in this early period. Another possibility is that these people were buried after the dozens who were cremated, and for this reason ended up at the periphery of the cemetery. The double burial shows a remarkable resemblance to the double burial at Lent, which is thought to date from the 6th century BC. In both cases the first individuals were deposited on their sides or in a prone position, after which the second were laid down next to them on their backs, with their feet near the head of the first. But whereas at Lent this opposition coincides with a difference in sex, the burial of Oosterhout is thought to contain the remains of two men.

The latter observation immediately prompts comparison with the two men preserved as a pair of bog bodies near Weerdinge, in Drenthe (fig. S1). The fact that they were excluded from the cremation ritual and were buried at a remote location could be explained by them having held an unacceptable position in the local community which ended with a death sentence.[8] But even if this is correct, punishment can-

not be the general explanation for inhumation in the Early Iron Age, so much is evident from the frequency and spatial distribution of the inhumation burials in the cemetery of Lent.

If the inhumation burials from this early period are indeed restricted to the small region in which they have now come to light, they could be the graves of a group of immigrants from an area where inhumation was the common burial practice. If so, the aforementioned hair rings suggest the Middle Rhine region as a likely area of origin. But we are then faced with the question as to how the simultaneous practice of cremation and inhumation is to be interpreted. The urns are unmistakably Lower Rhine in style, so not foreign imports. The complete absence of peripheral structures around the graves is not a foreign feature either, because this was common in this part of the Betuwe from the beginning of the Late Bronze Age onwards.[9] If the two forms of burial were indeed simultaneously practised, they could well reflect assimilation of indigenous and foreign people. Such a process is not inconceivable. Something similar must indeed have taken place at the end of the Iron Age, when a group of immigrants from Hessen (Germany) mixed with the local population, after which the two groups within a short time, in an archaeologically invisible process, merged to form a new ethnic unit, which we know as the Batavi.

Different developments?

We may therefore tentatively conclude that the Iron Age inhumation burials which have in the past few years widened the scope of Dutch archaeology, and of which several dozen have meanwhile come to light, reflect two different impulses: a local impulse resulting from the settlement of immigrants, followed by larger-scale cultural influence from northern France, the first signs of which we had already identified in the material culture.

This deviant burial tradition may however also have even older, and possibly also different, roots from those unearthed above: [14]C dates obtained for the skeleton in grave 3 in the aforementioned barrow near Meteren point to the Late Bronze Age.[10] So the different funerary practice could also represent an indigenous development. Future discoveries will have to show whether the inhumation burials may even reflect a tradition that extended as far back as the Middle Bronze Age.

The clustering of inhumation burials in the Betuwe could be partly attributable to the relatively good preservation conditions of the local clay soil, which favour the survival of bone. Inhumation may have been practised more often to the north and south of the river district than we now assume. Indeed,

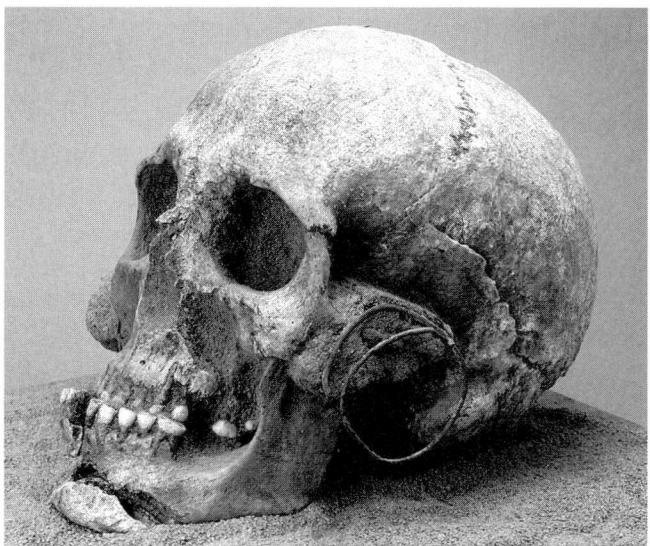

fig. R4

A woman aged 25-40 who was buried face downwards in the cemetery of Lent-Steltsestraat wore two bronze rings near her head. They may have been suspended from a hair band.

empty pits in cemeteries in the sandy areas with their poor preservation conditions are not readily identified as inhumation burials unless they contain imperishable grave goods or are found in such large numbers as at Geldermalsen or Lent. But no such concentrations of pits are known in the sandy areas. That would mean that the Betuwe is indeed to be seen as a central area in the distribution of the inhumation rite. This is also the conclusion that can be drawn from elite burials from the first half of the Middle Iron Age that have been found elsewhere in the river district. Surprisingly, precisely the people who had the most intensive and direct contacts with the Celtic culture of northern France were nevertheless cremated.[11] This holds for both the notable person who was given a chariot for his journey into the netherworld (Nijmegen-Traianusplein) and the important regional figure who was buried near Overasselt accompanied by bronze drinking vessels, various arms and harness fittings (chapter 28).

Whatever the motives for the inhumation burials may have been, this alternative burial rite was clearly practised for only a limited length of time. When, in the course of the 4th century BC, the southern cultural influences came to a fairly abrupt end, the flames of the pyre once again flared up at the end of every lifetime in the Betuwe, too.

Notes

1 The burials in question date from the Middle and Late Iron Age. Examples are known from Middelstum-Boerdamsterweg, Tritsum, Tzum and Englum, and Rockanje in the western coastal area. A larger number seem to date from the last decades BC and the Roman period. Burials from the latter period are also known from the river district (e.g. Wijk bij Duurstede – De Horden). See also Hessing 1993b.

2 Hulst 1999. A substantial number of other burials at this site definitely date from the Roman period and later times.

3 Van den Broeke 2001b, 142-144; see also Van den Broeke 2002a, 22.

4 Meijlink 2001, individuals 5 and 6.

5 Kortlang 1999, 150.

6 Van den Broeke 2000; 2002a, 28.

7 At the time when this cemetery was first mentioned (Van den Broeke 2002a, 27) only a small part of it had been investigated. No ^{14}C dates are yet available.

8 From Tacitus we know that death through burial in peat or a bog was the fate of, amongst others, homosexuals (Germania, 12). As far as the inhumation burials containing the remains of two individuals are concerned – they are incidentally not as exceptional as they may seem: cremation burials also frequently contain the remains of several persons, the most extreme case so far known being an urn that was found at Beegden in Limburg, which contained the remains of seven or more individuals (Hoogland 1999). For explanations of multiple inhumation burials in the Bronze Age and Iron Age, see e.g. Lohof 1991, 234-235, and Spindler 1996, 191-195.

9 Van den Broeke 2001b, 136.

10 Meijlink 2001, 429. This author suggests an alternative date in the Middle Bronze Age on the basis of other considerations.

11 The cases discussed here could also reflect influence from the Middle Rhine area, where inhumation had by this time also become common practice. For a comparison of elite burials in the two areas, see Diepeveen-Jansen 2001.

29 Gifts to the gods
Rites and cult sites in the Bronze Age and the Iron Age

Peter van den Broeke

PROFANE OR SACRED?

Material objects of many different kinds have proved valuable sources of information on such matters as prehistoric economy and technological knowledge. However, as appears from the groups of unused, precious objects that occasionally come to light in areas of former swamps, material objects can enhance our understanding of prehistoric societies in other fields, too. Those objects embrace views and customs relating to spiritual powers; they unlock the doors to religion and the sacred. In other contexts the term *magic* is more appropriate, namely there where man attempted to achieve his aims by invoking impersonal powers. We have, for example, written evidence from historical times describing the protective powers of certain types of wood against diseases and demons. This knowledge was borne in mind in interpreting the different kinds of wood that were used to construct the Early Iron Age house Q in the Assendelver polders. It was found that buckthorn wood – not the most obvious choice of wood for building purposes in this area – had been used in significant parts of the living area[1] (see also feature O). But whether this particular kind of wood had been selected because it was believed to possess the same magic protective powers with which it was endowed in the historical sources two thousand years later we do not know.

Another find of an intriguing nature is the earthenware mask with male features that was found at the Iron Age settlement of Middelstum-Boerdamsterweg (fig. 29.1). This object is commonly assumed to have served a ritual function mainly on the basis of the fact that in relatively uncomplex societies disguises are virtually always used in sacred-ritual contexts.[2]

In the literature, a few criteria and indicators have been suggested for distinguishing between sacred and profane phenomena in the archaeological record.[3] Some of the indicated forms of evidence are absent in the Lower Rhine area, in particular iconographic evidence of the kind that has been found in Scandinavia and other areas; Scandinavian rock art and miniature art are important keys to Bronze Age thought and religion.[4] Another disadvantage in the Lower Rhine region is the scarcity of remains of marked sacred areas, where evidence of religious ceremonies is more easily recognised. In this region, archaeologists interested in prehistoric religious practices therefore focus mainly on the nature and composition of votive deposits and their environmental contexts. The aforementioned collections of valuable objects such as bronze swords, axes and ornaments that were deposited in watery contexts are good examples of the kind of evidence that is available in the Lower Rhine region. However, not all such deposits can be interpreted in religious terms, as will become apparent below.

The disadvantages in terms of the scarcity of archaeological evidence for religious practices in the Lower Rhine region are to some extent compensated by the advantage of the availability of information relating to the period around the close of prehistory from historical sources, in particular the works of Caesar and Tacitus. These sources give us some idea of the motives behind particular rites, the

fig. 29.1

Part of an earthenware mask from the Middelstum-Boerdamsterweg settlement dating from the 5th century BC. Scale approx. 1:2.

nature of the sacred sites and the persons involved in the rites. They are particularly useful in interpreting archaeological evidence from the Late Iron Age. Most of these written sources however relate to the more spectacular, mass ceremonies; what religious and magic practices took place in and around the farmsteads is more difficult for us to infer. Among the few of such practices about which we do have some information are construction rituals, the best-known of which is the building sacrifice.

BUILDING SACRIFICES

In late prehistoric society the longhouse constituted both the base of the economy and the household's only sheltered, heated area. We may assume that the construction of a new farm, which must have been an important event for a family, was surrounded by various rites. There is one aspect of such rites for which we have clear evidence and that is the deposition of votive offerings during the building operations. The small vessels that are occasionally found at the bottom of postholes must have been placed there at some time during the building's construction. The impression that they were deposited during some rite is further strengthened by the vessels' significant positions (beneath a doorpost or a central roof support; at a corner of a room). Two approximately 3-cm-high cups were for example found to have been deposited in the hole of an interior post of the Late Bronze Age house plan that was unearthed at Hoogkarspel. A similar cup was found in the hole of a doorpost in the short northwest wall of an overlapping plan of what is believed to have been the building's successor (fig. 29.2).[5] This phenomenon has been observed at other sites, too, for example at Haps, where a vessel was found standing in an upright position in the hole that had contained the central roof support of a Middle Iron Age house.[6] A larger number of examples of this custom are known from the Roman period.[7] The vessels probably contained food or drink: the actual offerings. The fact that evidence for such building offerings is not observed as commonly as would be expected may be partly due to the perishable nature of the offerings. It is quite possible that the builders and/or occupants also poured out libations or offered other foodstuffs that have vanished without trace. The custom of offering objects, such as coins, seems to have become popular only in the Roman period.

Some of the written sources describing the motives for similar customs that have come down to us from historical times suggest that those customs originated before Christianisation; they may explain the above examples. According to those sources, most of the offerings were intended for household spirits that lived in, for example, the woodwork and had power over the occupants' wellbeing. The offerings intended for the powers of the building site, whose peace was disturbed by the building activities, were of a more placatory nature. Their aim was to ensure

fig. 29.2

A complete cup was found in the hole that held one of the posts of a door of a farm at Hoogkarspel. The predecessor of this Late Bronze Age farm contained two similar vessels buried in a posthole inside the house. The cups probably contained food or beverages deposited as votive offerings during the two farms' construction. House plan scale 1:200, cup scale 1:2.

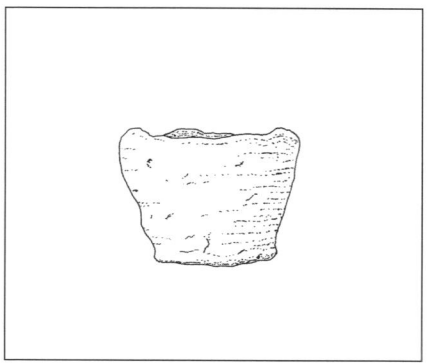

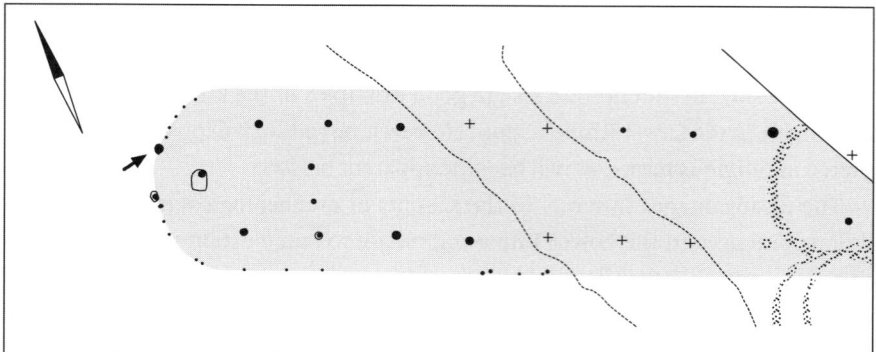

fig. 29.3
Against one of the wattle walls of the oldest known farm whose remains were incorporated in the *terp* of Ezinge lay large parts of the skeletons of a horse, a cow and a dog. They may represent a building sacrifice.

that the earth spirits would not oppose the construction of the farm and would not bring on misfortune later on.

Not only vessels are known as remains of building sacrifices; animals and human beings, too, have been given a place in or below new constructions. According to West European tradition, however, the live animals or human beings that were sometimes sacrificed during building rites were not all intended as votive offerings. Several were sacrificed for the specific purpose of creating a spirit that would protect the building, town walls, dam or bridge under construction. Apparently it was not always essential to actually kill a human being or an animal; in some cases it sufficed to use certain dead bodies that were believed to possess particular powers, for example the bodies of children. However, the human beings whose remains were buried at significant positions in Iron Age *oppida* may very well have been sacrificed for the specific purpose of securing the community's welfare. This fate befell a young man at the powerful Maiden Castle in southern Britain when that *oppidum*'s defensive bank system was expanded.[8] The round pit containing his skeleton was dug into the original bank and was covered with the soil that was thrown up to expand the bank. Whether he was sacrificed as an offering or for the purpose of creating a protective spirit to reinforce the defences with alternative means is not clear. That the occupants of this site believed in protective spirits is apparent from the fact that a dog was buried, with its head facing outwards, in the middle of one of the two entrances to the eastern part of the site.[9] We may assume that the six-year-old child that was buried at the *oppidum* of Manching in southern Germany served a similar purpose. The child was found lying with its face turned towards the gate and the interior of the enclosure, beneath the *oppidum*'s eastern gatehouse; it was probably buried there when the old gate was replaced by a new one.[10]

There is no evidence to suggest that people were sacrificed for buildings in the Netherlands. That is not surprising, because from ethnohistorical sources we know that the value of offerings tended to be proportional to a structure's size, or rather to the interest of the community as a whole in that structure, and virtually all the structures known from late prehistoric times in the Netherlands are farms; fortifications are rare. The large skeletal parts of a horse, a bovine animal and a dog that were found at the foot of the outside wall of the oldest known farm at Ezinge (fig. 29.3) are quite remarkable in this context.[11] If they are the remains of animals that were sacrificed during the farm's construction,[12] then the occupants of this farm must have made an exceptionally large investment in their welfare. The – numerous – examples of animal sacrifices known from the adjacent parts of northern Germany and Denmark are all of later, Roman dates.[13] Also noteworthy are the burials of infants and children, some showing traces of violence, that have occasionally been found inside farmsteads. They will certainly not all have been building offerings; some may have been household offerings of a different kind or may relate to customs of a more magic nature. In the western Netherlands, too, pre-Roman evidence for ritual practices in and around the house is scarcer than Roman evidence.[14]

DEPOSITS OUT IN THE OPEN (2000-100 BC)

The different classes of bronze deposits

For many years it has been generally assumed that a distinction is to be made between different classes of bronze deposits, namely between those that were buried for safekeeping, such as founder's hoards and merchant's hoards, and those that were buried for non-profane reasons. The latter category comprises those deposits that are found in locations that suggest that the objects were never to be recovered. In principle, all the Dutch peats outside the coastal plain may be regarded as such locations as they were uninhabited. But the best examples are watery contexts like swamps, fens and stream valleys.[15] Rivers may also be classed as such contexts, but as the objects that are found in rivers are always recovered in dredging operations their character is not always clear and it is impossible to determine what or which objects were deposited together.[16]

The environmental context and the composition of the deposits are the main criteria in distinguishing between profane and sacred – or at least ceremonial – deposits.[17] Sometimes there appears to be little doubt about the nature of a deposit. Large, homogeneous hoards like that comprising eighteen bronze palstaves and a chisel

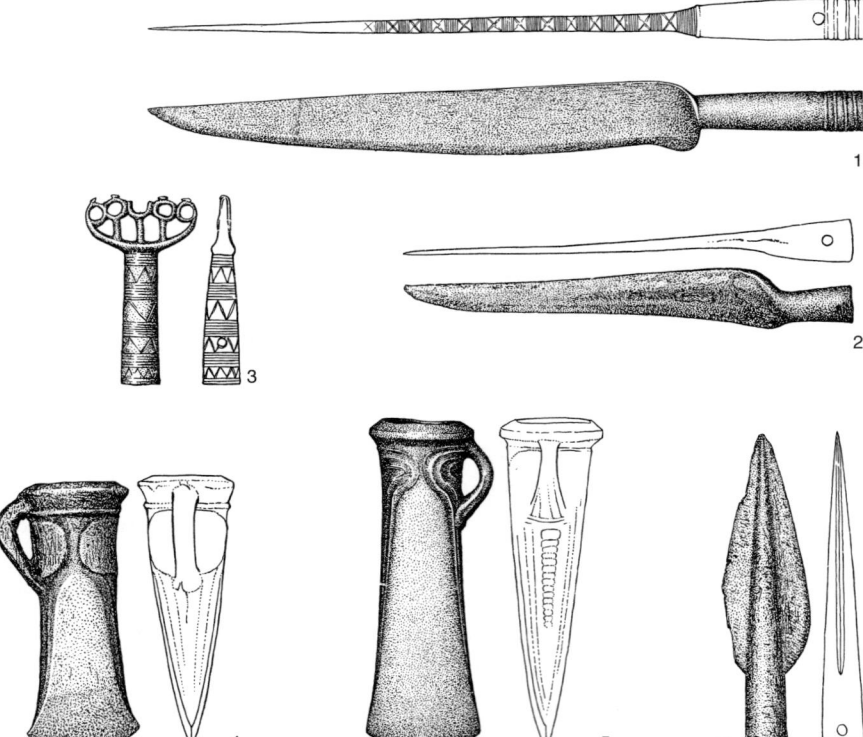

fig. 29.4
The Schoonebeek bronze hoard comprising two socketed knives (1-2), a unique socketed ornament (3), two locally produced socketed axes (4-5) and a spearhead (6). The two knives (so-called 'urnfield knives') are characteristic elements of Late Bronze Age northern hoards. Scale 1:3.

which was found at Voorhout (plate 27A)[18] may have been the stocks of smiths or traders, while a find like that from the Drouwenerveld (fig. 27.2), a vessel containing mainly scrap metal, may have been a founder's precious working material. Buried deposits including semi-finished articles besides finished ones are also assumed to be the hoards of (merchant) smiths; the hoard of Wageningen (fig. 17.8) is a good example. Of a different category are the hoards that consist exclusively of a varied range of end products, like that which was found at Schoonebeek, which comprised socketed axes, socketed knives, a spearhead and an ornament (fig. 29.4). Having been found in peat, this hoard may be regarded as a votive hoard.

A subcategory of finished objects are those that cannot possibly have been intended for everyday use, being far too small or too light or, on the contrary, exceptionally large or heavy or of particularly fine workmanship. Such showpieces were certainly not produced locally; they indicate the existence of far-reaching exchange networks, which were probably controlled by local leaders. Well-known examples of such showpieces in the Low Countries are the large sword of Ommerschans (fig. 17.15), the 42-cm-long spearhead of Exloërmond (plate 28) and the ceremonial axe that is believed to have come from the Meuse near Maaseik (Belgium).[19] The custom of depositing unusual objects of the above kind can in fact be traced back to the Neolithic, when the objects in question were mainly flint axes.

The aforementioned examples all concern deposits about whose character there appears to be no doubt. However, as the following cases illustrate, those examples are extremes on a sliding scale. We do not know the exact findspot of the large sword of Ommerschans, but we do know that it was recovered from peat, together with objects that are usually associated with bronze working, such as bronze chisels, a few grinders and some scrap metal. The sword itself was not ground.[20] Near Enter, also in Overijssel, in a peat that had already yielded several undisputed votive deposits, a deposit containing a few semi-finished bronze ornaments and three amber beads was found beneath a small boulder, which will have served to mark the deposit's position.[21] Are deposits of this kind also to be classed as votive offerings? And if so, which deposits found buried in the ground may we then regard as hoards that were hidden there for safekeeping? It is quite conceivable that, besides finished objects, any objects of a valuable material, including ingots, semi-finished articles and scrap bronze,[22] were considered suitable votive offerings, as is indeed suggested by the severely worn bronze objects that are occasionally encountered in votive deposits.[23]

The above examples make it plausible that single objects were also deposited as votive offerings; the valuable stray artefacts of the same nature that have repeatedly been recovered from the same specific contexts as the composite deposits may very well be such single offerings, especially those whose spatial distribution does not correspond to the pattern that would be expected in the case of profane use or loss. For example, virtually all of the bronze spearheads that have come to light in the area between the Meuse, the Demer and the Scheldt were recovered from stream beds or peat. All of the bronze spearheads that have been found in Overijssel came from similar contexts.[24]

Early deposits

In Northern Europe, including the northern part of the Netherlands, the custom of depositing objects in the ground or in water or swamps originated in the Neolithic. It became widespread throughout a much larger part of Europe in the Bronze Age, but there are considerable regional and chronological differences in the intensity of the depositions.[25] The number of composite deposits found in the Netherlands is fairly small compared with that of Germany, southern Scandinavia and Britain, and the same holds for the size of those deposits. This is particularly true of the deposits from the Early and Middle Bronze Age. In the Netherlands, the earliest known deposits after the very early Wageningen deposit date from the Middle Bronze Age period B.[26] Bronze axes prevail in these deposits. Other common objects are spearheads, pins and sickles. In addition to these collections of bronze objects, other objects were deposited in this period, too, for example strings of beads. The earliest bog bodies date from this same period; many of these bodies may actually be regarded as deposits, too (see feature S).

The Late Bronze Age, in particular the last part of this period (roughly speaking the 9th century BC), saw a sudden increase in the number of depositions in the Netherlands.[27] No fewer than sixteen composite deposits are known from this period. The majority of the objects in all of these deposits are of bronze; most are axes, knives and bracelets (figs. 29.4 and 29.5). The knives and bracelets are almost exclusively limited to the northern part of the Netherlands, the most common finds in the southern part, where far fewer deposits have come to light, being gouges and chisels. The largest deposits, of more than ten objects, were found in Drenthe (Drouwen urnfield, Drouwen-Drouwenerveld) and Limburg (Berg en Terblijt).[28]

The increase in the number of deposits after the Middle Bronze Age period B coincided with a decrease in the number and quality of the grave goods. This same trend has been observed elsewhere in Northern and Western Europe, too. Occasionally a deposit is found in the peripheral structures of barrows, such as the two

fig. 29.5

The relatively large Late Bronze Age bronze hoard from Berg en Terblijt comprising two spearheads (1-2), parts of bracelets (3-4), bronze wire (5-11), a socketed axe (12), a chisel (13), three sickles (14-16) and two winged axes (17-18). Scale 1:3.

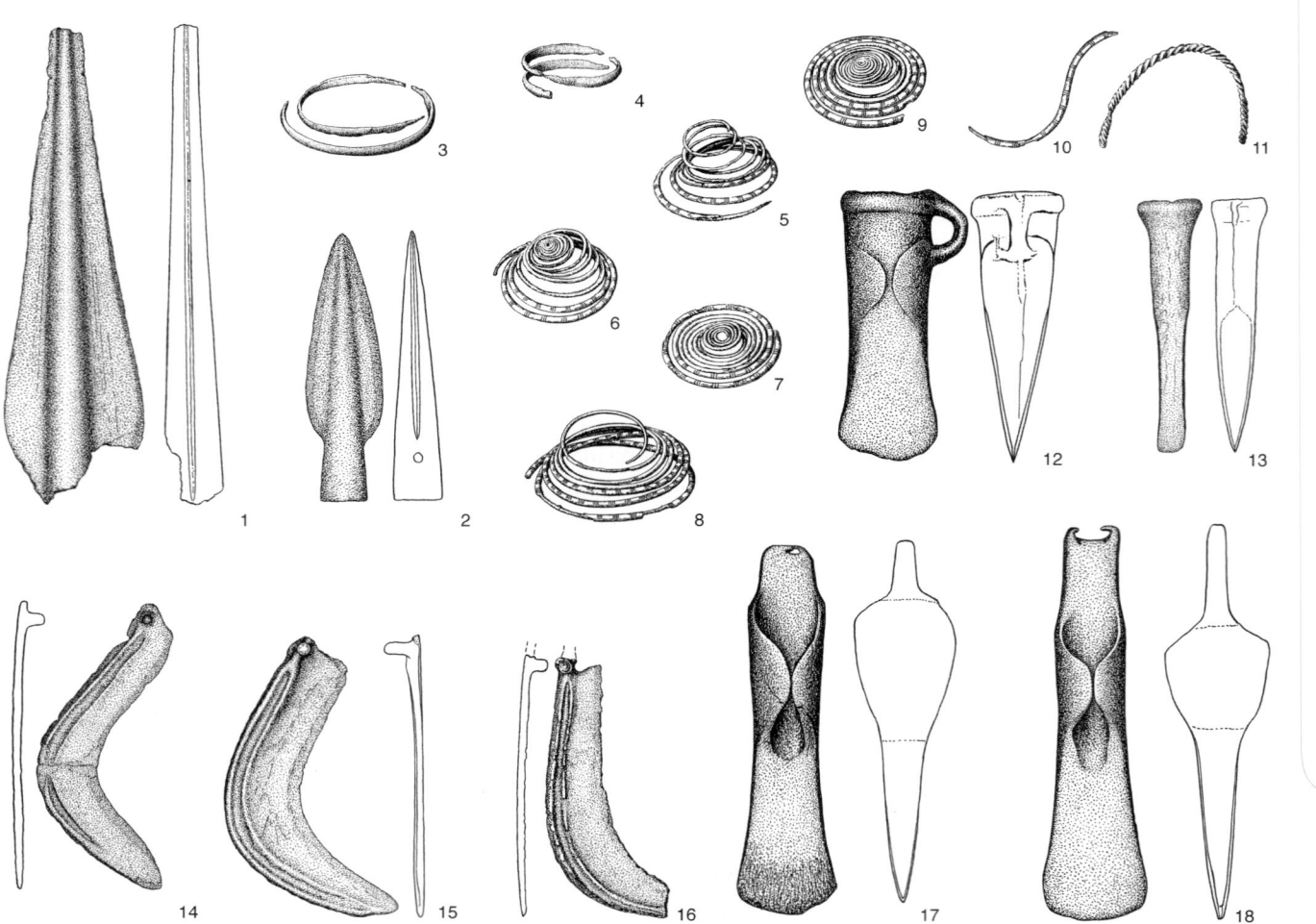

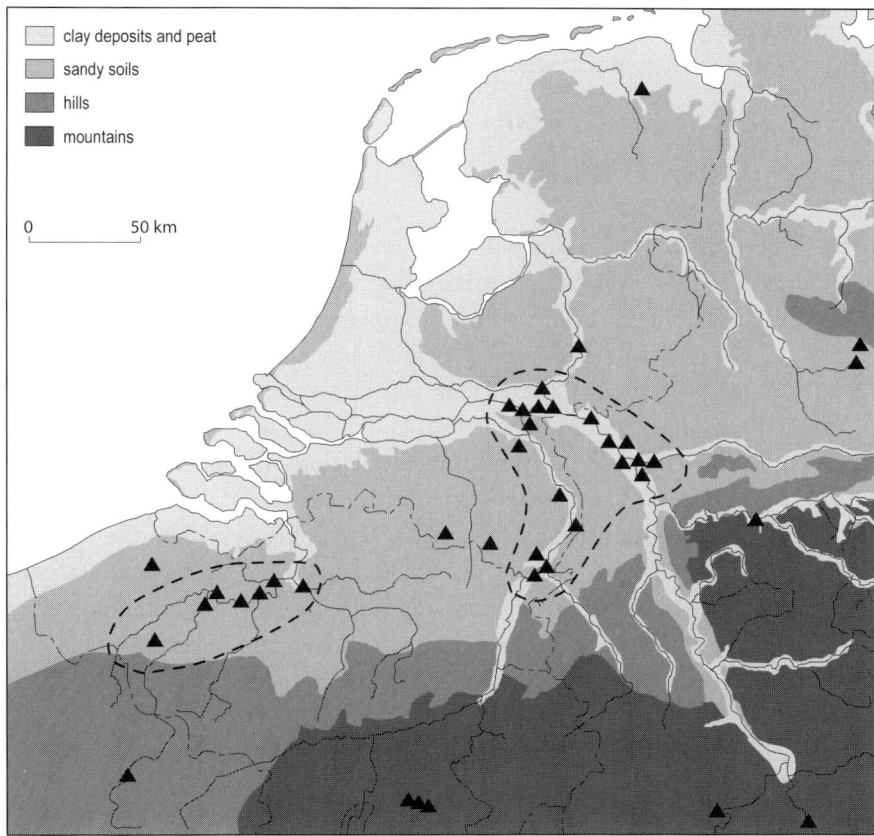

fig. 29.6
Distribution of different sword types from the last phase of the Late Bronze Age (Ha B2/3) in the Lower Rhine plain. The most important regional concentrations are indicated by dashed lines.

sickles and a bronze spearhead datable to the Middle Bronze Age period B that were discovered in the flank of a barrow at Holset.[29] As sickles are very rarely encountered as grave goods, this deposit must be a votive hoard that was buried in an unusual context, probably an offering to the deceased. A similar interpretation is conceivable for the deposit that was found in the circular ditch surrounding a burial at Drouwen. Besides a decorated hanging bowl made from bronze sheet, it comprised mainly ornaments (fig. 28.6).[30] This funerary deposit makes this the only Late Bronze Age burial in the Netherlands that could be classed as a 'rich' burial.

For a long time it escaped notice that an exceptionally large proportion of the bronze objects that have come to light in Belgium, the Netherlands and the Lower Rhine region of Germany had been found in rivers. Besides objects datable to the Late Bronze these river finds also include artefacts of Middle Bronze Age date.[31] These objects may have been deposited in groups, too, but that can no longer be ascertained as most were found during dredging operations. For this same reason we may assume that small objects will be underrepresented. The majority of the river finds are axes, spearheads and swords.[32]

In spite of the evidence being biased, a noteworthy observation has been made and that is that almost all of the weapons from the end of the Late Bronze Age that have been found in the Netherlands were recovered from rivers. The objects that were buried in the ground or deposited in swamps and fens around this time include virtually no weapons whatsoever;[33] weapons are even almost totally absent from graves, too. The majority of the dozens of swords known from this period were found in the Meuse, the Waal and the Rhine, within the triangle defined by Tiel, Duisburg and Roermond. A second concentration was found in the lower reaches of the Scheldt (fig. 29.6). In other nearby areas, for example in the Middle Rhine region, swords have been found both in hoards and in rivers. This led

665

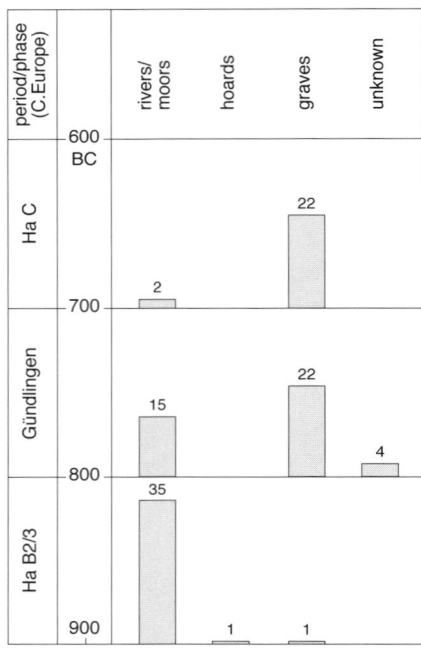

fig. 29.7

The contexts of the findspots of swords
dating from the period from 900 until
600 BC in the Netherlands and its wide
surroundings. A distinct shift is observable
from watery areas to burials. The figures give
absolute numbers.

Roymans to conclude that the custom of depositing weapons in this particular
environmental context was a peculiarity of the Lower Rhine area.[34]

The end of the bronze deposits

In the 8th century BC major changes took place in the deposition customs. In the
southern half of the Lower Rhine area the number of objects deposited in all of the
aforementioned contexts (rivers, swamps, soil) decreased considerably. Whereas
virtually no swords whatsoever had been buried along with the deceased since the
Middle Bronze Age, they now started to be placed in graves more frequently again.
In fact, almost all of the 7th-century swords that have been found in the Lower
Rhine region came from graves.[35] (fig. 29.7) By this time, iron had started to replace
bronze. The diffusion of iron technology from the core area of the Hallstatt culture
in Central Europe appears to have coincided with the spread of a warrior ideology,
characterised by individual leadership and competition. Apparently, the status of
those leaders was to be expressed after their death, too: status markers started to
be buried in graves instead of being consigned to water, fens or swamps.

Some of the other grave goods found in a few of the 7th-century graves that
yielded swords, i.e. those of Oss and Wijchen, reveal close links with the contemporary elite culture of Central Europe, too. The aforementioned ideological changes and the disappearance of the traditional bronze exchange network may both
have precipitated the extinction of the custom of depositing offerings. The same
decrease in the number of deposits has been observed in all of the aforementioned
parts of Europe. In the southern part of the Netherlands no hoards whatsoever or
even single objects appear to have been deposited until in the Late Iron Age.

The northern part of the Netherlands after the Bronze Age

In the northern part of the Netherlands things were different. As also observed
elsewhere in Northern Europe, there is a marked contrast between the large quantities of bronze objects from the Bronze Age and the much poorer finds from the
Early Iron Age; moreover, weapons and tools disappeared from the deposits. In
the northern part of the Netherlands, too, the deposits from after the Bronze Age
comprise mainly ornaments. Fine examples are the two neck rings from Uddel-
erveen (plate 42A), the neck ring from the Onstwedder Barlage peat (plate 47A)
and the neck ring, two bracelets and string of amber beads that were found in the
peat of Nieuw-Weerdinge (plate 28).[36] The deposit from a peat near Enter, which
included a semi-finished *Spatenkopfnadel* and amber beads, has already been mentioned above. The typological characteristics of the ornaments indicate that in this
area the custom of depositing offerings continued until in the 6th century BC.

Other deposits

Only in the northern half of the Netherlands have a large number of deposits consisting of objects made from materials other than bronze come to light besides
deposits of exclusively bronze objects. The only relatively large deposits are those
containing flint 'sickles', the majority of which were found in peat or in stream
valleys. The collection of at least five of such sickles that was found at Buren,[37] in
the rivers area of Gelderland, is the southernmost deposit. What could be called

a 'concentration' of such deposits, in relative terms, has been found in the northeast part of the Netherlands.[38] Another four of these artefacts were found together with a bronze sickle, possibly of Middle Bronze Age B date,[39] at Heiloo (plate 41C). Many of these deposits, which also include several used artefacts, will be of later dates, of up to the end of the Early Iron Age.

Besides the strings of beads already mentioned above, the finds recovered from the raised bogs and cauldron bogs of Drenthe,[40] which have not yet been properly inventoried, also include a few wooden ard shares. A ^{14}C date has shown that two of those shares, which were found together beneath a heap of stones at Echten, were deposited some time in the Early Iron Age. An ard share recovered from a well at Erm dates from the same period. No date has yet been obtained for the share that was found lying on a cobble floor in a cauldron bog near Loon.[41]

The large numbers of stone hammer axes of the Baexem and Muntendam types (fig. 29.8), primarily datable to the Late Bronze Age and the Early Iron Age, should also be mentioned in this context. Many are surface finds, but there are also several dozens that were recovered from bogs, while a few come from stream valleys and rivers. The largest numbers of these objects have come to light in the northeast of the Netherlands; a second, smaller, but nevertheless remarkable concentration has been found in the eastern rivers area.[42] Considering the large numbers of hammer axes that have come to light, it is remarkable that they have never been found in groups or in assemblages, but always as individual finds. Also noteworthy is the fact that about a quarter of the hammer axes are broken. It has been suggested that these hammer axes are therefore to be seen not as votive offerings, but as tools that were used for utilitarian purposes; the authors maintain that the reason why so many have been found in peats, stream valleys and similar contexts is that they were used as cold chisels for extracting bog iron ore. However, the curvature of the hammer axes of the Baexem type will have made them unsuitable for use as cold chisels.[43] What should be added here is that the three known specimens with unfinished sockets were all found in peats, too; this makes it more likely that these artefacts were deposited as offerings than that they were used for practical purposes.[44] Here we find ourselves faced with a problem that holds for other objects, too, i.e. the problem that one tool, weapon or ornament of a particular type may have been used exclusively for utilitarian purposes, whereas another – new or unused – tool, weapon or ornament of that same type may have been deposited as a votive offering.

No deposits consisting of groups of objects of bronze or any other metal from after the Early Iron Age are known in the Netherlands. In fact, deposits in general from before the 1st century BC are virtually unknown, but this may be partly due to the lack of surveys. The fact that the only three fibulae datable to the period between 400 and 100 BC that have been found in Overijssel were recovered from peat and the valley of the Vecht[45] indicates that the custom of depositing objects in watery contexts continued on a regional level at least.

The meaning of the votive deposits

The specific environmental contexts suggest that many of the deposited objects were votive deposits, in particular offerings. But a conclusion that a particular custom had a sacred background, even if generally accepted as correct, does not necessarily fully explain that custom. It is known that persons who give away or sacrifice valuable goods win prestige by doing so. A theory that has found much support over the past decades is that the votive deposits may be seen to reflect the spirit of social competition that characterised Bronze Age and Iron Age societies

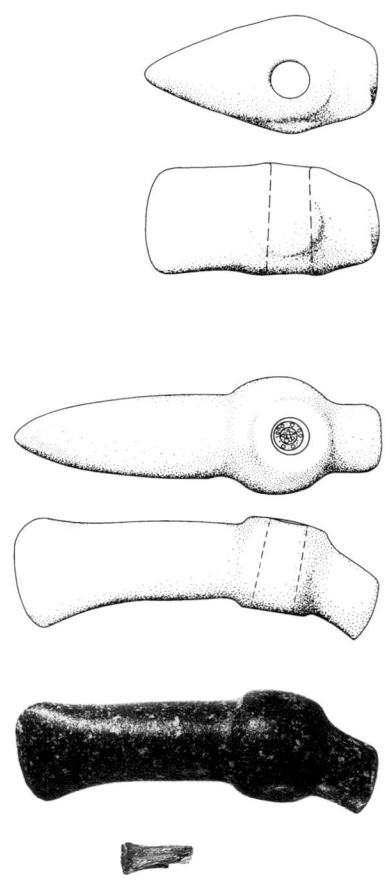

fig. 29.8
Stone hammer axes of the robust Muntendam type (top) and the slenderer Baexem type (bottom). Both were found in characteristic contexts, notably at the transition from sand to peat at Marum and in the Leubeek stream near Haelen. The top of the wooden handle had survived in the handle hole of the bottom axe. It was crowned with two concentric bronze rings and a few bronze pins. Scale 1:3.

in large parts of Europe.[46] From ethnographic sources we know that the destruction of goods and other demonstrations of wealth are the centre of social attention and ceremonial activities among communities of a complexity comparable with that of the Bronze Age communities of Western and Northern Europe. This has been observed for example along the northwest coast of America (potlatch) and in Burma. These sources also show what economic investments and social rivalry such ceremonies may involve.

Bradley has proposed a development from purely votive rites to votive customs governed by competition in the Late Bronze Age.[47] By generously fulfilling religious obligations, the prominent members of a community could enhance their own prestige, and possibly also that of their family, lineage or tribe. Moreover, giving gifts to the gods entailed fewer obligations than giving gifts to other members of the community, because the latter always implied the commitment of offering gifts or favours in return. This could also explain why, in the Early Iron Age, male attributes started to be placed in graves instead of being offered as votive deposits. The appearance of influences of the Hallstatt culture in the southern part of the Netherlands coincides with the emergence of patron-client relationships, in communities of a distinctly martial nature.[48] For the elite, giving away gifts and organising banquets, possibly with Mediterranean wine,[49] were ideal ways of securing the loyalty and services of their followers, whether or not organised in a following (*Gefolgschaft*). Such communities will not have removed prestige items from circulation primarily by offering them as votive gifts. The weapons of early dates suggest that such a martial culture may have existed in the Bronze Age already, but, if so, it will probably have been directed somewhat more to the benefit of the community than in the Iron Age, when martial *individuals* forced themselves to the foreground.[50]

The same kind of contexts that yielded the precious articles mentioned above have also yielded objects of less value. These objects cannot have been deposited for reasons associated with prestige; it is more likely that they had purely symbolic functions. Good examples are the aforementioned ard shares that were found in peat at Echten and Loon. Similar stray shares, but also several dozens of entire

fig. 29.9
Decorative gold-plated silver disc from the peat near Helden. This object, featuring a man struggling with a lion, was probably manufactured in Thrace (Bulgaria/Rumania). Scale 1:2.

ards – from prehistoric as well as later times – have been found in Danish peats. Most of them were old or even unfit for ploughing.[51] They may have ended up in that particular environment having played evocative parts in (fertility) rites associated with supernatural powers that resided in the wilderness.[52]

LATER DEPOSITS

Bog finds

The number of depositions started to increase drastically again around the beginning of the Christian era. Whereas many questions regarding the character of the older deposits still remain unanswered, we have at least some understanding of the motives behind the customs of the Late Iron Age thanks to written evidence relating to Gaul and Germany.

It has been known for some time that objects – and people, whose remains are known as 'bog bodies' – were being deposited in bogs in the northeast part of the Netherlands in the centuries around the beginning of the Christian era. From recently obtained evidence we now know that a similar custom was practised in the western and southern parts, too. Research at Velsen, in the western part of the country, has shown that the custom of depositing offerings in peat bogs started in the Late Iron Age and continued for several centuries, in spite of the fact that the formation of a spit of drifted dune sand and the deposition of sediments on the peat caused marked changes in the environmental conditions. The scarce deposits from the Late Iron Age include an iron chisel with a wooden handle and an iron spearhead. Some of the many dozens of objects of other metals are of pre-Roman date, but the majority certainly date from the Roman period. Most are ornaments, Roman coins and military attributes. Animal bones have also been found.[53]

By itself, the gold-plated decorative silver disc that was recovered from the peat at Helden in Limburg[54] (fig. 29.9 and plate 48A) would be insufficient evidence for concluding that the custom of depositing objects in watery environments existed in the south, too, at the end of the Iron Age. However, the three bronze objects (belt hook, belt decoration and a fibula) that have since then come to light only a short distance from this site, in a fen near Heel,[55] indicate that the aforementioned find is not an exception. What may very well be important in this context is that peat started to be cut at an earlier date – and hence under less archaeological supervision – in some areas in the southern part of the Netherlands than in the north.

River finds

It appears that, around the beginning of the Christian era, people in the southern part of the Netherlands tended to deposit objects in running water rather than in bogs, like they had done in the Bronze Age. Swords have been found at several sites and a richly varied assemblage of finds was recovered in dredging operations between Rossum and Lith, where the Meuse and the Waal almost touch one another. Besides a few socketed iron axes, bronze bracelets, bronze cauldrons and other objects, this assemblage included dozens of fibulae and Celtic coins and a considerable number of swords, scabbards and belt hooks[56].

The unsatisfactory contextual information available on the river finds – including, of course, those from earlier periods – has made many archaeologists doubt whether these objects were intentionally deposited. Alternative interpretations are

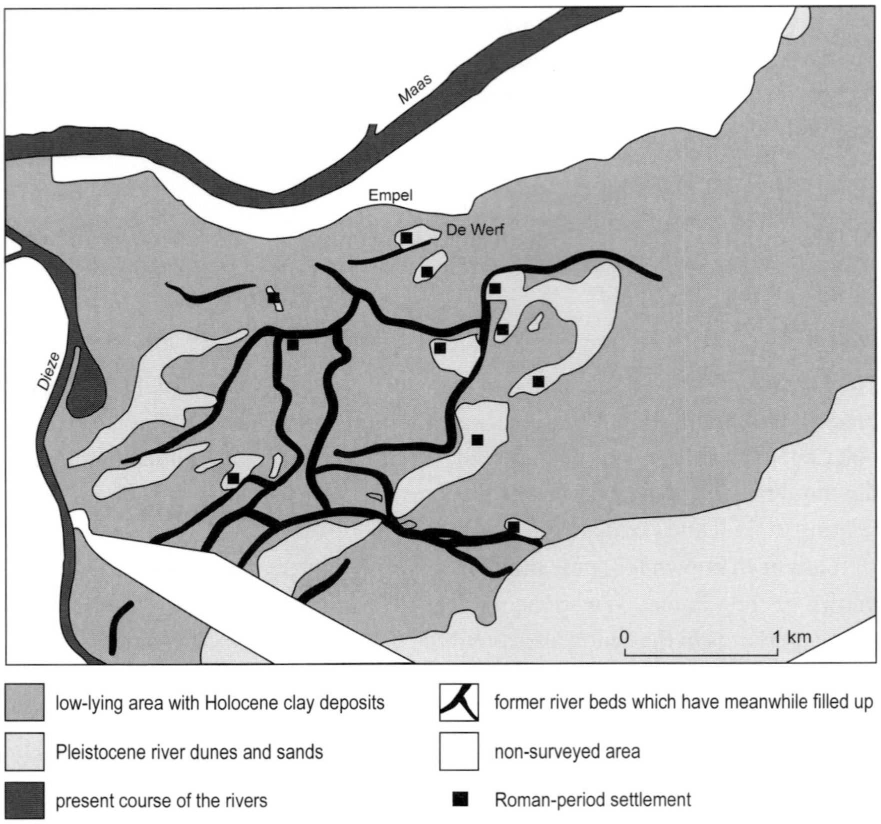

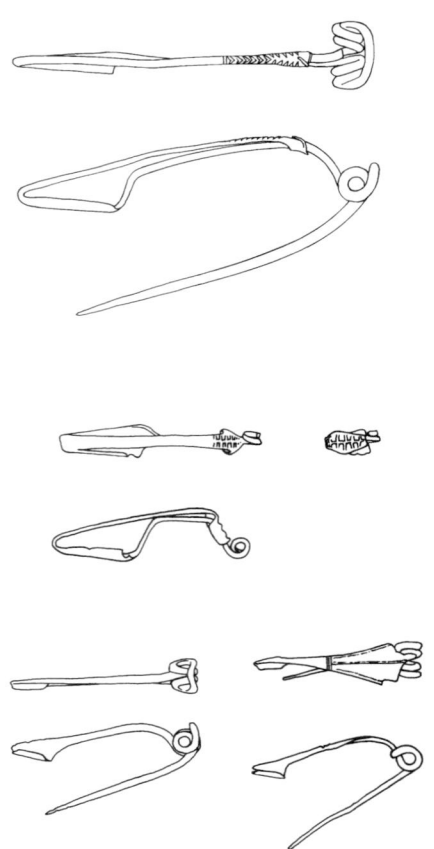

fig. 29.10

Geological map of the fluviatile landscape around the cult site at Empel. From the Meuse, the cult site must have been visible as the nearest stand of oaks rising from the alder carr.

low-lying area with Holocene clay deposits

Pleistocene river dunes and sands

present course of the rivers

former river beds which have meanwhile filled up

non-surveyed area

Roman-period settlement

fig. 29.11

Late Iron Age *fibulae* from the Empel cult site. The top *fibula* is of the earliest type found at this site (middle La Tène) and may date from before the 1st century BC. Scale 1:2.

that they are grave goods washed away from their original contexts or objects fallen from capsized boats or dropped at fords. On the other hand, there are several arguments for regarding most river finds from the 1st century BC as votive offerings.[57] A first major argument is the evidence in the historical sources relating to the Germanic and Celtic worlds. From these sources we know for example what the Cimbri, the Teutoni and their Gallic allies did with the booty they took from the Romans after they had defeated them at Arausio (Orange) in 105 BC: they tore up clothing, slashed armour to pieces, cast gold and silver into the river, destroyed harness fittings and drowned the horses in the river.[58]

The custom of rendering offerings – especially weapons – unsuitable for profane purposes that has frequently been observed in different parts of Europe is also attested in the Netherlands. The clearest evidence for this custom is provided by the finds of folded swords. Most of the fifteen La Tène III swords that were recovered from the water between Rossum and Lith were either broken or folded.[59] From written evidence we know that rivers and springs were associated, or sometimes even identified, with gods and goddesses in the Celtic world. Significant in this context is the fact that in the Roman period a sanctuary where the goddess Rura was venerated stood near Roermond, at the point where the river Roer flows into the Meuse and where five swords dating from the 1st century BC have been dredged from the water.[60] That armour need not necessarily be regarded as offered booty[61] will be illustrated in the next section.

The votive offerings of Empel

The environmental conditions of the findspot near Empel (North Brabant), the site that yielded the most impressive and widest range of deposits in the southern part of the Netherlands, differ from those of the sites described above. Although this

670

findspot also lies along a river, *viz* the Meuse (fig. 29.10), the finds were recovered from a relatively high point, namely a sandy knoll which, with its vegetation dominated by oaks, will in prehistoric times have formed a marked contrast with the surrounding landscape. The earliest deposits found at this site include a large proportion of Celtic gold coins that are known to have been issued by the Eburones. They show that there was a cult site of this tribe here from about 100 BC onwards. In the course of the first century BC the site became a Batavian cult site without any archaeologically visible interruptions. A Romano-Celtic stone temple was erected here probably some time before the beginning of the 2nd century AD. The main god worshipped here was Hercules Magusanus, the supreme god of the Batavians (fig. 30.3).[62] The site was used most intensively in the Roman period, as is evident from the fact that the majority of the approximately 2000 metal objects found here are of Roman date. These finds are only a fraction of the original number of offerings, which have disappeared over the ages in digging operations on the knoll.

Some hundred metal objects are of pre-Roman date. They represent a range comparable with that of the river finds of Rossum/Lith: twenty bronze fibulae (fig. 29.11), seven bronze belt hooks (plate 47B), a few fragments of swords and about seventy Celtic coins. Coins constitute the best represented find category at this site, too (fig. 29.12).

Coins and ornaments were also frequently encountered among the votive offerings found at sanctuaries from around the beginning of the Christian era in Belgium and northern France.[63] They are regarded as fairly 'neutral' offerings, donated by the worshippers to consolidate their personal ties with the deities, express their desires (supplicatory offerings) or their gratitude (thanks offerings). Weapons and other items of warrior equipment, such as belt hooks, are usually assumed to have had a specific meaning, as already briefly mentioned above with respect to the river finds. Several passages in classical texts referring to Gaul and Germany are devoted to the custom of offering booty after a victory over a tribe or a sub-tribe (*pagus*). Tacitus mentions this custom in relation to the Chatti and the Hermunduri in central Germany. Before they waged war on one another, in AD 58, they promised their gods 'Mars' and 'Mercury' that they would sacrifice all their adversaries along with their horses and possessions if their god would grant them victory.[64] From Caesar we know that, before a decisive battle, the Gauls would usually promise to donate all the booty to 'Mars'. If they then won the battle they would sacrifice the captured animals and pile up all the other spoils taken from the enemy. The Roman leader came across many such piles of booty at sacred sites during his campaigns through tribal territories.[65] Numerous deposits found in France are associated with these practices.[66]

The weapons and belt hooks that were found at the cult site of Empel, however, are not believed to be associated with the spectacular, collective rites that attracted the classical authors' attention, but are seen as offerings of a different, more private character. The warrior attributes are of types that are known almost exclusively from the rivers area in the east of the Netherlands. They are thought to have been the personal possessions of the Batavians, who lived in this area, rather than spoils taken from a tribe from elsewhere. These objects may have served a similar purpose as the weapons, harness fittings and other military objects that were deposited at the temple site in the Roman period, that is: they may have been offered during a rite of passage intended to symbolically confirm the return to civilian life of Batavian soldiers who had survived their 25 years of service in the Roman army.[67] Be that as it may, the great majority of both the pre-Roman and the Roman finds of Empel are definitely of a masculine, even martial, nature.

The thousands of animal bones that were found at this site – probably the re-

fig. 29.12

The three most common Celtic coin types from the period 70-15 BC found at the Empel cult site; top: gold *stater* thought to have been issued by the Eburones; middle: silver coin from central or eastern Gaul bearing the legend TOGIRIX; bottom: silver *triquetrum* coin of the Lith group assumed to have been issued by the Batavi. The TOGIRIX coins from Empel are the only coins of this type known to the north of France. They are thought to represent the pay of Batavian cavalrymen who served in the Roman army in Gaul and returned to the Lower Rhine area after their term of service. Scale 3:2.

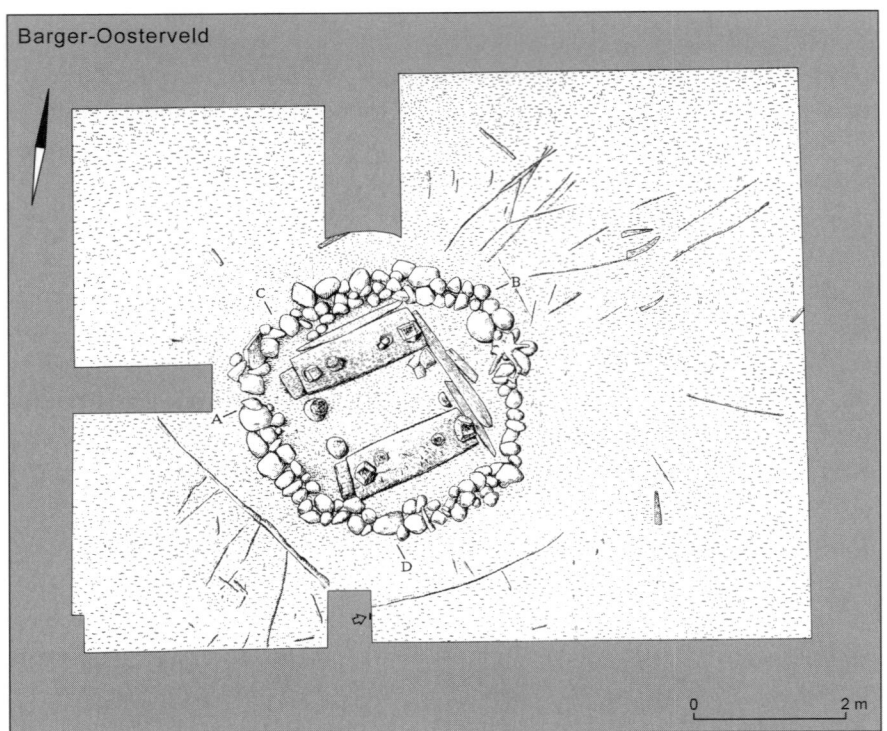
Barger-Oosterveld

0   2 m

fig. 29.13

Plan of the excavation of the Middle Bronze
Age wooden cult structure that was found in
the peat near Barger-Oosterveld.

mains of offerings and ritual banquets – have all been dated to the Roman period. As animal bones have been found at sanctuaries from the last centuries BC in
northern France,[68] the absence of bones of pre-Roman date at Empel could simply
be due to poor preservation conditions combined with a less intensive use of the
site in this period.

CULT SITES: TYPES, CLASSES AND USE

The northern part of the Netherlands

The aforementioned cult sites and other sacred areas have been identified as such
purely on the basis of the presence of votive offerings. As far as the northern part
of the Netherlands is concerned, when we consider the evidence provided by the
classical authors, this seems to be the only possible way of identifying such sites.
Tacitus, for example, informs us that the Germans regarded groves and forests as
sacred areas, the domiciles of the gods; it would have been an insult to the majestic
nature of their gods to have confined them between walls.[69] In view of this evidence and the evidence for the deposition of offerings in rivers discussed above,
it is not surprising that in the northern part of the Netherlands a wide variety of
deposits have come to light in bogs, fens, stream valleys, rivers and similar, unmarked places devoid of structures, away from the settlements.

fig. 29.14

Reconstruction of the cult structure of
Barger-Oosterveld in the archaeological
theme park Archeon in Alphen aan den Rijn.

The only exception concerns the timber Middle Bronze Age structure that was
found in the peat of the Bourtangerveen near Barger-Oosterveld (Drenthe). A ring
of boulders was arranged around this structure of heavy posts, whose sides measured only 2 m (fig. 29.13). Horn-shaped pieces of wood may have adorned the upper part of the structure (fig. 29.14).[70] Over a period of several thousands of years
a large number of votive offerings, including various unusual objects, were deposited in this part of the Bourtangerveen (fig. 29.15). Many of the finds date from the
same period as this structure, which appears to have been a cult building. In this
period the nearby sandy region around Emmen was densely occupied. Against all

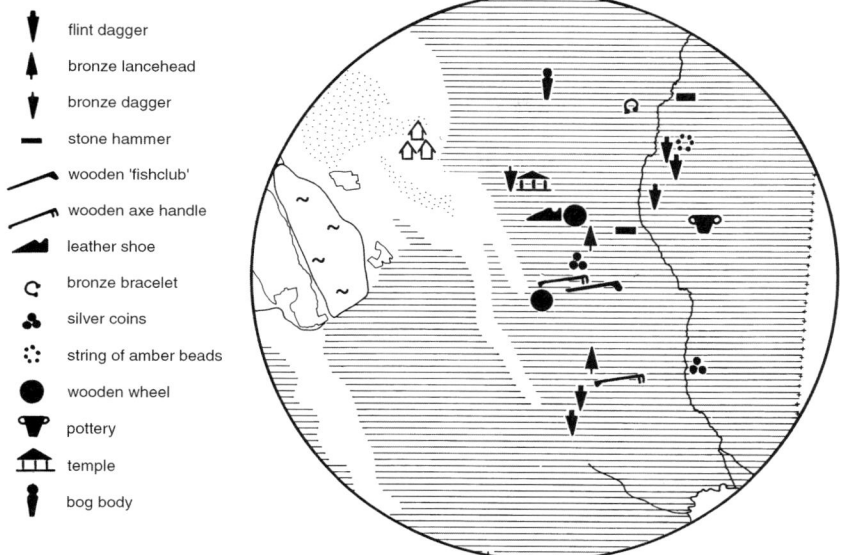

flint dagger
bronze lancehead
bronze dagger
stone hammer
wooden 'fishclub'
wooden axe handle
leather shoe
bronze bracelet
silver coins
string of amber beads
wooden wheel
pottery
temple
bog body

fig. 29.15
Objects from the Bronze Age and other periods found in the peat near the Barger-Oosterveld sanctuary. The houses on the Hondsrug elevation represent the Bronze Age settlement of Angelslo/Emmerhout. The surveyed area has a diameter of 12 km.

expectations, no deposits were found at the site of the building itself. The hypothesis that it was a sacred building is hence based mainly on its location.[71]

The southern part of the Netherlands

Unlike in Northern Europe, in Central and Western Europe, including Britain, many cult sites of the La Tène culture have been identified as such because of their association with a ditch, bank or palisade, or a combination of such structures, separating the sacred area from the profane outside world. These – invariably rectangular – enclosures have frequently been found to contain pits or a deep shaft

fig. 29.16
Square Middle Iron Age cult site at Oss adjoining a smaller funerary structure with cremated remains at its centre. Scale 1:400. *Cf.* fig. 23.8

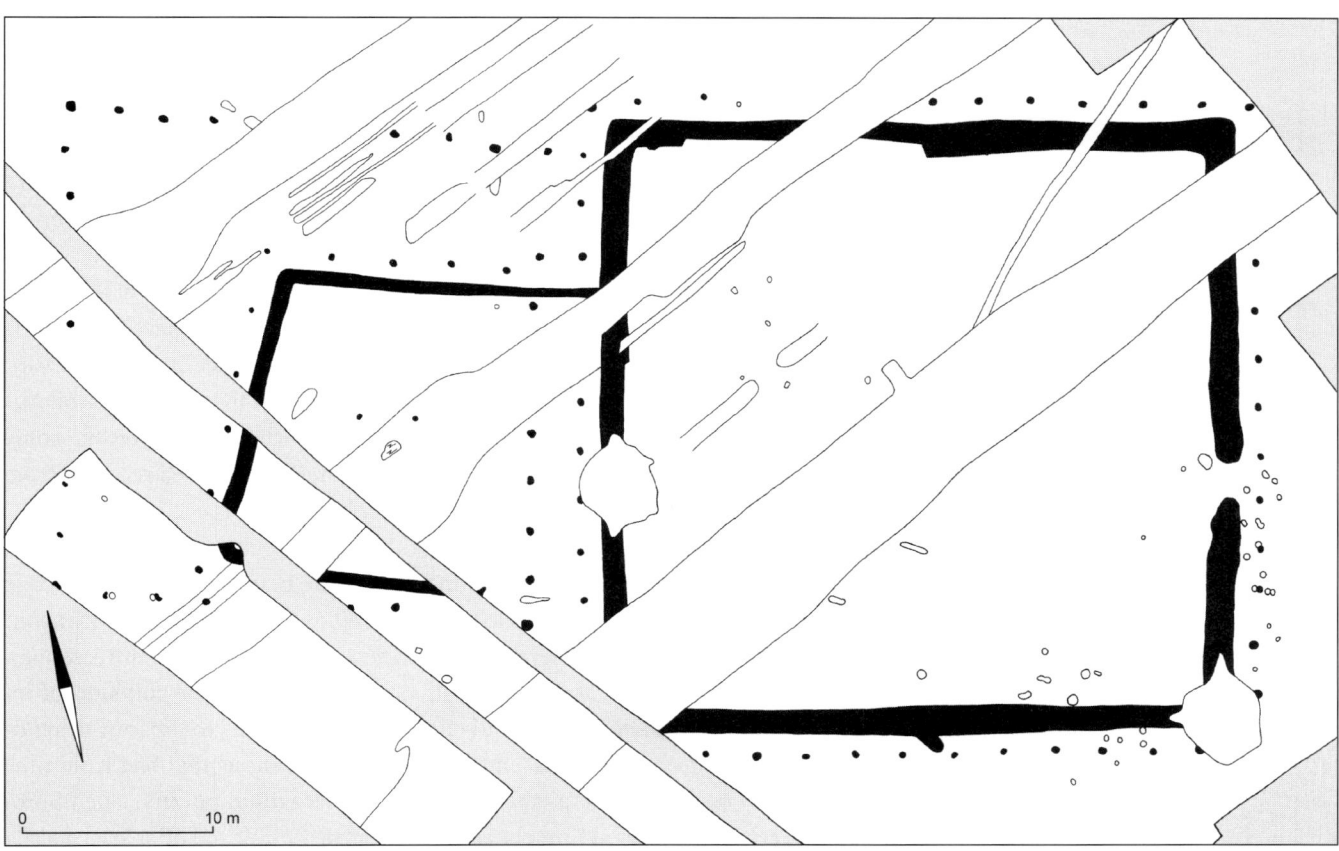

0   10 m

in which votive offerings were deposited, and sometimes also the plan of a small building. The majority of these structures date from the 2nd or 1st century BC. No consensus has yet been reached concerning the development of these enclosures, which are generally referred to as *Viereckschanzen* or *enclos cultuels*, but the impression is that they have a funerary background.[72]

The southern part of the Netherlands cannot be classed as part of the distribution area of the La Tène culture; at most it could be regarded as the northwestern-most extension of this culture's sphere of influence on the Continent. Nevertheless, the square enclosure from around 300 BC that was discovered at Oss-Ussen may throw some light on the development of these rectangular enclosures.[73] The approximately 33-m-long ditches marking the sides of the enclosure were accompanied by a row of postholes on the outside; there was an entrance in the southeast (fig. 29.16). Adjoining the western side of this enclosure was a smaller enclosure. The pile of cremation remains that were found at the centre of this smaller enclosure suggests that it was a funerary monument. A few less conspicuous cremation burials came to light at the northern side of this annex. The rectangular setting of postholes that was found to overlap this funerary monument is believed to represent the predecessor of the large enclosure; it measured 25 x 25 m.[74] The fact that the large enclosure was constructed in different phases, its large dimensions and the presence of two pits that were dug into the ditches at the time that those ditches were dug, all suggest that this enclosure was not a funerary monument but a cult site. The occupants of the farms scattered around the enclosure will have met here when they buried the cremated remains of the deceased; they may also have visited the site at regular intervals for some form of ancestor worship.[75]

Different types of cult sites, gods and social groups

Evidence for at least two more rectangular ditched enclosures from the same occupation period was found a few hundred metres from the cult site in the cemetery of Oss-Ussen. Because of their shape, they too are believed to have been cult sites. They were however somewhat smaller and were situated closer to the farms than the large enclosure. Their situation recalls that of the square cult sites from the Roman period that have been found at Oss-Ussen and elsewhere in the southern part of the Netherlands and also in native settlements further south.[76] However, no evidence of continuity has so far been found.

If the small ditched enclosures were also cult sites, the differences in their sizes and relative positions may relate to differences in use. There may have been different rites for communicating with ancestors and for communicating with the various deities that are known to us from written sources from the end of the Iron Age onwards. We know that those deities were endowed with different powers: some were believed to grant the worshippers fertility, others guaranteed recovery from sickness, protection, success in warfare or other benefits.

There were also differences in the social contexts within which religious ceremonies took place in Northwest Europe around the beginning of the Christian era: some were conducted within local communities, others within a tribal context or even on a supra-tribal level.[77] It is hence conceivable that the different ceremonies were conducted at different cult sites, varying from the cult sites of local communities, situated within the settlements themselves, to those of tribes or larger social units, at central assembly points or at locations that had from time immemorial been regarded as the domains of supernatural powers. The Eburonian-Batavian sanctuary at Empel may be classed as the cult site of at least a *pagus* (sub-tribe). The fact that woods were considered sacred places in Germany and Gaul[78] adds a deeper meaning to the oak vegetation of the sandy knoll at Empel.

FLUCTUATIONS AND DIVERSITY: AN EVALUATION

The years around the beginning of the Christian era saw a sudden increase in the number of cult sites and votive offerings all over Western and Northern Europe. This is often associated with the social tensions, unrest and uncertainty that characterised this period. It is true that there was a good deal of unrest in the Lower Rhine region, especially when Caesar and later Roman generals led their campaigns into this region. If we may indeed assume that the two phenomena are connected, we must ask ourselves whether the earlier peak, in the Late Bronze Age, can also be associated with social tension. Bradley has pointed out that fortifications started to appear in several parts of Europe in this period and that there are also indications of more frequent warfare.[79] However, nothing about the deposits found in the Low Countries suggests increased social unrest. What may be relevant in this context is the evidence concerning the deposition of swords in a few rivers in the Late Bronze Age. If the custom of offering booty to the deities originated several centuries before the accounts were written from which it is known to us, those swords could possibly be related to that custom. Another possibility is that the swords were deposited in the rivers as tokens of the valour of elite members of the communities, perhaps as substitutes for actual battles.[80] Alternatively, the increase in the number of depositions in the Late Bronze Age could be the consequence of fiercer competition in the deposition of valuable objects in general.

It is likely that the appeals, appeasements and thanks offerings were not all directed at a single deity, but at many different spiritual powers, ranging from household spirits to tribal gods, each with its own domicile and each requiring different offerings. This would explain why so many different types of cult sites have been found, and why the nature of the deposits sometimes differs per context, as emphasised by the swords from the rivers.

A final point that should be repeated here is that not all deposits were offerings. First of all, it is very difficult to distinguish between founder's hoards and votive hoards. Secondly, some deposits that we may consider sacred cannot really be interpreted as offerings. The ard shares, for example, are more likely to have served a purely symbolic purpose in the swampy domain of the deities. And several of the individuals whose remains have been recovered as bog bodies will have ended up in the bogs because they committed crimes.[81] The line between the sacred and the profane will have been less clear-cut in prehistory than may have been suggested by the above discussion of this subject and our decision to devote a separate chapter to it.[82]

NOTES

1 Garthoff-Zwaan 1987; Therkorn *et al.* 1984.

2 Dieck has published reports mentioning masks of a different kind. The masks were made from the – very hairy – skin of male upper legs; they have been found in several peats in Europe (Dieck 1975-'76). The accuracy of various details of the recorded find contexts is doubtful (*cf.* Van der Sanden 1993). Most of the indicated dates are late prehistoric. One of the dates given for the two Dutch finds, which are said to have come from find-spots in the peat in the eastern part of Groningen, is implausible (Onstwedde; Early Neolithic), the other (Vlagtwedde-Jipsinghuizerveld) is unknown.

3 Colpe 1970; Renfrew/Bahn 1991, 359-360.

4 *Cf.* Gelling/Ellis Davidson 1969; Malmer 1981.

5 Bakker *et al.* 1968; Van den Broeke 1977, 49-50.

6 Van den Broeke 1977, 50-51; Verwers 1972, *Abb.* 51:436.

7 Van den Broeke 1977; Van der Sanden 1987g, 98-99.

8 Wheeler 1943, 38 and 346.

9 Wheeler 1943, 115.

10 Gensen 1965.

11 An unusual burial of a man was found alongside the byre of a Late Iron Age farm at Rockanje (Van Trierum 1992, 80), but it is not known at what moment the man was buried there.

12 Van Giffen 1963.

13 Harck 1984b.

14 Bloemers 1978, 183; Van Londen 1992; Therkorn 1987a, 217-218.

15 But we must allow for the possibility of changes in environmental conditions as a result of which areas that were originally dry may have become waterlogged and covered with a layer of peat at some later time in history.

16 This does not hold for the many votive deposits that have been found in the Lesse in Belgium; they were recovered in underwater research in the cave of Han-sur-Lesse, where this rivulet rises to the surface (for a preliminary survey see O'Connor 1980, No. 194).

17 For other criteria see e.g. Levy 1982, 19 ff; Willroth 1985, 224 ff.

18 Butler 1990, 78-84. The author suspects that these bronzes were imported from northern Wales en bloc, but possibly as scrap metal, considering the poor condition of most of the objects.

19 Van Impe/Verlaeckt 1992.

20 Butler 1990, 86-91.

21 Verlinde 1980, 4-5.

22 Cf. Bradley 1990, 26.

23 E.g. Assendorp 1975.

24 Beex 1989 and Verlinde 1980, respectively.

25 Bradley 1990; O'Connor 1980, maps 22, 36, 46 and 75.

26 Butler 1990.

27 Ha B2/3 and Montelius' period V. See especially Butler 1986, 135, for the absolute dates.

28 Butler 1979b, 1986; O'Connor 1980, 412 ff. A few very large deposits have also been found just across the Belgian/Limburgian border, namely at Geistingen (more than 20 socketed axes; Butler 1973) and at Maaseik-Heppeneert (at least 48 socketed axes and a spearhead; Van Impe 1994).

29 Butler 1990, 98-100.

30 Butler 1986, figs. 20-22.

31 Roymans 1991, 20 ff; Van Impe/Verlaeckt 1992; Verlaeckt 1993; Warmenbol 1991.

32 Roymans 1991, table 1.

33 Roymans 1991, 20 ff.

34 Roymans 1991, 24.

35 Roymans 1991; Warmenbol 1988.

36 Assendorp 1975, Butler 1984-'85 and Remouchamps 1925, respectively. It is not clear whether the ornaments were specifically female attributes. From later, Iron Age representations from Northern and Western Europe we know that neck rings in particular were also worn by men.

37 Hulst 1987.

38 Butler 1990, 94.

39 Butler 1990, 92-94.

40 See Van der Sanden 1990, 216 ff, for a preliminary survey.

41 Van der Sanden 1993-'94.

42 Achterop/Brongers 1979. According to the authors, however, various records of finds in this area, especially from the Waal near Nijmegen, are unreliable.

43 Groenendijk 1993, 104.

44 Achterop/Brongers 1979, nos 2, 31 and 40. The specific find contexts are however unknown.

45 Verlinde 1982a; a fourth fibula from Overijssel, dating from the first century BC, has been found in the valley of the Vecht.

46 E.g. Bradley 1990; Parker Pearson 1984.

47 Bradley 1990, 142.

48 Roymans 1992.

49 Cf. Diepeveen-Jansen 1992.

50 Roymans 1992.

51 Kunwald 1970.

52 It has been suggested that the bronze sickles that have been encountered in deposits also played a symbolic part in rituals (Levy 1982, 81-82). See also Von Brunn 1980, 122 ff.

53 Bosman/Bosman 1992; Bosman/Therkorn 1993.

54 De Grooth 1987a.

55 Roymans 1988a.

56 Roymans 1990, 85.

57 Roymans 1990, 89; see also e.g. Zimmermann 1970.

58 Orosius, Historiarum adversum paganos: 5, 16, 1-7 (M.-P. Arnaud-Lindet, Paris 1991).

59 Roymans 1990, 85. Older examples of evidence for this custom (with the same meaning?) are the swords that are sometimes encountered in Early Iron Age elite burials, for example those which were found at Meerlo (Limburg) (Verwers s.a.) and Oss, where the valuable sword had been bent in order to make it fit into the bronze situla in which the cremated remains were buried (Modderman 1964b).

60 Bogaers 1962-'63; Roymans 1990, 85.

61 Research is currently being carried out into the connection between metal objects and animal bones – and also parts of human skeletons, including many skull fragments – that have been dredged from waters in the central part of the Netherlands (N. Roymans, pers. com.).

62 Roymans/Derks 1990, 1994b.

63 Brunaux 1991; Roymans 1990, 75 ff; Slofstra/Van der Sanden 1987.

64 Annales, XIII, 57.

65 De Bello Gallico, VI, 17.

66 In particular: Brunaux 1991; Méniel 1992. Most of the southern Scandinavian hoards of loot date from after the first century AD (Fabech 1991).

67 Roymans/Derks 1994b, 28-29.

68 Méniel 1992.

69 Germania, 9.

70 Waterbolk/Van Zeist 1961.

71 The aforementioned authors have pointed out a few details that could indicate that the building served a ritual purpose. No indis-

putable evidence for Bronze Age cult sites within settlements has so far been found in the Netherlands, although it has been claimed that two configurations of postholes at Zwolle-Ittersumerbroek are the remains of posts that served as orientation points for significant positions of the sun (De Jong/Wevers 1994). However, these configurations were distilled out of a dense mass of features after the excavation had been completed and various factors argue against the above interpretation, such as an unacceptable degree of variation in the cross-sections of the postholes (see also Fokkens 1994).

72 Brunaux 1991; Reichenberger 1993; Slofstra/Van der Sanden 1987.

73 The same holds for the square ditched enclosure of Kooigem Bos (Belgian province of West-Vlaanderen), which was situated on a natural elevation. There was a small building in one of the corners of this enclosure; the western ditch contained a funerary or votive deposit that included burned bone and a set of at least seven items of unusual earthenware dating from between 350 and 275 BC (Van Doorselaer 1989; Termote 1987, 1990). A recent discovery made on the Kops Plateau at Nijmegen should also be mentioned here, although the remains in question appear to date from the Bronze Age. They comprise a SW-NE-oriented straight course of boulders leading from a group of circular (funerary?) features, comprising cobble floors and rings of stones, to the northeast corner of what was probably a square enclosure, also consisting of courses of boulders. The three excavated sides were oriented E-W and N-S. The only side that was still intact measured 25 m. The impression that this quite exceptional enclosure marks a cult site is further strengthened by the fact that a bronze socketed axe was found just above the point at which the long course links up with the northeast corner of the square enclosure (H. van Enckevort/D. Fontijn, pers. com.).

74 Van der Sanden 1987e, 1994b; Slofstra/Van der Sanden 1987, 156.

75 The cult site was not recognisable as such on the basis of the pres- ence of indisputable deposits. The majority of the more than 3000 sherds found in the ditches of the square enclosure came from the secondary fill of the pit in the corner. They were all of ordinary settlement pottery. The numbers of fragments found in the two pits are not exceptional compared with those found in other pit fills at Oss-Ussen.

76 Cf. Slofstra/Van der Sanden 1987.

77 Roymans 1990, 49 ff.

78 See the survey in Roymans 1990, 63.

79 Bradley 1990, 137 ff.

80 Cf. Bradley 1990, 139.

81 Cf. Tacitus' *Germania*, 12. They may have been put to death to placate the deities.

82 Greater interest in spiritual aspects of prehistoric life has since the conclusion of this contribution led to a number of notable publications, especially in the field of ritual deposition. It has been found that not only bronzes (Essink/Hielkema 1997-'98; Fontijn 2003), but also other categories of objects, some quite unexpected, ranging from cattle horn sheaths to balls of wool, were systematically deposited in wet contexts (for an introduction see Van der Sanden 1995b, 1997, 1998a, 2002a); see also Van den Broeke 2001a, Van Hoof 2001, Jansen *et al.* 2002, Ter Schegget 1999, Verhart/Roymans 1998. Other publications focus on structures associated with ritual activities, such as rectangular cult sites (Fontijn 2002; Fontijn/Cuijpers 1998-'99; Van der Sanden 1998b [= Van der Sanden 1994b, English version]), the Barger-Oosterveld temple (Van der Sanden 2000) and the (secondary) meaning of funerary and non-funerary post-circles (Harsema 2001 and Waterbolk 1995, 135-136). A general survey of structures in wet contexts is to be found in Van der Sanden 2002c. For ritual practices in and around the house see especially Van den Broeke 2002b, Van Hoof 2002, Gerritsen 2001 and Jongste 2002.

S   Bog bodies
Human remains from the northern part of the Netherlands

Wijnand van der Sanden

If there is any group of finds of which it can sadly be said that they were discovered far too early it is the bog bodies that have come to light in the northern part of the Netherlands. The term 'bog bodies' includes all human bodies and skeletons that have been found in bogs, both raised bogs and fen peat. The 'classic' bog bodies were all found in raised bogs. In the acidic, non-calcareous conditions of raised bogs soft tissues usually survive whereas bones dissolve. The opposite holds for fen peats, in which the soft tissues decompose and only the skeleton is preserved. Both types of human remains will here be referred to as 'bog bodies'.

Most of the bog bodies that have so far been found were discovered in Northwest Europe. In the Netherlands, bog bodies have come to light in the northern provinces only: several dozen of bodies are reported to have been found in Groningen, Friesland and Drenthe.[1] We know that a small number of these are of medieval or later date. The other bodies certainly or probably date from prehistoric or Roman times. It is this last group that is of interest to us here.

'Paper' bog bodies and bog bodies proper

Unfortunately, the aforementioned bodies have not all been preserved; hence the uncertainty regarding the dates of the bog bodies and the above statement that they were discovered at an unfortunate time. Many of the bodies disappeared immediately after their discovery: they were indifferently thrown back into the bog or reburied in local cemeteries. The remains of only a few bog bodies have been preserved and are available for research. They vary from a single tuft of hair to large parts of the skin or the skeleton. The majority of the bodies are known to us from records only and they will hence be referred to as 'paper bodies' below.

The paper bodies include some very interesting finds, for example the so-called 'Roswinkel man'. The newspaper report (March 28, 1892) on its discovery reads as follows: 'It was clearly visible that it was the body of a person of firm stature. The length was about six feet; the outer skin was almost completely intact; one leg was cut off, but the skeleton had lost most of its strength, and the flesh as well. The colour of the skin was black. The nails were still clearly attached to the fingers and toes, but one might apparently say that the hands were covered with black leather gloves. The hair was longer than a decimetre, coloured dark red and still rather

sound. Nothing can be said with certainty about the age and the origin of this body, since nothing has been found on it.'[2] The man has been buried in the churchyard of Roswinkel, but it has not been documented where exactly.

Find-spots and finds

All of the bog bodies were discovered by pure chance. Most were found by peat cutters during turf cutting activities in the raised bogs. Bog bodies have come to light in the expansive raised bogs, such as Bourtanger Moor and the bogs along the border between the provinces of Drenthe and Overijssel, but also in smaller cauldron bogs. A few bog bodies were found in the valleys of the Voorste Diep, the Achterste Diep and the Runde; they are all skeletons or parts of skeletons.

Besides isolated finds, a *pair* of bog bodies has come to light. This is the so-called 'Weerdinge couple', the bodies of two adult men who had been deposited side by side, one with his arm extended behind the other's back (fig. S1).

Also noteworthy are both bog bodies found in the Terhaarster bog, in the immediate vicinity of the Iron Age remains of the so-called *Valtherbrug*, a timber trackway across the bog, dating from the Roman period (see feature I).

Most of the few objects that have been found in association with bog bodies are garments. Some of the reports of the paper bodies mention a woollen cloak and a fur cape.[3] Parts have been preserved of the clothing of the Emmer-Erfscheidenveen body and of the garments of the Yde girl, two bog bodies whose dates differ by more than a thousand years (feature Q).

The absence of clothing at the time of discovery does not necessarily mean that the body was buried without clothes. Any linen garments may have decomposed without trace in the peat.

Cause of death and season of death

The cause of death and the season of death are both very important for the interpretation of the phenomenon of bog bodies. If it were possible to excavate the bog bodies all over again, in the presence of several specialists, using modern excavation methods, then we would be able to say a good deal more about these two aspects than we can at present.

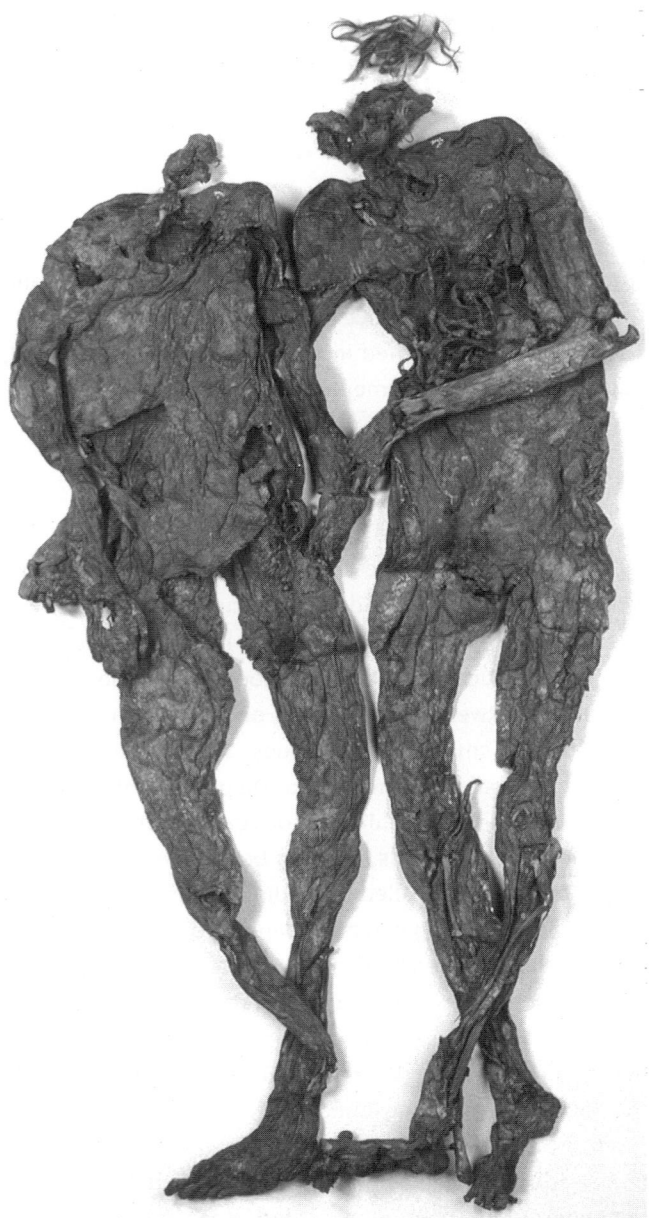

fig. S1

The 'Weerdinge couple', discovered in 1904. They were long taken for the 'Romeo and Juliet' of bog bodies, but we now know that these are the bodies of two men.

Now all that we have to rely on are the contents of old find reports and bodies that have dried out considerably since their discovery. In only very few cases has it proved possible to determine the cause and/or the season of death.

The running knot in the woollen band that was found around the neck of the approximately sixteen-year-old girl whose remains were found at Yde strongly suggests that she was strangled.[4] One of the two men of the 'Weerdinge couple' was presumably stabbed to death, judging from the gash in his chest through which his intestines had spilled out.[5]

It is even more difficult to determine the season in which the individuals met their death. The remains of a meal found in the intestines of the body from Exloërmond – barley and millet – provide no information whatsoever as to the season of death. The remains of a particular insect, a carabid beetle (*Carabus clatratus*), found on this body suggest that the man ended up in the peat some time between April and August, but this evidence is not entirely sound. More reliable is the evidence provided by the contents of the stomach of the bog body from Zweeloo, which dates from the Roman period. The blackberry seeds found in the body's stomach indicate that this adult female died some time between August and October.[6]

Dates

Only very rarely does a bog body yield information from which an accurate date can be obtained. The majority of the bodies found so far were not accompanied by diagnostic objects; the only way in which such bodies can be dated is via scientific methods. And as the results of pollen analysis of any peat that may be found adhering to a body are not always reliable, all that usually remains is radiocarbon analysis. The radiocarbon dating results show that the oldest bog body found in the Netherlands dates from the Middle Bronze Age, while the majority date from the centuries around the beginning of our era (fig. S2), which may hence be considered a peak period.[7] The records of the paper bodies contain relatively few indications concerning the dates of the bodies.

Interpretation

Most of the bodies that have been recovered from bogs are of men; a much smaller number are of women, while only very few bodies of children have been found. Apart from the possible odd exception, none of these bodies are the remains of individuals who lost their way and died in the bogs. Some of the bodies were found buried beneath a pile of branches, others showed indications of a violent death; this, and other evidence, signifies that the bodies were deliberately deposited in the peat. There is no doubt about it that this particular way of disposing of the dead differs markedly from the usual form of burial practised in pre- and protohistoric times. Whereas their contemporaries were buried in the cemeteries of the settlements where they had lived, these individuals were deposited in bogs.

Other finds besides bodies have been recovered from raised bogs, such as weapons, tools, parts of wagons, jewellery, clothing, pottery, *etc*. These objects can only be interpreted as votive offerings. They tell us that from the Neolith-

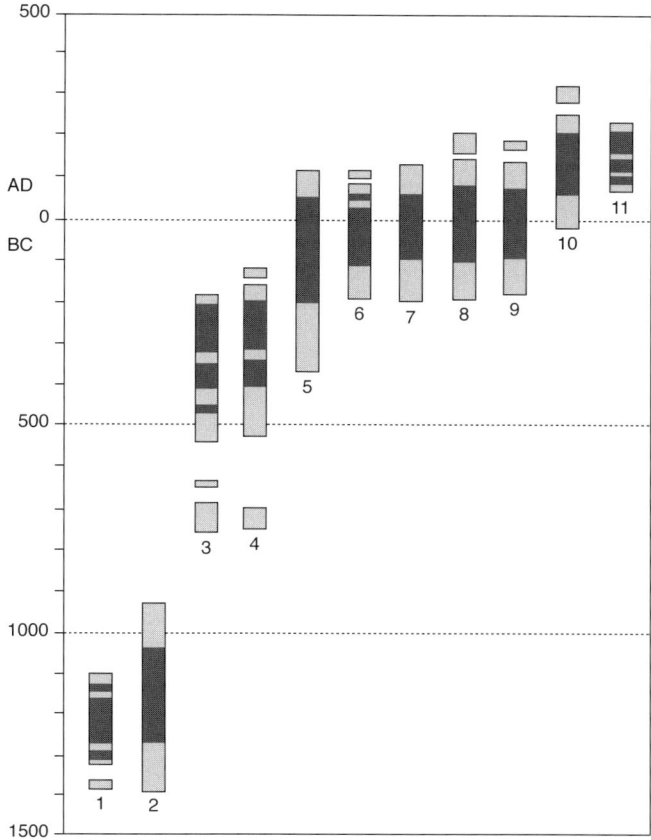

fig. S2

Survey of the calibrated ¹⁴C dates obtained for Dutch bog bodies. Grey bar sections: 2 standard deviations; black bar sections: 1 standard deviation.

1   Emmer-Erfscheidenveen 1938
2   Weerdinger Aschbroeken 1931
3   southeast Drenthe 1920-1930
4   Exloërmond 1914
5   Borger 1975
6   Terhaarsterveen 1891
7   Buinen 1985
8   Yde 1897
9   Weerdinge 1904
10 north Drenthe?
11 Zweeloo 1951

ic until at least the early Middle Ages the expansive raised bogs and smaller cauldron bogs must have been regarded as liminal places, sacred environments where people could communicate with the supernatural world. Further evidence supporting this view is the Bronze Age timber temple whose remains were found at Barger-Oosterveld. The many remarkable finds that have been recovered from river valleys suggest that they, too, were considered sacred areas. In this context it seems very plausible to regard the human bodies that were deposited in the raised bogs and river valleys as votive offerings, too. The fact that the hair of some of the bog bodies had been cut may be seen as an indication that some of the individuals who were offered to the deities were selected for sacrifice because of some crime that they had committed during their lives.[8]

Many questions still remain unanswered, for example the question regarding the cause of the peak in the frequency of sacrifices around the beginning of our era. The (scarce) data available for the part of Lower Saxony adjoining the Netherlands show a similar peak around the same time in that area, too. Another question is whether the human sacrifices were made during cyclic rites, as Glob has suggested for the Danish bog bodies.[9] Unfortunately, the data required to be able to answer this question, i.e. the contents of stomachs and intestines and associated insects, are almost completely lacking. Research on the other categories of bog finds might throw more light on this problem.[10]

Notes

1   From the number of 66 (Van der Sanden 2002b, 180-182) more than 20 should be subtracted, since recent research has shown that these relate to fictitious find reports (Van der Sanden forthcoming).
2   Van der Sanden 2002b, 175-176.
3   Van der Sanden 1990, 209, see also Van der Sanden 2002b, 180-182.
4   Especially Van der Sanden 1994a.
5   For Yde and Weerdinge see Uytterschaut 1990, 129-131.
6   For Exloërmond and Zweeloo see Van der Sanden 1990, 151-157; Hakbijl 1990, 169-170, 172; Troostheide 1990, 158-161. For Zweeloo and Weerdinger Aschbroeken see Van der Sanden et al. 1991-'92. It has recently been established that the Zweeloo body is of a woman.
7   Van der Sanden 1995 and 2002b, 180-182; Van der Plicht et al. 2004.
8   Van der Sanden 1990b, 216-225; Van der Sanden 1995a.
9   Glob 1977.
10 Van der Sanden 2002a.

30 Increasing diversity: synthesis

Peter van den Broeke

In the previous chapters the emphasis has been on the information that is currently available on individual aspects of society at the end of prehistory. We will now try to briefly integrate those aspects and to look beyond regional boundaries. That will give us the opportunity to consider aspects that have received only little attention so far, such as the degree of social differentiation. Although the period discussed here covers only just over one millennium, we are nevertheless able to trace various developments in this relatively short time span and to catch a glimpse of what was to follow in the subsequent Roman period.

We will also glimpse into another future, namely the future of prehistoric research, to see what questions regarding late prehistoric society must still be answered and how the information required to answer those questions can be obtained.

SETTLEMENT FORMS

In the first millennium BC the Netherlands comprised a richly varied mosaic of occupied environments. Besides in the areas that had already been occupied for many centuries, such as the dunes, the rivers area, the sandy soils and the loess region, there were now – since the Early Iron Age – also settlements in the coastal peat zones and, for the first time in the history of the Netherlands, the bare salt marshes were occupied on a large scale. The settlements in those distinct environments were however rather uniform. Some consisted of isolated farmsteads, others of several scattered farms forming open hamlets. Hamlets of nucleated farms were only to be found in areas with repeated flooding, on natural elevations (*e.g.* Bovenkarspel, Haps) or on artificial mounds built from sods and manure (*terpen*). Settlements of that kind were occupied for several centuries or – for example the Ezinge *terp* – even several thousands of years.

Where there were no major physical restrictions people did not originally feel tied to a particular location. The evidence obtained in the sandy regions shows that solitary farmsteads or the individual farms of open hamlets were constantly rebuilt at different locations within a territory of several square kilometres. The lifespan of 20-30 years that is assumed for the timber farms suggests that they were rebuilt once every human generation. Evidence obtained at Oss-Ussen and in the Celtic field of Hijken suggests that people returned to previously occupied sites after a few such movements. We may therefore speak of 'settlement cycles'. The cemetery in which the family or families buried their dead formed a fixed landmark within the territory, at least in the Late Bronze Age and the Early Iron Age (fig. 30.1, left).

It was only around the beginning of the Christian era that the first nucleated hamlets started to appear on the sandy soils, too. This trend towards nucleation was to continue in the Roman period (*cf.* Oss-Ussen, Noordbarge). At Oss-Ussen the distance over which the settlements moved was moreover found to have decreased over the centuries (fig. 30.1, right). Here the contraction in settlement (the development of nucleated hamlets) appears to have coincided with an increase in

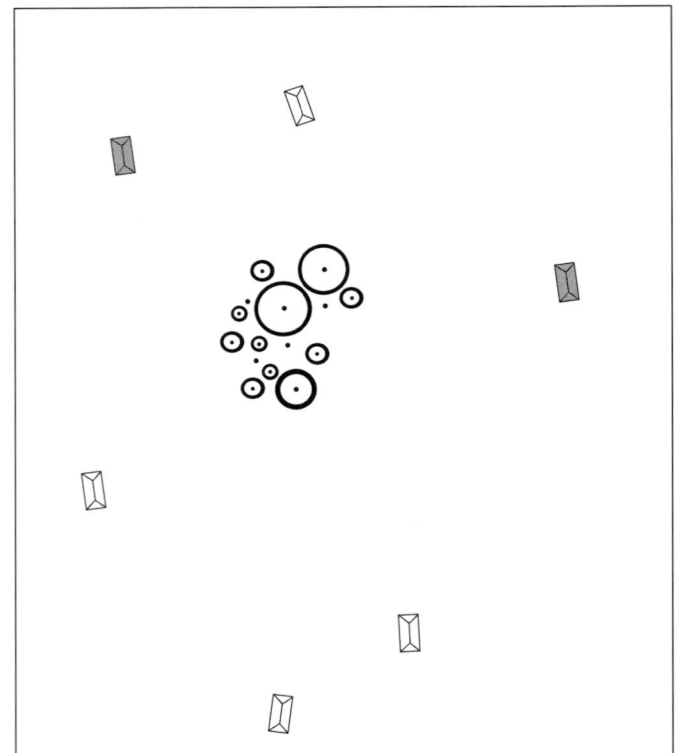
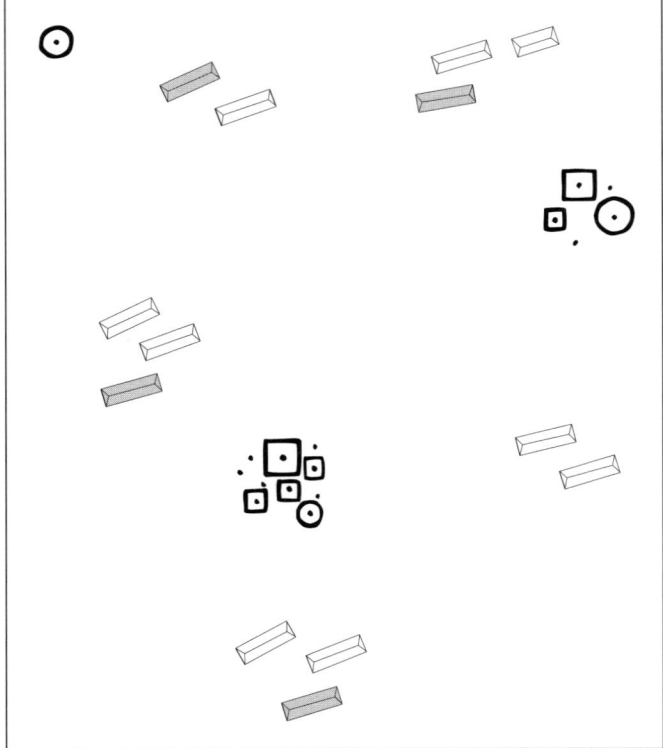

fig. 30.1

Left: model of the settlement pattern in the higher parts of the
Netherlands in the Late Bronze Age and Early Iron Age. The open hamlet
comprises only two occupied farms (grey), built at some distance from
their predecessors from two earlier occupation phases (white). The
constant factor in this form of 'unsettled settlement' was the urnfield.

Right: model of the settlement pattern in the higher parts of the
Netherlands in the Late Iron Age, in particular in the central and
southern parts of the country. Over the centuries, settlement has become
denser and the farms (grey) have now been built in the yards of their
predecessors (white). The cemeteries are smaller than in the urnfield
period. It is not yet possible to say how representative this model is, as
coherent information on occupation and burials is still restricted to a
few sites only.

the length of time spent at each site; in other words, people began to feel more
strongly tied to a particular location. By the end of the Iron Age a settlement pattern had emerged here – and probably in many other regions, too – that had previously existed only in environments abounding in water.

It is difficult to identify the factors and motivations responsible for these changes in settlement forms. There where palisades or banks were erected or ditches
were dug (for example in some places in northern Drenthe and in southern Limburg and the adjacent hills around the beginning of the Christian era) the occupants' safety was clearly a major consideration. In times of unrest it is safer to live
close together in hamlets – whether or not fortified – than in scattered farmsteads.
But there are other factors that may have been partly responsible for the observed
changes in settlement pattern on the Pleistocene soils, for example demographic
factors (fig. 30.2).

POPULATION

The population densities that have been calculated for the sandy soils in the Late
Bronze Age and the Early Iron Age all range from about 2 to 5 persons per km². The
substantial decrease in our most important sources of information on population

densities (the cemeteries) after that period is to be attributed not to a decrease in population, but to the poorer archaeological visibility of the burials. In view of the exceptionally large scale of the settlement research carried out at Oss-Ussen we have used the evidence obtained at this site as a basis for a model of the demographic developments on the (southern) sandy soils. The calculated figures increase from about 4 persons per km² in the Early Iron Age to at least 18 in the Late Iron Age. That the rivers area in the central part of the Netherlands was also very densely occupied in the Late Iron Age is most apparent from the glass bracelets that have been found in many places in this area; occupation remains are fairly rare here. The coastal peats were intermittently occupied, but they, too, were the most densely occupied after the Early Iron Age. In the *terpen* area, however, the increase in the population figures must be associated with the (temporary) decrease in the population of the adjacent plateau of Friesland and Drenthe.

Our earliest written records relating to population densities date from the 1st century BC. It is not inconceivable that Caesar exaggerated the number of opponents he faced in the Gallic war for personal ends, but even if we don't believe every word he wrote we may still assume that the region between the Rhine, the Ardennes and the North Sea was occupied by many tens of thousands of people around the end of the Iron Age.[1]

Caesar's accounts moreover show that it is still very difficult for us to archaeologically detect substantial, brief fluctuations in population figures. We have, for example, no archaeological evidence to demonstrate the void that Caesar left behind him in the southern part of the Netherlands. The archaeological proposition that certain categories of finds from the rivers area in the eastern Netherlands, in particular the silver *triquetrum* coins, indicate the arrival of a new group (the Batavians) would probably never have been advanced without historical sources. Indeed, the observed continuity in the use of a sacred site like that of Empel-De Werf (fig. 30.3) and the uninterrupted cultural development attested in that same area, with the possible exception of the layout of the houses (*cf.* Oss-Ussen), would never have suggested such a conclusion. Any demographic catastrophes or ethnic shifts that may have taken place before the middle of the first century BC may still be eluding us. Only the colonisation of previously uninhabited areas, such as the coastal peats and the salt marshes in the north of the country, is self-evident.

It should be added that hypotheses of the kind that were advanced a few decades ago, in which changes in cultural patterns were invariably attributed to the arrival of conquerors or immigrants, can no longer stand the test of criticism. We may not allow ourselves to be deluded by for example the exotic contents of the rich burials of Oss and Wijchen into neglecting the fact that the local burial rite was practised here.

ECONOMY

The economy was primarily based on agriculture. Hunting and fishing were hardly important at all after the first centuries of the Bronze Age. The previously unoccupied environments (the northern salt marshes and western coastal peat) were colonised for agricultural purposes, although the different ecological conditions of those environments will probably have forced the colonists to adapt the composition of their livestock and their range of crops. All the evidence indicates that the households were more or less self-sufficient within a subsistence economy based on a symbiotic ratio of crop cultivation and animal husbandry. Only in the coastal peat region is there some doubt about the possibilities of local crop cultivation,

fig. 30.2

The most densely populated areas in the Iron Age.

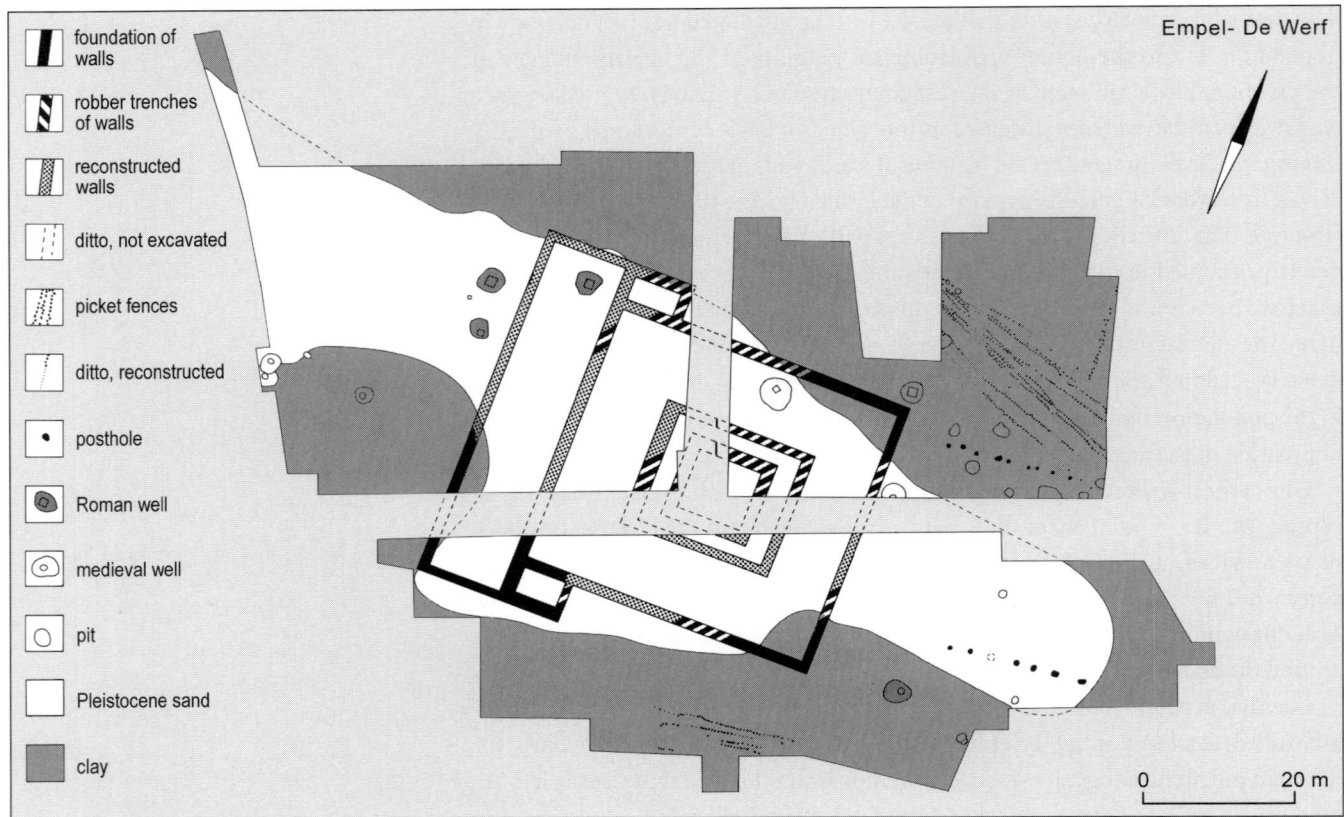

Empel- De Werf

foundation of walls

robber trenches of walls

reconstructed walls

ditto, not excavated

picket fences

ditto, reconstructed

• posthole

◉ Roman well

◎ medieval well

○ pit

Pleistocene sand

clay

0   20 m

fig. 30.3

From the end of the 1st century AD onwards, the temple of Empel was the stone crowning glory of a cult site that had originated as an open-air sanctuary in the Late Iron Age. The continuity in the sacred use of the site obscures the ethnic shifts that occurred in the eastern part of the rivers area.

partly on account of the fact that the earliest storage facilities known in this region date from the Roman period, whereas several storage facilities have been found in the ecologically much less versatile salt marshes. The occupants of the coastal regions will probably have been dependent on the hinterland mainly for material goods, such as timber.

Cattle dominated the stock system of the Lower Rhine region to what was by European standards an exceptionally high extent. Similarly to what was established for the settlement form above, environmental factors had only a minor effect on the composition of the stock, although the degree of the domination of cattle does vary slightly from one region to another. At some sites in the dunes sheep (and goats) occupied a prominent second position.

If we relate the prevalence of cattle to the size of the longhouses we must conclude that the stalls were intended for cattle. But why? In a temperate climate it is by no means essential to stall cattle continuously throughout the winter; winter stalling moreover involves the drawback of having to collect large quantities of fodder. The cattle may have been stalled to enable their owners to collect their manure. The occupants of areas of less fertile soils, especially those of the marginal sandy soils, had to rely on their cattle's manure to keep their fields fertile, especially in the period when population growth led to increased pressure on the most fertile soils.[2] However, if we continue along this line of reasoning it is very odd that thick layers of manure were used to raise the floors of houses in the peat regions (Midden-Delfland). This manure was evidently not used to fertilise the fields which are assumed to have surrounded those houses.

Although horses ranked among the regular stock at the farms in the Iron Age, they were virtually never used for farm work. All the heavy work was done by oxen. It would seem that horses were primarily the attributes of the elite, who used them to draw their ceremonial wagons (Wijchen and possibly Oss) or, in a different period, their war chariots (Nijmegen). They may also have used them as riding animals, whether or not in conflicts. As riding animals, horses may have enhanced the status of the occupants of many farms, too. It is moreover possible that horses had an important ritual meaning and/or that the occupants of the farms felt emotionally attached to these animals, as suggested by the fact that bones with cut marks are underrepresented in the faunal samples.

Besides the development of the Celtic field system, the first millennium BC witnessed another clearly observable change in farming practices. Around the transition from the Bronze Age to the Iron Age, for the first time since the introduction of crop cultivation, the range of cultivated crops was considerably expanded. Millet, and probably also oat, started to be grown on a permanent basis. Also conspicuous is the diversity of crops yielding oil-bearing seeds that were grown in the Iron Age (linseed, gold of pleasure, rape); legumes (pea, Celtic bean) were also grown. The wide range of cultivated crops may have encouraged the colonisation of new environments or may at least have reduced the risks involved in colonisation.[3] It is still very difficult for us to estimate in what quantities these new crops were grown and how they related to the traditional crops barley and wheat.

A factor that is even more difficult for us to assess, but that will sometimes have been of overriding importance with respect to starvation or survival, are the crops' yields. If the crop yield ratios gradually increased over the centuries, they may well have contributed to some of the changes observed in for example the locations selected for occupation, settlement mobility and population growth.

THE FARM AS THE CENTRE OF EXISTENCE

Within the territory comprising the farmyard, the fields and the pastures, the longhouse formed the centre of existence. The marked differences in the house plans from the Early Iron Age onwards between the southern part of the Netherlands and the northern and western parts (two-aisled plans vs. three-aisled plans) will undoubtedly have played a part in the occupants' awareness of their cultural identity. However, in spite of these differences – to which archaeologists, in the absence of other remains of the houses, have paid a good deal of attention – both types of house plans reflect a socio-economic development that took place at more or less the same rate all over the Netherlands: at some point, probably around the 10th century BC, the length of the plans decreased, in particular – so it seems – the length of the byre. Why this change took place is not clear;[4] neither do we know whether it coincided with or was related to the development of the Celtic field system and the assumed associated intensification of crop cultivation. Did people start to keep fewer animals because they had found new ways of enriching their soils, for example by mixing them with sods? Another possibility that has been suggested is that the need for a large byre for the cattle may have disappeared because people had started to keep more sheep (and pigs). But no such changes are indicated by the ratios of the different types of animals in the faunal samples, although it should be added that we don't know what changes may have taken place on the higher sandy soils because too few bones have survived for analysis in those areas. An entirely different possibility is that the decrease in the length of the farms is attributable to a decrease in the size of the households, which would have meant that fewer animals would have sufficed to support each farm.[5]

Large farms were to reappear only in the Late Iron Age. They stood alongside much smaller farms at some settlements, for example at Oss-Ussen and Ezinge – two settlements in entirely different environments. As the sizes of the byre also differed considerably, especially at the latter site, we may regard this as evidence for economic as well as social differentiation. According to Roman authors, status among Germanic and Celtic tribes was essentially dependent on the possession of livestock.

The small amount of settlement evidence so far obtained for the southeast of the Netherlands seems to indicate a different trend, more akin to the developments in the adjacent part of Germany. In this part of the Netherlands, no longhouses whatsoever are known from the last centuries BC, but only small structures. Here the animals may have been stalled in byres detached from the houses or they may not have been stalled at all.

PRODUCTION AND EXCHANGE

The uniformity in the settlements and buildings and the fact that objects like spindle whorls have been found at all of the sites both suggest that agricultural production was organised predominantly on a household basis. The individual households supported themselves with the products of their fields (food crops, flax for linen), their livestock (meat, milk, dairy products, wool, leather, bones) and what additional foodstuffs (fruit, fish) and materials (wood, fibres, clay, antler, stone, *etc.*) could be obtained from their natural surroundings. Some regions, especially the salt marshes, were however poor in natural resources. The occupants of those regions had to obtain their timber and stone via exchange or by making regular expeditions into other regions.

Flint sickles and the later querns of tephrite from the Eifel are among the few categories of goods that were exchanged on a fairly common basis; they have been found at sites all over the Netherlands. But they are not the only objects for which most households had to produce a surplus. Some households may have been unable to afford metal ornaments or weapons, but they will all have possessed tools (*e.g.* axes). The raw materials for bronze were not available in the Netherlands, but as people could melt down scrap metal to produce new tools, they were dependent on imports from elsewhere to a limited extent only.

Although the raw material for iron was available in the Netherlands in the form of high-quality bog iron ore, the scarcity of indications of iron production and the assumed high proportion of imports among the early iron swords suggest that only little use was made of it. Prestigious metal objects will have been primarily exchange objects, whereas everyday implements were produced and repaired on a more common basis, probably by an occupant of a hamlet who was skilled in forging or by a regionally operating smith. The smith's craft was probably one of the few – full-time or part-time – specialisations in the agriculturally oriented society. Whether there were actual merchants before the Roman period we don't know. What we do know for sure is that coined money didn't play a part in the exchanges of these early days. The coins that are known from the 1st century BC are not to be regarded as everyday currency, but as special purpose money.

The goods that were offered in exchange for both the elementary commodities (querns, axes) and the more prestigious articles will have been essentially agricultural products, woven clothing, leather and the like. The occupants of the coastal region and the areas bordering estuaries were moreover able to offer sea salt. This wide diversity of products will also have been used to obtain the unusual objects found in hoards, such as the ceremonial swords and axes. However, this does not hold for all the unusual finds. The four-wheeled ceremonial wagon of Wijchen is in several respects an exception. This vehicle cannot possibly have made its way into the eastern rivers area via ordinary exchange or trade. In the first place, Wijchen lies several hundreds of kilometres outside the distribution area of such vehicles and, secondly, in Central Europe it was only the elite that possessed such vehicles. It is more likely that we are to regard the wagon as a kind of 'diplomatic gift' presented by a member of one elite to a member of another elite many miles away. But what may have formed the basis for such a relationship with a member of an elite in the eastern Netherlands we do not know. From several other exotic articles from this same period that have been found at equally remote sites, such as the sword inlaid with gold that came to light at Oss, the *situla* that was found in the same grave and the similar finds recovered from other graves in the eastern rivers area, we know that this ceremonial wagon was not a unique case.

Valuable goods did not always change hands according to such a harmonious model of gift and exchange. From Caesar's accounts we know that native tribes raided one another and were constantly exacting tributes from one another. The occupants of the Kempen region – the Eburones – for example, had to pay tribute to their southern neighbours, the Aduatuci.[6]

SOCIAL AND POLITICAL ORGANISATION

The burials of the periods preceding and succeeding the Early Iron Age show no evidence of the social differentiation that is reflected by the aforementioned burials. This is due to the constant changes that took place in the way in which the elite treated their possessions. They seem to have offered many of their riches to their gods in the Late Bronze Age, enhancing their status in the process. The leaders of the Late Iron Age are archaeologically invisible, certainly in the northern part of the Netherlands. In view of Tacitus' comments on the little distinction that the Germanic tribes made between nobles and the rest of the community in their burial rite, this is not surprising. According to Tacitus, the only distinction was that a different kind of wood was used for the pyres of the nobles.[7]

In the southern part of the Netherlands the size of the funerary monument may have reflected a social difference, as it had done before, in the Early Iron Age. From Caesar's accounts we know that there were persons whom he referred to as 'kings', but that, in the south of the Netherlands and surrounding areas, there were no prominent, or even established, positions of power. The leadership of the Eburones was shared by Ambiorix and Catuvolcus, each of whom was the 'king' of his half of the tribe. In actual fact, the 'king' was the leader of the tribal community in times of war only. The sub-tribes (*pagi*) constituted separate political units, comprising families of nobles who were the tribal leader's rivals rather than his loyal followers. To maintain his position he had to compete with those nobles by organising sumptuous banquets and by giving away his possessions.[8] A similar situation may very well have existed in the Early Iron Age already.

As will be evident from what has been said above, no evidence of socio-political differentiation has so far been encountered in the settlements. A *Herrensitz* like that which came to light on the Kemmelberg in West Flanders (Belgium), with its own craft centre and a material culture differing from that of the surrounding rural areas, is unknown in the Netherlands. All that could be mentioned in this context are the – much later – concentrations of storage structures (at fortified sites in the north of Drenthe) and the substantial local differences in the size of the byres. However, in assessing the size of the stock – in principle an important indicator of wealth and status – we must also consider the size of the household.

In summary, we may conclude that in socio-political, economic and cultural terms, the communities in the Netherlands in the first millennium BC were living on the sidelines of the developments that were taking place in Central Europe among societies with a greater degree of differentiation and hence a somewhat more complex organisation.

AFTER THE IRON AGE

The arrival of the Romans did not cause any immediate changes in the main characteristics of the native communities described above.[9] It is believed that the first, disastrous confrontations, between 56 and 51 BC, did not end with the Romans asserting their control. However, things changed in 12 BC, when, under the reign of the emperor Augustus, the Romans started to use the eastern part of the rivers area as a base for their conquests with which they aimed to expand the Roman empire up to the Elbe. Then the Netherlands did pass under Roman control. When in AD 47 the Romans decided to abandon their Elbe project, and the Rhine consequently came to mark the northern border of the Roman empire, it was the population of the southern part of the Netherlands that felt the impact of the Roman dominion the most.

The reason why even then only minor, gradual social changes took place in that part of the Netherlands is that the Romans never aimed at complete integration of the areas they occupied. What actually happened is that an imperial political-military machinery, with military posts, villages and cities, was extended to embrace a tribal society with small rural settlements.

The Roman occupiers tried to formalise the existing tribal territories into administrative units (*civitates*) with the fewest possible changes. The native elite was used as a link in this process. The Romans won this elite over with luxury goods and Mediterranean wine and with 'cheap' but status-enhancing prerogatives, such as Roman family names and Roman civil rights. It is this elite that made the rural settlements of this period appear more differentiated than those of the Iron Age, partly because they emulated Roman building styles and Roman architecture. They started to cover their roofs with Roman tiles instead of reeds or straw, they plastered their walls and decorated them with wall-paintings and sometimes they even installed central heating. Although the burial practices did not change fundamentally, Roman influences are also observable in the grave goods that were buried with the cremated remains, for example in a suckling pig served on Roman crockery. The native men who returned to their communities after serving as mercenaries in the Roman army will have played an active part in the process of Romanisation. As the Romans also recruited mercenaries from the Germanic areas that were not under Roman control, 'foreign' customs will slowly have been assimilated in those areas too, as will Roman imports, introduced via trade and exchange. Illustrative in this context are the concentrations of all kinds of Roman objects, including pottery, coins and figurines of Roman deities, which have been found in the *terpen* of Friesland.

Agriculture remained the basis of the economy of the native settlements. The encampment of thousands of soldiers in the border region will of course have created a great demand for agricultural products, part of which at least was met by the local population via the imposed taxes. The other part was evidently produced on a voluntary basis. From the rapid increase in the numbers of Roman articles in the settlements in the south of the Netherlands we may infer that the occupants of those settlements were producing for the Roman market besides for their own support. The gradual replacement of a large part, or even all, of the local, domestically produced pottery by Roman ware is moreover one of the clearest signs that the degree of specialisation increased in this part of the country after the Iron Age.

WHAT NEXT?

The relatively large degree of uniformity that appears to characterise pre-Roman society in the Netherlands may be deceptive. The above conclusion that considerable differences in personal status existed in some periods but that the settlements were fairly uniform need not reflect the actual situation. On the basis of observations made elsewhere in Europe it has for example been suggested that the settlements where the elite lived may have been situated at strategic points in the network of long-distance trade contacts, in particular at the confluences of rivers. At some of such points along the lower reaches of the Rhine and along the Meuse conspicuous numbers of bronze objects – mainly weapons – have been found, namely at Roermond, Nijmegen and Wesel (Germany). Elite residences are assumed to comprise for example indications of unusual craft activities (in particular metal working), exceptionally large storage facilities (pits, granaries) or unusual ditched enclosures.[10] It may prove possible to locate such settlements in specific surveys. The discovery of such settlements would certainly affect our current picture of a settlement system characterised by a minimum degree of differentiation.[11]

In an economic respect, too, there may have been a greater degree of differentiation between the individual settlements than would now appear. Various archaeologists have suggested that some Early Iron Age settlements, especially in the salt marshes (Middelstum-Boerdamsterweg) and the coastal peat zone, may have been exponents of transhumance – the agricultural counterparts of the earlier extraction camps. Although it is quite conceivable that transhumance was practised in this period, it should be added that each of the settlements in question comprised a longhouse (or a building of that size). Byres would seem to be particularly superfluous in a system of transhumance, there being no need to collect manure in the absence of fields.[12] It is highly unlikely that people will have gone to the trouble of building large summer residences in the treeless salt marshes.

What seems to constitute far more convincing evidence of differences in the functions of individual settlements is the plan of a flimsy Middle Iron Age house that was unearthed in The Hague. The plan, which measured no more than 6 x 3 m and comprised foundation trenches and a hearth, was situated at the transition from the coastal barriers to the zone of clay and peat, on the inside of a bend in a creek, at the highest point of a marshy area. The land around the house was not suitable for crop cultivation, but hoof impressions show that cattle could be pastured there. The small site also comprised a pit containing fish remains, which is very unusual for the Iron Age. The presence of only one spindle whorl and no loom weights whatsoever among the more than ten thousand sherds of earthenware vessels also suggests that this settlement served a specific function.[13] From the large quantities of pottery we may infer that the house was used repeatedly (on a seasonal basis) or for a long period of time, possibly by the occupants of a base settlement elsewhere. The chance of such small sites being discovered is far smaller and far more dependent on fortuitous circumstances than that of ordinary settlements. But not many ordinary settlements have come to light in this particular environmental zone either.

A source of information that has not yet been tapped, but which may help to answer the question whether settlements were occupied on a seasonal basis in a transhumance system, is pottery. Pottery assemblages of summer settlements will differ in composition from the assemblages of the home bases. We may for example expect more types associated with cheese production at summer settlements.[14] If the salt marshes were indeed occupied on a seasonal basis, the greater part of the earthenware will have been made from clay obtained from the beds of streams on the higher grounds. This could be verified in diatom research.

Material studies in general may yield some answers to the many questions that still remain. The possibilities of archaeometric research are still increasing; they could prove most valuable in this respect. The analysis of microwear traces on stone hammer axes, for example, may show whether these artefacts were indeed used in iron production, as some archaeologists have suggested. But even our current macroscopic research may yield answers to elementary questions, for example regarding specialisation in production. The sites in the wetlands, which are such valuable sources of ecological information, too, may play a key role in answering such questions. A factor of crucial importance is that in the coastal peat zones, for example in the Assendelver polders and around the Meuse estuary, pottery sherds have been preserved in situ inside house plans. When dendrochronological research will have reached a stage enabling us to determine which farms within a particular region were simultaneously occupied, detailed comparison of decorative motifs on pottery combined with thin-section analysis will undoubtedly yield an answer to the question whether each household produced its own pottery.

What we must not forget is that in order to be able to reconstruct a single aspect of prehistoric society – let alone any developments it may have undergone – we have to approach that aspect from different angles and through different fields of research. As we have seen above, such a holistic approach is essential, especially in the case of questions regarding social differentiation and the size of the population. Research into burials and grave goods alone led to a picture that varied considerably over the ages, but a far more balanced picture emerged when that burial evidence was supplemented with evidence from settlements and from off-site deposits. It was then found that the burial evidence from which, until only a few decades ago, archaeologists had had to form an impression of late prehistory had in fact led to a distorted image of pre-Roman society. This is not to say that the synthesis presented in this book will remain valid for all eternity.[15]

NOTES

1   De Bello Gallico, II, 4. Caesar specifies figures of 9000 men for the troops of the Menapii, who are believed to have lived in Flanders and Zeeland, and 40,000 able-bodied men for the Eburones and some smaller nearby tribes, who lived in an area extending roughly from the territory of the Menapii to the Rhine in the east.

2   The need to stall the animals to protect them from predators seems to have disappeared almost completely by the Iron Age. It is far more likely that the risk of cattle being stolen by hostile groups necessitated preventive measures.

3   Cf. Louwe Kooijmans 1993a.

4   For a recent discussion see Fokkens 1998.

5   Roymans/Fokkens 1991, 9-10.

6   De Bello Gallico, V, 27.

7   Germania, 27. This was however not the case everywhere.

8   Roymans 1990, 34.

9   A good survey is to be found in Van Es 1981.

10   Roymans/Fokkens 1991, 14.

11   Waterbolk (1985, 73-74) suggests that there may have been a few other regional centres in the sandy region in the north of the Netherlands besides the fortified settlements in northern Drenthe, namely near Rolde (Balloërkuil) and near Havelte (Bisschopsberg).

12   But it may be assumed that transhumance did not preclude the cultivation of summer crops.

13   Waasdorp/Stuurman 1992, and information provided by A. Carmiggelt, P. Stuurman and J.A. Waasdorp.

14   The finds recovered from the aforementioned findspot in The Hague include no evidence of cheese production.

15   After completion of this synthesis a survey concerning food production in the greater part of Northwestern Europe was delivered (De Hingh 2000). In the meantime N. Roymans has published several works on the roots and identity of the native Roman community (1995a, 1996a, 1998, 2001).

Conclusion

31 The Netherlands in prehistory: retrospect

Leendert Louwe Kooijmans

THE LONG-TERM PERSPECTIVE

We have come to the end of a long, joint struggle to combine the evidence provided by finds, features and samples unequally distributed in terms of space and time into a more or less balanced story. In this struggle we had little other choice than to adopt a periodic approach and describe the past step by step. Processes embracing long time spans have been cut up into bits. More or less fixed structures and patterns have in each step been described in the specific ways in which they occur in successive phases. In the present conclusion we intend to take a more thematic look at our prehistory in its entirety, and describe a number of trends, developments on a very long term, embracing all of the individual periods. In other words, we intend to view things from the perspective which the famous French historian Braudel[1] called the *longue durée*, a perspective in which time virtually stands still and in which fixed contexts such as geography, climate and ecology are the main determining factors. A prehistorian's perspective however embraces a much longer time span than a historian's, and in that perspective even those factors are not constant. Over the millennia they, too, underwent distinct changes, some of which were even caused by man.

Our decision to leave the long, earliest period before the last glacial maximum out of consideration in this conclusion is in many respects justifiable. In the first place, that is an era involving problems all of its own, a comparatively extremely long era which saw several major environmental and geographical changes, the last phase of the physical development of man and the emergence of social and cultural differentiation. This long time span has been adequately summarised in chapters 5 and 9.

Around 13,000 years ago, when the last glacial came to an end, northern Europe was reoccupied and a more dynamic period began, in which changes occurred within an otherwise continuous development. The Magdalenian and Hamburgian hunters who moved into northern Europe were entirely 'modern', that is, physically the same as us, and in material and organisational terms comparable with subrecent arctic hunters. They were – apparently – no less developed in social and ideological terms either. Their arrival in the Netherlands marked the beginning of social developments and the use and organisation of land that were to become ever more specifically 'Dutch'.

Dry land and wetland

In this long time span, embracing more than 10,000 years, the Low Countries constituted a culturally fairly inconspicuous region, often even a backwater, outside the leading centres of development. With only a few exceptions, the Netherlands is in all periods poorly represented by material 'treasures' and visible monuments. Our part of the world did however see drastic environmental changes. It is largely in this period that the land that is now confined by the Dutch borders was shaped and moulded. The deposition of large quantities of sediments at the outlets of the major rivers led to the formation of a vast wetland complex, which gave the Netherlands an entirely original identity. Dutch archaeology has almost inevitably focused far more on settlement and environmental aspects than on material analysis. Those aspects evolved into typically Dutch specialisations and they have hence played prominent parts in the preceding contributions.

The story of Dutch prehistory is a modest account featuring hunters followed by simple farmers living in small hamlets. Life revolved around securing the daily and annual needs in the endless cycle of the seasons. Life in the higher, sandy parts of the Netherlands was very similar to that modelled for a wide area extending beyond the Dutch frontiers, but typically Dutch themes are the vast, dynamic wetlands in the lower parts of the country and life in those parts. Dutch prehistory is characterised not by major events, but by social developments that gained momentum from time to time. We tend to emphasise those – often subtle – changes, which to outsiders will probably seem constant variations on the same themes. Does that make our work boring, or is there also an intriguing, sometimes even exciting, side to it? What we would really like to know is how happy people were, what they believed and what they feared, but those questions we are unable to answer. We will have to make do with more materialistic and descriptive images of our past.

Trends

The following long-term processes characterised social developments in Dutch prehistory, or determined their course:
- population growth and the emergence of modest social differentiation;
- a chain of simple, but nevertheless highly essential innovations: the axe, the plough, the wheel and the wagon, spinning and weaving, bronze and iron metallurgy;
- constant, fundamental changes in subsistence patterns: adaptation to the drastic environmental changes that occurred around 10,000 years ago, the adoption of crop cultivation and stock keeping followed by the development of specific north European farming methods that enabled sustainable exploitation of the marginal sandy soils;
- a continuous process of conquering 'the wild' and consciously shaping the land, in which the intimate relationship between a territory and its occupants was expressed by simple burial monuments. In other spheres offers were made to higher powers. Besides the cosmos, the land and people's ancestors seem to have played important parts in spiritual life, too;
- the expression of ethnic identity in designing objects, and the marking of social rank through the possession of unusual exotic objects and their use in ritual deposition. Weapons played a modest, but central part in this respect.

It is difficult, if not impossible, to indicate straightforward cause-and-effect relations between these processes. One thing that is certain, however, is that they were not autonomous processes, but were on the contrary closely linked.

All the visible processes of change seem to have been indigenous processes, that is, they seem to have been based on ethnic continuity. Foreign ideas and inventions were introduced and accepted without much foreign human intervention. There are two exceptional cases of relatively large-scale immigration: the arrival of the first reindeer hunters, who moved into the northern plains from Central Europe some 13,000 years ago, and that of the first farmers, who settled on the loess

6000 years later. The latter event marks the only major break in the entire time span considered here.

POPULATION

An extremely important factor that affected all developments in prehistoric society was the growth of the population (fig. 31.1). This was made possible in the hunting communities for the first time after the end of the last glacial by the much higher carrying capacity of the early Holocene environment. The reliance on natural food resources came to an end with the transition to food production, which laid the basis for a much greater increase in population. This later population growth was associated with the creation of clearances in the forest, improvements in the farming system and technical innovations with which the adverse environmental consequences in particular could be compensated. The expanding population can be said to have been responsible for the increasing impact on the environment, the continuous culturing of the wild and the emergence of social differentiation.

Stone age: from 1000 to 10,000 individuals

For estimates of population figures in the Palaeolithic and Mesolithic we are greatly dependent on ethnographic evidence relating to comparable societies and conditions. Microliths of Wommersom quartzite provide some archaeological clues. They have been found in the southern part of the Netherlands, a large part of Belgium and a small part of northern France. If we assume that their distribution area corresponds to the territory of a dialectic tribe, no more than about 2000 individuals will have lived in what is now the Netherlands, i.e. at most one person per 10 km². Even fewer people will have lived in the late glacial tundras: perhaps only one inhabitant per 100 km².[2]

In the *Bandkeramik* period the native Mesolithic population expanded after the arrival of a farming community which in four centuries grew from 200-300 to about 1500 individuals.[3] The TRB population of Drenthe will have comprised 2000

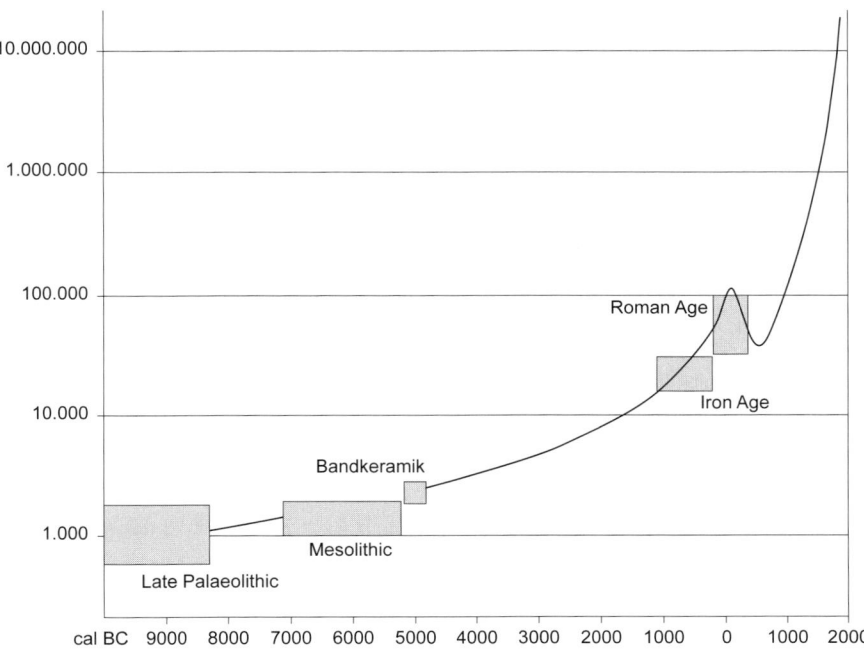

fig. 31.1
Population curve for the Netherlands since the end of the last glacial based on estimates or calculations for the periods marked with a block, and extrapolated to the present. The vertical scale is logarithmic.

697

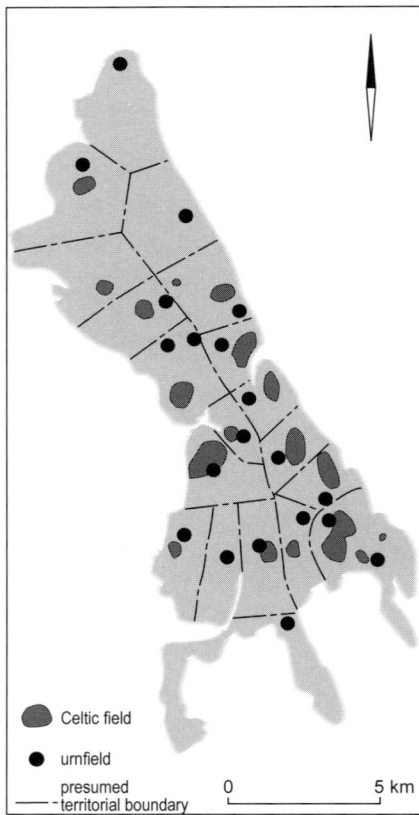

fig. 31.2

The Emmen-Odoorn microregion in the southeasternmost part of Drenthe. This is a settlement area (the southern part of the Hondsrug elevation) entirely enclosed by peat with well-preserved archaeological remains, making it very suitable as a basis for population calculations.

to 3000 individuals if the isolated *hunebedden* and the clusters of these monuments indeed represent kinship groups of 50-100 persons.[4] The whole of the Netherlands is thought to have had fewer than 10,000 occupants in this period.[5] Unfortunately the barrows from the Beaker period and the Bronze Age are not very suitable for calculating population figures, as they represent only an unknown, very small portion of the population.

Bronze Age and Iron Age: from 10,000 to 100,000 individuals

The urnfields and the Celtic fields of Drenthe constitute a sound basis for calculations for the end of prehistory. An urnfield from the Late Bronze Age or the Early Iron Age represents 1-4 households, or 6-24 persons. The associated territories in nucleated occupation areas measure 2.7-6.5 km². That implies 2-5 inhabitants per km².[6] In Drenthe, in particular the Emmen-Odoorn microregion, we may assume a link between a single urnfield (or two successive urnfields) and a Celtic field within a single territory of about 10 km² (fig. 31.2).[7] It is difficult to estimate on the basis of exploitation models how many households each Celtic field will have supported, but with 3-6 households the results are still a little higher than those obtained in calculations based on the urnfields. This difference could be attributable to chronological differences and the expansion of the population. The Celtic fields as they appear to us now date from the last phase of their development, at the end of the Iron Age, whereas urnfields are on average of a considerably earlier date. Evidence supporting population growth was obtained in the settlement analysis of the Oss microregion. This evidence also points to a increase in population in this period, notably from 3-6 inhabitants per km² in the Early Iron Age to 18 inhabitants per km² in the Late Iron Age.[8]

The oldest series of Dutch aerial photographs – taken during large-scale land reclamations in the late 1920s – show parts of most, or possibly even all, of the Celtic fields in Drenthe.[9] They indicate that the entire plateau of Drenthe was divided into roughly 130 territories of on average 10 km². If we assume 15 inhabitants per territory for the first occupation phase and 30 inhabitants for the final phase, we arrive at 2000-4000 inhabitants for the whole of Drenthe.[10] Rough extrapolation to the whole of the Netherlands leads to 15,000-30,000 inhabitants, or 1-2 inhabitants per km².

These figures apply only to the parts of the country that were fit for occupation, so they do not include areas of water or peatland, which then covered half of the Netherlands.[11] The latter values seem to be rather low compared with estimates for the mid-Roman period, which amount to about 150,000 inhabitants.[12]

The above are of course only general figures. We must also allow for local – and temporary – concentrations of people in special areas, such as the salt marshes of Westfrisia in the Bronze Age, the *terpen* area in the north and the peat district to the north of the Meuse estuary in the Iron Age.

We must bear in mind that population figures such as those presented above are based on very limited evidence, and have broad margins of uncertainty. The trend and the level of the population curve are however clear, as are incidental conspicuous concentrations. The archaeological basis for more subtle fluctuations, such as an assumed growth at the end of the Mesolithic, a substantial expansion of the population at the beginning of the Middle Bronze Age and a decrease in the Middle Iron Age, is rather hypothetical, as are the explanations for these fluctuations.[13]

As the population grew, the economic system became increasingly dependent on food production. There was no way back and no alternative, because the carrying capacity of the occupied area was in a short space of time exceeded. By the Bronze Age already, the natural food resources had come to play an entirely subordinate role. The development of food production, in particular farming, is well traceable in the archaeological record and can be split up into different steps or phases. There are clear links with various technical innovations and with the growth of the population and its impact on the environment.

The most important sources of information on subsistence are zoological and botanical remains. The studies of these remains are separate disciplines, which is why these sources of information have been summarised in two separate chapters (14 and 22). In the Netherlands, zoological evidence is unfortunately largely restricted to the wetlands, but botanical remains have been found in carbonised form at many dry sites, too. Biological evidence can only be interpreted correctly in the context of the available archaeological evidence: *ard* marks and features of byres, the implements used for hunting, fishing and crop cultivation, information on settlement types and settlement systems. Subsistence-related activities have been referred to in many of the preceding chapters, as well, because subsistence is of course directly related to many other aspects of society.

From specialised hunting to a broad-spectrum economy

Largely on the basis of a few key sites outside the Netherlands such as those at Gönnersdorf and Ahrensburg, we assume that the Upper Palaeolithic subsistence system was based on specialised hunting. The hunted animals were reindeer and/ or horses, which in large herds moved to and fro between the vast northern tundra in summer and the sheltered valleys and basins of the low mountains in winter. The transition to warmer conditions in the Holocene forced the foragers to adapt their subsistence strategies drastically and fairly quickly, in order to be able to exploit the vastly expanded biomass, the – highly diverse – range of resident animals, the greater number of edible plants available – root vegetables, tubers, onions, leaf vegetables, fruits and nuts – and aquatic resources, such as fish, waterfowl and molluscs. The Mesolithic subsistence system is not without reason called a 'broad-spectrum' economy. The contrast between the Late Palaeolithic and the Mesolithic, incidentally, might possibly be somewhat exaggerated. We can only speculate about the potential exploitation of the coastal areas, because the later rise in sea level has made them inaccessible to us. Nevertheless, the resources of the coastal areas will have made for greater diversity and a wider economic basis in both periods. On the other hand, red deer still played a fairly prominent part in the Mesolithic, comparable with that of reindeer at the end of the glacial period.

Unlike in the Near East, in northern Europe the transition to food production through the adoption of crop cultivation and/or stock keeping was not an independent development. We do, however, assume that people started nurturing and controlling certain species of wild animals and plants towards the end of the Mesolithic, practising what could be termed a form of small-scale cultivation. Only one animal was truly domesticated: the dog.

Via the *Bandkeramik* colonists the native hunter-gatherers were unexpectedly confronted with something entirely new: the 'agricultural package' from the Near East, which, by the time it reached the Low Countries, had been adjusted somewhat to European conditions.[14] This complete, balanced, but also fairly specialised farming system was based on the exploitation of a naturally and permanently fertile soil, namely loess. The new arrivals practised hoe agriculture in permanent, non-manured fields and pastured cattle in the relatively lush valleys. Their arrival marks the beginning of a second long-term process. From this moment onwards, c. 5300 BC, a farming system entirely adapted to northern conditions was to evolve step by step. This process was virtually unaffected by environmental changes, but it did force people to devise measures to prevent exhaustion of the soil so as to render the system sustainable.

Neolithisation

From the *Bandkeramik* agricultural package the native communities selected those elements that suited them best, adding them to their own subsistence system to create an 'extended broad-spectrum economy', combining cereal, cattle and pig and the wide range of natural resources.[15] Exactly when these developments began we do not yet know, but it was definitely before 4100 BC. Although the hunter-gatherers must have been familiar with the management of wild animals and the nurturing of plants, it took them a very long time to switch to the new farming way of life. This could imply that there was no great need for them to adopt the new system. Another possible explanation – as far as crop cultivation is concerned – could be the major differences in soil conditions that existed between the fertile loess and the marginal sandy soils. Perhaps the considerable investments in time and energy demanded by crop cultivation on the sandy soils put people off for a long time.

We assume that the successors of these native (Swifterbant) communities – or perhaps they themselves – developed a crop-cultivation system of their own. Their system was based not on a permanently fertile soil, but on exhaustion of the soils that had formed on top of the sand below the deciduous forests over many centuries.[16] After short periods of cultivation, the forest was given the opportunity to regenerate in part at least. This system of shifting cultivation[17] was probably first used slightly earlier in the south (Michelsberg culture)[18] than in the north and in the coastal part of the delta (TRB culture and Vlaardingen group, respectively).[19] It was combined with the pasturing of cattle in the forest, which had already been practised by the *Bandkeramik* population, but also with the traditional, native exploitation of the rich natural resources by means of hunting, fowling, fishing and gathering. Although this subsistence system was very varied, it would be incorrect to describe it as 'mixed farming'.[20] The various activities seem to have been practised separately and independently, and were not united in a single system. We know for certain that cattle were not yet being stalled, so dung was not being collected either; only the pastures will have benefited from the animals' dung. There is no evidence for ploughing until the end of this phase.

The shifting cultivation system could be improved only after the introduction of farming techniques developed elsewhere, comprising elements of the 'secondary products revolution'.[21] Traction animals (oxen) and the plough (fig. 31.3) made work on a larger scale, and hence lower yields per hectare, rewarding.[22] They thus contributed towards further exhaustion of the soil. Wagons created the possibility of bulk transport and expanded the farmer's radius of action. These elements are the main characteristics of the 'initial mixed farming' of the Beaker period, in which fowling and fishing continued to play a part.[23]

The typical north European mixed farming system seems to have been fully established only by (the beginning of) the Middle Bronze Age. Its dominant elements were cattle and cereal, which were now integrated in a single system. The cattle yielded the traction for ploughs and wagons and their dung was systematically used.[24] This was indeed necessary, for large areas of the sandy soils had within a relatively short time become severely exhausted.[25] Another, opportunistic, solution to this problem was the exploitation of the fertile, recently formed salt marsh deposits in Westfrisia. The principal characteristic of this mixed farming system is the farm incorporating stalls for the cattle, or *longhouses* which – we assume – were bedded with straw from the fields. It is, incidentally, unlikely that the animals were stalled in winter, because it was not yet technically feasible for these farmers to create a sufficient supply of winter fodder.[26] There is moreover no evidence for the large storage facilities that this would have necessitated.

In this way a form of sustainable agriculture that yielded sufficient food to support the expanding population had evolved step by step after all. This system was characterised by fairly permanent fields, manuring and possibly crop rotation with short fallow periods. It also comprised dairying and wool processing (spinning and weaving). This means that the division of tasks within the farming family had changed drastically since the *Bandkeramik* period.

In the Iron Age, expansion of the range of crops and greater variation in the livestock made the system more sustainable and more versatile. Plants like gold of pleasure (*Chenopodium*), Celtic bean (*Vicia faba*) and rape (*Brassica rapa*) could be successfully rotated with cereals. The farmer's range of implements seems to have expanded, too.[27] On the higher soils the Celtic fields now constituted permanent plots of manured land surrounded by expanses of poor sandy soil that was an easy prey to the wind.[28] In the lower parts of the Netherlands, landscapes that had not been occupied since the Vlaardingen period were recolonised.[29] Although the more favourable conditions in the estuaries will have been an important factor,[30] this is above all seen as a sign of the use of more flexible and more varied farming meth-

fig. 31.3

The prehistoric *ard* did not turn over the soil like present-day ploughs, but merely cut a furrow through it. The oldest type, the crook *ard*, was made from a thick branch with part of the trunk attached. A steering stick was clamped in a cavity. The illustrated specimen was found near Walle (Ostfriesland) in 1927. It has been dated to the beginning of the Bronze Age, making it one of the oldest known *ards*.

ods. The options open to farmers had apparently increased substantially. There may even have been strategic alliances for the exchange of basic food resources between communities living in different environmental zones, which would imply the end of the formerly entirely self-sufficient economy.[31]

MAN AND THE ENVIRONMENT

Much attention in this book has been paid to the relations between man and the land, in particular to the land as the basis of existence: the *use* of the land, the types of locations selected for settlement, the relations between farming and soil conditions, and – as a consequence of all this – the organisation of the land. Incidental references have been made to the impact that the modest, but nevertheless growing population had on the environment. On the higher soils man's activities had far-reaching consequences for his surroundings, but in the wetlands the impact on the environment was negligible on account of the land's natural fertility and its constant rejuvenation.

Sources

The many pollen diagrams that have been made in the Low Countries provide beautiful records of the natural development of the vegetation and of the ways in which it was affected by human occupation over the ages. Samples from extensive peat regions reflect the general development of the vegetation on the surrounding higher soils, while samples from small bogs near ancient settlements betray the specific influence of those settlements' occupants.[32] It should, however, be borne in mind that reconstructions of the former vegetation based on such pollen diagrams are not accurate in every respect; as with any other ancient remains, there is a complex relationship between what we see today and the way things actually were in the past.

Even more difficult to assess is prehistoric man's influence on the animal world, for our only evidence in this respect are the butchering remains that have been found at settlement sites, and the information they yield is not very systematic and is moreover very biased as a result of human selection. Very general information on the range of species and numbers of animals available can be obtained from reconstructions of the former environment and vegetation,[33] while man's impact on the soil can be studied in dated fossil soils, in particular those preserved beneath burial monuments or drift sand deposits.[34]

Hunter-gatherers

We can only speculate on the way in which hunter-gatherers may have interfered with the environment. Their small-scale activities are not visible in pollen diagrams. It has been suggested that they made the ecology more versatile, and hence enabled the number of animals to increase, by regularly burning the vegetation. But first of all it will have been rather difficult to ignite the natural vegetation of the Low Countries and, secondly, no evidence for this practice has so far been found in the Netherlands.[35] It has also been proposed that the vegetable component of the Mesolithic diet was in fact much greater than can be inferred from the archaeological remains. We assume that the hunter-gatherers had built up a native knowledge system, that covered an intimate knowledge of all plants, and that they hence knew how to manage or even grow them.[36]

While cave art and rock carvings outside the Netherlands show that animals, too, were assigned a symbolic meaning at an early stage already, the hunter's relation to the animal world will have been primarily that of a predator. As hunting methods became more systematic and specialised, the hunters will have progressively reduced the numbers of rival animals of prey, thus contributing towards their ultimate disappearance. But at the same time man appears to have practised some form of 'faunal management', in particular through the selective 'cropping' of the most important game on which he was entirely dependent for his survival.[37] The suggestion that man was responsible for the extinction of many large mammals – such as mammoth, woolly rhinoceros and giant deer – at the end of the last glacial is not compatible with this 'selective cropping' theory. A far more important factor in these animals' extinction seems to have been the large-scale disappearance of the expansive 'mammoth steppe'.

Farmers in the forest

The impact on the environment of the activities of the first farmers will have appeared impressive to the hunter-gatherers, but in actual fact it was still fairly limited. The farmers created large clearances in the forests on the loess for their settlements and their fields. The consequences of this are, however, visible only in the pollen diagrams of areas that were relatively densely occupied, such as the lower Rhine region. In other areas the consequences are virtually undetectable even in the settlements' immediate surroundings. The – scarce – pollen diagrams from the loess belt reflect closed forests until the end of the Neolithic. This agrees well with the assumption that the occupants of this area continued to practise hoe agriculture in small communities, in spite of all the archaeological differences. The environment did not deteriorate or suffer adverse effects from man's activities; it was on the contrary rather enhanced by them, for the clearances made the forest a more attractive biotiope for large wild animals such as red deer and roe. From an environmental viewpoint, prehistoric man seems to have practised a sustainable form of exploitation.[38]

On the sandy soils – almost all the higher parts of the Netherlands – things were somewhat different. The first clearances of the TRB culture were likewise fairly small; they, too, are visible only in the scarce pollen records obtained for samples from the immediate surroundings of former fields.[39] The Beaker period saw a major change, both in the loess region and in the central part of the Netherlands, which can be directly related to new farming methods.[40] The clearing of the primeval forest then 'suddenly' becomes clearly visible in the pollen diagrams of peat deposits (fig. 31.4) and ancient soils preserved beneath Beaker barrows.[41] The agricultural developments outlined above evidently had fairly destructive consequences for the vulnerable ecosystems of the sandy soils. Those developments included the introduction of ploughing, but also the pasturing of cattle in the forests. It is not surprising that people began to colonise also – or perhaps even preferably – less vulnerable environments, such as the desalinated former salt marshes of Westfrisia in the Middle Bronze Age and the northern salt marshes and the tidal flats in the provinces of South and North Holland in the Iron Age. They moreover began to grow their crops in Celtic fields in order to counter their adverse effects on the environment. If the soil in those fields was indeed enriched with sods, this will have led to further deterioration of the surrounding land, where more soil will

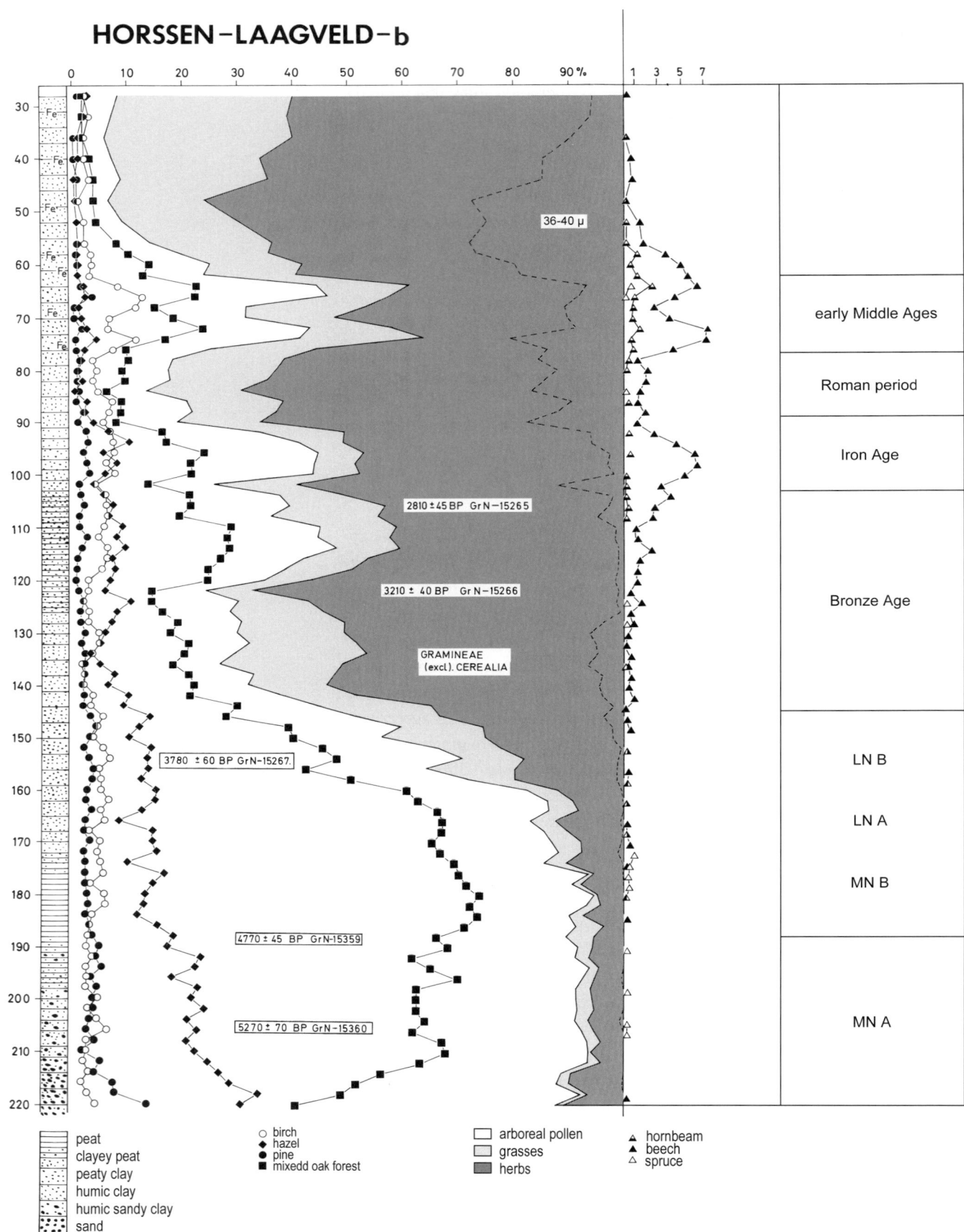

HORSSEN-LAAGVELD-b

fig. 31.4

Pollen diagram from the Land van Maas en Waal region. It illustrates the influence of prehistoric reclamation on the vegetation. Around 2200 BC (3780 BP) there was a strong increase in grass species (Gramineae) at the expense of trees. The forest recovered temporarily in the early Middle Ages (top peak in the tree curve). The vegetation changes will be partly caused by increased flooding, but the same trend is shown by other diagrams.

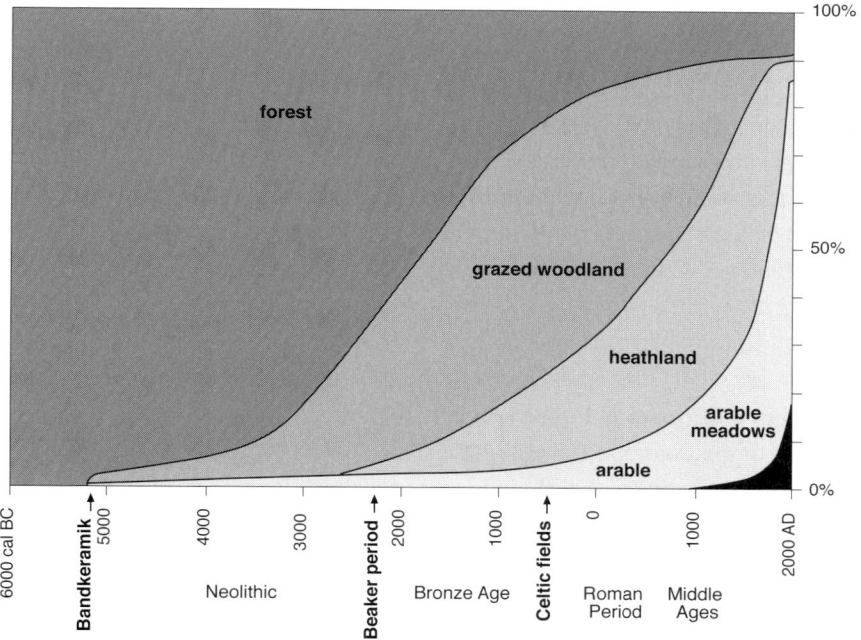

fig. 31.5
Schematic representation of the environmental changes that took place in the landscape of the Dutch loess and sandy zones in later prehistoric and historic times. Builtup area in black (lower right corner).

consequently have been blown away.[42] So man more and more left his mark on the land, both by slowly but surely interfering with the original landscape and by organising the land to an ever-increasing extent (fig. 31.5).

This first assault on the forest was made possible by a single tool: the axe, a simple stone blade hafted in a wooden handle. The hunters had not been entirely unfamiliar with axes, but stone axes are nevertheless regarded as the characteristic tool of the Neolithic, in which period they were also greatly perfected. They were used not only for felling trees to create clearances, but also for building houses, canoes, wagons and bog trackways. Axes were indeed such important tools that they were often made from special, exotic types of stone, buried in graves along with their owners or used as votive offerings. The axe symbolised man's power over nature.[43]

Farmers and livestock

Surprisingly enough, the prehistoric communities, especially from the Middle Bronze Age onwards, spent little time hunting large wild animals or fowling, even in the wetlands, which will for a very long time have been real bird paradises. All the faunal assemblages from Bronze Age and Iron Age settlements contain very few remains of game or birds. Fishing does seem to have been important for the Bronze Age farmers, but remains of fish and waterfowl are conspicuously absent from very wet Iron Age sites, such as the farming settlements in the Midden-Delfland region.[44] This seems to be attributable to three factors. The first is an evident lack of interest in these nevertheless readily accessible food resources, especially fish. Secondly, the wild animals could simply no longer support the greatly expanded population to the same extent as in the past. There were roughly twenty times as many mouths to feed as in the Mesolithic. If the numbers of animals available and the percentages killed had remained the same, this will automatically have implied a reduction of down to a 5% contribution to the meat, required by the population. And, thirdly, the wild animals will have been supplanted by cattle in a manner comparable with that observed in later times on a much larger scale in Africa and in the colonisation of the west of North America. It should be borne in mind that the ideal areas for colonisation by prehistoric farmers coincided precisely with the biotopes most favourable for large wild animals, in particular red deer. Calculations of the size of the population and the average areas available for stalling animals in the longhouses – at least 16 heads of cattle per household of six individuals – lead to livestock figures of at least 37,000 in the higher parts of the Netherlands in the Late Bronze Age and Early Iron Age, increasing to over 74,000 in the Iron Age, which corresponds to 4 heads of cattle per km². In spite of the differences in their feeding habits, these domestic animals, grazing freely in forests and pastures, will have meant severe competition for the large wild animals. These animals, especially the red deer, will in the Bronze Age already have been greatly reduced in numbers and forced to move to marginal areas as a result of the destruction of their biotope and possibly also overhunting.[45]

Large-scale destruction of the landscape and the vegetation is reflected not only in the pollen records, but also in the acidification of the soil caused by leaching, and in the formation of humic iron podzols all over the sandy area in the Early and Middle Bronze Age. Another clear sign of this destruction is the large-scale drifting of sand in these periods and especially afterwards, in the Iron Age.[46]

THE 'CULTURING' OF THE WILD

The land and the landscape were not only used, but also experienced. For the hunters, the landscape was the unchanging context of their daily existence. For the farmers, it more and more evolved into a basis which they themselves shaped. The expanding population, with ever more, if still simple, technical means at its disposal, became capable of leaving its mark on the land in which it lived to an ever-increasing extent. Prehistoric man slowly began to organise the land, to 'culture' the wild, in a literal sense. This was not an autonomous process, but clearly a derivative of developments in farming practices and of the territorial division of the land. It was moreover never a matter of starting with a clean slate: there was always a monument or some ancient remains or myths associated with direct or distant ancestors that determined the further layout of the land, through either confirmation or negation of old values. The 'investments' in the existing layout of the land (reclamation of wasteland, the laying out of fields, *etc.*), but also the emotional bond with it and the significance attributed to it, played a part in shaping new structures. Indeed, if we assume complete or partial long-term ethnic continuity we must regard the organisation of the land as a single, protracted and continuous process, over and above the boundaries of our traditional, archaeological cultures. The archaeologists' task is to write the first chapters of the history of the cultivation of the landscapes on the basis of the material remains and visible monuments at their disposal.

Hunters in their landscape: the experienced land

There was not yet any question of conscious shaping of the land among the hunter-gatherer communities. We do, however, assume that they attached importance to fixed, recognisable points at a remarkably early stage already. We can speculate about name giving or assigned symbolic meanings to certain elements in the landscape.[47] Certain large sites that have yielded vast quantities of finds from different, successive cultural phases must have been fixed points in the annual cycles for many centuries, if not several millennia. There will also have been fixed migration routes and – certainly in the Mesolithic – a network of paths providing access to different parts of the territories and linking individual camps.

a

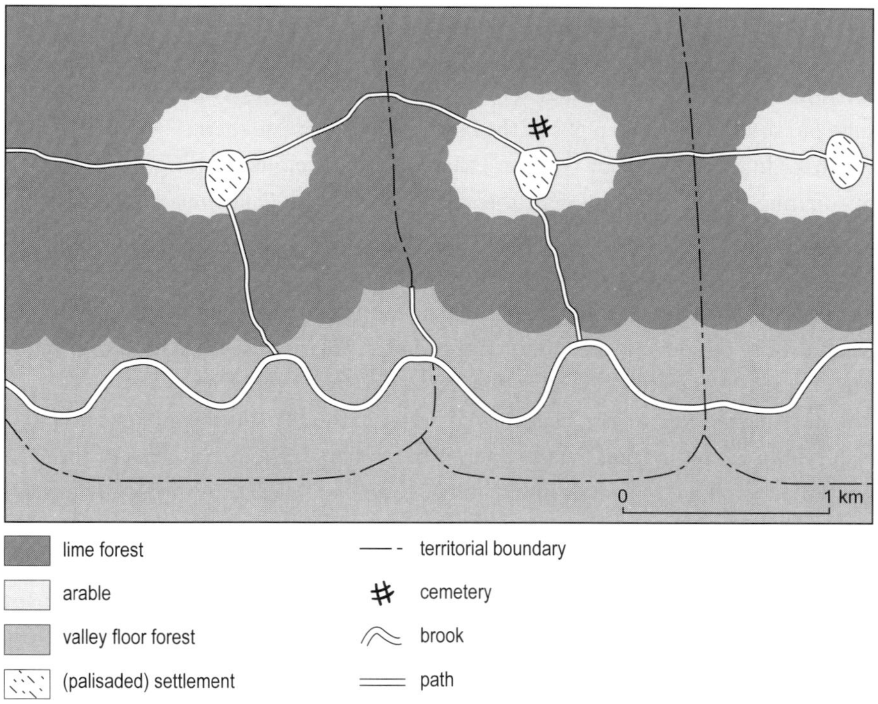
0
1 km
lime forest
arable
valley floor forest
(palisaded) settlement
territorial boundary
cemetery
brook
path

b

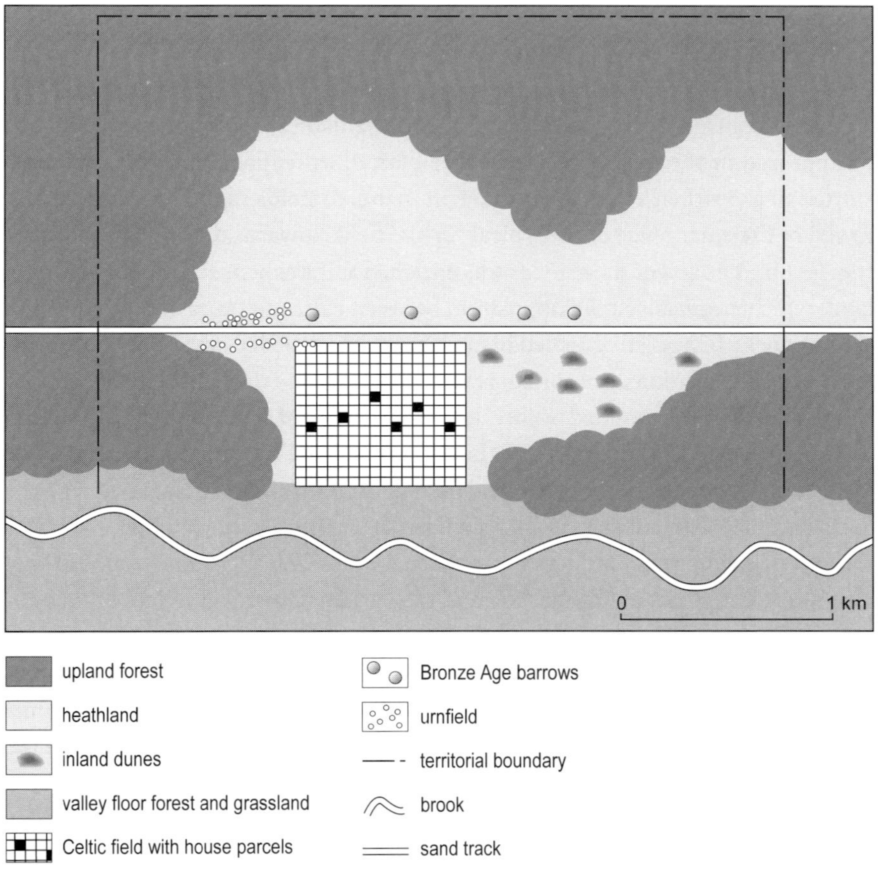
0
1 km
upland forest
heathland
inland dunes
valley floor forest and grassland
Celtic field with house parcels
Bronze Age barrows
urnfield
territorial boundary
brook
sand track

fig. 31.6
Schematic representation of the layout of an Early Neolithic *Bandkeramik* territory on the loess in Limburg (a) and that of an Iron Age Celtic field on the coversand of the Drenthe plateau (b), showing the increase in the opening of the forests.

But although elements like a fixed pattern of *use*, large-scale territoriality and the assigning of specific meanings to prominent locations are already observable among the hunter-gatherer communities, it is only in the Neolithic that we see the first efforts to actually *organise* the land. It is then that people began to reclaim the virgin forest. From then onwards the unity of man and nature began to give way to increasing opposition between culture and nature. Hodder has called this process the 'domestication of Europe'.[48] After millennia of straightforward life in large territories with little more than certain rights of use, groups of farmers began to take possession of small parts of the land, and to organise them.[49]

This 'domestication' of the land, that is, its conscious shaping by its human occupants, began abruptly with the settlement of the *Bandkeramik* farmers (fig. 31.6a). They created pockets of cultivated land in clearances in the wilderness. But there was as yet no continuity: in the Rössen period the *Bandkeramik* settlement pattern was to be replaced by an entirely new infrastructure[50] and the subsequent Michelsberg period saw the emergence of large, enclosed sites, also in previously unoccupied regions, representing the centres of larger social units.[51]

These developments can be followed better in the Northern Plain, in particular around the Veluwe region, where a series of primary settlement nuclei of the TRB people have been attested along the lower courses of brooks. From those stream valleys the clearances later expanded to the higher parts of the land. Long rows of barrows mark out a long-distance network of roads or paths dating from this expansion period.[52] From here onwards the process of reclamation is more difficult to follow, but we assume that the clearances surrounding these primary centres were gradually expanded and that the settlement territories became ever more distinct, not only in and around the Veluwe region, but also elsewhere, in particular in Drenthe. As the population further expanded, territories will have been split up, or new territories established in 'no man's land', until the entire area fit for occupation had been divided.[53]

We assume that at the time of the first, small clearances in particular, there was a marked contrast between the cultural and the natural. This contrast gradually disappeared in the course of the Beaker period, to reappear later when people started to grow their crops in permanent, manured fields in the Bronze Age, followed by the emergence of the typical 'Celtic' fields towards the end of prehistory (fig. 31.6b). The soil of these fields was enriched at the expense of the surrounding land, which emphasised the opposition between cultivated land and 'wasteland'. Three zones can be distinguished in those times: first of all central zones at specifically selected locations, comprising the settlements and the fields laid out around them. They were surrounded by forests, moors with drift sand deposits and stream valleys. These areas were exploited, but not organised. And finally there were the raised bogs, which were from the very time of their formation associated with the supernatural.[54] No landscape was organised in an entirely free manner. Man's efforts to shape his surroundings were dictated by visible, ancestral structures, but also by the natural layout of the land and the patterns of stream valleys or, in sedimentation areas, those of stream deposits.[55]

The organisation of the landscape of the higher parts of the country forms a marked contrast with the situation in the lowlands, where all efforts to obtain a more permanent layout were time and time again thwarted by the dynamics of the natural environment: by the growth of peat, by marine ingressions and the related formation of creek systems and deposition of clay, and by sedimentation by the rivers. These phenomena were all dictated by the strict regime of the rising sea level and the alternation of transgressions and regressions.

Territorial markers

From the very outset, the farmers marked their clearances as their territories, so as to be able to claim the right of using, if not possessing, the land.[56] The *Bandkeramik* and Rössen farmers marked their territories with their monumental farms,[57] the Michelsberg people with their large enclosures. Groups of TRB farmers in Drenthe were the first to visualise the triangular relationship between occupants, ancestors and the land by jointly erecting monumental collective burial chambers. Individual barrows later took over the function of these collective burials, after which the burial rite and this manifestation of territory were gradually 'socialised' again.[58] The final resting places of the dead constituted fixed points and markers legitimising the use of the land and the territorial claims, above all because they were associated with ancestral rights.

In Drenthe in particular, where modern, large-scale agricultural practices were introduced only very recently, the earliest development of the organisation of the land and its territorial division are clearly visible, especially in specific microre-

fig. 31.7

The Noordse Veld near Zeijen, in the north of the province of Drenthe. It is situated between the valleys of the Oostervoortsche Diep (left) and the Grote Masloot (right) and is an example of a prehistoric landscape that was organised and used for a long period of time. The sequence starts with a *hunebed* and flat graves of the TRB culture. These were succeeded by barrows from the Beaker period and the Bronze Age, cinerary mounds, a Celtic field and Late Iron Age defended settlements.

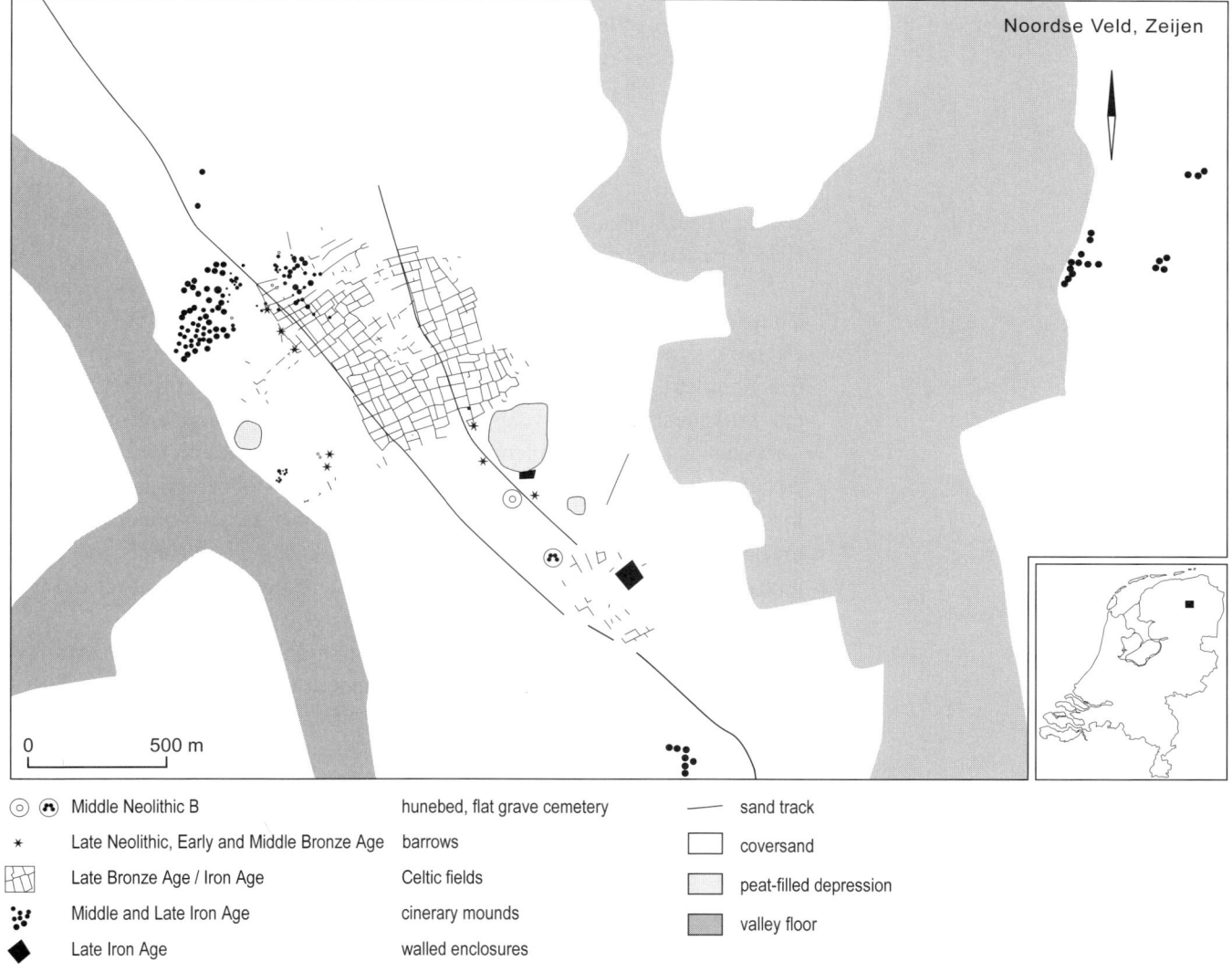

Noordse Veld, Zeijen

⊙ ⋒	Middle Neolithic B	hunebed, flat grave cemetery	—	sand track
✳	Late Neolithic, Early and Middle Bronze Age	barrows	☐	coversand
⊞	Late Bronze Age / Iron Age	Celtic fields	☐	peat-filled depression
⦂	Middle and Late Iron Age	cinerary mounds	▨	valley floor
◆	Late Iron Age	walled enclosures		

0   500 m

709

gions and at various excavated sites. Waterbolk even claimed to be able to trace the development of the present villages in this area through the Middle Ages all the way back to the Iron Age.[59]

Ritual landscapes

Some landscapes and certain parts of the territories seem to have been assigned specific meanings. They are the landscapes that were used for the deposition of offerings: raised bogs, low-lying swamps, stream valleys and rivers. People also created new ritual sites by erecting burial monuments, at which they venerated their ancestors. Areas with high densities of such monuments may be classed as 'ritual landscapes', though none of those in the Netherlands are as imposing as some of the areas known elsewhere in Europe. The Hondsrug hills with their groups of *hunebedden* are an example of such a ritual landscape in the Netherlands. Others are areas containing groups of barrows like the Noordse Veld near Zeijen (fig. 31.7), the Rechte Heide near Goirle and various moors in the Veluwe region.

In identifying such 'ritual landscapes' we must bear in mind that they are extremes within what was otherwise a continuum. The landscape as a whole will have held many different meanings in the occupants' perception of it, even the parts which we would regard as 'profane'. But thinking in terms of oppositions like that between 'ritual' and 'profane' is typical of our modern Western view of the world. On the other hand, only a few random parts of the overall prehistoric landscape are visible to us. When we speak of 'ritual landscapes' we are usually referring to microregions of which we see only the ritual aspects.

HOME AND HEARTH

Within the territories, the settlements were the centres of human activity. Much archaeological research consequently focuses on settlement sites, because they tend to contain many features and yield useful information on prehistoric societies. House plans in particular tell us much about the organisation and the size of social groups and the degree of differentiation within and between local communities. Almost all our information on prehistoric economy comes from settlements, too. Settlement *systems*, however, are very difficult to grasp, because people had the – archaeologically inconvenient – custom of using certain locations for long periods of time or on different occasions, which in almost all periods resulted in the formation of 'palimpsests': complex accumulations of remains and features embracing long time spans that are virtually impossible for us to analyse. They make it very difficult for us to form an impression of the settlement systems represented by those sites. This holds for the whole span of prehistory.

From the static settlement evidence we try to form an image of the occupants' mobility. In the case of hunter-gatherers we make a distinction between the movement of base camps – what is referred to as 'residential mobility' – and the activities carried out outside these central sites, during expeditions of a portion of the population that lasted for one or more days, called 'logistic mobility'.[60] These concepts can also be applied up to a point to the later farming communities.

Migrating hunters

The specialised late glacial hunters were extremely mobile. We assume that they moved across their vast territories in seasonal cycles, covering hundreds of kilometres, along more or less fixed routes between fixed, strategically situated locations. Clusters of sites or large accumulations of artefacts were formed at those locations, but we also know of base camps that were used only once, and of small special activity camps that were used for short periods of time as bases for hunting expeditions in their surroundings.[61]

The drastic changes that occurred in the environmental conditions, and in the hunting strategies adjusted to them, must in the Mesolithic have led to a substantial decrease in the former long-distance residential mobility. This is, however, virtually invisible in the archaeological record. People continued to camp at the same types of locations as in the past, with a preference for certain coversand ridges. So no distinct archaeological changes are observable, except that the large Late Mesolithic sites seem to suggest that people returned to specific locations more often than in the past.[62] All in all we assume that the interregional mobility of the Late Palaeolithic slowly gave way to seasonal migrations between different ecological zones within much smaller areas. The varied ecosystems of the valleys and lowlands must have played a crucial role in the latter migrations, but unfortunately we have little archaeological information on those parts owing to later sedimentation.[63]

Settled farmers

Around 5300 BC this mobile system comprising functionally different sites was confronted with an entirely different settlement concept: the stationary Bandkeramik 'hamlets' within well-defined territories that were occupied on a long-term and permanent basis. This form of settlement persisted into the Rössen period, after which it became the standard across large parts of Europe, but seems to have disappeared in the Lower Rhine Basin. The early farming settlements on the loess in the Netherlands hence represent an interlude with a fundamentally different pattern.

Wandering yards

Virtually no break whatsoever is observable in the sandy part of the Netherlands, not even when the occupants of this area switched to the farming way of life. Although features, especially house plans, are scarce, we know that the settlements remained small and that life in these regions continued to be characterised by a high degree of mobility. This is true especially for the Swifterbant and Vlaardingen groups, but also for communities that can otherwise be classed as fully Neolithic, such as the TRB groups.[64] Nevertheless, we do assume that the residential mobility decreased, both spatially and above all also in terms of frequency. The old logistic mobility, however, remained an aspect of the settlement system until in the late Beaker period. Hunting and fishing stations are virtually unrecognisable in the sandy regions, although they have been identified in the delta, especially in Westfrisia, where we know of several such camps of the Single Grave culture. Another site, of a slightly later date, is Oldeboorn, which was found on top of a low dune in the valley of the Boorne in Friesland. A few very small sites near Vlaardingen and

Hekelingen that yielded some sherds of Bell Beakers or Barbed Wire Beakers and a few flints are also to be interpreted as such camps.[65]

An important issue as far as this period is concerned is the relationship between the 'upland' and the wetlands. There are reasons to assume that the settlement system of the contemporary mobile communities with their broad spectrum of activities embraced both landscapes, in other words, that small 'task groups' of fishermen or hunters, or entire households set out to exploit the resources of the lowlands in certain seasons. With the exception of the coastal dune zone, which can actually be seen as a large, high and dry island surrounded by swamps, the lowlands were not occupied on a permanent basis until in the late Beaker period.

When, in the Middle Bronze Age, people began to enrich the soil of their fields with manure, they will have relocated their farms even less, and the bond between the farmers and their more permanent arable land will have intensified. It is thought that people may then have moved around in fixed cycles between a small number of favoured locations.[66] It is only in the Iron Age that we obtain clear evidence for this assumed decrease in mobility, in the form of the more visible system of 'Celtic' fields. Even then, the settlements retained the open structure of a hamlet, at least in the higher regions. Truly permanent, more nucleated settlements emerged in a few cases only, under special conditions: in the Middle Bronze Age on the fertile clay of Westfrisia and in the Iron Age on the artificial dwelling mounds or *terpen*, the largest of which we may class as 'villages'.[67]

From the Middle Bronze Age onwards a 'standard' settlement comprised two or three farmyards, each measuring a quarter of a hectare, with at the centre a longhouse surrounded by a few granaries, usually a few pits, possibly a shed or an outbuilding and sometimes a water well. Barrows and urnfields lay close by in some cases, and at a considerable distance from the settlement in others. The associated arable land, comprised several dozens of hectares, a major part of which being fallow.[68] At Oss a process of nucleation culminating in six houses per 36 hectares took place in the Late Iron Age. This is thought to illustrate the ubiquitous expansion of the population in this time span. By this time, the farms were being relocated much less often and the settlement pattern had consequently acquired a more permanent character.[69]

Around the end of the Iron Age we see the first indications of hierarchical relations between permanent settlements. The *terp* settlements on the northern salt marshes clearly differed from one another in terms of size.[70] The walled enclosures that emerged on the northern periphery of the plateau of Drenthe seem to have played key parts in the exchange of goods between the communities living on the sandy soils and those in the clay regions.[71] In the southern part of the Netherlands there were at this time a few fortified sites that are thought to have been peripheral phenomena of the distinctly hierarchically structured settlement system of the Celtic area further south.[72] Generally speaking, however, all the settlements were equal until the Roman period.

So all in all, from the reindeer hunters of the last glacial onwards, Dutch prehistory is characterised by a constant decrease in residential mobility, from a nomadic way of life to the limited movements of farmsteads within the narrow bounds of the 'Celtic' field system. The developments in logistic mobility are more difficult for us to follow, but this form of mobility seems to have largely disappeared, or at least to have become invisible, by the end of the Neolithic. It will definitely have been greatly restricted by the constantly decreasing extent of the territories.

Although the farmsteads still lay fairly far apart, we must nevertheless assume that the *people* were united by kinship ties and social networks.[73]

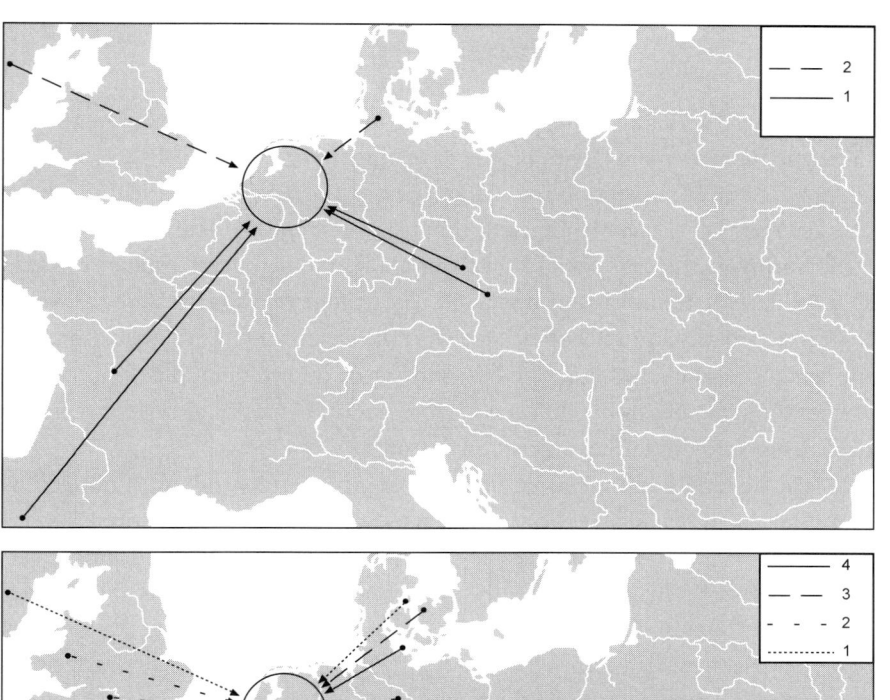

a Beaker period (Late Neolithic)

　2 gold (Ireland), amber (Scandinavia)

　1 Grand Pressigny daggers, wrist guards; copper (SE Europe)

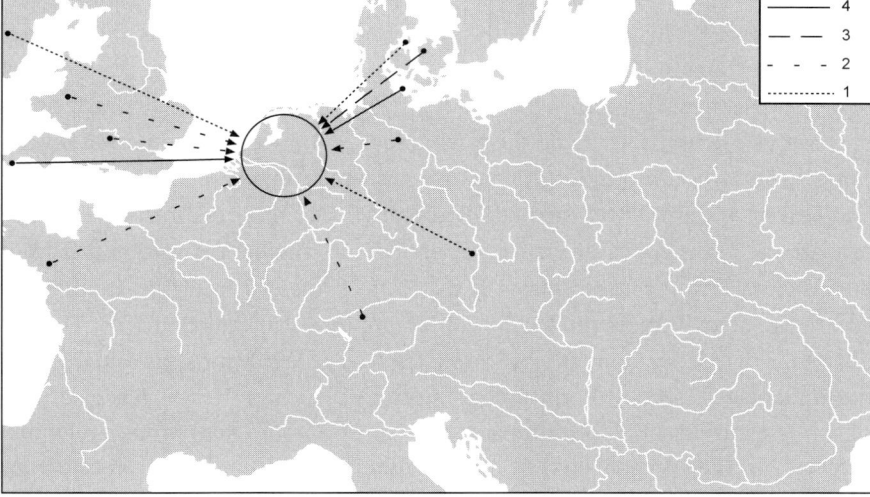

b Bronze Age

　4 general tin (Cornwall), amber (Scandinavia)

　3 Late e.g. Drouwen

　2 Middle e.g. Ommerschans, Voorhout, Weerdinge

　1 Early e.g. Wageningen, Roermond; Irish axes, Scandinavian flint daggers

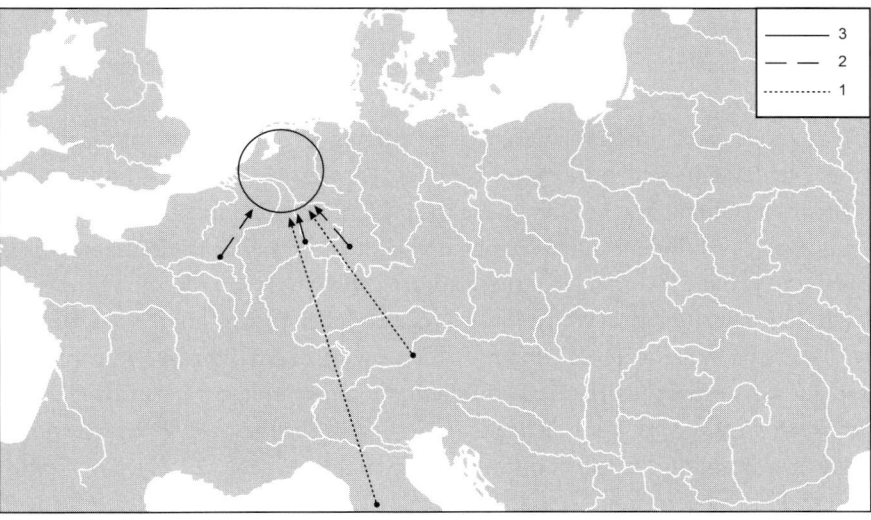

c Iron Age

　3 general tephrite querns (Eifel)

　2 Late Celtic coins (northern France, Hessen)

　1 Early Gündlingen and Mindelheim swords, situlae (circum-alpine region), axle caps Wijchen (Italy)

fig. 31.8
Contacts between prehistoric communities of the Netherlands and distant societies, as reflected by 'exotic' materials found at settlements and in burials in the sequence of later prehistoric periods and phases. See fig. 15.6 for the Early and Middle Neolithic.

A fully-fledged agricultural population, living in scattered small, undifferentiated, independent settlements, without the development of any central sites, without concentrations of population and without power or market centres. Those are the characteristics of a *segmentary* society, consisting of small, self-sufficient units.[74] It is not surprising that the social ladder was short, and that developments towards social differentiation were very restricted. The changes we observe in the archaeological record are primarily associated with the expansion of the population and the organisation of the land. The best sources of information on social ranking are not the settlements, but differences observable in burials, and evidence on exchange networks and ritual deposition customs.

Exotic materials and the associated exchange networks (fig. 31.8) played important parts in visualising social differences from the first farmers until the end of prehistory. These exotic materials – flint and other types of stone, amber, jet, copper, bronze, gold, glass and iron – were used to make prestigious objects such as tools, weapons and ornaments. There will also have been many status markers of perishable materials, which now elude us. For men, there was from early times onwards also a martial element: the ostentatious, prestigious presentation as warriors.[75] The earliest indications of this are the unusually shaped hammer axes or 'battle axes' of the Michelsberg and TRB cultures. Of a more distinctly martial nature are the grave goods of the Beaker period and, finally, the objects that were buried along with deceased males in the Bronze Age and Iron Age, though the latter were actually quite modest by contemporary European standards. The deliberate, ritual deposition, attested from the Neolithic onwards, of valuable and prestigious tools and weapons in bogs, stream valleys and rivers is likewise to be seen as a manifestation of prominent social positions and not only as a religious expression.[76] The organisation of major building projects, such as the construction of *hunebedden* and bog trackways, must have involved planning and hence also a certain form of leadership.

The social implications of evidence of this kind have been extensively discussed in the previous chapters, in the context of questions like: what can the evidence tell us about social differentiation, gender differences, differences within and between settlements and local and/or supralocal leadership? These all proved to be difficult questions, first of all because the evidence is often incomplete, and secondly because different sources frequently seem to contradict one another. This is due largely to the fact that what these sources show us is not the social structure itself, but only the way in which it was expressed, whether or not deliberately. All we have to go by are material remains, which, owing to different factors, moreover present a distorted picture. Social differentiation may indeed be expressed in the archaeological record, but this need not necessarily be the case. What may originally have been indications of differentiation may have been destroyed by formation and/or recovery processes. So the absence of archaeological differences does not need to be significant. This is why much research appears to focus more on understanding the whys and wherefores of the expression of differences (or its absence) than on the underlying social reality.

On the basis of anthropological arguments we assume that the hunter-gatherers lived in egalitarian tribes comprising kinship bands, whose members' tasks depended on their age and sex, with temporary leadership based on personal achievements. The Dutch evidence, however, factually tells us hardly anything about the organisation of hunter-gatherer communities. The very modest differences observable in the Swifterbant S2 cemetery reveal an almost complete lack of social ranking at the end of the Mesolithic.[77]

The social organisation of the first farmers, on the contrary, is remarkably well known to us thanks to the differentiated, complete archaeological record that is available for them, with the results of analyses of houses and burials agreeing very well with one another. Keen research has resulted in the most detailed picture of society, perhaps in the whole of Dutch prehistory. There appear to have been different levels of social organisation: from house and household, via hamlet and settlement to settlement cluster, with leadership on a settlement level and a certain equality of men and women.[78] After this, things become less clear. The differentiated, rather strict structure of *Bandkeramik* society gradually dissolved, that is, the social order becomes progressively less archaeologically visible in the subsequent Rössen and Michelsberg periods.

We assume that the northern farming communities that succeeded the Swifterbant groups showed only a modest degree of differentiation; social hierarchy changed very little in the long time span from the TRB culture to the end of the Iron Age.

TRB society is thought to have been characterised by kinship groups that cooperated with one another in the construction of the *hunebedden* of Drenthe, which will have required some planning and leadership.[79] The networks via which flint axes and rare, copper ornaments were obtained, the use of those objects in (ritual) deposition and finds of prestigious objects such as knob-butted axes also imply a certain amount of leadership and authority.[80]

With the Beaker cultures the emphasis shifted from collective units to smaller groups like (extended) families, and to personal positions. A small portion of the population – in particular men – emphatically distinguished themselves with conspicuous individual burials and status symbols. The size and design of the barrows and the exceptional grave goods of these cultures imply status positions and authority on a regional level.[81] The 'socialisation' of the burial rite in the course of the Middle Bronze Age, and the emergence of equal positions for men and women need not necessarily imply a less hierarchical social structure. In the Urnfield period the 'elite' manifested itself through the deposition of bronzes in peat bogs and rivers, in the Early Iron Age through a small number of conspicuously prestigious burials and in the Late Iron Age again through deposition.

These constantly changing manifestations may be clear to us, but we actually know less about the underlying social reality. Until the end of prehistory supralocal positions of power were rare, and not bound to specific locations (cemeteries).[82] Was the Early Bronze Age warrior of Drouwen a tribal leader – if we may use this term at all – of the Late Barbed Wire Beaker community of Drenthe, and was the 'prince' of Oss the leader of the Maaskant region in the Early Iron Age? Although we tend to use the term 'elite' to refer to comparatively prominent individuals, the picture that emerges from the evidence is nevertheless one of a modestly stratified society.

The settlements show virtually no signs of any social differentiation whatsoever. They at least include no special houses that may have been the homes of 'leaders'. The houses of the individual periods, and especially the individual phases, differed so little from one another in terms of size that we must assume that the various households were self-sufficient, economically independent and – in this respect – equal. Only the houses of the *terp* settlements, especially Ezinge, showed fairly large differences in size.

The slight differences that are observable in the lengths of the houses of the individual occupation phases – especially the lengths of the parts that were used for stalling cattle – must be connected with minor differences in the sizes of the families and/or the numbers of animals kept.[83] The assumed positions of power were apparently not based on economic differences. The lengths of the houses, especially again the byres, however did change considerably over the ages. It is thought that these differences reflect primarily the varying importance of stock keeping, though some may be related to changes in the composition of the households: extended as opposed to nuclear families.[84]

Large settlements and a degree of social differentiation that was distinctly higher than that of the first farmers were to reappear only in the Roman period. The Netherlands clearly lagged behind developments in the surrounding areas.[85]

STYLES AND TRIBES

It is generally assumed that prehistoric society, too, comprised large social units – tribes[86] and chiefdoms – of the kinds known from ethnographic studies all over the world. An important question that has busied archaeologists' minds for a long time is whether certain *archaeological* spatial patterns may be seen to reflect such regional or supraregional *social* units. In this book it has frequently implicitly, and sometimes more explicitly, been assumed that they may. We must now concern ourselves with how to interpret the continuities and discontinuities observable in these spatial patterns. If we assume that design and style are related to identity, then what we call 'style provinces' can be regarded as areas whose occupants had a certain communal group identity which differed from that of similar groups elsewhere. Such areas are distinguished predominantly on the basis of materials that were produced, used and discarded locally and that show distinct stylistic features, such as pottery and to a lesser extent also flint, but also on the basis of house plans and burial traditions.[87]

In the case of some periods our information is limited to the distribution of a single type of artefact, whereas in others we have well-defined distribution patterns of *assemblages* from burials and settlements. On the basis of such evidence we distinguish archaeological 'cultures' and subdivisions within such cultures. The aforementioned distribution patterns are incidentally determined not only by the artefacts' original use, but also by a wide range of processes, collectively known as 'formation processes'. They include deposition and disposal customs of the prehistoric people themselves, but also later natural processes such as erosion and sedimentation.[88] Another important factor is the intensity of archaeological research. But even when we make due allowance for all these factors, we are still able to distinguish large, original spatial patterns or 'style provinces'. The archaeological and social units vary in both scale and dimensions. It is not so easy to link the two, especially because of the fundamental social differences between the various periods.

In the Low Countries, few artefacts with distinct stylistic features have come down to us from the Late Palaeolithic and Mesolithic hunter-gatherers with their very low population densities and their high degree of mobility. The style provinces of these groups are hence perforce based on a single type of artefact or distinguishing feature. The distribution areas of the Ahrensburgian tanged points (at least 75,000 km²), artefacts of Wommersom quartzite (30,000 km²) and the Mesolithic *feuilles de gui* could reflect the territories of dialect tribes and the same could be said of the distribution areas of some types of barbed bone and antler points.[89]

The later prehistoric societies were small, sedentary farming communities living in smaller territories with much higher population densities. They were consequently able to contact groups of a sufficient size within a much smaller area. Thanks to, in particular, the stylistic differences observable in their pottery, we are able to distinguish units that vary considerably in size. Very large, highly distinct cultural units with a high degree of material uniformity, such as the *Bandkeramik*, the Rössen culture and the Single Grave culture, represent communities with a communal style, but they also reflect those communities' shared ideas and shared way of life. These units do not yet show any signs of social or political coherence. They represent segmentary communities without central authority or centralistic structures whose settlements functioned as independent, self-sufficient units.

Expressions of group identity are observable at a lower – regional – level, too, in the form of variations in style within small, clearly limited style provinces, such as that of the Veluwe Bell Beakers. Generally speaking, it is however impossible to determine the precise social meaning of such style provinces. Neither can they be related to the 'elite' distinguished in the Bronze Age and Iron Age. There are clear differences in scale. The areas within which the elites manifested themselves, such as the Maaskant region and the plateau of Drenthe, seem to have been smaller than the smallest cultural units, which makes it difficult for us to assess the scale of martial aspects on warriorship and the related tribal warfare.[90] We know for certain that there were violent conflicts between groups from the *Bandkeramik* onwards. The indications of conflicts increase as we proceed through prehistory, though they remain as modest as those of many other aspects of social life. Armed conflicts can likewise have been little more than small-scale, poorly organised encounters on a local rather than a regional level until the end of prehistory.

From the late glacial hunters until the farmers at the end of prehistory, and even in early historical times, there was constantly a conspicuous contrast between a northern and a southern cultural area in the Low Countries. At some times the boundary between these two areas was more distinct than at others, from time to time its position shifted to the south or to the north, and occasionally it disappeared for a relatively short period of time, that is, in those periods the boundary is archaeologically invisible. The latter holds in particular for the Early Mesolithic, a large part of the Beaker period and the beginning of the Iron Age. Many aspects of this north-south contrast can be seen in a much wider context. Most northern 'cultures' formed part of North European cultural phenomena encountered all over the North German Plain, with close ties in regions even further away. The majority of the southern groups belonged to a Rhineland – and in a wider sense Central European – tradition. A few cultures, like the Hilversum culture, show more western influences.

The various cultural units also differed from one another in their individual development: changes were constantly – if gradually – taking place within them. These changes did not in any way affect the unit's cultural or ethnic continuity. Even abrupt changes between successive 'cultures' are nowadays explained predominantly in social and ideological terms and are no longer attributed to movements of peoples as in the past. The continuity and stability of the cultural patterns can be seen as indications of a very long ethnic continuity, within which changes in material and stylistic expression, some gradual, others abrupt, constantly occurred. The only striking break in this continuum is the appearance of the Early Neolithic *Bandkeramik*.

We hence see the many millennia of our prehistory as a period of social developments in which the foundations for later society were laid. The population grew, the farming way of life acquired a sustainable basis in spite of its destructive impact on the environment, the land was organised and the first signs of social ranking and spatial grouping appeared. These are all largely indigenous developments. The many changes observable in material culture and people's customs and in the relationship between man and the land all took place within a context of substantial ethnic continuity. The arrival of the Romans and the establishment of *Germania Inferior* put an end to this long period of comparative peace. In a manner far more intrusive than in the case of the arrival of the *Bandkeramik* farmers 5300 years earlier, the native population was confronted with a new, and this time rather dominant, culture. The Romanisation that was inevitably to follow marked the end of prehistory in the Netherlands.

NOTES

1 Braudel 1969; Ankersmit 1986, 233.

2 See chapters 8 and 9. The knowledge that the natural environment became less varied – and hence less rich in resources – in the course of the Atlantic is a warning against assuming population growth in the Late Mesolithic.

3 See chapter 11. In my estimation the initial population will have been somewhat larger.

4 See chapter 13. For (originally) 100 *hunebedden*, divided between 30 sites/clusters, the extremes of the calculation are 30 x 50 = 1500 inhabitants, and 100 x 100 = 10,000 inhabitants. The latter figure is exorbitantly high in the light of the very limited environmental changes, and of the population figures calculated for later periods.

5 Louwe Kooijmans 1983b.

6 See chapters 28 and 30. Extremes have been left out of consideration here. Such regional figures can of course not be simply extrapolated to the whole of the Netherlands!

7 See chapter 24 and also Louwe Kooijmans 1995; Brongers 1976a; Kooi 1979; Harsema 1980a.

8 See chapter 23.

9 Brongers 1976a, 14.

10 See chapter 24. An area of approximately 1300 km², excluding the raised bogs, was fit for occupation.

11 Harsema assumed slightly higher figures in chapter 24: 3-4 inhabitants per km² and an overall population of 5000 in Drenthe.

12 Van Es (1981, 137, 207) maintained that the four cities (Nijmegen, Forum Hadriani, Maastricht and Heerlen) had only a few thousand inhabitants (Nijmegen 4000, Forum Hadriani 1000?). *Castella* and *vici* will have accounted for about 20,000 individuals (Van Es 1981, 231). Bloemers (1978, 111, 124) arrived at figures of 6500-19,000 for the Cananefates[AL1], Willems (1986a, 235) calculated 30,000-40,000 Batavi in 1000-1500 settlements of four households each on the basis of military recruitment figures. As for the Frisians: in an area of 200 km² in Westergo alone 300 *terpen* were occupied in the Roman period (chapter 25). If we assume that this corresponds to 10,000 inhabitants, there will have been about as many Frisians as Batavi. An estimate of 50,000 for the rest of the Netherlands (especially Limburg and North Brabant) brings us to 150,000 inhabitants in the mid-Roman period, which implies a considerable increase since the end of prehistory. From the expansion of the settlement at Rijswijk Van Es (1981, 231) inferred a three- or two-fold growth of the native Cananefates population in the Roman period. If we assume a similar growth elsewhere, too, and we allow for the presence of Roman soldiers and the Roman administrative machinery, we arrive at figures close to those based on the Celtic fields for the population at the beginning of the Roman occupation.

13 Roymans 1991, 70-71. For criticism see: Fontijn 1996c, Fokkens 1998b. The decrease in the number of cemeteries will be largely attributable to the decrease in the numbers of (datable) grave goods. There seems to be too little evidence to support a 'stagnating agricultural economy'.

14 See chapters 10 and 14.

15 See chapters 12 and 14 for Swifterbant and chapters 13 and 14 for Vlaardingen.

16 The brown forest soils or *holtpodzolen*; see also chapters 3 and 10.

17 See chapter 15. Whether or not this was done via the slash-and-burn method will be left aside here. See also chapter 14.

18 Chapter 12.

19 Chapter 14.

20 See chapter 14.

21 See chapters 15 and 16.

22 The large-scale, systematic use of the ard seems to have been preceded by a long period of experimentation and development. There is no sense in using an ard unless the land is more or less free of stumps (Fokkens 1986; 1991a, 106; 1998b). See also chapters 14 and 15.

23 See chapter 20. See feature J for fowling and fishing at the sites of Westfrisia. Special activity camps have been found at for example Vlaardingen, Hekelingen, Oldeboorn: Louwe Kooijmans 1993a; Fokkens 1991a, 116-119. For bone fish hooks recovered from a burial in an agricultural context at Molenaarsgraaf see chapter 14 and Louwe Kooijmans 1974, 250.

24 See chapters 16, 18 and 20.

25 See feature K for degradation of the soil. The stalling of cattle implies manuring and manuring means the end of shifting crop cultivation.

26 See chapter 30.

27 See chapter 27.

28 See chapter 24.

29 See chapters 25 and 26 and also feature N.

30 The formation of expansive tidal creek systems during the Dunkirk I transgression led to substantial drainage of the peripheries of many raised bogs in the western Netherlands in particular.

31 See chapter 24 and also Louwe Kooijmans 1993a, 100, 104-105.

32 On the development of the natural vegetation see chapters 7, 8 and 10, for the effects of human interference see chapters 14 and 21.

33 See chapter 10 and also Louwe Kooijmans 1985, 29.

34 See feature K.

35 See chapter 7. For fire ecology see Mellars 1976; for British pollen data see Simmons *et al.* 1989. Nowadays natural fires occur in pine forests and on moors, especially on the Veluwe; the fire implied here would have burned deciduous forests on moist soils.

36 See Clarke 1976 and Zvelebil 1994 for the role of plants in the Mesolithic in general. Unfortunately the views presented in those works cannot all be empirically substantiated with results of botanical research: (carbonised) plant remains, in particular seeds, only rarely survive and man's influence on the vegetation is not visible in pollen diagrams. The construction of trackways/paths and the felling mentioned in the above works can have been small-scale activities only. The evidence obtained at Milheeze seems to show the effects of activities at the camp sites themselves, but no consequences of any large-scale clearance of the forest (see chapter 7).

37 Bay-Petersen 1978.

38 See chapters 14 and 15 and also Kalis 1988; Kalis/Meurers-Balke 1988; Bakels 1988b (Wange).

39 Behre/Kučan 1986, 1994.

40 Kalis 1988, Kalis/Meurers-Balke 1988; Teunissen 1990.

41 Casparie/Groenman-van Waateringe 1980.

42 Fokkens 1991a, 128-129.

43 See chapter 15.

44 See chapter 22. A sample from the fill of a ditch at Bovenkarspel (Late Bronze Age) contained 790 fish remains per litre (IJzereef 1981, 119). It is not so easy to determine the importance of fish. Fish produce large amounts of remains, but those remains are extremely vulnerable, they survive only under special conditions and they can be reliably collected only if special measures (sieving) are taken during excavation.

45 Louwe Kooijmans 1995. The assumption that plenty of wild animals were available in 'unspoilt' prehistoric times is primarily based on intuition!

46 Waterbolk 1979, 1982.

47 See chapter 5.

48 Hodder 1990.

49 See chapter 20.

50 See chapter 15.

51 See chapters 12 and 15.

52 Bakker 1976, 1982; Modderman 1962-63a; Klok 1979. See also chapters 15, 16 and 19 and feature K.

53 The view expressed here may rightly be termed somewhat speculative. If we however assume that a community's behaviour was to a great extent determined by the 'context' of structures already present, the continuity outlined here is inevitable. We do not yet have sufficient evidence to support all the steps in this development, but on the other hand this view is not in any way disputed either; quite the contrary: if we accept this view, we find that many isolated observations suddenly fit into a pattern.

An argument favouring long continuity of patterns of use is the presence of features embracing a long time span at a single site, as for example observed at Hijken, Noordbarge and Angelslo (all of which lie in Drenthe), Haps and Oss in the southern part of the Netherlands, Hazendonk and Velserbroek in the west.

54 See chapters 16 and 29.

55 See for example chapter 18.

56 See chapter 20.

57 See chapter 15.

58 See chapters 19 and 20.

59 Waterbolk 1979, 1982. Direct comparison of the historical boundaries with much older archaeological patterns in the whole of Drenthe (1979) is however hampered by serious methodological problems. On a microregional scale (1982) there is far more archaeological evidence for this continuity and the transition from the relocation of settlements to life in permanent villages in the Middle Ages. The foundations for the territorial division of the land will have been laid in the TRB period, and will have been passed down via the Beaker period and the Middle Bronze Age.

60 Binford 1982.

61 For the Magdalenian and Hamburgian cultures see chapter 6, for the Mesolithic chapters 5 and 8, and for a summary chapter 9.

62 Especially within the De Leien-Wartena Group, like the Bergumermeer site. See also chapter 4.

63 See chapters 7 and 9.

64 See chapter 13. Settlement sites of the TRB culture measure 0.5-5 ha; the largest are undoubtedly the consequence of the frequent relocation of houses.

65 See chapters 16 and 18. For Oldeboorn also Fokkens 1991a, 116-120, 125.

66 See chapter 30.

67 See chapters 24 and 30. Ezinge comprised about 15 houses in the Late Iron Age.

68 See chapter 18.

69 See chapter 23.

70 See chapter 25.

71 See chapter 24.

72 See chapter 23.

73 See chapter 20.

74 Renfrew/Bahn 1991, 145, 155.

75 See chapters 17 and 29.

76 See chapters 20 and 30.

77 See chapters 9 and 12.

78 See chapter 11.

79 See chapter 13. The unequal distribution incidentally raises more complex questions (*cf.* chapter 20 and Fokkens 1991a, 101-102).

80 See chapter 15. For the TRB culture: chapter 13 (deposits in bogs,

construction of *hunebedden* and down-the-line exchange of exotic objects). It does not seem entirely correct to speak of egalitarian communities.

81 See chapter 19. Most burials are of men, such as the Sögel burial of Drouwen and a few large ring ditches.

82 See chapters 19 and 28.

83 See chapters 23 (southern and central parts of the Netherlands), 24 (northern sandy soils; one house at Hijken is an exception), 25 (northern clay; lengths 10-20 m), 26 (western Netherlands) and 30.

84 See chapter 12 for Rössen and chapter 18 for the Middle Bronze Age. Exceptions are a few very long Middle Bronze Age plans, such as those found at Angelslo and Dalfsen, which are the results of the construction of extensions and rebuilding.

85 See chapter 30.

86 The term 'tribe' is here used in a very general sense, to refer to a large, regional social unit. See also chapter 15.

87 They are hence based on local materials, not materials that were imported from distant sources in exchange systems, such as exotic types of stone and bronzes.

88 See chapter 1.

89 See chapter 8, feature B and Clark 1975, 70.

90 See feature L and chapters 17 and 29.

Abbreviations

AAC	Amsterdam Archaeological Centre, University of Amsterdam / Amsterdams Archeologisch Centrum, Universiteit van Amsterdam
APL	*Analecta Praehistorica Leidensia*
ASLU	Archaeological Studies Leiden University
BAI	Biologisch-Archaeologisch Instituut, Rijksuniversiteit Groningen
BAR	British Archaeological Reports
BOOR	Archaeological dept. Municipality of Rotterdam / Bureau Oudheidkundig Onderzoek van Gemeentewerken Rotterdam
BROB	*Berichten van de Rijksdienst voor het Oudheidkundig Bodemonderzoek*
ERAUL	Etudes et Recherches Archéologiques de l'Université de Liège
FdAL	Faculty of Archaeology, Leiden University / Faculteit der Archeologie, Universiteit Leiden
GIA	Groningen Institute of Archaeology; formerly known as BAI, State University of Groningen / Groninger Instituut voor Archeologie, Rijksuniversiteit Groningen
GNBA	Archaeological dept. Municipality of Nijmegen / Gemeente Nijmegen, Bureau Archeologie
IPL	Instituut voor Prehistorie, Universiteit Leiden, since 1997: FdAL
IPP	Instituut voor Pre- en Protohistorische Archeologie, Universiteit van Amsterdam, since 2002: AAC
MRGD	*Mededelingen van de Rijks Geologische Dienst*
NAR	Nederlandse Archeologische Rapporten
NITG	Nederlands Instituut voor Toegepaste Geowetenschappen
NDV	*Nieuwe Drentse Volksalmanak*
OMROL	*Oudheidkundige Mededelingen uit het Rijksmuseum van Oudheden te Leiden*
PPS	*Proceedings of the Prehistoric Society*
PSHAL	*Publications de la Société Historique et Archéologique dans le Limbourg*
RAAP	Regionaal Archeologisch Archiveringsproject
RAM	Rapportage Archeologische Monumentenzorg
RMO	National Museum of Antiquities / Rijksmuseum van Oudheden, Leiden
ROB	State Service for Archaeological Investigations / Rijksdienst voor het Oudheidkundig Bodemonderzoek, Amersfoort
UvA	University of Amsterdam / Universiteit van Amsterdam
VU	Free University / Vrije Universiteit, Amsterdam

Literature

Note: for author's names like S.J. *De Laet* and L. *Van Impe* see *Laet, S.J. De* and *Impe, L. Van.*

Aaris-Sørensen, K., 1988: *Danmarks forhistoriske dyreverden*, Copenhagen.

Abbink, A.A., 1989: Maasland: Foppenpolder, in: D.P. Hallewas, 322-326.

Abbink, A.A., 1990: Midden-Delfland: Foppenpolder/Aalkeetbuitenpolder, in: W.A.M. Hessing, 336-338.

Abbink, A.A., 1993a: The Midden-Delfland project: Iron Age occupation, *Helinium* 33, 253-301.

Abbink, A.A., 1993b: Dwelling on peat; fissures as a recurrent feature of (pre)historic structures built on peat in the Western Netherlands, *APL* 26, 59-82.

Abbink, A.A. / R. Frank 1991: Midden-Delfland 2: Aalkeetbuitenpolder site 16.59, in: W.A.M. Hessing 1991b, 334-336.

Abrahamse, J., *et al.* (eds.) 1985²: *Het Drentse landschap*, Assen.

Achterop, S.H., 1957: De vuurstenen dolk van Wollingboermarke, *Groningse Volksalmanak 1957*, 152-159.

Achterop, S.H., 1960: Een depot van vuurstenen bijlen van de Reemst, *NDV* 78, 179-180.

Achterop, S.H., 1961: Een depot van bijlen uit Boerakker, gem. Marum, *Groningse Volksalmanak*, 158-164.

Achterop, S.H. / J.A. Brongers 1979: Stone cold chisels with handle (*Schlägel*) in the Netherlands, *BROB* 29, 255-356.

Acsádi, G. / J. Nemeskéri 1970: *History of human life span and mortality*, Budapest.

Addink-Samplonius, M., 1968: Neolithische stenen strijdhamers uit Midden-Nederland, *Helinium* 8, 209-240.

Addink-Samplonius, M. (eds.) 1983: *Urnen delven*, Dieren.

Adriani, M.J., *et al.* 1980: *Ontdek de duinen*, Amsterdam (Nederlandse landschappen, 3).

Aerts-Bijma, A. / J.N. Lanting / J. van der Plicht 1999: Een verrassende wending: gecremeerd been blijkt wel ¹⁴C-dateerbaar!, *Paleo-aktueel* 10, 64-67.

Aimé, G. / C. Jeunesse 1986: Le niveau 5 des abris sous roches de Bavans (Doubs) et la transition Mésolithique récent Néolithique dans la moyenne vallée du Doubs, in: *Actes du Xe Colloque interrégional sur le Néolithique, Revue Archéologique de l'Ouest*, I, Caen (*Revue Archéologique de l'Ouest*, Suppl. 1), 31-40.

Aitken, M.J., 1990: *Science-based dating in archaeology*, London.

Albrethsen, S.E. / E. Brinch Petersen 1976: Excavation of a mesolithic cemetery at Vedbaek, Denmark, *Acta Archaeologica* 47, 1-28.

Allain, J., 1989: La fin du paléolithique supérieur en region Centre, in: J.-Ph. Rigaud (eds.), 93-214.

Allsworth-Jones, P., 1986: *The Szeletian and the transition from middle to upper palaeolithic in Central Europe*, Oxford.

Ammerman, A.J. / L.L. Cavalli-Sforza 1973: A population model for the diffusion of early farming in Europe, in: C. Renfrew (eds.), 343-357.

Amsden, C.W., 1977: *A quantitative analysis of Nunamiut Eskimo settlement dynamics: 1898 to 1969*, Albuquerque (Ph.D. thesis).

Amtmann, G. / W. Schwellnus 1987: Luft- und Bodenprospektion. Ein neues Erdwerk der Michelsberger Kultur bei Jülich, Kr. Düren, *Das Rheinisches Landesmuseum Bonn* 4/87, 53-56.

Andersen, K. / S. Jørgensen / J. Richter 1982: Maglemose hytterne ved Ulkestrup Lyng, *Nordiske Fortidsminder* Ser. B. 7.

Andersen, S.H., 1973: Ringkloster. En jysk inlandsboplads med Ertebøllekultur, *Kuml* 1973-'74, 10-108.

Andersen, S.H., 1985: Tybrind Vig. A preliminary report on a submerged Ertebølle settlement on the West coast of Fyn, *Journal of Danish Archaeology* 4, 52-59.

Andersen, S.H., 1987: Tybrind Vig: A submerged Ertebølle settlement in Denmark, in: J.M. Coles / A.J. Lawson (eds.), 253-280.

Andersen, S.H., *et al.*1990: Making cultural ecology relevant to mesolithic research: I. A data base of 413 mesolithic fauna assemblages, in: P.M. Vermeersch / P. Van Peer (eds.), 23-51.

Andersen, S.T., 1993: Early agriculture, in: S. Hvass / B. Storgaard (eds.), 88-91.

Anderson, P.C. (ed.) 1992: *Préhistoire de l'agriculture: nouvelles approches expérimentales et ethno-graphiques*, Valbonne (Monographie du CRA, 6).

Ankersmit, F.R., 1986: *Denken over geschiedenis*, Groningen.

Ankersmit, F.R., 1993: *De historische ervaring*, Groningen (rede).

Anscher, T.J. ten, 1990: Vogelenzang I, a Hilversum-1 settlement, *Helinium* 29, 44-78.

Anscher, T.J. ten, forthcoming: *Neolithicum en bronstijd in de Noordoostpolder*, Amsterdam (Ph.D. thesis).

Anscher, T.J. ten / E.F. Gehasse 1991: Archeologisch onderzoek op kavel P14, in: *Archeologische kroniek van Flevoland, En het land was niet langer woest en ledig. Cultureel Jaarboek voor Flevoland*, 119-125.

Anscher, T.J. ten / E. Gehasse 1993: Neolithische en vroege bronstijd-bewoning langs de benedenloop van de Overijsselse Vecht, in: J.H.F. Bloemers / W. Groenman-van Waateringe / H.A. Heidinga (eds.), 25-44.

Anscher, T.J. ten / E. Gehasse / J.A. Bakker 1994: A pre-megalithic TRB and Late Swifterbant complex at P14-Schokland, Gemeente Noordoostpolder, The Netherlands, in: J. Pavúk (ed.), 460-466.

Anthony, D.W. / D.R. Brown 1991: The origins of horseback riding, *Antiquity* 65, 22-38.

Arjaans, J., 1990: Terpafgravingen in Friesland, *Historisch-Geografisch Tijdschrift* 8, 54-62.

Arora, S.K., 1974: Ein verziertes Knochenstück vom mesolithischen Fundplatz Gustorf, Kr. Gre-venbroich, *Archäologisches Korrespondenzblatt* 4, 299.

Arora, S.K., 1976: Die Mittelsteinzeit im westlichen Deutschland und in den Nachbargebieten, *Rheinische Ausgrabungen* 17, 1-65.

Arora, S.K., 1979: Mesolithische Rohstoffversorgung im westlichen Deutschland, *Rheinische Aus-grabungen* 19, 1-51.

Arora, S.K. / J.H.G. Franzen 1987: Simpelveld vuursteen: een nieuw type vuursteen, *Archeologie in Limburg* 32, 23-27.

Arps, C.E.S., 1978: Petrography and possible origin of adzes and other artefacts from prehistoric sites near Hienheim and Elsloo, Sittard and Stein, in: C.C. Bakels, 202-228.

Arps, C.E.S., 1990: Bandkeramische dissels van Centraal-Europa: gesteentesoorten en herkomst, in: H. Kars (ed.), 11-28.

Arts, N., 1984: Waubach: a Late Upper Palaeolithic / Mesolithic lithic raw material procurement site in Limburg, the Netherlands, *Helinium* 24, 209-220.

Arts, N., 1986: Tilburg, Lepelare Zand, in: W.J.H. Verwers, 14-16.

Arts, N., 1987a: Vroegmesolithische nederzettingssporen en twee versierde hertshoornen arte-fakten uit het Maaskantgebied bij 's-Hertogenbosch, *Brabants Heem* 39, 2-22.

Arts, N., 1987b: Mesolithische jagers, vissers en voedselverzamelaars in noordoost België en zui-doost Nederland, *Het Oude Land van Loon* 42, 27-85.

Arts, N., 1988: A survey of final Palaeolithic archaeology in the Southern Netherlands, in: M. Otte (ed.), 287-356.

Arts, N., 1989: Archaeology, environment and the social evolution of later band societies in a lowland area, in: C. Bonsall (ed.), 291-312.

Arts, N. / J. Deeben 1977: Een Laat-Mesolithische nederzetting bij het Steenven te Netersel (Gem. Bladel c.a.), in: N. Roymans et al. (eds.), 33-41.

Arts, N. / J. Deeben 1978: Een Federmesser nederzetting te Oostelbeers: een rapport betreffende de noodopgravingen in 1976, Brabants Heem 30, 60-75.

Arts, N. / J. Deeben 1981: Prehistorische jagers en verzamelaars te Vessem: een model, Eindhoven (Bijdrage tot de studie van het Brabants Heem, 20).

Arts, N. / J. Deeben 1983: Archeologisch onderzoek in een Late Magdalénien-nederzetting te Sweikhuizen, gemeente Schinnen, Archeologie in Limburg 16, 2-5.

Arts, N. / J. Deeben 1987a: On the Northwestern border of Late Magdalenian territory: Ecology and archaeology of Early Late Glacial band societies in Northwestern Europe, in: J.M. Burdukiewicz / M. Kobusiewicz (eds.), 25-66.

Arts, N. / J. Deeben 1987b: De opgraving, analyse en interpretatie van een Magdalénien nederzetting bij Sweikhuizen, provincie Limburg, Amsterdam (internal report AAC).

Arts, N. / M. Hoogland 1987: A Mesolithic settlement area with a human cremation grave at Oirschot V, municipality of Best, the Netherlands, Helinium 27, 172-189.

Arts, N., et al. 1990: Rendierjagers. Prehistorische tentenkampen nabij de Maas, Tongeren (Publicaties van het Provinciaal Gallo-Romeins Museum, 43).

Ashbee, P., 1960: The Bronze Age round barrow in Britain, London.

Asmussen, P.S.G. / J. Moree 1987: De Ewijkse velden, Leiden (internal report FdAL).

Assendorp, J.J., 1975: Twee bronzen halsringen uit het Uddeler veen, Westerheem 24, 150-155.

Assendorp, J.J., 1987: Eine Siedlung der Trichterbecherkultur bei Penningbüttel, Berichte zur Denkmalpflege in Niedersachsen 7, 140-141.

Audouze, F., 1987: The Paris Basin in Magdalenian times, in: O. Soffer (ed.), 183-200.

Audouze, F. / J. Enloe 1991: Subsistence strategies and economy in the Magdalenian of the Paris Basin, France, in: N. Barton / A.J. Roberts / D.A. Roe (eds.), 63-71.

Auguste, P., 1988: Apports paléontologiques et archéozoologiques de l'étude de la faune des grands mammifères de Biache-St-Vaast (Pas-de-Calais), Actes du Colloque International 'Cultures et industries paléolithiques en milieu loessique', Revue Archéologique de Picardie 1/2, 63-68.

Baart, J.M., 1990: Amsterdam, gewestelijke stad in de middeleeuwen, wereldstad in de Gouden Eeuw, in: H. Sarfatij (ed.), 152-162.

Bailey, G.N. (ed.) 1983: Hunter-gatherer economy in prehistory. An European perspective, Cambridge.

Baillie, M.G.L. / J.R. Pilcher 1983: Some observations on the high-precision calibration dates, in: B.S. Ottaway (ed.), 51-63.

Bakel, M.A. van / R.R. Hagesteijn / P. van de Velde (eds.) 1986: Private politics – Multi-disciplinary approach to 'big-man' systems, Leiden (Studies in Human Society, 1).

Bakels, C.C., 1975: Pollen spectra from the late Bronze Age urnfield at Hilvarenbeek-Laag Spul, Prov. Noord-Brabant, Netherlands, APL 8, 45-51.

Bakels, C.C., 1978: Four Linearbandkeramik settlements and their environment: A paleoecological study of Sittard, Stein, Elsloo and Hienheim, Leiden (Ph.D. thesis; = APL 11).

Bakels, C.C., 1981: Neolithic plant remains from the Hazendonk, Province of Zuid-Holland, The Netherlands, Zeitschrift für Archäologie 15, 141-148.

Bakels, C.C., 1982a: Der Mohn, die Linearbandkeramik und das westliche Mittelmeergebiet, Archäologisches Korrespondenzblatt 12, 11-13.

Bakels, C.C., 1982b: The settlement system of the Dutch Linearbandkeramik, APL 15, 31-45.

Bakels, C.C., 1982c: Zum wirtschaftlichen Nutzungsraum einer bandkeramischen Siedlung, in: Siedlungen der Kultur mit Linearkeramik, Nitra, 9-16.

Bakels, C.C., 1983: L'exploitation par l'homme du Rubané de son milieu naturel et en particulier des sources minérales, in: S.J. De Laet (ed.), 17-19.

Bakels, C.C., 1986: Akkerbouw in het moeras? in: M.C. van Trierum / H.E. Henkes (eds.), 1-6.

Bakels, C.C., 1987a: On the adzes of the northwestern Linearbandkeramik, APL 20, 53-87.

Bakels, C.C., 1987b: Oss-Ussen en de tuinboon, in: W.A.B. van der Sanden / P.W. van den Broeke (eds.), 137-139.

Bakels, C.C., 1988a: Hekelingen, a Neolithic site in the swamps of the Meuse estuary, in: H. Küster (ed.), 155-161.

Bakels, C.C., 1988b: On the location of the fields of the Northwestern Bandkeramik, in: M. Bierma / O.H. Harsema / W. van Zeist (eds.), 49-57.

Bakels, C.C., 1990a: Graan, het oude goud, Natuur en Techniek 58, 240-249.

Bakels, C.C., 1990b: The crops of the Rössen culture: significantly different from their Bandkeramik predecessors – French influence?, in: D. Cahen / M. Otte (eds.), 83-87.

Bakels, C.C., 1991a: Tracing crop processing in the Bandkeramik culture, in: J. Renfrew (ed.), 281-288.

Bakels, C.C., 1991b: Western continental Europe, in: W. van Zeist / K. Wasylikowa / K.-E. Behre (eds.), Progress in Old World palaeoethnobotany, 279-298.

Bakels, C.C., 1992a: Het Neolithicum, in: Speurwerk, archeologische monumentenzorg in de Euregio Maas-Rijn, Mainz, 58-79.

Bakels, C.C., 1992b: Research on land clearance during the Early Neolithic in the loess regions of The Netherlands, Belgium and northern France, in: B. Frenzel et al. (eds.), 47-56.

Bakels, C.C., 1994: Vruchten en zaden uit de ijzertijd-nederzettingen te Oss-Ussen; in: K. Schinkel, 219-232.

Bakels, C.C. / M.J. Alkemade / C.E. Vermeeren 1993: Botanische Untersuchungen in der Rössener Siedlung Maastricht-Randwijck, in: A.J. Kalis / J. Meurers-Balke (eds.), 35-48.

Bakels, C.C. / R.W.J.M. van der Ham 1980: Verkoold afval uit een Midden-Bronstijd en een Midden-IJzertijd nederzetting op de Hooidonksche Akkers, gem. Son en Breugel, prov. Noord-Brabant, APL 13, 81-91.

Bakels, C.C. / J. Lüning 1990: Pioneer farmers, in N. Calder (ed.), 132-138.

Bakels, C.C. / R. Rousselle 1985: Restes botaniques et agriculture du néolithique ancien en Belgique et aux Pays Bas, Helinium 25, 37-57.

Bakels, C.C. / P. van de Velde 2002: Beek Geverikerveld, een noodopgraving in een prehistorisch boerendorp. Leiden.

Bakker, J.A., 1959: Veenvondsten van de trechterbekercultuur, in: J. Bogaers et al. (eds.), 93-99.

Bakker, J.A., 1976: On the possibility of reconstructing roads from the TRB period, BROB 26, 63-91.

Bakker, J.A., 1979b: Protection, acquisition, restoration and maintenance of the Dutch hunebeds since 1734: an active and often exemplary policy in Drenthe (I), BROB 29, 143-183.

Bakker, J.A., 1979a: The TRB West Group. Studies in the chronology and geography of the makers of the hunebeds and Tiefstich pottery, Amsterdam (Ph.D. thesis; = Cingula, 5).

Bakker, J.A., 1980: Einige Bermerkungen über die niederländische Grosssteingräber und deren Erbauer, Nachrichten aus Niedersachsens Urgeschichte 49, 31-59.

Bakker, J.A., 1982: TRB settlement patterns on the Dutch sandy soils, APL 15, 87-124.

Bakker, J.A., 1988: A list of the extant and formerly present hunebedden in the Netherlands, Palaeohistoria 30, 63-77.

Bakker, J.A., 1992: The Dutch hunebedden: megalithic tombs of the Funnel Beaker Culture, Ann Arbor (Archaeological Series, 2).

Bakker, J.A / W. Groenman-van Waateringe 1988: Megaliths, soils and vegetation on the Drenthe plateau, in: W. Groenman-van Waateringe / M. Robinson (eds.), 143-181.

Bakker, J.A. / H.A. Luijten 1990: 'Service sets' and other 'similarity groups' in western and northern TRB pottery, Revue Archéologique de l'Ouest, suppl. 2, 173-187.

Bakker, J.A. / J.D. van der Waals 1973: Denekamp-Angelslo: cremations, collared flasks and a corded ware sherd in Dutch final TRB context, in: G. Daniel / P. Kjaerum (eds.), 17-50.

Bakker, J.A. / Ph. J. Woltering / W.J. Manssen 1968: Opgravingen te Hoogkarspel (V), West-Frieslands Oud en Nieuw 35, 192-199.

Bakker, J.A., *et al.* 1977: Hoogkarspel-Watertoren: towards a reconstruction of ecology and archaeology of an agrarian settlement of 1000 BC, in: B.L. van Beek / R.W. Brandt / W. Groenman-van Waateringe (eds.), 187-225.

Bakker, J.P. / A. Bohmers / J.J. Spahr van der Hoek (eds.) 1961: *Boven-Boorngebied; rapport betreffende
het onderzoek van het Lânskip-genetysk Wurkforbân van de Fryske Akademy*, Drachten (Wâldrige, 9).

Bakker, J.T., 1982: Een bronzen brilfibula en een bronzen speerpunt uit het Rijksmuseum van
Oudheden te Leiden, Leiden (internal report FdAL).

Band, A.P. van den / E.H.P. Cordfunke (eds.), 2001: *Archeologie in veelvoud. Vijftig jaar Archeologische
Werkgemeenschap voor Nederland*, Utrecht .

Barendsen, G.W., 1955: *Ouderdomsbepaling met radioactieve koolstof*, Den Haag (Ph.D. thesis).

Bartelheim, M. / E. Pernicka / R. Krause (eds.) 2002: *Die Anfänge der Metallurgie in der alten Welt / The
beginnings of metallurgy in the Old World*, Rahden.

Barton, N. / A.J. Roberts / D.A. Roe (eds.) 1991: *The Late Glacial in north-west Europe: human adaptation and environmental change at the end of the Pleistocene*, Oxford (CBA Research Report, 77).

Bauchhenß, G. (ed.) 1983: *Archäologie in den Rheinischen Lößbörden, Beiträge zur Siedlungsgeschichte im
Rheinland* (Rheinische Ausgrabungen, 24).

Bauerochse, A., / A. Metzler 2001: Landschaftswandel und Moorwegenbau im Neolithikum in
der südwestlichen Dümmer-Region, *Telma* 31, 105-133.

Bay-Petersen, J.L., 1978: Animal exploitation in Mesolithic Denmark, in: P. Mellars (ed.), 115-
145.

Bazelmans, J. (ed.) 1992: *Krijgshaftigheid in de pre- en protohistorische samenlevingen van Noordwest-
Europa*, Amsterdam.

Beck, H., *et al.* (eds.) 1976: *Reallexikon der Germanischen Altertumskunde von Joh. Hoops*, Berlin.

Becker, C.J., 1947: *Mosefundne lerkar fra yngre stenalder, studier over tragtbaegerkulturen i Danmark*, Kopenhagen.

Becker, C.J., 1970: Eine Kerbspitze der Hamburger Stufe aus Jütland, in: K. Gripp / R. Schütrumpf
/ H. Schwabedissen (eds.), 362-364.

Beckers, H.J. / G.A.J. Beckers 1940: *Voorgeschiedenis van Zuid-Limburg*, Maastricht.

Beek, B.L. van, 1990: *Steentijd te Vlaardingen, Leidschendam en Voorschoten*, Amsterdam (Ph.D. thesis
UvA).

Beek, B.L. van / R.W. Brandt / W. Groenman-van Waateringe (eds.) 1977: *Ex Horreo*, Amsterdam
(Cingula, 4; *Festschrift* W. Glasbergen).

Beek, R. van, 1988: Rondbouwhuizen uit de Midden-Bronstijd in Spoolde, gem. Spoolde, *Overijsselse Historische Bijdragen* 103, 5-17.

Beek, R. van, 1991: Nog steeds Elp, *NDV* 108, 118-127.

Beemster, D.C.M / R.W. Brandt 1986: Velsen, in: P.J. Woltering, 280-282.

Beerenhout, B. / T. van der Mast / O. Odé 1990: Onderzoek aan het Laat-Paleolithische vondstma-
teriaal van 'De Banen', gem. Nederweert (L.), Amsterdam (internal report AAC).

Beets, D.J. / M.M. Fischer / W. de Gans 1996: Introduction: Ten papers on the coastal evolution of
the Netherlands, *MRGD* 57, 5-9.

Beets, D.J. / A.J.F. van der Spek 2000: The Holocene evolution of the barrier and the back-barrier
basins of Belgium and The Netherlands as a function of late Weichselian morphology, relative sea-level rise and sediment-supply, *Geologie en Mijnbouw* 79, 3-16.

Beets, D.J. / A.J.F. van der Spek / L. van der Valk 1994: *Holocene ontwikkeling van de Nederlandse kust*,
Haarlem (Rijks Geologische Dienst, rapport 40.016-Project Kustgenese).

Beets, D.J. / L. van der Valk / M.J.F. Stive 1992: Holocene evolution of the coast of Holland, *Marine
Geology* 103, 423-443.

Beex, G., 1964: Ringwalheuvel te Alphen, prov. Noord-Brabant, *BROB* 14, 53-65.

Beex, G. / R.S. Hulst 1968: A Hilversum-culture settlement near Nijnsel, municipality of St.
Oedenrode, North -Brabant, *BROB* 18, 117-129.

Beex, G. / H. Roosens 1967: Een urnenveld te Achel-Pastoorsbos, Brussel (Archaeologia Belgica,
96).

Beex, W.F.M., 1989: Oud nieuws – Archeologische vondsten en vindplaatsen uit de Vroege en Midden Bronstijd in het Maas-Demer-Schelde-gebied, Amsterdam (internal report AAC).

Behre, K.-E., 1970: Die Entwicklungsgeschichte der natürlichen Vegetation im Gebiet der unteren Ems und ihre Abhängigkeit von den Bewegungen des Meeresspiegels, in: *Probleme der Küstenforschung im südlichen Nordseegebiet*, 9, Hildesheim, 13-47.

Behre, K.-E., 1976: Beginn und Form der Plaggenwirtschaft in Nordwestdeutschland nach pollenanlytischen Untersuchungen in Ostfriesland, *Neue Ausgrabungen und Funde in Niedersachsen* 10, 197-224.

Behre, K.-E., (ed.) 1986: *Anthropogenic indicators in pollen diagrams*, Rotterdam.

Behre, K.-E. / D. Kučan 1986: Die Reflektion archäologisch bekannter Siedlungen in Pollendiagrammen verschiedener Entfernung – Beispiele aus der Siedlungskammer Flögeln, Nordwestdeutschland, in: K.-E. Behre (ed.), 95-114.

Behre, K.-E. / D. Kučan, 1994: Die Geschichte der Kulturlandschaft und des Ackerbaus in der Siedlungskammer Flögeln, Niedersachsen, seit der Jungsteinzeit, *Probleme der Küstenforschung im südlichen Nordseegebiet*, 21, Hildesheim.

Behrens, G. / J. Werner (eds.) 1950: *Reinecke Festschrift*, Mainz.

Bekhuis, J., *et al.* 1987: *Atlas van de Nederlandse vogels*, Arnhem.

Bell, M., 1990: *Brean Down excavations 1983-1987*, London (English Heritage Archaeological Report, 15).

Bellier, C. / P. Cattelain (eds.) 2000: *La chasse dans la préhistoire, Actes du Colloque international de Treignes 3-7 octobre 1990*, Liège (ERAUL, 51).

Bender, B., 1978: Gatherer-hunter to farmer: a social perspective, *World Archaeology* 10, 204-210.

Bennema, J., 1954: Bodem- en zeespiegelbewegingen in het Nederlandse kustgebied, *Boor en Spade* 7, 1-96.

Bennike, P. / K. Ebbesen 1986: The bog find from Sigersdal, human sacrifice in the early neolithic, *Journal of Danish Archaeology* 5, 85-115.

Berendsen, H.J.A., 1984: Problems of lithostratigraphic classification of Holocene deposits in the perimarine area of the Netherlands, *Geologie en Mijnbouw* 63, 351-354.

Berendsen, H.J.A. / E. Stouthamer 2001: *Palaeogeographic development of the Rhine-Meuse delta, The Netherlands*, Assen.

Bérenger, D., 1989: L'âge du bronze moyen en Westphalie, in: *Dynamique du Bronze Moyen en Europe occidentale*, Paris, 99-101.

Berg, M.W. van den / D.J. Beets 1987: Saalian glacial deposits and morphology in the Netherlands, in: J.J.M. van der Meer (ed.), 235-251.

Berg, M.W. van den / C. den Otter 1993: *Toelichtingen bij de Geologische kaart van Nederland 1:50.000, Blad Almelo Oost / Denekamp (28 O / 29)*, Haarlem.

Berg, P.L. Van, 1987a: Céramique de La Hoguette à Sweikhuizen, *Helinium* 22, 332.

Berg, P.L. Van, 1987b: Identification de potiers dans le Rubané récent de Hesbaye (Province de Liège, Belgique), *Actes du 14e Colloque interrégional sur le Néolithique Blois 1987*, 247-256.

Berg, P.L. Van, 1990: La céramique néolithique ancienne non-Rubanée dans le Nord-Ouest de l'Europe, *Bulletin de la Société de la Préhistoire du Luxembourg* 12, 107-124.

Berg, P.L. Van / J.P. Van Roeyen / L.H. Keeley 1991: Le site mésolithique à céramique de Melsele (Flandre-orientale), campagne de 1990, *Notae Praehistoricae* 10, 37-47.

Berger, A. (ed.) 1984: *Milankovitch and climate*, Hingham, Massachusetts.

Bergmann, J., 1970: *Die ältere Bronzezeit Nordwestdeutschlands*, Marburg (Kasseler Beiträge zur Vor- und Frühgeschichte, 2).

Berke, H. / J. Hahn / C.J. Kind (eds.) 1984: *Upper palaeolithic settlement patterns in Europe*, Tübingen.

Berkel, G.J.W. van, 1987: *Het namenlandschap van de provincie Groningen*, z.p. (ETC-reeks, 5).

Bernhardt, G., 1986: Die Linearbandkeramische Siedlung von Köln-Lindenthal, eine Neubearbeitung, *Kölner Jahrbuch* 18/19, 7-166.

Bertaux, J.-P., 1977: Das Briquetage an der Seille in Lothringen, *Archäologisches Korrespondenzblatt* 7, 261-272.

Besteman, J.C., et al. (eds.) 1999: *The excavations at Wijnaldum.Reports on Frisia in Roman and Medieval times*, I, Rotterdam/Brookfield.

Besteman, J.C. / J.M. Bos / H.A. Heidinga 1992: *Graven naar Friese Koningen – De opgravingen in Wijnaldum*, Franeker.

Bettinger, R.L., 1991: *Hunter-gatherers. Archaeological and evolutionary theory*, New York.

Beukema, J.J. / W.J. Wolff / J.W.M. Brouns (eds.) 1990: *Expected effects of climatic change on marine coastal ecosystems*, Dordrecht (Developments in Hydrology, 57).

Beuker, J.R., 1981: Een vindplaats met primair bewerkt vuursteenmateriaal bij Uffelte, gemeente Havelte, NDV 98, 99-111.

Beuker, J.R., 1983: *Vakmanschap in vuursteen*, Assen (Museumfonds Publicatie, 8).

Beuker, J.R., 1986: De import van Helgoland-vuursteen in Drenthe, NDV 103, 111-135.

Beuker, J.R., 1989: Mesolithische bewoningssporen op een zandopduiking te Nieuw-Schoonebeek, NDV 106, 117-186.

Beuker, J.R., 1990: Het gebruik van Helgoland-vuursteen in N.W.-Europa in de steen- en bronstijd, in: A.T.L. Niklewicz-Hokse / C.A.G. Lagerwerf (eds.), 74-81.

Beuker, J.R., 1991: De pijlen van een stamhoofd, NDV 108, 97-108.

Beuker, J.R. / M.J.L.Th. Niekus 1994: Neanderthalers in Drenthe: enkele opzienbarende nieuwe vondsten, NDV 111, 95-110.

Beuker, J.R. / W.A.B. van der Sanden / V.T. van Vilsteren 1991: *Zorg voor de doden – Vijfduizend jaar begraven in Drenthe*, Assen (Archeologische Monografieën van het Drents Museum, 3).

Beuker, J.R. / W.A.B. van der Sanden / V.T. van Vilsteren 1993: *Wonen en werken – Honderdduizend jaar dagelijks leven in Drenthe*, Assen (Archeologische Monografieën van het Drents Museum, 4).

Beuker, J.R., et al. 1992: De stenen bijlen en hamerbijlen van het Drents Museum: een onderzoek naar de gebruikte steensoorten, NDV 111-139.

Beuker, J.R. et al. 2001: Nogmaals de grafheuvel 'de Ketenberg' te Eext: over de dodenhouding in graven van de klokbekercultuur in Nederland, *Nieuwe Drentse Volksalmanak* 118, 109-118.

Beyries, S. (ed.) 1988: *Industries lithiques – Tracéologie et technologie*, Oxford (BAR International Series, 411).

Bienenfeld, P., 1988: Stone tool use and the organization of technology in the Dutch Neolithic, in: S. Beyries (eds.), 219-230.

Bierma, M. / O.H. Harsema / W. van Zeist (eds.) 1988: *Archeologie en landschap*, Groningen.

Bierma, M., et al. (eds.) 1988: *Terpen en wierden in het Fries-Groningse kustgebied*, Groningen.

Bilgi, Ö., 1984: Metal objects from Ikiztepe-Turkey, *Beiträge zur Allgemeinen und Vergleichenden Archäologie* 6, 31-83.

Bilgi, Ö., 1990: Metal objects from Ikiztepe-Turkey, *Beiträge zur Allgemeinen und Vergleichenden Archäologie* 9-10, 119-219.

Binford, L.R., 1965: Archaeological systematics and the study of culture process, *American Antiquity* 31, 203-210.

Binford, L.R., 1968: Post-Pleistocene adaptations, in: S.R. Binford / L.R. Binford (eds.), 313-341.

Binford, L.R., 1978a: *Nunamiut ethnoarchaeology*, New York.

Binford, L.R., 1978b: Dimensional analysis of behavior and site structure: learning from an Eskimo hunting stand, *American Antiquity* 43, 330-361.

Binford, L.R., 1980: Willow smoke and dogs' tails: hunter-gatherer settlement systems and archaeological site formation, *American Antiquity* 45, 4-20.

Binford, L.R., 1982: The archaeology of place, *Journal of Anthropological Archaeology* 1, 5-31.

Binford, S.R. / L.R. Binford (eds.) 1968: *New perspectives in archaeology*, Chicago.

Bintliff, J. (ed.) 1984: *European social evolution: archaeological perspectives*, Bradford.

Bintliff, J. / D.A. Davidson / E.C. Grant (eds.) 1988: *Conceptual issues in environmental archaeology*, Edinburgh.

Birdsell, J. B., 1973: A basic demographic unit, *Current Anthropology* 14, 337-356.

Blanchet, J.C. / B. Lambot 1977: Les dragages de l'Oise de 1973 à 1976. Première partie, *Cahiers Archéologiques de Picardie* 4, 61-88.

Bloch, M., 1971: *Placing the dead*, London.

Bloch, M., 1975a: Property and the end of affinity, in: M. Bloch (ed.), 203-228.

Bloch, M. (ed.) 1975b: *Marxist analysis and social anthropology*, London.

Bloemers, J.H.F., 1968: Flintdolche vom skandinavischen Typus in den Niederlanden, BROB 18, 47-110.

Bloemers, J.H.F., 1972: Drie Rössenscherven uit Nederlands-Limburg, *Helinium* 12, 47-52.

Bloemers, J.H.F., 1975: Archeologische kroniek van Limburg over de jaren 1973-1974, PSHAL 111, 7-51.

Bloemers, J.H.F., 1978: *Rijswijk (Z.H.), 'De Bult' – Eine siedlung der Cananefaten*, Groningen (Ph.D. thesis; = Nederlandse Oudheden, 8).

Bloemers, J.H.F., 1983: Heijen, in: W.J.H. Willems 1983b, 238-240.

Bloemers, J.H.F., 1986: A cart burial from a small Middle Iron Age cemetery in Nijmegen, in: M.A. van Bakel / R.R. Hagesteijn / P. van de Velde (eds.), 76-95.

Bloemers, J.H.F. (ed.) 1988: *Archeologie en oecologie van Holland tussen Rijn en Vlie*, Assen (Studies in Prae- en Protohistorie, 2).

Bloemers, J.H.F., 1990: *Weert-Boshoverheide, 'een voorhistorische doodenakker'*, Amersfoort (Archeologische Monumenten in Nederland, 13).

Bloemers, J.H.F., 1993: Een urnenveld in een stuifzandgebied. Het onderzoek op de Boshoverheide bij Weert, in: N. Roymans / F. Theuws (eds.), 12-21.

Bloemers, J.H.F. / T. van Dorp (eds.) 1991: *Pre- en protohistorie van de Lage Landen*, Heerlen.

Bloemers, J.H.F. / W. Groenman-van Waateringe / H.A. Heidinga (eds.) 1993: *Voeten in de aarde; een kennismaking met de moderne Nederlandse archeologie*, Amsterdam.

Bloemers, J.H.F. / R.S. Hulst 1983: Mitteleisenzeitliche Keramik von zwei Siedlungen zu Ressen und aus einem Töpferofen zu Bemmel, BROB 33, 107-151.

Bloemers, J.H.F. / L.P. Louwe Kooijmans / H. Sarfatij 1981: *Verleden Land; archeologische opgravingen in Nederland*, Amsterdam.

Boddeke, R., 1971: *Vissen en vissen*, Amsterdam.

Bodegraven, N. van, 1991: Nederzettingssporen uit de late bronstijd en de vroege ijzertijd op de Everse Akkers in St.-Oedenrode, in: H. Fokkens / N. Roymans (eds.), 129-139.

Boe, G. De, 1985: De opgravingscampagne 1984 te Neerharen-Rekem, *Archaeologia Belgica* I-2, 53-62.

Boeles, P.C.J.A., 1927: *Friesland tot de elfde eeuw*, 's-Gravenhage.

Boeles, P.C.J.A., 1951²: *Friesland tot de elfde eeuw*, 's-Gravenhage.

Boelicke, U., 1982: Gruben und Häuser: Untersuchungen zur Struktur bandkeramischer Hofplätze, in: *Siedlungen der Kultur mit Linearkeramik in Europa*, Nitra, 17-28.

Boelicke, U., 1988a: Die Gruben, in: U. Boelicke *et al.* (eds.), 300-394.

Boelicke, U., 1988b: Das Erdwerk, in: U. Boelicke *et al.* (eds.), 395-427.

Boelicke, U., 1988c: Sonstige Befunde, in: U. Boelicke *et al.* (eds.), 428-437.

Boelicke, U., *et al.* (eds.) 1977: Untersuchungen zur neolithischen Besiedlung der Aldenhovener Platte 7, *Bonner Jahrbücher* 177, 481-559.

Boelicke, U., *et al.* 1988a: Struktur und Entwicklung des Siedlungsplatzes, in: U. Boelicke *et al.* (eds.), 891-932.

Boelicke, U., *et al.* (eds.) 1988b: *Der bandkeramische Siedlungsplatz Langweiler 8, Gemeinde Aldenhoven, Kreis Düren*, Köln (Rheinische Ausgrabungen, 28).

Boer, P.L. de / A. van Gelder / S.-D. Nio (eds.) 1988: *Tide-influenced sedimentary environments and facies*, Dordrecht.

Boersma, J.W. (ed.) 1972²: *Terpen, mens en milieu*, Haren.

Boersma, J.W., 1976: Ringvormige aardewerken voorwerpen en haardkragen, *Westerheem* 25, 182-188.

Boersma, J.W., 1983: De opgraving Middelstum-Boerdamsterweg in een notedop, in: P.B. Kooi 1983b, 31-35.

Boersma, J.W., 1988a: De datering van een vuurstenen sikkel uit Middelstum-Boerdamsterweg, in: M. Bierma *et al.* (eds.), 31-35.

Boersma, J.W., 1988b: Een voorlopig overzicht van het archeologisch onderzoek van de wierde Heveskesklooster (Gr.), in: M. Bierma *et al.* (eds.), 61-87.

Boersma, J.W., 1991: Archeologisch onderzoek van terpen: verleden, heden, toekomst, *Jaarverslagen van de Vereniging voor Terpenonderzoek 75* (= 75 jaar Terpenonderzoek 1916-1991), 24-44.

Boersma, J.W., 1999: Back to the roots of Ezinge, in: H. Sarfatij / W.J.H. Verwers / P.J. Woltering (eds.), 87-96.

Bogaers, J.E., 1962-'63: Ruraemundensia, *BROB* 12-13, 57-86.

Bogaers, J.E., 1966: Opgravingen te Cuijk, 1964-1966, *Brabants Heem* 18, 122-136.

Bogaers, J.E., *et al.* (eds.) 1959: *Honderd eeuwen Nederland*, Den Haag.

Bogucki, P.I., 1984: Ceramic sieves of the Linear Pottery Culture and their economic implications, *Oxford Journal of Archaeology* 3, 15-31.

Bogucki, P.I., 1988: *Forest farmers and stockherders. Early agriculture and its consequences in Northcentral Europe*, Cambridge.

Bogucki, P.I. (eds.) 1993: *Case studies in European prehistory*, Boca Raton.

Bohmers, A., 1947: Jong-palaeolithicum en vroeg-mesolithicum, in: H.E. van Gelder *et al.* (eds.), 129-201.

Bohmers, A., 1951: *Die Höhlen von Mauern. Teil 1. Kulturgeschichte der Altzeinzeitlichen Besiedlung*, Groningen (= *Palaeohistoria* 1).

Bohmers, A., 1956: Statistics and graphs in the study of flint assemblages. II. A preliminary report on the statistical analysis of the Younger Palaeolithic in Northwestern Europe, *Palaeohistoria* 5, 8-25.

Bohmers, A. / P. Houtsma 1961: De praehistorie, in: J.P. Bakker / A. Bohmers / J.J. Spahr van der Hoek (eds.), 126-151.

Bohmers, A. / A.M. Wouters 1956: Statistics and graphs in the study of flint assemblages. III. A preliminary report on the statistical analysis of the Mesolithic in Northwestern Europe, *Palaeohistoria* 5, 27-38.

Bohmers, A. / A.M. Wouters 1962: Belangrijke vondsten van de Ahrensburg-cultuur in de gemeente Geldrop, *Brabants Heem* 14, 3-20.

Bohncke, S.J.P., 1991: *Paleohydrological changes in the Netherlands during the last 13.000 years*, Amsterdam (Ph.D. thesis VU).

Bohncke, S.J.P., *et al.* 1988: The Late-Glacial infill of three lake successions in The Netherlands: regional vegetational history in relation to NW European vegetational developments, *Boreas* 17, 385-402.

Bokelmann, K., 1971: Duvensee, ein Wohnplatz des Mesolithikums in Schleswig-Holstein, und die Duvenseegruppe, *Offa* 28, 5-26.

Bokelmann, K., 1979: Rentierjäger am Gletscherrand in Schleswig-Holstein? Ein Diskussionsbeitrag zur Erforschung der Hamburger Kultur, *Offa* 36, 12-22.

Bokelmann, K., 1986: Rast unter Bäumen. Ein ephemerer mesolithischer Lagerplatz aus dem Duvenseer Moor, *Offa* 43, 149-163.

Bokelmann, K., 1990: Eine mesolithische Kieferrindenmatte aus dem Duvenseer Moor, *Offa* 46, 17-22.

Bokelmann, K., 1991a: Duvensee, Wohnplatz 9. Ein präborealzeitlicher Lageplatz in Schleswig-Holstein, *Offa* 48, 75-114.

Bokelmann, K., 1991b: Some new thoughts on old data on humans and reindeer in the Ahrensburgian tunnel valley in Schleswig-Holstein, Germany, in: N. Barton / A.J. Roberts / D.A. Roe (eds.), 72-81.

Bokelmann, K. / F.-R. Averdieck / H. Willkomm 1981: Duvensee, Wohnplatz 8. Neue Aspekte zur Sammelwirtschaft im frühen Mesolithikum, *Offa* 38, 21-40.

Bokelmann, K. / F.-R. Averdieck / H. Willkomm 1985: Duvensee, Wohnplatz 13, *Offa* 42, 13-33.

Bolus, M., 1992: *Die Siedlungsbefunde des späteisenzeitlichen Fundplatzes Niederbieber (Stadt Neuwied)*, Bonn.

Bonifay, E. / B. Vandermeersch (eds.) 1991: *Les Premiers Européens*, Paris.

Bonsall, C., 1980: The coastal factor in the Mesolithic settlement of Northern-West England, in: B. Gramsch (eds.), 451-474.

Bonsall, C. (ed.) 1989: *The Mesolithic in Europe. Papers presented at the Third International Symposium Edinburgh 1985*, Edinburgh.

Bordaz, J., 1970: *Tools of the Old and New Stone Age*, Newton Abott.

Borman, R., 1980: *Oude beschavingen van de Lage Landen*, Amsterdam.

Bos, J.A.A. / C.R. Janssen 1996: Local impact of Palaeolithic man on the environment during the end of the last Glacial in the Netherlands, *Journal of Archaeological Science* 23, 731-739.

Bos, J.M., 1985: *Archeologische streekbeschrijving; een handleiding*, Vlaardingen (AWN-monografieën, 4).

Bosinski, G., 1978: Der Poggenwischstab, *Bonner Jahrbücher* 178, 83-92.

Bosinski, G., 1979: *Die Ausgrabungen in Gönnersdorf 1968-1976 und die Siedlungsbefunde der Grabung 1968*, Band 3, Wiesbaden.

Bosinski, G., 1981: *Gönnersdorf, Eiszeitjäger am Mittel-Rhein*, Koblenz.

Bosinski, G., 1982: *Die Kunst der Eiszeit in Deutschland und in der Schweiz*, Bonn.

Bosinski, G., 1987: Die grosse Zeit der Eiszeitjäger: Europa zwischen 40.000 und 10.000 v. Chr., *Jahrbuch des Römisch-Germanischen Zentralmuseums Mainz*, 34, 1-139.

Bosinski, G., 1992: *Eiszeitjäger im Neuwieder Becken. Archäologie des Eiszeitalters im Mittelrhein*, Koblenz (Archäologie am Mittelrhein und Mosel, 1).

Bosinski, G. / G. Fischer 1980: *Mammut- und Pferdedarstellungen von Gönnersdorf*, Der Magdalénien Fundplatz Gönnersdorf, Band 5, Wiesbaden.

Bosinski, G. / J. Hahn 1972: Der Magdalenien-Fundplatz Andernach (Martinsberg), *Rheinische Ausgrabungen* 11, 81-257.

Bosinski, G., *et al.* 1986: Altsteinzeitliche Siedlungsplätze auf den Osteifel-Vulkanen, *Jahrbuch des Römisch-Germanischen Zentralmuseums Mainz* 33, 97-130.

Bosman, A.V.A.J. / W. Bosman 1992: Velsen: Velserbroekpolder, in: P.J. Woltering, 323-326.

Bosman, A.V.A.J. / L.L. Therkorn 1993: Velsen: Velserbroekpolder B6, in: P.J. Woltering / J.-K.A. Hagers, 302-305.

Bosman, W.J., 1989: Velsen: Hofgeest, in: P.J. Woltering, 285-286.

Bosman, W.J., forthcoming: *Archeologisch Monumentenrapport Velsen*.

Bosman, W.J. / C. Soonius 1990: Bronstijdboeren met hun schaapjes op het droge in Velsen, *Westerheem* 39, 1-6.

Bosscha Erdbrink, D.P., 1982: Red deer keratic artefacts in Dutch collections, *BROB* 32, 103-137.

Bottema, S., 1975: The use of gastroliths in archaeology, in: A.T. Clason (ed.), 397-406.

Bottema, S., *et al.* 1980: An agricultural experiment in the unprotected salt marsh, part II, *Palaeohistoria* 22, 127-140.

Bourdieu, P., 1972: *Outline of a theory of practice*, Cambridge.

Bourgeois, J., 1984: Aperçu sur le second Age du Fer en Flandre orientale, in: A. Cahen-Delhaye *et al.* (eds.), 85-97.

Bourgeois, J., 1990: Nécropoles et 'sanctuaires' de La Tène en Flandre, in: G. Leman-Delerive (ed.), 117-119.

Bourgeois, J., 1991a: Nederzettingen uit de late bronstijd en vroege ijzertijd in westelijk België: Sint-Denijs-Westrem en Sint-Gillis-Waas, in: H. Fokkens / N. Roymans (eds.), 171-179.

Bourgeois, J., 1991b: Enclos et nécropole du second âge du fer à Kemzeke (Stekene, Flandre orientale). Rapport provisoire des fouilles 1988, in: Scholae archaeologicae, 12, Gent, 3-28.

Bourgeois, J., *et al.* (eds.) 1994: *Lunula, II*, Han-sur-Lesse.

Bourgeois, J., *et al.* (eds.) 2001: *Een duik in het verleden – Schelde, Maas en Rijn in de pre- en protohistorie*, Zottegem (Publicaties van het Provinciaal Archeologisch Museum van Zuid-Oost-Vlaanderen – site Velzeke, 4).

Braat, W.C., 1936: Een urnenveld te Knegsel (gem. Vessem), OMROL 17, 38-46.

Bradley, R., 1984: *The social foundations of prehistoric Britain*, London.

Bradley, R., 1990: *The passage of arms – An archaeological analysis of prehistoric hoards and votive deposits*, Cambridge.

Bradley, R. / M. Edmonds 1993: *Interpreting the axe trade. Production and exchange in Neolithic Britain*, Cambridge.

Braidwood, R.J. / G. Willey 1962a: Conclusions and afterthoughts, in: R.J. Braidwood / G. Willey (eds.), 330-359.

Braidwood, R.J. / G. Willey (eds.) 1962b: *Courses towards urban life*, Chicago.

Brandt, K., 1967: *Neolithische Siedlungsplätze im Stadtgebiet von Bochum*, Bonn (Quellenschrifte zur westdeutschen Vorgeschichte, 8).

Brandt, D. von, 1988: Die Häuser, in: U. Boelicke *et al.* (eds.), 36-289.

Brandt, K., 1984: Langwurten, ihre Topographie und ihre Funktion, in: H. Jankuhn / K. Schietzel / H. Reichstein (eds.), 100-113.

Brandt, K.-H., 1967: *Studien über steinerne Äxte und Beile der jüngeren Steinzeit und der Stein-Kupferzeit Nordwestdeutschlands*, Hildesheim (Münstersche Beiträge zur Vorgeschichte, 2).

Brandt, K.-H., 1971: Eine neue kulturell bestimmbare Hammeraxt, *Jahresschrifte für mitteldeutsche Vorgeschichte* 55, 65-78.

Brandt, R.W., 1988a: Aardewerk uit enkele Bronstijd-nederzettingen in West-Friesland, in: J.H.F. Bloemers (ed.), 206-267.

Brandt, R.W., 1988b: Nieuwe landschappen en kolonisatie: de rol van perceptie, in: M. Bierma / O.H. Harsema / W. van Zeist (eds.), 59-77.

Brandt, R.W. / A.L. van Gijn 1986: Bewoning en economie in het oer-IJ estuarium, in: R.W. Brandt / S.E. van der Leeuw / M.J.A.N. Kooijman (eds.), 61-75.

Brandt, R.W. / W. Groenman-van Waateringe / S.E. van der Leeuw (eds.) 1987: *Assendelver Polder papers 1*, Amsterdam (Cingula, 10).

Brandt, R.W. / G.J. van der Horst / J.J. Stolp (eds.) 1983: *De Zaanstreek archeologisch bekeken*, Zaanstad (= *Westerheem* 32, 51-176).

Brandt, R.W. / G.F. IJzereef 1980: West-Friesland in de Bronstijd – Leven en sterven 'binnen de grenzen van een model', in: M. Chamalaun / H.T. Waterbolk (eds.), 47-62.

Brandt, R.W. / S.E. van der Leeuw / M.J.A.N. Kooijman (eds.) 1986: *Gedacht over Assendelft*, Amsterdam (IPP Working Paper, 6).

Brandt, R.W. / S.E. van der Leeuw / L.H. van Wijngaarden-Bakker 1984: Transformations in a Dutch estuary: research in a wet landscape, *World Archaeology* 16, 1-17.

Brandt, R.W. / J. Slofstra (eds.) 1983: *Roman and Native in the Low Countries*, Oxford (BAR International Series, 184).

Braudel, F., 1966: *La Méditerranée et le monde méditerranéen à l'époque de Philippe II*, Paris.

Braudel, F., 1969: *Ecrits sur l'histoire*, Paris.

Breest, K., 1988: Ein Schuhleistenkeil von einem mittelsteinzeitlichen Fundplatz in der Gemarkung Schletau. Ldkr. Lüchow-Dannenburg, *Die Kunde* 39, 53-62.

Breuil, H., 1912: Les subdivisions du paléolithique supérieur et leur signification, *Comptes Rendus du 14e congrès international d'anthropologie et d'archéologie préhistorique*, Genève, 165-238.

Breunig, P., 1985: Bandkeramische Phasen und ^{14}C-Datierung – ein Vergleich, *Archäologisches Korrespondenzblatt* 15, 139-145.

Breunig, P., 1987: ^{14}C-Chronologie des vorderasiatischen, südost- und mitteleuropäischen Neolithikums, Köln.

Briard, J., 2001: Armorique, Grande-Bretagne et pays-Bas à l'Age du Bronze, in: W.H. Metz / B.L. van Beek / H. Steegstra (eds.), 125-143.

Brinch Petersen, E., 1973: A survey of the Late Palaeolithic and Mesolithic of Denmark, in: S.K. Kozlowski (ed.), 77-127.

Brinch Petersen, E., 1988: Ein mesolithisches Grab mit acht Personen von Strøby Egede, Seeland, *Archäologisches Korrespondenzblatt* 18, 121-125.

Brindley, A.L., 1983: The finds from hunebed G3 on the Glimmer Es, mun. of Haren, Prov. of Groningen, the Netherlands, *Helinium* 23, 209-236.

Brindley, A.L., 1986a: Typochronology of TRB West Group pottery, *Palaeohistoria* 28, 93-107.

Brindley, A.L., 1986b: Hunebed G2: excavation and finds, *Palaeohistoria* 28, 27-92.

Brindley, A.L. / J.N. Lanting 1991-'92: A re-assessment of the hunebedden O1, D30 and D40, *Palaeohistoria* 33/34, 97-140.

Brinkhuizen, D.C., 1979: Preliminary notes on fish remains from archaeological sites in the Netherlands, *Palaeohistoria* 25, 84-90.

Brinkhuizen, D.C., 1989: *Ichtyo-archaeologisch onderzoek: methoden en toepassing aan de hand van Romeins vismateriaal uit Velsen (Nederland)*, Groningen (Ph.D. thesis).

Brinkkemper, O., 1992: Het botanisch onderzoek, site 15.04, Foppenpolder en site 16.59, Aalkeetbuitenpolder, Leiden (internal report FdAL).

Brinkkemper, O., 1993: *Wetland farming in the area to the south of the Meuse estuary during the Iron Age and Roman period. An environmental and palaeo-economic reconstruction*, Leiden (Ph.D. thesis; = APL 24, 1991).

Brinkkemper, O., 1994: De botanische macroresten uit de profieldammen van vindplaats 11.17 in de Duifpolder (Midden-Delfland), Leiden (internal report FdAL).

Brinkkemper, O. / C. Vermeeren 1992: Het hout van een aantal nederzettingen uit de IJzertijd en de Romeinse Tijd op Voorne-Putten, in: A.B. Döbken (ed.), 103-117.

Broadbent, N., 1975-'77: Perforated stones, antlers and stone picks. Evidence for the use of the digging stick in Scandinavia and Finland, *Tor* 1975-1977, 63-106.

Broeke, P.W. van den, 1977: Bouwoffer en archeologie, Leiden (internal report FdAL).

Broeke, P.W. van den, 1979: Een depot met vuurstenen bijlen uit het Eenerveld bij Een, gem. Norg, *NDV* 96, 105-115.

Broeke, P.W. van den, 1980a: Bewoningssporen uit de IJzertijd en andere perioden op de Hooidonksche Akkers, gem. Son en Breugel, prov. Noord-Brabant, *APL* 13, 7-80.

Broeke, P.W. van den, 1980b: Een rijk gevulde kuil met nederzettingsmateriaal uit de IJzertijd, gevonden te Geleen, prov. Limburg, *APL* 13, 102-113.

Broeke, P.W. van den, 1982: Kustprodukten uit de IJzertijd en de Romeinse tijd in het Zuidnederlandse achterland, *Westerheem* 31, 242-249.

Broeke, P.W. van den, 1983: Neolithic bone and antler objects from the Hazendonk near Molenaarsgraaf (prov. South Holland), *OMROL* 64, 163-195.

Broeke, P.W. van den, 1984: Nederzettingsvondsten op De Pas, gem. Wijchen, prov. Gelderland, *APL* 17, 67-107.

Broeke, P.W. van den, 1985: Oud zout – Prehistorische winning en handel, *Natuur en Techniek* 53, 410-425 (= *Vondsten uit het verleden; oudheidkundig bodemonderzoek – Archeologisch Jaarboek 1986*, Maastricht, 66-81).

Broeke, P.W. van den, 1986: Zeezout: een schakel tussen West- en Zuid-Nederland in de IJzertijd en de Romeinse tijd, in: M.C. van Trierum / H.E. Henkes (eds.), 91-114.

Broeke, P.W. van den, 1987a: De dateringsmiddelen voor de ijzertijd van Zuid-Nederland, in: W.A.B. van der Sanden / P.W. van den Broeke (eds.), 23-43.

Broeke, P.W. van den, 1987b: Oss-Ussen: het handgemaakte aardewerk, in: W.A.B. van der Sanden / P.W. van den Broeke (eds.), 101-119.

Broeke, P.W. van den, 1987c: De Maas, een handelsweg van belang in de IJzertijd, *Het Oude Land van Loon* 42, 19-26.

Broeke, P.W. van den, 1990a: Midden-Delfland, in: W.A.M. Hessing, 338-339.

Broeke, P.W. van den, 1990b: De archeologische begeleiding van de reconstructie van Midden-Delfland, *Terra Nigra* 112, 3-17.

Broeke, P.W. van den, 1991: Nederzettingsaardewerk uit de late bronstijd in Zuid-Nederland, in: H. Fokkens / N. Roymans (eds.), 193-211.

Broeke, P.W. van den, 1993: A crowded peat area; observations in Vlaardingen-West and the Iron Age habitation of southern Midden-Delfland, *APL* 26, 59-82.

Broeke, P.W. van den, 1995: Iron Age sea salt trade in the Lower Rhine area, in: J.D. Hill / C. Cumberpatch (eds.), 149-162.

Broeke, P.W. van den, 1996a: Turfwinning en zoutwinning langs de Noordzeekust. Een verbond sinds de ijzertijd?, *Tijdschrift voor Waterstaatsgeschiedenis* 5, 48-59.

Broeke, P.W. van den, 1996b: Southern sea salt in the Low Countries; a reconnaissance into the land of the Morini, in: M. Lodewijckx (ed.), *Archaeological and historical aspects of West-European societies – Album amicorum André Van Doorselaer*, Leuven (Acta Archaeologica Lovaniensia, Monographiae, 8), 193-205.

Broeke, P.W. van den, 2000: Een tweede ijzertijd-grafveld in Lent, *Jaarverslag AWN-afdeling Nijmegen en omstreken*, 11-13.

Broeke, P.W. van den, 2001a: The inconspicuous continuation of bronze deposition in Dutch wet contexts after the Early Iron Age, in: W.H. Metz / B.L. van Beek / H. Steegstra (eds.): 161-168.

Broeke, P.W. van den, 2001b: Een gordel van macht en pracht – Het Midden-Nederlandse rivierengebied in het 1ste millennium v.Chr., in: J. Bourgeois *et al.* (eds.), 131-156.

Broeke, P.W. van den, 2002a: *Vindplaatsen in vogelvlucht – Beknopt overzicht van het archeologische onderzoek in de Waalsprong 1996-2001*, Nijmegen (Archeologische Berichten Nijmegen, Rapport 1).

Broeke, P.W. van den, 2002b: Een vurig afscheid? – Aanwijzingen voor verlatingsrituelen in ijzertijdnederzettingen, in: H. Fokkens / R. Jansen (eds.), 45-61.

Broeke, P.W. van den, forthcoming: *Het handgemaakte aardewerk uit de ijzertijd en de Romeinse tijd van Oss-Ussen – Studies naar typochronologie, technologie en herkomst*, Leiden (Ph.D. thesis).

Brongers, J.A., 1972: *Vaassen, een akkercomplex uit de IJzertijd*, Amersfoort (Archeologische Monumenten in Nederland, 3).

Brongers, J.A., 1972-'73: Berend Willem Cranssen, een Groninger amateur-archeoloog van grote klasse (1779-1860), *Groningse Volksalmanak*, 133-136.

Brongers, J.A., 1973a: *1833: Reuvens in Drenthe. Dagboek van een archeologische exploratie tocht door de provincie Drenthe*, Bussum.

Brongers, J.A., 1973b: Het Genootschap ter beoefening en opheldering der oudheden en geschiedenissen van Drenthe (1819-1822) in: W.A. van Es *et al.* (eds.), 459-468.

Brongers, J.A., 1974: An early nineteenth-century excavation in the Netherlands, *BROB* 24, 191-194.

Brongers, J.A., 1976a: *Air photography and Celtic field research in the Netherlands*, Groningen (Ph.D. thesis; = Nederlandse Oudheden, 6).

Brongers, J.A., 1976b: Material for a history of Dutch archaeology up to 1922, *BROB* 26 7-62.

Brongers, J.A., 1980: Vondsten uit grafheuvels als impuls tot de oprichting van museum Flehite in 1878, *Flehite* 12, 26-35.

Brongers, J.A., 2002: Een vroeg begin van de moderne archeologie. Leven en werken van Cas Reuvens (1793-1835), Amersfoort (NAR, 23).

Brongers, J.A. / P.J. Woltering 1978: *De prehistorie van Nederland; economisch-technologisch*, Bussum.

Brounen, F.T.S., 1985: HVR 183, vroeg-, midden- en laat-neolithische vondsten te Echt-Annendaal, *Archeologie in Limburg* 24, 66-71.

Brounen, F.T.S., 1988: Mergelland-Oost, een archeologische kartering, inventarisatie en waardering, Leiden (internal report FdAL).

Brounen, F.T.S., 1995a: Neolithic flint extraction at Valkenburg aan de Geul, *Archaeologia Polonia* 33, 444-453.

Brounen, F.T.S., 1995b: Verrassende vondsten uit Vogelzang, in: *Randwyck ondergronds, de resultaten van 10 jaar archeologisch bodemonderzoek*, Maastricht, 12-19.

Brounen, F.T.S. / J.P.M. de Jong 1988: Opmerkelijke vroegneolithische vondsten bij Gassel, *Westerheem* 37, 183-192.

Brounen, F.T.S. / H. Pisters / P. Ploegaert, 1993: In het hol van 'De Leeuw': een kalksteenwand met prehistorische vuursteenmijnen in Valkenburg aan de Geul, *Historische en Heemkundige Studies in en rond het Geuldal*, Jaarboek 1993, 7-35.

Brounen, F.T.S. / P. Ploegaert, 1992: A tale of the unexpected: Neolithic shaft mines at Valkenburg aan de Geul (Limburg, The Netherlands), APL 25, 189-223.

Brounen, F.T.S. / H. Vromen 1990: A find of La Hoguette pottery at Geleen (South Limburg, the Netherlands), Helinium 30, 36-43.

Brugmans, H., (ed.) 1935: Geschiedenis van Nederland, I, Amsterdam.

Bruin, D. de, et al. 1987: Ooievaar – De toekomst van het rivierengebied, Arnhem.

Brun, P., 1991: Le Bronze atlantique et ses subdivisions culturelles: essai de définition, in: C. Chevillot / A. Coffyn (eds.), 11-24.

Brunaux, L. (ed.) 1991: Les sanctuaires celtiques et leurs rapports avec le monde méditerranéen, Paris.

Brunn, W.A. von, 1980: Eine Deutung spätbronzezeitlicher Hortfunde zwischen Elbe und Weichsel, Berichte der Römisch-Germanischen Kommission 61, 91-150.

Brunnacker, K., 1978: Geowissenschaftliche Untersuchungen in Gönnersdorf, Der Magdalénien-Fundplatz Gönnersdorf, Band 4, Wiesbaden.

Brunsting, H., 1947: Het grafheuvelonderzoek, in: H.E. van Gelder et al. (eds.), 223-253.

Brunsting, H. / G.J. Verwers 1975: Het urnenveld bij Valkenswaard, prov. Noord-Brabant, APL 8, 53-77.

Büchner, M., 1986: Kieselgeoden im Wiehengebirge als Rohstoff steinzeitlicher Artefakte ('Wiehengebirgs-Lydit'), Berichten der Naturwissenschaftlichen Verein Bielefeld und Umgegend 28, 139-171.

Buchvaldek, M., 1967: Die Schnurkeramik in Böhmen, Praha (Acta Universitatis Carolinae Philosophica et Historica Monographia, 19).

Buchvaldek, M. / C. Strahm (eds.) 1992: Die kontinentaleuropäischen Gruppen der Kultur mit Schnurkeramik. Schnurkeramik-Symposium 1990, Praha (Praehistorica, 19).

Buchwald, V.F. / P. Leisner 1990: A metallurgical study of 12 prehistoric bronze objects from Denmark, Journal of Danish Archaeology 9, 64-102.

Bult, E.J., 1983: Midden-Delfland, een archeologische kartering; inventarisatie, waardering, bewoningsgeschiedenis, Amersfoort (NAR, 2).

Bult, E.J. / D.P. Hallewas (eds.) 1987: Graven bij Valkenburg II; het archeologisch onderzoek in 1986, Delft.

Bult, E.J. / D.P. Hallewas / P. van Rijn 1989: Het praetorium van Valkenburg, Natuur en Techniek 57, 194-205.

Bult, E.J. / D.P.Hallewas (eds.) 1990: Graven bij Valkenburg III; het archeologisch onderzoek in 1987 en 1988, Delft.

Bunnik, F. / A.J. Kalis / J. Meurers-Balke 1993: Mens en vegetatie in het Rijnland gedurende het Holoceen, Frankfurt am Main.

Burch jr., E.S., 1972: The caribou / wild reindeer as a human resource, American Antiquity 37, 339-368.

Burdukiewicz, J.M., 1986: The Late Pleistocene shouldered point assemblages in western Europe, Leiden.

Burdukiewicz, J.M., 1987: Zum Forschungsstand der Hamburger Kultur, Jahrbuch des Römisch-Germanischen Zentralmuseums Mainz 34, 143-167.

Burdukiewicz, J.M. / M. Kobusiewicz (eds.) 1987: Late Glacial in Europe: culture and environment, Wroclaw, 25-66.

Burkitt, M.C., 1932: A Maglemose harpoon dredged up recently from the North Sea, Man 32, 118.

Bursch, F.C., 1928: Microlithen, OMROL 9, 80-81.

Bursch, F.C., 1929: Een Germaansche nederzetting bij Kotten, OMROL, N.R. 10, 43-49.

Bursch, F.C., 1934: Heuvelonderzoekingen te Soesterberg, OMROL 15, 54-64.

Bursch, F.C., 1937: Grafheuvels te Oss, OMROL 18, 1-3.

Bush, M.B., 1988: Early Mesolithic disturbance: a force on the landscape, Journal of Archaeological Science 15, 453-462.

Butler, J.J., 1959: Vergeten schatvondsten uit de bronstijd, in: J.E. Bogaers et al. (eds.), 125-142.

Butler, J.J., 1961a: A looped spearhead converted to a pegged spearhead, from 's-Hertogenbosch (North Brabant), *Helinium* 1, 54-55.

Butler, J.J., 1961b: De Noordnederlandse fabrikanten van bijlen in de late bronstijd en hun produkten, *NDV* 79, 199-233.

Butler, J.J., 1963a: Bronze Age connections across the North Sea, *Palaeohistoria* 9.

Butler, J.J., 1963b: An Early Bronze Age spearhead from De Zilk (South Holland), *Helinium* 3, 241-245.

Butler, J.J., 1963c. Ook in de oudere bronstijd bronsbewerking in Noord-Nederland?, *NDV* 81, 181-212.

Butler, J.J., 1964: The bronze rapier from Zwaagdijk, gemeente Wervershoof, Prov. North-Holland, *BROB* 14, 37-43.

Butler, J.J., 1965: Ook eens iets voor dames, *NDV* 83, 163-198.

Butler, J.J., 1973: Einheimische Bronzebeilproduktion im Niederrhein-Maasgebiet, *Palaeohistoria* 15, 319-343.

Butler, J.J., 1979a: Rings and ribs: the copper types of the 'ingot hoards' of the Central European Early Bronze Age, in: M. Ryan (ed.), 345-362.

Butler, J.J., 1979b²: *Nederland in de Bronstijd*, Haarlem.

Butler, J.J., 1980: Metaalbewerking in de prehistorie, in: M. Chamalaun / H.T. Waterbolk (eds.), 113-130.

Butler, J.J., 1984-'85: De IJzertijd-halsring uit Onstwedder Barlage (Gr.), *Groningse Volksalmanak*, 146-159.

Butler, J.J., 1986: Drouwen: end of a 'Nordic' rainbow?, *Palaeohistoria* 28, 133-168.

Butler, J.J., 1987a: Bronze Age connections: France and the Netherlands, *Palaeohistoria* 29, 9-34.

Butler, J.J., 1987b: Drouwen: Het einde van de Noordse regenboog?, *NDV* 104, 103-150.

Butler, J.J., 1990: Bronze Age metal and amber in the Netherlands (I), *Palaeohistoria* 32, 47-110.

Butler, J.J., 1995-'96: Bronze Age metal and amber in the Netherlands (II:1), catalogue of flat axes, flanged axes and stopridge axes, *Palaeohistoria* 37/38, 159-243.

Butler, J.J. / J.A. Bakker 1961: A forgotten middle Bronze Age hoard with a Sicilian razor from Ommerschans (Overijssel), *Helinium* 1, 193-210.

Butler, J.J. / J.W.H. Hogestijn 1988: The Tollebeek spearhead, *Palaeohistoria* 30, 109-123.

Butler, J.J. / J.N. Lanting / J.D. van der Waals 1972: Annertol III: a four period Bell Beaker and Bronze Age barrow at Schuilingsoord, gem. Zuidlaren, Drente, *Helinium* 12, 225-241.

Butler, J.J. / H. Sarfatij 1970-'71: Another bronze ceremonial sword by the Plougrescant-Ommerschans smith, *BROB* 20-21, 301-309.

Butler, J.J. / H. Steegstra 1997-'98: Bronze Age metal and amber in the Netherlands (II:2): catalogue of the palstaves, *Palaeohistoria* 39/40, 163-275.

Butler, J.J. / H. Steegstra 1999-2000: Bronze Age metal and amber in the Netherlands (III:1), catalogue of the winged axes, *Palaeohistoria* 41/42, 127-148.

Butler, J.J. / H. Steegstra 2001-'02: Bronze Age metal and amber in the Netherlands (III:2): catalogue of the socketed axes, part A, *Palaeohistoria* 43/44, 263-319.

Butler, J.J. / J.D. van der Waals 1966: Bell Beakers and early metal-working in the Netherlands, *Palaeohistoria* 12, 44-139.

Buttler, W. / W. Haberey 1936: Die bandkeramische Ansiedlung bei Köln-Lindenthal, Leipzig (Römisch-Germanische Forschungen, 11).

Butzer, K.W., 1971: The significance of agricultural dispersal into Europe and northern Africa, in: S. Struever (ed.), 313-334.

Butzer, K.W., 1982: *Archaeology as human ecology. Method and theory for a contextual approach*, Cambridge.

Buurman, J., 1979: Cereals in circles. Crop processing activities in Bronze Age Bovenkarspel (the Netherlands), in: U. Körber-Grohne (ed.), 21-37.

Buurman, J., 1986: Graan in IJzertijd-silo's in Colmschate, in: R.M. van Heeringen (ed.), 67-73.

Buurman, J., 1988: Economy and environment in Bronze Age West-Friesland, Noord-Holland (from wetland to wetland), in: P. Murphy / C. French (eds.), 267-292.

Buurman, J., 1990: Verkoolde eikeltjes uit de IJzertijd, *Nieuwsblad Monumentenzorg en Archeologie* (Amersfoort) 22, 3-4.

Buurman, J. / J.P. Pals 1974: Some remarks on prehistoric flax in the Netherlands, BROB 24, 107-111.

Byvanck, A.W., 1941: *De voorgeschiedenis van Nederland*, Leiden.

Cahen, D. / J.P. Caspar / M. Otte 1986: *Industries lithiques danubiennes de Belgique*, Liège (ERAUL, 21).

Cahen, D. / J. Docquier, 1985: Présence du Groupe de Blicquy en Hesbaye Liégeoise, *Helinium* 25, 94-122.

Cahen, D. / P. Haesaerts (eds.) 1984: *Peuples chasseurs de la Belgique préhistorique dans leur cadre naturel*, Bruxelles.

Cahen, D. / L.H. Keeley / F.L. Van Noten 1979: Stone tools, toolkits and human behavior in prehistory, *Current Anthropology* 20, 661-683.

Cahen, D. / M. Otte (eds.) 1990: *Rubané et Cardial*, Liège (ERAUL, 39).

Cahen, D., *et al.* 1981-'82: Eléments non-Rubanés du néolithique ancien entre les vallées du Rhin inférieur et de la Seine, *Helinium* 21, 31-32.

Cahen, D., *et al.* 1985: Le village rubané de Darion (province de Liège, Belgique), *Bulletin de la Société Royale Belge d'Anthropologie et du Préhistoire* 96, 5-86.

Cahen, D., *et al.* 1990: Trois villages fortifiés du Rubané récent en Hesbaye Liégeoise, in: D. Cahen / M. Otte (eds.), 125-147.

Cahen-Delhaye, A., *et al.* (eds.) 1984: Les Celtes en Belgique et dans le nord de la France (*Revue du Nord*, numéro spécial).

Calder, N. (ed.) 1990: *Scientific Europe*, Maastricht.

Callow, P. / J.M. Cornford (eds.) 1986: *La Cotte de St.Brélade, Jersey. Excavations by C.B.M. McBurney 1961-1978*, Norwich.

Campbell, J.B., 1977: *The upper palaeolithic of Britain: a study of man and nature in the Ice Age*, Oxford.

Capitan, L. / D. Peyrony 1928: *La Madeleine; son gisement, son industrie, ses oeuvres d'art*, Paris.

Carasso, D.G. / M. Carasso-Kok (eds.) 1985: *Abcoude en Baambrugge 900 jaar*, Amsterdam.

Carbonell, E., *et al.* 1995: Lower Pleistocene hominids and artifacts from Atapuerca-Td6 (Spain), *Science* 269, 826-830.

Cartmill, M., 1990: Human uniqueness and theoretical content in palaeoanthropology, *International Journal of Primatology* 11, 173-192.

Case, H., 1984: The Beaker Culture in Britain and Ireland, in: J. Guilaine (ed.), 37-51.

Caspar, J.-P., 1984: Matériaux lithiques de la préhistoire, in: D. Cahen / P. Haesaerts (eds.), 107-114.

Caspar, J.P., *et al.* 1993: Nouveaux éléments dans le Groupe de Blicquy en Belgique: le site de Vaux-et-Borset 'Gibour' et 'à la croix de Marie-Jeanne', *Helinium* 33, 67-79.

Casparie, W.A., 1972: *Bog development in southeastern Drenthe (the Netherlands)*, Groningen (Ph.D. thesis).

Casparie, W.A., 1984: The three Bronze Age footpaths XVI(Bou), XVII(Bou) and XVIII(Bou) in the raised bog of Southeast Drenthe (the Netherlands), *Palaeohistoria* 26, 41-94.

Casparie, W.A., 1987: Bog trackways in the Netherlands, *Palaeohistoria* 29, 35-65.

Casparie, W.A., 1991: Bergumermeer-De Leijen: het ontstaan van een mesolithisch wetland, in: *21e Congres van Nederlandse Archeologen 'De Reuvensdagen'*, Assen, 14.

Casparie, W.A., 1992: Neolithic deforestation in the region of Emmen (the Netherlands), *Paläoklimaforschung* 8, 115-127.

Casparie, W.A. / W. Groenman-van Waateringe 1980: Palynological analyses of Dutch barrows, *Palaeohistoria* 22, 7-65.

Casparie, W.A., *et al.* 1977: The palaeobotany of Swifterbant, *Helinium* 17, 28-55.

Casparie, W.A., *et al.* 2004: De veenweg van Nieuw-Dordrecht – onvoltooid en niet gebruikt, NDV 121, 114-141.

Ceunynck, R. De / J. Termote 1987: Een zoutwinningssite uit de Midden-Laat-La Tène-periode te Veurne, *Westvlaamse Archaeologica* 3, 73-82.

Chamalaun, M. / H.T. Waterbolk (eds.) 1980, *Voltooid verleden tijd? Een hedendaagse kijk op de prehistorie*, Amsterdam.

Champion, T., e.a 1984: *Prehistoric Europe*, London.

Chapman, J., 1988: Putting pressures on population: social alternatives to Malthus and Boserup, in: J. Bintliff / D.A. Davidson / E.C. Grant (eds.), 291-310.

Chapman, R., 1981: The emergence of formal disposal areas and the problem of megalithic tombs in prehistoric Europe, in: R. Chapman / I. Kinnes / K. Randsborg (eds.), 71-81.

Chapman, R. / I. Kinnes / K. Randsborg (eds.) 1981: *The archaeology of death*, Cambridge.

Charbonnier, G., 1961: *Entretiens avec Claude Lévi-Strauss*, Paris.

Charles, J.A., 1984: The Middle Bronze Age iron punch of Southeast Drenthe, *Palaeohistoria* 26, 95-99.

Charles, R., 1993: Towards a new chronology for the Belgian Late Glacial: recent radiocarbon dates from the Oxford AMS-systeem, *Notae Praehistoricae* 12, 59-62.

Chase, P. / H.L. Dibble 1987: Middle palaeolithic symbolism: a review of current evidence and interpretations, *Journal of Anthropological Archaeology* 6, 263-296.

Chevillot, C. / A. Coffyn (eds.) 1991: *L'Age du Bronze Atlantique : ses faciès, de l'Ecosse à l'Andalousie et leurs relations avec le Bronze continental et la Méditerranée*, Beynac-et-Cazenac.

Childe, V.G., 1942: *What happened in history*, Baltimore.

Childe, V.G., 1957⁶: *The dawn of European civilization*, London.

Childe, V.G., 1959: *De prehistorie der Europese samenleving*, Utrecht.

Chmielewski, W., 1961: *Civilisation de Jerzmanowice*, Warsaw.

Chronologie..., 1986: *Chronologie – Archäologische Daten der Schweiz*, Basel (Antiqua, 15).

Clark, G.A. / M. Neeley, 1987: Social differentiation in European Mesolithic burial data, in: P. Rowley-Conwy / M. Zvelebil / P. Blankholm (eds.), 121-127.

Clark, J.D., 1991: Early copper-mining and smithing methods on the Zambezi / Congo watershed, in: H. Thoen *et al.* (eds.), 7-13.

Clark, J.G.D., 1936: *The mesolithic settlement of Northern Europe*, Cambridge.

Clark, J.G.D., 1954: *Excavations at Star Carr, an early mesolithic site at Seamer, near Scarborough, Yorkshire*, Cambridge.

Clark, J.G.D., 1975: *The earlier stone age settlement of Scandinavia*, Cambridge.

Clarke, D.L., 1976: Mesolithic Europe: the economic basis, in: G. de G. Sieveking / I.H. Longworth / K.E. Wilson (eds.), 449-481.

Clarke, D.L., 1968, 1978²: *Analytical archaeology*, London.

Clason, A.T. (ed.) 1975: *Archaeozoological studies*, Amsterdam. 6

Clason, A.T., 1967: *Animal and man in Holland's past*, Groningen (Ph.D. thesis; = Palaeohistoria 13).

Clason, A.T., 1977a: Bouqras, Gomolava en Molenaarsgraaf, drie stadia in de ontwikkeling van de veeteelt, *Museologia* 7, 69-82.

Clason, A.T., 1977b: *Jacht en veeteelt van prehistorie tot middeleeuwen*, Haarlem.

Clason, A.T., 1980: Jager, visser, veehouder, vogellijmer, in: M. Chamalaun / H.T. Waterbolk (eds.), 131-146.

Clason, A.T., 1985: Worked and unworked antlers and bone tools from Spoolde, de Gaste, the IJsselmeerpolders and adjacent areas, *Palaeohistoria* 25, 77-130.

Clason, A.T., 1990: Ewijk, an inland Vlaardingen settlement; Archaeozoology and the amateur archaeologist, in: J. Sedlemeier / H. Spycher (eds.), 63-75.

Clason, A.T / D.C. Brinkhuizen 1993: Bergschenhoek, in: A.T. Clason / S. Payne / H.P. Uerpmann (eds.), 61-73.

Clason, A.T. / S. Payne / H.P. Uerpmann (eds.) 1993: *Skeletons in her cupboard, Festschrift for Juliet Clutton-Brock*, Oxford (Oxbow Monograph, 34).

Cleveringa, J., 2000: *Reconstruction and modelling of Holocene coastal evolution of the western Netherlands*, Utrecht (Ph.D. thesis University of Utrecht).

Clevis, H. / J. de Jong (eds.) 1993: *Archeologie en bouwhistorie in Zwolle 1*, Zwolle.

Clevis, H. / J. de Jong (eds.) 1994: *Archeologie en bouwhistorie in Zwolle 2*, Zwolle.

Clevis, H. / J. de Jong (eds.), 1995: *Archeologie en Bouwhistorie in Zwolle 3*, Zwolle.

Clevis, H. / A.D. Verlinde, 1991: *Bronstijdboeren in Ittersumbroek. Opgraving van een Bronstijdnederzetting in Zwolle*, Kampen.

Coblenz, W. / F. Horst (eds.), 1978: *Mitteleuropäische Bronzezeit. Beiträge zur Archäologie und Geschichte*, Berlin.

Coles, B. (ed.) 1992: *The wetland revolution in prehistory*, Exeter.

Coles, J.M., 1987a: *Meare Village East – The excavations of A. Bulleid and H. St George Gray 1932-1956*, Exeter (Somerset Levels Papers, 13).

Coles, J.M., 1987b: Preservation of the past: the case for wet archaeology, in: J.M. Coles / A.J. Lawson (eds.), 1-21.

Coles, J.M., 1991: *From the waters of oblivion*, Assen (C.J.C. Reuvens-lezing, 2).

Coles, J.M. / A.J. Lawson (eds.) 1987: *European wetlands in prehistory*, Oxford.

Coles, J.M., *et al.* 1975-'89: *Somerset Levels Papers 1-15*, Hertford.

Collis, J., 1984: *The European Iron Age*, London.

Colpe, C., 1970: Theorethische Möglichkeiten zur Identifizierung von Heiligtümern und Interpretation von Opfern in ur- und parahistorischen Epochen, in: H. Jankuhn (ed.), 18-39.

Coninx, Y., 1984: Oker en zijn relatie tot de mens van de steentijd, *Archaeologische Berichten 15*, 131-144.

Conkey, M.W., 1985: Ritual communication, social elaboration and the variable trajectories of Palaeolithic material culture, in: T.D. Price / J.A. Brown (eds.), 299-323.

Constandse-Westerman, T.S. / C. Meiklejohn 1979: The human remains from Swifterbant (Swifterbant Contributions, 12), *Helinium 19*, 235-260.

Constandse-Westermann, T.S. / R.R. Newell, 1989: Social and biological aspects of the Western European Mesolithic population structure: A comparison with the demography of North American Indians, in: C. Bonsall (ed.), 106-115.

Constantin, C., 1985: *Fin du Rubané, céramique du Limbourg et post-Rubané – le néolithique le plus ancien en Bassin Parisien et en Hainaut*, Oxford (BAR International Series, 273).

Coope, G.R., 1977: Fossil coleopteran assemblages as sensitive indicators of climatic changes during the Devensian (Last) cold stage, *Philosophical Transactions of the Royal Society of London B280*, 313-337.

Corbey, R., 1989: *Wildheid en beschaving: de Europese verbeelding van Afrika*, Baarn.

Corbey, R. / W. Roebroeks (eds.) 2001: *Studying human origins, disciplinary history and epistemology*, Amsterdam.

Corbey, R. / B. Theunissen (eds.) 1995: *Ape, man, apeman: changing views since 1600*, Leiden.

Cordy, J.-M., 1980: Le paléokarst de Belle Roche (Sprimont, Liège): premier gisement paléontologique et archéologique du Pléistocène moyen en Belgique, *Comptes rendus Acad. Sc. Paris 291 (D)*, 749-752.

Cordy, J.-M., 1981: Découverte d'un gisement karstique du Paléolithique inférieur à la carrière de la Belle Roche, commune de Sprimont, *Activités 80 S.O.S. Fouilles 2*, 92-98.

Cordy, J.-M., 1991: Palaeoecology of the Late Glacial and early Postglacial of Belgium and neighbouring areas, in: N. Barton, A.J. Roberts / D.A. Roe (eds.), 40-47.

Cordy, J.-M. / M. Stassart 1984: La faune omalienne de la Place Saint-Lambert à Liège, in: M. Otte (ed.), 235-237.

Cordy, J.-M. / M. Ulrix-Closset 1981: La grotte de la Belle Roche à Sprimont. Un gisement à galets aménagés du Pléistocène moyen ancien, *Notae Praehistoricae 1*, 30.

Cox, M. / V. Straker / D. Taylor (eds.) 1995: *Wetlands, archaeology and nature conservation*, London.

Crabtree, D.E., 1972: *An introduction to the technology of flint tools*, Idaho.

Creemers, G. / P.M. Vermeersch 1986: Het jong-mesolithisch site van Meeuwen-In den Damp 1, *Notae Prehistoricae* 6, 107-112.

Creemers, G. / P.M. Vermeersch 1989: Meeuwen-Donderslagheide: A Middle Neolithic site on the Limburg Kempen Plateau (Belgium), *Helinium* 29, 206-226.

Crew, P. / S. Crew 1990: *Early mining in the British Isles: Proceedings of the Early Mining Workshop at Plas Tan y Bwlch 1989), Maentwrog (Plas Tan y Bwlch Occasional Paper, 1).

Criado Boado, F., 1989: We, the post-megalithic people, in: I. Hodder (ed.), 79-89.

Cuijpers, A.G.F.M., 1990: Analyse van de crematieresten van het grafveld te Deventer-'t Bramelt, Amersfoort (ROB internal report 1990/8).

Cunliffe, B.W., 1993: *Fertility, propitiation and the gods in the British Iron Age*, Amsterdam (15e Kroon-voordracht).

Cziesla, E., 1992: Betrachtungen zur Kulturgeschichte des 6. vorchristlichen Jahrtausends in Südwestdeutschland, *Bulletin de la Société Préhistorique Luxembourgeoise* 13, 15-35.

Cziesla, E., *et al.* (eds.) 1990: *The big puzzle. International symposium on refitting stone artefacts*, Bonn.

d'Acy, E., 1893: Marteaux casse-têtes et gaines de hache néolithiques en bois de cerf ornamentés, *l'Anthropologie* 4, 385-401.

Daniel, G., 1967: *The origin and growth of archaeology*, Harmondsworth.

Daniel, G. / P. Kjaerum (eds.) 1973: *Megalithic graves and ritual. Papers presented at the III Atlantic Colloquium, Moesgard 1969*, Moesgard.

Deckers, P.H., 1979: The flint material from Swifterbant, earlier neolithic of the Northern Netherlands, I. sites S-2, S-4 and S-51 (Final reports on Swifterbant, II), *Palaeohistoria* 21, 143-180.

Deckers, P.H., 1982: Preliminary notes on the Neolithic flint material from Swifterbant, *Helinium* 22, 33-39.

Deckers, P.H. / J.P. de Roever / J.D. van der Waals 1980: Jagers, vissers en boeren in een prehistorisch getijdengebied bij Swifterbant, *ZWO Jaarboek 1980*, 111-145.

Deeben, J., 1988: The Geldrop sites and the Federmesser occupation of the Southern Netherlands, in: M. Otte (ed.), 357-398.

Deeben, J., 1990: Geldrop, in: W.J.H. Verwers, 15-20.

Deeben, J., 1994: De laatpaleolithische en mesolithische sites bij Geldrop (N.Br.). Deel 1, *Archeologie* 5, 3-57.

Deeben, J. / J.A.A. Bos 1989: De overgang van het Laat-Paleolithicum naar het Mesolithicum in Zuid-Nederland, in: *Archon jaarverslag over 1988*, Den Haag, 45-55.

Dehn, W., 1950: Älterlatènezeitliche Marnekeramik im Rheingebiet, in: G. Behrens / J. Werner (eds.), 33-50.

Deichmüller, J., 1969: Die neolithische Moorsiedlung Hüde I am Dümmer, Kreis Grafschaft Diepholz, Vorläufiger Abschlussbericht, *Neue Ausgrabungen und Forschungen in Niedersachsen* 4, 28-36.

Dennell R. / W. Roebroeks 1996: The earliest colonization of Europe: the short chronology revisited, *Antiquity* 70, 535-542.

Desittere, M., 1968: *De urnenveldenkultuur in het gebied tussen Neder-Rijn en Noordzee (periodes Ha A en B)*, Brugge (Dissertationes Archaeologicae Gandenses, 11).

Desse, J., 1984: Les restes de poissons dans les fosses omaliennes, in: M. Otte (ed.), 239-240.

Dewez, M., 1987: *Le Paléolithique supérieur récent dans les grottes de Belgique*, Louvain-La-Neuve (Publications d'Histoire de l'Art et d'Archéologie de l'Université Catholique de Louvain, 57).

Dewez, M., *et al.* 1974: Nouvelles recherches à la grotte de Remouchamps, *Bulletin de la Société royale belge d'Anthropologie et de Préhistoire* 85, 5-161.

Dieck, A., 1975-'76: Gesichtsmasken aus menschlicher Oberschenkelhaut im vor- und frühgeschichtlichen Europa, *Die Kunde* 26/27, 77-86.

Diepeveen-Jansen, M., 1992: Martialiteit en drinkgelag in het Vroeg-La Tène Midden-Rijngebied, in: J. Bazelmans (ed.), 35-45.

Diepeveen-Jansen, M., 2001: *People, ideas and goods – New pespectives on 'Celtic barbarians' in Western and Central Europe (500-250 BC)*, Amsterdam 2001 (Amsterdam Archaeological Studies, 7).

Dijk, J. van, 1992: Melkboeren in Midden Delfland, Leiden (internal report FdAL).

Dijkman, W., 1989: *Een vindplaats uit de IJzertijd te Maastricht-Randwyck*, Amersfoort (NAR, 8).

Dijkman, W. / R. Hulst 2000: Het urnenveld van Maastricht-Vroendael, *Archeologie in Limburg* 84, 19-26.

Dillehay, T.D. / D.J. Meltzer (eds.) 1991: *The First Americans: Search and Research*, Boca Raton.

Dimbleby, G.W., 1985: *The palynology of archaeological sites*, London.

Dockum, S.G. van, forthcoming: A situla burial in Rhenen (prov. of Utrecht), BROB.

Döbken, A.B. (ed.) 1992: *BOORbalans 2: Bijdragen aan de bewoningsgeschiedenis van het Maasmondgebied*, Rotterdam.

Dohrn-Ihmig, M., 1973: Gruppen in der jüngeren nordwestlichen Linienbandkeramik, *Archäologisches Korrespondenzblatt* 3, 279-287.

Dohrn-Ihmig, M., 1974: Untersuchungen zur Bandkeramik im Rheinland, *Rheinische Ausgrabungen* 15, 51-142.

Dohrn-Ihmig, M., 1979: Bandkeramik an Mittel und Niederrhein, *Rheinische Ausgrabungen* 19 (Beiträge zur Urgeschichte des Rheinlandes, 3), 191-363.

Dohrn-Ihmig, M., 1983a: *Neolithische Siedlungen der Rössen Kultur in der Niederrheinischen Bucht*, München (Materialen zur allgemeinen und vergleichenden Archäologie, 21).

Dohrn-Ihmig, M., 1983b: Das bandkeramische Gräberfeld von Aldenhoven-Niedermerz, Kreis Düren, in: G. Bauchhenß (ed.), 47-190.

Doorselaer, A. Van, 1989: Un site fortifié de l'âge du Fer avec enclos cultuel à Kooigem, commune de Courtrai (Flandre Occidental), in: M. Ulrix-Closset / M. Otte (eds.), 357-359.

Doorselaer, A. Van, 1990: Le mont Kemmel, une fortification celtique, in: G. Leman-Delerive (ed.), 39-42.

Doorselaer, A. Van, et al. 1987: *De Kemmelberg, een Keltische bergvesting – Voorstelling van het aarden vaatwerk*, Kortrijk (Westvlaamse Archeologica Monografieën, 3).

Dorenbos, O., 1988: De continuïteit van de akkerbouw gedurende de Late IJzertijd en de Romeinse Tijd, bestudeerd aan de hand van botanische macroresten uit waterputten uit de nederzetting 'Westerveld' in Oss-Ussen, Leiden (internal report FdAL).

Drenth, E., 1990: Een onderzoek naar aspecten van de symbolische betekenis van Grand-Pressigny- en pseudo-Grand-Pressigny-dolken in graven van de enkelgrafcultuur in Nederland, in: A.T.L. Niklewicz-Hokse / C. Lagerwerf (eds.), 100-121.

Drenth, E., 1992: Flat graves and barrows of the Single Grave Culture in the Netherlands in social perspective: An interim report, in: M. Buchvaldek / C. Strahm (eds.), 207-214.

Drenth, E., 1994: Tradition and change in the interpretation of burial practices, *Archaeological Dialogues* 1, 119-121.

Drenth, E. / A.E. Lanting 1991: De chronologie van de enkelgrafcultuur in Nederland: Enkele voorlopige opmerkingen, *Paleo-aktueel* 2, 42-46.

Drenth, E. / W.A.M. Hessing / E. Knol (eds.) 1993: *Het tweede leven van onze doden*, Amersfoort (NAR, 15).

Driessens, J.E., 1982: Ongebruikelijke jong-paleolithische vondsten uit Noord-Limburg, wijzend op Aurignacien, Perigordien en Magdalenien en kanttekeningen daarbij, *Archaeologische Berichten* 11/12, 93-103.

Drijver-de Haas, J.S. / O. Smit (eds.) 1992: *Geologie rondom ijstijden*, Heerlen.

Dumont, J.V., 1988: *A microwear analysis of selected artefact types from the Mesolithic sites of Star Carr and Mount Sandel*, Oxford (BAR British Series, 187).

Dupont, Ed., 1872: *L'homme pendant les ages de la pierre dans les environs de Dinant-sur-Meuse*, Brussel.

Ebbesen, K., 1993: Sacrifices to the powers of nature, in: S. Hvass / B. Storgaard (eds.), 122-125.

Ebbing, J.H.J. / H.J.T. Weerts / W.E. Westerhoff 2003: Towards an integrated land-sea stratigraphy of the Netherlands, *Quaternary Science Reviews* 22, 1579-1587.

Eckert, J., 1972: Untersuchungen zur neolithischen Besiedlung der Aldenhovener Platte 2, *Bonner Jahrbücher* 172, 344-394.

Eckert, J., 1986: Ein mittel- und jungneolithischer Siedlungsplatz bei Nottuln, Kreis Coesfeld, *Ausgrabungen und Funde in Westfalen-Lippe* 4, 39-63.

Eckert, J. / U. Eisenhauer / A. Zimmermann (eds.), 2003: *Archäologische Perspektiven, Analysen und Interpretationen im Wandel, Festschrift für Jens Lüning zum 65. Geburtstag*, Rahden.

Edelman, C.H., *et al.* 1950: *Een bodemkartering van de Bommelerwaard boven den Meidijk*, Wageningen.

Edmonds, M. / C. Richards (eds.) 1998: *Understanding the Neolithic of North-western Europe*, Glasgow.

Eggers, H.J., 1959: *Einführung in die Vorgeschichte*, München (= *Inleiding tot de wetenschap der Prehistorie*, Utrecht 1961).

Eibner, C., 1982: Kupfererzbergbau in Österreichs Alpen, in: B. Hänsel (ed.), 399-408.

Eisma, D. / W.G. Mook / C. Laban 1981: An early Holocene tidal flat in the Southern Bight, in: S.-D. Nio *et al.* (eds.), 229-237.

Ellis, Chr.J. / N. Ferris (eds.) 1990: *The Archaeology of Southern Ontario to A.D. 1650*, London, Ontario.

Eluère, C., 1982: *Les ors préhistoriques*, Paris (L'âge du bronze en France, 2).

Elzinga, G., 1962: Prehistorische werktuigen van edelhert- en elandgewei uit Drenthe, *NDV* 80, 185-219.

Enckevort, H. van, 2001: Bemerkungen zum Besiedlungssystem in den südöstlichen Niederlanden während der späten vorrömischen Eisenzeit und der römischen Kaiserzeit, in: Grünewald Th. (eds.), 336-396.

Engelen, F.H.G. (ed.), 1981: *3e Internationale Symposium over vuursteen – 3rd International Symposium on flint. Maastricht 1979*, Heerlen (Staringia, 6).

Ente, P.J., 1976: The geology of the northern part of Flevoland in relation to the human occupation in Late Atlantic time, *Helinium* 16, 15-35.

Es, W.A. van, 1965-'66: Friesland in Roman times, *BROB* 15-16, 37-68. (= Friezen en Romeinen, in: J.J. Kalma / J.J. Spahr van der Hoek / K. de Vries (eds.), 48-94.)

Es, W.A. van, 1968: Paddepoel, excavations of frustrated terps, 200 B.C.-250 A.D., *Palaeohistoria* 14, 187-352.

Es, W.A. van, 1972: The origins and development of the State Service for Archaeological Investigations in the Netherlands, *BROB* 22, 17-71.

Es, W.A. van, 1981³: *De Romeinen in Nederland*, Haarlem.

Es, W.A. van, 1982: Ländliche Siedlungen der Kaiserzeit in den Niederlanden, *Offa* 39, 139-154.

Es, W.A. van, n.d.: *Terpen*, Kampen (serie Dichterbij).

Es, W.A. van / W.A. Casparie, 1968: Mesolithic wooden statuette from the Volkerak, near Willemstad, North Brabant, *BROB* 18, 111-116.

Es, W.A. van / W.A.M. Hessing (eds.) 1994, *Romeinen, Friezen en Franken in het hart van Nederland: van Traiectum tot Dorestad 50 v.Chr. – 950 n.Chr.*, Utrecht/Amersfoort.

Es, W.A. van / H. Sarfatij / P.J. Woltering (eds.) 1988: *Archeologie in Nederland – De rijkdom van het bodemarchief*, Amsterdam.

Es, W.A. van / W.J.H. Verwers 1973: Het beenderdelven te Wijk bij Duurstede in de winter van 1841/42, in: W.A. van Es *et al.* (eds.), Bussum, 477-494.

Es, W.A. van, *et al.* (eds.) 1973: *Archeologie en historie. Opgedragen aan H. Brunsting bij zijn zeventigste verjaardag*, Bussum.

Essink, M. / J. Hielkema 1997-'98: Rituele depositie van bronzen voorwerpen in Noord-Nederland, *Palaeohistoria* 39/40: 277-321.

Eynde, G. van den / R. Berkvens 2001: Bronstijd- en ijzertijdbewoning op Moskes te Breda, prov. Noord-Brabant (Nl.): opgravingscampagnes 1997-2000, *Lunula* 9, 32-35.

Fabech, C., 1991: Booty sacrifices in Southern Scandinavia: a reassesment, in: P. Garwood *et al.* (eds.), 88-99.

Fabech, C. / J. Ringtved (eds.) 1999: *Settlement and Landscape. Proceedings of a conference in Århus, Denmark, May 4-7 1998*, Højbjerg.

Faegre, T., 1979: *Tents. Architecture of the nomads*, London.

Fagnart, J.P., 1988: *Les industries lithiques du Paléolithique Supérieur dans le nord de la France*, Amiens.

Farizy, C. D. / J. Jaubert 1994: *Hommes et bisons du Paléolithique Moyen à Mauran (Haute-Garonne)*, Paris.

Féblots-Augustins, J., 1993: Mobility strategies in the Late Middle Palaeolithic of Central Europe and Western Europe: elements of stability and variability, *Journal of Anthropological Archaeology* 12, 211-265.

Felder, P.J., 1980: Feuersteinbergbau in Rijckholt-St. Geertruid (NL1) und Grime's Graves (GB13) – ein Vergleich, in: Weisgerber *et al.* (eds.), 120-124.

Felder, P.J., 1998: Overzicht van de prehistorische vuursteenexploitaties binnen het Krijtgebied tussen Aken-Heerlen-Luik-Maastricht en Tongeren, in: P.C.M. Rademakers (ed.), 169-192.

Felder, P.J. / P.C.M. Rademakers / M.E.Th. de Grooth (eds.), 1998: *Excavations of Prehistoric Flint Mines at Rijckholt-St. Geertruid (Limburg, The Netherlands)*, Bonn (Achäologische Berichte, 12).

Feldman, J., *et al.* 1990: *Tribal treasures, cosmic reflections in stone, wood and gold*, Delft.

Feldtkeller, A. / H. Schlichtherle 1987: Jungsteinzeitliche Kleidungsstücke aus Ufersiedlungen des Bodensees, *Archäologische Nachrichten aus Baden* 38/39, 74-83.

Ferdière, A. (ed.) 1993: *Monde des morts, monde des vivants en Gaule rurale*, Tours (Revue Archéologique du Centre de la France, supplement 6).

Feustel, R., 1974: *Die Kniegrotte, Eine Magdalénien-Station in Thüringen*, Weimar.

Fiedler, L., 1979: Formen und Techniken neolithischer Steingeräte aus dem Rheinland, *Rheinische Ausgrabungen* 19, 53-190.

Finke, W., 1989: *Neujahrsgruss Westfälisches Museum für Archäologie, Amt für Bodendenkmalpflege Münster*, 20.

Finke, W., 1990: *Neujahrsgruss Westfälisches Museum für Archäologie, Amt für Bodendenkmalpflege Münster*, 39-42.

Fischer, A., 1987: Stenalderbopladsen på Argusgrunden, *Antikvarisk Studier* 8, 11-58.

Fischer, A., 1991: Pioneers in deglaciated landscapes: the expansion and adaptation of late palaeolithic societies in Southern Scandinavia, in: N. Barton / A.J. Roberts / D.A. Roe (eds.), 100-121.

Fischer, A., (ed.) 1995: *Man and sea in the Mesolithic: coastal settlement above and below present sealevel*, Oxford (Oxbow Monograph, 53).

Fischer, A. / H. Tauber 1986: New ^{14}C-datings of late palaeolithic cultures from Northwestern Europe, *Journal of Danish Archaeology* 5, 7-14.

Flamman, J., 1993: De reconstructie van een IJzertijd-oven uit MD 15.04. Experimenten in bouw en gebruik, Leiden (internal report FdAL).

Floss, H., 1987: Silex-Rohstoffe als Belege für Fernverbindungen im Paläolithikum des nordwestlichen Mitteleuropa, *Archäologische Informationen* 10, 151-161.

Floss, H., 1990: *Rohmaterialversorgung im Paläolithikum des Mittelrheingebietes*, Köln.

Fokkens, H., 1982: Late neolithic occupation near Bornwird (province of Friesland), *Palaeohistoria* 24, 91-113.

Fokkens, H., 1986: From shifting cultivation to short fallow cultivation: Late Neolithic change in the Netherlands reconsidered, in: H. Fokkens / P.M. Banga / M. Bierma (eds.), 5-21.

Fokkens, H., 1991a: *Verdrinkend landschap; archeologisch onderzoek van het westelijk Fries-Drents Plateau 4400 BC tot 500 AD*, Groningen (Ph.D. thesis).

Fokkens, H., 1991b: Nederzettingssporen uit de bronstijd en de vroege ijzertijd in Oss-Ussen, wijk Mikkeldonk, in: H. Fokkens / N. Roymans (eds.), 93-109.

Fokkens, H., 1993: *Oss, verleden aan het licht. De voorgeschiedenis van Oss, 2500 vóór tot 250 na Christus*, Oss.

Fokkens, H., 1994: Palencirkels in Ittersumerbroek: hutten, schaapskooien, zonnekalenders of gewoon fantasie?, *Spiegel Historiael* 29, 176-178.

Fokkens, H., 1996: The Maaskant project. Continuity and change of a regional research project, *Archaeological Dialogues* 3, 196-215.

Fokkens, H., 1997: From barrows to urnfields: economic crisis or ideological change? *Antiquity* 71, 360-373.

Fokkens, H., 1998a: *Drowned landscape – The occupation of the western part of the Frisian-Drentian plateau, 4400 BC – AD 500*, Assen/Amersfoort.

Fokkens, H., 1998b: From the collective to the individual: some thoughts about culture change in the third millennium BC, in: M. Edmonds / C. Richards (eds.), 481-491.

Fokkens, H. (ed.) 1998c: *The Ussen project – The first decade of excavations at Oss*, Leiden (= APL 30).

Fokkens, H., 1999: Cattle and martiality: changing relations between man and the landscape in the Late Neolithic and the Bronze Age, in: C. Fabech / J. Ringtved (eds.), 35-43.

Fokkens, H., 2001: The periodisation of the Dutch Bronze Age: a critical review, in: W.H. Metz / B.L. van Beek / H. Steegstra (eds.), 241-262.

Fokkens, H., 2002: Vee en voorouders: centrale elementen uit het dagelijks leven in de bronstijd, in: H. Fokkens / R. Jansen (eds.), 125-148.

Fokkens, H. / P. Banga / M. Bierma (eds.) 1986: *Op zoek naar mens en materiële cultuur*, Groningen.

Fokkens, H. / A.L. van Gijn, forthcoming: *A Late Neolithic and Middle Bronze Age encampment near Oldeboorn, prov. Friesland.*

Fokkens, H. / R. Jansen (eds.) 2002: *2000 Jaar bewoningsdynamiek. Brons- en ijzertijdbewoning in het Maas-Demer-Scheldegebied*, Leiden.

Fokkens, H. / N. Roymans (eds.) 1991: *Nederzettingen uit de bronstijd en de vroege ijzertijd in de Lage Landen*, Amersfoort (NAR, 13).

Fokkens, H. / C. Schinkel 1990: Neolithische slijpstenen uit de provincie Friesland, *De Vrije Fries* 70, 39-52.

Fokkens, H. / L. Smits 1989: Een grafveldje uit de Late Bronstijd bij Groot-Linden (gem. Beers), *Westerheem* 38, 11-15.

Fontijn, D.R., 1996a: De bewoning krijgt vorm – Nederzettingssporen uit de Bronstijd en de IJzertijd op de Leestense enk, in: M. Groothedde, 37-48.

Fontijn, D.R., 1996b: Het eerste Eme? Bewoning in de Late IJzertijd en Romeinse tijd in de Ooijerhoek; in: M. Groothedde, 49-56.

Fontijn, D.R., 1996c: Socializing landscape. Second thoughts about the cultural biography of urnfields, *Archaeological Dialogues* 3, 77-87.

Fontijn, D.R., 2001: Rethinking ceremonial dirks of the Plougrescant-Ommerschans type. Some thoughts on the structure of the of metalwork exchange, in: W.H. Metz / B.L. van Beek / H. Steegstra (eds.), 263-280.

Fontijn, D.R., 2002: Het ontstaan van rechthoekige 'cultusplaatsen', in: H. Fokkens / R. Jansen (eds.), 149-172.

Fontijn, D.R., 2003: *Sacrificial landscapes. Cultural biographies of persons, objects and 'natural' places in the Bronze Age of the southern Netherlands, c. 2300-600 BC*, Leiden (Ph.D. thesis; = APL 33/34 [2001-'02]).

Fontijn, D.R. / A.G.F.M. Cuijpers 1998-'99: Prehistoric stone circles, stone platforms and a ritual enclosure from Nijmegen, *BROB* 43, 33-67.

Fontijn, D.R. / H. Fokkens / R. Jansen 2002: De gietmal van Oss-Horzak en de inheemse bronsproductie in de Midden-Bronstijd. Enkele voorlopige resultaten, in: H. Fokkens / R. Jansen (eds.), 63-72.

Formsma, W.J., et al. (eds.) 1976: *Historie van Groningen, Stad en Land*, Groningen.

Forsberg, L.L., 1985: *Site variability and settlement patterns. An analysis of the hunter-gatherer settlement system in the Lule River Valley, 1500 B.C.-B.C./A.D.*, Umeå (Archaeology and Environment, 5).

Först, E., 1991: *Zur Besiedlungsgeschichte der Flussmarsch im Kreis Wesermarsch*, Hildesheim (Veröffentlichungen der urgeschichtlichen Sammlungen des Landesmuseums zu Hannover, 37).

Frangipane, M., 1985: Early developments of metallurgy in the Near East, in: *Studi di paletnologia in onore di Salvatore M. Puglisi*, Rome, 215-228.

Franken, H.J. / J. Kalsbeek 1984: Iron Age pottery from Haren, *Newsletter Department of Pottery Technology Leiden* 2, 17-26.

Franssen, C.J.H. / A.M. Wouters 1978: Beknopt voorlopig verslag over het Oud-Palaeolithicum in Nederland. I. Gelderse en Utrechtse stuwwallen, *Archaeologische Berichten* 4, 4-38.

Frenzel, B., *et al.* (eds.) 1992: *Evaluation of land surfaces cleared from forests by prehistoric man in Early Neolithic times and the time of migrating Germanic tribes*, Stuttgart.

Fuhlrott, C., 1859: Menschliche Überreste aus einer Felsengrotte des Düsselthals, *Verhandlungen des naturhistorischen Vereins des preußischen Rheinlande und Westphalens* 16, 134.

Gallay, A., 1976: The Bell-Beaker civilisation of Petit-Chasseur, in: J.N. Lanting / J.D. van der Waals (eds.), 279-306.

Gamble, C.S., 1983: Culture and society in the Upper Palaeolithic of Europe, in: G.N. Bailey (ed.), 201-211.

Gamble, C.S., 1986: *The Palaeolithic settlement of Europe*, Cambridge.

Gamble, C.S., 1987: Man the Shoveller: alternative models for Middle Pleistocene colonization and occupation in northern latitudes, in: O. Soffer (ed.), 81-98.

Gamble, C.S., 1993a: *Timewalkers. The prehistory of global colonization*, Gloucesthire.

Gamble, C.S., 1993b: Exchange, foraging and local hominid networks, in: C. Scarre / F. Healy (eds.), 35-44.

Gamble, C.S., 1994: Time for Boxgrove man, *Nature* 369, 275-276.

Gamble, C.S., 1995: The earliest occupation of Europe: the environmental background, in: W. Roebroeks / T. van Kolfschoten (eds.), 279-295.

Gardiner, J. (ed.) 1993: *Flatlands and wetlands: current themes in East Anglian archaeology*, Norwich (East Anglian Archaeology Report, 50).

Garthoff-Zwaan, P., 1987: An ethnohistorical perspective in archaeology, in: R.W. Brandt / W. Groenman-van Waateringe / S.E. van der Leeuw (eds.), 333-338.

Garwood, P., *et al.* (eds.) 1991: *Sacred and profane – Proceedings of a conference on archaeology, ritual and religion. Oxford, 1989*, Oxford (Oxford University Committee for Archaeology Monograph, 32).

Gaudzinski, S., 1995: Wallertheim revisited: a re-analysis of the fauna from the middle-paleolithic site of Wallertheim (Rheinhessen, Germany), *Journal of Archaeological Science* 22, 51-66.

Gebers, W., 1984: *Das Endneolithikum im Mittelrheingebiet. Typologische und chronologische Studien*, Bonn (Saarbrücker Beiträge zur Altertumskunde, 27).

Geel, B. van / J. Buurman / H.T. Waterbolk 1997: Abrupte veranderingen in delta ¹⁴C rond 2700 BP in paleo-klimatologisch en archeologisch perspectief, in: Hallewas / G.H. Scheepstra / P.J. Woltering (eds.), 153-173.

Geel, B. van / E. Kolstrup 1978: Tentative explanation of the Late Glacial and early Holocene climatic changes in North-Western Europe, *Geologie en Mijnbouw* 57, 87-89.

Geel, E A. van, 1980: Sweikhuizen, *Archeologie in Limburg* 9, 14.

Gehasse, E.F., 1992: The response of man to environmental changes at P14 (Noordoostpolder, the Netherlands) during the Neolithic and Early Bronze Age, *Archaeozoologica* 5, 63-78.

Gehasse, E.F., 1995: *Ecologisch-archeologisch onderzoek van het Neolithicum en de Vroege Bronstijd in de Noordoostpolder met de nadruk op vindplaats P14*, Amsterdam (Ph.D. thesis UvA).

Gehasse, E., 2001: Aartswoud: an environmental approach of a Late Neolithic site, in: R.M. van Heeringen / E.M. Theunissen (eds.), 161-201.

Gehlen, B. / M. Heinen / A. Tillmann (eds.) 2001: Zeit-Räume, Gedenkschrift für Wolfgang Taute, Bonn.

Gelder, H.E. van, *et al.* (eds.) 1947: *Een kwart eeuw oudheidkundig bodemonderzoek in Nederland*, Meppel.

Gelder-Ottway, S.M. van, 1988: Animal bones from a pre-Roman Iron Age coastal marsh site near Middelstum (province of Groningen, the Netherlands), *Palaeohistoria* 30, 125-144.

Gelissen, E., 1992: Geleen-Krawinkel; een botanische kijk op een vindplaats uit de vroege ijzertijd, Leiden (internal report FdAL).

Gelling, P. / H.R. Ellis Davidson 1969: *The chariot of the sun and other rites and symbols of the northern Bronze Age*, London.

Gendel, P.A., 1982: The distribution and utilization of Wommersom quartzite during the Mesolithic, in: A. Gob / F. Spier (eds.), 21-50.

Gendel, P.A., 1984: *Mesolithic social territories in Northwestern Europe*, Oxford (BAR International Series, 218).

Gendel, P.A., 1987: Socio-stylistic analysis of lithic artefacts from the Mesolithic of Northwestern Europe, in: P. Rowley-Conwy / M. Zvelebil / H.P. Blankholm (eds.), 65-73.

Gendel, P.A., 1989: The analysis of lithic styles through distributional profiles of variation: examples from the Western European Mesolithic, in: C. Bonsall (ed.), 40-47.

Gendel, P.A. / H. Van de Heyning / G. Gijselings 1985: Helchteren-Sonnisse Heide 2: a mesolithic site in the Limburg Kempen (Belgium), *Helinium* 25, 2-22.

Geneste, J.M., 1985: *Analyse lithique d'industries moustériennes du Périgord: une approche technologique du comportement des groupes humaines au Paléolithique moyen*, Bordeaux (Ph.D. thesis).

Geneste, J.M., et al. 1989: *Les hauts lieux de la préhistoire en France*, Paris.

Gensen, R., 1965: Manching III. Die Ausgrabungen des Osttores in den Jahren 1962 bis 1963, *Germania* 43, 49-62.

Gerrets, D.A. / E.E.B. Bulten / J.M. Pasveer 1988: *De Laat-Neolithische vindplaats 'Zeewijk'*, Groningen (Internal report dept. Physical Geography and Soil Science, 25).

Gerritsen, F.A., 1999: The cultural biography of Iron Age houses and the long-term transformation of settlement patterns in the southern Netherlands, in: C. Fabech / J. Ringtved (eds.), 139-148.

Gerritsen, F.A., 2001: *Local identities – Landscape and community in the late prehistoric Meuse-Demer-Scheldt region*, Amsterdam (Ph.D. thesis VU).

Gerritsen, H. / C.W.J. Berentsen 1998: A modelling study of tidally indiced equilibrium sand balances in the North Sea during the Holocene, *Continental Shelf Research* 18, 151-200.

Geurts, P.A.M., et al. (eds.) 1986: *Horster Historiën – Fragmenten uit dertig eeuwen*, Horst.

Gibert, J. / P. Palmquist / B. Martinez-Navarro 1994: Los primeros europeo, *Investigacion y Ciencia* Diciembra, 28-29.

Giffen, A.E. van, 1910: Het dalingsvraagstuk der Alluviale Noordzeekusten in verband met de terpen, *Tijdschrift voor geschiedenis, land- en volkenkunde* 25, 258-294.

Giffen, A.E. van, 1913: *Die Fauna der Wurten*, Leiden (Ph.D. thesis Groningen).

Giffen, A.E. van, 1925-'27: *De hunebedden in Nederland*, Utrecht.

Giffen, A.E. van, 1930: *Die Bauart der Einzelgräber. Beitrag zur Kenntnis der älteren individuellen Grabhügelstrukturen in den Niederlanden*, Leipzig.

Giffen, A.E. van, 1937a: Twee grafvelden uit den hunebedden- en bekertijd in het Kruidhaarsveld bij Sleen, gem. Sleen, *NDV* 55, 8-11.

Giffen, A.E. van, 1937b: Tumuli-opgravingen in Gelderland 1935/1936, *Gelre* 40, 3-18.

Giffen, A.E. van, 1937c: *Opgravingen in de provincie Noord-Brabant 1935, Bouwsteenen van de Brabantsche Oergeschiedenis*, 's-Hertogenbosch.

Giffen, A.E. van, 1938a: Continental bell or disc barrows in Holland with special reference to tumulus I at Rielsch Hoefke, *PPS* 4, 258-71.

Giffen, A.E. van, 1938b: Een kringgreppelurnenveld te Meppen, gem. Zweelo, *NDV* 56, 101-103.

Giffen, A.E. van, 1939: De zgn. heidensche legerplaats te Zuidveld bij Sellingen, gem. Vlachtwedde, *Verslag Museum van Oudheden Groningen*, 86-93.

Giffen, A.E. van, 1943a: Opgravingen in Drente, in: J. Poortman (ed.), 392-564.

Giffen, A.E. van, 1943b: Oudheidkundige aanteekeningen over Drentsche vondsten (X): Een urnenveld te Drouwen, *NDV* 61, 93-139.

Giffen, A.E. van, 1945: Oudheidkundige aanteekeningen over Drentsche vondsten XII, *NDV* 63, 69-121.

Giffen, A.E. van, 1947: *Oudheidkundige perspectieven, in het bijzonder ten aanzien van de Vaderlandsche Prae- en Protohistorie*, Amsterdam (inaugural speech).

Giffen, A.E. van, 1948: Een rendierjagersstation tussen Eext en Gasselte, Gemeente Gasselte, NDV 66, 85-104.

Giffen, A.E. van, 1949: Oudheidkundige aanteekeningen over Drentsche vondsten XVI, NDV 67, 93-148.

Giffen, A.E. van, 1953: Onderzoek van drie Bronstijd-grafheuvels bij Grootebroek, gem. Grootebroek, Noord-Holland, *West-Frieslands Oud en Nieuw* 20, 1-32.

Giffen, A.E. van, 1961: Een gereconstrueerd hunebed, NDV 79, 189-198.

Giffen, A.E. van, 1962: Grafheuvels uit de midden-bronstijd met nederzettingssporen van de Klokbekercultuur bij Oostwoud, *West-Frieslands Oud en Nieuw* 29, 199-209.

Giffen, A.E. van, 1963: Het bouwoffer uit de oudste hoeve te Ezinge (Gr.), *Helinium* 3, 246-253.

Giffen, A.E. van, 1973: Nogmaals Ezinge, in: W.A. van Es *et al.* (eds.), 49-86.

Giffen, A.E. van / M. Addink-Samplonius / W. Glasbergen 1971: Een grafheuvel te Putten, *Helinium* 11, 105-123.

Giffen, A.E. van, *et al.* 1951: Oudheidkundige aantekeningen over Drentse vondsten (XVIII), NDV 69, 97-157.

Gijn, A.L. van, 1986: Fish polish, fact and fiction, *Early Man News* 9/10/11, 13-27.

Gijn, A.L. van, 1987: Site N; Assendelver Polders, in: R.W. Brandt / W. Groenman-van Waateringe / S.E. van der Leeuw (eds.), 99-113.

Gijn, A.L. van, 1988: The use of Bronze Age flint sickles in the Netherlands: a preliminary report, in: S. Beyries (ed.), 197-218.

Gijn, A.L. van, 1989: A functional analysis of the Belvédère flints, in: W. Roebroeks, 151-157.

Gijn, A.L. van, 1990: *The wear and tear of flint. Principles of functional analysis applied to Dutch Neolithic assemblages*, Leiden (Ph.D. thesis) (= APL 22 [1989]).

Gijn, A.L. van, 1992: The interpretation of 'sickles': a cautionary tale, in: P.C. Anderson (ed.), 363-372.

Gijn, A.L. van, 1998: Craft activities in the Dutch Neolithic: a lithic viewpoint, in: M. Edmonds / C. Richards (eds.), 328-350.

Gijn, A.L. van / M. Verbruggen 1992: Brandwijk – Het Kerkhof, in: W.A.M. Hessing, 349-352.

Gijn, A.L. van / H.T. Waterbolk 1984: The colonization of the salt marshes of Friesland and Groningen: the possibility of a transhumant prelude, *Palaeohistoria* 26, 101-122.

Gilman, A., 1981: The development of social stratification in Bronze Age Europe, *Current Anthropology* 22, 1-23.

Gilot, E., 1984: Datations radiométriques, in: D. Cahen / P. Haesaerts (eds.), 115-125.

Ginkel, E. van, 1988: *Hunebedden: gids en geschiedenis van Nederlands oudste monumenten*, Assen.

Ginkel, E. van / J.W.H. Hogestijn 1997: *Bekermensen aan zee*, Abcoude.

Glasbergen, W., 1954: *Barrow excavations in the Eight Beatitudes, the Bronze Age cemetery between Toterfout & Halve Mijl, North Brabant*, Groningen (Ph.D. thesis; = Palaeohistoria 2, I: 1-134 / Palaeohistoria 3, II: 1-204).

Glasbergen, W., 1956: De dolk van Bargeroosterveld I, NDV 74, 191-198.

Glasbergen, W., 1957: De gesteelde stenen hamerbijl van Emmercompascuum, NDV 75, 16-18.

Glasbergen, W., 1960: De dolk van Bargeroosterveld II, NDV 78, 190-198.

Glasbergen, W. 1969: *Nogmaals HVS/DKS*, Haarlem (Haarlemse voordrachten, 28).

Glasbergen, W., 1971: *Graves containing beakers with a protruding foot*, Inventaria Archaeologica, The Netherlands 1. set, Bonn.

Glasbergen, W. / M. Addink-Samplonius 1965: Laat-neolithicum en bronstijd te Monster (Z.H.), *Helinium* 5, 97-117.

Glasbergen, W. / W. Groenman-van Waateringe (eds.) 1961: *In het voetspoor van A.E. van Giffen*, Groningen.

Glasbergen, W. / W. Groenman-van Waateringe (eds.) 1966²: *In het voetspoor van A.E. van Giffen*, Groningen.

Glasbergen, W., *et al.* 1961: De neolithische nederzettingen te Vlaardingen (Z.-H.), in: W. Glasbergen / W. Groenman-van Waateringe (eds.), 41-65.

Glasbergen, W., *et al.* 1967: Settlements of the Vlaardingen culture at Voorschoten and Leidschendam, *Helinium* 7, 3-31, 97-120.

Glob, P.V., 1970: *The mound people*, London.

Glob, P.V., 1977: *The bog people; Iron-Age man preserved*, London.

Gob, A., 1976: Le mésolithique du gisement inférieur de la Roche-aux-Faucons (Plainevaux), *Bulletin de la Société Royale de la Belgique* 87, 45-76.

Gob, A., 1981: *Le Mésolithique dans le bassin de l'Ourthe*, Liège.

Gob, A., 1985: Extension géographique et chronologique de la culture Rhein-Meuse-Schelde (RMS), *Helinium* 25, 23-36.

Gob, A. / F. Spier (eds.) 1982: *Le mésolithique entre Rhin et Meuse*, Luxembourg.

Gotjé, W., 1993: *De Holocene laagveenontwikkeling in de randzone van de Nederlandse kustvlakte (Noordoostpolder)*, Amsterdam (Ph.D. thesis VU).

Goubitz, O., 2001: *Stepping through time – Archaeological footwear from prehistoric times until 1800*, Zwolle.

Graaf, K. van der, 1988: De mesolithische vindplaatsen in het zuidlimburgse lössgebied, Leiden (internal report FdAL).

Graaf, K. van der, 1989: *Centraal Plateau – Een archeologische kartering, inventarisatie en waardering*, Amsterdam (RAAP-rapport, 19).

Gramsch, B. (ed.) 1980: *Mesolithikum in Europa. 2e Internationales Symposium Potsdam, 3-8 april 1978*, Bericht, Berlin (Veröffentlichungen des Museums für Ur und Frühgeschichte Potsdam, 14/15).

Green, S.W. / S.M. Perlman (eds.) 1985: *The archaeology of frontiers and boundaries*, New York.

Gregory, C.A., 1982: *Gifts and commodities*, London.

Griede, J.W. / W. Roeleveld 1982: De geologische en paleogeografische ontwikkeling van het noordelijk zeekleigebied, *Geografisch Tijdschrift* 16, 439-455.

Gripp, K. / R. Schütrumpf / H. Schwabedissen (eds.) 1970: *Frühe Menschheit und Umwelt, Teil I*, Köln, (Fundamenta, A/2).

Groenendijk, H.A., 1987: Mesolithic hearth-pits in the Veenkoloniën (prov. Groningen, the Netherlands): defining a specific use of fire in the Mesolithic, *Palaeohistoria* 29, 85-102.

Groenendijk, H.A., 1988: Archeologie en landschap: drie voorbeelden uit Oost-Groningen, in: M. Bierma / O.H. Harsema / W. van Zeist (eds.), 9-30.

Groenendijk, H.A., 1993: *Landschap en bewoningsontwikkeling in het Herinrichtingsgebied Oost-Groningen, 8000 BC – 1000 AD*, Groningen (Ph.D. thesis).

Groenendijk, H.A., in press: Middle Mesolithic occupation on the extensive site NP3 in the peat reclamation district of Groningen, The Netherlands, in: *Proceedings of the XIVth Congress of the UISPP, Liège 2001*.

Groenendijk, H.A. / J.L. Smit 1984-'85: Een mesolithische vindplaats bij Wildervank, *Groningse Volksalmanak*, 131-145.

Groenendijk, H.A. / J.L. Smit, 1990: Mesolithische Herdstellen: Erfahrungen eines Brennversuchs, *Archäologischen Informationen* 13, 213-220.

Groenewoudt, B., 1984: IJzertijdvondsten uit Colmschate (gemeente Deventer) – De inhoud van een zestal afvalkuilen, *Westerheem* 33, 46-63.

Groenewoudt, B.J., 1989: Colmschate, gem. Deventer, in: A.D. Verlinde, 167-169.

Groenewoudt, B.J., 1994: *Prospectie, waardering en selectie van archeologische vindplaatsen: een beleidsgerichte verkenning van middelen en mogelijkheden*, Amersfoort (NAR, 17).

Groenewoudt, B.J., *et al.* 1998: *Raalte-Jonge Raan: de geschiedenis van een Sallandse bouwlandkamp*, Amersfoort (RAM, 58).

Groenewoudt, B.J. / A.D. Verlinde 1989: Ein Haustypus der NGK und eine Vorratsgrube aus der frühen Eisenzeit in Colmschate, Gem. Deventer, *BROB* 39, 269-295.

Groenman-van Waateringe, W., 1961: Palynologisch onderzoek van drie laat-neolithische tumuli van St. Walrick bij Overasselt (Gld.), in: W. Glasbergen / W. Groenman-van Waateringe (eds.), 72-80.

Groenman-van Waateringe, W., 1966: Nederzettingen van de Hilversumcultuur te Vogelenzang (N.H.) en Den Haag (Z.H.), in: W. Glasbergen / W. Groenman-van Waateringe (eds.), 81-92.

Groenman-van Waateringe, W., 1970: Pre- en (proto)historisch schoeisel uit Drenthe, NDV 88, 241-262.

Groenman-van Waateringe, W., 1986: Grazing possibilities in the Neolithic of the Netherlands based on palynological data, in: K.-E. Behre (ed.), 187-202.

Groenman-van Waateringe, W., 1988a: Palynologisch onderzoek van het urnenveld te Weert, in: J.M. van Mourik (ed.), 139-156.

Groenman-van Waateringe, W., 1988b: Lokale bosbestanden en houtgebruik in West-Nederland in IJzertijd, Romeinse tijd en Middeleeuwen, in: J.H.F. Bloemers (ed.), 133-153.

Groenman-van Waateringe, W., 1990: De kledingstukken van leder en bont, in: W.A.B. van der Sanden (ed.), 174-180.

Groenman-van Waateringe, W., 1991: Wederom prehistorisch schoeisel uit Drenthe, NDV 108, 128-135.

Groenman-van Waateringe, W., 2001: Prehistoric footwear, in: O. Goubitz, 379-396.

Groenman-van Waateringe, W. / R. Goedecker-Ciolek 1992: The equipment made of hide and leather, in: F. Höpfel / W. Platzer / K. Spindler (eds.), 410-418.

Groenman-van Waateringe, W. / M.J. Jansma 1969: Diatom and pollen analysis of the Vlaardingen creek, a revised interpretation, Helinium 9, 105-117.

Groenman-van Waateringe, W. / M. Robinson (eds.) 1988: Man-made soils, Oxford (BAR International Series, 410).

Groenman-van Waateringe, W. / A. Voorrips / L.H. van Wijngaarden-Bakker 1968: Settlements of the Vlaardingen Culture at Voorschoten and Leidschendam (ecology), Helinium 8, 105-130.

Grönnow, B., 1985: Meiendorf and Stellmoor revisited; an analysis of late palaeolithic reindeer exploitation, Acta Archaeologica 56, 131-166.

Gronenborn, D., 1990a: Eine Pfeilspitze vom ältestbandkeramischen Fundplatz Friedberg Bruchenbrücken in der Wetterau, Germania 68, 223-232.

Gronenborn, D., 1990b: Mesolithic-Neolithic interactions, the lithic industry of the Earliest Bandkeramik Culture site at Friedberg Bruchenbrücken, Wetteraukreis (West Germany), in: P.M. Vermeersch / Ph. Van Peer (eds.), 173-183.

Gronenborn, D., 1992: Beilklingen aus Lousberg-Feuerstein in Hessen, Archäologisches Korrespondenzblatt 22, 183-190.

Grood, J.N.M. de, 1984: De belangrijkste archeologische aktiviteiten van de AWN-afdeling 17: Zuid-Veluwe en Oost-Gelderland, Westerheem 33, 195-206.

Groot, D.J. de, 1988: Hunebed D9 at Annen, gem. Anlo, Province of Drenthe, the Netherlands, Palaeohistoria 30, 73-108.

Grooth, M.E.Th. de, 1987b: The organisation of flint tool manufacture in the Dutch Bandkeramik, APL 20, 27-52.

Grooth, M.E.Th. de, 1987a: De sierschijf van Helden, OMROL 67, 67-84.

Grooth, M.E.Th. de, 1990: Technological and socio-economic aspects of Bandkeramik flint working, in: E. Cziesla et al. (eds.), 197-210.

Grooth, M.E.Th. de, 1991: Socio-economic aspects of neolithic flint mining: a preliminary study, Helinium 31, 153-189.

Grooth, M.E.Th. de / G.J. Verwers 1984: Op goede gronden, de eerste boeren in Noordwest- Europa, Leiden.

Grünewald (ed.), Th., 2001: Germania inferior – Besiedlung, Gesellschaft und Wirtschaft an der Grenze der römisch-germanischen Welt, Berlin/New York (Ergänzungsbände zum Reallexikon der Germanischen Altertumskunde, 28).

Guilaine, J. (ed.) 1980: L'âge du cuivre européen: civilisations à vases campaniformes, Paris.

Gusinde, M., 1931: Die Feuerland Indianer, Band I. Die Selk'nam. Vom Leben und Denken eines Jägervolkes auf der grossen Feuerland Insel, Mödling bei Wien.

Guthrie, R.D., 1990: Frozen fauna of the mammoth steppe. The story of Blue Babe, Chicago.

Haan Hettema, M. de, 1846: Opgraving en bewaring van oudheden, *Vrije Fries* 5, 1-21.

Haaren, H.M.E. van / P.J.R. Modderman 1973: Ein mittelneolithischer Fundort unter Konings-
bosch, prov.Limburg, *APL* 6, 1-49.

Haarnagel, W., 1969: Die Ergebnisse der Grabung auf der ältereisenzeitlichen Siedlung Boom-
borg/Hatzum, Kreis Leer, in den Jahren von 1965 bis 1967, *Neue Ausgrabungen und Forschungen
in Niedersachsen* 4, 58-97.

Haarnagel, W., 1979: *Die Grabung Feddersen Wierde. Methode, Hausbau, Siedlungs- und Wirtschaftsformen
sowie Sozialstruktur (Feddersen Wierde II)*. Wiesbaden.

Haarnagel, W., 1984: Güterproduktion, 5, in: G. Kossack / K.-E. Behre / P. Schmid (eds.), 298-
301.

Haesaerts, P. / J. de Heinzelin 1979: *Le site paléolithique de Maisières-Canal*, Brugge (Dissertationes
Archaeologicae Gandenses, 19).

Haffner, A., 1976: *Die westliche Hunsrück-Eifel-Kultur*, Berlin (Römisch-Germanische Forschungen,
36).

Hahn, J., 1974: Die jungpaläolithische Station Lommersum, Gemeinde Weilerswist, Kreis
Euskirchen, *Rheinische Ausgrabungen* 15, 1-50.

Hahn, J., 1986: *Kraft und Aggression; die Botschaft der Eiszeitkunst im Aurignacien süddeutschlands?* Tübingen.

Hakbijl, T., 1990: Insekten, in: W.A.B. van der Sanden (ed.), 168-173.

Halbertsma, H., 1963: *Terpen tussen Vlie en Eems*, Groningen.

Hald, M., 1980: *Ancient Danish textiles from bogs and burials*, Copenhagen.

Hallewas, D.P., 1989: Archeologische kroniek van Holland over 1988, II Zuid-Holland, *Holland*
21, 318-348.

Hallewas, D.P. / G.H. Scheepstra / P.J. Woltering (eds.) 1997: *Dynamisch landschap; archeologie en
geologie van het Nederlandse kustgebied*, Amersfoort.

Halstead, P. / J. O'Shea (eds.) 1989: *Bad year economics: cultural responses to risk and uncertainty*, Cambridge.

Hamal-Nandrin, J. / J. Servais 1909: Contribution à l'étude du Préhistorique dans la Campine
Limburgeoise, *Annales de la Fédération Archéologique et Historique de Belgique* 21, 202-225.

Hamal-Nandrin, J. / J. Servais 1923: La station néolithique de Sainte-Gertrude (Limbourg hol-
landais), *Revue anthropologique* 33, 348-492.

Hammen, T. van der / T.A. Wijmstra / W.H. Zagwijn 1971: The floral record of the Late Cenozoic
of Europe, in: K.K. Turekian (ed.), 391-424.

Hammond, F., 1981: The colonization of Europe: the analysis of settlement processes, in: I. Hodder / G. Isaac / N. Hammond (eds.), 211-249.

Hänsel, B. (ed.) 1982: *Südosteuropa zwischen 1600 und 1000 v.Chr.*, Berlin (Prähistorische Archäologie in Südosteuropa, 1).

Harck, O., 1972: *Nordostniedersachsen vom Beginn der jüngeren Bronzezeit bis zum frühen Mittelalter*, Hildesheim (Materialhefte zur Ur- und Frühgeschichte Niedersachsens, 7).

Harck, O., 1984a: Güterproduktion, 4, in: G. Kossack / K.-E. Behre / P. Schmid (eds.), 295-298.

Harck, O., 1984b: Bauopfer und Kultplätze, in: G. Kossack / K.-E. Behre / P. Schmid (eds.), 343-
349.

Harck, O., 1987: Archäologisches zur Kenntnis des vor- und frühgeschichtlichen Ackerbaus, in:
G. Kossack / O. Harck / J. Reichstein (eds.), 1-50.

Harris, D. / G.C. Hillman (eds.) 1989: *Foraging and farming; the evolution of plant exploitation*, London.

Harrison, R.J., 1980: *The Beaker Folk*, London.

Harsema, O.H. (ed.) 1983: Kroniek van opgravingen en vondsten in Drenthe in 1980 en 1981, *NDV*
100, 203-217.

Harsema, O.H., 1976: Noordbarge, *BKNOB* 75, 52-55.

Harsema, O.H., 1978: Mesolithische vuurstenen bijlen in Drenthe, *NDV* 95, 161-186.

Harsema, O.H., 1979a: *Maalstenen en handmolens in Drenthe van het neolithicum tot ca. 1300 A.D.*, Assen (Museumfonds Publicatie, 5).

Harsema, O.H., 1979b: Het neolithisch vuursteendepot gevonden in 1940, bij Een, gem. Norg, NDV 96, 117-128.

Harsema, O.H., 1980a: *Drents boerenleven van de bronstijd tot de middeleeuwen*, Assen (Museumfonds publicatie, 6).

Harsema, O.H., 1980b: Het Drents plateau; de latere prehistorische bewoning, in: M. Chamalaun / H.T. Waterbolk (eds.), 83-102.

Harsema, O.H., 1980c: De reconstructie van een ijzertijdhuis te Orvelte, gem. Westerbork, NDV 97, 149-175.

Harsema, O.H., 1982: Settlement site selection in Drenthe in later prehistoric times: criteria and considerations, APL 15, 145-159.

Harsema, O.H., 1985: Het verleden herbouwd – Boerderijconstructies in Nederland in prehistorie en middeleeuwen, in: K.J. Steehouwer / A.H.C. Warringa (eds.), 208-224.

Harsema, O.H., 1987: Change and continuity in rural settlement in Drenthe from the Neolithic onwards: a reconsideration of traditional and current opinions, Palaeohistoria 29, 103-118.

Harsema, O.H., 1990: Drenthe's plaats en rol in de ijzertijd, NDV 107, 169-179.

Harsema, O.H., 1991: De bronstijd-bewoning op het Hijkerveld bij Hijken, in: H. Fokkens / N. Roymans (eds.), 21-29.

Harsema, O.H., 1992: *Geschiedenis in het landschap. Hoe het Drentse landschap werd gebruikt, van de toendratijd tot in de 20e eeuw*, Assen.

Harsema, O.H., 1994: Zes dagen in juni op de es van Noordbarge, Palaeo-aktueel 5, 69-73.

Harsema, O.H., 2001: Over de betekenis van precisie in de uitvoering van paalkransen in de Nederlandse midden-bronstijd, in: W.H. Metz / B.L. van Beek / H. Steegstra (eds.), 321-335.

Hartmann, A., 1970, 1982: *Prähistorische Goldfunde aus Europa (I,II)*, Berlin (Studien zu den Anfängen der Metallurgie 3 / 5).

Hartmann, A., 1979: Irish and British gold types and their West European counterparts, in: M. Ryan (ed.), 215-228.

Hassan, F.A., 1977: The dynamics of agricultural origins in Palestine: a theoretical model, in: Ch. Reed (ed.), 589-609.

Hassan, F.A., 1981: *Demographic archaeology*, New York.

Hayden, B., 1981: Research and development in the stone age: technological transitions among hunter-gatherers, Current Anthropology 22, 519-548.

Hayen, H., 1985: Bergung, wissenschaftliche Untersuchung und Konservierung moorarchäologischer Funde, *Archäologische Mitteilungen aus Nordwestdeutschland 8*, 1-43.

Hayen, H., 1987: New light on the history of transport, Endeavour, New Series 11(4), 209-216.

Hayen, H., 1989: Bau und Funktion der hölzernen Moorwege: Einige Fakten und Folgerungen, *Untersuchungen zu Handel und Verkehr der vor- und frühgeschichtlichen Zeit in Mittel- und Nordeuropa 5*, 11-82.

Healey, C.J., 1990: *Maring hunters and traders. Production and exchange in the Papua New Guinea Highlands*, Berkeley.

Heemskerck Düker, W.F. van / P. Felix 1943: *Wat aarde bewaarde, vondsten uit onze vroegste geschiedenis*, Den Haag.

Heeringen, R.M. van, 1985: Typologie, Zeitstellung und Verbreitung der in die Niederlande importierten vorgeschichtlichen Mahlsteine aus Tephrit, *Archäologisches Korrespondenzblatt 15*, 371-383.

Heeringen, R.M. van, 1986a: Een stenen armband uit de late ijzertijd uit Sint Maartensdijk, Tholen, in: R.M. van Heeringen (ed.), 61-65.

Heeringen, R.M. van (ed.) 1986b: *Voordrachten gehouden te Middelburg ter gelegenheid van het afscheid van ir. J.A. Trimpe Burger als provinciaal archeoloog van Zeeland*, Amersfoort (NAR, 3).

Heeringen, R.M. van, 1988a: De bewoning van Zeeland in de IJzertijd, *Archief, Mededelingen van het Koninklijk Zeeuwsch Genootschap der Wetenschappen*, 1-43.

Heeringen, R.M. van, 1988b: Natte voeten, droge voeten. Bewoningsmogelijkheden in de midden- en late ijzertijd in Holland en Zeeland, in: M. Bierma / O.H. Harsema / W. van Zeist (eds.), 79-96.

Heeringen, R.M. van, 1992: *The Iron Age in the Western Netherlands*, Amersfoort (Ph.D. thesis VU Amsterdam; ook verschenen in BROB 31 [1981], 37 [1987] en 39 [1989]).

Heeringen, R.M. van, 1998-'99: Burial with Rhine view: the Hallstatt situla grave on the Koerheuvel at Rhenen, BROB 43, 69-97.

Heeringen, R.M. van / R.C.G.M. Lauwerier / H.M. van der Velde 1998: *Sporen uit de IJzertijd en de Romeinse tijd in de Hoeksche Waard – Een aanvullend Archeologisch Onderzoek te Westmaas-Maaszicht, gem. Binnenmaas*, Amersfoort (RAM, 56).

Heeringen, R.M. van / E.M. Theunissen (eds.) 2001: *Kwaliteitsbepalend onderzoek ten behoeve van duurzaam behoud van neolithische terreinen in West-Friesland en de Kop van Noord-Holland*, Amersfoort (NAR, 21).

Heeringen, R.M. van / H.M. van der Velde / I. van Amen 1998: Een tweeschepige huisplattegrond uit de vroege bronstijd te Noordwijk, provincie Zuid-Holland, Lunula 6, 15-18.

Heesters, W., 1971: Een mesolithische nederzetting te Sint-Oedenrode, Brabants Heem 23, 94-115.

Heesters, W. / A.M. Wouters 1968: Een vroeg-mesolithische kultuur te Nijnsel, Brabants Heem 20, 98-108.

Heesters, W. / A.M. Wouters 1970: De Tjongerkultuur in de Rips (gem. Bakel), Brabants Heem 22, 2-20.

Heidinga, H.A. / E. Vreenegoor 1990: Beers, Gassel IV, in: W.J.H. Verwers 1990a, 71-75.

Heinzelin, J. de, 1977: Un artefact de la terrasse de Sint-Pietersberg (Halembaye, Commune de Haccourt, Prov. de Liège), Helinium 17, 231-234.

Hendriks, J. / F. van Nuenen 1989: Prehistorische bewoningssporen langs de Leij: wonen en werken aan een beekdal, Westerheem 38, 69-79.

Hendrix, W.P.A.M., 1999: De bandkeramische nederzetting Stein-Heidekampweg. Archeologie in Limburg 80, 21-24.

Heringa, J., et al. (eds.) 1985: *Geschiedenis van Drenthe*, Meppel.

Hermannn, F.R. / A. Jockenhövel 1975: Bronzezeitliche Grabhügel mit Pfostenringen bei Edelsberg, Kreis Limburg-Veilburg, Fundberichte aus Hessen 15, 87-127.

Hessing, W.A.M., 1989: Wijk bij Duurstede 'De Horden': Besiedlung und Bestattungen aus der frühen Eisenzeit, BROB 39, 297-344.

Hessing, W.A.M., 1990: Archeologische kroniek van Holland over 1989, II: Zuid-Holland, Holland 22, 332-362.

Hessing, W.A.M., 1991a: Bewoningssporen uit de midden-bronstijd en de vroege ijzertijd op 'De Horden' te Wijk bij Duurstede, in: H. Fokkens / N. Roymans (eds.), 41-52.

Hessing, W.A.M., 1991b: Archeologische kroniek van Holland over 1990, II Zuid-Holland, Holland 23, 329-367.

Hessing, W.A.M., 1992: Archeologische Kroniek van Holland over 1991, II Zuid-Holland, Holland 24, 348-388.

Hessing, W.A.M., 1993a: Nécropoles indigènes de la zone alluviale des Pays-Bas (50 av. J.-C. – 300 ap. J.-C.), in: A. Ferdière (ed.), 105-112.

Hessing, W.A.M., 1993b: Ondeugende Bataven en verdwaalde Friezinnen?; enkele gedachten over de onverbrande menselijke resten uit de ijzertijd en de Romeinse tijd in West- en Noord-Nederland, in: E. Drenth / W.A.M. Hessing / E. Knol (eds.), 17-40.

Hessing, W.A.M., 1993c: Archeologische kroniek van Holland over 1992, II Zuid-Holland, Holland 25, 329-369.

Hessing, W.A.M. / R. Steenbeek 1990: Landscape and habitation history of 'De Horden' at Wijk bij Duurstede: an overview, BROB 40, 9-28.

Heymans, H. / P.M. Vermeersch 1983: Siedlungsspuren aus Mittel- und Spätneolithikum, Bronzezeit und Eisenzeit in Geistingen, Huizerhof (Provinz Limburg), in: *Miscellanea archaeologica in honorem H. Roosens*, Brussel (Archaeologia Belgica, 255), 15-64.

Heynowski, R., 1991: Zum Schläfenschmuck in der älteren Hunsrück-Eifel-Kultur, *Trierer Zeitschrift* 54, 43-64.

Heynowski, R., 1992: *Eisenzeitlicher Trachtschmuck der Mittelgebirgszone zwischen Rhein und Thüringer Becken*, Mainz (Archäologische Schriften des Instituts für Vor- und Frühgeschichte der Johannes Gutenberg-Universität Mainz, 1).

Hielkema, J.B., 2001: Bronze finds in the Middle Bronze Age settlement at Eigenblok, in: W.H. Metz / B.L. van Beek / H. Steegstra (eds.), 337-344.

Higgs, E.S. (ed.) 1975: *Palaeoeconomy II. Papers in Economic Prehistory*, Cambridge.

Hijszeler, C.C.W.J., 1952: Grave-mounds near Knegsel (Province of Noord-Brabant), *BROB* 3, 26-27.

Hijszeler, C.C.W.J., 1970: De pre- en protohistorie van Twente, in: B.H. Slicher van Bath (ed.), 37-57.

Hill, J.D. / C. Cumberpatch (eds.) 1995: *Different Iron Ages: studies on the Iron Age in temperate Europe*, Oxford (BAR International Series, 602).

Hillier, B. / J. Hanson 1984: *The social logic of space*, Cambridge.

Hillman, G., 1984: Interpretation of archaeological plant remains: The application of ethnographic models from Turkey, in: W. van Zeist / W.A. Casparie (eds.), 1-41.

Hingh, A.E. de, 2000: *Food production and food procurement in the Bronze Age and Early Iron Age (2000-500 BC). The organisation of a diversified and intensified agrarian system in the Meuse-Demer-Scheldt region (The Netherlands and Belgium) and the region of the river Moselle (Luxemburg and France)*, Leiden (Ph.D. thesis; = ASLU, 7).

Hinz, H., 1964: Einige naturwissenschaftliche Untersuchungsergebnisse an niederrheinischen Fundstellen, *Bonner Jahrbücher* 164, 233-245.

Hinz, H., 1974: Die Ausgrabungen auf dem Friedhof der vorrömischen Eisenzeit von Veen, Kreis Moers, *Rheinische Ausgrabungen* 15, 243-346.

Höckmann, O., 1972: Andeutungen zu Religion und Kultus in der bandkeramischen Kultur, in: *Aktuelle Fragen der Bandkeramik*, Székesfehérvár (Alba Regia, 12), 197-209.

Hodder, I., 1977: The distribution of material culture items in the Baringo district, Kenya, *Man* 12, 239-269.

Hodder, I., 1982a: Sequences of structural change in the Dutch neolithic, in: I. Hodder (ed.), 162-177.

Hodder, I., 1982b: *Symbols in action*, Cambridge.

Hodder, I. (ed.) 1982c: *Symbolic and structural archaeology*, Cambridge.

Hodder, I., 1985: Boundaries as strategies: an ethnoarchaeological study, in: S.W. Green / S.M. Perlman (eds.), 141-159.

Hodder, I., 1986: *Reading the past. Current approaches to interpretion in archaeology*, Cambridge.

Hodder, I. (ed.) 1987: *The archaeology of contextual meanings*, Cambridge.

Hodder, I. (ed.) 1989: *The meaning of things – material culture and symbolic expression*, London.

Hodder, I., 1990: *The domestication of Europe – structure and contingency in Neolithic societies*, Cambridge.

Hodder, I. / G. Isaac / N. Hammond (eds.) 1981: *Pattern of the past: studies in honour of David Clarke*, Cambridge.

Hodder, I., et al. (eds.) 1995: *Interpreting Archaeology. Finding meaning in the past*, London.

Höpfel, F. / W. Platzer / K. Spindler (eds.) 1992: *Der Mann im Eis*, Innsbruck (Veröffentlichungen der Universität Innsbruck, 187)

Hoffecker, J.F. / G. Baryshnikov / O. Potapova 1991: Vertebrate remains from the Mousterian Site of Il'Skaya I (Northern Caucasus, U.S.S.R.): New Analysis and Interpretation, *Journal of Archaeological Science* 18, 113-147.

Hogestijn, J.W.H., 1990: From Swifterbant to TRB in the IJssel-Vecht Basin; some suggestions, in: D. Jankowska (ed.), 163-180.

Hogestijn, J.W.H., 1991: Resten van neolithische bewoning bij Schokkerhaven, *Cultuur historisch jaarboek voor Flevoland* 1, 114-115.

Hogestijn, J.W.H., 1992: Functional differences between some settlements of the Single Grave culture in the northwestern coastal area of the Netherlands, in: M. Buchvaldek / C. Strahm (eds.), 199-205.

Hogestijn, J.W.H. / G. van Haaff 1991: Hoogwoud Mienakker, *Jaarverslag ROB 1990*, 34-36.

Hogestijn, J.W.H. / J.H.M. Peeters 2001: *De mesolithische en vroeg-neolithische vindplaats Hoge Vaart-A27 (Flevoland)*, Amersfoort (RAM, 79).

Hogestijn, J.W.H. / P.J. Woltering 1990: 'Het woiffie van Soibekarspel': een Laat-Neolithisch vrouwengraf te Sijbekarspel, *West-Frieslands Oud en Nieuw* 57, 152-164.

Hogestijn, J.W.H., *et al.* 1991: Slootdorp, *ROB Jaarverslag 1990*, 36.

Hogestijn, J.W.H., *et al.* 1995: Bewoningsresten uit de steentijd langs een voormalige loop van de Eem in Zuidelijk Flevoland; de voltooiing van de A27 en de archeologie, *Cultuurhistorisch Jaarboek voor Flevoland 1994*, 83-102.

Hollstein, E., 1976: Dendrochronologische Datierung von Hölzern aus der Wallanlage von Kanne, Caster, in: *Conspectus 1975*, Brussel (Archaeologia Belgica, 186), 59-61.

Hollstein, E., 1980: *Mitteleuropäische Eichenchronologie*, Mainz (Trierer Grabungen und Forschungen, 11).

Holm, J. / F. Rieck 1983: Jels I the first Danish site of the Hamburgian Culture; a preliminary report, *Journal of Danish Archaeology* 2, 7-11.

Holm, J. / F. Rieck 1987: Die Hamburger Kultur in Dänemark, *Archäologisches Korrespondenzblatt* 17, 151-168.

Holwerda, J.H., 1910: Opgravingen in de Hertekamp bij Vaassen, *OMROL* 4, 1-30.

Holwerda, J.H., 1925: *Nederlands vroegste geschiedenis*, Amsterdam.

Holwerda, J.H., 1935: De prae-historie en de oude geschiedenis, in: H. Brugmans (ed.), 13-104

Holwerda, J.H., n.d.: *Das Gräberfeld von 'de Hamert' bei Venlo*, Leiden.

Hoof, D., 1970: *Die Steinbeile und Steinäxte im Gebiet des Niederrheins und der Maas*, Bonn (Antiquitas Reihe 2, Band 9).

Hoof, L.G.L. van, 2001: Speciaal metaal? Enige aantekeningen over depositiepraktijken in het Limburgse Maasdal, *Lunula* 9, 19-22.

Hoof, L.G.L. van, 2002: 'En zij begroeven zich een huis'. Structuur en levensloop van een ijzertijd-erf in de Zuid-Limburgse lösszone, in: H. Fokkens / R. Jansen (eds.), 73-93.

Hoogland, M.L.P., 1985: Fysisch-antropologisch onderzoek van het skeletmateriaal van de opgraving Hekelingen III, Leiden (internal report FdAL).

Hoogland, M.L.P., 1999: Physical-anthropological study of the cremation remains, in: F. Theuws / N. Roymans (eds.), 74-77.

Horst, F., 1985: *Zedau – Eine jungbronze- und eine eisenzeitliche Siedlung in der Altmark*, Berlin (Schriften zur Ur- und Frühgeschichte, 36).

Hoskins, J.A., 1986: So my name shall live: stone-dragging and grave-building in Kodi, West Sumba, *Bijdragen tot de Taal-, Land- en Volkenkunde* 142, 31-51.

Housley, R.A., 1991: AMS dates from the Late Glacial and early Postglacial in north-west Europe: a review, in: N. Barton / A.J. Roberts / D.A. Roe (eds.), 25-39.

Houtsma, P. / E. Kramer / R.R. Newell 1990: De jong-paleolithische vindplaats Haule V: van opgravingsrapport naar een reconstructie van Federmesser-nederzettingspatroon en -landgebruik, in: A.T.L. Niklewicz-Hokse / C.A.G. Lagerwerf (eds.), 40-44.

Houtsma, P., *et al.* 1996: *The Late Glacial habitation of Haule V: from the site report to the reconstruction of Federmesser settlement patterns and land-use*, Assen.

Hübner, K.-D. / R. Saur / H. Reichstein 1988: Die Säugetierknochen der neolithischen Seeufersiedlung Hüde I am Dümmer, Landkreis Diepholz, Niedersachsen, *Göttinger Schriften zur Vor- und Frühgeschichte* 23, 35-142.

Hülle, W., 1977: *Die Ilsenhöhle unter Burg Ranis*, New York.

Huijbers, T., 1990: Beek en Donk, in: W.J.H. Verwers 1990b, 143-146.

Huijts, C.S.T.J., 1992: *De voor-historische boerderijbouw in Drenthe; reconstructiemodellen van 1300 vóór tot 1300 na Chr.*, Arnhem.

Huiskes, B., 1988: Tietjerk-Lutse Geast I: A reconstruction of a Mesolithic site from an anthropological perspective, *Palaeohistoria* 30, 29-62.

Hulst, R.S., 1964: Een grafveld uit de voor-Romeinse IJzertijd te Nijnsel, gem. St. Oedenrode, prov. Noord-Brabant, BROB 14, 74-83.

Hulst, R.S., 1973: A contribution to the study of Bronze Age and Iron Age house-plans: Zijderveld, BROB 23, 103-107.

Hulst, R.S., 1986: Archeologische kroniek van Gelderland 1985, *Bijdragen en mededelingen van de Vereniging Gelre* 77, 141-158.

Hulst, R.S., 1987: Archeologische kroniek van Gelderland 1986, *Bijdragen en mededelingen van de Vereniging Gelre* 78, 207-224.

Hulst, R.S., 1989: Archeologische kroniek van Gelderland 1988, *Bijdragen en mededelingen van de Vereniging Gelre* 80, 141-160.

Hulst, R.S., 1991: Nederzettingen uit de midden-bronstijd in het rivierengebied: Zijderveld en Dodewaard, in: H. Fokkens / N. Roymans (eds.), 53-60.

Hulst, R.S., 1999: Geldermalsen: an Early La Tène cemetery – Diffusion or convergence?, in: H. Sarfatij / W.J.H. Verwers / P.J. Woltering (eds.), 41-49.

Hulst, R.S. / A.D. Verlinde 1976: Geröllkeule aus Overijssel und Gelderland, BROB 26, 93-126.

Hulst, R.S. / A.D. Verlinde 1979: Spitzhauen aus den Niederlanden, BROB 29, 185-207.

Hurtrelle, J., *et al.* 1989: *Les débuts du second âge du fer dans le Nord de la France*, Liévin (Les dossiers de Gauheria, 1).

Huyge, D. / P.M. Vermeersch 1982: Late Mesolithic settlement at Weelde-Paardsdrank, *Studia Prehistorica Belgica* 1, 116-209.

Hvass, S. / B. Storgaard (eds.) 1993: *Digging into the past. 25 Years of archaeology in Denmark*, Aarhus.

IJsseling, M.A. / A. Scheygrond 1956: *Gewervelde dieren*, Zutphen.

IJzereef, G.F., 1981: *Bronze Age animal bones from Bovenkarspel; the excavation at Het Valkje*, Amsterdam (Ph.D. thesis UvA; = Nederlandse Oudheden, 10).

IJzereef, G.F., 1983: Boeren in de bronstijd, *Spiegel Historiael* 18, 635-643.

IJzereef, G.F. / F.J. Laarman / R.C.G.M. Lauwerier 1992: Animal remains from the Late Bronze Age and the Iron Age found in the Western Netherlands, in: R.M. van Heeringen, 341-351 (= BROB 39, 257-267).

IJzereef, G.F. / J.F. van Regteren Altena 1991: Nederzettingen uit de midden- en late bronstijd te Andijk en Bovenkarspel, in: H. Fokkens / N. Roymans (eds.), 61-81.

Ille, P., 1991: *Totenbrauchtum in der älteren Bronzezeit auf den dänischen Inseln*, Buch am Erlbach (Internationale Archäologie, 2), 1-154.

Imbrie, J. , *et al.* 1984: The orbital theory of Pleistocene climate: support from a revised chronology of the marine ?[18]O record, in: A. Berger (ed.), Part I, 269-305.

Impe, L. Van, 1976: Ringwalheuvels in de Kempense bronstijd: typologie en datering, Brussel (*Archaeologia Belgica*, 190), 5-21.

Impe, L. Van, 1991: Nederzettingssporen uit de ijzertijd te Donk (België), in: H. Fokkens / N. Roymans (eds.), 181-191.

Impe, L. Van, 1994: Bronsdepots in de Maasvallei, in: J. Bourgeois *et al.* (eds.), 13-14.

Impe, L. Van / G. Creemers 1991: Aristokratische graven uit de 5de/4de eeuw v.Chr. en Romeinse cultusplaats op de 'Rieten' (gem. Meeuwen-Gruitrode) – Interimverslag, *Archeologie in Vlaanderen* 1, 55-73.

Impe, L. Van / K. Verlaeckt 1992: Een ceremoniële bijl uit het Maasgrind – Een bijdrage over Noord-Europese invloeden in de Bronstijd der Lage Landen, *Archeologie in Vlaanderen* 2, 21-39.

Ingold, T., 1981: The hunter and his spear: notes on the cultural mediation of social and ecological systems, in: J.A. Sheridan / G. Bailey (eds.), 119-130.

Ingold, T. / D. Riches / J. Woodburn (eds.) 1988: *Hunters and gatherers*, Oxford.

Iterson Scholten, F.R. van, 1977: Rope and fishing tackle, in: B.L. van Beek *et al.* (eds.), 135-143.

Iterson Scholten, F.R. van / W.H. de Vries-Metz 1981: A late neolithic settlement at Aartswoud I, *Helinium* 21, 105-135.

Iversen, J., 1941: *Landnam i Danmarks Stenalder*, København (Danmarks Geologiske Undersøgelse IV. Rk 4,3).

Jacobi, R.M., 1973: Aspect of the 'Mesolithic Age' in Great Britain, in: S.K. Kozlowski (eds.), 237-266.

Jacobi, R.M., 1976: Britain inside and outside Mesolithic Europe, *PPS* 42, 67-84.

Jacobi, R.M., 1990: Leaf-points and the British Early Upper Palaeolithic, in: J.K. Kozlowski (eds.), 271-289.

Jacobi, R.M., 1991: The Creswellian, Creswell and Cheddar, in: N. Barton / A.J. Roberts / D.A. Roe (eds.), 128-140.

Jadin, I., 1990: Economie de production dans le Rubané récent de Belgique, approche comparative des industries lithiques de trois villages, in: D. Cahen / M. Otte (eds.), 147-160.

Jadin, I. / D. Cahen 1992: Darion: twee naburige dorpen, in: *Speurwerk, Archaeologische monumentenzorg in de Euregio MaasRijn*, Mainz (Führer des Rheinischen Landesmuseums Bonn und des Rheinischen Amtes für Bodendenkmalpflege, 136), 509-526.

Jadin, I., *et al.* 1989: Omaliens et Blicquiens face à face, fouille d'urgence d'un établissement et d'un sépulture du Groupe de Blicquy à Darion-Colia (Geer, prov. de Liège), *Notae Praehistoricae* 9, 61-68.

Jager, S.W., 1982: Duntoppige vuurstenen bijlen uit Oudemolen, gem. Vries en Gees, gem. Oosterhesselen, *NDV* 99, 115-123.

Jager, S.W., 1985: A prehistoric route and ancient cart-tracks in the gemeente of Anloo (Province of Drenthe), *Palaeohistoria* 27, 185-245.

Jager, S.W. / P.J. Woltering 1990: Archeologische kroniek van Holland over 1989, I Noord-Holland, *Holland* 22, 296-331.

Jankowska, D. (ed.) 1990: *Die Trichterbecherkultur, neue Forschungen und Hypothesen*, Poznan.

Jankuhn, H. (ed.) 1970: *Vorgeschichtliche Heiligtümer und Opferplätze in Mittel- und Nordeuropa*, Göttingen (Abhandlungen der Akademie der Wissenschaften in Göttingen, Philologisch-Historische Klasse, Dritte Folge, 74).

Jankuhn, H. / K. Schietzel / H. Reichstein (eds.) 1984: *Archäologische und naturwissenschaftliche Untersuchungen an ländlichen und frühstädtischen Siedlungen im deutschen Küstengebiet vom 5.Jahrhundert v. Chr. bis zum 11.Jahrhundert n. Chr., 2: Handelsplätze des frühen und hohen Mittelalters*, Weinheim.

Jansma, E., 1995: *RemembeRINGs – The development and application of local and regional tree-ring chronologies of oak for the purposes of archaeological and historical research in the Netherlands*, Amsterdam (Ph.D. thesis UvA; = NAR, 19).

Janssen, C.R., 1974: *Verkenningen in de palynologie*, Utrecht.

Janssen, M. / L. van der Valk (eds.) 1987: *Duinen bij Den Haag,... de moeite waard, Duin* (supplement).

Jansen, R. / H. Fokkens 1999: *Bouwen aan het verleden – 25 jaar archeologisch onderzoek in de gemeente Oss*, Leiden.

Jansen, R. / H. Fokkens / C. van der Linde 2002: Lith-Oijensche Hut en Haren-Spaanse Steeg. Lokale riviercultusplaatsen uit de Late IJzertijd in de Brabantse Maaskant, in: H. Fokkens / R. Jansen (eds.), 173-205.

Jelgersma, S., 1961: *Holocene sea-level changes in the Netherlands*, Leiden (Ph.D. thesis; = *Mededelingen Geologische Stichting* CVI-7).

Jelgersma, S., 1979: Sea-level changes in the North Sea basin, in: E. Oele / R.T.E. Schüttenhelm / A.J. Wiggers (eds.), 233-248.

Jelgersma, S. / P.J. Ente 1977: Genese van het Holoceen, in: C.J. van Staalduinen (ed.), 23-33.

Jelgersma, S., *et al.* 1970: The coastal dunes of the western Netherlands; geology, vegetational history and archeology, *MRGD*, nieuwe serie, 21, 93-167.

Jensen, H.J., 1986: Unretouched blades in the Late Mesolithic of South Scandinavia. A functional study, *Oxford Journal of Archaeology* 5, 19-33.

Jensen, H.J. / E. Brinch Petersen 1985: A functional study of lithics from Vaenget Nord, a Mesolithic site at Vedbaek, *Journal of Danish Archeology* 4, 40-51.

Jensen, J., 1987a: Bronze Age research in Denmark 1970-1985, *Journal of Danish Archaeology* 6, 155-174.

Jensen, J., 1987b: Christian Jürgensen Thomsen: an appreciation in the bicentennial of his birth, *Acta Archaeologica* 58, 1-15.

Jeunesse, C., 1986: Rapports avec le Néolithique ancien d'Alsace de la céramique 'Danubienne' de La Hoguette (à FontenayLeMarmion, Calvados), in: *Actes du Xe Colloque interrégional sur le Néolithique, Caen (Revue Archéologique de l'Ouest, Suppl. 1)*, 41-50.

Jeunesse, C., 1987: La céramique de La Hoguette, un nouvel 'élément nonrubané' du Néolithique ancien de l'Europe du NordOuest, *Cahiers Alsaciens d'Archéologie, d'Art et d'Histoire* 30, 533.

Jeunesse, C., *et al.* 1991: Nouveaux temoins d'âge néolithique ancien entre Rhône et Rhin, *Jahrbuch der schweizerischen Gesellschaft für Ur- und Frühgeschichte* 74, 43-78.

Joachim, H.-E., 1970: Späthallstattzeitliche Hügelgrabfunde aus Wirfus, Kreis Cochem – Zur Verbreitung und Funktion einiger späthallstättischer Typen und Typenmerkmale im Rheinischen Gebirge, *Bonner Jahrbücher* 170, 36-70.

Joachim, H.-E., 1980: Jüngerlatènezeitliche Siedlungen bei Eschweiler, Kr. Aachen, *Bonner Jahrbücher* 180, 355-441.

Joachim, H.-E., 1985: Schmuck und Tracht der Eisenzeit – Zu einer Schautafel mittelrheinischer Späthallstatt-Trachten, *Das Rheinische Landesmuseum – Berichte aus der Arbeit des Museums* 2/85, 17-19.

Jochim, M.A., 1976: *Hunter-gatherer subsistence and settlement – A predictive model*, New York.

Jochim, M.A., 1983: Palaeolithic cave art in ecological perspective, in: G.N. Bailey (ed.), 212-219.

Jockenhövel, A., 1991: Räumliche Mobilität von Personen in der mittleren Bronzezeit des westlichen Mitteleuropa, *Germania* 69, 49-62.

Jodlowski, A., 1976: *Technika produkcji soli na terenie Europy w pradziejach i wczesnym sredniowieczu – Studium archeologiczne*, Wieliczka (Studia i materialy do dziejów zup solnych w polsce, 5).

Johansson, L., 1981: Bistoft LA 11. Siedlungs- und Wirtschaftsformen im frühen Neolithikum Norddeutschlands und Südskandinaviens, *Offa* 38, 91-129.

Jong, J. de / H. Wevers 1994: Cirkels en zonnekalenders in Zwolle-Ittersumerbroek, in: H. Clevis / J. de Jong (eds.), 74-93.

Jongste, P.F.B., 2002: De verlaten erven van Eigenblok. Deposities van metalen voorwerpen op twee erven uit de Midden-Bronstijd in de Betuweroute, in: H. Fokkens / R. Janssen (eds.), 95-108.

Jongste, P.F.B. / B.H.F.M. Meijlink / H.M. van de Velde 2001: Enkele huisplaatsen uit de vroege Bronstijd (2000-1800 v.Chr.), ADC-info 4ᵉ kwartaal 2001, 9-17.

Jongste, P.F.B. / G.J. van Wijngaarden (eds.) 2002: *Het erfgoed van Eigenblok. Nederzettingsterreinen uit de Bronstijd te Rumpt, gemeente Geldermalsen*, Amersfoort (RAM, 86).

Jope, E.M., 1961: Daggers of the Early Iron Age in Britain, PPS 27, 307-343.

Joussaume, R., 1985: *Des dolmens pour les morts, les mégalithes à travers le monde*, Parijs.

Jovanovič, B., 1982: *Rudna Glava*, Bor.

Jürgens, A., 1979: Die Rössener Siedlung Aldenhoven, Kreis Düren, *Rheinische Ausgrabungen* 19, 385-505.

Julien, M., 1982: *Les harpons magdaléniens*, Paris (Gallia Préhistoire, supplément 17).

Julien, M., 1984: L'usage du feu à Pincevent (Seine-et-Marne), in: H. Berke / J. Hahn / C.-J. Kind (eds.), 161-168.

Jungerius, E. / E. Smits 1988: Een groepsbegraving te Wassenaar, *Westerheem* 37, 71-74.

Junghans, S. / E. Sangmeister / M. Schroeder 1968: *Kupfer und Bronze in der frühen Metallzeit Europas*, Berlin, (Studien zu den Anfängen der Metallurgie, 2).

Junghans, S. / E. Sangmeister / M. Schroeder 1974: *Kupfer und Bronze in der frühen Metallzeit Europas*, Berlin, (Studien zu den Anfängen der Metallurgie, 4).

Junk, M. / R. Krause / E. Pernicka 2001: Ösenringbarren and classical Ösenring copper, in : W.H. Metz / B.L. van Beek / H. Steegstra (eds.), 353-366.

Kalis, A.J., 1988: Zur Umwelt der frühneolithischen Menschen: ein Beitrag der Pollenanalyse, in: H. Küster (ed.), 125-137.

Kalis, A.J. / A. Zimmermann 1988: An integrative model for the use of different landscapes in Linearbandkeramik times, in J. Bintliff / D.A. Davidson / E.C. Grant (eds.), 145-152.

Kalis, A.J. / J. Meurers-Balke (eds.) 1993: *7000 Jahre bäuerliche Landschaft: Entstehung, Erforschung, Erhaltung*, Köln (Archaeo-Physika, 13).

Kalis, A.J. / J. Meurers-Balke 1988: Wirkungen neolithischer Wirtschaftsweisen in Pollendiagrammen, *Archäologische Informationen* 11, 39-53.

Kalma, J.J / J.J. Spahr van der Hoek / K. de Vries (eds.) 1968: *Geschiedenis van Friesland*, Drachten.

Kampffmeyer, U., 1983: Der neolithische Siedlungsplatz Hüde I am Dümmer, in: G. Wegner (ed.), 119-134.

Kampffmeyer, U., 1991: *Die Keramik der Siedlung Hüde I am Dümmer, Untersuchungen zur Neolithisierung des Nordwestdeutschen Flachlandes*, Göttingen (Ph.D. thesis).

Karsten, P., 1994: *Att kasta yxan i sjön*, Stockholm (Acta Archaeologica Lundensia, 23).

Kars, E A.K. / H. Kars 1992: Natuursteen uit ijzertijdvindplaatsen in het Maasmondgebied, in: A.B. Döbken (ed.), 121-130.

Kars, H. (ed.) 1988: *Archeometrie in Nederland. Een overzicht. De mogelijkheden*, 's-Gravenhage.

Kars, H. (ed.) 1990: *Archeometrie in Nederland – wat voorbeelden*, Amersfoort (NAR, 9).

Karsten, J.W., 1819: Verslag wegens het oude planken voetpad tusschen ter Apel en Valthe, *Algemeene Konst- en Letterbode*, 3-20.

Kasteleijn, H.W., 1982: Archeozoölogische vondsten van de opgraving in Oldeboorn 1980, Groningen (internal report GIA).

Keeley, L.H., 1978: Preliminary microwear analysis of the Meer assemblage, in: F. Van Noten (ed.), 73-86.

Keeley, L.H. / D. Cahen 1989: Early Neolithic forts and villages in NE Belgium: a preliminary report, *Journal of Field Archaeology* 16, 157-176.

Kelly, R.L., 1992: Mobility/sedentism concepts, archaeological measures and effects, *Annual Review of Anthropology* 21, 43-66.

Kersten, W., 1948: Die Niederrheinische Grabhügelkultur, *Bonner Jahrbücher* 148, 5-81.

Ketelaar, F.C.J. (ed.) 1987: *De historie herzien; vijfde bundel 'Historische Avonden'*, Hilversum.

Kielman, D., 1986: The postholes of Kolhorn (Northern site): preliminary data analysis and pattern recognition, in: H. Fokkens / P.M. Banga / M. Bierma (eds.), 21-36.

Klein, R.G., 1973: *Ice-Age Hunters of the Ukraine*, Chicago.

Klok, R.H.J., 1979: Ontmoetingen met onze vroegste cultuurhistorie: prehistorische grafheuvels op de Veluwe (2), *Tijdschrift van de Koninklijke Nederlandsche Heide Maatschappij* 90, 18-32.

Klok, R.H.J., 1988: Prehistoric barrows on the Veluwe, BROB 32, 1-91.

Knip, A.S., 1974: Late Neolithic skeleton finds from Molenaarsgraaf (Z.H.), in: L.P. Louwe Kooijmans, 379-395.

Knippels, B., 1991: Bewoningssporen uit de IJzertijd te Maastricht-Randwyck, *Archeologie in Limburg* 49, 43-48.

Knöll, H., 1959: *Die Nordwestdeutsche Tiefstichkeramik und ihre Stellung im Nord- und Mitteleuropäischen Neolithikum*, Münster.

Knörzer, K.-H., 1991: Deutschland nördlich der Donau, in: W. van Zeist / K. Wasylikowa / K.-E. Behre (eds.), 189-206.

Knol, E., 1983: Farming on the banks of the river Aa. The faunal remains and bone objects of Paddepoel 200 BC – 250 AD. *Palaeohistoria* 25, 145-182.

Knol, E., 1991: Op weg naar systematisch terpenonderzoek; 1897-1913, *Jaarverslagen van de Vereniging voor Terpenonderzoek* 75, 69-85.

Knol, E., 1993: *De Noordnederlandse kustlanden in de vroege middeleeuwen*, Groningen (Ph.D. thesis VU).

Kobusiewicz, M., 1983: Le problème des contacts des peuples du Paléolithique final de la plaine européenne avec le territoire français, *Bulletin de la Societé Préhistorique Française* 80, 308-321.

Körber-Grohne, U. (ed.) 1980: *Festschrift Maria Hopf*, Bonn (Archaeo-Physika, 8).

Körner, G. / F. Laux 1980: *Ein Königreich an der Luhe*, Lüneburg.

Kolfschoten, T. van, 1981: On the Holsteinian? and Saalian mammal fauna from the ice-pushed ridge near Rhenen (the Netherlands), *MRGD* 35, 223-251.

Kolfschoten, T. van, 1990: The evolution of the mammal fauna in the Netherlands and the Middle Rhine area (Western Germany) during the late Middle Pleistocene, *MRGD* 43(3), 1-69.

Kolfschoten, T. van / W. Roebroeks (eds.) 1985: Maastricht-Belvédère: stratigraphy, palaeoenvironment and archaeology of the Middle and Late Pleistocene deposits, *MRGD* 39, 1-121.

Kolfschoten, T. van / W. Roebroeks / J. Vandenberghe 1993: The Middle and Late Pleistocene sedimentary and climatic sequence at Maastricht-Belvédère: the type locality of the Belvédère Interglacial, *MRGD* 47, 81-91.

Kolstrup, E., 1982: Late-glacial pollen diagrams from Hjelm and Draved Mose (Denmark) with a suggestion of drought during the Earlier Dryas, *Review of palaeobotany and palynology* 36, 35-63.

Kooi, P.B., 1979: *Pre-Roman urnfields in the north of the Netherlands*, Groningen (Ph.D. thesis).

Kooi, P.B., 1982: *De urnenvelden in Drenthe*, Assen (Museumfonds Publicatie, 7).

Kooi, P.B., 1983a: A remarkable Iron Age grave in Darp (municipality of Havelte, the Netherlands), *OMROL* 64, 197-208.

Kooi, P.B., 1983b: Leven langs de Fivel, van Helwerd tot Zwart Lap, in: *Middelstum-Kantens. Bijdragen tot de plattelandsgeschiedenis met een beschrijving van de boerderijen en hun bewoners*, Kantens, 9-35.

Kooi, P.B., 1991: Een nederzetting uit de midden-bronstijd op het Huidbergsveld bij Dalen, *NDV* 108, 104-117.

Kooi, P.B., 1991-'92: Project Peelo – Het onderzoek in de jaren 1977, 1978 en 1979 op de es, *Palaeohistoria* 33/34, 165-285.

Kooi, P.B. / G.J. de Langen 1987: Bewoning in de vroege ijzertijd op het Kleuvenveld te Peelo, gem. Assen, *NDV* 104, 151-165.

Kooistra, L.I., 1990: *Houtskoolanalyse van een grafveld te Deventer uit de Vroege IJzertijd*, Amersfoort (ROB internal reports, 1990/2).

Koot, C.W., 1993: Midden-Delfland 2: Maasland, Duifpolder (vindplaatsen 11.17 en 11.07), in: W.A.M. Hessing 1993c, 331-332.

Koot, C.W. / C. Vermeeren 1993: Natural wood resources and human demand: use of wood in Iron Age houses in the wetlands of Midden-Delfland, *APL* 26, 99-110.

Koot, J.M., 1994: *In kannen en kruiken, veertig jaar archeologisch onderzoek in Rijswijk*, Rijswijk (Rijswijkse Historische Reeks, 11).

Koot, H. / B. van der Have 2001: *Graven in Rijswijk. De Steentijdmensen van Ypenburg*, Rijswijk.

Kortlang, F., 1987: *De Dommelvallei. Een archeologische inventarisatie*, 's-Hertogenbosch.

Kortlang, F., 1999: The Iron Age urnfield and settlement from Someren-'Waterdael', in: F. Theuws / N. Roymans (eds.), 133-197.

Kossack, G. / K.-E. Behre / P. Schmid (eds.) 1984: *Archäologische und naturwissenschaftliche Untersuchungen an ländlichen und frühstädtischen Siedlungen im deutschen Küstengebiet vom 5.Jahrhundert v.Chr. bis zum 11.Jahrhundert n.Chr.*, 1: *Ländliche Siedlungen*, Weinheim.

Kossack, G. / O. Harck / J. Reichstein (eds.) 1987: *Archsum auf Sylt*, 2: *Landwirtschaft und Umwelt in vor- und frühgeschichtlicher Zeit*, Mainz am Rhein (Römisch-Germanische Forschungen, 44).

Kosse, K., 1990: Group size and social complexity: thresholds in the long-term memory, *Journal of Anthropological Archaeology* 9, 275-303.

Koster, E A. 1992: Duin- en dekzandvorming in 'koude woestijnen', *Grondboor & Hamer* 4/5/6, 81-92.

Kozlowski, J.K. (ed.), 1990: *Feuilles de pierre; les industries à pointes foliacées du Paléolithique supérieur européen*, Liège (ERAUL, 42).

Kozlowski, S.K. (ed.) 1973: *The Mesolithic in Europe*, Warsaw.

Kozlowski, S.K., 1975: *Cultural differentiation of Europe from 10th to 5th millenium BC*, Warsaw.

Kramer-Clobus, G.M.C., 1978: L.J.F. Janssen (1806-1869): an inventory of his notes on archaeological findspots in the Netherlands, BROB 28, 441-544.

Kramer, E. / P. Houtsma / J. Schilstra 1985: The Creswellian site Siegerswoude II (Gemeente Opsterland, province of Friesland, the Netherlands), *Palaeohistoria* 27, 67-88.

Krause, A., 1988: *Die endneolithische und frühbronzezeitliche Grabfunde von Singen am Hohentwiel I*, Stuttgart (Forschungen und Berichte zur Vor- und Frühgeschichte in Baden-Württemberg, 32).

Krause, E.-B., 1989: Zur Hallstattzeit an Mosel, Mittel- und Niederrhein – Kulturelle Beziehungen zwischen der Laufelder Gruppe und dem Niederrhein während der frühen Eisenzeit, in: M. Ulrix-Closset / M. Otte (eds.), 93-110.

Krause, E.-B. / B. Mecke (eds.) 1992: *Ur-Geschichte im Ruhrgebiet* (Festschrift Arno Heinrich), Bottrop.

Kreuz, A.M., 1991: *Die ersten Bauern Mitteleuropas – eine archäobotanische Untersuchung zu Umwelt und Landwirtschaft der ältesten Bandkeramik*, Leiden (Ph.D. thesis; = APL 23 [1990]).

Kristiansen, K., 1984: Krieger und Häuptlinge in der Bronzezeit Dänemarks, *Jahrbuch des Römisch-Germanischen Zentralmuseums Mainz* 31, 187-209.

Kristiansen, K., 1989: Prehistoric migrations – The case of the Single Grave and Corded Ware cultures, *Journal of Danish Archaeology* 8, 211-225.

Kristiansen, K. / C. Paludan-Müller (eds.) 1978: *New directions in Scandinavian archaeology*, Kopenhagen.

Kroezenga, P., *et al.* 1991: Vondsten van de Swifterbantcultuur uit het Voorste Diep bij Bronneger (Dr.), *Paleo-aktueel* 2, 32-36.

Kroll, H.J., 1987: Vor- und frühgeschichtliche Ackerbau in Archsum auf Sylt: Eine botanische Grossrestanalyse, in: G. Kossack / O. Harck / J. Reichstein (eds.), 51-158.

Kromer, B. / B. Becker 1993: German oak and pine ¹⁴C calibration, 7200-9439 BC, *Radiocarbon* 35, 231-237.

Krüger, B., *et al.* 1988⁵: *Die Germanen, I: Von den Anfängen bis zum 2. Jahrhundert unserer Zeitrechnung*, Berlin.

Kruk, J., 1980: *The Neolithic settlement of Southern Poland*, Oxford (BAR International Series, 93).

Kuijper, W.J., 1981: Molluscs, in: G.F. IJzereef, 127-130.

Kunwald, G., 1970: Der Moorfund im Rappendam, Seeland, Dänemark, in: H. Jankuhn (ed.), *Vorgeschichtliche Heiligtümer und Opferplätze in Mittel- und Nord-Europa*, Göttingen (Abhandlungen der Akademie der Wissenschaften in Göttingen, Philologisch-Historische Klasse, Dritte Folge, 74), 100-118.

Kuper, R., *et al.* 1974: Untersuchungen zur neolithischen Besiedlung der Aldenhovener Platte 4, *Bonner Jahrbücher* 174, 424-508.

Kuper, R., *et al.* 1975: Untersuchungen zur neolithischen Besiedlung der Aldenhovener Platte 5, *Bonner Jahrbücher* 175, 191-230.

Kuper, R., *et al.* 1977: Der bandkeramische Siedlungsplatz Langweiler 9, *Rheinische Ausgrabungen* 18.

Kuper, R. / J. Lüning, 1985: Untersuchungen zur neolithischen Besiedlung der Aldenhovener Platte, in: *Ausgrabungen in Deutschland*, Teil I, Mainz, 85-97.

Küster, H. (ed.) 1988: *Der prähistorische Mensch und sein Umwelt, Festschrift für Udelgard Körber-Grohne zum 65. Geburtstag*, Stuttgart (Forschungen und Berichte zur Vor- und Frühgeschichte in Baden-Württemberg, 31).

Laet, S.J. De, 1974: *Prehistorische kulturen in het zuiden der Lage Landen*, Wetteren.

Laet, S.J. De (ed.) 1976: *Acculturation and continuity in Atlantic Europe, mainly during the Neolithic period and the Bronze Age; papers presented at the IV Atlantic Colloquium, Ghent 1975*, Brugge (Dissertationes Archaeologicae Gandenses, 16).

Laet, S.J. De, 1979²: *Prehistorische kulturen in het zuiden der Lage Landen*, Wetteren.

Laet, S.J. De (ed.) 1983: *Progrès récents dans l'étude du néolithique ancien*, Brugge.

Laet, S.J. De / W. Glasbergen 1959: *De voorgeschiedenis der Lage Landen*, Groningen.

Lambot, B., 1988: Les coupes à bord festonné du Bassin parisien et du Nord de la France, *Bulletin de la Société Archéologique Champenoise* 81, 31-83.

Langen, G.J. de / H.T. Waterbolk 1982-'88: De archeologie van Ezinge. De nederzettings- en onderzoeksgeschiedenis van een Gronings terpdorp, *Jaarverslagen van de Vereniging voor Terpenonderzoek* 66-72, 78-111.

Lanting, A.E., 1969: Iets over de grafgebruiken van de Standvoetbeker-cultuur, *NDV* 87, 165-178.

Lanting, J.N., 1969a: Twee grafheuvels in de Emmerdennen, gem. Emmen, *NDV* 87, 179-89.

Lanting, J.N., 1969b: Verspreiding en datering van wikkeldraadaardewerk, *NDV* 87, 191-210.

Lanting, J.N. 1973: Laat-Neolithicum en Vroege Bronstijd in Nederland en N.W.-Duitsland: continue ontwikkelingen, *Palaeohistoria* 15, 215-317.

Lanting, J.N., 1992: Aanvullende ¹⁴C-dateringen, *Paleo-aktueel* 3, 61-63.

Lanting, J.N. / W.G. Mook 1977: *The pre- and protohistory of the Netherlands in terms of radiocarbon dates*, Groningen.

Lanting, J.N. / J. van der Plicht 1993-'94: ¹⁴C-AMS: pros and cons for archaeology, *Palaeohistoria* 35/36, 1-12.

Lanting, J.N. / J. van der Plicht 1995-'96: De ¹⁴C-chronologie van de Nederlandse pre- en protohistorie, I: Laat-Paleolithicum, *Palaeohistoria* 37/38, 71-125.

Lanting, J.N. / J. van der Plicht 1997-'98: De ¹⁴C-chronologie van de Nederlandse pre- en protohistorie, II: Mesolithicum, *Palaeohistoria* 39/40, 99-162.

Lanting, J.N. / J. van der Plicht 1999-2000: De ¹⁴C-chronologie van de Nederlandse pre- en protohistorie, III: Neolithicum, *Palaeohistoria* 41/42, 1-110.

Lanting, J.N. / J. van der Plicht 2001-'02: De ¹⁴C-chronologie van de Nederlandse pre- en protohistorie, IV: bronstijd en vroege ijzertijd, *Palaeohistoria* 43/44, 117-262.

Lanting, J.N. / A. Ufkes 1989: Klokbekervondsten bij Dalen (Dr.), *Paleo-aktueel* 1, 45-47.

Lanting, J.N. / J.D. van der Waals 1974: Oudheidkundig onderzoek bij Swalmen. I. De praehistorie, opgravingen in de jaren 1936-38 en 1968-73, *OMROL* 55, 1-111.

Lanting, J.N. / J.D. van der Waals 1976a: Beaker cultures in the Lower Rhine Basin, in: J.N. Lanting / J.D. van der Waals (eds.), 1-80.

Lanting, J.N. / J.D. van der Waals (eds.) 1976b: *Glockenbecher Symposium Oberried 1974*, Haarlem.

Larsson, L., 1983: Mesolithic settlement on the sea floor in the Strait of Öresund, in: P.M. Masters / N.C. Flemming (eds.), 283-301.

Larsson, L. 1984: The Skateholm Project – A late Mesolithic settlement and cemetery complex at a South Swedish Bay, *Meddelanden fran Lunds Universitets Historiska Museum* 1983-1984, 5-38.

Larsson, L., 1990: Dogs in fraction – symbols in action, in: P.M. Vermeersch / P. Van Peer (eds.), 153-160.

Larsson, L. et al. (eds.) 2003: *Mesolithic on the move. Papers presented at the Sixth International Conference on the Mesolithic in Europe, Stockholm 2000*, Oxford.

Lauwerier, R.C.G.M. / G.F. IJzereef 1994: Vee en vlees in de nederzettingen in Oss-Ussen (800 v.Chr.-250 na Chr.), in: K. Schinkel, 233-243.

Lauwers, R., 1988: Le gisement Tjongerien de Rekem (Belgique). Premier bilan d'une analyse spatiale, in: M. Otte (ed.), 217-234.

Laux, F., 1971: *Die Bronzezeit in der Lüneburgerheide*, Hildesheim (Veröffentlichungen der urgeschichtlichen Sammlungen des Landesmuseums zu Hannover, 18).

Laux, F., 1989, Zur älteren und mittleren Bronzezeit in Niedersachsen, in: *Beiträge zur mitteleuropäischen Bronzezeit*, Berlin, 275-294.

Leach, F. / J. Davidson (eds.) 1981: *Archaeological studies of Pacific stone sources*, Oxford (BAR International Series, 104).

Leacock, E.B. / R.B. Lee (eds.) 1982: *Politics and history in band societies*, Cambridge.

Lech, J., 1990: The organization of silicious rock supplies to the Danubian early farming communities (LBK): Central European examples, in: D. Cahen / M. Otte (eds.), 51-60.

Lee, R.B, 1992: Art, science or politics? The crisis in hunter-gatherer studies, *American Anthropologist* 94, 31-54.

Lee, R.B. / I. DeVore (eds.) 1968: *Man the hunter*, Chicago.

Leeuw, S.E. van der / A.J. Spruijt / V.A. Shelton-Bunn 1987: Ceramic production, in: R.W. Brandt et al. (eds.), 225-264.

Leeuwaarden, W. van, 1982: *Palynological and macropalaeobotanical studies in the development of the vegetation mosaic in eastern Noord-Brabant (The Netherlands) during Late-Glacial and Early Holocene times*, Utrecht (Ph.D. thesis).

Lehmann, L.Th., 1963: Het partiële onderzoek van tumulus 1 in de gemeente Enkhuizen, *West-Frieslands Oud en Nieuw* 30, 234-242.

Lehmann, L.Th., 1965: Placing the potbeaker, *Helinium* 5, 3-31.

Lehmkühler, S., 1991: Heiratskreise in der Vorgeschichte, *Archäologische Informationen* 14, 155-159.

Leman-Delerive, G. (ed.) 1990: *Les Celtes en France du Nord et en Belgique VIer-Ier siècle avant J.-C.*, Valenciennes.

Leroi-Gourhan, A., 1982: *The dawn of European art*, Cambridge.

Leroi-Gourhan, A., 1983: Une tête de sagaie à armature de lamelles de silex à Pincevent (Seine-et-Marne), *Bulletin de la Société Préhistorique Française* 80, 154-156.

Leroi-Gourhan, A. / M. Brézillon 1966: L'habitation magdalénienne no. 1 de Pincevent près Montereau (Seine-et-Marne), *Gallia Préhistoire* 9, 263-385.

Leroi-Gourhan, A. / M. Brézillon 1972: *Fouilles de Pincevent, essai d'analyse ethnographique d'un habitat magdalénien*, Paris (Gallia Préhistoire, suppl. 7).

Leroi-Gourhan, A. / R.M. Jacobi 1986: Analyse pollinique et matériel archéologique de Gough's Cave (Cheddar, Somerset), *Bulletin de la Société Préhistorique Française* 83, 83-90.

Leroi-Gourhan, A., et al. 1979: *Lascaux inconnu*, Paris (Gallia Préhistoire, suppl. 12).

Lévêque, F. / B. Vandermeersch 1980: Découverte de restes humains dans un niveau castelperronien à Saint-Césaire (Charente-Maritime), *Comptes rendus de l'académie des sciences de Paris*, series 2, 291, 187-189.

Lévi-Strauss, C., 1962: *La pensée sauvage*, Paris.

Levy, J.E., 1982: *Social and religious organization in Bronze Age Denmark – An analysis of ritual hoard finds*, Oxford (BAR International Series, 124).

Lewin, R., 1994: Human origins: the challenge of Java's skulls, *New Scientist* 1924 (7 May 1994), 36-40.

Lier, J. van, 1760: *Oudheidkundige brieven : bevattende eene verhandeling over de manier van begraven, en over de lykbusschen, wapenen, veld- en eertekens, der oude omslag, Germanen, en in het byzonder de beschryving van eenen alouden steenen grafkelder, met de daarin gevondene lykbusschen, donderkeilen en donderbylen, enz. by het boerschap Eext, in het landschap Drenthe, ontdekt : in welke beschryvinge zekere brief, over byzondere Nederlandsche oudheden, zo opgehelderd als wederlegd word*, 's-Gravenhage.

Liere, W.J. van, 1948: *De bodemgesteldheid van het Westland*, Wageningen (De bodemkartering van Nederland, 2).

Liversage, D., 2001: Riddles of the ribs, in: W.H. Metz / B.L. van Beek / H. Steegstra (eds.), 377-398.

Liversage, D. / M. Liversage 1989: A method for the study of the composition of early copper and bronze artifacts. An example from Denmark, *Helinium* 29, 42-76.

Lock, G. / Z. Stančič (eds.) 1995: *Archaeology and Geographical Information Systems: A European Perspective*, London.

Löbert, H.W., 1982: Die Keramik der vorrömischen Eisenzeit und der römischen Kaiserzeit von Hatzum/Boomborg (Kr. Leer), in: *Probleme der Küstenforschung im südlichen Nordseegebiet*, 14, Hildesheim, 11-122.

Loecker, D. De, 1992: Site K: a Middle Palaeolithic site at Maastricht Belvédère (Limburg, The Netherlands), *Archäologisches Korrespondenzblatt* 22, 449-460.

Löhr, H., 1972: Betrachtungen zu den neolithischen Steingeräten der Aldenhovener Platte 1, in: Eckert *et al.* (eds.), 389-391.

Löhr, H., 1974: Betrachtungen zu den neolithischen Steingeräten der Aldenhovener Platte 2, in: Kuper *et al.* (eds.), 475-482.

Löhr, H., 1977: Betrachtungen zu den neolithischen Steingeräten der Aldenhovener Platte 3, in: U. Boelicke *et al.* (eds.), 533-544.

Löhr, H., 1979: *Der Magdalenien-Fundplatz Alsdorf, Kreis Aachen-Land; ein Beitrag zur Kenntnis der funktionalen Variabilität jungpaläolithischer Stationen*, Tübingen (Ph.D. thesis).

Loewe, G., 1971: *Kreis Kempen-Krefeld*, Düsseldorf (Archäologische Funde und Denkmäler des Rheinlandes, 3).

Loftus, J., 1984: Der spätpaläolithische Fundplatz Niederbieber Fläche 33 / 32-38 / 39, Köln (internal report).

Loftus, J., 1985: Der spätpaläolithische Fundplatz Niederbieber Fläche 64 / 74-81 / 77, Köln (internal report).

Lohof, E., 1991: *Grafritueel en sociale verandering in de bronstijd van Noordoost-Nederland*, Amsterdam (Ph.D. thesis UvA).

Lohof, E., 1992: Hoofdmannen in de bronstijd van Noord-Nederland?, *Profiel* 4-4, 16-24.

Lohof, E., 1994: Tradition and change. Burial practices in the Late Neolithic and Bronze Age in the north-eastern Netherlands, *Archaeological Dialogues* 1, 98-118.

Londen, H. van, 1992: Midden-Delfland 8: Maasland, Oude Campsweg, in: W.A.M. Hessing, 358-359.

Loon, A.J. van, 1982: Problems of Holocene lithostratigraphy; with examples from the central Netherlands, *Geologie en Mijnbouw* 60, 353-361.

Louwe Kooijmans, L.P., 1970-'71: Mesolithic bone and antler implements from the North Sea and the Netherlands, BROB 20-21, 27-73.

Louwe Kooijmans, L.P., 1974: *The Rhine/Meuse Delta; four studies on its prehistoric occupation and Holocene geology*, Leiden (Ph.D. thesis; = OMROL 53-54 [1972-1973] en APL 7 [1974]).

Louwe Kooijmans, L.P., 1976a: Local developments in a borderland, OMROL 57, 227-298.

Louwe Kooijmans, L.P., 1976b: The Neolithic at the Lower Rhine – Its structure in chronological and geographical respect, in: S.J. De Laet (ed.), 150-173.

Louwe Kooijmans, L.P., 1980: The Middle Neolithic assemblage of Het Vormer near Wijchen and the culture pattern around the Southern North Sea, OMROL 61, 113-208.

Louwe Kooijmans, L.P., 1983a: Tussen SOM en TRB, enige gedachten over het laat-neolithicum in Nederland en België, *Bulletin des Musées Royaux d'art et d'histoire* 54, 55-67.

Louwe Kooijmans, L.P., 1983b: *De autheuren der antiquiteten*, Leiden (speech).

Louwe Kooijmans, L.P., 1985: *Sporen in het land; de Nederlandse delta in de prehistorie*, Amsterdam.

Louwe Kooijmans, L.P., 1986: Het loze vissertje of boerke Naas? Het een en ander over het leven van de steentijdbewoners van het Rijnmondgebied, in: M.C. van Trierum / H.E. Henkes (eds.), 7-25.

Louwe Kooijmans, L.P., 1987: Neolithic settlement and subsistence in the wetlands of the Rhine/ Meuse delta of the Netherlands, in: J.M. Coles / A.J. Lawson (eds.), 227-251.

Louwe Kooijmans, L.P., 1988: Een Rössen-nederzetting te Maastricht-Randwyck, *Notae Praehistoricae* 8, 67-71.

Louwe Kooijmans, L.P., 1990: Bronstijdstrijd, slachtoffers van een oeroorlog, *Natuur en techniek* 58, 748-759.

Louwe Kooijmans, L.P., 1991-'92: An Early Bandkeramic settlement and a Roman cremation cemetery at Geleen-Janskamper Veld, *Notae Praehistoricae* 11, 63-65.

Louwe Kooijmans, L.P., 1993a: Wetland exploitation and upland relations of prehistoric communities in the Netherlands, in: J. Gardiner (ed.), 71-116.

Louwe Kooijmans, L.P., 1993b: The Mesolithic/Neolithic transformation in the Lower Rhine Basin, in: P. Bogucki (ed.), 95-145.

Louwe Kooijmans, L.P., 1993c: An Early/Middle Bronze Age multiple burial at Wassenaar, the Netherlands, APL 26, 1-20.

Louwe Kooijmans, L.P., 1995: Prehistory or paradise? Prehistory as a reference for modern nature development, the Dutch case, MRGD 52, 415-424 (= M. Cox / V. Straker / D. Taylor (eds.), 3-17).

Louwe Kooijmans, L.P., 1998: Understanding the Mesolithic/Neolithic Frontier in the Lower Rhine Basin, 5300-4300 cal. BC, in: M. Edmonds / C. Richards (eds.), 407-427.

Louwe Kooijmans, L.P. (ed.) 2001a: Hardinxveld-Giessendam, Polderweg. Een jachtkamp uit het Laat-Mesolithicum, 5500-5000 v. Chr., Amersfoort (RAM, 83).

Louwe Kooijmans, L.P. (ed.) 2001b: Hardinxveld-Giessendam, De Bruin. Een jachtkamp uit het Laat-Mesolithicum en het begin van de Swifterbant-cultuur, 5500-4450 v. Chr. Amersfoort (RAM, 85).

Louwe Kooijmans, L.P., 2003: The Hardinxveld sites in the Rhine/Meuse delta, 5500-4450 cal BC, in: Larsson et al. (eds.), 608-624.

Louwe Kooijmans, L.P. / H. Kamermans / I.A. Schute 1992: Bandkeramische nederzetting, IJzertijdsporen en een Romeins crematiegrafveld op het Janskamperveld te Geleen, in: H. Stoepker (ed.), 250-255.

Louwe Kooijmans, L.P. / E. Smits 1985: Wessem, in: W.J.H. Willems, 165-167.

Louwe Kooijmans, L.P. / L.B.M. Verhart 1990: Een middenneolithisch nederzettingsterrein en een kuil van de Stein-groep op de voormalige Kraaienberg bij Linden, gemeente Beers (N.Br.), OMROL 70, 49-108.

Lowe, J.J. / J.M. Gray 1980: The stratigraphic subdivision of the Lateglacial of Northwestern Europe: a discussion, in: J.J. Lowe / J.M. Gray / J.E. Robinson (eds.), 157-175.

Lowe, J.J. / J.M. Gray / J.E. Robinson (eds.) 1980: Studies in the Lateglacial of North-West Europe, Oxford.

Lubbock, J. (Lord Avebury) 1865: Prehistoric times, as illustrated by ancient remains, and the manners and customs of modern savages, London.

Lüning, J., 1968: Die Michelsberger Kultur. Ihre Funde in zeitlicher und räumlicher Gliederung, Berichte der Römisch-Germanischen Kommission 48, 1-350.

Lüning, J. (ed.) 1972: Die Anfänge des Neolithikums vom Orient bis Nordeuropa, Tiel 5a: westliches Mitteleuropa, Köln (Fundamenta Reihe A, Band 3).

Lüning, J. (ed.), 1978: Untersuchungen zur neolithischen Besiedlung der Aldenhovener Platte 8, Bonner Jahrbücher 178, 299-362.

Lüning, J. (ed.), 1980a: Untersuchungen zur neolithischen Besiedlung der Aldenhovener Platte 10, Bonner Jahrbücher 180, 275-303.

Lüning, J., 1980b: So bauten die Zimmerleute der Steinzeit, Bild der Wissenschaften 8, 44-59.

Lüning, J., 1982a: Research into the bandkeramik settlement of the Aldenhovener Platte in the Rhineland, APL 15, 1-31.

Lüning, J., 1982b: Siedlung und Siedlungslandschaft in Bandkeramischer und Rössener Zeit, Offa 39, 9-33.

Lüning, J., 1988a: Zur Verbreitung und Datierung bandkeramischer Erdwerke, Archäologisches Korrespondenzblatt 18, 155-158.

Lüning, J., 1988b: Frühe Bauern in Mitteleuropa im 6. und 5. Jahrtausend v.Chr., Jahrbuch des Römisch-Germanischen Zentralmuseums Mainz 35, 27-93.

Lüning, J. / U. Kloos / S. Albert 1989: Westliche Nachbarn der bandkeramischen Kultur: die Keramikgruppen La Hoguette und Limburg, Germania 67, 350-420.

Lüning, J. / P. Stehli 1989: Die Bandkeramik in Mitteleuropa: von der Natur- zur Kulturlandschaft, Spektrum der Wissenschaft April 1989, 78-90.

Luttropp, A. / G. Bosinski 1971: Der altsteinzeitliche Fundplatz Reutersruh bei Ziegenhain in Hessen, Köln.

Maarleveld, Th.J., 1985: Been en tand als grondstof in de Vlaardingen-cultuur, Leiden (internal report FdAL).

MacNeish, R.S., 1991: *The origins of agriculture and settled life*, Norman.

Madsen, T., 1982: Settlement systems of early agricultural societies in east Jutland, Denmark: a regional study of change, *Journal of Anthropological Archaeology* 1, 197-236.

Madsen, T., 1986: Where did all the hunters go? An assessment of an epoch-making episode in Danish prehistory, *Journal of Danish Archaeology* 5, 229-247.

Magendans, J.R., 1987: Zand erover, in: M. Janssen / L. van der Valk (eds.), 23-26.

Malinowski, B., 1922: *Argonauts of the Western Pacific. An account of native enterprise and adventure in the archipelagoes of Melanesian New Guinea*, London (reprint 1992).

Malmer, M.P., 1981: *A chorological study of North European rock art*, Stockholm (Antikvariska Serien, 32).

Mannion, A.M., 1991: *Global environmental change – A natural and cultural environmental history*, Harlow, Essex.

Mariën, M.E., 1987: *Het vorstengraf van Eigenbilzen*, Tongeren (Publikaties van het Provinciaal Gallo-Romeins Museum Tongeren, 37).

Masters, P.M. / N.C. Flemming (eds.) 1983: *Quartenary coastlines and marine archaeology*, New York.

Masuch, A. / K.H. Ziessow 1985: Reconstructing Linear Culture houses: theoretical and practical contributions, *Helinium* 25, 58-93.

Mauser, P.F., 1970: *Die jungpaläolithische Höhlenstation Petersfels im Hegau*, (Badener Fundberichte, Sonderheft 13).

Mauss, M., 1950: *The gift. The form and reason for exchange in archaic societies*, London (reprint 1990).

McBryde, I. / D. Harrison 1981: Valued good or valuable stone? Consideration of the distribution of greenstone artefacts in south-eastern Australia, in: F. Leach / J. Davidson (eds.), 183-208.

McCormick, F., 1987: *Stockrearing in Early Christian Ireland*, Belfast (Ph.D. thesis The Queen's University of Belfast).

McCormick, F., 1992: Early faunal evidence for dairying, *Oxford Journal of Archaeology* 11, 201-209.

Meehan, B. / R. Jones (eds.): *Archaeology with ethnography: an Australian perspective*, Canberra.

Meer, J.J.M. van der (ed.) 1987: *Tills and glaciotectonics*, Rotterdam.

Meier Arendt, W., 1966: *Die bandkeramische Kultur im Untermaingebiet*, Bonn.

Meijer, T., 1985: The pre-Weichselian non-marine molluscan fauna from Maastricht-Belvédère (Southern-Limburg, The Netherlands), *MRGD* 39-1, 75-104.

Meijlink, B.H.M.F., 2001: The barrow of 'De Bogen', in: W.H. Metz / B.L. van Beek / H. Steegstra (eds.), 405-430.

Meijlink, B.H.F.M., 2002: Ouderwets puzzelen: een gecompliceerde grafheuvel op 'de Bogen', in: H. Fokkens / R. Jansen (eds.), 207-232.

Meijlink, B.H.F.M. / P. Kranendonk 2002: *Boeren, erven en graven. De boerengemeenschap van De Bogen bij Meteren (2450-1250 v.Chr.)*, Amersfoort (RAM, 87).

Meiklejohn, C., 1978: Ecological aspects of population size and growth in the Late-Glacial and early Postglacial north-western Europe, in: P. Mellars (ed.), 65-79.

Meiklejohn, C. / T.S. Constandse-Westermann 1978: The human skeletal material from Swifterbant, Earlier Neolithic of the Northern Netherlands, *Palaeohistoria* 20, 39-89.

Mellars, P.A. 1970: An antler harpoon-head of 'Obanian' affinities from Whitburn, County Durham, *Archaeologia Aeliana* 48, 337-346.

Mellars, P.A., 1973: The character of the Middle-Upper Palaeolithic transition in Southwest France, in: C. Renfrew (ed.), 255-276.

Mellars, P.A., 1976: Fire ecology, animal populations and man: a study of some sociological relationships in prehistory, *PPS* 42, 15-45.

Mellars, P.A. (ed.), 1978: *The Early Postglacial settlement of Northern Europe*, London.

Mellars, P.A., 1989: Major issues in the emergence of modern humans, *Current Anthropology* 30, 349-385.

Mellars, P.A. (ed.), 1990: *The emergence of modern humans; an archaeological perspective*. Edinburgh.

Mellars, P.A. / C. Stringer (eds.) 1989: *The human revolution; behavioural and biological perspectives on the origins of modern humans*, Edinburgh.

Meltzer, D., 1993: *Search for the first Americans*, Washington DC.

Méniel, P., 1992: *Les sacrifices d'animaux chez les Gaulois*, Paris.

Mensch, P.J.A. van, 1975: Dierenresten uit de polder Achthoven (gem. Leiderdorp), *Westerheem* 24, 111-116.

Metz, W.H. / B.L. van Beek / H. Steegstra (eds.) 2001: *Patina – Essays presented to Jay Jordan Butler on the occasion of his 80th birthday*, Groningen/Amsterdam.

Metzler, J., *et al.* (eds.), 1995: *Integration in the Early Roman West – The role of culture and ideology*, Luxembourg (Dossiers d'Archéologie du Musée National d'Histoire et d'Art, 4).

Meurers-Balke, J., 1981: Steinzeitlicher Aalstecher. Zur funktionalen Deutung einer Holzgerätform, *Offa* 38, 131-151.

Meurers-Balke, J., 1985: Experimente zum Anbau und zur Verarbeitung prähistorischer Getreidearten, *Archäologische Informationen* 8, 8-17.

Meyer-Christian, W., 1976: Die Y-Pfostenstellung in Häusern der älteren Linearbandkeramik, *Bonner Jahrbücher* 176, 125.

Midgley, M.S., 1992: *TRB culture. The first farmers of the North European Plain*, Edingburgh.

Miedema, M., 1983: *Vijfentwintig eeuwen bewoning van het terpenland ten noordwesten van Groningen*, Amsterdam (Ph.D. thesis).

Milikowski, E., 1985: Archeologische luchtkartering van het gebied Eersel-Riethoven-Bergeijk in de Kempen, in: J. Slofstra / H.H. van Regteren Altena / F. Theuws (eds.), 79-85.

Miller, D. / C. Tilley (eds.) 1984: *Ideology, power and prehistory*, Cambridge.

Milojkovic, J. / D.C. Brinkhuizen 1984: Bones from a terp remnant near Kimswerd, *Helinium* 24, 240-246.

Minc, L.D., 1986: Scarcity and survival: The role of oral tradition in mediating subsistence crises, *Journal of Anthropological Archaeology* 5, 39-113.

Minc, L.D. / K.P. Smith 1989: The spirit of survival: Cultural responses to resource variability in North Alaska, in: P. Halstead / J. O'Shea (eds.), 8-39.

Mithen, S., 1994: From domain specific to generalized intelligence: a cognitive interpretation of the Middle/Upper Palaeolithic transition, in: C. Renfrew / E.B.W. Zubrow (eds.), 29-39.

Modderman, P.J.R., 1945: *Over de wording en de beteekenis van het Zuiderzeegebied*, Groningen (Ph.D. thesis).

Modderman, P.J.R., 1949: Enkele aantekeningen over de bewoningsgeschiedenis van het Westland, *Boor en Spade* 3, 201-212.

Modderman, P.J.R., 1953: Een neolithische woonplaats in de polder Vriesland onder Hekelingen (eiland Putten) (Zuid-Holland), *BROB* 4, 1-26.

Modderman, P.J.R., 1954: Grafheuvelonderzoek in Midden-Nederland, *BROB* 5, 7-44.

Modderman, P.J.R., 1955a: Woonsporen uit de bronstijd en de ijzertijd op de Margijnen Enk onder Deventer, *BROB* 6, 22-31.

Modderman, P.J.R., 1955b: Laat bekeraardewerk met indrukken van een wikkeldraadstempel, *BROB* 6, 32-43.

Modderman, P.J.R., 1957: Een dodenhuis op de Gelpenberg bij Aalden, *NDV* 75, 19-22.

Modderman, P.J.R., 1958-'59: Die bandkeramische Siedlung von Sittard, *Palaeohistoria* 6/7, 33-120.

Modderman, P.J.R., 1960-'61a: De Spanjaardsberg; voor- en vroeghistorische boerenbedrijven te Santpoort, *BROB* 10-11, 210-262.

Modderman, P.J.R., 1960-'61b: Een polychroom versierde pot uit Bergeijk, Noord-Brabant, *BROB* 10-11, 548-551.

Modderman, P.J.R., 1960-'61c: Een slijpsteen bij Slenaken, *BROB* 10-11, 542-545.

Modderman, P.J.R., 1962-'63a: De verspreiding van de bekerculturen op de Veluwe, *BROB* 12-13, 7-24.

Modderman, P.J.R., 1962-'63b: Een grafheuvel met paarsgewijs gestelde palenkrans van het urnenveld op het Philips kampeerterrein, gem. Someren, Noord-Brabant, BROB 12-13, 571-575.

Modderman, P.J.R., 1964a: Middle bronze age graves and settlement traces at Zwaagdijk, gemeente Wervershoof, Prov. North-Holland, BROB 14, 27-36.

Modderman, P.J.R., 1964b: The chieftain's grave of Oss reconsidered, Bulletin van de Vereeniging tot Bevordering der Kennis van de Antieke Beschaving 39, 57-62.

Modderman, P.J.R., 1964c: The Neolithic burial vault at Stein, APL 1, 3-16.

Modderman, P.J.R., 1970: Linearbandkeramik aus Elsloo und Stein, APL 3.

Modderman, P.J.R., 1972: Die Hausbauten und Siedlungen der Linienbandkeramik in ihrem westlichen Bereich, in: J. Lüning (ed.), 77-84.

Modderman, P.J.R., 1974: Die Limburger Keramik von Kesseleyk, Archäologisches Korrespondenzblatt 4, 5-11.

Modderman, P.J.R., 1984: Intermediaire standgreppels in grafheuvels? Nee!, APL 17, 57-64.

Modderman, P.J.R., 1985: Die Bandkeramik im Graetheidegebiet, Niederländisch Limburg, Berichte der Römisch-Germanischen Kommission 66, 26-121.

Modderman, P.J.R., 1987: Limburger aardewerk uit Sweikhuizen, gem. Schinnen, prov. Limburg, APL 20, 87-94.

Modderman, P.J.R., 1988: The Linear Pottery Culture: diversity in uniformity, BROB 38, 63-140.

Modderman, P.J.R. / L.P. Louwe Kooijmans 1966: The Heibloem, a cemetery from the Late Bronze Age and Early Iron Age between Veldhoven and Steensel, prov. Noord-Brabant, APL 2, 9-26.

Modderman, P.J.R. / M.J.G.Th. Monforts 1991: Archeologische kroniek van Gelderland 1970-1984, Bijdragen en Mededelingen Vereniging Gelre 82, 143-188.

Mohen, J.-P., 1989: The world of megaliths, London.

Molen, J. van der / B. van Dijck 2000: The evolution of the Dutch and Belgian coasts and the role of sand supply from the North Sea, Global and planetary change 27, 223-244.

Montet-White, A. / S. Holen (eds.) 1991: Raw material economies among prehistoric hunter-gatherers, Lawrence (Kansas).

Mook, W.G. / H.T. Waterbolk 1985: Radiocarbon dating, Strasbourg (Handbooks for Archaeologists, 3).

Mook-Kamps, E. / S. Bottema 1987: Palynological investigations in the northern Netherlands (The Drenthe Plateau), Palaeohistoria 29, 169-172.

Moore, A.M.T., 1989: The transition from foraging to farming in Southwest Asia: present problems and future directions, in: D.R. Harris / G.C. Hillman (eds.), 620-631.

Mooren, S., 1993: Een vondstcomplex uit de Bischheimfase van de Rössen-cultuur te Ven-Zelderheide, Noord-Limburg, Leiden (internal report FdAL).

Mordant, D. / C. Mordant 1992: Noyen-sur-Seine: a mesolithic waterside settlement, in: B. Coles (ed.), 55-64.

Mortillet, G. de, 1903: Musée préhistorique: album de 105 planches, Paris.

Moss, E.H., 1983: The functional analysis of flint implements; Pincevent and Pont d'Ambon: two case studies from the French Final Palaeolithic, Oxford (BAR International Series, 296).

Moss, E.H., 1988: Techno-functional studies of the Hamburgian from Oldeholtwolde, Friesland, the Netherlands, in: M. Otte (ed.), 399-426.

Mourik, J.M. van (ed.) 1988: Landschap in beweging; ontwikkeling en bewoning van een stuifzandgebied in de Kempen, Amsterdam (Nederlandse Geografische Studies, 74).

Mulder, E.F.J. de / J.H.A. Bosch 1982: Holocene stratigraphy, radiocarbon datings and palaeogeography of central and northern North-Holland (The Netherlands), MRGD 36-3, 11-160.

Mulder, E.F.J. de, et al. (eds.) 2003: De ondergrond van Nederland, Groningen.

Murphy, P. / C. French (eds.) 1988: The exploitation of wetlands, Oxford (BAR British Series, 186).

Murray, T., 1988: Ethnoarchaeology or Palaeoethnology? in: B. Meehan / R. Jones (eds.), 1-16.

Musch, J.E., 1974: Reconstructie van een jong paleolithische wooneenheid in het Hoornseveld te Buinen, gem. Borger, NDV 91, 139-160.

Musch, J.E., 1981: Mesolithische behuizing uit Havelte, *Archaeologische Berichten* 9, 132-133.

Musée de préhistoire d'Ile-de-France, 1987: *Le feu apprivoisée; le feu dans la vie quotidienne des hommes préhistoriques*, Nemours.

Myers, A., 1989: Reliable and maintainable technological strategies in the Mesolithic of mainland Britain, in: R. Torrence (ed.), 78-91.

Narr, K.J., 1968: *Studien zur älteren und mittleren Steinzeit der niederen Lande*, Bonn (Antiquitas, Reihe 2, Band 7).

Needham, S., 1990: Middle Bronze Age ceremonial weapons from Oxborough, Norfolk and Essex/Kent, *Antiquaries Journal* 70, 239-252.

Neeley, M.P. / G.A. Clark, 1990: Measuring social complexity in European Mesolithic, in: P.M. Vermeersch / P. Van Peer (eds.), 127-137.

Neer, W. Van, 1982: Faunal analysis, in: P.M. Vermeersch (ed.), 143-144.

Neijenhuis, C., 1983: Huissens oudste bewoning, in: *Jaarverslag AWN-afdeling Nijmegen e.o. 1983*, 25-26.

Nenquin, J., 1961: *Salt – A study in economic prehistory*, Brugge (Dissertationes Archaeologicae Gandenses, 6).

Newell, R.R., 1970a: *The mesolithic affinities and typological relations of the Dutch Bandkeramik flint industry*, London (Ph.D. thesis).

Newell, R.R., 1970b: Een afslagbijl uit Anderen, Gem. Anloo en zijn relatie tot het Atlantisch Mesolithicum, *NDV* 88, 177-184.

Newell, R.R., 1970c: The flint industry of the Dutch Linearbandkeramik, in: P.J.R. Modderman, 144-183.

Newell, R.R., 1973: The Post-glacial adaptations of the indigenous people of the Northwest European Plain, in: S.K. Kozlowski (ed.), 399-440.

Newell, R.R., 1975: Mesolithicum, in: G.J. Verwers (ed.), 39-54.

Newell, R.R., 1980: Mesolithic dwelling structures: fact and fantasy, in: B. Gramsch (ed.), 235-284.

Newell, R.R., 1984: On the Mesolithic contribution to the social evolution of Western European society, in: J. Bintliff (ed.), 69-82.

Newell, R.R. / A.A. Dekin 1978: An integrative strategy for the definition of behaviorally meaningful archaeological units, *Palaeohistoria* 20, 7-38.

Newell, R.R. / A.P.J. Vroomans 1972: *Automatic artifact registration and systems for archaeological analysis with the Philips P1100 computer: a Mesolithic test-case*, Oosterhout.

Newell, R.R., et al. 1990: *An inquiry into the ethnic resolution of mesolithic regional groups: a study of their decorative ornaments in time and space*, Leiden.

Nielsen, P.O., 1977: Die Flintbeilen der frühen Trichterbecherkultur in Dänemark, *Acta Archaeologica* 48, 61-138.

Niklewicz-Hokse, A.T.L., 1990; Voorlopig verslag van het onderzoek naar de schelpconcentraties in de laat-Neolithische vindplaats Kolhorn, provincie Noord-Holland, in: A.T.L. Niklewicz-Hokse / C.A.G. Lagerwerf (eds.), 122-136.

Niklewicz-Hokse, A.T.L. / C.A.G. Lagerwerf (eds.) 1990: *Bundel van de steentijddag 1 april 1989*, Groningen.

Nio, S.-D. / R.T.E. Schüttenhelm / Tj. C.E. van Weering (eds.) 1981: *Holocene marine sedimentation in the North Sea Basin*, Oxford (Int. Ass. Sediment. Spec. Publ., 5).

Noort, G. van / A.M. Wouters 1987: De jagers/verzamelaars van de Ahrensburgkultuur, *Archaeologische Berichten* 18, 63-138.

Noten, F. Van (ed.) 1978: *Les chasseurs de Meer*, Brugge.

O'Connor, B., 1980: *Cross-Channel relations in the Later Bronze Age – Relations between Britain, North-Eastern France and the Low Countries during the Later Bronze Age and the Early Iron Age, with particular reference to the metalwork*, Oxford (BAR International Series, 91).

O'Kelly, M.J. / C.A. Shell 1979: Stone objects and a bronze axe from Newgrange, Co. Meath, in: M. Ryan (eds.), 127-144.

O'Shea, J. / M. Zvelebil 1984: Oleneostrovski mogilnik: reconstructing the social and economic organization of prehistoric foragers in northern Russia, *Journal of Anthroplogical Archaeology* 3, 1-40.

Obermaier, H., 1925: *Der Mensch der Vorzeit*, Berlin.

Odé, O., 1990: *Het gebruik van oker tijdens het Laat Paleolithicum en Mesolithicum*, Amsterdam (internal report AAC).

Odell, G.H., 1977: *The application of microwear analysis to the lithic component of an entire prehistoric settlement: methods, problems and functional reconstructions*, Cambridge (Ph.D. thesis Harvard University).

Odell, G.H., 1980: Toward a more behavioral approach to archaeological lithic concentrations, *American Antiquity* 45, 404-431.

Oele, E. / R.T.E. Schüttenhelm / A.J. Wiggers (eds.) 1979: *The Quaternary History of the North Sea*, Uppsala (Acta Univ. Ups., Symp. Univ. Ups. Annum Quingentesium Celebrantis, 2).

Oliva, M., 1990: La signification des pointes foliacées dans l'Aurignacien morave et dans le type de Miskovice, in: Kozlowski, J.K. (ed.), 223-232.

Oosting, W.A.J., 1936: *Bodemkunde en bodemkartering, in hoofdzaak van Wageningen en omgeving*, Wageningen (Ph.D. thesis).

Oppenheim, R., 1926: Neolithicum in stuifterreinen, *OMROL* 7, 90-91.

Oppenheim, R., 1929: Steinzeitliches aus Zuid-Limburg, *OMROL* Nieuwe Reeks 10, 21-29.

Orme, B., 1981: *Anthropology for archaeologists – an introduction*, Ithaca, New York.

Oswalt, W.H., 1976: *An anthropological analysis of foodgetting technology*, New York.

Ottaway, B.S. (ed.) 1983: *Archaeology, dendrochronology and the radiocarbon calibration curve*, Edinburgh (University of Edinburgh Occasional Paper, 9).

Otte, M., 1984: Le Paléolithique supérieur en Belgique, in: D. Cahen / P. Haesaerts (eds.), 157-179.

Otte, M., 1985: *Les industries à pointes foliacées et à pointes pédonculées dans le nord-ouest européen*, Viroinval (Artefacts, 2).

Otte, M. (ed.) 1988: *De la Loire à l'Oder. Les civilisations du Paléolithique final dans le Nord-Ouest européen*, Oxford (BAR International Series, 444).

Otte, M., 1990a: L'occupation moustérienne de Sclayn (Belgique), *Ethnographisch-Archäologische Zeitschrift* 31, 78-101.

Otte, M., 1990b: The northwestern European Plain around 18000 BP, in: O. Soffer / C. Gamble (eds.), 54-68.

Otte, M., et al. 1984: Maldegem et le paléolithique récent du nord-ouest européen, *Helinium* 24, 105-126.

Otterbein, K.F., 1969: *The evolution of war, a cross-cultural study*, New Haven (2nd ed. 1985).

Oude Rengerink, H., 1991: *De Rössen komen, een midden-neolithische needrzetting te Maastricht-Randwyck*, Leiden (internal report FdAL).

Oudemans, T.F.M. / J.J. Boon 1993: Traces of ancient vessel use: investigating prehistoric usage of four pot-types by organic residue analysis, using pyrolysis mass spectrometry, *APL* 26, 221-234.

Overmars, W., 1987: Ooibossen, een nieuw perspectief voor de uiterwaarden, in: D. de Bruin *et al.*, 47-58.

Paddayya, K., 1971: The Late Palaeolithic of the Netherlands – a review, *Helinium* 11, 257-270.

Pals, J.P., 1984: Plant remains from Aartswoud, a Neolithic settlement in the coastal area, in: W. van Zeist / W.A. Casparie (eds.), 313-322.

Pals J.P., 1988: *Phyto-archeologische studies*, Amsterdam (Ph.D. thesis UvA).

Paludan-Müller, C., 1978: High Atlantic food gathering in Northwestern Zealand: ecological conditions and spatial representation, in: K. Kristiansen / C. Paludan-Müller (eds.), 120-157.

Pare, C.F.E., 1987: Der Zeremonialwagen der Hallstattzeit: Untersuchungen zu Konstruktion, Typologie und Kulturbeziehungen, in: *Vierrädrige Wagen der Hallstattzeit – Untersuchungen zu Geschichte und Technik*, Mainz, (Monographien Römisch-Germanisches Zentralmuseum, 12), 189-248.

Pare, C.F.E., 1991: *Swords, wagon-graves, and the beginning of the Early Iron Age in Central Europe*, Marburg (Kleine Schriften aus dem Vorgeschichtlichen Seminar Marburg, 37).

Pare, C.F.E., 1992: *Wagons and wagon-graves of the Early Iron Age in Central Europe*, Oxford (Oxford University Committee for Archaeology, 35).

Parés, J.M. / A. Pérez-González 1995: Paleomagnetic age for hominid fossils at Atapuerca archaeological site, Spain, *Science* 269, 830-832.

Parker Pearson, M., 1984: Economic and ideological change: cyclical growth in the pre-state societies of Jutland, in: D. Miller / C. Tilley (eds.), 69-92.

Pasveer, J.M. / H.T. Uytterschaut 1992: Twee Laat-Neolithische skeletten uit Noord-Holland, een fysisch-anthropologisch onderzoek, *Westerheem* 41, 268-275.

Pavúk, J. (ed.), 1993: *Actes du XIIe Congrès International des Sciences Préhistoriques et Protohistoriques à Bratislava, 1-7 september 1991, deel 2*, Nitra.

Pearson, G.W. / M. Stuiver 1986: High-precision radiocarbon time-scale calibration from 500 BC to 2500 BC, *Radiocarbon* 28, 839-862.

Pearson, G.W. / M. Stuiver 1993: High-precision bidecadal calibration of the radiocarbon time scale, 500-2500 BC, *Radiocarbon* 35, 25-33.

Peddemors, A., 1975: Latèneglasarmringe in den Niederlanden, *APL* 8, 93-145.

Peeters, H. / J. Musch / A. Wouters 1988: Les plus anciennes industries des Pays-Bas, *L'Anthropologie* 92, 649-676, 1093-1136.

Perger, T.M / H. Hendrichs 1991: Velsen: Velserbroekpolder, in: P.J. Woltering 1991a, 302-305.

Peters, F.J.C. / J.H.M. Peeters 2001: *De opgraving van de mesolithische en neolithische vindplaats Urk-E4 (Domineesweg, gemeente Urk)*, Amersfoort (RAM, 93).

Picardt, J., 1660: *Korte beschryvinge van eenige vergetene en verborgene Antiquiteten der Provintien en Landen tusschen de Noord-Zee, de Yssel, Emse en Lippe*, Amsterdam.

Pierpoint, S., 1980: *Social patterns in Yorkshire prehistory*, Oxford (BAR British Series, 74).

Plaetsen, P. Van der / J.-P. Parent / J. Vanmoerkerke 1985: Mesolithische en neolithische vondsten aan de Donk te Oudenaarde (Oost-Vlaanderen), *Notae Praehistoricae* 5, 143-146.

Plassche, O. van de, 1982: *Sea-level change and water-level movements in the Netherlands during the Holocene*, Amsterdam (Ph.D. thesis VU; = MRGD 36-1).

Pleyte, W., 1877-1903: *Nederlandsche oudheden van de vroegste tijden tot Karel de Groote*, Leiden.

Plicht, J. van der, 1993: The Groningen radiocarbon calibration program, *Radiocarbon* 35, 231-237.

Plicht, J. van der / W.G. Mook 1987: Automatic radiocarbon calibration: illustrative examples, *Palaeohistoria* 29, 173-182.

Plicht, J. van der, *et al.* 2004: Dating bog bodies by means of ^{14}C-AMS, *Journal of Archaeological Science* 31, 471-491.

Poel, J.G.M. van der, 1960-'61: De landbouw in het verste verleden, *BROB* 10-11, 125-194.

Pollard, A.M., / R.G. Thomas / P.A. Williams 1990: Experimental smelting of arsenical copper ores, in: P. Crew / S. Crew, 72-74.

Polman, S., 1993: *Frans vuursteen uit het Rijksmuseum van Oudheden. Romigny-Lhéry- en Grand Pressigny vuursteen in Nederland*, Leiden (internal report FdAL).

Pons, L.J., 1992: Holocene peat formation in the lower parts of the Netherlands, in: J.T.A. Verhoeven (ed.), 7-79.

Pool, M.A., 1992: *Modelmatige, grootschalige profielanalyse van centraal Hollandse kustsecties*, Utrecht (Report Faculty Geo-Sciences State University of Utrecht).

Poortman, J., (ed.) 1943: *Drente, een handboek voor het kennen van het Drentsche leven in voorbije eeuwen (deel I)*, Meppel.

Popping, H.J., 1929: De praehistorische vuursteen-werkplaatsen in Friesland, *De Vrije Fries* 29, 1-36.

Price, T.D., 1975: *Mesolithic settlement systems in the Netherlands*, Ann Arbor (Ph.D. thesis).

Popping, H.J., 1931: Een Magdalénien-station op de Veluwe, *De Levende Natuur* 11, 340-349.

Poulsen, J. (ed.), 1989: *Regionale forhold i Nordisk Bronzealder. 5. Nordiske Symposium for Bronzealderforskning på Sandbjerg Slot 1987*, Aarhus (Jysk Arkæologisk Selskabs Skrifter, 24).

Pressmar, E., 1979: *Elchinger Kreuz, Landkr. Neu-Ulm, Siedlungsgrabung mit urnenfelderzeitlichem Töpferofen*, Kallmünz (Kataloge der Prähistorischen Staatssammlung, 19).

Price, T.D., 1978: Mesolithic settlement systems in the Netherlands, in: P.A. Mellars (ed.), 81-113.

Price, T.D., 1980: The Mesolithic of the Drents Plateau, *BROB* 30, 11-63.

Price, T.D., 1981: Regional approaches to human adaptation in the Mesolithic of the North European Plain, in: B. Gramsch (ed.), 217-234.

Price, T.D., 1987: The Mesolithic of Western Europe, *Journal of World Prehistory* 1, 225-305.

Price, T.D., 1989: The reconstruction of Mesolithic diets, in: C. Bonsall (ed.), 48-59.

Price, T.D. / J.A. Brown (eds.) 1985: *Prehistoric hunter-gatherers. The emergence of cultural complexity*, Orlando.

Price, T.D., *et al.* 1974: Mesolithic sites near Havelte, Prov. of Drenthe (Netherlands), *Palaeohistoria* 16, 7-61.

Primas, M., 1977: Untersuchungen zu den Bestattungssitten der ausgehenden Kupfer- und frühen Bronzezeit, *Bericht der Römisch-Germanischen Kommission* 58, 1-160.

Prummel, W., 1979: Environment and stock-raising in Dutch settlements of the Bronze Age and Middle Ages, *Palaeohistoria* 21, 91-107.

Prummel, W., 1987: The faunal remains from the Neolithic site of Hekelingen III, *Helinium* 27, 190-258.

Prummel, W., 1989: Iron Age animal husbandry, hunting, fowling and fishing on Voorne-Putten (The Netherlands), *Palaeohistoria* 31, 235-265.

Prummel, W., 1992: Veeteelt, jacht en visserij op Voorne-Putten in de IJzertijd, in: A.B. Döbken (ed.), 131-144.

Rademakers, P.C.M. (ed.) 1998: *De prehistorische vuursteenmijnen van Ryckholt-St.Geertruid*, Maastricht.

Raemaekers, D.C.M., *et al.* 1997: Wateringen 4: a coastal settlement of the Middle Neolithic Hazendonk 3 group, *APL* 29, 143-191.

Raemaekers, D.C.M., 1999: *The articulation of a 'New Neolithic'. The meaning of the Swifterbant culture for the process of neolithisation in the western part of the North European Plain (4900-3400 BC)*, Leiden (Ph.D. thesis; = ASLU, 3).

Raemaekers, D.C.M., 2001: De Vlaardingen-groep als de laatste schakel in het neolithisatieproces?, *Terra Nigra* 151, 45-52.

Raftery, B., 1990: *Trackways through time*, Dublin.

Raftery, B., 1996: *Trackway excavations in the Mount Dillon Bogs, Co. Longford, 1985-'91*, Dublin (Transactions of the Irish Archaeological Wetland Unit, 3).

Randsborg, K., 1974: Social stratification in early Bronze Age Denmark: a study in the regulation of cultural systems, *Prähistorische Zeitschrift* 49, 38-61.

Rappol, M. / C.M. Soonius (eds.) 1984: *In de bodem van Noord-Holland; geologie en archeologie*, Amsterdam.

Rau, P. / B. Willing 1991: Statistische und archäologische Bearbeitung von prähistorischen Kupferanalysen. Ein neues Stuttgarter Analysenprojekt, *Archäologisches Korrespondenzblatt* 21, 357-367.

Rech, M., 1979: *Studien zu Depotfunde der Trichterbecher- und Einzelgrabkultur des Nordens*, Neumünster (Offa-Bücher, 39).

Reed, Ch., (ed.) 1977: *Origins of agriculture*, Den Haag.

Regteren Altena, J.F. van, 1970: Archaeology, in: S.J. Jelgersma *et al.*, 133-146.

Regteren Altena, J.F van, 1977: Polder Grootslag en Bovenkarspel, in: Woltering 1977, 187-192.

Regteren Altena, J.F. van, 1980: Mens en duin, een archeologsch beeld, in: M.J. Adriani *et al.*, 48-63.

Regteren Altena, J.F. van / J.A. Bakker 1961: De neolithische woonplaats Zandwerven (N.H.), in: W. Glasbergen / W. Groenman-van Waateringe (eds.), 33-40.

Regteren Altena, J.F. van, *et al.* 1962-'63: The Vlaardingen culture I-III, *Helinium* 2, 1-41, 97-103, 215-235.

Regteren Altena, J.F. van, *et al.* 1964: The Vlaardingen culture IV-V, *Helinium* 3, 39-57, 97-119.

Reichenberger, A., 1993: Bemerkungen zur Herleitung und Entstehung der spätkeltischen Viereckschanzen, *Acta Praehistorica et Archaeologica* 25, 186-210.

Reinerth, H., 1939: Ein Dorf der Grosssteingräberleute, *Germanen-Erbe* 4, 226-242.

Remouchamps, A.E., 1925: Een vondst uit Nieuw-Weerdinge (Drenthe), *OMROL* 6, 32-35.

Renfrew, C. (ed.) 1973: *The explanation of culture change: models in prehistory*, London.

Renfrew, J. (ed.) 1991: *New light on early farming*, Edinburgh.

Renfrew, C. / P. Bahn 1991: *Archaeology – Theories, methods and practice*, London.

Renfrew, C. / E.B.W. Zubrow (eds.) 1994: *The ancient mind. Elements of cognitive archaeology*, Cambridge.

Rensink, E., 1986: Een jong-paleolithische vindplaats te Mesch-Steenberg. Voorlopig bericht over de opgravingsresultaten juni-juli 1986, *Archeologie in Limburg* 29, 173-176.

Rensink, E., 1991: L'observation du gibier et le débitage des nucléus: un poste de quet du Magdalénien à Mesch (Limbourg, Pays-Bas), *Helinium* 31, 5-59.

Rensink, E., 1992: Eyserheide: A late Magdalenian site on the fringe of the northern loessbelt (Limburg, the Netherlands), *Archäologisches Korrespondenzblatt* 22, 315-327.

Rensink, E., 1993: *Moving into the north: Magdalenien occupation and exploitation of the loess landscapes of northwestern Europe*, Leiden (Ph.D. thesis).

Rensink, E., 1995: On Magdalenian mobility and land use in north-west Europe, some methodological considerations, *Archaeological Dialogues* 2, 85-104.

Rensink, E. / J. Kolen / A. Spieksma 1991: Patterns of raw material distribution in the Upper Pleistocene of Northwestern and Central Europe, in: A. Montet-White / S. Holen (eds.), 141-159.

Rensink, E. / A. Smit / A. Verpoorte 1991: Bewoningssporen uit het late Magdalénien in Nederlands Limburg: Eyserheide, *Archeologie in Limburg* 49, 37-42.

Reuvens, C.J.C., 1819: *Oratio de laudibus archaeologiae*, 24 october 1818, Leiden.

Reuvens, C.J.C. / C. Leemans / L.J.F. Janssen 1845: *Romeinsche, Germaansche of Gallische Oudheden gevonden in Nederland, België en een gedeelte der aangrenzende landen*, Leiden.

Reynolds, P., 1974: Experimental Iron Age storage pits: an interim report, *PPS* 40, 118-131.

Reynolds, P., 1992: Crop yields of the prehistoric cereal types emmer and spelt: the worst option, in: P.C. Anderson (ed.), 383-393.

Rigaud, J.-Ph. (ed.) 1989: *Le Magdalénien en Europe*, Liège (ERAUL, 38).

Rijn, P. van, 2001: Palen uit Borssele en een verdronken bos, *Zeeland* 10/2, 41-46.

Roberts, M.B. / C.B. Stringer / S.A. Parfitt 1994: A hominid tibia from Middle Pleistocene sediments at Boxgrove, UK *Nature* 369, 311-313.

Roe, D. (ed.), 1986: *Studies in the Upper Palaeolithic of Britain and NW Europe*, Oxford (BAR International Series, 296).

Roebroeks, W., 1980: De 'middenpaleolithische' vindplaats Sint-Geertruid (L). Hypothesen voor nader onderzoek, *Archaeologische Berichten* 8, 7-37.

Roebroeks, W., 1981: Ein mittelpaläolithischer Fundplatz bei Sint-Geertruid (Süd-Limburg, Niederlande), *Archäologisches Korrespondenzblatt* 11, 289-293.

Roebroeks, W., 1986a: On the 'Lower Paleolithic' site La Belle Roche: an alternative interpretation, *Current Anthropology* 27, 369-371.

Roebroeks, W., 1986b: Eindhoven, in: W.J.H. Verwers, 13-14.

Roebroeks, W., 1989: *From find scatters to early hominid behavior. A study of middle paleolithic river side settlements at Maastricht-Belvédère (The Netherlands)*, Leiden (Ph.D. thesis; = APL 21 [1988]).

Roebroeks, W., 1990a: Waar komen wij vandaan?, *Spiegel Historiael* 25, 528-534.

Roebroeks, W., 1990b: *Oermensen in Nederland – De archeologie van de oude steentijd*, Amsterdam.

Roebroeks, W., 1995: 'Policing the boundary'? Continuity of discussions in 19th and 20th century paleoanthropology, in: R. Corbey / B. Theunissen (eds.), 173-180.

Roebroeks, W., 2001: Hominid behaviour and the earliest occupation of Europe: an exploration, *Journal of Human Evolution* 41, 437-461.

Roebroeks, W. / J. Kolen / D. De Loecker 1988: Planning depth, anticipation and the organization of Middle Paleolithic technology: the 'archaic natives' meet Eve's descendants, *Helinium* 28, 17-34.

Roebroeks, W. / N.J. Conard / T. van Kolfschoten 1992: Dense forests, cold steppes and the Palaeolithic settlement of Northern Europe, *Current Anthropology* 33, 551-586.

Roebroeks, W. / T. van Kolfschoten 1994: The earliest occupation of Europe: a short chronology, *Antiquity* 68, 489-503.

Roebroeks, W. / T. van Kolfschoten (eds.) 1995a: *The Earliest Occupation of Europe. Proceedings of the European Science Foundation Workshop at Tautavel (France), 1993*, Leiden.

Roebroeks, W. / T. van Kolfschoten 1995b: The earliest occupation of Europe: A reappraisal of artefactual and chronological evidence, in: W. Roebroeks / T. van Kolfschoten (eds.), 297-316.

Roebroeks, W., *et al.* 1992: 'A veil of stones': on the interpretation of an early Middle Palaeolithic low density scatter at Maastricht-Belvédère (The Netherlands), *APL* 25, 1-16.

Roebroeks, W., *et al.* 1993: On the archaeology of the Belvédère pit, *MRGD* 47, 69-79.

Roebroeks, W., *et al.* 1997: 'Site J': An Early Weichselian (Middle Palaeolithic) flint scatter at Maastricht-Belvédère, the Netherlands, *Paleo* 9, 143-172.

Roeleveld, W., 1974: The holocene evolution of the Groningen marine-clay district, *BROB* 24, supplement.

Roep, Th.B. / J.F. van Regteren Altena 1988: Paleotidal levels in tidal sediments (3800-3635 BP); compaction, sea level rise and human occupation (3275-2620 BP) at Bovenkarspel, NW Netherlands, in: P.L. de Boer / A. van Gelder / S.-D. Nio (eds.), 215-231.

Roep, Th.B. / L. van der Valk / D.J. Beets 1991: Strandwallen en zeegaten langs de Hollandse kust, *Grondboor en Hamer* 45, 115-124.

Roever, J.P. de, 1979: The pottery from Swifterbant – Dutch Ertebølle? (Swifterbant contribution 11) *Helinium* 19, 13-36.

Roever, J.P. de, 1986: Scherven per vierkante meter: problemen met de verspreidingskaarten en het kwantificeren van aardewerk, aan de hand van de opgravingen bij Swifterbant, in: M. Bierma *et al.* (eds.), 59-72.

Roever-Bonnet, H. de, *et al.* 1979: Helminth eggs and gregarines from coprolites from the excavations at Swifterbant, *Helinium* 19, 7-12.

Rolland, N., 1992: The Palaeolithic colonization of Europe: an archaeological and biogeographic perspective, *Trabajos de Prehistoria* 49, 69-111.

Roossens, H., 1962: Gebouwen van een bandkeramische nederzetting op de Staberg te Rosmeer, in: *Miscellanea archaeologica in honorem J. Breuer*, Brussel (Archaeologia Belgica, 61), 121-144.

Roosens, H., 1975: Oude versterking te Kanne-Caster, in: *Conspectus 1974*, Brussel (Archaeologia Belgica, 177), 32-36.

Roosens, H., 1976: De oude versterking te Caster, in: *Conspectus 1975*, Brussel (Archaeologia Belgica, 186), 54-58.

Roussot-Larroque, J., 1990: Rubané et Cardial: le poids de l'Ouest, in: D. Cahen / M. Otte (ed.), 315-360.

Rowlands, M.J., 1971: The archaeological interpretation of prehistoric metalworking, *World Archaeology* 3, 210-223.

Rowlands, M.J., 1973: Modes of exchange and the incentives for trade, with reference to later European prehistory, in: C. Renfrew (ed.), 589-600.

Rowley-Conwy, P., 1983: Sedentary hunters: the Ertebølle example, in: G.N. Bailey (ed.), 111-126.

Rowley-Conwy, P., 1984: The laziness of the short-distance hunter: the origins of agriculture in western Denmark, *Journal of Anthropological Archaeology* 4, 188-195.

Rowley-Conwy, P. / M. Zvelebil / H.P. Blankholm (eds.) 1987: *Mesolithic Northwest Europe: recent trends*, Sheffield.

Roymans, N., 1977: IJzertijdceramiek in een depotvondst te Bladel (N.-Br.), in: N. Roymans *et al.* (eds.), 71-80.

Roymans, N., 1982: Een veekraal uit de ijzertijd en een inheems-Romeins grafveldje op de Kriekeschoor bij Bladel, in: J. Slofstra *et al.* (eds.), 94-101.

Roymans, N., 1985: Nederzettingssporen uit de Midden-IJzertijd op de Kerkakkers bij Dommelen, in: J. Slofstra / H.H. van Regteren Altena / F. Theuws (eds.), 81-88.

Roymans, N., 1988a: Eine spätlatènezeitliche Gürtelgarnitur aus dem 'Heelderpeel' in Heel (Limburg, Niederlande), *Archäologisches Korrespondenzblatt* 18, 279-284.

Roymans, N., 1988b: Beegden; nederzetting en grafveld uit de IJzertijd en Romeinse Tijd, in: H. Stoepker (ed.), 346-363.

Roymans, N., 1990: *Tribal societies in Northern Gaul – An anthropological perspective*, Amsterdam (Cingula, 12).

Roymans, N., 1991: Late Urnfield societies in the Northwest European Plain and the expanding networks of Central European Hallstatt groups, in: N. Roymans / F. Theuws (eds.), 9-89.

Roymans, N., 1992: Elite-ideologie, martialiteit en de rituele depositie van wapens – een archeologisch perspectief, in: J. Bazelmans (ed.), 21-34.

Roymans, N., 1993: Het Pionierproject 'Macht en elite', in: J.H.F. Bloemers / W. Groenman-van Waateringe / H.A. Heidinga (eds.), 83-96.

Roymans, N., 1994: Keltische munten en de vroegste geschiedenis van het heiligdom, in: N. Roymans / T. Derks (eds.), 112-131.

Roymans, N., 1995a: Romanization, cultural identity and the ethnic discussion. The integration of Lower Rhine populations in the Roman Empire, in: J. Metzler *et al.* (eds.), 47-64.

Roymans, N., 1995b: The cultural biography of urnfields and the long-term history of a mythical landscape, *Archaeological Dialogues* 2, 2-24.

Roymans, N. (ed.) 1995c: *Opgravingen in de Molenakker te Weert; campagne 1994*, Amsterdam (Zuidnederlandse Archeologische Rapporten, 1).

Roymans, N., 1996a: The sword or the plough. Regional dynamics in the romanisation of Belgic Gaul and the Rhineland area, in: N. Roymans (ed.), 9-126.

Roymans, N. (ed.), 1996b: *From the sword to the plough – Three studies on the earliest romanisation of northern Gaul*, Amsterdam (Amsterdam Archaeological Studies, 1)

Roymans, N., 1996c: Vrouwendracht uit de Late IJzertijd: glazen armbanden van de Weertse opgravingen, in: N. Roymans / A. Tol (eds.), 57-61.

Roymans, N., 1996d: The South-Netherlands project. Changing perspectives on landscape and culture, *Archaeological Dialogues* 3, 231-245.

Roymans, N., 1998: *Romeinse frontierpolitiek en de etnogenese van de Bataven*, Amsterdam (inaugural speech VU).

Roymans, N., 2001: The Lower Rhine Triquetrum coinages and the ethnogenesis of the Batavi, in: Th. Grünewald (ed.), 93-145.

Roymans, N., n.d.: Lith (NB), baggergat 'De Bergen', Amsterdam (internal report AAC).

Roymans, N. / T. Derks 1990: Ein keltisch-Römischer Kultbezirk bei Empel (Niederlande), *Archäologisches Korrespondenzblatt* 20, 443-451.

Roymans, N. / T. Derks (eds.) 1994a: *De tempel van Empel – Een Hercules-heiligdom in het woongebied van de Bataven*, 's-Hertogenbosch.

Roymans, N. / T. Derks 1994b: Het heiligdom te Empel. Algemene beschouwingen, in: N. Roymans / T. Derks (eds.), 10-38.

Roymans, N. / H. Fokkens 1991: Een overzicht van veertig jaar nederzettingsonderzoek in de Lage Landen, in: H. Fokkens / N. Roymans (eds.), 1-19.

Roymans, N. / H. Hiddink 1991: Nederzettingssporen uit de bronstijd en de vroege ijzertijd op de Kraanvensche Heide te Loon op Zand, in: H. Fokkens / N. Roymans (eds.), 111-127.

Roymans, N. / F. Kortlang 1993: Bewoningsgeschiedenis van een dekzandlandschap langs de Aa te Someren, in: N. Roymans / F. Theuws (eds.), 22-41.

Roymans, N. / F. Kortlang 1999: Urnfield symbolism, ancestors and the land in the Lower Rhine region, in: F. Theuws / N. Roymans (eds.), 33-61.

Roymans, N. / T. van Rooijen 1993: De voorromeinse glazen armbandproduktie in het Neder-rijnse gebied en haar culturele betekenis, *Vormen uit vuur* 1993/3, 2-10.

Roymans, N. / W.A.B. van der Sanden 1980: Celtic coins from the Netherlands and their archaeological context, *BROB* 30, 173-254.

Roymans, N. / F. Theuws (eds.) 1991: *Images of the past; studies on ancient societies in Northwestern Europe*, Amsterdam (Studies in Prae- en Protohistorie, 7).

Roymans, N. / F. Theuws (eds.) 1993: *Een en al zand: twee jaar graven naar het Brabantse verleden*, 's-Hertogenbosch.

Roymans, N. / A. Tol 1993: Noodonderzoek van een dodenakker te Mierlo-Hout, in: N. Roymans / F. Theuws (eds.), 42-56.

Roymans, N. / A. Tol (eds.), 1996: *Opgravingen in Kampershoek en de Molenakker te Weert; campagne 1995*, Amsterdam (Zuidnederlandse Archeologische Rapporten, 4).

Roymans, N. / A. Tol / H. Hiddink, 1998: *Opgravingen in Kampershoek en de Molenakker te Weert; campagne 1996-1998*, Amsterdam (Zuidnederlandse Archeologische Rapporten, 5).

Roymans, N., et al. (eds.) 1977: *Brabantse Oudheden*, Eindhoven (Bijdragen tot de studie van het Brabantse heem, 16).

Rozoy, J.G., 1978: *Les derniers chasseurs. L'Epipaleolithique en France et en Belgique. Essai de synthèse*, Charleville.

Rulf, J. (ed.), 1989: *Bylany Seminar 1987, Collected Papers*, Praha.

Runia, L.T., 1985: Gebruik van strontium, andere spoorelementen en stabiele isotopen als voedingsindicatoren in de archeologie, *Voeding* 46, 368-375.

Runia, L.T., 1987: *The chemical analysis of prehistoric bones. A paleodietary and ecoarcheological study of Bronze Age West-Friesland*, Amsterdam (Ph.D. thesis; = BAR International Series, 363).

Ruppel, T., 1985: Zum Beginn der Spätbronzezeit im niederrheinischen Raum, *Ausgrabungen in Westfalen-Lippe* 3, 9-25.

Ruppel, T., 1990: *Die Urnenfelderzeit in der Niederrheinischen Bucht*, Köln (Rheinische Ausgrabungen, 30).

Rust, A., 1937: *Das altsteinzeitliche Rentierjägerlager Meiendorf*, Neumünster.

Rust, A., 1943: *Die alt- und mittelsteinzeitlichen Funde von Stellmoor*, Neumünster.

Rust, A., 1951: Eine jungpaläolithische Gesichtsplastik aus Ahrensburg-Poggenwisch, *Hammaburg* 3, 1-3.

Rust, A., 1958: *Die jungpaläolithischen Zeltanlagen von Ahrensburg*, Neumünster.

Rust, A., 1962: *Vor 20.000 Jahren; Rentierjäger der Eiszeit*, Neumünster.

Ryan, M. (ed.) 1979: *The origins of metallurgy in Atlantic Europe: Proceedings of the Fifth Atlantic Colloquium (Dublin)*, Dublin.

Ryder, M.L., 1993: Wool at Danebury: a speculation using evidence from elsewhere, *Oxford Journal of Archaeology* 12, 305-320.

Sahlins, M., 1972: *Stone age economics*, London.

Sainty, J., et al. 1983: Cuisson expérimentale d'une série de quarante poteries néolithiques rubanées, *Cahiers Alsaciens d'Archéologie, d'Art et d'Histoire* 26, 31-39.

Sanden, W.A.B. van der, 1981: The urnfield and the Late Bronze Age settlement traces on the 'Haagakkers' at St. Oedenrode (Province of North Brabant), *BROB* 31, 307-328.

Sanden, W.A.B. van der, 1986: Houtsnijwerk uit de Late IJzertijd uit een waterput in Oss-Ussen, in: H. Fokkens / P. Banga / M. Bierma (eds.), 73-84.

Sanden, W.A.B. van der, 1987a: De regio in landschappelijk, geologisch en archeologisch perspectief, in: W.A.B. van der Sanden / P.W. van den Broeke (eds.), 1-10.

Sanden, W.A.B. van der, 1987b: Het project Oss-Ussen, in: W.A.B. van der Sanden / P.W. van den Broeke (eds.), 11-22.

Sanden, W.A.B. van der, 1987c: Dendrochronologie en het archeologisch onderzoek op de zuidelijke zandgronden, in: W.A.B. van der Sanden / P.W. van den Broeke (eds.), 45-52.

Sanden, W.A.B. van der, 1987d: Oss-Ussen: de nederzettingen, in: W.A.B. van der Sanden / P.W. van den Broeke (eds.), 53-67.

Sanden, W.A.B. van der, 1987e: Oss-Ussen: de grafvelden, in: W.A.B. van der Sanden / P.W. van den Broeke (eds.), 69-80.

Sanden, W.A.B. van der, 1987f: Oss-Ussen: ecologie en economie, in: W.A.B. van der Sanden / P.W. van den Broeke (eds.), 81-89.

Sanden, W.A.B. van der, 1987g: Oss-Ussen: de materiële cultuur, in: W.A.B. van der Sanden / P.W. van den Broeke (eds.), 91-100.

Sanden, W.A.B. van der, 1987h: Oss-Ussen: een interpretatie, in: W.A.B. van der Sanden / P.W. van den Broeke (eds.), 121-129.

Sanden, W.A.B. van der, 1987i: The Ussen project: large-scale settlement archaeology of the period 700 BC-AD 250, a preliminary report, APL 20, 95-123.

Sanden, W.A.B. van der (ed.) 1990: Mens en moeras – Veenlijken in Nederland van de bronstijd tot en met de Romeinse tijd, Assen (Archeologische Monografieën van het Drents Museum, 1; = Ph.D. thesis Leiden).

Sanden, W.A.B. van der, 1992a: Mens en moeras: het vervolg, NDV 109, 140-154.

Sanden, W.A.B. van der, 1992b: Anloo, NDV 109, 177-178.

Sanden, W.A.B. van der, 1993-'94: Early Iron Age ard shares from Drenthe, the Netherlands, Tools and Tillage VII 2-3, 103-106.

Sanden, W.A.B. van der, 1993: Alfred Dieck und die niederländischen Moorleichen: einige kritische Randbemerkungen, Die Kunde 44, 127-139.

Sanden, W.A.B. van der, 1994a: Het meisje van Yde, Assen.

Sanden, W.A.B. van der, 1994b: De funeraire en aanverwante structuren, in: K. Schinkel, 199-218.

Sanden, W.A.B. van der, 1995a: Bog bodies on the continent: developments since 1965, with special reference to the Netherlands, in: R.C. Turner / R.G. Scaife (eds.), 146-165.

Sanden, W.A.B. van der, 1995b: Veenvondsten in Drenthe, Nieuwe Drentse Volksalmanak 112, 79-83.

Sanden, W.A.B. van der, 1996: Through nature to eternity; the bog bodies of northwest Europe, Amsterdam.

Sanden, W.A.B. van der, 1997: Veenvondsten in Drenthe (2): over potten, herten en wielen, Nieuwe Drentse Volksalmanak 114, 117-121.

Sanden, W.A.B. van der, 1998a: Veenvondsten in Drenthe (3): van maalstenen, wolkluwens, bronzen potten en veenlijken, Nieuwe Drentse Volksalmanak 115, 103-106.

Sanden, W.A.B. van der, 1998b: The funerary and related structures; in: H. Fokkens (ed.), The Ussen project – The first decade of excavations at Oss, Leiden (= Analecta Praehistorica Leidensia 30), 307-336.

Sanden, W.A.B. van der, 2000: Het tempeltje van Barger-Oosterveld, Nieuwe Drentse Volksalmanak 117, 135-143.

Sanden, W.A.B. van der, 2002a: Veenvondsten in Drenthe (4): over oude kranten met nieuwe vondsten, Nieuwe Drentse Volksalmanak 119, 96-100.

Sanden, W.A.B. van der, 2002b: Mens en moeras 3: nieuwe veenlijkvondsten in Noord-Nederland, Nieuwe Drentse Volksalmanak 119, 168-185.

Sanden, W.A.B. van der, 2002c: Structuren in het Drentse veen, Nieuwe Drentse Volksalmanak 119, 186-216.

Sanden, W.A.B. van der, 2002d: Veenwegen in Drenthe: enkele nieuwe dateringen, *NDV* 119, 101-112.

Sanden, W.A.B. van der / P.W. van den Broeke (eds.) 1987: *Getekend zand; tien jaar archeologisch onderzoek in Oss-Ussen*, Waalre (Bijdragen tot de studie van het Brabantse heem, 31).

Sanden, W.A.B. van der / C. Haverkort / J. Pasveer 1991-'92: Een menselijk skelet uit de Aschbroeken bij Weerdinge (Drenthe) – Reconstructie van een misverstand, *Palaeohistoria* 33/34, 155-163.

Sangmeister, E. / K. Gerhardt 1965: *Schnurkeramik und Schnurkeramiker in Südwestdeutschland*, Freiburg (Badische Fundberichte Sonderheft, 8).

Sarfatij, H. (ed.) 1990: *Verborgen steden – Stadsarcheologie in Nederland*, Amsterdam.

Sarfatij, H. / W.J.H. Verwers / P.J. Woltering (eds.) 1999: *In discussion with the past – Archaeological studies presented to W.A. van Es*; Zwolle/Amersfoort.

Scarre, C. / F. Healy (eds.), 1993: *Trade and exchange in prehistoric Europe*, Oxford (Oxbow Monograph, 33).

Schaaffhausen, H., 1888: Die vorgeschichtliche Ansiedelung in Andernach, *Bonner Jahrbücher* 86, 1-41.

Schatorjé, J.M.C.W., 1985: Ontstaan, bloei en ondergang van de Romeinse villae in het Maasdal, *Archeologie in Limburg* 25, 86-88.

Schatorjé, J.M.C.W., 1986: IJzertijdvondsten uit Meterik, in: P.A.M. Geurts *et al.* (eds.), 13-34.

Schegget, M.E. ter, 1999: Late Iron Age human skeletal remains from the river Meuse at Kessel: a river cult place?, in: F. Theuws / N. Roymans (eds.), 199-240.

Schelvis, J. / C. Koot 1995: Sheep or goat? Damalinia deals with the dilemma, *Proceedings of the Section Experimental and Applied Entomology of the Netherlands Entomological Society (NEV)* 6, 161-162.

Schiffer, M.B., 1972: Archaeological context and systemic context, *American Antiquity* 37, 156-165.

Schiffer, M.B., 1976: *Behavioral Archaeology*, New York.

Schiffer, M.B., 1987: *Formation processes of the archaeological record*, Albuquerque.

Schinkel, K., 1994: *Zwervende erven; bewoningssporen in Oss-Ussen uit bronstijd, ijzertijd en Romeinse tijd; opgravingen 1976-1986*, Leiden (Ph.D. thesis).

Schinkel, C., 1998: Unsettled settlement, occupation remains from the Bronze Age and the Iron Age at Oss-Ussen. The 1976-1986 excavations; in: H. Fokkens (ed.), 5-305.

Schirnig, H. 1979a: Das 'Huntedorf' bei Lembruch am Dümmer, in: H. Schirnig (ed.), 235-238.

Schirnig, H. (ed.), 1979b: *Grosssteingräber in Niedersachsen*, Hildesheim.

Schlanger, N., 1994: Mindful technology: unleashing the *chaîne opératoire* for an archaeology of mind, in: C. Renfrew / E.B.W. Zubrow (eds.), 143-151.

Slicher van Bath, B.H. (ed.) 1970: *Geschiedenis van Overijssel*, Deventer.

Schlichtherle, H. / B. Wahlster 1986: *Archäologie aus Seen und Mooren*, Stuttgart.

Schmerling, C., 1833-'34: *Recherches sur les ossements fossiles découverts dans les cavernes de la Province de Liège*, Liège.

Schmid, P., 1984: Siedlungsstrukturen, in: G. Kossack / K.-E. Behre / P. Schmid (eds.), 193-244.

Schmider, B., 1979: Un nouveau faciès du Magdalénien du Bassin Parisien: l'industrie du gisement de Pré-des-Forges à Marsangy (Yonne), in: *La fin des temps glaciaires en Europe*, Bordeaux, 763-771.

Schmider, B., 1984: Les habitations Magdaléniennes de Marsangy (Vallée de Yonne), in: H. Berke / J. Hahn / C.-J. Kind (eds.), 169-180.

Schmider, B., 1989: Le Magdalénien dans le centre du Bassin Parisien: les gisements, l'industrie lithique, in: J.-Ph. Rigaud (ed.), 219-235.

Schmidt, B., 1992: Holzfunde des Jahres 1991, ein dendrochronologischer Bericht, in: *Archäologie im Rheinland 1991*, 166-169.

Schneider, W. / G. Schwarz-Mackensen 1983: Wo liegen die Hauptliefergebiete für das Rohmaterial donauländischer Steinbeile und -äxte in Mitteleuropa ?, *Archäologisches Korrespondenzblatt* 13, 305-314.

Schoenfelder, U., 1992: *Untersuchungen an Gräberfeldern der späten Bronze- und beginnenden Eisenzeit am unteren Niederrhein*, Bonn (Studies in modern archaology, 5).

Schoneveld, J., 1988: *Grafheuvelonderzoek in de omgeving van Borger*, Borger (Flint'nhoesreeks, 3).

Schoneveld, J. / P. Kranendonk 2001: *Drie erven uit de Midden-Bronstijd bij Lienden*, Amersfoort (RAM, 89).

Schoneveld, J. / E. Gehasse (eds.) 2001: *Boog C-noord, een vindplaats bij Meteren op de overgang van Neolithicum naar Bronstijd*, Amersfoort (RAM, 84).

Schreurs, J., 1992: The Michelberg site Maastricht-Klinkers, a functional interpretation, *APL* 25, 129-171.

Schreurs, J., 1994: Een functionele interpretatie van de Michelsberg-site Maastricht-Klinkers, *Notae Praehistoricae* 14, 165-73.

Schreurs, J., forthcoming: *Een functionele interpretatie van enkele Michelsberg-sites*, Leiden (Ph.D. thesis).

Schrire, C., 1984a: Wild surmises on savage thoughts, in: C. Schrire (ed.), 1-25.

Schrire, C. (ed.), 1984b: *Past and present in hunter-gatherer studies*, Orlando.

Schröder, M., 1991: Die Stuttgarter Gruppe. 40 Jahre Metallanalysen vor- und frühgeschichtlicher Bodenfunde, *Fundberichte aus Baden-Württemberg* 16, 1-26.

Schut, P., 1987: *Een inventarisatie van Neolithische vondsten uit de Achterhoek, Gelderland*, Amersfoort (NAR, 4).

Schut, P., 1988: Poteries du Néolithique ancien à Ede (Prov. de Gueldre), *Helinium* 28, 223-231.

Schut, P., 1991: *Een inventarisatie van neolithische bijlen uit Gelderland ten noorden van de Rijn*, Amersfoort (NAR, 11).

Schut, P. / H. Kars / J.M.A.R. Wevers 1987: Jade axes in the Netherlands: A preliminary report, *Helinium* 27, 71-87.

Schute, I.A., 1992: *Geleen-Janskamperveld 1990-1991 – een beschrijving en analyse van de Lineair bandkeramische huisplattegronden*, Leiden (internal report FdAL).

Schütz, C., *et al.* 1991: Ausgrabungen in der Wilhelma von Stuttgart – Bad Cannstatt: die erste Siedlung der altneolithischen La-Hoguette-Kultur, *Archäologische Ausgrabungen in Baden Württemberg* 1991, 45-49.

Schwabedissen, H., 1954: *Die Federmesser Gruppen des Nordwesteuropäischen Flachlandes. Zur Ausbreitung des Spät-Magdalenien*, Neumünster.

Schwantes, G., 1933: Die ältesten Bewohner des mittleren Norddeutschland, *Forschungen und Fortschritte* 9, 261-262.

Schwantes, G., 1958: *Die Urgeschichte. Geschichte Schleswig-Holsteins, Band 1*. Neumünster.

Schwarz, W., 1990: *Besiedlung Ostfrieslands in ur- und frühgeschichtlicher Zeit*, Aurich (Abhandlungen und Vorträge zur Geschichte Ostfrieslands, 71).

Schwarz, W., *et al.* 1993: Fundchronik 1992 für den Regierungsbezirk Weser-Ems, *Archäologische Mitteilungen aus Nordwestdeutschland* 16, 86-87.

Schwellnus, W., 1979: *Wartberg-Gruppe und hessische Megalithik. Ein Beitrag zum späten Neolithikum des Hessischen Berglandes*, Wiesbaden.

Schwellnus, W., 1983: Archäologische Untersuchungen im Rheinischen Braunkohlengebiet 1977-1981, in: G. Bauchhenß (ed.), 1-33.

Schwellnus, W., 1985: Systematische Oberflächenprospektion von Kleinlandschaften, Probleme der Interpretation ihrer Ergebnisse, *Archäologische Informationen* 8, 117-124.

Sedlemeier, J. / H. Spycher (eds.) 1990: *Beiträge zur Archäozoologie, Archäologie, Anthropologie, Geologie und Paläontologie*, Helbring.

Shackleton, N.J. / A. Berger / W.R. Peltier 1990: An alternative astronomical calibration of the lower Pleistocene timescale based on ODP Site 677, *Transactions of the Royal Society of Edinburgh: Earth Sciences* 81, 251-261.

Shalev, S. / J.P. Northover 1993: The metallurgy of the Nahal Mishmar hoard reconsidered, *Archaeometry* 34, 35-41.

Shanks, M. / I. Hodder 1995: Processual, postprocessual and interpretive archaeologies, in: Hodder *et al.* (eds.), 3-29.

Shell, C.A., 1979: The early exploitation of tin deposits in South West England, in: M. Ryan (ed.), 251-263.

Shennan, S., 1977: The appearance of the Bell Beaker assemblage in Central Europe, in: R. Mercer (ed.), 51-70.

Shennan, S., 1986: Interaction and change in the third millennium BC in western and central Europe, in: C. Renfrew / J.F. Cherry (eds.), 137-148.

Sheridan, J.A. / G. Bailey (eds.), 1981: *Economic archaeology*, Oxford (BAR International Series, 96).

Sherratt, A., 1981: Plough and pastoralism: aspects of the secondary products revolution, in: I. Hodder / G. Isaac / N. Hammond (eds.), 261-305.

Sherratt, A., 1983: The secondary exploitation of animals in the Old World, *World Archaeology* 15, 90-104.

Sherratt, A., 1986: The Radley 'earrings' revised, *Oxford Journal of Archaeology* 5, 61-66.

Sherratt, A., 1987: 'Earrings' again, *Oxford Journal of Archaeology* 6, 119.

Sherratt, A., 1990: The genesis of megaliths: monumentality, ethnicity and social complexity in Neolithic north-west Europe, *World Archaeology* 22, 147-167.

Shott, M., 1986: Technological organization and settlement mobility: an ethnographic examination, *Journal of Anthropological Research* 42, 15-51.

Siebinga, J., 1944: Overzicht van de voorgeschiedenis van de gemeente Smallingerland, *Smellingerland*, 3-31.

Siemen, P., 1992: Social structure of the Elbe-Saale Corded Ware Culture – a preliminary model, in: M. Buchvaldek / C. Strahm (eds.), 207-214.

Sieveking, G. de G. / I.H. Longworth / K.E. Wilson (eds.) 1976: *Problems in economic and social archaeology*, London.

Sigaut, F., 1992: Rendements, semis et fertilité: signification analytique des rendements, in: P.C. Anderson (ed.), 395-403.

Simmons, I.G. / J. Turner / J.B. Innes, 1989: An application of fine-resolution pollen analysis to later Mesolithic peats of an English upland, in: C. Bonsall (ed.), 206-217.

Simons, A., 1987: Archäologischer Nachweis eisenzeitlichen Salzhandels von der Nordseeküste ins Rheinland, *Archäologische Informationen* 10, 8-14.

Simons, A., 1989: *Bronze- und eisenzeitliche Besiedlung in den Rheinischen Lössbörden – Archäologische Siedlungsmuster im Braunkohlengebiet*, Oxford (BAR International Series, 467).

Skaarup, J., 1973: *Hesselø-Sølager. Jagdstationen der südskandinavischen Trichterbecherkultur in Dänemark*, København.

Slager, S. / L. van der Plas / J.D.J. van Doesburg 1978: Examination of LBK potsherds from Hienheim, in: C.C. Bakels, 193-201.

Slicher van Bath, B.H., 1978: *Bijdragen tot de agrarische geschiedenis*, Utrecht.

Slicher van Bath, B.H., 1987[6]: *De agrarische geschiedenis van West-Europa 500-1850*, Utrecht.

Slofstra, J., 1991: Een nederzetting uit de vroege ijzertijd op de Heesmortel bij Riethoven, in: H. Fokkens / N. Roymans (eds.), 141-151.

Slofstra, J., 1994: Recent developments in Dutch archaeology, *Archaeological Dialogues* 1, 9-33.

Slofstra, J. / H.H. van Regteren Altena / F. Theuws (eds.) 1985: *Het Kempenprojekt, 2 – Een regionaal-archeologisch onderzoek in uitvoering*, Waalre (Bijdragen tot de studie van het Brabantse heem, 27).

Slofstra, J. / W. van der Sanden 1987: Rurale cultusplaatsen uit de Romeinse tijd in het Maas-Demer-Scheldegebied, *APL* 20, 125-168.

Slofstra, J., et al. (eds.) 1982: *Het Kempenproject; een regionaal-archeologisch onderzoeksprogramma*, Waalre (Bijdragen tot de studie van het Brabants heem, 22).

Smith, A.G., et al. 1989: Mesolithic and Neolithic activity and environmental impact on the south-east fen-edge in Cambridgeshire, *PPS* 55, 207-249.

Smith, C., 1992: *Late stone age hunters of the British Isles*, London.

Smith, I., 1961: An essay towards the reformation of the British Bronze Age, *Helinium* 1, 97-118.

779

Soffer, O. (ed.), 1987: *The Pleistocene Old World. Regional perspectives*, New York.

Soffer, O. / C. Gamble (eds.) 1990: *The World at 18000 BP. Volume 1: High latitudes*, London.

Solway, J.S. / R.B. Lee 1990: Foragers, genuine or spurious?, *Current Anthropology* 31, 109-146.

Spek, A.J.F. van der, 1994: *Large-scale evolution of Holocene tidal basins in the Netherlands*, Utrecht (Ph. D. thesis).

Spek, T., 1992: The age of plaggensoils, in: A. Verhoeve / J.A.J. Vervloet (eds.), 72-91.

Spiess, A.E., 1979: *Reindeer and caribou hunters; an archaeological study*, New York.

Spindler, K., 1983: *Die frühen Kelten*, Stuttgart.

Spindler, K., 1996³: *Die frühen Kelten*, Stuttgart.

Staalduinen, C.J. van (ed.) 1977: *Geologisch onderzoek van het Nederlandse Waddengebied*, Haarlem.

Stapel, B., 1988: *Die Geschlagene Steingeräte der Siedlung Hüde I am Dümmer*, Münster.

Stapert, D., 1976: Some natural surface modifications on flint in the Netherlands, *Palaeohistoria* 18, 7-41.

Stapert, D., 1979a: Preliminary report on the presumed Creswellian site 'Op de Hees' (Municipality of Meerlo-Wanssum, province of Limburg, the Netherlands), *BROB* 29, 133-141.

Stapert, D., 1979b: Zwei Fundplätze von übergang zwischen Paläolithikum und Mesolithikum in Holland, *Archäologisches Korrespondenzblatt* 9, 159-166.

Stapert, D., 1981a: Handaxes in Southern Limburg (The Netherlands) – How Old?, in: F.H.G. Engelen (ed.), 107-113.

Stapert, D., 1981b: Archaeological research in the Kwintelooyen pit, municipality of Rhenen, The Netherlands, *MRGD* 35, 204-222.

Stapert, D., 1981c: A site of the Hamburg tradition on the Wadden island of Texel (province of North Holland, the Netherlands), *Palaeohistoria* 23, 1-27.

Stapert, D., 1982: A site of the Hamburg tradition with a constructed hearth near Oldeholtwolde (province of Friesland, the Netherlands); first report, *Palaeohistoria* 24, 53-89.

Stapert, D., 1985a: Jagers en verzamelaars, in: J. Abrahamse *et al.* (eds.), 26-31.

Stapert, D., 1985b: A small Creswellian site at Emmerhout (province of Drenthe, the Netherlands), *Palaeohistoria* 27, 1-65.

Stapert, D., 1986a: On the 'Lower Paleolithic' site La Belle Roche: an alternative interpretation, *Current Anthropology* 27, 370-371.

Stapert, D., 1986b: Two findspots of the Hamburgian tradition in the Netherlands dating from the Early Dryas Stadial: stratigraphy, *Contributions to Tertiary and Quaternary Geology* 23, 21-41.

Stapert, D., 1987: A progress report on the Rhenen industry (Central Netherlands) and its stratigraphical context, *Palaeohistoria* 29, 219-243.

Stapert, D., 1989: Een vindplaats van de Ahrensburg-traditie bij Oudehaske (Fr.), *Paleo-aktueel* 1, 16-20.

Stapert, D., 1990: Middle paleolithic dwellings: fact or fiction? Some applications of the ring and sector method, *Palaeohistoria* 32, 1-19.

Stapert, D., 1992a: *Rings and sectors: intrasite spatial analysis of Stone Age sites*, Groningen (Ph.D. thesis).

Stapert, D., 1992b: Een bladspitsfragment van de Aardjesberg (Hilversum, N.H.): bewoning tijdens het Midden-Pleniglaciaal?, *Paleo-aktueel* 3, 29-32.

Stapert, D., 2000: The Late Palaeolithic in the northern Netherlands, in: B. Valentin / P. Bodu / M. Christiansen (eds.), 175-195.

Stapert, D. / E. Drenth / J. Hulst 1993: Een bladspits van de Leusderheide (prov. Utrecht), *Paleo-aktueel* 4, 15-19.

Stapert, D. / L. Johansen 1999: Flint and pyrite: making fire in the Stone Age, *Antiquity* 73, 765-777.

Stapert, D. / L. Johansen 2001: The Creswellian site at Zeijen (prov. of Drenthe, the Netherlands): an encampment with a probable tent ring, in: W.H. Metz / B.L. van Beek / H. Streegstra (eds.), 503-526.

Stapert, D. / J.S. Krist / A.L. Zandbergen 1986: Oldeholtwolde, a Late Hamburgian site in the Netherlands, in: D. Roe (ed.), 187-226.

Stapert, D. / J.S. Krist 1990: The Hamburgian site of Oldeholtwolde (the Netherlands); some results of the refitting analysis, in: E. Cziesla *et al.* (eds.), 371-404.

Stapert, D. / H.J. Veenstra 1988: The section at Usselo; brief description, grain-size distributions, and some remarks on archaeology, *Palaeohistoria* 30, 1-28.

Starling, N., 1985: Social change in the later Neolithic of central Europe, *Antiquity* 59, 30-38.

Startin, W., 1978: Linear Pottery Culture houses: reconstruction and manpower, *PPS* 44, 143-159.

Steehouwer, K.J. / A.H.C. Warringa (eds.) 1985: *Archeologie in de praktijk – Methoden en technieken voor de (amateur-)archeoloog*, Weesp.

Stehli, P., 1974: *Bagger und Bandkeramiker: Steinzeitforschungen im rheinischen Braunkohlengebiet*, Bonn.

Stehli, P., 1982: Zur Methode der chronologischen Gliederung des bandkeramischen Siedlungsplatzes Langweiler 8, in: *Siedlungen der Kultur mit Linearkeramik in Europa (Nitra 1981 Symposium)*, Nitra, 271-278.

Stehli, P., 1989a: Merzbachtal – Umwelt und Geschichte einer bandkeramischen Siedlungskammer, *Germania* 67, 51-76.

Stehli, P., 1989b: Zur relativen und absoluten Chronologie der Bandkeramik, in: J. Rulf (ed.), 69-78.

Stehli, P. / A. Zimmermann 1980: Zur Analyse neolithischer Gefäßformen, *Archäo-Physika* 7, 147-177.

Stein, A., *et al.* 1991: Chemical homogeneity and representativeness of prehistoric pottery sherds relative to their assemblage, *Journal of Quantitative Anthropology* 3, 261-277.

Steuer, H. / U. Zimmermann (eds.) 1993: *Alter Bergbau in Deutschland*, Stuttgart (*Archäologie in Deutschland*, Sonderheft).

Stiles, D., 1992: The hunter-gatherer 'revisionist' debate, *Anthropology Today* 8, 13-17.

Stodiek, U., 1987: Fussgönheim zwei spätjungpaläolithische Fundplätze in der Vorderpfalz, *Archäologisches Korrespondenzblatt* 17, 31-41.

Stodiek, U., 1993: *Zur Technologie der jungpaläolithischen Speerschleuder*, Tübingen.

Stoepker, H. (ed.) 1988: Archeologische kroniek van Limburg over 1987, *PSHAL* 124, 345-425.

Stoepker, H. (ed.) 1990: Archeologische kroniek van Limburg over 1988 en 1989, *PSHAL* 126, 194-254.

Stoepker, H. (ed.), 1992: Archeologische kroniek van Limburg over 1991 (*PSHAL* 128, 246-318).

Stoepker, H. (ed.), 1993: Archeologische kroniek van Limburg over 1992 en 1993, (*PSHAL* 129, 283-334).

Stolp, J.J., 1983: Assendelft 32, een huis uit de Late IJzertijd, *Westerheem* 32, 98-111.

Stolzenbach, L. / O. Stolzenbach 1991: Twee mesolithische hakken en een halffabrikaat uit de Noordzee, *Archeologie* 3, 94-98.

Storch, H.-P., 1985: Frühneolithische Bestattungssitten – ein Beitrag zur Urgeschichte des südlichen Oberrheins, *Acta Praehistorica et Archaeologica* 16/17, 23-53.

Strahl, E., 2001: Rodenkirchen, in: *Fundchronik Niedersachsen 2000*, Nr. 121 (*Nachrichten aus Niedersachsens Urgeschichte*, Beiheft 6), 99-104.

Strahm, Ch., 1991: L'introduction de la métallurgie en Europe Centrale, in: *Le chalcolithique en Languedoc, Colloque International Hommage au Dr. Jean Arnal* (= *Archéologie en Languedoc 1990-1991*), 15-25.

Street, M., 1989a: Ein frühmesolithischer Hund und Hundeverbiss an Knochen vom Fundplatz Bedburg-Königshoven, Niederrhein, *Archäologische Informationen* 12, 203-215.

Street, M., 1989b: *Jäger und Schamanen. Bedburg-Königshoven ein Wohnplatz am Niederrhein vor 10000 Jahren*, Mainz.

Street, M., 1991: Bedburg-Königshoven: a Pre-Boreal Mesolithic site in the Lower Rhineland (Germany), in: N. Barton / A.J. Roberts / D.A. Roe (eds.), 256-270.

Street, M. / M. Baales / B. Weniger 1994: Absolute Chronologie des späten Paläolithikums und des Frühmesolithikums im nördlichen Rheinland, *Archäologisches Korrespondenzblatt* 24, 1-28.

Streurman, H.J. / E. Taayke 1989: Vegetation horizons and 'frustrated terps': new radiocarbon ages from the Paddepoel area near Groningen, *BROB* 39, 345-356.

Strien, H.-C. / A. Tillmann, 2001: Die La-Hoguette-Fundstelle Stuttgart – Bad Cannstatt: Archäologie, in B. Gehlen / M. Heinen / A. Tillmann (eds.), 673-681.

Stringer, C. / C. Gamble 1993: *In search of the Neanderthals: solving the puzzle of human origins*, London.

Stringer, C. / C. Gamble 1994: Review Feature. In search of the Neanderthals: solving the puzzle of human origins, *Cambridge Archaeological Journal* 4, 95-119.

Struever, S. (ed.), 1971: *Prehistoric agriculture*, Garden City.

Stuiver, M. / G.W. Pearson 1986: High-precision radiocarbon time-scale calibration from the present to 500 BC, *Radiocarbon* 28, 805-838.

Stuiver, M. / G.W. Pearson 1993: High-precision bidecadal calibration of the radiocarbon time scale, AD 1950-500 BC and 2500-6000 BC, *Radiocarbon* 35, 1-23.

Sturdy, D.A., 1975: Some reindeer economies in prehistoric Europe, in: E.S. Higgs (ed.), 55-95.

Sudholz, G., 1964: *Die ältere Bronzezeit zwischen Niederrhein und Mittelweser*, Hildesheim (Münstersche Beiträge zur Vorgeschichteforschung, 1).

Swisher, C.C., *et al.* 1994: Age of the earliest known hominids in Java, Indonesia, *Science* 263, 1118-1121.

Taayke, E., 1988: Terpenaardewerk uit de ijzertijd en de Romeinse tijd, in: M. Bierma *et al.* (eds.), 50-60.

Taayke, E., 1990a: Die einheimische Keramik der nördlichen Niederlande 600 v.Chr. bis 300 n.Chr.: Vorbericht, *BROB* 40, 101-108.

Taayke, E., 1990b: Die einheimische Keramik der nördlichen Niederlande, 600 v.Chr. bis 300 n.Chr., Teil I: Westergo (Friesland), *BROB* 40, 109-222.

Taayke, E., 1991: Inheems aardewerk in Westergo, 600 vC – 300 AD, *Jaarverslagen van de Vereniging voor Terpenonderzoek* 75, 104-117.

Taayke, E., 1995: Die einheimische Keramik der nördlichen Niederlande, 600 v.Chr. bis 300 n.Chr., Teil II: Drenthe, *BROB* 41, 9-102.

Taayke, E., 1996: *Die einheimische Keramik der nördlichen Niederlande, 600 v.Chr. bis 300 n.Chr.*, Groningen (Ph.D. thesis; also in BROB 40, 41 and 42).

Tackenberg, K., 1978: Kleine Beiträge zur Ur- und Frühgeschichte Nordwestdeutschlands 2, der Goldfund von Lorup, Kr. Emsland, *Nachrichten aus Niedersachsens Urgeschichte* 47, 1-76.

Tackenberg, R., 1970: Die Geröllkeulen in Nordwestdeutschland, *Quartär* 21, 81-92.

Tauber, H., 1981: ^{13}C Evidence for dietary habits of prehistoric man in Denmark, *Nature* 292, 332-333.

Taute, W., 1968: *Die Stielspitzen-Gruppen im Nördlichen Mitteleuropa. Ein Beitrag zur Kenntnis der späten Altsteinzeit*, Köln.

Taute, W., 1973-'74: Neue Forschungen zur Chronologie von Spätpaläolithikum und Mesolithikum in Süddeutschland, *Archäologischen Informationen* 2/3, 59-66.

Tegtmeier, U., 1993: *Neolithische und bronzezeitliche Pflugspuren in Norddeutschland und den Niederlanden*, Bonn (Archäologische Berichte, 3)

Tent, W.J. van, 1988: *Archeologische kroniek van de provincie Utrecht over de jaren 1980-1984*, Utrecht.

Termote, J., 1987: De Keltische hoogtenederzetting van Kooigem Bos. De opgravingscampagne 1986, *Westvlaamse Archaeologica* 3/2, 61-72.

Termote, J., 1990: Un site fortifié de l'Age du Fer à Kooigem, commune de Courtrai (Flandre occidentale), in: M. Leman-Delerive (ed.), 43-46.

Testart, A., 1982: The significance of food storage among hunter-gatherers: residence patterns, population densities and social inequalities, *Current Anthropology* 23, 523-538.

Teunissen, D., 1990: *Palynologisch onderzoek in het oostelijk rivierengebied: een overzicht*, Nijmegen (Mededelingen van de afdeling Biogeologie van de Discipline Biologie van de Katholieke Universiteit van Nijmegen, 16).

Thanos, C., 1995: Caberg-Maastricht, opgravingen door het Rijksmuseum van Oudheden 1925-1935, Leiden (internal report FdAL).

Therkorn, L.L., 1987a: The structures, mechanics and some aspects of inhabitant behaviour, in: R.W. Brandt / W. Groenman-van Waateringe / S.E. van der Leeuw (eds.), 177-224.

Therkorn, L.L., 1987b: The inter-relationships of materials and meanings: some suggestions of housing concerns within Iron Age Noord-Holland, in: I. Hodder (ed.), 101-110.

Therkorn, L.L., 1987c: Velsen, Velserbroekpolder, in: P.J. Woltering, 292-294.

Therkorn, L.L., 1988: The excavation at Schagen-Lagedijk, 1978, in: J.H.F. Bloemers (ed.), 186-205.

Therkorn, L.L., 1989: Uitgeest: Uitgeesterbroekpolder 1, in: P.J. Woltering, 290-294.

Therkorn, L.L., 1991: De empirische cyclus in werking: Het Assendelver Polder-Project, in: J.H.F. Bloemers / T. van Dorp (eds.), 157-170.

Therkorn, L.L. / A.A. Abbink 1987: Seven levee sites: B, C, D, G, H, F and P, in: R.W. Brandt / W. Groenman-van Waateringe / S.E. van der Leeuw (eds.), 115-167.

Therkorn, L.L. / H. van Londen 1990: Velsen: Velserbroekpolder, in: S.W. Jager / P.J. Woltering, 303-305.

Therkorn, L.L., *et al.* 1984: An early Iron Age farmstead: site Q of the Assendelver Polders Project, *PPS* 50, 351-373.

Theunissen, E.M., 1990: Prehistorische bewoning op de Caberg (groeve Klinkers), in: H. Stoepker (ed.), 211.

Theunissen, E.M., 1999: *Midden-bronstijdsamenlevingen in het zuiden van de Lage Landen. Een evaluatie van het begrip 'Hilversum-cultuur'*, Leiden (Ph.D. thesis).

Theuws, F. / N. Roymans (eds.), 1999: *Land and ancestors – Cultural dynamics in the Urnfield period and the Middle Ages in the southern Netherlands*, Amsterdam (Amsterdam Archaeological Studies, 4).

Thieme, H., 1983: *Der paläolithische Fundplatz Rheindahlen*, Köln (Ph.D. thesis).

Thieme, H., 1997: Lower Palaeolithic hunting spears from Germany, *Nature* 385, 807-810.

Thieme, H. / K. Brunnacker / E. Juvigné 1981: Petrographische und urgeschichtliche Untersuchungen im Lössprofil von Rheindahlen/Niederrheinische Bucht, *Quartär* 31/32, 41-69.

Thieme, H. / S. Veil 1985: Neue Untersuchungen zum eemzeitlichen Elefanten-Jagdplatz Lehringen, Ldkr. Verden, *Die Kunde* 36, 11-58.

Thissen, J., 1989: Ein Fundplatz des Magdalénien am linken Niederrhein bei Kamphausen, Gemeinde Jüchen, Kreis Neuss, *Archäologisches Korrespondenzblatt* 19, 315-323.

Thoen, H. (ed.) 1987: *De Romeinen langs de Vlaamse kust*, Koksijde.

Thoen, H., 1990: La production du sel à l'époque romaine, in: G. Leman-Delerive (ed.), 182-190.

Thoen, H., *et al.* (eds.) 1991: *Studia Archaeologica – Liber Amicorum Jacques A.E. Nenquin*, Gent.

Thomas, J., 1988: Neolithic explanations revisited: the mesolithic-neolithic transition in Britain and South Scandinavia, *PPS* 54, 59-66.

Thomas, J., 1991: *Rethinking the Neolithic*, Cambridge.

Tixier, J. / M.L Inizan / H. Roche 1980: *Préhistoire de la pierre taillée, 1: terminologie et technologie*, Bordeaux.

Törnqvist, T.E. / H.J.T. Weerts / H.J.A. Berendsen 1994: Definition of two new members in the Upper Kreftenheye and Twente formations (Quaternary, The Netherlands): a final solution to persistent confusion?, *Geologie en Mijnbouw* 72, 251-264.

Tol, A., 1999: Urnfield and settlement traces from the Iron Age at Mierlo-Hout, in: F. Theuws / N. Roymans (eds.), 87-132.

Tol, A., *et al.* (eds.) 2000: *Twee urnenvelden in Limburg – Een verslag van opgravingen te Roermond en Sittard, 1997-1998*, Amsterdam (Zuidnederlandse Archeologische Rapporten, 6).

Torrence, R. (ed.) 1989: *Time, energy and stone tools*, Cambridge.

Toth, N., 1991: The material record, in: T.D. Dillehay / D.J. Meltzer (eds.), 53-76.

Trier, B., 1989: Bericht über die Tätigket des Westfälischen Museums für Archäologie – Amt für Bodendenkmalpflege – im Jahre 1988, *Neujahrsgruss 1989*, Munster.

Trierum, M.C. van, 1986: Landschap en bewoning rond de Bernisse in de IJzertijd en de Romeinse Tijd, in: M.C. van Trierum / H.E. Henkes (eds.), 49-77.

Trierum, M.C. van, 1992: Nederzettingen uit de IJzertijd en de Romeinse Tijd op Voorne-Putten, IJsselmonde en een deel van de Hoekse Waard, in: A.B. Döbken (ed.), 15-102.

Trierum, M.C. van / A.B. Döbken / A.J. Guiran 1988: Archeologisch onderzoek in het Maasmondgebied 1976-1986, in: BOORbalans 1 – *Bijdragen aan de bewoningsgeschiedenis van de Maasmond*, Rotterdam, 11-105.

Trierum, M.C. van / H.E. Henkes (eds.) 1986: *Landschap en bewoning rond de mondingen van de Rijn, Maas en Schelde*, Rotterdam (Rotterdam Papers, 5).

Trigger, B.G. 1989: *A history of archaeological thought*, Cambridge.

Trimpe Burger, J.A., 1977: Brabers bij Haamstede, een opgraving, 1956-1957, *Kroniek van het Land van de Zeemeermin*, 40-53.

Trinkaus, E., 1989: *The emergence of modern humans: biological adaptations in the later Pleistocene*, Cambridge.

Trinkaus, E. / P. Shipman, 1993: *The Neanderthals: changing the image of mankind*, New York.

Tromnau, G., 1975a: *Neue Ausgrabungen im Ahrensburger Tunneltal. Ein Beitrag zur Erforschung des Jungpaläolithikums im nordwest-europäischen Flachland*, Neumünster (Offa Bücher, 33).

Tromnau, G., 1975b: *Die Fundplätze der Hamburger Kultur von Heber und Deimern, Kreis Soltau*, Hildesheim.

Tromnau, G., 1984: Rentierjagd während des Spätpaläolithikums von Booten aus?, *Hammaburg* N.F. 6, 29-37.

Tromnau, G., 1992: Anmerkungen zur Rengeweih-Harpune von Meiendorf, in: E.-B. Krause / B. Mecke (eds.), 79-83.

Troostheide, C.D., 1990: De laatste maaltijd (2): de stuifmeelkorrels, in: W.A.B. van der Sanden (ed.), 158-161.

Tuck, J.A., 1971: The Iroquois Confederacy, *Scientific American* 224, 32-42.

Tuffreau, A. / J. Sommé (eds.) 1988: *Le gisement paléolithique moyen de Biache-Saint-Vaast (Pas-de-Calais). Vol. I. Stratigraphie, environnement, études archéologiques*, Paris (Mémoires de la Société Préhistorique, 21).

Tuohy, C., 1992: Long-handled 'weaving combs' in the Netherlands, PPS 58, 385-387.

Turekian, K.K. (ed.) 1971: *The Late Cenozoic glacial age*, New Haven.

Turner, R.C. / R.G. Scaife (eds.) 1995: *Bog bodies; new discoveries and new perspectives*, London.

Tylecote, R.F., 1992: *A history of metallurgy* , London.

Ulrix-Closset, M., 1975: *Le Paléolithique moyen dans le bassin Mosan en Belgique*, Wetteren.

Ulrix-Closset, M. / M. Otte (eds.) 1989: *La civilisation de Hallstatt; bilan d'une rencontre, Liège 1987*, Liège (ERAUL, 36).

Urban, B., 1995: Palynological evidence of younger Middle Pleistocene Interglacials (Holsteinian, Reinsdorf and Schöningen) in the Schöningen open cast lignite mine (eastern Lower Saxony, Germany), MRGD 52, 175-185.

Usinger, H., 1985: Pollenstratigraphische, Vegetations- und Klima-geschichtliche Gliederung des 'Bølling-Allerød Komplexes' in Schleswig-Holstein und ihre Bedeutung für Spätglazial-Stratigraphie in Benachbarten Gebieten, *Flora* 177, 1-43.

Uslar, R. von (ed.) 1965: *Studien aus Alteuropa 2*, Köln (Beihefte der Bonner Jahrbücher 10-11).

Uytterschaut, H.T., 1990: Trauma en pathologie, in: W.A.B. van der Sanden (ed.), 129-135.

Valentin, B. / P. Bodu / M. Christiansen (eds.) 2000: *L'Europe centrale et septentrionale au Tardiglaciaire*, Nemours.

Valk, L. van der / F. Beekman / R.M. van Heeringen 1997: Stuivend zand over boerenland. Geologie, archeologie en historische geografie van het duingebied op Schouwen in de provincie Zeeland, in: D.P. Hallewas / G.H. Scheepstra / P.J. Woltering (eds.), 131-152.

Vandenberghe, J. / W. Roebroeks / T. van Kolfschoten (eds.) 1993: Maastricht-Belvédère: stratigraphy, palaeoenvironment and archaeology of the Middle and Late Pleistocene deposits. Part II, MRGD 47, 1-91.

Vanderhoeven, A., 1991: Botanisch onderzoek van de vroege ijzertijd-nederzetting op de Heesmortel bij Riethoven, in: H. Fokkens / N. Roymans (eds.), 154-162.

Vang Petersen, P., 1984: Chronological and regional variation in the Late Mesolithic of Eastern Denmark, Journal of Danish Archaeology 3, 7-18.

Vasbinder, A. / H. Fokkens 1987: Een bronstijdhuis uit Oss-Ussen, in: W.A.B. van der Sanden / P.W. van den Broeke (eds.), 131-135.

Veen, M. van der / J.N. Lanting 1989: A group of tumuli on the 'Hooghalen' estate near Hijken (municipality of Beilen, province of Drenthe, the Netherlands), Palaeohistoria 31, 191-234.

Veen, M.M.A. van, 1989: Voorschoten-De Donk, Leiden (internal report FdAL).

Veil, S., 1984: Siedlungsbefunde vom Magdalenien-Fundplatz Andernach. Zwischenbericht über die Grabungen 1979-1983, in: H. Berke / J. Hahn / C.J. Kind (eds.), 181-193.

Velde, H.M. van der, 1998: Archeologisch onderzoek in de Maasbroeksche Blokken te Boxmeer, Amersfoort (RAM, 64).

Velde, P. van de, 1973: Rituals, skins and homer : the Danubian 'tan-pits', APL 6, 50-65.

Velde, P. van de, 1976: Ein paradigmatisches Klassifikationsschema zur Verzierung der Bandkeramik in Bayern, Archäologisches Korrespondenzblatt 6, 109-116.

Velde, P. van de, 1979a: The social anthropology of a neolithic graveyard in the Netherlands, Current Anthropology 20, 37-58.

Velde, P. van de, 1979b: On bandkeramik social structure, Leiden (Ph.D. thesis; = APL 12).

Velde, P. van de, 1990: Bandkeramik social inequality – a case study, Germania 68, 19-38.

Velde, P. van de, 1995: Dust and ashes: the two Neolithic cemeteries of Elsloo and Niedermerz compared, APL 25, 173-188.

Velde, P. van de, 1997: Much ado about nothing: Bandkeramik funerary ritual, APL 29, 83-90.

Veltkamp, A. / M.W. van den Berg 1993: Three-dimensional modelling of Quaternary fluvial dynamics in a climo-tectonic dependent system – A case study of the Maas record (Maastricht, The Netherlands), Global and Planetary Change 8, 203-218.

Ven, G.P. van de (ed.) 1993: Leefbaar laagland – Geschiedenis van de waterbeheersing en landaanwinning in Nederland, Utrecht.

Venema, H.J. / H. Doing / I.S. Zonneveld 1970: Vegetatiekunde als synthetische wetenschap, Wageningen (Miscellaneous Papers Landbouwhogeschool, 5).

Verbruggen, M., 1992a: Alblasserwaard: Donkenproject, in: W.A.M. Hessing, 348-349.

Verbruggen, M., 1992b: Geoarchaeological prospection of the Rommertsdonk, APL 25, 117-128.

Verbruggen, M., forthcoming: Het Neolithicum op de donken; een geologische prospectie naar archeologische lagen rond de donken in het Nederlandse Rivierengebied Leiden (Ph.D. thesis).

Verhagen, A.J.C.E., 1991: 'De Hoogaard' een kultusplaats in Maaspoort, Den Bosch, Archeologie 3, 99-129.

Verhagen, M., 1990: Ver voordat de Romeinen kwamen, II: dierlijk botmateriaal van het Marktveld te Valkenburg (Z.H.) uit de vroege ijzertijd, in: E.J. Bult / D.P. Hallewas (eds.), 47-51.

Verhagen, M. / E. Esser 1992: Rockanje 1990, object 08-52; zoölogisch onderzoek, Rotterdam (BOOR-rapporten, 13).

Verhart, L.B.M., 1983: Het vuursteen uit de opgraving Hekelingen III, Leiden (internal report RMO).

Verhart, L.B.M., 1988: Mesolithic barbed points and other implements from Europoort, the Netherlands, OMROL 68, 145-194.

Verhart, L.B.M., 1989: Nederzettingssporen uit het Midden-Neolithicum langs de Pater Berthierstraat te Grave, Westerheem 38, 190-197.

Verhart, L.B.M., 1990: Stone Age bone and antler points as indicators for 'social territories' in the European Mesolithic, in: P.M. Vermeersch / Ph. Van Peer (eds.), 139-151.

Verhart, L.B.M., 1992: Settling or trekking? The late neolithic house plans of Haamstede-Brabers and their counterparts, OMROL 72, 73-99.

Verhart, L.B.M., 1995: Fishing for the Mesolithic. The North Sea: A submerged Mesolithic landscape, in: A. Fischer (ed.), 291-302.

Verhart, L.B.M., 2000a: Times fade away. The neolithization of the southern Netherlands in an anthropological perspective, Leiden (Ph.D. thesis; = ASLU, 6).

Verhart, L.B.M., 2000b: The function of Mesolithic bone and antler points, in: C. Bellier / P. Cattelain (eds.), 114-123 (= Anthropologie et Préhistoire 111, 114-123).

Verhart, L.B.M. / L.P. Louwe Kooijmans, 1989: Een midden-neolithische nederzetting bij Gassel, gemeente Beers [N.-Br.], OMROL 69, 75-117.

Verhart, L.B.M. / N. Roymans, 1998: Een collectie La Tène-vondsten uit de Maas bij Kessel, gemeente Lith (prov. Noord-Brabant), OMROL 78, 75-91.

Verhart, L.B.M. / M. Wansleeben 1990: Tussen America en Siberië: Enkele aspecten van het Maasdalproject, in: A.T.L. Niklewicz-Hokse / C.A.G. Lagerwerf (eds.), 45-54.

Verhart, L.B.M. / M. Wansleeben 1991a: Steentijdbewoning in het Vlootbeekdal, Roerstreek '91, jaarboek Heemkundevereniging 'Roerstreek' 23, 119-128.

Verhart, L.B.M. / M. Wansleeben 1991b: Het Maasdalproject en de activiteiten van mesolithische jagers en verzamelaars in het dal van de Loobeek bij Merselo, gemeente Venray, Archeologie in Limburg 46, 48-52.

Verhoeve, A. / J.A.J. Vervloet (eds.) 1992: The transformation of the European rural landscape: methodological issues and agrarian change 1770-1914, Brussels.

Verhoeven, J.T.A. (ed.) 1992: Fens and bogs in the Netherlands: vegetation, history, nutrient dynamics and conservation, Dordrecht.

Verlaeckt, K., 1993: Metalen voorwerpen uit de Bronstijd gevonden op het grondgebied van de provincie Oost-Vlaanderen, in: Archeologisch Jaarboek Gent over 1992, Gent, 49-130.

Verlinde, A.D., 1973: Two barrows from the Middle Bronze Age at Gammelke, municpality of Weerselo, province of Overijssel, BROB 23, 109-122.

Verlinde, A.D., 1974: A mesolithic settlement with cremation at Dalfsen, BROB 24, 113-117.

Verlinde, A.D., 1980: Prehistorische depots uit het Enterveen en Elsener Broek in West Twente, 't Inschrien 12, 17-25.

Verlinde, A.D., 1982a: Archeologische kroniek van Overijssel over 1980/1981, Overijsselse Historische Bijdragen 97, 167-208.

Verlinde, A.D., 1982b: Bronstijd: Rechteren, gem. Dalfsen, in: A.D. Verlinde 1982a, 182-185.

Verlinde, A.D., 1986: Deventer-Holterweg, Jaarverslag ROB, 67-70.

Verlinde, A.D., 1987: Die Gräber und Grabfunde der späten Bronzezeit und frühen Eisenzeit in Overijssel, Leiden (Ph.D. thesis; ook verschenen in BROB 28 [1978], 29 [1979], 30 [1980] en 35 [1985]).

Verlinde, A.D., 1989: Archeologische kroniek van Overijssel over 1988, Overijsselse Historische Bijdragen 104, 165-192.

Verlinde, A.D., 1991: Huizen uit de bronstijd en de vroege ijzertijd te Colmschate, in: H. Fokkens / N. Roymans (eds.), 31-40.

Verlinde, A.D., 1993a: Een nederzetting uit de vroege ijzertijd en middeleeuwse ontginningsgreppels te Enschede, Westerheem 42, 62-68.

Verlinde, A.D., 1993b: Bronstijdbewoning in Zwolle-Ittersumerbroek, site 6, in: H. Clevis / J. de Jong (eds.), 33-47.

Verlinde, A.D., 1994: Een grafveld uit de 5e eeuw v.Chr. te Raalte, in: Over Salland en de Sallanders, Zwolle, 10-16.

Verlinde, A.D., 1999: Isolated houses in Overijssel during the transition from prehistory to protohistory, in: H. Sarfatij / W.J.H. Verwers / P.J. Woltering (eds.), 77-86.

Verlinde, A.D. / R.R. Newell, in press: A multi-component complex of Mesolithic settlements with Late Mesolithic grave pits at Mariënberg in Overijssel, Amersfoort (NAR).

Vermeersch, P.M., 1980: Quelques idées sur l'origine de la hache polie en silex en Europe occidentale, *Helinium* 20, 260-288.

Vermeersch, P.M. (ed.), 1982a: *Contributions to the study of the Mesolithic of the Belgian lowland*, Tervuren (Studia Praehistorica Belgica, 1).

Vermeersch, P.M., 1982b: Quinze années de recherches sur le Mesolithique en basse Belgique. Etat de question, in: A. Gob / F. Spier (eds.), 343-351.

Vermeersch, P.M., 1984: Du Paleolithique final au Mesolithique dans le nord de la Belgique, in: D. Cahen / P. Haesaerts (eds.), 181-193.

Vermeersch, P.M., 1987-'88: Le Michelsberg en Belgique, *Acta Archeologica Lovaniensia* 26/27, 1-20.

Vermeersch, P.M., 1989: Ten years' research on the Mesolithic of the Belgian lowland: results and prospects, in: C. Bonsall (ed.), 284-290.

Vermeersch, P.M., 1990: La transition du Mésolithique au Néolithique en Basse et Moyenne Belgique, in: D. Cahen / M. Otte (eds.), 96-105.

Vermeersch, P.M. / D. Huyge / R. Foblets 1980: Weelde and the Final Mesolithic of the Belgian Campine. A preliminary report on the excavations of a mesolithic site at Weelde (North Belgium), *Veröffentlichungen des Museums für Ur- und Frühgeschichte, Potsdam* 14/15, 323-328.

Vermeersch, P.M. / R. Lauwers / Ph. Van Peer 1985: Un site magdalénien à Kanne (Limbourg), *Archaeologia Belgica* 1, 17-54.

Vermeersch, P.M. / A.V. Munaut / E. Paulissen 1974: Fouilles d'un site du Tardenoisien final à Opglabbeek-Ruiterskuil (Limbourg Belge), *Quartär* 25, 85-104.

Vermeersch, P.M. / Ph. Van Peer (eds.) 1990: *Contributions to the Mesolithic in Europe*, Leuven.

Vermeersch, P.M. / R. Walter, 1980: *Thieusies, Ferme de Hosté, site Michelsberg*, Bruxelles (Archaeologia Belgica, 230).

Vermeersch, P.M., et al. 1987: Orp, site magdalénien de plein air, *Archaeologia Belgica* 3, 7-56.

Vervloet, J.A.J., 1974: *Marken, een terpen-zwerm uit de Late Middeleeuwen*, Bussum (Archeologische Monumenten in Nederland, 4).

Verwers, G.J., 1966a: Tumuli at the Zevenbergen near Oss, gemeente Berghem, province of North Brabant, *APL* 2, 27-32.

Verwers, G.J., 1966b: Non-circular monuments in the southern Dutch urnfields, *APL* 2, 49-57.

Verwers, G.J., 1972: *Das Kamps Veld in Haps in Neolithikum, Bronzezeit und Eisenzeit*, Leiden (Ph.D. thesis; = APL 5).

Verwers, G.J. (ed.) 1975: *Noord-Brabant in pre- en protohistorie*, Oosterhout.

Verwers, G.J., n.d.: *Het vorstengraf van Meerlo*, Maastricht.

Verwers, G.J. / J. Ypey 1975: Six iron swords from the Netherlands, *APL* 8, 79-91.

Verwers, W.J.H., 1981: *Archeologische Kroniek van Noord-Brabant 1974-1976*, Eindhoven.

Verwers, W.J.H. 1986: *Archeologische kroniek van Noord-Brabant 1981-1982*, Waalre.

Verwers, W.J.H., 1988: *Archeologische Kroniek van Noord-Brabant 1983-1984*, Waalre.

Verwers, W.J.H., 1990a: *Archeologische kroniek van Noord-Brabant 1985-1987*, Waalre.

Verwers, W.J.H., 1990b: Archeologische kroniek van Noord-Brabant 1988-1989, *Brabants Heem* 42, 135-162.

Verwers, W.J.H., 1991: Bewoningssporen uit de vroege ijzertijd aan de Kloosterstraat te Den Dungen, in: H. Fokkens / N. Roymans (eds.), 163-170.

Verwers, W.J.H. / G.A.C. Beex 1978: *Archeologische Kroniek van Noord-Brabant 1977-1978*, Eindhoven.

Verwers, W.J.H. / P.W. van den Broeke 1986: Het Bossche Broek opgerold – Een archeologisch onderzoek in Den Dungen, in: E. Verzandvoort / R. van Nuland / L. van Minderhout (eds.), 11-21.

Verzandvoort, E. / R. van Nuland / L. van Minderhout (eds.) 1986: *Den Dungen omgeploegd – Bijdragen tot de geschiedenis van Den Dungen*, Den Dungen.

Villa, P., 1991: Middle Pleistocene prehistory in southwestern Europe: the state of our knowledge and ignorance, *Journal of Anthropological Research* 47, 193-217.

Vilsteren, V. van, 1989: Heilige huisjes. Over de interpretatie van vierpalige structuren bij grafvelden, *Westerheem* 38, 2-10.

Vink, T., 1954: *De rivierstreek*, Baarn.

Voerman, G.H., 1937: Nieuwe vondsten van jong-palaeolithische artefacten in de gemeente Havelte, *De Levende Natuur* 42, 109-116.

Vogel, J.C. / H.T. Waterbolk 1964: Groningen radiocarbon dates V, *Radiocarbon* 6, 349-369.

Vons-Comis, S.Y., 1980: Laat-middeleeuwse textielvondsten in het Brinkmann-complex te Haarlem, *Haarlems Bodemonderzoek* 12, 59-65.

Vons-Comis, S.Y., 1990: De wollen kleding, in: W.A.B. van der Sanden (ed.), 181-197.

Vos, P.C., 1983: De relatie tussen de geologische ontwikkeling en de bewoningsgeschiedenis in de Assendelver polders vanaf 1000 v.Chr., in: R.W. Brandt / G.J. van der Horst / J.J. Stolp (eds.), 54-80.

Vos, P.C. / R.M. van Heeringen 1997: Holocene geology and occupation history of the province of Zeeland (SW Netherlands), *Mededelingen Nederlands Instituut voor Toegepaste Geowetenschappen TNO* 59, 5-109.

Voss, J.A., 1982: A study of western TRB social organisation, *BROB* 32, 9-102.

Vries, F. de, 1988: Luttenberg. Een Hamburg / Creswell basiskamp met een woonconstructie en een haard, Groningen (internal report GIA).

Vries, L.S. de 2001: De faunaresten van Zeewijk, een laat-neolithische nederzetting in de Groetpolder, in: R.M. van Heeringen / E.M. Theunissen (eds.), 281-332.

Vromen, H., 1982: Lineairbandkeramische graven in Haesselderveld-West te Geleen, *Archeologie in Limburg* 14, 10-14.

Waals, J.D. van der, 1961: De zool van Tumulus XIII bij 'De Ark', gemeente Wervershoof, *West-Frieslands Oud en Nieuw* 28, 52-96.

Waals, J.D. van der, 1963a: Een huisplattegrond uit de vroege ijzertijd te Een, gem. Norg, *NDV* 81, 217-229.

Waals, J.D. van der, 1963b: Kroniek van opgravingen en vondsten in Drenthe in 1961, *NDV* 81, 248-261.

Waals, J.D. van der, 1964a: *Prehistoric disc wheels in the Netherlands*, Groningen (Ph.D. thesis).

Waals, J.D. van der, 1964b: Een klokbekergraf met crematieresten bij Hoog Buurlo (gemeente Apeldoorn), *Bijdragen en Mededelingen der vereniging Gelre* 61, 69-76.

Waals, J.D. van der, 1969: *Prehistorie en mythevorming*, Utrecht (speech).

Waals, J.D. van der, 1972: Die durchlochten Rössener Keile und das frühe Neolithikum in Belgien und den Niederlanden, in: J. Lüning (ed.), 3-27.

Waals, J.D. van der, 1973: 'In opdracht van Hare Majesteit', in: W.A. van Es *et al.* (eds.), 509-520.

Waals, J.D. van der, 1976: Continuity and discontinuity in prehistory: some comments on definitions, demonstrability and interpretations, in: S.J. De Laet (ed.), 257-260.

Waals, J.D. van der, 1977: Excavations at the natural levee sites S2, S3/5 and S4, *Helinium* 17, 3-2

Waals, J.D. van der, 1984: Discontinuity, cultural evolution and the historic event, *Proceedings of the society of Antiquaries of Scotland* 114, 1-14.

Waals, J.D. van der, 1987: *De kolonisatie van het terpengebied; een ethno-archeologische benadering*, Amsterdam (Tiende Kroon-voordracht).

Waals, J.D. van der, 1988: Polderperspectieven, enkele gedachten bij Swifterbant en Kolhorn, *Westerheem* 37, 44-56.

Waals, J.D. van der, 1989a: Excavation of two Beaker domestic sites near Kolhorn: general introduction, *Palaeohistoria* 31, 139-150.

Waals, J.D. van der, 1989b: Kolhorn, Southern Site: The well – General description, *Palaeohistoria* 31, 151-156.

Waals, J.D. van der, 2001: De 'ijzerslak' van Emmerhout, in: W.H. Metz / B.L. van Beek / H. Steegstra (eds.), 605-610.

Waals, J.D. van der / J.J. Butler 1976: Bargeroosterveld, in: H. Beck et al. (eds.), Band II, 54-58.

Waals, J.D. van der / W. Glasbergen 1955: Beaker types and their distribution in the Netherlands, *Palaeohistoria* 4, 5-46.

Waals, J.D. van der / H.T. Waterbolk 1973: The middle palaeolithic finds from Hogersmilde, *Palaeohistoria* 15, 35-166.

Waals, J.D. van der / H.T. Waterbolk 1976: Excavations at Swifterbant – discovery, progress, aims and methods (Swifterbant contributions 1), *Helinium* 16, 3-14.

Waasdorp, J.A. / P. Stuurman 1992: 's-Gravenhage: Lozerlaan/Erasmusweg, in: W.A.M. Hessing, 353-354.

Währen, M., 1987: Das Brot in der Bronzezeit und älteren vorrömischen Eisenzeit nördlich der Alpen unter besonderer Berücksichtigung von Brotfunden aus Kreisgrabenfriedhöfen des Münsterlandes, *Ausgrabungen und Funde in Westfalen-Lippe* 5, 23-71.

Wahl, J. / H.G. König 1987: Anthropologisch-traumatologische Untersuchungen der menschlichen Skelettreste aus dem bandkeramischen Massengrab bei Talheim, Kreis Heilbronn, *Fundberichte aus Baden-Württemberg* 12, 65-193.

Wamser, L., 1980: Eine gefäßtragende Idolfigur der frühen Linearbandkeramik aus Mainfranken, *Jahresbericht der Bayerischen Bodendenkmalpflege* 21, 26-38.

Wansleeben, M., 1987: Spatial analysis of late mesolithic and neolithic surface scatters, a test case of the Roerstreek (Middle Limburg), *APL* 20, 11-27.

Wansleeben, M. / L.B.M. Verhart 1990: The Meuse Valley Project: the transition from the Mesolithic to the Neolithic in the Dutch Meuse Valley, in: P.M. Vermeersch / Ph. Van Peer (eds.), 389-402.

Wansleeben, M. / L.B.M. Verhart 1992: The Meuse Valley Project: GIS and site location statistics, *APL* 25, 99-108.

Wansleeben, M. / L.B.M. Verhart 1995: GIS on different spatial levels and the Neolithization process in the south-eastern Netherlands, in: G. Lock / Z. Stančič (eds.), 153-169.

Ward, R.H. / K.M. Weiss (eds.) 1976: *The demographic evolution of human populations*, London.

Warmenbol, E., 1988: Broken bronzes and burned bones; the transition from Bronze to Iron Age in the Low Countries, *Helinium* 28, 244-270.

Warmenbol, E., 1989: La dynamique du bronze moyen en Belgique, in: *Dynamique du Bronze Moyen en Europe occidentale*, Paris, 502-513.

Warmenbol, E., 1991: Le Bronze Final atlantique entre côte et Escaut, in: C. Chevillot / A. Coffyn (eds.), 89-110.

Warren, S.H., 1920: A natural 'eolith' factory beneath the Thanet sand, *Quarterly Journal Geological Society* 76, 238-253.

Waterbolk, H.J. / H.T. Waterbolk 1991: Amber on the coast of the Netherlands, in: H. Thoen et al. (eds.), 201-209.

Waterbolk, H.J. / H.T. Waterbolk 1992: Barnsteen in het waddengebied, *Waddenbulletin* 27, 70-77.

Waterbolk, H.T., 1954: *De praehistorische mens en zijn milieu*, Assen (Ph.D. thesis Groningen).

Waterbolk, H.T., 1957: Een kringgrepurnenveld te Wapse, *NDV* 75, 42-67.

Waterbolk, H.T., 1958-'59: Die bandkeramische Siedlung von Geleen, *Palaeohistoria* 6/7, 121-162.

Waterbolk, H.T., 1959a: De prehistorie van Nederland in absolute getallen, in: *Honderd eeuwen Nederland*, 's-Gravenhage (Antiquity and Survival vol. II, no. 5-6), 12-26.

Waterbolk, H.T., 1959b: Nieuwe gegevens over de herkomst van de oudste bewoners der kleistreken, *Akademiedagen* 11, 16-37.

Waterbolk, H.T., 1960: Preliminary report on the excavations at Anlo in 1957 and 1958, *Palaeohistoria* 8, 59-90.

Waterbolk, H.T., 1962: Hauptzüge der eisenzeitlichen Besiedlung der nördlichen Niederlande, *Offa* 19, 9-46.

Waterbolk, H.T., 1964: The Bronze Age settlement of Elp, *Helinium* 4, 97-131.

Waterbolk, H.T., 1965-'66: The occupation of Friesland in the prehistoric period: BROB 15-16, 13-35. (= Van rendierjagers tot terpbewoners), in: J.J. Kalma / J.J. Spahr van der Hoek / K. de Vries (eds.), 13-47.

Waterbolk, H.T. 1965: Ein eisenzeitliches Gräberfeld bei Ruinen, Provinz Drenthe, Niederlande, in: R. von Uslar (ed.), 34-53.

Waterbolk, H.T., 1970a: ¹⁴C en de archeologie, Spiegel Historiael 5, 324-334.

Waterbolk, H.T., 1970b: Die Deutung der Wurten in historischer Sicht, in: Probleme der Küstenforschung im Südlichen Nordseegebiet, 9, Hildesheim, 1-12.

Waterbolk, H.T., 1975: Evidence of cattle stalling in excavated pre- and protohistoric houses, in: A.T. Clason (ed.), 383-394.

Waterbolk, H.T., 1977a: Opgravingen rond het Witteveen op het Noordse Veld bij Zeijen, gem. Vries (1949-1953), NDV 94, 177-203.

Waterbolk, H.T., 1977b: Walled enclosures of the Iron Age in the North of the Netherlands, Palaeohistoria 19, 97-172.

Waterbolk, H.T., 1979: Siedlungskontinuität im Küstengebiet der Nordsee zwischen Rhein und Elbe, in: Probleme der Küstenforschung im südlichen Nordseegebiet, 13, Hildesheim, 1-21.

Waterbolk, H.T., 1981: Archaeology in the wetlands: delta archaeology, World Archaeology 13, 240-254.

Waterbolk, H.T., 1982: Mobilität von Dorf, Ackerflur und Gräberfeld in Drenthe seit der Latènezeit, Offa 39, 97-137.

Waterbolk, H.T., 1985a: Archeologie, in: J. Heringa et al. (eds.), 15-90.

Waterbolk, H.T., 1985b: The Mesolithic and Early Neolithic settlement of Northern Netherlands in the light of radiocarbon evidence, Jahrbuch des Bernischen Historischen Museums 1983-1984, 273-281.

Waterbolk, H.T., 1986: Elp, in: H. Beck et al. (eds.), Band 7, 163-175.

Waterbolk, H.T., 1987: Terug naar Elp, in: F.C.J. Ketelaar (ed.), 183-215.

Waterbolk, H.T., 1988: Zomerbewoning in het terpengebied?, in: M. Bierma et al. (eds.), 1-19.

Waterbolk, H.T., 1989: Siebzig Jahre Siedlungsforschung durch das Biologisch-Archäologische Institut der Universität Groningen. Unter besondere Berücksichtigung der Untersuchungen Albert Egges van Giffen in der Provinz Drenthe, Siedlungsforschung. Archäologie-Geschichte-Geographie 7, 285-320.

Waterbolk, H.T., 1990a: Elp (Pays-Bas): données nouvelles sur la chronologie du village du Bronze moyen et final, in: Un monde villageois – Habitat & milieu naturel en Europe de 2000 à 500 av. J.-C., Lons-le-Saunier, 17-23.

Waterbolk, H.T., 1990b: Zeventig jaar archeologisch nederzettingsonderzoek in Drenthe, NDV 107, 137-168.

Waterbolk, H.T., 1995: De prehistorische nederzetting van Zwolle-Ittersumerbroek, in: H. Clevis / J. de Jong (eds.), 123-173.

Waterbolk, H.T. / J.W. Boersma 1976: Bewoning in vóór- en vroeg-historische tijd – het kleigebied, in: W.J. Formsma et al. (eds.), 33-74.

Waterbolk, H.T. / J.J. Butler 1965: comments on the use of metallurgical analysis in prehistoric studies, Helinium 5, 227-252.

Waterbolk, H.T. / W. van Zeist 1961: A Bronze Age sanctuary in the raised bog at Bargeroosterveld (Dr.), Helinium 1, 5-19.

Wegner, G. (ed.), 1983: Frühe Bauernkulturen in Niedersachsen, Oldenburg. (Archäologische Mitteilungen aus Nordwestdeutschland, Beiheft 1).

Weiner, A.B., 1988: The Tobrianders of Papua New Guinea, Fort Worth.

Weiner, A.B., 1992: Inalienable posessions; the paradox of keeping-while-giving, Berkeley.

Weiner, J., 1992a: Der früheste Nachweis der Blockbauweise; zum Stand der Ausgrabung des bandkeramischen Holzbrunnens, in: Archäologie im Rheinland 1991, 30-33.

Weiner, J., 1992b: De oudste bewaard gebleven houten konstruktie ter wereld; een waterput uit de Bandkeramiek in Erkelenz-Kückhoven / der älteste erhaltene Holzbau der Welt; ein

Brunnen der Bandkeramik aus Erkelenz-Kückhoven, in: *Speurwerk, archeologische monumentenzorg in de Euregio Maas-Rijn*, Mainz (Führer des Rheinischen Landesmuseums Bonn und des Rheinischen Amtes für Bodendenkmalpflege, 136), 432-438.

Weisgerber, G. / R. Slotta / J. Weiner (eds.) 1980: *5000 Jahre Feuersteinbergbau; die Suche nach dem Stahl der Steinzeit*, Bochum.

Wels-Weyrauch, U., 1989: Mittelbronzezeitliche Frauentrachte in Süddeutschland, in: *Dynamique du Bronze Moyen en Europe occidentale*, Paris, 117-34.

Wesselingh, D.A., 1993: Oss-IJsselstraat: Iron Age graves and a native-Roman settlement, *APL* 26, 111-138.

Wesselingh, D.A., 2000: *Native neighbours – Local settlement system and social structure in the Roman period at Oss (The Netherlands)*, Leiden (Ph.D. thesis; = APL 32).

Westendorp, N. 1819: *Antiquiteiten: een oudheidkundig tijdschrift*, Groningen (vol. 1 June 1819).

Westerhoff, W.E. / P. Cleveringa 1990: Sea-level rise and coastal sedimentation in central Noord Holland (The Netherlands) around 5500 BP: a case study of changes in sedimentation dynamics and sediment distribution patterns, in: J.J. Beukema / W.J. Wolff / J.W.M. Brouns (eds.), 133-138.

Westerhoff, W.E. / E.F.J. de Mulder / W. de Gans 1987: *Toelichtingen bij de Geologische Kaart van Nederland 1: 50 000, Blad Alkmaar West en Alkmaar Oost (19 W en 19 O)*, Haarlem.

Westerhoff, W.E. / T.E. Wong / E.F.J. de Mulder 2003: Opbouw van de ondergrond, in: E.F.J. de Mulder et al. (eds.), 247-352.

Wheeler, R.E.M., 1943: *Maiden Castle, Dorset*, Oxford.

White, R., 1982: Rethinking the middle/upper paleolithic transition, *Current Anthropology* 23, 169-192.

Whittle, A., 1985: *Neolithic Europe, a survey*, Cambridge.

Wiessner, P., 1983: Style and social information in Kalahari San projectile points, *American Antiquity* 48, 253-276.

Wiessner, P., 1984: Reconsidering the behavioural basis for style: a case study among the Kalahari San, *Journal of Anthropological Archaeology* 3, 190-234.

Wijngaarden-Bakker, L.H. van, 1970: Dierenresten uit het castellum te Zwammerdam; voorbericht over de opgravingscampagnes 1968 en 1969, *Helinium* 10, 274-278.

Wijngaarden-Bakker, L.H. van, 1985: De voorgeschiedenis van Baambrugge en Abcoude, in: D.G. Carasso / M. Carasso-Kok (eds.), 10-17.

Wijngaarden-Bakker, L.H. van, 1986: Trace elements in prehistoric environment and food chains, *Mitteilungen der Berliner Gesellschaft für Anthropologie, Ethnologie und Urgeschichte* 7, 25-29.

Wijngaarden-Bakker, L.H. van, 1988: Zoöarcheologisch onderzoek in de west-Nederlandse delta 1983-1987, in: J.H.F. Bloemers (ed.), 154-185.

Wilford, J.N., 1994: Prehistorische tinmijn verklaart Bronstijd in Midden-Oosten, *De Volkskrant*, 5 February 1994, 1.

Wilhelmi, K., 1971: Neuartige Funde des Jungneolithikums auf der Osterwicker Platte (West-Westfalen), *Archäologisches Korrespondenzblatt* 1, 33.

Wilhelmi, K., 1977a: West-Westfalen zwischen Michelsberger und Trichterbecher-kultur, *Archäologisches Korrespondenzblatt* 7, 9-21.

Wilhelmi, K., 1977b: Zur Funktion und Verbreitung dreieckiger Tongewichte der Eisenzeit, *Germania* 55, 180-184.

Wilhelmi, K., 1982: Erste Eisengewinnung, Hohenbefestigungen und Münzen vom Sieger- bis zum Weserbergland, in: G. Krause (ed.), *Vor- und Frühgeschichte des unteren Niederrheins*, Bonn (Quellenschriften zur Westdeutschen Vor- und Frühgeschichte, 10), 217-239.

Willems, W.J.A., 1935: *Een bijdrage tot de kennis der voor-romeinsche urnenvelden in Nederland*, Maastricht.

Willems, W.J.H., 1983a: Romans and Batavians: regional developments at the imperial frontier, in: R.W. Brandt / J. Slofstra (eds.), 105-125.

Willems, W.J.H., 1983b: Archeologische kroniek van Limburg over de jaren 1980-1982, *PSHAL* 119, 197-291.

Willems, W.J.H., 1984: Archeologische kroniek van Limburg over 1983, *PSHAL* 120, 354-393.

Willems, W.J.H., 1985: Archeologische kroniek van Limburg over 1984, *PSHAL* 121, 146-196.

Willems, W.J.H., 1986a: *Romans and Batavians. A regional study in the Dutch Eastern River Area*, Amsterdam (Ph.D. thesis UvA; also in *BROB* 31 [1981] and 34 [1984]).

Willems, W.J.H., 1986b: Archeologische kroniek van Limburg over 1985, *PSHAL* 122, 203-246.

Willems, W.J.H. / L.I. Kooistra 1988: De Romeinse villa te Voerendaal, opgraving 1987, *Archeologie in Limburg* 37, 137-147.

Willms, C., 1982: *Zwei Fundplätze der Michelsberger Kultur aus dem Westlichen Münsterland, Gleichzeitig ein Beitrag zum Neolithischen Silexhandel in Mitteleuropa*, Hildesheim (Münstersche Beiträge zur Ur- und Frühgeschichte, 12).

Willms, C., 1985: Neolithischer Spondylusschmuck, hundert Jahre Forschung, *Germania* 63, 331-343.

Willroth, K.-H., 1985: *Die Hortfunde der Älteren Bronzezeit in Südschweden und auf den dänischen Inseln*, Neumünster (Offa-Bücher, 55).

Willroth, K.-H., 1989: Nogle betragninger over de regionale forhold i Slesvig og Holsten i bronzealderens periode II, in: J. Poulsen (ed.), 89-100.

Wilmsen, E.N. / J.R. Denbow 1990: Paradigmatic history of San-speaking peoples and current attempts at revision, *Current Anthropology* 31, 489-524.

Wimmers, W.H., 1988: Het urnenveld op de Westerheide bij Hilversum, *OMROL* 68, 117-143.

Wind, C., 1973: De ijzertijd, in: *Van steurvisser tot stedeling*, Vlaardingen, 74-108.

Windl, H., 1996: *Rätsel um Gewalt und Tod vor 7000 Jahren*. Asparn an der Zaya (exhibiton catalogue).

Winter, D., 1986: *Der spätpaläolithische Fundplatz Niederbieber Fläche 50 / 14-56 / 20*, Köln (internal report).

Wobst, H.M., 1973: Boundary conditions for palaeolithic social systems: a simulation approach, *American Antiquity* 39, 147-148.

Wobst, H.M., 1976: Locational relationships in Palaeolithic society, in: R.H. Ward / K.M. Weiss (eds.), 49-58.

Wobst, H.M., 1978: The archaeo-ethnology of hunter-gatherers, or the tyranny of the ethnographic record in archaeology, *American Antiquity* 43, 303-309.

Woltering, P.J., 1975: Occupation history of Texel, I: the excavations at Den Burg: preliminary report, *BROB* 25, 7-36.

Woltering, P.J. 1977: Archeologische Kroniek van Noord-Holland over 1976, *Holland* 9, 182-211.

Woltering, P.J., 1979: Occupation history of Texel, II: the archaeological survey: preliminary report, *BROB* 29, 7-114.

Woltering, P.J., 1981: Archeologische kroniek van Holland over 1980, I Noord-Holland, *Holland* 13, 201-229.

Woltering, P.J., 1985: Prehistorie en Romeinse tijd in West-Friesland, *West-Frieslands Oud en Nieuw* 52, 199-232.

Woltering, P.J., 1986: Archeologische kroniek van Holland over 1985, I Noord-Holland, *Holland* 18, 276-303.

Woltering, P.J., 1987: Archeologische kroniek van Holland over 1986, I Noord-Holland, *Holland* 19, 284-310.

Woltering, P.J., 1989: Archeologische kroniek van Holland over 1988, I Noord-Holland, *Holland* 21, 280-317.

Woltering, P.J., 1991a: Archeologische kroniek van Holland over 1990, I Noord-Holland, *Holland* 23, 296-328.

Woltering, P.J., 1991b: Nederzettingen uit de bronstijd en de vroege ijzertijd bij Den Burg, Texel, in: H. Fokkens / N. Roymans (eds.), 83-92.

Woltering, P.J., 1992: Archeologische kroniek van Holland over 1991, I Noord-Holland, *Holland* 24, 313-347.

Woltering, P.J., 1994: Texel – Landschap en bewoning van Midden Bronstijd tot Vroege Middeleeuwen, in: M. Rappol / C.M. Soonius (eds.), 189-217.

Woltering, P.J., 2000: *The archaeology of Texel; four studies on settlement and landscape (1350 BC – AD 1500)*, Amersfoort (Ph.D. thesis VU; also in BROB 25 [1975], 29 [1979], 42 [1996-'97] and 44 [2000]).

Woltering, P.J. / J.-K.A. Hagers 1993: Archeologische kroniek van Holland over 1992, I Noord-Holland, *Holland* 25, 287-328.

Woude, J.D. van der, 1981: *Holocene palaeoenvironmental evolution of a perimarine fluviatile area – Geology and paleobotany of the area surrounding the archaeological excavation at the Hazendonk river dune (western Netherlands)*, Amsterdam (Ph.D. thesis VU; = APL 16 [1983]).

Wouters, A.M., 1952-'53: Het palaeolithicum en mesolithicum in Limburg, *PSHAL* 88/89, 1-18.

Wouters, A.M., 1957: Een nieuwe vindplaats van de Ahrensburgcultuur onder de gemeente Geldrop, *Brabants Heem* 9, 2-12.

Wouters, A.M., 1980: De middenpaleolithische vindplaats Sint-Geertruid (L), *Archaeologische Berichten* 8, 38-107.

Wouters, A.M., 1983: Uit de oude doos, Magdalenien uit het Peelgebied, *Archaeologische Berichten* 14, 99-108.

Wouters, A.M., 1985: Nogmaals: bewoningssporen uit het Magdalenien van Sweikhuizen, *Archeologie in Limburg* 23, 51-53.

Wouters, A.M., 1990: 'Budel II'. Vindplaats van een epigravettien uit Budel-Dorplein, *Archeologie* 2, 14-39.

Wouters, A.M., 1991: Lijngraveringen op artefacten van de Jongpaleolithische vindplaats 'De Fransman', *Rondom het Leudal* 16, 82-91.

Wüstemann, H., 1978: Zur Sozialentwicklung der Bronzezeit im Norden der DDR, in: W. Coblenz / F. Horst (eds.), 195-209.

Yener, K.A., / H. Özbal 1987: Tin in the Turkish Taurus mountains: the Bolkardag mining district. *Antiquity* 61, 220-226.

Zagwijn, W.H., 1961: Vegetation, climate and radiocarbon datings in the Late Pleistocene of the Netherlands. I. Eemian and Early Weichselian, *Mededelingen Geologische Stichting*, nieuwe serie, 14, 15-45.

Zagwijn, W.H., 1975: De paleogeografische ontwikkeling van Nederland in de laatste drie miljoen jaar, *Geografisch Tijdschrift* 9, 181-201.

Zagwijn, W.H., 1983: Sea-level changes in the Netherlands during the Eemian, *Geologie en Mijnbouw* 62, 437-450.

Zagwijn, W.H., 1985: An outline of the Quaternary stratigraphy of the Netherlands, *Geologie en Mijnbouw* 64, 17-24.

Zagwijn, W.H., 1986: *Nederland in het Holoceen*, 's-Gravenhage (Geologie van Nederland, 1).

Zagwijn, W.H., 1989: The Netherlands during the Tertiary and the Quaternary: a case history of coastal lowland evolution, *Geologie en Mijnbouw* 68-1, 107-120.

Zagwijn, W.H., 1992: The beginning of the ice age in Europe and its major subdivisions, *Quaternary Science Reviews* 11, 583-591.

Zagwijn, W.H., 1994: Reconstruction of climate change during the Holocene in western and central Europe based on pollen records of indicator species, *Vegetation History and Archaeobotany* 3, 65-88.

Zagwijn, W.H. / J.W.Chr. Doppert 1978: Upper Cenozoic of the Southern North Sea Basin: palaeoclimatic and palaeogeographic evolution, *Geologie en Mijnbouw* 57, 577-588.

Zagwijn, W.H. / C.J. van Staalduinen (eds.) 1975: *Toelichting bij geologische overzichtskaarten van Nederland*, Haarlem.

Zalieznjak, L.L., 1989: *Ochotniekie na sjewjernogo oljenja oekraienskogo lolesja èpochja fienaljnogo paljeo-lieta*, Kiev.

Zandstra, J.G., 1971: Geologisch onderzoek in de stuwwal van de oostelijke Veluwe bij Hattem en Wapenveld, MRGD, nieuwe serie 22, 215-260.

Zeiler, J.T., 1986: Swifterbant: dwelling place for a season or throughout the whole year? An archaeozoological contribution, in: M. Bierma *et al.* (eds.), 85-95.

Zeiler, J.T., 1987: The exploitation of fur animals in Neolithic Swifterbant and Hazendonk (Central and Western Netherlands), *Palaeohistoria* 29, 245-263.

Zeiler, J.T., 1989: Archeozoölogisch onderzoek van de laat-neolithische vindplaats Kolhorn (N.-H.), *Paleo-aktueel* 1, 25-30.

Zeiler, J.T., 1991: Hunting and animal husbandry at Neolithic sites in the western and central Netherlands; interaction between man and the environment, *Helinium* 31, 60-125.

Zeiler, J.T., 1997: *Hunting, fowling and stock-breeding at Neolithic sites in the Western and Central Netherlands*, Groningen (Ph.D. thesis).

Zeist, W. van, 1955: *Pollen analytical investigations in the northern Netherlands, with special reference to archaeology*, Amsterdam (Ph.D. thesis UvA).

Zeist, W. van, 1957: De mesolithische boot van Pesse, NDV 75, 4-11.

Zeist, W. van, 1958: De Valtherbrug, NDV 76, 21-49.

Zeist, W. van, 1968: Prehistoric and early historic food plants in the Netherlands, *Palaeohistoria* 14, 41-173.

Zeist, W. van, 1970: Betrekkingen tussen palynologie en vegetatiekunde, in: Venema / H. Doing / I.S. Zonneveld (eds.), 127-140.

Zeist, W. van, 1976: Two early rye finds from the Netherlands, *Acta Botanica Neerlandica* 25, 71-79.

Zeist, W. van, 1977: De eerste landbouw. Archeologisch onderzoek in het Nabije Oosten, *Natuur en Techniek* 45, 668-683.

Zeist, W. van, 1989: Plant remains from a middle Iron Age coastal-marsh site near Middelstum. An intriguing cereal grain find, *Helinium* 29, 103-116.

Zeist, W. van / W.A. Casparie (eds.) 1984: *Plants and ancient man*, Rotterdam.

Zeist, W. van / R.M. Palfenier-Vegter 1981: Seeds and fruits from the Swifterbant S3 site, *Palaeohistoria* 23, 105-168.

Zeist, W. van / K. Wasylikowa / K.-E. Behre (eds.) 1991: *Progress in Old World palaeoethnobotany*, Rotterdam.

Zeist, W. van / H.T. Waterbolk 1960: Een houten gebouwtje uit de bronstijd in het veen bij Barger-oosterveld, NDV, 199-204.

Zeist, W. van, *et al.* 1976: An agricultural experiment in the unprotected salt marsh, *Palaeohistoria* 18, 111-153.

Zich, B., 1992: Besuch aus Niedersachsen in Schleswig-Holstein, *Archäologie in Deutschland* 3, 54.

Ziegler, A., 1990: Festive space, territories and feasts in the south of Nias, in: J. Feldman *et al.*, 78-96.

Zimmermann, A., 1982: Zur Organisation der Herstellung von Feuersteinartefakten in bandkeramischen Siedlungen, in: *Siedlungen der Kultur mit Linearkeramik in Europa (Nitra 1981 Symposium)*, Nitra, 319-323.

Zimmermann, A., 1988: Steine, in: U. Boelicke *et al.* (eds.), 569-787.

Zimmermann, A., 1991: *Austauschsysteme von Silexartefakten in der Bandkeramik Mitteleuropas*, Frankfurt am Main (Ph.D. thesis).

Zimmermann, U., 1993: Urgeschichtlicher Metallerzbergbau in Mitteleuropa, in: H. Steuer / U. Zimmermann (eds.), 48-54.

Zimmermann, W.H., 1970: Urgeschichtliche Opferfunde aus Flüssen, Mooren, Quellen und Brunnen Südwestdeutschlands, *Neue Ausgrabungen und Forschungen in Niedersachsen* 6, 53-92.

Zimmermann, W.H., 1980: Ein Hausgrundriss der Trichterbecherkultur von Flögeln – Im Örtjen, Kreis Cuxhaven, in: *Beiträge zur Archäologie nordwestdeutschlands und Mitteleuropas (Festschrift K.*

Raddatz), Hildesheim (Materialhefte zur Ur- und Frühgeschichte Mitteldeutschlands, 16), 474-489.

Zimmermann, W.H., 1984: Nahrungsproduktion, I, in: G. Kossack / K.-E. Behre / P. Schmid (eds.), 246-263.

Zohary, D., 1992: Domestication of the neolithic Near Eastern crop assemblage, in: P.C. Anderson (ed.), 81-86.

Zoller, D., 1963: Vorläufiger Bericht über eine Rentierjägerstation der Hamburger Stufe bei Querenstede, Kr. Ammerland, *Die Kunde* N.F. 14, 17-25.

Zoller, D., 1977: Eine Siedlung der vorrömischen Eisenzeit bei Meppen, Kr. Emsland, *Nachrichten aus Niedersachsens Urgeschichte* 46, 233-239.

Zoller, D., 1981: Neue jungpaläolithische und mesolithische Fundstellen im nordoldenburgischen Geestgebiet, *Archäologische Mitteilungen aus Nordwestdeutschland* 4, 1-12.

Zschocke, K. / E. Preuschen 1932: *Das urzeitliche Bergbaugebiet von Mühlbach-Bischofshofen*, Wien (Materialien zur Urgeschichte Österreichs, 6).

Zvelebil, M., 1986a: Mesolithic prelude and Neolithic revolution, in: M. Zvelebil (ed.), 5-15.

Zvelebil, M. (ed.), 1986b: *Hunters in transition: mesolithic societies of temperate Europe and their transition to farming*, Cambridge.

Zvelebil, M., 1994: Plant use in the Mesolithic and its role in the transition to farming, *PPS* 60, 35-74.

Location maps of regions and sites

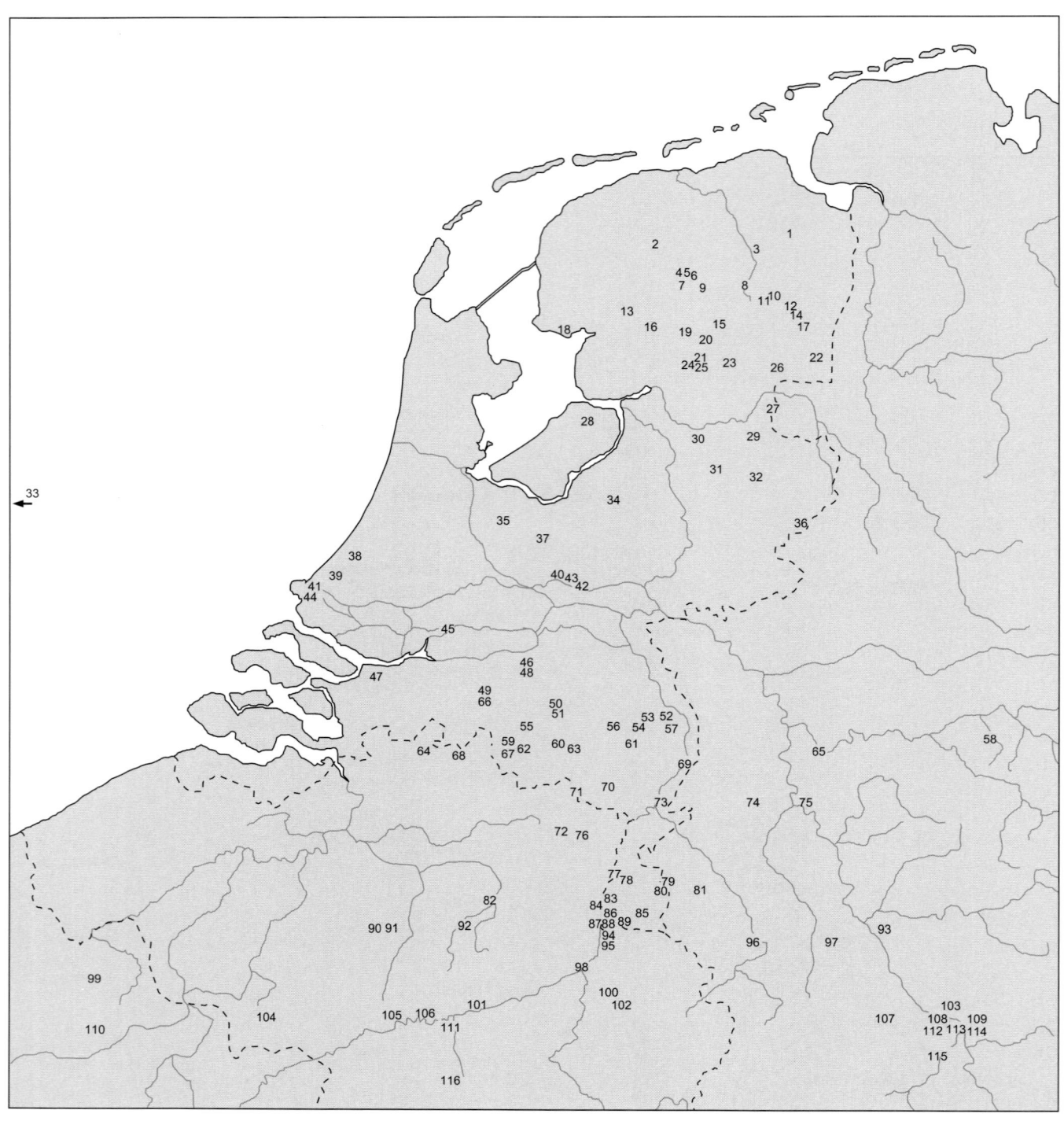

Site locations Part I

Site locations Part II

Site locations Part III

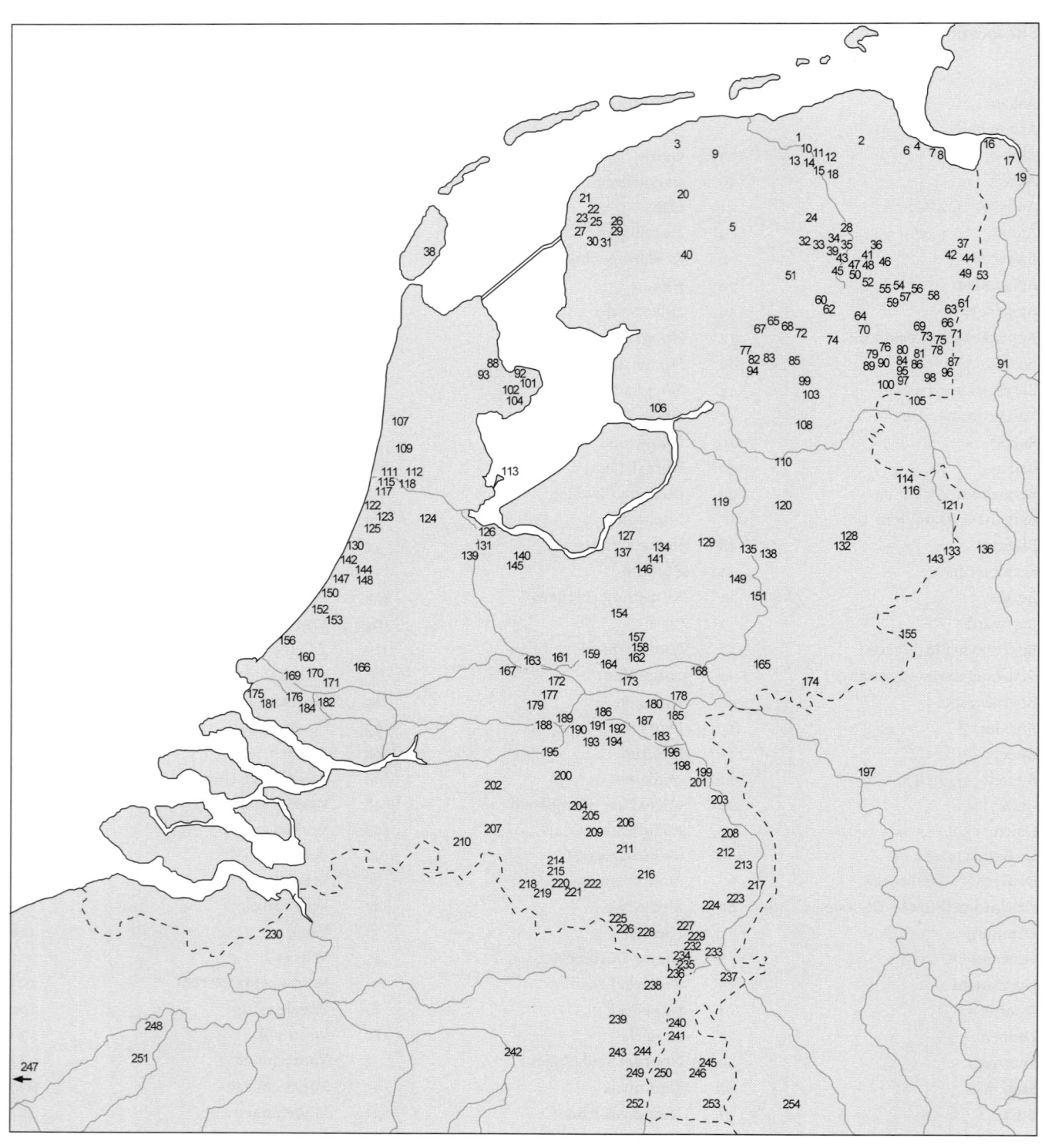

Site locations Part IV

Site index

References to figures and Plates in *italics*

Thematical index

References to figures and Plates in *italics*

floods   69, 71, 478, 491, 557-559, 583

flounder *(Platichthys flesus)*   331

Flussmarsch   561

Fochteloo, house type   571

fodder   504, 510, 563, 598
 leaf hay   322
 winter foddering   334, 497, 502, 504, 511

foliage plants   *see* legumes

Font Robert type points   116

food
 cooking   *see* cooking stones
 drying   127, 431

food remains   680
 preparation and conservation   180

footpaths, wooden   *401-403, 482, 666, pl. 31*

forest exploitation   230, 404-405, 477-478

forest management   405

forests, as sacred places   672, 675

fowl, domestic *(Gallus domesticus)*   506

fowling
 Palaeolithic, Mesolithic   123, 152, 154
 Neolithic   318, *324*, 326, 328, 331
 metal ages   408, *493*, 504

fox *(Vulpes vulpes)*   123, 161, 170, *323*, 326

fresh water quarzite   118, 123

Frisian culture   *480-481*

frost cracks   57

frost wedges   48, 55, *57*

fruits, wild
 Mesolithic   154, 161, 170, 184
 Neolithic   274, 313, 317-318, 326-332
 metal ages   511, 680

Fuchsberg phase   211

Funnel Beaker culture   211, 266, *277-293*, 347, 463, 697, 708
 chronology   *207, 282-284*
 distribution   *281, 290*
 artefacts   *277-280, 282-287, 303-304, pl. 20B-C*
 settlements   *287-289,* 409
 burials   *288-290, 307-310, pl. 22*
 environment   63, 206-207, *321-322, 457, pl. 4*
 subsistence   322, 457
 organisation   291-292, 462
 ritual   *289*-291, *pl. 20C*
 trackways   *401-402,* 404

fur animals   298-299, 316, 326, 329, 331

gabbro   277, 280

Galeriegräber   281

Gallic war   519

Gallo-Roman   671

game, stock of   494, 705

garganey *(Anas querquedula)*   *324,* 331

gastroliths   129

geese   123, *324,* 504

Geest   563

Gefolgschaft   668

Geistingen type socketed axe   *382-383, 603-*604

Gelderland group (urnfields)   633

Gemeinschaftshalle   *575*

Germania inferior   718

Germans / German   670-672, 688, 690

Geröllkeule   *165,* 167, *170,* 266

giant deer *(Cervus giganteus)*   99, 102

giants   *33,* 309

glacial cycle   50

glacials   46, 51

glass   379, 574, *612-614, 621-622, 642-643, 685, pl. 41A*

gneiss   286

goats *(Capra hircus) see* sheep/goats
 coprolites   502
 stabling of   502

gods   *see* spirits

gold   377, 380, 467, 713-714
 Celtic coins   *671, pl. 41B*
 leaf-gold   607, 644, 689, *pl. 45A*
 ornaments   386, 389, *440, 443-445, 447, 448-449,* 622, *pl. 42B*

golden eye *(Bucephala clangula)*   184, *324*

gold of pleasure   501-502, 504, *506-507, 510,* 521, 593, 600-601, 687, 701

goosander *(Mergus merganser)*   184, *324*

goosefoot   313, 496

Gorkum deposits   *65, 66-*67

gouges, bronze   664

grain   203, 251, 263, 274, *see also* barley, millet, oats, rye, wheat
 threshing waste   501
 impressions in pottery   *311,* 313, 322, 500-*501*
 pollen   *61-62, 321-*322, 332
 winter cereal   501, 507
 seed grain   509
 summer cereal   493, 501, 507

grain/cereal ricks   567, 571

granaries
 Bronze Age   411, 413, *419-427,* 544
 Iron Age   504, 521-523, 525, 530, 533-534, 540, 546, *550-552, 563-567,* 570, 574, *585-586,* 590, 656, *pl. 37A*

Grand-Pressigny daggers, flint   *347-348,* 351, *393, 443-*444, 447, *713-*714, *pl. 29*

granite   126, 146, *285, 396,* 618

grates, ceramic   *see* kilns

graves   *see* inhumation burials *and* cremation burials

Gravette points   129, *144-145*

grazing of cattle   230, 463, 477, 565, 703

Grenzhorizont   63

Griendtsveen Formation   63

Griffzungenschwerter   *387*

Grimston bowls   259

grinding stones   228, 256, *286, 396,* 443, 618, *pl. 16B*
 grooved   146

grip, ornamental piece   *662-663*

Grobkeramik   607

Großgartach culture   207, 209, *239-240,* 250

groundwater rise   183, 478, 543, *see also* sea level rise

Gündlingen sword type   *387, 713*

gyttja   141, 144

haddock *(Gadus aeglefinus)*   331, 429, 431

haematite   *see* red ochre

hair comb   620-*621*

hair dress   620

hair, plaits   *26*

hair rings   *see also* ear rings
 bronze   605, *656, 662, pl. 46*
 gold   386, *440,* 444-445, 449

halberds, bronze or copper   *377-379, 380, pl. 28*

Hallstatt culture   480-482, 516, 607, 643, 645, 666, 668

Hamburg culture   85, *116-117, 124-130,* 192, 695

hammer axes
 copper   380
 stone
  typology   *394-395*
  Middle Neolithic   257, *285-286,* 303, 715
  Late Neolithic   304, 371, *390-396, 443-448,* 463, 714
  metal ages   606, 666-667, 692

hammers
 antler   136, 296
 stone   379, 396, *673, see also* hammer stones
 wood   *268*

hammer stones
 flint   227
 quartzite, sandstone   *136,* 260, 574, 618-*619*

hand axes   *80, 87,* 95-100, 105, 138, 194, *pl. 8A-C*

hand axe tradition   84

Rixheim sword type *387*
roads *see also* trackways
    Neolithic 309, 434, 708
    Bronze Age *288*, 417, 645-*646*
    Iron Age *647*
road-system 403, 645, 708
Rocourt soil horizon *101*
rodents, small 52, 102, 495-*496*
roe *(Capreolus capreolus)*
    Palaeolithic 102
    Mesolithic 161, 184-*185*
    Neolithic 207, 313, 320, *323*, 325
    metal ages 429, 494
Rollenkopfnadel 620-*621*
Romanisation 718
Roman period 478-479, 482, 504-505,
    510, 530, 549, 553, 575, 608, 624, 633,
    651, 660-662, 670-671, 674, 679, 683,
    686, 690, 718
Romigny-Léhry flint 254, 257, *347-349*,
    pl. 29
rope 228, 268-269, 296, *see also* fish-traps
rose hips 317
Rosnoën sword type 386, *388*
Rössen culture 209, *239*
    chronology *207*, *343*
    distribution *215*, *249*, *343*
    artefacts *252-258*, *343*, *348*, pl. 17
    settlements 250-251, 338-339
    subsistence 314-*315*, *319*
rowan-wood *390*-391
rubber tree *(Eucommia)* 54
rubbing stones *619*
Ruinen-Wommels pottery 481
    Ruinen-Wommels I 482, 562-563,
        612, 641
Rullen flint *239*, 254, *348*, *pl. 17A*
Rura 670
rye *61*, *507*, 574

Saale ice sheet 53-54, 105
Saalian, Saale glacial *53-55*, 59, *pl. 1B*
sacred areas 659, 672-673
sacrifices *see* depositions *and* building
    sacrifices
saddle roofs *529*
salmon *(Salmo salar)* 184-*185*, 330, 429,
    494
salt 247, 431, 594, 620, 640, *see also*
    briquetage
    mines 515
    pottery 514, *515*, 609
    production *513*, 514, *516*, 574, 601
    semi-cylinders *513*, 514, 515,640, *pl.*
        36A
    trade 515-516, 594, 613, 688

salt marshes 66, 70, 418, 477, 543,
    561
    occupation of salt marshes 70, 417-
        418, 478, 505-506, 558-575, 587,
        600, 685
    settlements on the marsh sur-
        face 558, *562-566*, 567-571
salt marsh ridges 70, 558-559
sand drift 63-64, 477-478, 519, 543, 563,
    591, 597, 704, 706, 708
sandstone 120, 126, 146, 149, 196
Santpoort style group 593
Sauveterrian-Tardenoisian 164
scabbards
    swords, bronze 623, 669
    daggers, iron *622*
Scandinavian flint daggers 351, 386,
    393, *395*, *713*, *pl. 28*
scavenging 106, 110, 193
Schoonrewoerd stream ridge 409
Schräghals pots 612, 641
Schrägrand pots 641
Schuhleistenkeile, perforated *255*
scrapers
    Palaeolithic *97*, *105*, *116*, *118-119*, *125*,
        131, *144*-145, *194*
    Mesolithic *163*, 165, 173
    Neolithic 227, 254, 266, 285, *294*-
        295, 301, *366*, 442
    metal ages *615*
sea connections 279, 616
sea level curve *60*
sea level rise
    Holocene 46, 60-63, 66-69, 83, 141,
        157, 183, 212, 357, 408, 543, *see also*
        groundwater rise
    Pleistocene 93, 129, 157
sea mammals 194, 207, 299, 313, 318,
    323, 495, 505
sea salt *see* salt
seal, common *(Phoca vitulina)* 207, *323*
seal, grey *(Halichoerus gryphus)* 207, 318,
    323, 495, 505
season, establishment of 184-*185*, *193*,
    263
seasonal activities 430, 516, *see also* an-
    nual cycle
seasonal camps 184-*185*, 263, 293, 333,
    340, 492-*493*
seasonal exploitation 299, 493
seasonal migration 123, 128, 130, 153, *see*
    also transhumance
seasonal occupation 124, 263, 297, 299,
    317-319, 320, 332, 338, 430, 585, 691
seasonal (summer) grazing 487, 502-
    505, 567, 594, 691

secondary interments 436, 439, *441-442*,
    447, 451, 455, 466, 637, 651, *pl. 34B*
secondary products revolution 346, 358,
    701
sedentism, increasing in Mesolithic 196
Seemarsch 561
Segel earrings *621*, 651
Seine-Oise-Marne culture 207, 247, *281*,
    293, 303, 462-463
semi-permanent settlements 317, 332
settlement forms
    Gehöftsiedlung 563, 567
    Gruppensiedlung 567
    hamlet 537, 554, 683
    Herrensitz 689
    single farm 554, 597-598, 649
    village 230, 233, 558, 569, 575, 711
settlements *see also* sites
    clusters 347, 389
    continuity of place 229, *537-539*, 559
    distribution patterns 215, 292, 417,
        429, 538, 558, 581, 590-591, 597,
        698
    extent 522, 525-526, 549, 554
    locations *212*, *261*, *292*, *429*, 465,
        519, *537*, 543, 545, 583, 589
settlement systems
    Palaeolithic and Mesolithic 81, 108-
        109, 150, 170-176, 189-191
    Neolithic 263, 338-340, 347, 430
    Bronze Age 426-427
    Iron Age *536-539*, 548, 649-650, 683-
        684, 712
shad *(Alosa alosa)* 494
shaft hole axes *see Arbeitsäxte, Breitkeile*,
    hammer axes, *Schuhleistenkeile*,
    Spitzhauen
sheep *(Ovis aries)* *see* sheep/goat
sheep/goat
    Neolithic 186, 204, 235, 312, 316,
        323, 326, 328, 330, 332, 408, 410
    Bronze Age 427, 493-499, 511
    Iron Age 493-494, *500-505*, 511, 521,
        574, 594, 599-600, 686
shell layers *362*, 408, *430*, *pl. 23A*
shell ornaments 223, 228, 256, *347*, 349
shoes 614-615, 620, *627-628*, *673*, *pl.*
    43A
shouldered points 85, *125*, 130
sickles
    bronze *604*, *617*, *664*, 667, *pl. 41C*
    flint
        one piece sickles *486*, 562-563,
            574, 615-*618*, 666, 688, *pl. 41C*
        sickle gloss 260, 286
        sickle knife *227*, 269, 301, 311, *314*

Index of persons

References to figures in *italics*

Acknowledgement of the sources of illustrations

Medy Oberendorff (Faculty of Archaeology, Leiden University) took care of the final editing of the illustrations.

Many line drawings have been redrawn, when no original or digital version was available, by the following draughtspersons:

FdALeiden	6.3, 4; 7.2; 8.3; 10.3; 11.1; 13.1; 16.2; 22.3, 4, 7, 10, 11, 14.
Harry Fokkens	18.1, 9, 13.
Peter Heavens	16.3.
Petra de Jong	1.5, 10; 4.7; 10.7; 15.7; 16.7; 19.7; 21.2, 3; 29.2, 6, 7; 30.1; N2, S2-3.
Hans Kamermans	11.6.
Henk de Lorm	6.1, 2, 16, 17; 12.16; 13.5, 17; 14.5; 29.16.
Medy Oberendorff	1.6; 4.2; 6.18; 7.7, 8, 10; 8.4, 11-13; 9.7; 10.9-10; 11.2, 3, 7, 10, 16, 21; 12.11-13; 13.10, 12, 13, 20; 15.2-4, 6; 17.17, 20, 21; 18.4, 5, 8, 10, 15; 19.12; 20.2; 23.17, 18; 24.1, 6, 8-10; 25.4, 5; 26.9, 12, 13; 28.9, 10; 29.10, 13; 30 3; 31.7, 8; C1; E1, 2; I2; J1, 2; K1, M1.
P. van den Broeke	29.2l.
K. van Gijssel	3.1-7, 10-17; B1.
M. Hense	1.7, 9; 27.9; 30.1r; G2.
J.E. Dilz	17.1; 22.2, 6, 15; 27.6, 7, 8, 10, 12, 14, 17, 19; 28.2, 3a, 3b; P3, Q4.
A.M. Numan	19.16.
R. Mols	21.4; 23.22; O3, R1; plate 4-7.

Most drawings and photo's have been published once or more than once. They were placed at our disposal by the authors.
In the case of drawings reference is made to a/the previous publication.
Substantial additions to or changes in the original drawings are indicated as 'after …' .
For photos reference is made to the institute and/or photographer.
For abbreviations used see the list at the head of the bibliography.

cover   photo FdAL (J. Pauptit)

figures

1.1	photo FdAL (J. Pauptit)	1.8	photo Drents Museum, Assen	3.1	Zagwijn/Doppert 1978
1.2	photo ROB	1.9	after Pearson/Stuiver 1993 and Stuiver/ Pearson 1993	3.2	Zagwijn/Van Staalduinen 1975
1.3	photo Leeuwarder Courant	1.10	designed by the editors	3.3	design by K. van Gijssel
1.4	photo FdAL (Menno Hoogland)			3.4	after Van der Hammen et al.1971
1.5	after Clarke 1968	2.1	Picardt 1660	3.5	Drijver-de Haas/Smit 1992
1.6	after drawing by Ben van Mierlo in: Kortlang 1987	2.2	photo FdAL	3.6	Zagwijn/Van Staalduinen 1975
		2.3	photo RMO	3.7	Van den Berg/Den Otter 1993
1.7	after Coles 1987b	2.4	photo RMO	3.8	photo P. Paris
		2.5	photo FdAL (H. Fokkens)	3.9	photo GIA
				3.10	Jelgersma 1979
				3.11	after Zagwijn 1986

13.1 designed by the editors
13.2 Brindley 1986b
13.3 photo RMO
13.4 photo FdAL (W. Meuzelaar)
13.5 Waterbolk 1960
13.6 photo AAC (F. Gijbels)
13.7 photo Drents Museum, Assen
13.8 photo FdAL (J. Pauptit)
13.9 Zimmermann 1980
13.10 Waterbolk 1960
13.11 photo Drents Museum Assen
13.12 Harsema 1992
13.13 Louwe Kooijmans 1986
13.14 Glasbergen et al. 1961
13.15 Van Gijn 1990
13.16 photo FdAL (J. Pauptit)
13.17 Maarleveld 1985
13.18 Louwe Kooijmans 1985, Schlichtherle/ Wahlster 1986 (canoe)
13.19a Louwe Kooijmans 1986
13.19b photo RMO (L.B.M. Verhart)
13.20 Verhart 1992
13.21 photo ROB
13.22 photo RMO
13.23a photo AAC (F.Gijbels)
13.22b Bakker/Van der Waals 1973

14.1 photo FdAL (J.Pauptit)
14.2 photo FdAL (J. Pauptit)
14.3 photos FdAL (J.Pauptit)
14.4a Van Gijn 1990
14.4b photo FdAL (A.L. van Gijn)
14.5 design C.C. Bakels
14.6 photo FdAL (J. Pauptit)
14.7 Zeiler 1997
14.8 photo FdAL (J. Pauptit)
14.9 photo FdAL (J. Pauptit)
14.10 Behre/Kučan 1986
14.11 photo FdAL (W. Meuzelaar)
14.12 photo AAC
14.13 Boddeke 1971
14.14 r photo FdAL (J.Pauptit)
14.14 l IJsseling/Scheygrond 1956
14.15 photo Gemeente Groningen (G.L.G.A. Kortekaas)
14.16 photo FdAL (W. Meuzelaar)
14.17 photo RMO (M. Vinkesteyn)
t. 14.1 design C.C. Bakels
t. 14.2 design J. Zeiler/L.P. Louwe Kooijmans
t. 14.3 design J. Zeiler/L.P. Louwe Kooijmans

15.1 after Lüning 1982b
15.2 Zvelebil 1986a
15.3 Zvelebil 1986a
15.4 Sherratt 1990
15.5 Louwe Kooijmans 1993b, 1998
15.6 designed by the editors
15.7 designed by the editors
15.8 photo FdA (L.P. Louwe Kooijmans)
15.9 Louwe Kooijmans 1985

16.1 Van der Waals 1964
16.2 designed by the editors
16.3 designed by the editors
16.4 l photo AAC
16.4 r photo ROB
16.5 photo AAC (L. Therkorn)
16.6 photo RMO
16.7 Klok 1979
16.8 l Theunissen 1999
16.8 r photo ROB

17.1 Lanting/Van der Waals 1976a
17.2 photo FdA (W. Meuzelaar)
17.3 photos ROB
17.4 FdAL (1-3), Van Giffen et al. 1971 (4), Fokkens 1991a (5), Lanting 1973 (6)
17.5 Butler 1969 (1); De Laet/Glasbergen 1959 (2)
17.6 FdAL (J.P. Boogerd)
17.7 Bakker et al. 1977
17.8 Butler 1990
17.9 Fontijn et al. 2002
17.10 Butler 1995-'96; Butler/Steegstra 1997-'98, 1999-2000, 2001-'02.
17.11 ROB (1), GIA (2-7)
17.12 Modderman 1964a (1), Butler 1990 (2), Meijlink 2001 (3)
17.13 photo RMO
17.14 H. Steegstra
17.15 Butler/Sarfatij 1970-'71 (1, 2), de Mortillet 1903 (3), Needham 1990 (4)
17.16 H. Steegstra (1-2), Butler 1990 (3)
17.17 Glasbergen 1957
17.18 FdAL (drawing Medy Oberendorff)
17.19 Louwe Kooijmans 1986 (1), Lanting/ Van der Waals 1976 (2, 3), Butler 1986 (4)
17.20 Glasbergen 1971 (1), Lanting/Van der Waals 1976 (2, 3), Achterop 1957 (4)
17.21 after Drenth/Lanting 1991, Lanting 1973, Achterop/Brongers 1979
17.22 Brongers/Woltering 1978

18.1 Louwe Kooijmans 1974, Jongste et al. 2001
18.2 Louwe Kooijmans 1974
18.3 Fokkens in Fokkens/Jansen 2002
18.4 Waterbolk 1964
18.5 Harsema 1991
18.6 Kooi 1991, Verlinde 1982b
18.7 IJzereef/Van Regteren Altena 1991
18.8 IJzereef 1983
18.9 Van Regteren Altena 1977
18.10 Hessing 1991a
18.11 photos FdAL
18.12 FdAL (drawing H.Fokkens)
18.13 FdAL (drawing H.Fokkens)
18.14 Fokkens 1993, Schinkel 1994 (1), photos FdAL (2-6)
18.15 Theunissen 1999
18.16 Theunissen 1999
18.17 Roymans/Hiddink 1991

19.1 Louwe Kooijmans 1974
19.2 photo GIA
19.3 designed by the authors after data in Lohof 1994, 235, Theunissen 1999, 84,
19.4 Waterbolk 1985
19.5 photo AAC
19.6 Bosman/ Soonius 1990
19.7 design H. Fokkens after data in Lanting/Van der Waals 1974
19.8 photo GIA
19.9 Lanting/Van der Waals 1976
19.10 Lanting/Van der Waals 1976
19.11 Butler 1990
19.12 Hijszeler 1970
19.13 Butler 1990
19.14 Lohof 1994
19.15 Beuker et al. 1991

20.1 Fokkens 2002
20.2 design H. Fokkens
20.3 Fokkens 1999

21.1 photo L. van der Valk
21.2 designed by the editors
21.3 designed by the editors et al.
21.4 after Roymans 1991
21.5 photo FdAL (H. Fokkens)
21.6 photo FdAL (A.L. van Gijn)

22.1 photo W. Overmars
22.2 Overmars 1987

835

22.3 after data in Gehasse 1995

22.4 after data in Clason 1977b, 1980, IJz-
ereef *et al.* 1992, Roymans 1990, *s.a.*,
Verhagen 1990, Van Wijngaarden-
Bakker 1988

22.5 photo J. Fielmich

22.6 IJzereef 1981

22.7 after data in IJzereef 1981

22.8 photo ROB

22.9 IJzereef 1981

22.10 after data in IJzereef 1981

22.11 after data in Clason 1967, IJzereef *et al.*
1992

22.12 photo FdAL (J. Pauptit)

22.13 photo FdAL (J. Pauptit)

22.14 after data in: Clason 1967, Van Dijk
1992, IJzereef *et al.* 1992, Prummel
1989

22.15 Krüger *et al.* 1988

22.16 Van Gelder-Ottway 1988

22.17 Brongers 1972

22.18 photo ROB (J. Buurman)

t. 22.1 Bakels 1991b

t. 22.2 Runia 1987

t. 22.3 after data in Therkorn *et al.* 1984,
Brinkkemper 1992, 1993, 1994

t. 22.4 after Van Zeist *et al.* 1976, Bottema *et al.*
1980

t. 22.5 after data in Bakels 1994, Bakels/Van
der Ham 1980, Buurman 1986, Roy-
mans 1985, Van Zeist 1968, 1976

t. 22.6 after data in Gelissen 1992, Annual Report ROB 1990

23.1 photos FdAL

23.2 photo FdAL (J.Pauptit)

23.3 Schinkel 1998

23.4 Fokkens 1991b

23.5 Schinkel 1998

23.6 Fokkens 1991b

23.7 Schinkel 1998

23.8 Schinkel 1998

23.9 Schinkel 1998

23.10 photo *Stichting Prehistorisch Huis*, Eindhoven

23.11 Schinkel 1998

23.12 Schinkel 1998

23.13 Schinkel 1998

23.14 Schinkel 1998

23.15 Schinkel 1998

23.16 Hulst 1989

23.17 Van Es/Hessing 1994

23.18 Zoller 1977

23.19 Van der Sanden 1987f

23.20 Verwers 1991

23.21 photos FdAL

23.22 Schinkel 1998

24.1 Waterbolk 1990a

24.2 Waterbolk 1987

24.3 after Verlinde 1993b

24.4 Harsema 1980a

24.5 photo Photo Service Province of Drenthe

24.6 Harsema 1980b

24.7 Huijts 1992

24.8 Harsema 1980a

24.9 Waterbolk 1977

24.10 Waterbolk 1977

24.11 photo Ordnance Survey (*Topografische
Dienst*), Emmen

25.1 GIA

25.2 GIA

25.3 Schmid 1984

25.4 Boersma 1999

25.5 GIA

25.6 Boersma 1988b

25.7 photo GIA

25.8 GIA

26.1 Van Heeringen 1992

26.2 Van Heeringen 1992

26.3 Vos 1983

26.4 Woltering 1991

26.5 Woltering 1991

26.6 Woltering 1991

26.7 Modderman 1960-'61a

26.8 photo FdAL (J. Pauptit)

26.9 Therkorn 1989

26.10 Van Trierum *et al.* 1986

26.11 Van Trierum 1992

26.12 Therkorn *et al.*1984

26.13 Van Trierum 1992

26.14 photo FdAL

26.15 Van Heeringen 1992

27.1 Roymans 1991

27.2 Butler 1986

27.3 Van Heeringen 1992, Van den Broeke
in prep.

27.4 photo ROB

27.5 Modderman 1960-'61a

27.6 Flamman 1993

27.7 Abbink, in prep.

27.8 design by P.W. van den Broeke

27.9 Roymans/Van Rooijen 1993

27.10 Schinkel 1998 (1-8, 10-11), Van Heeringen 1992 (9), Abbink in prep. (12)

27.11 photo FdAL (J. Pauptit)

27.12 Roymans 1988b

27.13 photo RMO

27.14 Miedema 1983 (1), Beuker *et al.* 1993
(2), Modderman 1960-'61a (3), Van
Trierum *et al.* 1988 (4), Van der Waals
1964a (5), Butler 1973 (6), doc. FdAL
(7).

27.15 photo FdAL (J.Pauptit)

27.16 photo AAC

27.17 after Bloemers 1983 (1), Harsema 1979
(2), Kars/Kars 1992 (3 en 4), Therkorn
1989 (5), Van den Broeke 1987b (6)

27.18 Roymans 1991

27.19 IJzereef 1981 (1), Van Heeringen 1992
and J.T. Bakker 1982 (2), Groenewoudt
1984 (3), Butler 1987a (4), Van Heeringen 1992 (5), Harsema 1983 (6), Woltering 1989 (7), Kooi 1979 (8), Remouchamps 1925 (9), Willems 1986b (10),
Assendorp 1975 (11), Wesselingh 1993
(12).

27.20 Verwers 1972

27.21 photo RMO

27.22 photo FdAL (J. Pauptit)

28.1 photo GIA

28.2 design W.A.M. Hessing

28.3a design P.B. Kooi / W.A.M. Hessing

28.3b design W.A.M. Hessing / P.B. Kooi

28.4 Roymans/Tol 1993

28.5 photo GIA

28.6 Butler 1990

28.7 photo ROB

28.8 FdAL (drawing B. Dekker)

28.9 GIA

28.10 Roymans 1988b

28.11 Kooi 1979

28.12 photo ROB

28.13 photo ROB

29.1 photo GIA

29.2 r Bakker *et al.*1968

29.2 l after photo AAC

29.3 photo GIA

29.4 Butler 1979

16A	FdAL (J. Pauptit)	26	RMO (P. Bomhof)	39B	FdAL (J. Pauptit)
16B	FdAL (L.P. Louwe Kooijmans)	27A	Henk Brandsen, Amsterdam	40A	RMO (P. Bomhof)
17A	FdAL (J. Pauptit)	27B	Henk Brandsen, Amsterdam	40B	RMO
17B	FdAL (L.P. Louwe Kooijmans)	28	Henk Brandsen, Amsterdam	41A	Henk Brandsen, Amsterdam
18A	FdAL (L.P. Louwe Kooijmans)	29	RMO (P. Bomhof)	41B	RMO (P. Bomhof)
18B	FdAL (L.P. Louwe Kooijmans)	30	FdAL (L.P. Louwe Kooijmans)	41C	RMO (P. Bomhof)
19A	RMO (L.P. Louwe Kooijmans)	31	GIA (W. Casparie)	42A	RMO (P. Bomhof)
19B	RMO (L.P. Louwe Kooijmans)	32A	Bob Brobbel, Hilversum	42B	RMO (P. Bomhof)
20A	RMO (P. Bomhof)	32B	Koen van der Velde, Den Andel	43A	RMO (P. Bomhof)
20B	Drents Musem, Assen	33A	FdAL (P.J.R. Modderman)	43B	Drents Museum, Assen
20C	FdAL (J. Pauptit)	33B	RMO (L.P. Louwe Kooijmans)	44A	GIA
21A	FdAL (J. Pauptit)	34A	FdA	44B	GIA
21B	FdAL (J. Pauptit)	34B	GIA	44C	GIA
21C	FdAL (C.C. Bakels)	35A	RMO	45A	RMO (P. Bomhof)
22A	FdA	35B	FdAL (J. Pauptit)	45B	RMO (P. Bomhof)
22B	L.P. Louwe Kooijmans	36A	FdAL (J. Pauptit)	46A	GNBA (R. Mols)
23A	FdAL (L.P. Louwe Kooijmans)	36B	Kelvin Wilson, Ridderkerk	46B	Kelvin Wilson, Ridderkerk
23B	GIA	37A	photo W.H. Metz, Huizen	47A	Groninger Museum
24A	Panorama	37B	S. Drost, Assen	47B	AAC
24B	Bob Brobbel, Hilversum	38A	GIA	48A	RMO (P. Bomhof)
25A	RMO (P. Bomhof)	38B	FdAL (J. Pauptit)	48B	Drents Museum, Assen
25B	FdAL (W. Meuzelaar)	39A	BOOR		

The authors

N. *Arts* (1954) studied cultural anthropology in Leiden and pre- and protohistory at the University of Amsterdam. He has been working as the municipal archaeologist of Eindhoven since 1989; in 1992 he was appointed the municipal archaeologist of Helmond, too. His specialisations are the Upper Palaeolithic and the Mesolithic of the southern Netherlands and the medieval history of occupation of towns and countryside in the southeast of North Brabant.

Prof. dr C.C. Bakels (1942) studied ecology and microbiology in Leiden and Delft. In 1968 she was appointed a lecturer at Leiden University and in 1988 professor of palaeoeconomy. She graduated in 1978 on an ecological-archaeological analysis of four *Bandkeramik* settlements in the Netherlands and Bavaria. Her specialisations are crop farming and environmental history.

Dr J.A. Bakker (1935) studied physical geography and prehistory in Amsterdam. He worked at the University of Amsterdam from 1959 until 2002, first as an assistant researcher, and later as a senior lecturer. He graduated in 1973 on a study of the West Group of the funnel beaker culture. His specialisations are the Neolithic, the Westfrisian Bronze Age, wetland archaeology and the history of archaeology.

J.R. Beuker (1952) was educated as a teacher of geography and history in Groningen. He has been working in the Museum of Drenthe since 1977, first as an archaeological field assistant, and since 1991 as the curator of the archaeological department, specialising in the Stone Age. He has done research into flint working and the occurrence of exotic flint in the northern Netherlands.

J.W. Boersma (1936) studied history and pre- and protohistory in Groningen. He was a lecturer at the Groningen Institute of Archaeology (GIA) of Groningen University from 1967 until 1999 and the curator of the archaeological department of the Groningen Museum from 1967 until 1993. He has directed several *terp* and church excavations in the northern Netherlands. *Terp* and church research is his main field of interest.

Dr O. Brinkkemper (1962) studied biology in Amsterdam and graduated in 1993 in Leiden on an archaeobotanical study of Voorne-Putten. He was appointed an archaeobotanist with the State Service for Archaeological Investigations (ROB) in 1994. His specialisation is archeaobotanical analysis of macroremains, wood and pollen. He is in charge of the RADAR database for botanical macroremains.

P.W. van den Broeke (1952) received a degree in cultural prehistory at Leiden University in 1978. Since then, he has specialised in the archaeology of the Iron Age of northwestern Europe. He is at present working for the archaeological department of the Municipality of Nijmegen as director of the archaeological investigations conducted in the context of the Waalsprong development scheme.

Dr J.A. Brongers (1933) studied chemistry in Leiden. He was the head of the science department of the State Service for Archaeological Investigations (ROB) from 1962 until 1990. He graduated in 1976 in Groningen on a study of aerial photography and Celtic field research. His specialisations are archaeometric research into ceramics (dilatometry and porosimetry) and the history of archaeology.

Dr J.J. Butler (1921) studied prehistoric archaeology at the University of London. He has been working as a (senior) lecturer at Groningen University since1975. He was later also appointed a senior lecturer at the University of Amsterdam. He graduated in 1958 in London on a study of the Bronze Age connections between Great Britain and continental Europe. His specialisations are the Bronze Age of the Netherlands and of Europe in general.

Dr W.A. Casparie (1930) studied biology in Groningen. He worked as a palaeobotanist at the Biological-Archaeological Institute in that town from 1958 until 1995. He graduated on a study of the development of Bourtanger Moor in the southeast of Drenthe. He has been active in archaeological peat research in Ireland since 1988. His specialisations are peat and wood archaeology.

J. Deeben (1955) studied social geography in Nijmegen and prehistory in Amsterdam. He was employed by the University of Amsterdam from 1988 until 1992, and has been working for the State Service for Archaeological Investigations (ROB) since 1995, since 2002 as head of the archaeological values department. His specialisations are the Upper Palaeolithic and the Mesolithic and archaeological predictive models.

E. Drenth (1962) studied pre-and protohistory in Groningen. He joined the State Service for Archaeological Investigations (ROB) in 1990. He has published various works mainly on Dutch prehistory, more specifically the Dutch Neolithic and Bronze Age.

Prof. dr H. Fokkens (1953) studied social geography at the Free University of Amsterdam and prehistory in Groningen. He was appointed a (senior) lecturer at Leiden University in 1982 and appointed to the chair of prehistory in 2005. He graduated 1991 in Groningen on a study of the history of occupation of the western part of the Friesland-Drenthe plateau. He specialises in late prehistory and is the director of an extensive field project around Oss in the Maasland region.

Dr A.L. van Gijn (1956) studied prehistory in Groningen and was appointed a (senior) lecturer at Leiden University in 1986. She graduated in 1990 on the analysis of use-wear traces on flint implements from Neolithic settlements. In her research she concentrates on the function of prehistoric tools made of stone, bone and antler, with special attention for the Neolithic.

K. van Gijssel (1957) studied physical geography in Amsterdam. He did research for the State Geological Survey,at Leiden University and elsewhere for more than ten years. He is now working as a GIS specialist with the Hollands Noorderkwartier Water Board. His specialisations are Quaternary geology and petrography.

Dr H.A. Groenendijk (1949) studied history of art in Utrecht and prehistory in Leiden. He has worked for various public authorities in the field of archaeological heritage and was appointed the provincial archaeologist of Groningen in 1991. He graduated in 1993 on the archaeology of the Groningen peat reclamation district. His study of the Mesolithic is a direct result of his involvement in the re-development of eastern Groningen.

Prof. dr W. Groenman-van Waateringe (1933) is an emeritus professor of ecological prehistory at the University of Amsterdam. She studied biology and ecological prehistory at that university and graduated on a thesis entitled 'Roman leatherwork from Valkenburg'. Her main research topics have been palynological investigations of barrows and other archaeological remains, the military occupation of the northwestern part of the *Imperium Romanum* and leather from archaeological contexts.

Dr M.E.Th. de Grooth (1948) studied prehistory, archaeology and history of art in Leiden. She has been the curator of the archaeological department of the Bonnefantenmuseum in Maastricht since 1978 and has since 2001 also been participating in the archaeological project team of the Meuse Works. She graduated in 1994 in Leiden on a study of Neolithic flint exploitation in the southern Netherlands and Germany. Her specialisations are the Neolithic, flint mining, museology.

O.H. Harsema (1939) studied geography and prehistory in Groningen. He worked as a lecturer at Groningen University until his early retirement in 2000 and combined his tasks in that capacity with those of curator of the archaeological department of the Museum of Drenthe in Assen from 1967 until 1983. His specialisations are settlements from the Bronze Age to the Middle Ages, prehistoric technology, construction and reconstruction of buildings.

Dr R.M. van Heeringen (1953) studied geology and archaeology in Leiden and Amsterdam. Since 1975 he has held various positions with the State Service for Archaeological Investigations (ROB). He has also been the provincial archaeologist of Zeeland (1987-'94) and South Holland (1995-'97). He graduated in 1992 on a study of Iron Age society in the coastal region of the western Netherlands. His interests are prehistoric pottery, wetland archaeology and the interaction between archaeology and heritage management.

W.A.M. Hessing (1957) studied history and prehistory in Leiden. From 1983 until 2000 he worked at the State Service for Archaeological Investigations (ROB), amongst others as the provincial archaeologist of South Holland en Head of the Department Research and Development. He has been director of *Vestigia Archeologie & Cultuurhistorie* consultancy since 2000. He is currently preparing a thesis on burial rites in the Late Iron Age and the Roman period. His interests are late prehistory and the Roman period, Roman frontier studies and heritage management.

J.W.H. Hogestijn (1955) studied biology, classical archaeology and history of art in Utrecht and cultural prehistory in Amsterdam. He has been working for the State Service for Archaeological Investigations (ROB) as the provincial archaeologist in the province of Flevoland since 1987. He is municipal archaeologist of Almere since 2001. He has directed a field programme focusing on the Neolithic occupation of the province of North Holland and specialises in Dutch early prehistory.

Dr P.B. Kooi (1943) studied biology and prehistory in Groningen. He has been working for Groningen University since 1976 and was the provincial archaeologist of Drenthe from 1983 until 1986. He graduated in 1979 on a study of Late Bronze Age and Iron Age urnfields in the northern Netherlands. His specialisations are agrarian settlements and the history of occupation of the three northern Dutch provinces.

J.M. Koot (1963) studied cultural pre- and protohistory at the University of Amsterdam after an undergraduate study in social geography. He received his degree in 1993 and was that same year appointed the municipal archaeologist of Rijswijk. His specialisations are wetland archaeology and late medieval and post-medieval archaeology.

Dr E. Lohof (1946) studied prehistory of Europe and western Asia at the University of Amsterdam, where he graduated in 1991 on a study of burial rites and social change in the Bronze Age of the northeastern Netherlands. He was involved in archaeological prospecting from 1992 until 1999, predominantly in the German Rhineland and Brandenburg, and has since 1999 been the field director of an archaeological excavation company.

Prof. dr L.P. Louwe Kooijmans (1940) studied physical geography in Utrecht and prehistory in Leiden. He was the curator of the prehistoric department of the National Museum of Antiquities in Leiden from 1966 until 1982 and has held the chair of prehistory at Leiden University since 1982. He graduated in 1974 on a study of the prehistory of the western Netherlands. His specialisations are the Neolithic and wetland archaeology.

Dr E. Rensink (1961) studied history of art in Utrecht and cultural prehistory in Leiden. He graduated in Leiden in 1993 on a study of Magdalenian hunter-gatherers. Until 1998 he was a member of the *Changing Views of Ice Age Foragers* (Leiden) pioneer project team and after that he worked for RAAP archaeological consultancy until 2000. He has been a senior investigator with the State Service for Archaeological Investigations (ROB) since 2000, specialising in early prehistory (Palaeolithic and Mesolithic).

Prof. dr J.W.M. Roebroeks (1955) studied history in Nijmegen and prehistoric archaeology in Leiden, where he was appointed a lecturer in 1982. He graduated in 1989 on his research at Belvédère quarry near Maastricht and has held a personal chair in Palaeolithic archaeology at Leiden University since 1997. His research focuses on the earliest occupation of Europe.

Dr W.A.B. van der Sanden (1953) studied history of art and classical archaeology in Nijmegen and cultural prehistory in Groningen. He was head of the archaeological department of the Museum of Drenthe in Assen from 1987 until 1996, after a temporary position at Leiden University. He has been the provincial archaeologist of Drenthe since 1997. He graduated in 1990 on his research into Dutch bog bodies. His specialisation is wetland archaeology.

Dr K. Schinkel (1962) studied history and prehistory in Leiden. He graduated in 1994 on the analysis of the prehistoric settlements at Oss-Ussen. He has been a smallholding farmer in central France since 1998.

Dr D. *Stapert* (1947) studied geology and prehistory in Groningen. He was appointed a lecturer at Groningen University in 1973, where he graduated in 1992 on the development of a new method for spatial analysis of Stone Age flint scatters. His specialisations are the Palaeolithic and spatial analysis.

M.C. *van Trierum* (1949) studied prehistory in Leiden and medieval archaeology in Amsterdam. In 1979 he joined the department of archaeological investigations of the Municipality of Rotterdam (BOOR), whose head he has been since 1986.

Dr L. *van der Valk* (1952) studied Quaternary geology at the Free University of Amsterdam. He started a geological investigation of the coastal barriers in the western Netherlands in 1984, which was concluded in 1992 with a doctoral thesis at the same university. In 1990 he joined the State Geological Survey of the Netherlands and since 1999 he has been working for Delft Hydraulics, mostly abroad. The archaeology of the western Netherlands retained his attention throughout this period.

Dr P. *van de Velde* (1940) was a merchant steersman (1958-'67) prior to his study of cultural anthropology and prehistory in Leiden (1966-'73). He graduated in 1980 on a social analysis of the *Bandkeramik* culture. He worked at Leiden University from 1990 until 2001, after a period of archaeological field research in Lower Saxony and Indonesia. One of his specialisations is the *Bandkeramik*. He is currently working on a publication on the Geleen-Janskamperveld excavation.

Dr L.B.M. *Verhart* (1952) studied cultural prehistory at Leiden University and graduated in 2000 on a study of the neolithisation process in the southern Netherlands. He was appointed the curator of the prehistoric department of the National Museum of Antiquities in Leiden in 1989 and has been combining his tasks in that capacity with the commercial production of TV programmes and involvement in cultural-historical tourism. His research focuses on the Mesolithic and Neolithic periods.

Dr A.D. *Verlinde* (1940) studied physical geography in Utrecht and prehistory in Leiden. He worked for the State Service for Archaeological Investigations (ROB) as the provincial archaeologist of Overijssel from 1969 until 1998. He graduated in 1987 on 'the urnfields of Overijssel'. His publications cover all archaeological periods.

C.E. *Vermeeren* (1960) studied biology in Leiden, specialising in archaeobotany. In 1968 she began to combine biology teaching with free-lance archaeobotanical research. She joined the BIAX *Consult* partnership in the year of its foundation, 1993. She is interested in all archaeobotanical remains, but most of all in the use of wood, and makes great efforts to transmit archaeobotanical knowledge to others.

Dr L.H. *van Wijngaarden-Bakker* (1940) studied biology and ecological prehistory at the University of Amsterdam. She worked as a (senior) lecturer at this university from 1965 until 2003; since then, she has been a guest researcher. She graduated in 1980 on a zooarchaeological study of an Early Bronze Age settlement at New Grange, Ireland. Her field of research is zooarchaeology, from the Mesolithic to subrecent times.

Dr J.T. *Zeiler* (1955) studied biology in Groningen. He graduated in 1997 on a study of hunting and animal husbandry in the Netherlands during the Neolithic. He was a research fellow at the Biological-Archaeological Institute in Groningen from 1984 until 1992, when he set up his own research bureau *ArchaeoBone*, in which he has since then been working as a free-lance archaeozoologist.